# The Art of Simple Food II

# THE ART OF
# SIMPLE
# FOOD II

## ALICE WATERS

with

Kelsie Kerr and Patricia Curtan

Illustrations by Patricia Curtan

Clarkson Potter / Publishers
New York

Also from Alice Waters and Chez Panisse

*40 Years of Chez Panisse*
*The Art of Simple Food*
*In the Green Kitchen*
*Chez Panisse Fruit*
*Chez Panisse Café Cookbook*
*Chez Panisse Vegetables*
*Fanny at Chez Panisse*
*Chez Panisse Cooking*
*Chez Panisse Desserts*
*Chez Panisse Pasta, Pizza, and Calzone*
*Chez Panisse Menu Cookbook*

Copyright © 2013 by Alice Waters
Illustrations © 2013 by Patricia Curtan

Published in the United States by Clarkson Potter/Publishers,
an imprint of the Crown Publishing Group,
a division of Random House, Inc., New York.
www.crownpublishing.com
www.clarksonpotter.com

CLARKSON POTTER is a trademark and POTTER with
colophon is a registered trademark of Random House, Inc.

Library of Congress Cataloging-in-Publication Data
is available upon request.

ISBN 978-0-307-71827-3
eISBN 978-0-7704-3347-5

Printed in the United States of America

Design by Patricia Curtan

10 9 8 7 6 5 4 3 2 1

First Edition

To Bob Cannard

# CONTENTS

## Part I: Flavor as Inspiration
### Varieties in the Garden—Recipes for the Kitchen

**My Kitchen Garden**    3
Growing What I Love to Eat

**Fragrant and Beautiful**    7
Herbs and Herb Flowers

**Tender Leaves**    35
Lettuce and Salad Greens

**Hidden Flavor**    51
Garlic, Onions, Leeks, and Shallots

**Growing Underground**    67
Roots and Tubers

**Crisp Stalks**    97
Fennel, Celery, Asparagus, Cardoons, and Rhubarb

**Fresh and Dried**    111
Peas, Fava Beans, Green Beans, Shell Beans, and Peanuts

**Meandering Vines**    135
Cucumbers, Melons, Summer Squash, and Winter Squash

**The Height of Summer**    157
Tomatoes, Eggplant, Peppers, Corn, and Okra

## Colorful Chicories 191
Frisée, Escarole, Radicchio, Belgian Endive, and Puntarelle

## Essential Greens 205
Kale, Collard Greens, Broccoli Rabe, Chard, Spinach, Amaranth,
and Asian Greens

## Heading into Winter 223
Cabbage, Broccoli, Cauliflower, Kohlrabi, and Brussels Sprouts

## Ripe Summer Fruit 243
Cherries, Apricots, Plums, Peaches, and Nectarines

## Just-Picked Berries 263
Strawberries, Raspberries, Blackberries, Blueberries,
Huckleberries, Mulberries, and Red Currants

## Autumn Fruits and Nuts 281
Figs, Grapes, Apples, Pears, Quince, Persimmons, Pomegranates,
Walnuts, Hazelnuts, and Almonds

## Sweet and Savory Citrus 307
Lemons, Limes, Oranges, Grapefruit, Kumquats, Mandarin Oranges,
and Citron

## Preserving Vegetables and Fruits 325
Home Canning, Pickles, Jams and Jellies, Candied Fruit, Liqueurs,
and Dried Fruit

# Part II: Seed to Seed
## Growing the New Kitchen Garden

## Plant Wherever You Are 359

## It's All About the Soil 361
Soil, Compost, Minerals, Cover Crops, Potting Soil

## Preparing the Beds 373
Garden Planning, Soil Beds, Extending the Seasons, Containers

## Seeds, Seedlings, and Healthy Plants 387
Sowing Seeds, Seedlings, Planting, Water, Plant Foods, Cultivation

## Harvesting Flavor 399
Peak Harvest, Curing and Storing, Saving Seeds

## Fruit in the Garden 403
Selecting Varieties, Planting, Pruning and Shaping, Harvest

## Tools and Resources 411

## Glossary 416

## Index 422

# Part I

# Flavor as Inspiration

## Varieties in the Garden—Recipes for the Kitchen

# My Kitchen Garden

## Growing What I Love to Eat

I STARTED MY KITCHEN GARDEN because I was longing for mesclun, that very particular French salad made of distinctive sweet and bitter greens and herbs. I had been daunted by the thought of growing food, but then, driven by the desire for that flavor from Nice, I turned my backyard into a salad garden for the restaurant. My success surprised and delighted me. I was so excited to have my yard filled with the lettuces I loved.

You do not need a large backyard to start a garden. There are many other underused locations waiting just for you: balconies and windowsills, rooftops, vacant lots—and schoolyards! Tragically, supermarkets have numbed us with the convenience of the same mass-produced fruits and vegetables year-round—to the point that most of us consider a garden unnecessary. Growing a few lettuces or tomatoes is pleasurable, but it is so much more than that—for the future of the planet, it is a necessity that we become caretakers of the land. Fortunately, this is easy to do—and affordable, too.

We have been thoroughly indoctrinated from childhood to think that we can't grow our own food—or cook, for that matter—because it is too much work and takes too much time, that the climate is not right, or that there isn't enough room. But that is not so. When I was very young, my family had a victory garden in our New Jersey backyard, and we were not alone. With Eleanor Roosevelt leading the charge with her garden on the White House lawn, more than twenty million victory gardens were planted during World War II, and they produced more than nine million tons of fresh vegetables. I find it incredibly inspiring that the White House has a kitchen garden again, after too many years—especially now, when so many of us want to grow beautiful edible plants instead of lawns.

The lettuce garden in my backyard moved to a farm long ago, but my kitchen garden continues to grow. The grassy area of my tiny yard gets smaller and smaller every year. But I couldn't live without my beds of lettuces! Herbs are planted throughout; I depend on them daily. I let rocket reseed itself all over the garden to eat young in salads, with its flowers sprinkled over, or wilted in pasta sauce when it matures. In summer, I grow cherry tomatoes and beans. In fall and winter, I have plots of chicories, kales, and chard. There is plenty of fruit, too—a dwarf apple and a large Gravenstein, a small Meyer lemon, a kumquat, a Fuyu persimmon, and a small thicket of raspberry canes. I tuck edible plants in among the roses, and they are as beautiful as their neighboring flowers. I have a couple of chairs and a small table, and a little grill is set up nearby so I can cook and eat right in the garden. I love to watch the ebb and flow of growth: tiny sprouts as they push up from the soil, blue borage flowers reaching out to bees and birds, the burgeoning harvest as it ripens. I feel connected to the whole cycle of life.

My own path to gardening has been through taste. I am forever falling in love with the fantastic range of varieties available for almost every food plant. Learning to discern these subtleties of texture and flavor—learning to distinguish an Elberta peach from a Sun Crest—is a thrill for me. Using hand-selected produce that is still full of life and vitality, just picked from the vine or pulled from the ground, is what makes cooking not just good, but irresistible.

Gardening has also taught me empathy for farmers and farm workers and respect for the hard work they do growing our food and taking care of the land. It makes us all remember that food is precious, and we are dependent on the land for our survival. It is all about the land. That's the reason I wanted to write this book. One of my most powerful gardening experiences has been watching the children at The Edible Schoolyard, a kitchen garden planted at Martin Luther King Jr. Middle School, a public school in Berkeley, California. Every time I see them measuring the vegetable beds for their math class, or harvesting ancient grains out in the garden for a history class, or stealing a taste of a ripe mulberry, I am reminded that there is nothing more transformational than the experience of being in nature. We have been separated from it, but as soon as we dig our hands into the soil and start watching things grow, we fall in love effortlessly—we realize we are a part of nature. I have seen this transformation happen in a school full of teenagers; I have seen it happen at the Homeless Garden Project in Santa Cruz; I have seen it happen with inmates in a jail. This connection to and respect for nature can be awakened in all of us.

The chapters of this book are filled with the experience of extraordinary farmers and cooks that I have met over the past forty years. It is with their collective knowledge that we have tried to demystify gardening, by providing recipes for cultivation and offering the most enticing dishes we make from our harvest. Each recipe celebrates the flavor of the delicious varieties of fruits and vegetables we have discovered in the fields of our farmer-gastronomes, heritage varietals that have been lost in the industrial farms in this country. Carlo Petrini, the founder of Slow Food International, has said that cooks need to be gardeners and gardeners need to be gastronomes in order to ensure the sustainability of our food system. Thomas Jefferson, our country's most celebrated farmer-gastronome, is an inspiring example. The garden was the passion of his life. He had an adventurous palate and a profound respect for agrarian values. He planned his garden for the pleasures of the table and combed the world for interesting and tasty plants to grow. I love knowing that he sowed a thimbleful of lettuce seeds every week to ensure there was fresh salad on the table every night. Today Monticello is more than a landmark; it is a national treasury of heirloom seeds, a place of enduring values, where the roots of our democracy still thrive.

Tending the soil, planting, and growing food in this way has had a long and important history in this country. If we let ourselves, we can easily return to this tradition. And what a revolutionary idea: That we can preserve the land by nurturing the vital link between taste, cooking, and gardening! It can be as simple as putting a seed in the ground and watching it grow.

# Fragrant and Beautiful

## Herbs and Herb Flowers

HERBS DEFINE MY COOKING. They provide the freshness—aliveness, really—and the beauty, fragrance, and flavor that inspire and compel me in the kitchen. Branches and bouquets of herbs flavor my stocks, soups, roasts, and stews; the leaves of tender herbs are tossed into salads; chopped herbs are stirred into sauces and scattered over any number of dishes to add a final burst of freshness. And finally, my favorite way to end a meal is with a glass of tisane—fresh herbs infused into boiling water. My yard is filled with a long list of varieties that give me a great sense of satisfaction and the security that I have something delicious to cook.

## Recipes

Parsley and Herb Salad  11

Basil Mayonnaise  13

Chilled Beet Soup with Dill  14

Herb Noodles  15

Wild Salmon Carpaccio with Chervil and
Green Coriander Seeds  16

Green Rice Pilaf with Cilantro and Onions  17

Black Bean and Epazote Tostadas  18

Sorrel Cream Sauce  19

Anise Hyssop and Cucumber Salad  20

Crab Salad with Tarragon and Red Belgian Endive  21

Roast Leg of Lamb with Spring Herbs  22

Marjoram, Garlic, and Marash Pepper Sauce  23

Pork Shoulder Braised in Milk with Sage  23

Thyme-Scented Baby Back Ribs  25

Lamb Kebabs with Oregano and Garlic  26

Fried Rosemary  27

Lovage Meatballs  28

Pounded Almond and Mint Pasta Sauce  29

Candied Mint Leaves  30

Borage Cocktail  31

Lemon Verbena Ice Cream  32

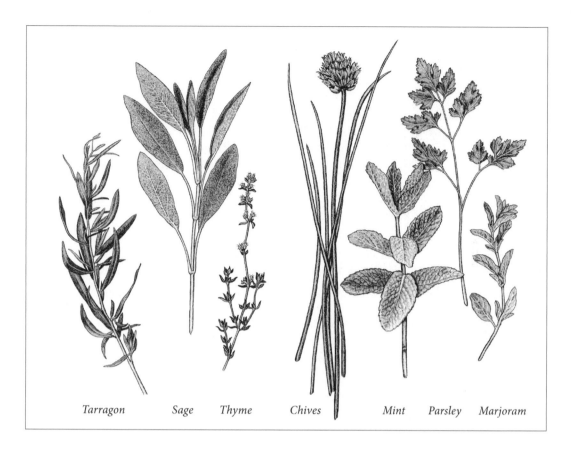

Tarragon    Sage    Thyme    Chives    Mint    Parsley    Marjoram

# Herbs in the Garden

If you only plant one thing, plant some herbs. They are easy to grow and offer so much in return. Basically, herbs are wild, primitive plants that require very little care. Throughout the summer and fall, they lend a wonderful palette of color and texture to the landscape. In spring, perennial herbs erupt in colorful blooms, and depending on where you live, many herbs stay green year-round. Scatter them throughout your garden to take advantage of their fragrance and beauty, and plant your favorites near the kitchen where they are easy to get to.

The leaves are not the only useful part of herbs; the flowers and seeds are quite tasty as well. Sprinkle them on salads, over pastas, soups, or anywhere else you would strew herbs. Tiny chervil and thyme blossoms, bell-shaped sage and rosemary blooms, and tender dill heads all lend sweet flavor and beauty. The flowering heads of cilantro and dill produce culinary seeds to harvest (coriander seed is from cilantro). Fresh green coriander seeds crushed in a mortar and pestle make a standout addition to an olive oil salsa or compound butter. Immature dill and fennel heads are a pickler's prize. Dried, the seeds make wonderful spices, much more pungent than those bought in a jar. Herb branches thrown on the embers of a grill or wood-fired oven subtly perfume foods. Toss them in during the last few minutes of cooking.

The herbs I grow the most of are the building blocks of French and Italian cuisine, but other cuisines prize different herbs. Plant your garden to reflect your tastes, and as your herb garden grows—as I am sure it will—I recommend looking through catalogs and cookbooks to discover other herbs to try both in the garden and the kitchen.

Herbs are mostly broken into two groups: annuals and perennials (with a subgroup of half-hardy perennials). The growing cycle of annual herbs is completed in a single season and they must be resown or planted each year. Their seeds are plentiful and quite easy to propagate. Sow them individually or as a patch. They do best in well-draining soil. Strategically placed, they make good use of the areas between slow-growing plants or under plants that tower over the ground. Parsley and chervil will tolerate some shade. Annuals are particularly easy to grow in containers outside or on a sunny windowsill.

Annual herbs include basil, borage, chervil, cilantro, dill, epazote, parsley, and shiso. These all grow rapidly—and they are all quick to bolt (grow tall, flower, and go to seed). To prolong their life, pinch off the bolting tips and flower buds. This also encourages bushy growth for a greater harvest. Consistent watering is important, as very dry soil will cause the plants to rush to seed. It is always worthwhile to let a few plants go through the stages of flowering and developing seeds. Save the seeds, or allow them to reseed or self-sow. They

will sprout again and again over the years, rewarding you with fresh herbs early in the season. In the spring, if you are not sure what is weed or herb, pinch off a leaf and taste it: even the first leaves of herbs will have a marked flavor. If you need to thin your plot, enjoy the thinnings as a flavorful, elegant garnish.

Perennial herbs include chives, garlic chives, hyssop, lovage, mint, sage, sorrel, tarragon, thyme, and winter savory. Half-hardy perennials include anise hyssop, bay laurel, lemon verbena, marjoram, oregano, and rosemary. These herbs will live for many years when grown in the proper conditions. Hardy perennials will overwinter in mild to cold winters; half-hardy herbs need a milder winter to survive, although in some areas they can be protected with a deep mulch and nursed through some cold. In very cold climates, plant perennial herbs in pots and bring them inside to a sunny spot during the cold months. Containers may also be the best bet for many herbs in hot and humid climates.

Perennials can be difficult to start from seeds. Try cuttings or divisions, or purchase seedlings. Be sure to choose a culinary variety; many widely available ornamental varieties are not at all good in the kitchen. Situate the plants in full sun and well-drained soil. Once established, perennial herbs thrive on a little benign neglect, and their aromatic nature makes them fairly impervious to pests. To help the plants keep their shape and vigor, prune them annually, right after they have flowered. Trim only soft new growth.

*Flowering parsley*

## Parsley (*Petroselinum crispum*)

Parsley is a staple in my kitchen for its bright green flavor and cleansing freshness. I use the stems to flavor broths and soups and use the leaves for sauces, as a salad with lemon and Parmesan, and, chopped and scattered, as a final garnish. Parsley and garlic are a perfect pair, the fresh green parsley counterbalancing the pungent spicy garlic. Many a pasta sauce is started or finished with a mix of the two. *Persillade* is the French name for a mixture of chopped parsley and garlic. Add some lemon zest and you have Italian *gremolata*. Each of them is a perfect last touch for many dishes. When you add olive oil to gremolata, along with capers and salt (or anchovies), you have *salsa verde*, a fantastic sauce to drizzle over meats, vegetables, and fish.

There are two varieties of parsley: flat leaf and curly leaf. I use and grow the flat-leaf variety the most. Curly parsley is classically used for tabbouleh and other Middle Eastern chopped green salads.

Parsley seed takes up to three weeks to germinate, so don't give up on it if you are starting from seed. Parsley plants need consistent watering to perform well and they like a feeding of compost now and then. In colder climates, parsley is planted as an annual, but it is a biennial herb, meaning that it goes to seed in the second year of its life. It will overwinter in mild climates, and once established, reseed easily. A good-size parsley patch is a welcome addition to any kitchen garden.

## Parsley and Herb Salad

In the spring, parsley is abundant and tender. It shoots up along with other spring herbs such as chervil, chives, and tarragon. I love to harvest them all together to make this fantastic salad. As the season progresses and the parsley becomes sturdier, other herbs, such as thyme, savory, and marjoram, have tender new growth and blossoms that you can pick and toss together. They are married into a delightful salad with lemon juice, olive oil, and Parmesan cheese. It can be piled up next to rich roasts or grilled fish and it makes a great standup appetizer tucked into a lettuce leaf. Shave in a little radish for color and zing.

Gather a small handful of parsley per person. Remove the leaves and tender stems from the main stalks. Toss the stalks into the compost (or nibble on them while you make the salad) and put the leaves in a bowl of cold water. Gather a large handful of other herbs—chervil, tarragon, cilantro, shiso, mint, or chives—pluck off the leaves and tender stems and add them to the water. Drain the leaves and dry well. Place them in a bowl and sprinkle with sea salt, a squeeze of lemon juice, a drizzle of extra-virgin olive oil, and a crack of pepper. Toss and taste. Add salt, lemon, or oil as needed. Using a sharp vegetable peeler, shave a few slices of Parmesan cheese into the bowl, enough so everyone gets a couple shavings, and toss gently. If they are available, scatter the salad with borage and nasturtium flowers. Serve.

## Basil  (*Ocimum basilicum*)

Basil tastes of summer to me. Tomato salads, pasta with pesto, and *soupe au pistou* jump to mind immediately. The spicy and warm, aromatic flavor of basil brightens anything it is added to—even cocktails and desserts. There are many different kinds of basil: large-leaf *Genovese*, tiny-leaf *Fino Verde*, reddish purple *Dark Opal* basil, and frilly *Purple Ruffles* are the varieties I use the most. Some others are *Thai* basil, *lemon* basil, and *lime* basil. *African Blue* basil is a gorgeous perennial, highly aromatic basil with greenish purple leaves on a tall, very hardy plant. The flavor is quite strong; I use it mostly for tisane and pick the branches for fragrant bouquets.

Basil will stay greener when torn or cut in a chiffonade instead of chopped. Stack a few leaves neatly and then roll them, lengthwise, into a cigar shape and cut across into thin (or thick) ribbons. The leaves will only oxidize and turn dark where they have been cut. Basil will quickly turn black when scattered over a hot dish. Stir it in instead and allow it to just heat through; it will stay green longer this way. When making vinaigrette, add a sprig to flavor the vinaigrette and then add a fresh chiffonade just before serving.

When harvesting basil, pick leaves and pinch off the tops to encourage bushier growth. As flowers develop, cut them off before they have the chance to mature and your plants will keep producing for quite some time. Basil is cold sensitive, so don't plant out too early, and water the plants consistently to keep them from bolting.

# Basil Mayonnaise

MAKES 1 CUP

Pounded basil makes a beautiful green mayonnaise. Serve it with grilled fish or a tomato salad.

Pick the leaves from:
> ½ **bunch of basil (about ½ cup lightly packed)**

Coarsely chop the leaves and pound them to a paste in a mortar with:
> **Salt**

Add:
> **1 egg yolk**
> **1 teaspoon water**

Whisk the yolk, water, and basil together. Into a cup with a pour spout, measure:
> **1 cup olive oil**

Very slowly dribble the oil into the egg yolk, whisking constantly. As the egg yolk absorbs oil, the sauce will thicken, lighten in color, and become opaque. This will happen rather quickly. Then you can add the oil a little faster, whisking all the while.

If the sauce is thicker than you like, thin it with a few drops of water. Taste and add more salt, if necessary.

VARIATIONS

• Substitute ½ teaspoon lemon juice in place of half the water.

• Instead of basil, use a mix of other tender herbs such as chervil, parsley, chives, tarragon, or very tender thyme or anise hyssop.

• Pound 1 or 2 cloves of garlic in the mortar before adding the basil leaves.

• If your olive oil is especially pungent, substitute vegetable oil for part of the total quantity.

# Dill (*Anethum graveolens*)

I avoided using dill for many years, but now I love it. I like the freshness and the deep, almost caraway-seed flavor it adds to food. When I am sick I crave chicken soup with a sprinkle of freshly cut leaves. Add dill to salads and soups, both chilled and hot, and use it to flavor pickles. Cucumbers and dill is a classic combination. Dill goes to seed quite readily, which is a good thing: the seeds are delicious. Fresh and dried seed heads have different flavors, so experiment with both.

Annual dill is quite beautiful in the garden and self-seeds quite readily. Keep it moist and protected from harsh, hot afternoons. Dill will grow quite tall as it goes to seed, so situate it where it won't make too much shade as it shoots up. Stagger sowings over the spring and summer to have fresh leaves and mature seeds throughout the growing season.

## Chilled Beet Soup with Dill

MAKES 6 CUPS

This soup is more like a liquid salad than a chilled soup. The beets can be roasted ahead. Roasting them with different spices will add to the flavor of the soup. Fennel seed and fenugreek is one of my favorite blends. If your beets still have their tops, steam or sauté them and add them to the soup, too. Or serve them marinated and wrapped in a piece of prosciutto alongside the soup with some crusty bread for a lovely light lunch.

Preheat the oven to 400°F. Trim the leaves from:

**1 bunch of beets**

Wash the beets well and put them in an ovenproof pan in a single layer. Add:

**¼ inch water**

**1 teaspoon whole spices (optional)**

Cover and roast until tender, around 45 minutes to an hour. Let the beets cool, then trim and peel them. Cut into a fine dice, or grate on the large holes of a box grater.

Mix together with:

**2 scallions, trimmed and cut fine**

**1 medium or 2 small cucumbers,
 peeled, seeded (if needed), and
 diced**

**2 tablespoons chopped fresh dill
 leaves**

**3 tablespoons crème fraîche or yogurt
Salt**

Stir in:

**2 cups buttermilk**

**A splash of red wine vinegar**

Chill thoroughly. Taste for salt and adjust as needed. Serve in chilled bowls with a sprinkle of chopped dill leaves.

VARIATIONS

- Garnish with chopped hard-cooked egg.
- Stir in chopped cooked beet greens.
- Purée the soup for a velvety bright pink soup. Use only half the dill when puréeing, and save the other half for a garnish.

## Chervil (*Anthriscus cerefolium*)

Chervil is a lacy tender herb with a mild licorice flavor. We use it a lot at Chez Panisse, whole or chopped, in salads, fresh sauces, and other cold dishes. It is a principal ingredient in the French herb mix known as *fines herbes*, along with chives, parsley, and tarragon. I use chervil whenever a delicate flavor and texture is called for and I always mix some into my mesclun baby salad mix. Sprigs scattered across a dish make a beautiful and flavorful garnish. I love it on poached and soft scrambled eggs. The tiny starry white flowers are lovely, too.

Chervil is an annual herb and very sensitive to heat. It thrives in spring and fall, self-seeds readily, and pops up again when weather conditions are favorable. It will grow in summer when protected from the heat of the afternoon.

# Herb Noodles

This is a fun way to make pasta. Whole herb leaves are pressed into the dough and as it is rolled out they can be seen silhouetted within the noodles. The herb flavor is more pronounced and distinct than it is in green pasta made with a purée of spinach and herbs. Cut the noodles extra wide or in *fazzoletti* ("handkerchief squares"). I like to serve them with the meat and juices of a tender braise, or with spring vegetables, butter, and Parmesan cheese. This pasta is tricky to use for ravioli or other stuffed pasta.

Make Farro Tagliatelle dough (page 313) (or make it using the same method, but with a different whole-grain flour—or all white flour). When the pasta has been rolled ⅛ inch thick, place clean, dry, whole chervil and parsley leaves (without stems) on half the length of the dough. Fold the other half over the herbs and press the two layers together. Continue rolling out the dough to the desired thickness. Cut the noodles in strips or shapes with a scalloped pastry cutter or a sharp knife.

Less tender herbs, such as rosemary and savory, should be chopped before being placed on the pasta, because whole leaves will tear the dough as it is rolled out.

## Cilantro (*Coriandrum sativum*)

Cilantro, also known as coriander, makes Mexican, Indian, and Chinese cuisines sing. Some people are sensitive to its flavor, but I love it. The tender leaves and stems are delicious both raw and cooked. Use it as a scattering herb to add a final touch of flavor, or chop or pound it into fresh sauces, salsas, and raitas. Cook it into pilafs, vegetable braises, and soups. The flowers and seeds are fantastic to cook with, too. The green, still-unripe seeds are a heady mix of fresh cilantro and coriander seed flavors. They are a real treat to cook with. Add whole coriander seeds to pickle brines and poaching liquids for sweet flavor. Eggplant and coriander are especially delicious together. Try seasoning your eggplant purée or eggplant caviar with pounded coriander seeds, either green or dried.

Cilantro is a tender annual and bolts quickly in hot weather. Stagger plantings every few weeks to have it around as long as the weather holds. Pinch back flowering stalks to help prolong production. Dry the mature seeds to cook with or to plant again next spring.

# Wild Salmon Carpaccio with Chervil and Green Coriander Seeds

4 SERVINGS

Wild salmon is very lean and fine, a true delicacy. When it is pounded thin, its color becomes beautifully translucent. Salmon carpaccio may sound difficult to make, but the flesh flattens readily and easily. Spread on a cold plate and decorated with herbs and blossoms, it is gorgeous—and packed with flavor. Pounded fresh coriander seeds are a revelation.

Put four 8- to 9-inch round salad plates in the refrigerator to chill.

Remove any pinbones (a pair of needle-nose pliers is a good tool to use) from:

**One 8-ounce wild salmon fillet, skin removed**

Slice the fish into 8 same-size pieces. Cut 8 pieces of parchment paper, slightly larger than the salad plates. (If you have round cake pan liners, they work perfectly for this.)

Pour into a ramekin or other small dish:

**1 tablespoon extra-virgin olive oil**

Brush a piece of parchment with oil and place 2 of the salmon slices side by side in the center of the paper, flat sides abutting each other. Brush another piece of parchment with oil and put it on top of the salmon. Make 3 more parchment-salmon "sandwiches" with the rest of the salmon. Put them all in the refrigerator to stay cold. Take one out of the refrigerator and use a meat pounder, a mallet and wide metal spatula, or the flat bottom of a frying pan to gently pound out the salmon round and thin. Pound with a downward and outward motion, forming the fish into a flat disk. Rotate the parchment as you pound and lift it to the light now and then to see whether the salmon is being flattened evenly. Make the circle of fish just smaller than the chilled plate. Repeat with all the pieces. Keep refrigerated until ready to serve.

Prepare the garnish ingredients. Remove the seeds from:

**A mature cilantro flower head**

Pound slightly using a mortar and pestle. Remove the blossoms from:

**A few sprigs of flowering herbs (such as chervil, cilantro, thyme, borage, rosemary, sage, or nasturtium)**

Gather:

**Salt**
**Fresh-ground black pepper**
**1 lemon, cut in half, seeds removed**
**Extra-virgin olive oil**
**Leaves from 4 large chervil sprigs**

When ready to serve, carefully peel the top sheet of parchment away from the fish and invert onto a cold plate. Peel off the other piece of paper. Season with salt and pepper. Squeeze lemon juice over and drizzle with olive oil. Scatter the crushed coriander and herb blossoms over and serve immediately.

VARIATIONS

◆ Other fish, such as halibut, make good carpaccio. Be sure to use the freshest of fish. Let your fishmonger know before you purchase the fish that you plan on eating it raw.
◆ Use dried coriander seeds if fresh are not available.
◆ Use chopped tender herbs if blossoms are not available. Try tarragon, basil, shiso, anise hyssop, or tiny nasturtium leaves.

# Green Rice Pilaf with Cilantro and Onions

4 SERVINGS

This rice is perfect to serve with Squash Blossom Quesadillas (page 149) or Chile Verde (page 181). The stems of cilantro have as much flavor as—or more than—the leaves, so be sure to use both in this recipe.

Measure:

**½ cup cilantro sprigs, tightly packed**
**½ cup parsley leaves, tightly packed**

Trim the stem from:

**1 poblano pepper**
**1 serrano pepper (optional)**

Cut the peppers in half lengthwise and remove the veins and seeds. Cut the peppers into smaller pieces.
Purée the herbs and peppers in a blender with:

**½ cup water**

Heat a heavy-bottomed pot over medium-high heat and pour in:

**2 tablespoons olive oil or vegetable oil**

Add:

**1 cup long-grain brown rice**

Cook, stirring now and then, for 5 minutes. Add:

**½ white onion, finely diced**
**2 garlic cloves, peeled and chopped**

Cook another 5 minutes. The onions should be softened and the rice lightly toasted. Pour in the herb and pepper purée along with:

**2 cups light chicken stock or water**
**Salt**

Bring to a boil and turn down to a bare simmer. Cover and cook for 45 minutes. All the liquid should be absorbed; if not, cook another few minutes. Let sit, covered, for 5 minutes. Gently stir the rice before serving.

VARIATIONS

◆ Substitute epazote, *hoja santa* (*Piper auritum*, a giant tropical Mexican herb), Mexican oregano, or spinach for some of the parsley.
◆ Chop the herbs and peppers instead of puréeing them.

## Epazote *(Chenopodium ambrosioides)*

Epazote flavors Mexican cuisine, especially beans, with a pungent intensity reminiscent of mint and tarragon. It adds zest to quesadillas and a pot of black beans is improved by a sprig.

Epazote is a hardy annual that takes hot, dry weather well. In mild climates, it easily reseeds itself.

# Black Bean and Epazote Tostadas

4 SERVINGS

Velvety soft black beans spread on a crispy fried tortilla are heavenly, alone or topped with a variety of vegetables and salsa. Epazote and fried onions add just the right touch of flavor to the beans.

Heat a low-sided, heavy-bottomed pot or pan over medium heat. Measure in:

> **1 tablespoon olive oil or fresh lard**

Swirl to coat the bottom of the pan and add:

> **½ white onion, diced**
> **2 small epazote sprigs**
> **1 smoked dried chile (optional)**

Cook, stirring now and then, until the onions soften, about 5 minutes.

Add:

> **3 cups cooked black beans**
> **1 cup bean cooking liquid**

Cook at a simmer for 5 minutes. Mash the beans coarsely (a potato or bean masher works well) and cook for another 5 minutes over very low heat. Add more bean liquid if the beans get too stodgy. Taste for salt and season as needed.

Heat, in a small cast-iron or other heavy pan:

> **1 inch vegetable oil**

Fry, 1 at a time:

> **8 tortillas**

Slip each tortilla gently into the hot oil and cook about 2 minutes, turn, and cook another minute or so. Remove to drain on absorbent paper or a towel, and season with salt. The tortillas should be lightly golden and crisp once cool. (Cook longer if they are leathery and not crispy.)

Gather any number of the following toppings:

> **Ripe avocado slices**
> **Thin crème fraîche**
> **Cilantro sprigs**
> **Sliced scallions**
> **Sungold Cherry Tomato Salsa (the variation with poblano) (page 165)**
> **Crumbled queso fresco or cotija cheese**
> **Thinly sliced jalapeño or serrano peppers**
> **Thinly sliced cabbage tossed with lime and salt**
> **Lime wedges**

When ready to serve, spread the warm beans on the crispy tortillas and garnish with the toppings.

# Sorrel (*Rumex acetosa*)

Sorrel has long green leaves that bring spinach to mind. After a bite, its bright lemon flavor banishes any thoughts of comparison. Mixed with cream it makes a classic sauce for fish that tastes quite good on pork and steamed vegetables, too. Use it raw in salads, salsa verde, or an omelet. Sauté it with spinach for a soup or a side dish. Use it where you would otherwise spritz a bit of lemon.

Sorrel's tender leaves belie its hardy constitution. Heat will not destroy it and it will winter over in quite harsh weather. Sorrel grows into a lovely dark green bush that can be picked throughout the growing season, which, in very mild climates, will be all year.

# Sorrel Cream Sauce

MAKES ½ CUP

This sauce marries luscious crème fraîche with tangy sorrel to make a light creamy sauce with spirit. I have loved this sauce ever since the first time I ate it in France, at the Maison Troisgros.

Remove and discard the stems from:
   **1 large bunch of sorrel**
Coarsely chop the leaves, or cut them into a chiffonade.
In a small pot or skillet over medium heat, melt:
   **1 tablespoon butter**
Add the sorrel and cook until wilted. Don't be surprised: it will turn a khaki green color. Transfer to a dish and set aside.
Wash out the pot and pour in:
   **¼ cup water**
   **¼ cup dry white wine**
Bring to a boil and cook for a few minutes to slightly reduce. Swirl in:
   **1 tablespoon butter, cut into small
      pieces**
   **3 tablespoons crème fraîche**
Simmer for 1 minute, turn off the heat, stir in the sorrel, and season with:
   **Salt**
   **Fresh-ground black pepper**

VARIATIONS
• Use court bouillon (vegetable stock seasoned with white wine) in place of the water and wine.
• You can use 2 teaspoons white wine vinegar instead of wine; just don't reduce.
• Dice a small shallot and cook it in the butter before adding the sorrel.

## Anise Hyssop (*Agastache foeniculum*)

Anise hyssop, though distantly related to common hyssop, tastes nothing like it. The tender serrated leaves have a light minty-licorice fragrance with a very sweet flavor. The purple blossoms are sweet and aromatic. Use both the leaves and flowers in salads, salsa verde, fish tartare, and carpaccio and also with mild vegetables, such as cucumbers and summer squash. I especially like it with melon.

Anise hyssop is a tender perennial that is easily grown from seed. The plants grow fairly tall, so relegate them to an area where their height won't create unwanted shade for other plants. Bees and other pollinators love the blossoms, too.

## Anise Hyssop and Cucumber Salad

This is a very simple and refreshing salad. Use as many kinds of cucumbers as you can find: lemon, Japanese, Persian, and Armenian make a tasty and pretty mix. Cut each variety into a different shape: wedges, roll-cut batons, slices, and so on. I don't bother with making a vinaigrette as the cucumbers taste best very lightly dressed.

Prepare the equivalent of ½ medium cucumber per person, peeling if needed. Cut into bite-size pieces and put them in a pretty serving bowl (with low sides, if possible). Count 2 small or 1 large anise hyssop leaf per person, stack them, and cut them crosswise into thin strips. Cut the strips in half if they are long. Toss with the cucumbers. Sprinkle the cucumbers lightly with red wine vinegar and salt and then with a light drizzle of extra-virgin olive oil. Toss and taste. Adjust as needed. If available, scatter a handful of anise hyssop blossoms over the top.

## Tarragon (*Artemisia dracunculus*)

Tarragon has an intensely aromatic and clear, licorice-like flavor. It is good to remember that a little is delightful, but a lot will quickly overwhelm a dish. Béarnaise sauce is not possible without tarragon, and a steak with béarnaise is a classic. Vinegar infused with tarragon has a wonderful light touch when used to dress salads, either with or without the addition of a few fresh leaves. I am fond of it combined with horseradish (see page 86). Look for *French* tarragon plants; *Russian* tarragon has little flavor.

Tarragon is a hardy deciduous perennial that will come back in the spring in all but the coldest climates. Mulch will keep the roots protected in winter and helps guarantee a spring return. Root division after a few years will result in stronger-flavored plants.

# Crab Salad with Tarragon and Red Belgian Endive

4 SERVINGS

On the Pacific coast, we enjoy large sweet Dungeness crab from late fall through early summer, but other types of crab will make delicious salad as well. Fresh tarragon enhances the clean sweet flavor of crab and other shellfish.

Bring a large pot of salted water to a boil. Add:

**1 live Dungeness crab (or enough other crab to yield about ½ pound picked meat)**

Cook for 13 minutes. Remove the crab and let it drain and cool. When cool enough to handle, pull off the large top shell and remove the fibrous lungs. Rinse lightly, pull off the legs and split the main body in half down the center. Crack the legs, and pick the crabmeat clean from the body and legs. Put the meat in a bowl. Gently go through the picked meat with your fingers to remove any last stray bits of shell. Refrigerate until ready to use.

Make the dressing. Mix together in a small bowl:

**1 shallot, finely diced**
**1 tarragon sprig**
**Zest of ½ lemon**
**2 teaspoons lemon juice**
**2 teaspoons white wine or Champagne vinegar**
**A pinch of cayenne (optional)**
**Salt**
**Fresh-ground black pepper**

Stir to dissolve the salt and let sit for 10 minutes or more to macerate. Whisk in:

**¼ cup extra-virgin olive oil**

Taste and adjust the salt and acid as needed. Cut the root ends from:

**2 heads of red Belgian endive**

Remove and discard any blemished leaves. Separate the rest of the leaves and put them in a large bowl. Pour in half the vinaigrette and:

**2 scallions, trimmed and sliced thin on a diagonal**

Arrange the leaves on a platter or individual plates. Remove the leaves from:

**A small tarragon sprig**

Take 8 or so leaves and stack them in a neat pile. Cut into a very fine chiffonade—at an acute angle, into long, very thin strips. Add three quarters of the leaves to the cleaned crabmeat and pour in the rest of the vinaigrette. Toss gently. Arrange on and around the endive. Sprinkle over the rest of the tarragon and, if desired, drizzle with:

**Thin crème fraîche (optional)**

# Marjoram *(Origanum majorana)*

Marjoram is addictive. If I am not careful, I find myself scattering it over or stirring it into almost everything I make: green beans, scrambled eggs, grilled fish, tomato sauces, salads, and more. I like to marinate squid or fish in a mixture of chopped marjoram, lemon zest, and dried chile flakes before grilling. The leaves are tender with a spicy, aromatic, mintlike flavor and are used raw or cooked. Marjoram is closely related to oregano but is more brightly flavored than its aggressive cousin. Tender leaves and stems tinged with red give it away.

Being a half-hardy perennial, marjoram is sensitive to cold and may need replanting and tending every year. It winters over well in mild climates. Pinch off the flowering stems as they appear, to keep growth tender and productive.

# Roast Leg of Lamb with Spring Herbs

8 SERVINGS

Season, the night before, if possible:

    **1 leg of pasture-raised lamb (about 7 pounds with bone in), boned and butterflied**

with:

    **Salt**
    **Fresh-ground black pepper**

The next day, remove the lamb from the refrigerator. Remove the leaves from

    **1 bunch of marjoram**
    **½ bunch of parsley**
    **¼ bunch of lemon thyme**

Chop. Mix with:

    **1 bunch of chives, chopped**

Open the leg of lamb, interior side up, and drizzle with:

    **Extra-virgin olive oil**

Sprinkle the chopped herbs over the lamb. Roll up the leg and tie securely with cotton twine. Let sit for ½ hour to come to room temperature.

Meanwhile, preheat the oven to 375°F. Strew over the bottom of a roasting pan that the leg of lamb will just fit in:

    **1 bunch of marjoram**
    **¼ bunch of lemon thyme**

Place the leg on top of the herbs and cook until done. This will take about 1 hour and 20 minutes for medium rare (125°F internal temperature). Check the roast after 1 hour, monitoring the internal temperature with an instant-read thermometer. When the lamb is done, remove it from the oven and let it rest for 20 minutes before slicing the meat. This allows the juice to stabilize and makes the roast more succulent.

When ready to serve, remove the strings from the roast. Collect the juices that accumulated while the roast was resting. Slice the meat, sprinkle with a bit of salt, and drizzle with the resting juices. If you like, serve with the marjoram sauce that follows.

## Marjoram, Garlic, and Marash Pepper Sauce

MAKES ¼ CUP

I don't often make sauces that involve reducing stocks and meat juices. Instead, I like to make combinations of herbs, spices, and olive oil to add freshness and bite to grilled or roasted meats and vegetables. Marash pepper is a mildly hot dried red chile, similar to the Aleppo pepper, with an earthy, fruity flavor. This sauce is especially good with lamb.

Mix together:

**2 tablespoons coarsely chopped marjoram leaves**
**1 teaspoon coarsely chopped capers**
**Zest of ½ lemon**
**A large pinch of Marash pepper**
**1 garlic clove, pounded to a paste**
**Salt**
**Fresh-ground black pepper**

Stir in:

**3 tablespoons oil**

Taste for salt and adjust as needed.

VARIATION

◆ Substitute 1 small green garlic stalk, chopped fine, for the pounded garlic.

## Sage (*Salvia officinalis*)

Sage's pebbly gray-green leaves have a strong, almost winey flavor. Pork and winter squash are both classic pairings with sage, and many consider it a necessity in stuffings for turkey and other fowl. American breakfast sausage would not be the same without sage to perfume it. A winter minestrone is warmed by its fragrance in a tasty base of sautéed onions and garlic. The leaves fry nicely for a garnish. And squash ravioli with sage brown butter is always good. Try flattening a couple of leaves onto your next grilled cheese sandwich and let them toast along with the bread.

Spring sage is tender in both flavor and texture, but as the season progresses the flavor becomes more pronounced and the leaves sturdier. Common sage and *Berggarten* are the varieties I recommend. Although they are gorgeous in the garden, avoid variegated and purple sages for cooking as they lend an overly bitter quality to food.

Sage is a beauty in the garden—the plants form soft gray mounds that shoot up stalks of purple trumpet flowers. It thrives with little more than sun and well-draining soil. A hardy perennial, sage will remain evergreen in all but the coldest climates. If allowed to, sage will become woody and rangy: annual pruning after flowering will keep it compact and bushy.

## Pork Shoulder Braised in Milk with Sage

4 SERVINGS

This is a homey, rustic, and utterly delicious way to serve pork. The milk sweetens and caramelizes while cooking, and the lemon and sage give lift and flavor. Any remains of the roast taste great the next day. Serve with soft polenta, roasted potatoes, or homemade pasta to soak up the sauce.

Season, the day before, if possible:

> **One 2½- to 3-pound pork shoulder
> roast, trimmed of excess fat**

with:

> **Salt**
>
> **Fresh-ground black pepper**

Cover and refrigerate for a few hours or overnight. Take the pork out 1 hour before cooking to come to room temperature.

Heat a heavy-bottomed pot in which the roast will fit fairly snugly over medium-high heat. Measure in:

> **1½ tablespoons olive oil or butter**

Add the roast and brown on all sides. Remove it from the pan, pour off all the fat, and add:

> **1 tablespoon butter**
>
> **5 garlic cloves, peeled**
>
> **4 large sage sprigs**

Cook for a couple of minutes to soften the garlic. Return the pork to the pot. Add:

> **3 to 4 cups whole milk**
>
> **2 strips of lemon zest, removed with a
> sharp vegetable peeler**

The milk should come up just over three quarters of the height of the roast. When the milk comes to a boil, turn it down to a bare simmer, and partly cover the pot. Cook at a slow simmer until the meat is tender, about 2 hours. Check the meat now and then, turning the roast and stirring the milk up from the bottom. Add more milk if the level drops below a couple of inches. The sauce will separate and curdle; don't worry, it is supposed to. Once the meat is done, set it aside. Skim the fat from the sauce and reduce it if it seems too thin. Slice the roast and reheat in the sauce. Serve on a warm platter with the sauce poured over.

*Common sage*

*Common thyme*

# Thyme (*Thymus vulgaris*)
# Lemon Thyme (*Thymus citriodorus*)

Thyme is the herb of French cuisine and one I use often. It has a deep, green flavor with a slightly piney aroma that adds depth and complexity without being overbearing. Thyme rarely takes the spotlight but is used to enhance and unify other flavors. I toss its scented leaves into braises, soups, and soufflés. I chop its leaves or strew sprigs into marinades and dry rubs. A bouquet garni, a tied-up bunch of herbs used to flavor stocks and many other preparations, is never without a sprig or two of thyme. I like to cut large bouquets to use as a garnish for a roast or other savory dish. The irregular, charming, curling growth adds the perfect visual touch. There are numerous varieties of thyme available, many of which are ornamental and not useful for cooking. For the kitchen garden, choose *English* and *French* thyme; both are frequently referred to as common thyme.

*Lemon* thyme has a light floral lemony scent. The flavor suits asparagus well. Try roasting spears tossed with olive oil and sprigs of lemon thyme. Court bouillon infused with lemon thyme is a lovely poaching liquid for fish and chicken breasts. After cooking, reduce some of the liquid and swirl in a pat or two of butter for a light and aromatic sauce.

Thyme is a hardy perennial. In cold climates, mulch the plants to help them make it through the winter. Thyme especially prefers well-draining soil. Spring brings a riot of tiny white or pink flowers across the low-growing bushy plants. Thyme plants are like old friends in the kitchen garden, a pleasure to have around.

# Thyme-Scented Baby Back Ribs

4 SERVINGS

Baby back ribs are the ribs on the backside of a pork loin. Their meat is tender and fine, like the loin itself. I like to cook the ribs only a short time, just until they are done. This simple marinade brings out their sweet flavor. If you can, season the ribs the night before.

Trim any excess fat from:

**4 pounds baby back ribs**

Season well with:

**Salt**

**Fresh-ground black pepper**

Drizzle with:

**Extra-virgin olive oil**

Crush using a mortar and pestle and sprinkle over the ribs:

**2 teaspoons coriander seeds**

**½ teaspoon fennel seeds**

Rinse and dry well:

**1 bunch of thyme (2 if bunches are small)**

Strew one quarter of the thyme over the bottom of a dish and lay in one rack of ribs. Strew with thyme. Repeat until all the ribs are in the dish, and refrigerate.

One hour before cooking, light the fire. Bring the ribs out of the refrigerator to come to room temperature. When the embers are medium hot, preheat, clean, and oil the grill. Pull the thyme off the ribs and set aside for later. Put the ribs on the grill, meaty side down, and cook for 7 minutes. Rotate the racks every few minutes for even coloring. Turn the ribs and cook for another 7 minutes. After 5 minutes throw the marinade herbs on the coals to perfume the ribs. When the ribs are done, let them rest for 5 minutes. Cut and serve.

VARIATIONS

◆ Use other herbs with the thyme such as savory, marjoram, rosemary, sage, or oregano.

◆ Cut thin slices of lemon and scatter on the ribs before strewing with the herbs.

◆ Add a pinch or two of cayenne to the salt-and-pepper seasoning.

## Oregano (*Origanum vulgare*)

Oregano is a stronger flavored cousin of marjoram. It is used extensively in Greek and Italian cooking. Many people prefer its flavor when it is dried; try it both ways, fresh and dried. Oregano complements tomatoes, meat sauces, and vegetable braises. There are many varieties of oregano; my choices for cooking are *Italian* and *Greek*. I also like another oregano, *za'atar* (*Origanum syriacum*), the oregano of Syria and Israel, which has fuzzier leaves and a deeper flavor. It is dried and mixed with sumac, sesame, and other herbs to make a condiment that is also called za'atar.

Oreganos are half-hardy perennials grown as annuals in colder climates. Dig up a plant and transplant to a container to bring inside over winter. Oregano needs little in the garden besides well-draining soil and sun.

*Mexican* oregano (*Lippia graveolens*) is not really an oregano but a hardy cousin of lemon verbena. It has a sharper, more pungent flavor than oregano that adds a distinct flavor to Mexican cuisine. Chile Verde (page 181) would not taste the same without it, nor would tortilla and chicken soup. Traditionally it is used dried, but if you grow it, experiment with using it fresh. It is a tender perennial that grows quite tall with fragrant white blossoms that attract bees and other beneficial garden insects. (*Lippia berlandieri* and *Poliomintha longiflora* are two similar plants also called Mexican oregano.)

# Lamb Kebabs with Oregano and Garlic

4 SERVINGS

Cooking over the fire makes everything taste better and these kebabs are no exception. Set out some freshly made Whole-Wheat Pita Bread (page 132), bowls of Yogurt (page 183), cucumber salad, diced tomatoes, purslane or other greens, mint leaves, chopped scallions, and some sumac and marash pepper for a fun outdoor meal. The kebabs taste best hot off the grill, splashed with a bit of extra marinade. Stuff them into some pita bread with any or all of the accompaniments. Add some summer squash, eggplant, and onions on the grill to complete the meal.

First make the marinade. Mix together:
**½ cup olive oil**
**½ cup lemon juice**
**1 teaspoon dried oregano or**
    **2 teaspoons chopped fresh**
**3 garlic cloves, pounded to a purée**
    **using a mortar and pestle**
**Salt**
Cut into 1½-inch cubes:
**1 to 1½ pounds lamb leg or shoulder**
Trim most of the fat away, but leave some on for flavor and juiciness. Season well with:
**Salt**
**Fresh-ground black pepper**
Thread 5 or 6 cubes of meat onto each skewer. Large, flat, metal skewers are the best, but bamboo work well, too. (Soak the bamboo skewers in water to help keep them from burning.) Lay out the skewers in a low-sided plate or pan and pour two thirds of the

marinade over them. Marinate for at least 1 hour, turning the skewers now and then.

Prepare a hot fire and clean and oil the grill. When the coals are ready and the grill is hot put the skewers on to cook. Turn to cook on all sides. They should be crispy and brown on the outside while still juicy and pink in the middle after 6 minutes or so. Brush the meat with the reserved marinade as it comes off the grill. Serve immediately.

VARIATIONS

✦ Use pork loin, flatiron steak, skinless chicken breast or thighs instead of lamb leg.
✦ Cook the kebabs under the broiler for the same amount of time.

## Rosemary (*Rosmarinus officinalis*)

Rosemary's needlelike leaves are rich in pungent oil with a pinelike flavor. I like to chop it and add it to fava bean purée or mix it into pasta dough. Creamy white beans flavored with rosemary, garlic, and olive oil are one of my winter staples. Nuts roasted with whole leaves are an addictive hors d'oeuvre. Fried rosemary leaves make a wonderful crunchy garnish that adds that *je ne sais quoi* to many a dish. Strewn in the bottom of a roasting pan, the branches make an aromatic bed for roast meat and fowl, and long branches stripped of their leaves (leaving the top leaves in place) make wonderful skewers for grilling poultry livers and tender bits of meat. I frequently light a sprig or branch of rosemary (or sage) with an ember or the flame of a burner to scent the air. The fragrance is uplifting and clean. I like to carry a sprig in my pocket as an aromatic touchstone on a flight or whenever I'm away from the kitchen or garden for a long time. There are a number of cultivars available; my favorite is common rosemary (*Rosmarinus officinalis*), which grows quite well where I live. *Arp* rosemary is exceptionally hardy and thrives in both hotter and colder climates, and *Barbeque* grows very long stems that make good skewers.

Rosemary is a cold-sensitive perennial that is treated as an annual in colder climates. In its native Mediterranean climate it will grow into an evergreen bush. It requires little to thrive. Planting in a container offers the possibility of moving the plants indoors when it gets cold.

## Fried Rosemary

I finish many dishes with fried herbs, on their own or mixed with breadcrumbs. I love the crunch and flavor that they add. Rosemary is my favorite herb to fry, followed by sage, thyme, and savory.

Remove the leaves from a medium sprig of rosemary. Discard the stem. Heat a small heavy-bottomed pan over medium-high heat. Pour in about ½ inch olive oil. When the oil is hot, add the leaves. Don't be surprised: the oil will bubble up when the leaves are added. Let them fry for 1 minute and then scoop out with a slotted spoon or fine strainer before they turn brown. Drain on absorbent paper or towel. Sprinkle with salt and a tiny pinch of cayenne if desired. They will stay crisp for a few hours.

## Lovage *(Levisticum officinale)*

I have a special fondness for lovage. It has a sweet celery flavor that adds a perfect note to meat, especially ground meat. Try it chopped into your next hamburger or added to meatballs. It is great in potato soup. A judicious quantity of young leaves is nice in salads—albacore salad, chicken salad, and cucumber salad with tomato aspic, to name a few.

Lovage is a large hardy perennial that looks like giant flat-leaf parsley. It can grow quite tall, up to eight feet, but it doesn't make it past four in its shaded spot in my garden. It grows best in moist, rich soil.

## Lovage Meatballs

4 SERVINGS

Remove the crust from:
   **2 thick slices crusty day-old bread**
Cut into cubes. You should have about 1 cup. Cover with water and let soak.
Measure into a large bowl:
   **½ pound ground pork**
   **½ pound ground chicken**
   **1 teaspoon salt**
   **¼ teaspoon fresh-ground black pepper**
   **1 tablespoon dry red wine**
   **1 egg**
   **¼ cup grated Parmesan cheese**
   **2 garlic cloves, pounded to a purée**
   **2 teaspoons chopped lovage**
   **2 teaspoons chopped parsley**
   **A pinch of dried chile flakes**
Squeeze the water from the soaking bread

and crumble it into the bowl. Mix gently, using stiff open fingers like a comb, until the ingredients are well combined. Take a small ball of the mixture and pat into a thin patty. Heat a small heavy-bottomed pan over medium-high heat. Add the patty and cook for 3 minutes on each side. Taste for salt and spices, and adjust as needed. Roll the mixture into small meatballs. Refrigerate until needed.

When ready to cook, heat a large pan over medium-high heat. Pour in:
   **Olive oil, enough to generously coat the bottom of the pan**
Carefully add the meatballs in a single layer. Cook until browned, about 5 minutes. Shake the pan to turn and continue to cook until browned on all sides, about another 5 minutes.

VARIATION
• Remove when slightly underdone and finish cooking in a batch of spicy tomato sauce (see page 166).

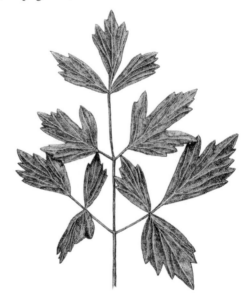

# Mint (*Mentha* spp.)

The refreshing perfume of mint enlivens many sweet and savory preparations. Mint goes well with melons, cucumbers, and summer squash. It is delicious with fresh or salt-cured anchovies. I like it in salsa verde and especially with spring lamb. While in Sicily, I discovered a pasta sauce of pounded almonds and mint that immediately became a household favorite. Infused in hot water, mint makes a delicious tisane. Infused in cream and milk, it makes dynamite mint chocolate-chip ice cream. A few leaves can flavor lemonade, ice tea, fruit spritzers, or refreshing cocktails. Dry some fresh mint at the end of the summer and discover how much better it is than store-bought. There is a vast array of mint varieties, but I find the best variety to cook with is *Spearmint*. Many others are overpowering or bitter. Taste a leaf before committing to planting.

Mint is a very hardy perennial, and it can be quite invasive. Plant it in its own bed, or plant it in a bottomless container sunk into the ground. It sends out runners and is eager to take up as much room as it can. That said, it is a welcome herb to have around and its purple blossoms are pretty in the landscape.

# Pounded Almond and Mint Pasta Sauce

4 SERVINGS (ABOUT 1½ CUPS)

This is an improvisation on basil pesto. I call it La Finca pasta, as I made it on a farm in Puerto Rico where there was lots of mint and no basil or Parmesan cheese. Mint, almonds, and garlic are pounded together with a touch of tomato for balance.

Peel, seed, and dice:
   **1 small tomato**
Blanch for 20 seconds in boiling water:
   **½ cup almonds**
Drain, cool, and slip off the skins.
Using a mortar and pestle, pound to a paste:
   **2 medium garlic cloves**
   **A pinch of salt**
Add the almonds a handful at a time, pounding all the while. Add the diced tomato and pound into the almonds. Remove the nut mixture from the mortar. Chop:
   **3 cups mint leaves**
Add the chopped leaves to the mortar with:
   **A large pinch of salt**
Pound the leaves to a paste. Return the pounded almond mixture to the mortar. Pound the mint and almond mixture together. Continue pounding as you gradually pour in:
   **¼ cup extra-virgin olive oil**
Taste for salt and adjust as needed. Toss the sauce with cooked pasta and a few tablespoons pasta cooking water. Finish the pasta with a drizzle of:
   **Extra-virgin olive oil**

# Candied Mint Leaves

MAKES ABOUT 20 LEAVES

Serve candied mint leaves with a cup of tea or as an after-dinner candy. Chopped, the leaves are fantastic sprinkled over ice cream, sorbet, or chilled melons.

Pick the leaves off:
> **1 bunch of mint**

Select the large, fresh, whole leaves for candying. Save the rest for another use.

Combine in a small bowl:
> **1 egg white (room temperature)**
> **1 teaspoon water**

Whisk the egg white and water together until frothy. With a small pastry brush, paint a thin layer of the egg white onto both sides of the mint leaves. Sprinkle the leaves all over with:
> **Sugar**

Place the sugared leaves on a rack to dry. This will take several hours or overnight. Use immediately or keep in an airtight container for up to a week.

VARIATIONS

◆ Dip one half of each candied mint leaf into melted chocolate. Let the chocolate harden before serving.

◆ To make candied rose petals: Select freshly cut, fragrant unsprayed roses. Before candying, refrigerate the roses so the petals stay firm and crisp. Serve candied rose petals as a candy or sprinkled on strawberry desserts or chocolate ice cream.

# Borage  (*Borago officinalis*)

Borage has beautiful bright blue, star-shaped flowers that complement cucumbers and melon and look gorgeous floating in a glass of lemonade (but be sure to remove the spiny sepals from behind the petals before using). The young leaves taste of cucumber and are good in salads and make a wonderful cocktail. Cook them briefly and chop them into ricotta for a Ligurian ravioli stuffing.

Borage is a tender annual that reseeds readily in temperate climates. Borage attracts bees to the garden like no other plant—they love it.

## Borage Cocktail

MAKES 2 DRINKS

The herb garden is a great place to look for cocktail ingredients. Many tonics and tinctures from medieval monastery gardens have become today's aperitifs and digestifs. This refreshing drink is much easier than making your own liqueur; it can be made at a moment's notice, with delicious and uplifting results.

Pull the tender blue petals away from the green sepals of:

**4 borage flowers**

Set aside.

Measure into a cocktail shaker:

**6 ounces gin (artisanal gin for the best flavor)**

**2 ounces lemon juice**

**4 teaspoons simple syrup (2 parts sugar to 1 part water)**

**2 handfuls of borage leaves (about 6 large or 8 to 10 smaller)**

**6 large ice cubes**

Shake for a full 30 seconds. Taste for sweetness and add more simple syrup or lemon juice as desired. Strain into 2 chilled cocktail glasses and float the borage flowers on top.

VARIATIONS

◆ Substitute gum syrup (simple syrup thickened with gum Arabic) in place of the simple syrup.

◆ Substitute 4 lemon verbena leaves or 3 lemon thyme sprigs for the borage leaves.

◆ Substitute lime juice for the lemon juice and use mint leaves instead of borage leaves.

## Winter Savory (*Satureja montana*)
## Summer Savory (*Satureja hortensis*)

Winter savory (*above*) is a hardy perennial. It is considered to be the herb to serve with beans, and it is indeed quite tasty added to a ragout of fava beans. The leaves have an earthy depth, with a slight bitterness. When very young they are good in salad. When more mature they are too strong to eat raw and are good used wherever thyme is used. Try winter savory in tomato sauce, a braise of duck legs, or a pot roast. In springtime, the bush becomes a soft hill of beautiful white blossoms.

Summer savory, an annual herb, has a wonderful deep earthy flavor with a touch of mint. The leaves are tender enough to use in a vinaigrette or scattered over a salad. I love it with fresh sliced tomatoes and roasted eggplant. Plant seeds or seedlings in early spring and keep the flowers trimmed back to prolong the life of the plants.

# Lemon Verbena *(Aloysia triphylla)*

The leaves of lemon verbena are a fragrant, lemony delight. Ice cream, custard, and roasted berries all achieve greater heights with a quick infusion of its leaves. You can easily flavor sugar syrup with it to add to drinks of all kinds, and it makes the most delightful tisane I know. The leaves are too tough to eat, so they are used to perfume dishes and then removed. When the days grow colder and shorter, dry the leaves before they start to turn yellow; the dried leaves make good tisane all winter long.

A tender annual, lemon verbena is deciduous, except in the far South, where stable day length will keep the leaves growing year-round. The bush will grow quite tall in its favored climate. Grow it in a pot for ease of transport indoors where cold weather would otherwise be its demise.

# Lemon Verbena Ice Cream

MAKES 1 QUART

Lemon verbena infuses tea, custards, and liqueurs with a heady, habit-forming aroma. I find that you get the best flavor after a short infusion of about 5 minutes in hot liquids. Steep the leaves any longer and the more delicate aromas tend to disappear. The ice cream goes beautifully with peaches, nectarines, and berries.

Separate:

    **3 eggs**

Whisk the yolks just enough to break them up.

Heat in a heavy-bottomed pot over medium heat:

    **¾ cup half-and-half**

    **⅓ cup sugar**

    **A pinch of salt**

    **1 cup loosely packed lemon verbena**
        **leaves**

Stir to dissolve the sugar. When the mixture starts to steam, turn off the heat and let the leaves steep for 5 minutes. Strain the mixture, return to the pan, and heat.

Whisk a little of the hot milk into the egg yolks and then whisk the warmed yolks into the hot milk. Cook over medium heat, stirring constantly until the mixture thickens and coats the back of the spoon. Do not allow to come to a boil. When thickened, remove from the heat and strain. Stir in:

    **¾ cup heavy cream**

Chill thoroughly. Freeze in an ice-cream maker according to the manufacturer's instructions. Scrape into a chilled container and place in the freezer to firm up.

## Hyssop  (*Hyssopus officinalis*)

I was first introduced to hyssop—and its brilliant blue flowers—while eating an amazing salad in Richard Olney's Provençal kitchen garden. Hyssop flowers and young tender leaves were his favorite summer salad garnish, regardless of what was in it. I was won over immediately. Hyssop offers a minty, slightly bitter pungency to salads, soups, pastas, and braises.

With their spiky leaves and colored blossoms, hyssop plants are quite pretty in the garden. Like most herbs, well-draining soil and sunshine are all it needs to thrive. The plants will last at least four years in climates where they can winter over. Divide the roots in spring to propagate.

## Chives  (*Allium schoenoprasum*)
## Garlic Chives  (*Allium tuberosum*)

The long thin stems of chives add a mild onion flavor to salads, sauces, soups, and eggs. Their sprightly purple-pink blossoms perk up the garden as well as a salad or soup.

Garlic chives are flatter in shape, with a garlicky bite, and can be used anywhere chives are used. They are a mainstay in many Asian cuisines and are used in dumplings, pancakes, and soups. The blossoms of garlic chives are white and every bit as good to eat as their purple cousins.

Both kinds of chive are hardy perennials, popping up in the garden long after you thought they were gone. Keep them watered through dry spells and they will thrive.

## Shiso  (*Perilla frutescens*)

The tender ruffled leaves of shiso have an intense spiced flavor somewhat reminiscent of cinnamon. It is the herb of Japanese sushi. I love its surprising flavor with cucumbers, melon, and tomatoes. Shiso is a natural flavoring for fish dishes such as carpaccio, tartare, sushi, and sashimi. The flowers and seeds are quite aromatic and tasty, too. There are green, red, and two-toned (leaves that are green on top and purple on the bottom) varieties. They are all ornamental annuals that will reseed freely in milder climates.

## Bay Laurel  (*Laurus nobilis*)

Bay leaves are a staple in the spice cabinet, but if you've only known dried bay leaves, fresh ones will be a revelation: thread them between meat and vegetables on skewers to grill; pound them with salt to make a pungent seasoning for pork loin; add a leaf to soups, stews, and sauces for aromatic flavor. Bay can scent custards and candies, too. A friend of mine makes a wonderful nut caramel that she sandwiches between bay leaves (peel off the leaves before eating). But make sure you are using true bay laurel; *California* bay (*Umbellularia californica*, also known as Oregon myrtle) has a fantastic fragrance but is too strong to cook with.

Bay laurel is a tender perennial tree that will grow quite tall in favorable Mediterranean climates. In colder zones, grow bay in a container and move it indoors when the temperature drops. Don't overwater.

# Tender Leaves

## Lettuce and Salad Greens

I NEVER GET TIRED OF MAKING AND EATING SALAD. The varied textures and colors of
fresh cut young lettuces are ravishing, but there is more to make salad with than just
baby lettuces. There are the mature heads of lettuce, both those with large loose leaves
(to be torn—or not—and tossed in lively vinaigrettes) and those that form tight crisp
balls (to be cut into wedges and napped with flavorful creamy dressings). And then there
are other leaves to mix in for flavor and spice—rocket, mâche, dandelion greens, garden
cress, miner's lettuce, and more. Vinaigrettes and dressings offer infinite possibilities—
with vinegars and citrus for acid; olive oils, nut oils, and cream for body; and herbs,
garlic, shallots, spices, and salt for heightening flavor.

# Recipes

Cut-and-Come-Again Salad  40

Garden Salad Tortilla  40

Little Gem Wedges with Fines Herbes and Shaved Radish  41

Red Romaine Salad with Sherry Vinegar and Garlic  42

Butter Lettuce Salad with Beets, Gruyère, and Walnuts  42

Rocket Salad with Babcock Peaches and Basil  44

Rocket Pesto  45

Wild Rocket with Balsamic Vinegar and Speck  46

Mâche with Pickled Cherries and Duck Liver Croutons  47

Garden Cress and Green Oak Leaf Lettuce Salad
with Chopped Egg  48

Dandelion Greens with Anchovies and Garlic Croutons  49

Miner's Lettuce Salad  50

# Lettuce and Salad Greens in the Garden

I love knowing that there are ancient Egyptian wall paintings depicting farmers harvesting lettuce and that the Romans served dressed greens as an appetizer to most of their meals. At my table, thousands of years later, the freshness and flavor of salad greens is a necessity at every meal. Salad greens taste the best when freshly harvested, which, for all intents and purposes, means they come from a local farmers' market or your own garden. Luckily, lettuce and salad greens are very easy to grow and quick to come to harvest. Healthy, well-drained soil and even moisture are about all they need. A good serving of compost will help, and sun is required, but they all can tolerate a fair amount of shade. Salad greens perform very well in containers, too, needing little soil for their shallow compact roots. I always have salad greens growing both in the ground and in containers. Best of all, when you grow your own salad greens there is a larger, more interesting, and tastier range of varieties to choose from than you will ever find in stores. (Chicories, the other family of delicious salad greens, can be found on page 191.)

Spring and fall are easy times to grow salad greens. Many greens bolt, or go to seed, in hot weather, but a plot or container well positioned to avoid the hottest sun of the day can extend the season. There are heat-tolerant varieties of lettuces to grow in summer; and a cold frame, tunnel, or greenhouse will keep cold-tolerant lettuces and other greens growing even in very cold weather. So in most climates it is possible to grow lettuces and other greens year-round.

Salad greens are also quite easy to start from seed. Seeds can be broadcast in patches to harvest in a cut-and-come-again manner (page 40) or sown strategically for mature heads. Many will self-seed if allowed to flower. Before sowing, cultivate the soil to create a fine, even texture, amend the soil with compost, and cover the seeds with just a scattering of fine soil or compost. Keep the soil moist until the seeds germinate, watering up to two times a day if needed.

Once up, the young sprouts are quite susceptible to the creeping and crawling denizens of the garden. Patrol nightly with a flashlight to find and remove any slugs and snails. Raised beds and containers discourage marauders. For tender sweet greens, water consistently. If the plants are left to dry out they become bitter and tough. A side dressing of compost or a drenching of compost tea will keep maturing heads well fed.

## Lettuce *(Lactuca sativa)*

There are an impressive number of varieties of lettuce available and more are being developed every year. The assortment of leaf shapes and colors is stunning. Lettuces can be planted separately, or in a mix. There are mixes that have been developed for hot weather, for cold weather, for color, and for flavor. Be creative in your plantings: plant single varieties as a border or divider or choose mixes that are mono-colored or multicolored. The possibilities are endless—and so delicious.

Lettuce varieties are divided into three groups: loose leaf, cos, and heading. Each has specific characteristics of growth, texture, and flavor. Choose varieties according to the season.

Loose-leaf lettuces, also referred to as salad bowl lettuces, do not form hearts or heads. Their leaf shapes vary from ruffled and curly to smooth and indented, and they come in a beautiful range of colors, from light green to bronze to stunning reds. Loose-leaf lettuces prefer cool weather. *Lolla Rosso*, both *Red* and *Green Oak Leaf*, *Marvel of Four Seasons*, *Deer Tongue*, *Tango*, and *Red Sails* are just a few that I love. These lettuces may be harvested over an extended period of time. Cut tiny leaves cut-and-come-again style, or harvest larger mature leaves from the outside in and allow the plant to keep growing.

Cos, or romaine, lettuces form tall upright heads of crisp, delicious, narrow leaves with a wide rib. These varieties take longer to mature, are slow to bolt, and tolerate extremes of both hot and cold. Some varieties can overwinter well. My favorite cos lettuce is *Little Gem*, a mini-romaine type. Its small size makes it easy to incorporate into many kinds of salads, and the leaves make perfect boats for all manner of hors d'oeuvres. Little Gem holds well in the garden and does not have to be harvested right away. *Freckles*, *Flashy Trout Back*, *Red Romaine*, *Rouge d'Hiver*, and *Winter Density* (similar to Little Gem) are very good, too. Cos lettuces can be harvested cut-and-come-again method or allowed to grow into mature heads.

The heading lettuces form round heads and include both crisphead varieties and the butterhead and Bibb varieties. Crispheads, as you can imagine, have crisp, juicy leaves. Iceberg lettuces are the most common crispheads; though frequently maligned, they are delicious fresh from the garden. My favorite is *Reine de Glace*, or *Ice Queen*. Crisphead lettuces do very well in the long hot days of summer. Give them lots of compost and water and they form dense sweet heads. Another crisphead type, the Batavia lettuces, have ruffled crisp, sweet leaves that start out loose then mature into tight heads. They also do well in hot weather. *Sierra* has charming red tips, *Mottistone*'s green leaves are speckled with burgundy, and *Nevada* is a pretty ruffled green. Batavia types' outer leaves can be harvested as they grow.

Butterhead and Bibb lettuces form billowy heads of tender, folded, mildly flavored leaves. There are green, red, and green and red varieties. These lettuces do well in the short cold days of winter, spring, and fall. *Buttercrunch*, mini–*Tom Thumb*, red-tipped *Skyphos*, green *Victoria*, and the oddly named *Drunken Woman Frizzy Headed* are all delicious. Grow heading lettuces as a cut-and-come-again crop or as mature heads.

When planting for mature heads, plant the seeds fairly close together to help control weeds. When the crop of young lettuce is two to three inches tall, thin the plants for a delectable tender salad. It is best to harvest in the morning or the evening when the lettuce is cool and crisp. For a constant supply of lettuce, plant successively in plots or containers every three to four weeks.

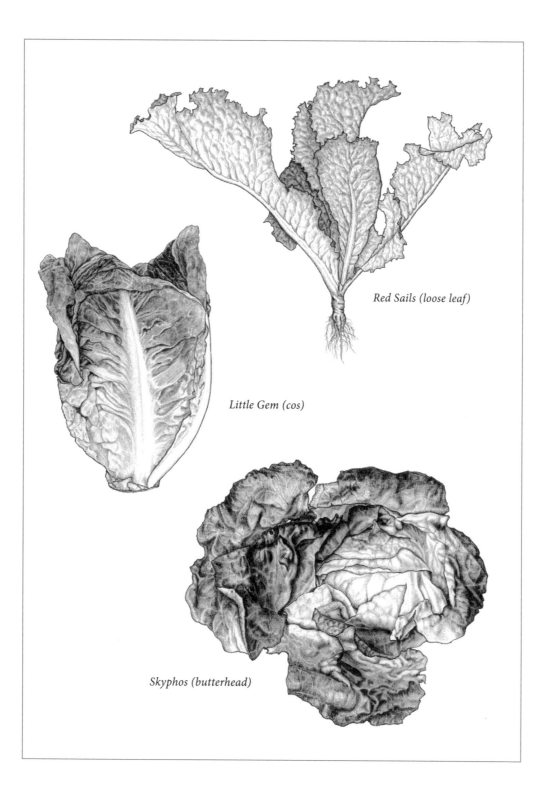

Red Sails (loose leaf)

Little Gem (cos)

Skyphos (butterhead)

## Cut-and-Come-Again Salad

My favorite salad is inspired by the mesclun of Provence—a vibrant, spicy blend of green and red lettuces, endive, rocket, and the young leaves of tender herbs. Over the years I have learned to sow the herbs and rocket apart from the lettuces because they grow at different rates. Harvest the leaves young, when they are about three to four inches tall. Cut just enough lettuces for your salad, an inch above the soil, in the cool of the morning or in the evening. Cut the bed in a methodical manner so it is easy to discern which greens needs to be harvested next, and which are growing in. It takes about a week for the lettuces to grow back for the next harvest. Keep harvesting the same bed until the lettuces become bitter or tough, anywhere from three to five harvests.

In the kitchen, wash the lettuces gently in cold water and dry them well. My favorite way to dress them is with a quick vinaigrette. I make mine directly in a little mortar—a pounded clove of garlic, a splash of vinegar, salt, pepper, and a drizzle of good olive oil. I vary the vinegar (red wine, white wine, sherry, etc.) and add some chopped herbs or a little diced shallot for variety. When I serve the greens alongside a main dish, I occasionally sprinkle them with a just a little salt and a touch of olive oil. Avoid heavy dressings, as these lettuces are very delicate and easily matted down.

## Garden Salad Tortilla

1 SERVING

My salad garden is the inspiration for a delicious lunch: fresh greens folded into a warm tortilla with seasoned yogurt. I make these differently each time, depending on what is available and what I choose to pick—tender spring lettuces, winter rocket, sweet cucumbers, bittersweet frisée, mint leaves, cilantro sprigs, or sliced radishes. A little slice of leftover roasted meat is good, too.

Gather, wash, and dry well:
> **1 handful of salad greens**
> **A few tender herb leaves**

In a small bowl mix together:
> **A spoonful of plain yogurt**
> **A sprinkle of salt**
> **A pinch of fresh-ground spices (cumin, coriander, nigella, or fennel)**

Heat directly over a gas burner or in a hot pan:
> **1 Whole-Wheat Tortilla (page 149)**

Put the warm tortilla on a plate, spoon the yogurt over half the tortilla, add the greens, and finish with:
> **A drizzle of good olive oil**

Fold the tortilla in half and it is ready to eat.

# Little Gem Wedges with Fines Herbes and Shaved Radish

4 SERVINGS

This salad brings together three of my favorite things: lettuce, herbs, and radishes. Little Gems are a wonderful variety of romaine lettuce. Fines herbes are a mix of tender tarragon, chervil, parsley, and chives. They are all in plentiful supply in my garden every spring. These tender herbs are easy to pound into a flavorful paste and add loads of flavor to this creamy dressing. Shaving a radish over the top adds color, texture, and a nice spicy note. If your radishes need thinning, pull up the tiny plants when you make this salad and add them, as well. They're delicious!

Closely trim the ends, taking off as little as possible, and remove any blemished outer leaves from:

**4 heads of Little Gem lettuce**

Cut the heads lengthwise into quarters and wash gently in cold water. Spin dry.

Put in a mortar:

**1 small green garlic stalk, trimmed and coarsely chopped**
**Salt**

Pound the garlic to a smooth paste and add:

**2 tablespoons chopped chervil**
**1 tablespoon chopped chives**
**1 tablespoon chopped tarragon**
**1 tablespoon chopped parsley**

Continue pounding until the herbs are a smooth purée. Stir in:

**1 egg yolk**
**Fresh-ground black pepper**
**1 tablespoon lemon juice**
**½ teaspoon white wine vinegar**

Once everything is well mixed, slowly dribble in, whisking constantly:

**¼ cup extra-virgin olive oil**

Once all the oil is incorporated, whisk in:

**¼ cup buttermilk**

Taste for salt and adjust as needed. Thinly slice:

**4 small or 2 larger trimmed radishes (such as French Breakfast or Easter Egg)**

Arrange the quartered Little Gems on a platter or individual plates. Sprinkle with a bit of salt and spoon some dressing over each wedge of lettuce. Scatter the radishes over the top of the salad.

You will have some dressing left. Save it for another salad or use it as a dipping sauce for crudités.

VARIATIONS

◆ Use 1 small ordinary garlic clove instead of the green garlic.

◆ Use other lettuces: loose-leaf varieties such as Red Oak Leaf; other varieties of romaine; or crisphead varieties, such as Reine de Glace, to name a few.

◆ Slice a ripe avocado and arrange the slices in between the wedges of lettuce before salting and dressing.

◆ Garnish with quarters of hard-cooked egg for a light lunch.

## Red Romaine Salad with Sherry Vinegar and Garlic

4 SERVINGS

I love the strikingly beautiful leaves of baby red romaine. And the dressing is strikingly flavored, too, with garlic, cumin, and paprika.

Trim the ends and remove any blemished outer leaves from:

**4 heads of baby red romaine**

Separate the leaves and wash and dry well. In the same water, wash:

**4 large cilantro sprigs**

**2 parsley sprigs**

Dry well. Remove the leaves, saving the cilantro stems.

Make the vinaigrette. Pound to a paste using a mortar and pestle:

**2 garlic cloves**

**A pinch of salt**

Stir in:

**1 tablespoon sherry vinegar**

**A pinch of cayenne**

**½ teaspoon paprika**

**¼ teaspoon cumin seeds, lightly toasted and crushed**

**Salt**

**Fresh-ground black pepper**

Add the stems from the cilantro and allow to sit for a few minutes to macerate. Whisk in:

**3 tablespoons extra-virgin olive oil**

Taste and adjust for salt and acid.

Trim the root ends and outer layer from:

**4 small or 2 medium scallions**

On a slight diagonal, finely slice the white and half the green leaves of each scallion. Remove the cilantro stems from the vin-aigrette. Toss the lettuce, herb leaves, and scallions with the dressing and serve.

VARIATIONS

◆ Use other tender leaves in place of the cilantro and parsley, such as anise hyssop, basil, chives, and young thyme.

◆ Garnish with wedges of hard-cooked egg or slices of roast chicken breast for a light meal. Reserve a bit of the dressing to drizzle over the eggs or meat.

## Butter Lettuce Salad with Beets, Gruyère, and Walnuts

4 SERVINGS

Preheat the oven to 375°F. Remove any leaves, leaving 1 inch of stem, from:

**1 bunch of baby beets**

Wash and drain and put them in a baking dish that will just hold them. Add:

**¼ inch water**

**Salt**

**A drizzle of olive oil**

**A pinch of fennel seeds (optional)**

Cover tightly and bake until tender, about 50 minutes. Let cool and peel, slipping the skins off with your fingers. Cut into wedges and season with:

**Salt**

**Red wine vinegar**

Let sit for a few minutes and taste for acid and salt. Add more as needed. Drizzle with:

**Extra-virgin olive oil**

While the beets are roasting, lay out on a baking sheet and toast until golden, about 10 minutes:

**¼ cup walnuts**

When cool, rub the nuts in your hands to remove their tannic skins. Crush or chop coarsely.

Meanwhile, separate the leaves from:

**1 head of butter lettuce**

Discard any blemished leaves. Wash and dry well the rest.

Prepare the vinaigrette. Mix together:

**1 teaspoon Dijon mustard**

**2½ teaspoons red wine vinegar**

**Salt**

**Fresh-ground black pepper**

Whisk in:

**3 tablespoons extra-virgin olive oil**

Dice:

**2 ounces Gruyère cheese**

Toss the lettuce, cheese, beets, and walnuts with the dressing. Arrange prettily on a plate. (If using red beets, toss the beets separately with a couple spoonfuls of the dressing and arrange them on top of the salad so they don't bleed and turn everything pink.)

Scatter over:

**1 tablespoon chopped chives**

Serve.

VARIATIONS

◆ Replace 1 tablespoon olive oil with 1 tablespoon crème fraîche.

◆ Use miner's lettuce in place of the butter lettuce.

scatter them on top of a pizza just out of the oven, serve them lightly dressed next to a roast, mix them into lettuces for added zing in a salad, or toss them on their own with toasted nuts and cheese or fruit. The larger, more mature leaves are spicier, with more texture and bite. Try them quickly sautéed or pounded into a zesty pesto. Don't overlook the ivory, purple-veined flowers that will inevitably appear—they are quite delicious and well worth harvesting for a sweet-spicy garnish to sprinkle on a salad or other dish.

## Rocket *(Eruca sativa)*

I eat a lot of rocket—or arugula, if you prefer. Nutty and spicy with a hint of sweetness, it adds an exciting flavor to everything. The dark green lobed leaves can be used as an herb or salad green. Fold them into pasta,

Rocket is gratifyingly easy to grow and yields large rewards in the kitchen. It germinates quickly and is quite productive. It can be ready to harvest as early as three weeks after planting and it grows right back after cutting up to five times. Like lettuce, it prefers a richly amended soil and even moisture. Though rocket can be sown from early spring through late fall, the cooler months produce the best crops. Hot and dry conditions create tougher, spicier leaves and send the plant rapidly to seed.

Sow successive plots every three weeks for a constant supply. Rocket is wonderful to intercrop among slower growing plants, or to use to quickly fill an open patch. Harvest young tender leaves once the plants are three inches high, using the cut-and-come-again method. Later, snip the spicier, mature leaves or cut the whole plant. Rocket seeds are easy to save. In fact, it naturalizes quite easily: if you would like to establish a permanent patch in your garden, just let the pods open to self-sow. Or tie the stalks of seeding plants together to keep the pods off the ground, and when they are brown and dry, harvest the seedpods to plant another time.

# Rocket Salad with Babcock Peaches and Basil

4 SERVINGS

Sun-ripened white-fleshed Babcock peaches mixed with basil and the nutty spice of rocket make a splendid summer salad. If you have any pickled cherries or other fruit in the larder, substitute the pickle brine for the vinegar in the dressing. Fino Verde (also called Piccolo Fino) basil has pretty little leaves that can be tossed into the salad whole.

Wash and dry well:
   **4 handfuls of rocket**
Make the vinaigrette. Mix together:
   **2 teaspoons red wine vinegar, or**
      **1 tablespoon fruit pickle brine**
   **1 large basil sprig, gently smashed**
   **Salt**
   **Fresh-ground black pepper**
Let sit for a few minutes, and whisk in:
   **3 tablespoons extra-virgin olive oil**
Taste for salt and acid and adjust as needed. Carefully peel:
   **1 large or 2 medium Babcock peaches**
If the peaches are fully ripe the peels should pull right off. Otherwise dunk them in a pot of boiling water for 5 seconds and then put them in ice water. If not using the peach right away, cover with a damp towel.
When ready to serve, toss the rocket with the dressing and:
   **1 tablespoon Fino Verde basil leaves or**
      **chiffonade of basil**
Arrange on a plate. Cut the peeled peach in two and twist the halves apart. Pry out the stone and slice the halves into ¼-inch slices. Arrange the slices in the rocket and serve.

# Rocket Pesto

MAKES ABOUT 1½ CUPS

Classic pesto is made with basil. In the winter at the Chez Panisse Café, when basil is no longer available, we make pesto from rocket and walnuts. It is very spicy and full flavored and it is delicious on whole-grain pasta and bean soups.

Wash and dry well:

**1 cup young rocket leaves, lightly packed**

Using a mortar and pestle, pound to a paste:

**2 garlic cloves, peeled**
**Salt**

Add and continue to pound:

**⅓ cup walnuts, lightly toasted**

Add:

**¼ cup grated Parmesan or pecorino cheese**

Transfer this mixture to a bowl. Coarsely chop the rocket and put it into the mortar. Pound the leaves to a paste. Return the pounded walnut mixture to the mortar. Pound the leaves and walnut mixture together. Continue pounding as you gradually pour in:

**½ cup extra-virgin olive oil**

Taste for salt and adjust as needed.

VARIATIONS

‣ Replace the rocket leaves with flat-leaf parsley leaves or wild rocket.

‣ Use pine nuts in place of walnuts.

‣ To make a traditional pesto, use basil leaves in place of the rocket, and ¼ cup pine nuts in place of the walnuts.

# Wild Rocket (*Diplotaxis muralis*)

The leaves of wild rocket are thinner, with deeper indentations and a fleshier texture than cultivated rocket. The taste is fantastic—slightly sweeter and juicier. Wild rocket is a perennial in mild climates and very easy to grow in any zone. It is hardier than garden rocket, so it can be planted earlier in the season, and it is very slow to bolt. The plants form low-growing, bushy clumps that sport tasty yellow flowers when in bloom. Start harvesting the leaves when the plants are three inches tall. The leaves will continue to grow back many times over. The bushes can become unruly and sprawl. Trim freely to shape them, they will grow back vigorously. Wild rocket will naturalize easily; just let a plant or two form seeds, and look for young sprouts in early spring.

# Wild Rocket with Balsamic Vinegar and Speck

4 SERVINGS

Wild rocket is a very sturdy green that stands up to rich full flavors. The sweet balsamic vinegar, tempered by a bit of sherry vinegar, brings out the nutty flavors of the rocket and the lightly smoked speck ham.

Wash and dry well:
**4 handfuls of wild rocket**
Make the vinaigrette. Mix together:
**2 teaspoons balsamic vinegar, as good quality as possible**
**2 teaspoons sherry vinegar**
**Salt**
**Fresh-ground black pepper**
Whisk in:
**3 tablespoons extra-virgin olive oil**
Taste for salt and acid and adjust as needed.
Cut:
**4 to 8 thin slices speck**
Toss the wild rocket with the dressing and arrange on a plate. Drape the slices of speck ham over the salad and serve.

VARIATIONS
✦ Scatter toasted, chopped hazelnuts over the salad before serving.
✦ Dribble a bit of traditional aged balsamic over the finished salad.
✦ Use prosciutto instead of the speck and add a few shavings of Parmesan.
✦ Use rocket, preferably mature leaves rather than tender young leaves, instead of wild rocket.

# Mâche (*Valerianella locusta*)

Mâche is a small, delicate green that tastes like roses to me. Others say it has a nutty flavor. I was surprised to find out how incredibly winter hardy it is. It can winter over in temperatures as low as −10°F. Mâche was originally a popular foraged green, collected in the wheat fields of England in early spring—thus its two other common names: corn salad (wheat was called corn in old England) and lamb's lettuce (lambs come in spring, the same time the green appeared wild). *Verte de Cambrai* has small leaves and *Large-Leaf Round*, as the name implies, has larger ones.

Sow mâche in fall and start to harvest leaves or whole rosettes in a couple of months. The plants will go to flower in spring. Allow a few to make seed and the plants will spontaneously grow again in fall creating an annual harvest of fall and winter salad.

# Mâche with Pickled Cherries and Duck Liver Croutons

4 SERVINGS

The delicate floral flavor of mâche goes well with fruit and the rich flavor of liver paste. Serve the rosettes whole for a pretty salad. Be sure to wash them well, as they may harbor a bit of grit.

First prepare the liver paste. Trim the fat from:

**¾ pound duck livers**

Gently separate the two lobes of each liver and remove any connecting veins. Season liberally with:

**Salt**

**Fresh-ground black pepper**

Heat a small heavy-bottomed skillet over medium-high heat. Add:

**Olive oil, enough to coat the pan**

**2 thin slices pancetta, chopped**

Cook for a minute and then add:

**1 large or 2 small shallots, sliced thin**

**1 thyme sprig, leaves only**

Cook until the shallot is softened, about 2 minutes. Remove from the pan and pour in:

**A bit more oil**

Add the livers in a single layer and cook 2 minutes on one side. Turn and continue to cook until just done and still pink in the center, about 2 more minutes. Carefully add and ignite:

**1 tablespoon Cognac or brandy**

Remove the livers from the pan and stir together with the cooked pancetta and shallots. When slightly cooled tip onto a cutting board and add:

**2 tablespoons butter**

Chop the livers and the butter with a sharp knife. The butter will meld with the livers. The paste is tastier when left a bit chunky. Taste for salt and pepper and adjust as needed.

For the salad, trim the root ends from and wash and dry well:

**4 handfuls of mâche**

Drain:

**10 Pickled Cherries (page 346)**

Remove the pits carefully by cutting each cherry in half and twisting away from the pits, or use a cherry pitter and cut in half. Try to preserve the halves intact.

Make the vinaigrette. Mix together in a small bowl:

**1 shallot, finely diced**

**1 tablespoon red wine vinegar**

**Salt**

**Fresh-ground black pepper**

Allow to sit for 10 minutes or so to macerate. Whisk in:

**3 to 4 tablespoons extra-virgin olive oil**

Taste for salt and acid and adjust as needed. Toast and cut in half:

**4 slices country-style bread**

When ready to serve, toss the greens with three quarters of the vinaigrette. Arrange on a plate and garnish with the pickled cherries. Spread the croutons with the duck liver paste and place them around the salad. Drizzle the rest of the dressing over the salad and croutons. Serve.

## Garden Cress (*Lepidium sativum*)

Garden cress has lovely delicate curly leaves and a definite spicy kick. It is a great green for adding color and spice to a dish. Sprinkle it on top or serve a little pile on the plate, lightly dressed in oil and salt. It is especially nice with rich dishes like roast duck, *salumi*, grilled steak, and tuna confit. A salad made completely of garden cress may be a bit too much, but it is fantastic mixed into a salad bowl of greens.

Garden cress is prolific and easily grown. Direct sow in spring or fall (it will quickly go to seed in hot weather) in well-amended moist soil. Provide adequate and regular water to keep the spiciness in check; hot and dry conditions make the leaves inedible. Garden cress grows to a maximum height of ten inches and thrives in borders or in between slower growing crops. Harvest by snipping the young leaves using the cut-and-come-again method; the leaves will quickly grow back four to five times. When the plants bloom, save some seed for the next season. Grow garden cress in a small container on the windowsill for some winter spice.

## Garden Cress and Green Oak Leaf Lettuce Salad with Chopped Egg

4 SERVINGS

This is a beautiful salad. The colors and flavors of the two greens are well matched and the chopped egg, with its bright color and richness, is the perfect foil for the spicy cress.

Bring a pot of water to a boil. Carefully add:
> **2 eggs**

Cook at a simmer for 8 minutes. Remove the eggs to a bowl of ice water to stop the cooking.
Trim the ends and separate the leaves from:
> **4 small or 2 larger heads of Green Oak Leaf lettuce**

Wash along with:
> **3 handfuls of garden cress**

Dry well.
Make the dressing. Mix together in a small bowl:
> **1 shallot, minced**
> **2 teaspoons red wine vinegar**
> **Salt**
> **Fresh-ground black pepper**

Let sit 10 minutes to macerate. Then whisk in:
> **2½ tablespoons extra-virgin olive oil**

Taste for salt and acid and adjust as needed. When ready to serve, peel the eggs and chop coarsely. Toss the lettuce and cress with the dressing, arrange on a plate, and scatter the chopped egg over the top.

VARIATIONS
• Scatter nasturtium or chive blossoms over the salad for color and sweet spicy flavor.

• Substitute other lettuces for some or all of the Green Oak Leaf. Red Oak Leaf and other red lettuces would be beautiful, too.

• Substitute young tender watercress for the garden cress.

## Dandelion *(Taraxacum officinale)*

Dandelion has been foraged as a wild green since the earliest of times. It was so well loved that cultivars were soon developed for the garden. The long, dark green, deeply serrated leaves are packed full of minerals and vitamins. Their bitter flavor goes well with strong flavors like garlic, anchovy, mustard, and smoky bacon. Eat the tender young leaves in salad or sautéed as a side dish with grilled or roasted meat.

Dandelion is hardy and can be sown very early in spring. Harvest the leaves when tender and young, as they become too bitter to eat as the plant matures. Dandelion is very easy to grow and can self-sow to the point of invasion. Consistent moisture will help keep the plants from going to seed. Pull out plants before they mature, or wait and pick the pretty yellow blossoms to make dandelion wine. (Italian dandelions are not dandelions at all but a type of chicory. Their blue flowers give them away.)

## Dandelion Greens with Anchovies and Garlic Croutons

4 SERVINGS

Preheat the oven to 375°F. Cut:

**2 thick slices country-style bread**

Cut the slices into cubes and toss them with:

**A drizzle of olive oil**
**Salt**
**Fresh-ground black pepper**

Spread the seasoned cubes on a baking sheet and bake, stirring now and then, until golden and crisp, 10 to 12 minutes. While still hot, tip them into a bowl and toss with:

**2 garlic cloves, finely minced**

Wash and dry well:

**4 handfuls of dandelion greens**

Soak and debone:

**2 salt-cured anchovies**

Chop the four fillets coarsely and coat with olive oil. Pound to a purée in a mortar:

**2 garlic cloves**
**A pinch of salt**

Add:

**2 teaspoons red wine vinegar**
**2 teaspoons Dijon mustard**
**Fresh-ground black pepper**

Mix well. Slowly whisk in:

**3 tablespoons extra-virgin olive oil**

Taste for salt and acid and adjust as needed. Stir in the chopped anchovies. Toss the dandelion greens and croutons with the dressing and serve.

# Miner's Lettuce

*(Claytonia perfoliata)*

Miner's lettuce, a native to the western United States, has light green, fleshy, heart-shaped leaves. During the California gold rush days, miners depended on the plant's high vitamin C content to ward off scurvy and keep them going. The mild-tasting leaves make a wonderful salad and add a juicy bite to a sandwich.

Miner's lettuce grows wild all over the western coastal lands and is easy to cultivate. It is quite cold hardy but cannot survive heat. Seed directly in spring or late summer in a moist spot in your garden, from full sun to slightly shady. The plants grow no higher than a foot and will winter over in milder climates. Harvest the leaves cut-and-come-again style, and they will grow back for a number of harvests. The little flowers that form at the center of the leaf are edible, too. For best flavor, cut the leaves before the flower stem begins to elongate. If you love miner's lettuce, let it go to seed and it will naturalize and come back every year. Any unwanted plants can easily be turned under for green compost.

# Miner's Lettuce Salad

4 SERVINGS

I like miner's lettuce with very simple vinaigrettes. It is such a mild green that I find strong flavors tend to overwhelm it. Any salad recipe that calls for butter lettuce or other mild greens will be a good fit for miner's lettuce.

Wash and dry well:
> **4 handfuls of miner's lettuce**

Make the dressing. Mix together in a small bowl:
> **Zest of 1 lemon**
> **1 tablespoon lemon juice**
> **Salt**
> **Fresh-ground black pepper**

Stir to dissolve the salt. Whisk in:
> **1 tablespoon walnut oil**
> **1 tablespoon extra-virgin olive oil**

Taste for salt and acid and adjust as needed. When ready to serve, toss the miner's lettuce with the dressing and serve.

VARIATIONS

◆ Add 1 or 2 teaspoons of whole-grain mustard to the dressing.

◆ Use only olive oil instead of half walnut and half olive oil.

◆ Add a few marinated beets and toasted walnuts to the salad.

# Hidden Flavor

## Garlic, Onions, Leeks, and Shallots

Hidden but not unnoticed! I cannot imagine cooking without the Allium family: garlic, onions, scallions, leeks, and shallots. So much of what I love to eat and make at home is started with a bit of onion or garlic, or both. Garlic is pounded into a smooth purée in vinaigrette and aïoli (garlic mayonnaise)—my two most beloved sauces. The compelling and comforting aroma of onions sautéed in butter or oil marks the beginning of countless soups, stews, sauces, pastas, and risottos. Onion tarts, pickled shallots, and sliced scallions in relishes are some other ways to enjoy this remarkable vegetable family.

Recipes

Garlic Mayonnaise (Aïoli) 55

Potato and Green Garlic Ravioli
with Fava Beans 56

Chicken with 40 Cloves of Garlic 57

Spring Onions in Cream 59

Grilled Scallions 60

Onion Rings 60

Onion Soup 61

Leek Tart with Crème Fraîche and Bacon 63

Braised Leeks with Chickpeas, Saffron,
and Dried Marjoram 64

Crispy Fried Shallots 65

Sweet-and-Sour Shallots 65

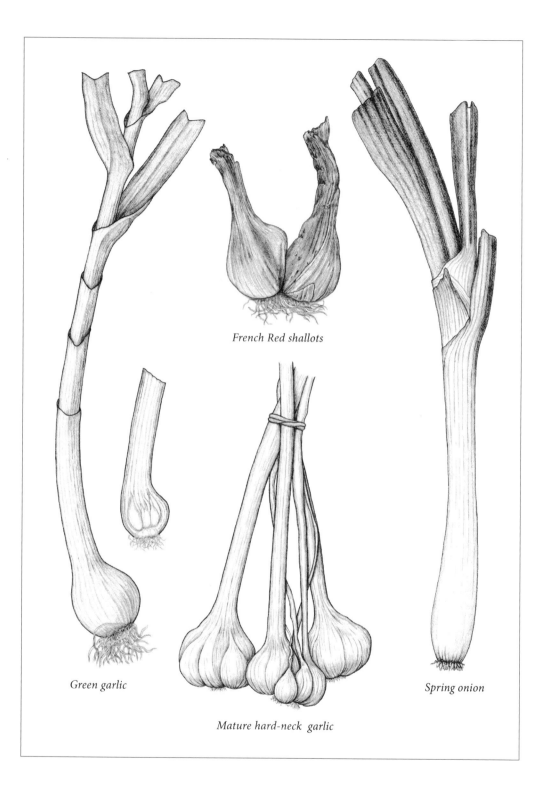

*French Red shallots*

*Green garlic*

*Mature hard-neck garlic*

*Spring onion*

## Alliums in the Garden

Where I live in northern California, we plant garlic and onions in the fall, and they slowly grow through the winter. This is true in many other zones throughout the country as well. Hard-neck garlic in particular can survive very cold temperatures. By early spring there will be young garlic to harvest, and spring onions and scallions not long after that. Early spring—as early as a few weeks before the last frost date—is the other time to plant garlic, onions, leeks, and shallots. They all like rich, loose soil. For good results add lots of compost to the ground where you plant them and water consistently, especially when they are just starting out. Alliums have shallow roots so deep watering is not as important as watering often. Feed with compost or water with compost tea every couple of months. Alliums do well interplanted among other quicker growing plants such as lettuce and other greens. Plant them where legumes such as peas and beans have grown; they will appreciate the extra nitrogen left in the soil.

Shallots, leeks, onions, and garlic taste delicious in all their stages of growth. Plant them thickly and harvest plants throughout the season. Browning lower leaves and flopping plants are the telltale signs that it's time to harvest. Loosen the soil around the bulbs and then pull. Let the freshly harvested plants sit in a dry, airy place until their outer papery skins have dried. Once cured, store in a cool dark place or they will soon start to sprout, spoiling their flavor and texture. Garlic, shallots, and smaller onions are also well suited to being grown in containers.

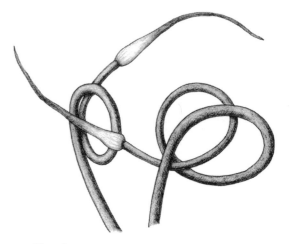

## Garlic  (*Allium sativum*)

I love eating garlic at every stage of its maturity. Green garlic arrives on the scene just as winter-stored garlic is starting to sprout and lose its fresh flavor. Use it as you would any other garlic: added to a pasta sauce, pounded into a paste to flavor a spring aïoli, or gently cooked and added to mashed potatoes. Its green flavor complements spring vegetables—little baby carrots, tender spinach, asparagus, peas, and fava beans. When bulbs have started to form, but the surrounding paper-thin skin is still moist and tender, slice the bulbs crosswise and poach them in chicken broth with a couple of sage leaves for a simple, fragrant soup. Or chop them whole to add to a vegetable stew or pasta sauce. In early summer, you will see the twisted, snakelike flower shoots. Garlic scapes, as they are called, are quite tasty. Sauté them for an omelet, pound them into a pesto, add them to a batch of dill pickles, or pickle them on their own. The rest of the year, fully mature garlic is a staple that I cook with every day. It is always in my kitchen. I even take it with me when I travel.

There are two types of garlic, hard neck and soft neck, and I grow both. Hard-neck varieties are quite cold hardy, they produce heads with fewer but larger cloves, and they have a central flowering stem. Soft-neck varieties have no such stem and produce heads with many smaller cloves that store well. Both types taste delicious and are grown in the same manner. Ask local farmers what varieties do best in your area, and plant those you think taste best. Some good soft-neck choices are *Inchelium Red*, *Italian Late*, and *Lorz Italian*; for hard neck, *Bogatyr*, *Siberian*, and *Spanish Roja*. There are many, many more to choose from.

There is a third type of garlic, called elephant garlic (*Allium ampeloprasum*), which has very large mild-flavored cloves, only a few to a head. I don't cook with it much, because it has such a mild flavor, but it is certainly easy to peel.

Garlic seed may be purchased from a catalog or nursery, but if you find a variety you like that comes from a known source with healthy soil, the cloves are well worth planting. Choose large cloves for large heads. Plant them blunt side down, about one inch deep. Fall is the best time to plant garlic. Mulch it well in freezing climates. When spring comes and the greens start to poke up, give them a healthy meal of compost and remulch. Early spring is the next best time to plant. The flower buds, or scapes, of hard-neck varieties should be cut before they open to bloom so the plant will concentrate on growing the bulb belowground. Harvest when two or three of the bottom leaves have turned brown. Eat right away or cure for storage.

# Garlic Mayonnaise (Aïoli)

MAKES ABOUT 1 CUP

This is one of the very few recipes that is in both volumes of *The Art of Simple Food*. In fact, this recipe is in every cookbook I have ever written. It has to be so. I adore garlic mayonnaise, or aïoli, as it called in Provence, where I learned to make and eat it. It is a luxurious sauce filled with flavor and richness that makes everything taste better. Make it as garlicky as you like. Use green garlic in spring, just freshly harvested mature garlic in summer, and delicious well-cured garlic in fall and winter. Even garlic mayonnaise has its seasons!

Peel:

**2 or 3 small garlic cloves**

Pound until smooth, using a mortar and pestle, along with:

**A pinch of salt**

Separate into a mixing bowl:

**1 egg yolk**

Add about half the garlic and:

**½ teaspoon water**

Mix well with a whisk. Into a cup with a pour spout, measure about:

**1 cup olive oil**

Slowly dribble the oil into the egg yolk, whisking constantly. As the egg yolk absorbs oil, the sauce will thicken, lighten in color, and become opaque. This will happen rather quickly. Then you can add the oil a little faster, whisking all the while.

If the sauce is thicker than you like, thin it with a few drops of water. Taste and add more salt and garlic, if necessary.

# Potato and Green Garlic Ravioli with Fava Beans

4 SERVINGS

Sweet, yellow-fleshed potatoes marry well with the bright fresh flavor of green garlic. This simple filling is easy to make and has the perfect texture for learning to fill ravioli.

Peel and cut into medium-size chunks:

**1 pound yellow-fleshed potatoes**

Place in a pot and cover with at least 2 inches of salted water. Bring to a boil, reduce the heat, and simmer until tender, about 6 minutes. There should be no resistance when pierced with a small sharp knife or skewer. Drain the potatoes well and put through a ricer or food mill to purée.

Meanwhile, trim away the root ends and any blemished outside layers of:

**4 green garlic stalks**

Slice into thin rings, including any lighter green stem. Discard the dark green leaves into the compost. Melt in a small heavy-bottomed skillet:

**1 teaspoon butter or olive oil**

Add the sliced garlic along with enough water to cover and:

**A pinch of salt**

Cook until soft, about 3 to 4 minutes. Be sure that the pan does not dry out and cause the garlic to stick and burn. When the garlic is cooked, stir it into the puréed potatoes with:

**2 tablespoons crème fraîche**

Season to taste with:

**Salt**

**Fresh-ground black pepper**

Put in the refrigerator to cool thoroughly.

To make ravioli, roll out fairly thin:

**1 recipe Farro Tagliatelle (page 313)**

Cut the pasta into sheets about 14 inches long. Keep the stack of well-floured extra sheets of pasta under a towel to keep them from drying. Along the lower third of the long side of each sheet of pasta, pipe or spoon tablespoonful-size blobs of the potato and green garlic filling, keeping about 1½ inches between each blob of filling. Spray very lightly with a fine mist of water. Fold the upper half of the pasta over the lower half. Starting at the fold, press the 2 layers of pasta together with your fingertips, gently coaxing all the air out of each ravioli. When the ravioli have been formed and pressed, cut off the bottom edge with a zigzag rolling cutter and cut between each bit of filling. Separate the ravioli and lay them out on a sheet pan sprinkled with flour; make sure they aren't touching each other or they will stick together. Cover with a towel or parchment paper and refrigerate right up to the time of cooking. This keeps the filling from seeping through the ravioli and causing them to stick to the pan.

Prepare the fava beans. Shell the beans from:

**2 pounds fava beans**

Blanch quickly in boiling water and then cool in ice water. Drain and pop the beans out of their skins. When ready to serve, bring a large pot of salted water to a boil. Melt in a heavy-bottomed pan:

**2 tablespoons butter**

**2 tablespoons olive oil**

Add:

**6 to 8 sage leaves**

**Salt**

Cook until the sage turns translucent, add the fava beans, and pour in a ladleful of boiling water. Taste for salt and adjust as needed. Cook the ravioli in the boiling water for 5 to 6 minutes, until the pasta is done. Drain or remove from the water with a slotted spoon or spider. Place on a platter, or in individual bowls, and spoon over the fava beans and their liquid. Sprinkle with:

**Freshly grated Parmesan cheese**
Serve immediately.

# Chicken with 40 Cloves of Garlic

4 SERVINGS

This recipe is a fantastic showcase for fresh mature garlic that has just been harvested and cured. The skins are papery and dry, but the cloves within are juicy and bursting with flavor. Don't peel the garlic; the skins keep it from melting into the sauce, and it is fun to squeeze the tender purée from the skins over the golden chicken or toasted bread. A big rocket salad is the perfect accompaniment.

Season the day before if possible:
**4 chicken legs, or 1 whole chicken, cut into 8 pieces**
with:
**Salt**
**Fresh-ground black pepper**
Preheat the oven to 375°F. Heat a large heavy-bottomed pan over medium-high heat. (Cast iron works very well.) Pour in:
**2 tablespoons olive oil**
Add the chicken legs, skin side down, and cook until crisp and brown, about 12 min-

utes. Turn and cook for another 4 minutes. Meanwhile, break apart:
**4 heads of garlic, about 40 cloves**
Remove any excess papery peel. (You may peel the cloves completely if you wish.) Put the garlic in a braising dish or casserole with a tight-fitting lid. Add:
**10 thyme sprigs, or 5 thyme sprigs and 5 savory sprigs**
**3 tablespoons extra-virgin olive oil**
**1 bay leaf**
Toss to coat well. Arrange the chicken legs over the garlic. Cover the pot with foil and then the lid. Cook on the middle shelf of the oven for 50 minutes. Remove the lid and foil and cook another 10 minutes to crisp the skin.

When the chicken is done, lay out on a baking sheet:
**4 thick slices crusty bread**
Toast in the oven, about 8 minutes. Spoon some of the oil from the chicken over the toasts. Serve the chicken with the garlic and toasted bread.

## Onions　(*Allium cepa*)

Onions, too, can be harvested throughout their growing cycle. When they are very young, eat them as scallions. In fact, although a true scallion is a specific type of onion, frequently called a bunching onion, many scallions on sale are simply baby onions that have yet to swell and bulb. As onions mature, they begin to bulb. Farmers' markets are full of such onions all through late spring and early summer. These spring onions are fresh and delicious and a real pleasure to cook with. I like to slice them thicker than I would cured onions and cook them a little less (but still all the way through) to capture their springtime sweetness. Use them in soups, pasta sauces, and tarts. They are divine paired with green garlic and spring vegetables in a ragout, or baked with a touch of luscious crème fraîche.

Onions are a fascinating plant to grow. They are photoperiodic, which means that their stages of growth are regulated by day length. Onion varieties are categorized as long day, short day, and day neutral. Each category is sensitive to where they are planted geographically, and to the time of year. A long-day onion planted in the South, where day length is fairly constant, will stay scallion size and produce no bulb; a short-day onion planted in the North will be confused by long summer days and will do the same. Day-neutral onions are exactly that and can be planted almost anywhere, but they still need to be in the ground at the right time to make a mature onion. This makes it sound hard, but really all it means is that you should be sure to choose the right onion for where you are gardening. Bunching onions, because they don't produce a bulb, are unaffected by day length. *Shimonita* and red *Deep Purple* are quite delicious. Use both the white (or red) part and the green leaves of scallions, especially when they are fresh from your own garden. They are delectable.

Where I live, day-neutral varieties are the onions most commonly grown. *Stockton Red*, mini *Purplette*, long red *Torpedo* (sometimes called *Long Red Florence*), and white *Gladstone* are a few favorites. Among the onions that are grown to maturity and cured to develop a tough, protective outer skin, there are sweet varieties, such as *Walla Walla* and *Vidalia,* and flat cipollini varieties, such as *Borettana*, as well as the classic red-, white-, and yellow-skinned types.

Onions are planted as seeds, seedlings, or sets. Seeds can be started early indoors to get a start on the season or direct seeded in spring. Seedlings are very convenient to plant and can be mail-ordered or found at local nurseries. Sets are baby onions ready to grow. In milder climates, onions can be planted in the fall and wintered over to get a jump on spring. In very cold climates, plant them in early spring, a few weeks before the last frost date. Plant them thickly and enjoy the thinnings in all the different stages. I don't have room to grow onions all the way to maturity, but I love having spring onions throughout the spring and summer and scallions to pull year-round.

# Spring Onions in Cream

4 SERVINGS

Trim away the green leaves and most of the roots from:

**1 bunch of spring onions (about
    3 large or 6 smaller onions)**

Cook in salted boiling water until tender, about 10 minutes. Remove the onions, reserving the water, and when they are cool enough to handle cut them in half lengthwise, cutting evenly through the root. If the onions are very large, cut in quarters, keeping an equal amount of root on each piece. (The root helps keep the onions together.) Meanwhile, heat in a heavy-bottomed pot:

**½ to ¾ cup crème fraîche**

Add ¼ cup of the reserved onion cooking water and season with:

**Salt
A pinch of cayenne pepper
Leaves from a marjoram or thyme
    sprig**

When you're ready to bake, preheat the oven to 375°F. Butter a baking dish that will just hold the onions in a single layer with:

**2 teaspoons softened butter**

Toss the onions gently with:

**A large pinch of salt
A few grinds of black pepper**

Arrange the onions in the buttered baking dish and pour over the seasoned cream.

Bake until hot, bubbling, and spotted with brown, about 25 minutes.

VARIATIONS

◆ Sprinkle the onions with ¼ cup grated Parmesan or Gruyère cheese before putting the dish in the oven.

◆ Use cream instead of crème fraîche, or make a light béchamel (follow the recipe on page 108 and substitute onion cooking liquid for the cardoon liquid).

◆ Add a few scrapings of nutmeg to the cream.

# Grilled Scallions

Grilled onions are delicious and grilled scallions are divine. Serve them draped over a piece of grilled fish, alongside slices of steak, stirred into a lentil salad, or simply eat them as they come off the grill. They are good with just about anything and are easy to make. Cut away any roots, trim the top inch of green leaves, and remove any dirty or blemished outer layers from 2 or 3 (or more!) scallions per person. Toss the cleaned scallions with salt and a drizzle of oil, and a little splash of water. Place on a hot grill over medium embers and cook, turning now and then until soft and golden brown. That is all there is to it. Having scallions in the garden to pull as you are lighting the grill is pretty close to heaven.

# Onion Rings

I love to make onion rings in the summer as all the freshly cured onions are coming to market. I scatter them over salads, grilled steak, or chicken. Sometimes I will fry some squid to serve together with the onions. Use fresh bulbing red onions for a special treat.

Set up 2 bowls. Fill one with:
**2 cups buttermilk**
Fill the other with:
**2 cups unbleached all-purpose flour**
**⅓ cup semolina**
Peel and cut crosswise into ¼-inch slices:
**4 red onions**
Gently separate the slices into rings. Put the rings in the buttermilk and stir to coat. Fill a tall-sided, heavy-bottomed pot (a cast-iron dutch oven works well) with:
**4 inches rice bran oil**
Make sure the oil goes no higher than half-way up the pot. Heat over medium high to 350°F. When the oil is close to temperature, scoop the rings out of the milk, drain them well, and add them to the flour. Toss to coat well and then shake off the excess flour. Carefully add the floured rings to the hot oil. Don't crowd the pot; fry in batches as necessary. Cook until golden brown, about 4 minutes. Drain on absorbent paper or a towel, season with:
**Salt**
and serve.

# Onion Soup

MAKES ABOUT 1 QUART

French onion soup frequently calls for a rich beef broth—not the easiest thing to make at home. This recipe calls for a roasted chicken broth, easily made with the meaty bones left from a roasted chicken. The toasty caramelized skin, bits of meat, and any herbs that were used to season the bird add wonderful flavor and richness to the simple broth. It is worthwhile to make a fair amount, as any excess can be frozen for another soup or stew. The bones can be collected in the freezer until you are ready to make the broth.

First make the broth. Put into a large soup pot:

**2 meaty roasted chicken carcasses**

Pour in water until the bones are covered by 1 inch. Bring to a boil and then reduce the heat to a simmer. Skim any foam that collects on the surface. Cook at a bare simmer for 1½ hours. Add:

**1 carrot, peeled and sliced into ½-inch coins.**

**1 thyme sprig (if none was used to season the roasted bird)**

**A few black peppercorns**

Simmer for another 45 minutes and then strain. Use straightaway, or refrigerate for 5 to 7 days or freeze for a few months. Meanwhile, peel and thinly slice:

**1½ pounds onions (about 4 cups sliced)**

Heat in a heavy-bottomed pan:

**3 tablespoons butter or olive oil**

Add the onions with:

**2 to 3 thyme sprigs**

Cook over medium-low heat until quite soft, about 30 minutes. When soft, turn up the heat slightly and cook the onions 15 to 20 minutes more, stirring frequently, until they are a deep, even caramel brown. Season with:

**Salt**

Cook another 1 or 2 minutes and then pour in:

**4 cups roasted chicken broth**

Bring the soup to a boil, then reduce the heat to a simmer and cook for 30 minutes. Taste for salt and adjust as needed.

VARIATIONS

◆ Garnish with garlic croutons (see page 49).

◆ For a crusty cheese topping: Select 4 ovenproof bowls. Cut ½-inch-thick slices of crustless bread that just fit inside the bowls. Toast the bread in a 350°F oven until dry, about 7 minutes. When the soup is done, ladle it into the bowls 1 inch below the rim. Place the toasted bread on top and cover each crouton with a few shavings of cold butter and ¼ cup grated Gruyère cheese. Place the bowls on a baking sheet and bake in a 450°F oven until the cheese is hot and bubbling.

◆ Substitute ½ cup dry white wine for the same amount of roasted chicken broth.

◆ Substitute beef broth for the roasted chicken broth.

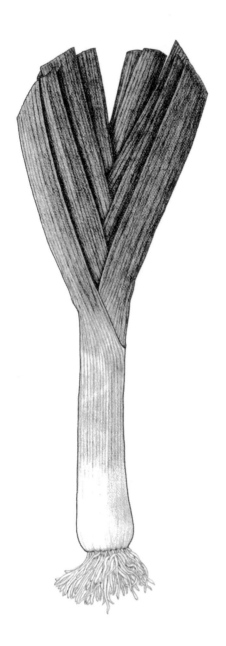

## Leeks (*Allium ampeloprasum* var. *porrum*)

Leeks have a mild sweet flavor that is perfect for soups and stews. The white part of the long stem is eaten and the green leaves are used to flavor stock or build the compost pile. Leeks are great steamed whole and served chilled with a mustard vinaigrette or heated on the grill and served warm with an herb and hard-cooked egg salsa. Wash leeks well to rid them of any soil or grit that might be caught between their layers. There are seasonal varieties of leeks. Cold-tolerant leeks have a shorter white shank (stem), while the spring and early summer ones are longer. *King Richard* is a fine early leek, slim and tall with a long sweet shank. It does not tolerate frost well. Tasty *Bleu de Solaise* is a winter-hardy leek with beautiful purple-tinted leaves.

Leeks are sold as seeds or plants. Cold-hardy varieties can be planted in late summer for fall and winter harvest. Other varieties are started in spring for summer harvest. Seedlings can be planted out before the last frosts; light frost will not harm them. Leeks have a particular cultivation—the delicately flavored white shank is developed by burying the growing plants in soil. Planting seedlings in a trench makes this easier. As the leeks grow, hill them—meaning pile up the soil around them. For best results, add compost as you hill. Harvest leeks at any size; pick strategically to allow others to grow larger. Winter-hardy leeks may be left in the ground; mulch thickly to keep the ground from freezing. Leeks will bolt in hot weather, so harvest at the first sign of flowering.

# Leek Tart with Crème Fraîche and Bacon

8 TO 10 SERVINGS

Serve this richly flavored tart with a mixed green salad. Make the dough at least an hour ahead or the night before.

To make the dough, have measured:

**¼ cup ice-cold water**

Mix together:

**1 cup unbleached all-purpose flour**
**¼ teaspoon salt (omit if using salted butter)**

Add:

**6 tablespoons cold butter, cut into small (¼-inch) cubes**

Cut or work the butter into the flour with a pastry blender or your fingertips. (Or mix, at medium-low speed, in a stand mixer fitted with the paddle attachment.) This will take about 1 minute. Pour in three quarters of the water, stirring all the while with a fork until the dough begins to form clumps. (In the mixer, turn the speed to low and pour the water down the sides of the bowl, mixing for 30 seconds or less.) Keep adding water as needed. Bring the dough together into a ball and wrap in plastic. Press the ball together and flatten into a disk. Refrigerate and allow to rest for 1 hour or longer.

For the filling, cut crosswise into ⅓-inch slices:

**4 slices bacon**

Heat a heavy-bottomed pan over medium-high heat and add the bacon pieces. Cook until the bacon is well rendered and just beginning to crisp. Remove from the pan and set aside.

Trim the root end and remove all but 1 inch of the green from:

**8 medium leeks, about 4 pounds**

Cut the leeks in half lengthwise and slice into ¼-inch half-moons. Rinse the sliced leeks well in water and lift them out into a colander to drain. Melt in a heavy-bottomed pan:

**4 tablespoons butter**

Add the leeks and:

**6 thyme sprigs**

Cook until soft, but not brown, about 10 minutes. Shake the pan occasionally to prevent sticking. Add some water if the pan is going dry before the leeks are done. Add the bacon and season with:

**Salt**
**Fresh-ground black pepper**

Let cool completely. Stir in:

**6 tablespoons crème fraîche**

Taste for salt and adjust as needed.

When ready to bake, preheat the oven to 375°F. Roll the dough out into a 14-inch circle. Brush off the excess flour and transfer the dough to a baking sheet lined with parchment paper and let it firm up in the refrigerator for 10 minutes or so. Spread the cooled leek mixture over the dough (removing the thyme branches as you do so), leaving a 1½-inch border around the circumference of the dough. Fold the border up over the leeks. For a shiny, more finished look, mix together and brush the rim of dough with:

**1 egg**
**1 tablespoon milk or water**

Bake in the lower third of the oven for 45 to 50 minutes, or until the crust is golden brown on the bottom. Slide the tart off the pan onto a rack to cool.

VARIATIONS

◆ Omit the bacon and stir ½ cup crumbled fresh goat cheese into the leek mixture before spreading on the tart.

◆ When cooking the leeks, substitute 2 tablespoons bacon fat for 2 tablespoons of the butter.

◆ Use spring onions instead of the leeks and cook for another 5 minutes or so to thoroughly soften.

# Braised Leeks with Chickpeas, Saffron, and Dried Marjoram

4 SERVINGS

Long cooking makes leeks taste luscious and sweet; combining them with freshly dried marjoram and saffron gilds the lily, so to speak. Serve with couscous or quinoa for a light yet very flavorful meal.

Trim the roots and all but 1 inch of the green from:

**4 medium or 8 small leeks (about 2 pounds)**

Cut the leeks lengthwise and wash. Swish the leeks well to dislodge any hidden grit. Drain and pat dry.

Crush, using a mortar and pestle:

**1 large pinch of saffron threads**

Add:

**½ cup warm water or light chicken stock**

**Salt**

**2 tablespoons extra-virgin olive oil**

Stir together and let sit.

Heat a heavy-bottomed pan large enough to hold the leeks in a single layer over medium heat. Pour in:

**1 tablespoon olive oil**

Add the leeks cut side down and cook until they begin to brown, about 6 minutes. Turn the leeks cut side up and sprinkle over:

**1 teaspoon marjoram, freshly dried if possible**

**Salt**

**A large pinch of dried chile flakes (optional)**

Pour in the saffron water or stock. The liquid should come up to the shoulders of the leeks but not cover them. Add water as needed, rinsing out the mortar with the extra water to get all of the saffron. Adjust the heat to a bare simmer and partly cover the pan. Cook until tender, about 12 minutes. Remove the lid for the last 5 minutes and allow the liquid to reduce. Meanwhile, heat together:

**2 cups cooked chickpeas**

**1 garlic clove, pounded to a purée**

When ready to serve, taste a leek and the braising liquid for salt and adjust as needed. Using a slotted spoon, spoon the chickpeas onto a serving platter or individual plates and then gently arrange the leeks over the chickpeas along with their braising juices. Drizzle with:

**Extra-virgin olive oil**

VARIATION

◆ Sauté a chopped chile pepper in olive oil before adding the chickpeas to the pot to heat.

## Shallots (*Allium cepa* var. *aggregatum*)

Shallots look like small reddish onions. They have a particular flavor, which some describe as cross between onions and garlic. To me they have a very refined onion flavor, without the harsh bite most onions have. There is a whole list of French sauces based on shallots and their fine flavor. I use them most often in vinaigrettes. Macerated in vinegar, they add depth and sweetness to a salad—especially one made with frisée. Many cuisines fry them to a crispy brown for a garnish. Try it! You will not be disappointed. *French Gray* is a French classic with dusty gray skin, and *French Red* is a larger variety with red skin. Both are quite tasty.

Shallots are very easy to grow. They mature rapidly and, like garlic, will create a bunch, or clump, of bulbs from a single planted bulb. Separate the bulbs and plant them, burying them root end down and covering with a good inch of soil. Harvest them all through their growing cycle. Their young greens are as tasty as the bulbs.

## Crispy Fried Shallots

Fried shallots make everything taste better. Like fried herbs, they add a burst of flavor. Try them as a garnish to puréed potatoes, celery root, and other vegetables or piled on steaks, chops, and fish. I love them scattered over an Indian rice pilaf. Large, juicy late-summer shallots are especially good fried.

Cut 1 or 2 large shallots in half lengthwise, then peel. Trim off the root end and slice the shallots ⅛ inch thick. Heat a small frying pan, and pour in olive oil or vegetable oil to a depth of about ¼ inch. When the oil is hot, add the shallots and cook 1 to 2 minutes, stirring frequently, until they are browned and crisp. Lift the shallots out of the oil, drain on paper towels, and serve immediately. Leeks are delicious fried the same way. Cut the white part of the leek into a fine julienne and fry as above.

## Sweet-and-Sour Shallots

4 SERVINGS

Preheat the oven to 375°F.
Peel, leaving the root end intact:

   **12 small or 8 medium shallots**
Arrange the shallots in a baking dish that will just hold them comfortably. If some of the shallots are larger than the others, cut them in half lengthwise. (Try to keep a bit of root end on each half so the layers stay together.) Season with:

   **2 teaspoons olive oil**
   **2 teaspoons butter, cut into shavings**
   **1 teaspoon sugar**
   **Salt**
   **Fresh-ground black pepper**
Toss together to coat evenly. Bake until the shallots begin to color and are almost tender, about 12 minutes. Shake the pan now and then to ensure even cooking. Pour over:

   **2 tablespoons balsamic vinegar**
   **2 teaspoons red wine vinegar**
Continue cooking until the vinegar is reduced and thick and the shallots are tender, another 10 minutes. Keep tossing the onions in the pan now and then. Serve warm or at room temperature.

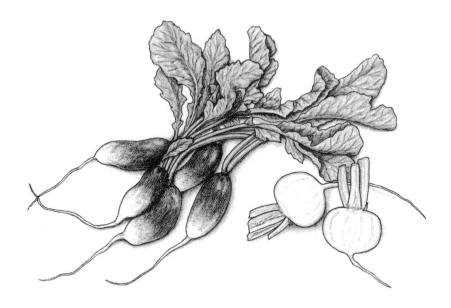

# Growing Underground

## Roots and Tubers

FARM AND GARDEN SOIL is filled with vegetables growing underground. Roots, tubers, and an occasional odd-fellow legume populate the agricultural underworld. In the kitchen, root vegetables are frequently relegated to the back of the refrigerator and thought of only as boring necessities. I heartily disagree. Freshly pulled red, pink, and golden beets; multicolored carrots; dazzling radishes of every size; and ravishing white and purple-topped turnips all inspire me. I love cooking with parsnips, rutabagas, turnips, celery root, and horseradish, too. When shaved in salads, served on a crudités plate, or made into zesty pickles, their sweet flavors and toothy bite are refreshing. When roasted, mashed into purées, baked in gratins, or glazed in butter, they are tender, luscious, and comforting. Potatoes need no introduction, they are beloved in all their guises—roasted, mashed, baked, fried, or in a gratin, soup, or salad. Sweet potatoes and sunchokes complete this subterranean roster, adding still more flavor and color to the kitchen and kitchen garden.

# Roots: Carrots, Radishes, Turnips, Beets, Celery Root, Parsnips, Rutabagas, Horseradish

## Recipes

Carrot Curls  71

Chicken Braised with Carrots and Coriander  72

Colorful Carrots with Butter and Honey  72

Spiced Carrot Raita  73

Shaved Watermelon Radish with Lime and Sea Salt  74

Sautéed French Breakfast Radishes  75

Daikon Radish Braised with Miso and Soy  75

Grilled Pork Sandwiches with Radishes, Carrots, and Chiles  76

Tokyo Turnip Pickles  77

Caramelized Purple Top Turnips  78

Scarlet Turnip Risotto with Red Wine  78

Chioggia Beet and Carrot Salad  80

Beets Cooked in the Coals  80

Celery Root Soup with Celery and Buttered Croutons  81

Parsnip Soup with Sage and Toasted Walnuts  83

Rutabaga and Parsnip Gratin  84

Rutabaga à la Greque  85

Fresh Horseradish and Tarragon Salsa  86

## Roots in the Garden

Root vegetables hide their brilliant colors and varied shapes under the soil while they grow, not to be seen until harvest. But many offer a quite a bit of charm above ground, too. Carrots have graceful feathery leaves that soften the texture of the garden landscape, and beets extend their tall, brilliantly colored greens and stems up into the air. Parsnips and parsley root, the most winter hardy of the bunch, retain a comforting, sturdy green even after the advent of frosts and snow. Radishes, when allowed to go to seed, send up delicate flowers and pointy, plump seedpods that claw the air; and both flowers and pods are tasty.

Root vegetables, especially larger varieties, prefer to grow in loose soil. If your garden's soil is heavy and clay-filled, adding a good layer of compost on the surface will encourage the worms to come and help loosen the soil as the seeds sprout and grow. For healthy, thriving roots, water consistently. Carrots and their cousins need relatively little nitrogen in their diet, so avoid adding any plant foods high in nitrogen to the soil.

Carrot, celery root, and parsnip seeds are tiny and sometimes take up to three weeks to germinate. Be patient; they will come up. Turnips and radish seeds, on the other hand, germinate quickly and the plants grow fast. Plant in early spring and late summer; cold weather makes roots turn sweet and tender, while heat makes their flesh woody and tough. Sow the seeds directly in the ground in blocks or in broad rows. Carrots, turnips, and radishes can be planted densely and thinned strategically. For the first thinnings, pull out the sprouting leaves, and later pull out enough young roots to allow those left behind to grow and expand. To gauge the roots' size, if their shoulders aren't peeking over the soil surface, scratch away enough dirt to get a look at the roots below. The little leafy thinnings and tiny roots are fabulous in salads, pastas, and soups, and on grilled fish.

Smaller varieties of the quick-growing roots, such as radishes, turnips, carrots, and beets, all grow well in containers. For best results, choose containers that are large and deep.

*Radish thinnings*

## Carrots *(Daucus carota)*

Carrots are so common they are easy to take for granted, but biting into a young carrot fresh from your garden or a nearby farm will bring carrots sharply back into focus. Sweet, juicy, and crisp, that first bite makes it clear why carrots are part of just about every cuisine. Carrot salads made with carrot curls of different colors bring flavor and flamboyance to a winter day. A simple cooked carrot glazed with butter and just a touch of honey is a revelation. And carrots are delicious pickled, roasted, and made into soup. In France and Italy, carrots join celery and onions to form the flavorful bases, known respectively as mirepoix and *soffritto,* that underlie many stews, soups, and sauces.

Not all carrots are orange. The varieties called *Purple* and *Atomic Red* are dark colored and bright; *Yellowstone* is tasty and yellow; and *Lunar White* is just that. *Little Finger* and *Tonda di Parigi (tonda* means "round" in Italian) are small, orange, and have the shapes their names suggest. *Scarlet Nantes* carrots are very sweet, crisp, and cylindrical, with a blunt tip. *Chantenay* carrots are sturdy, thick, and pointy, good for juicing and storing. When you grow carrots yourself, you can start eating them when they are tiny babies and continue until they are full-size. Carrot tops are edible, and recipes can be found for making them into soups and salads; but because they can be quite bitter, most often they get fed to the chickens or thrown on the compost heap.

## Carrot Curls

Sweet, crisp, and pretty, with bright colors and charming shapes, carrot curls show off all the best attributes of a carrot. Slicing carrots thinly enhances their flavor the way light enhances the colors of stained glass, and letting them soak in ice water makes them curl and a whole lot more fun to eat. Use as many carrot colors as you can find for your curls.

To make them, first peel the carrots with a swivel-bladed vegetable peeler. Use the same tool to cut long, thin strips from the length of the carrot. Soak the slices in ice water for a couple hours, or until they curl. Drain. That's it.

Toss the curls with colorful lettuces or chicories and dress them with vinaigrette for a fantastic salad. Kids love carrot curls as a snack or in a packed lunch. I used to send my daughter, Fanny, to school with carrot curls and a little jar of vinaigrette to dip them in. They always got eaten.

# Chicken Braised with Carrots and Coriander

4 SERVINGS

Sweet, mild coriander seeds add warmth and texture to a simple braise of carrots and chicken. If you grow cilantro, use the immature green seeds from bolting plants for a fresher, deeper flavor.

Trim:

**4 bone-in chicken thighs**

Season with:

**Salt**

**Fresh-ground black pepper**

This can be done the night before for even better flavor.

Heat a heavy skillet over medium-high heat (a cast-iron pan is great for this). When hot pour in:

**1 tablespoon olive oil**

Carefully add the thighs skin side down and cook until golden brown, about 10 minutes. If the skin starts to brown too quickly, turn down the heat. When the skin is crisp and brown, turn the thighs and brown the meat for a couple minutes. Remove the thighs from the pan and add:

**1 large or 2 small onions, peeled and diced coarse**

**1 tablespoon coriander seeds**

Cook for 5 minutes or so until the onions are softened. Add:

**4 large carrots, peeled and cut into large even-size pieces**

**A pinch of salt**

**1 small bay leaf**

Cook for a few minutes, then add the chicken thighs skin side up, and pour in:

**⅓ cup dry white wine**

Bring to a boil and reduce until almost gone. Pour in:

**1 cup chicken stock or water**

The liquid should reach just above the bottom of the chicken; add more if needed. Bring to a boil, and then turn down to a bare simmer. Cover and cook until the thighs are tender, about 20 minutes. Check the braise now and then to be sure it is not boiling hard and that there is enough liquid to keep the bottom of the pan from burning. Add more liquid if necessary. Serve garnished with:

**2 teaspoons chopped parsley**

VARIATIONS

✦ Use whole legs in place of the thighs; cut them in half at the joint.

✦ Substitute chicken breasts for the thighs. Follow the recipe, but don't add the breasts until the vegetables have cooked in the liquid for 10 minutes. After adding the breasts, cook until just done, about 10 minutes, to keep the tender meat from overcooking and drying out.

✦ Substitute parsnips or celery root for some—or all—of the carrots. If using all parsnips, try 1 teaspoon of cumin seeds instead of the 1 tablespoon of coriander seeds.

# Colorful Carrots with Butter and Honey

This is a simple recipe, and like all simple recipes, it requires the best ingredients. Most important of all are the carrots. Choose young carrots, vibrantly fresh and alive, in as many colors as are available—

red, orange, yellow, and purple. Depending on their size, count on 2 to 4 carrots per person. Cut off the greens, leaving a half inch of stem. Peel the carrots lightly, and wash them well. Cut large ones in half lengthwise, but leave small ones whole. Put a pan with ½ inch of water in it over high heat. Add the carrots, a small knob of butter per person, and salt to taste. Cover the pan and cook until the carrots are just tender. Remove the lid, lower the heat, add a small spoonful of honey, and cook until the water is mostly gone and the carrots are gilded with a shiny glaze of butter and honey. Remove from the pan and serve right away. If you like, strew some chopped chervil or dill on the top.

## Spiced Carrot Raita

MAKES ABOUT ⅔ CUP

Sweet, juicy, young, fresh carrots have the nicest texture for this *raita*. Serve it with Kohlrabi and Red Lentil Dal (page 239), Yogurt-Spiced Chicken Skewers (page 183), and basmati rice for an easy Indian-inspired meal. Or spoon it over a simple coleslaw for a delicious spin on an old classic.

Mix together:

**2 carrots, peeled and grated**
**½ teaspoon finely grated peeled ginger (a Microplane works well)**
**1 tablespoon chopped cilantro**
**½ cup Yogurt (page 183)**
**Salt**

Heat a small pan over medium-high heat and measure in:

**1½ teaspoons olive oil, ghee, or coconut oil**

**½ teaspoon black mustard seeds**
**5 ajwain seeds, crushed**
**¼ teaspoon nigella seeds (a small, sharp-tasting Indian spice; also called Kalonji)**

Cook until the seeds start to pop and then pour over the yogurt mixture. Mix and taste for salt. Finish with:

**A squeeze of lime juice**

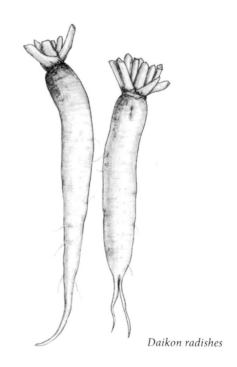

*Daikon radishes*

## Radishes (*Raphanus sativus*)

Radishes come small and large, pointy like carrots, or round or oval like turnips. They can be white, red, purple, pink, bicolored, black-skinned, green-skinned, and more. Some are very spicy; many are mild. *French Breakfast* radishes—bright ruby red with a snowy white tip—are sensational. I like them so much there is one on my business card. Round *Easter Egg* radishes—in hues of purple, pink, red, and white—are wonderful, too. Large round *Watermelon* radishes, also called *Red Meat* radish, are a beautiful magenta inside their ivory and green skin. *Daikon* is a long white radish that makes great kimchi. All radishes make great crudités—raw vegetables served as an hors d'oeuvre while waiting for dinner or drinking a glass of wine. Small French Breakfast and Easter Egg radishes are gorgeous lying on a plate with their delicate greens still attached. Serve them with buttered bread and a bowl of salt to dip them in. Slice large daikon and Watermelon radishes to make a quick pickle, or wrap a thin slice around a pinch of dressed herbs or greens. Thinly sliced small radishes add a colorful, peppery, pretty crunch to salads. Radishes are also good cooked. Sautéed, steamed, braised, or roasted, they add a mildly piquant touch to a dish.

The small varieties of radishes are quick to grow and do not need a lot of space. I like to grow them in the lettuce bed; they also do very well in containers. The larger radishes such as daikon and Watermelon radish are slower growing and need more space.

An interesting role in the garden for small radishes is that of a decoy or trap crop. They are in the same family as cabbage, kale, and the other brassicas and, when interplanted, will tempt the usual pests away from the larger, slower growing crops. It is good to know that although the leaves of radishes may have been nibbled on, the roots below are usually fine.

## Shaved Watermelon Radish with Lime and Sea Salt

Watermelon radishes are large, round, and unassuming-looking on the outside, with a dull taupe body and bright green shoulders. Cut open a ripe one and you will be greeted with brilliant magenta flesh ringed with white. Thinly slice them or make shavings with a swivel-bladed vegetable peeler, drizzle them with lemon or lime juice, and right before you serve them, sprinkle with salt. (If you salt them ahead, they will start to give off liquid and soften.)

Slices make good wraps, too. Salt thin slices, and when they are soft, wrap them around cilantro dressed with lime, olive oil, and salt—a perfect couple of bites, light and refreshing. Rocket with lemon and a few shavings of Parmesan is another good combination to wrap in radish slices.

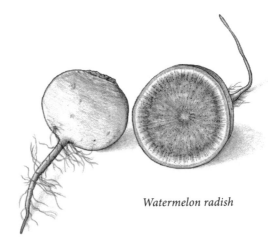

*Watermelon radish*

## Sautéed French Breakfast Radishes

Sautéed radishes make a good side dish, especially with fish. The pungent spice of the radish is tamed by cooking, and the lingering bite is delightful with the delicate flavor of fish. If the radish greens are young and tender, cook them along with the roots.

Wash the radishes well in an ample amount of cool water. If you are keeping the radish greens or tops on be sure to give them a good swish to remove any grit. Leave smaller radishes whole, and halve or quarter the larger ones. Heat a heavy-bottomed pan over medium-high heat, pour in enough oil to coat the bottom of the pan, and add the radishes with a large pinch of salt. Cook, tossing the pan now and then, until the radishes are lightly browned; turn the heat down, cover, and cook until the radishes are tender but not soft. Finish with a knob of butter or a drizzle of extra-virgin olive oil—or a spoonful of salsa verde.

I like radishes steamed, too. Toss them with a pinch of salt and steam over boiling water until tender. Finish as above.

## Daikon Radish Braised with Miso and Soy

4 SERVINGS

Daikon is milder in flavor than the smaller European varieties of radishes. It turns quite sweet when cooked, reminiscent of a young turnip.

Peel:
   **1 large daikon**
Cut into ¾-inch slices. Arrange the slices in a single layer in a small heavy-bottomed pot. Add cold water just to cover the daikon, about 1 cup. Add:
   **1 teaspoon soy sauce**
   **One 2-inch piece kombu seaweed**
Bring to a boil and immediately turn down to a simmer. Cover and cook until just tender, about 10 minutes. Test with a sharp knife or bamboo skewer. Turn off the heat, remove the kombu, and cut into a fine julienne.
Measure into a small bowl:
   **1 tablespoon miso, either light (shiro)**
      **or medium flavored**
Add 1 tablespoon cooking liquid and stir to mix well. Stir the miso into the daikon pot with:
   **½ teaspoon rice wine vinegar**
Bring up to a simmer and cook until the liquid is almost gone, about 10 more minutes. When done, remove the daikon to a warm dish. Add the kombu to the pan with:
   **¼ teaspoon sesame oil**
Reduce the sauce, if needed, until thick and spoon over the daikon and mix well. Serve warm or cold.

VARIATIONS
◆ Add 1 tablespoon hon mirin (sweet rice wine) with the rice wine vinegar.
◆ Substitute Tokyo turnips for the daikon. Turnips need a much shorter cooking time than radishes. Remove them when they are done and reduce the liquid more if necessary.
◆ Replace 2 tablespoons of the water with 2 tablespoons sake.

# Grilled Pork Sandwiches with Radishes, Carrots, and Chiles

4 SERVINGS

A *bành mí* sandwich is the result of a blend of French and Vietnamese cuisine—a crusty light baguette filled with crispy grilled marinated pork, pickled daikon and carrots, mayonnaise, cilantro, and jalapeño peppers. If you want to be even more traditional, add a slice of fine-textured pâté. The flavors meld into one of the best-tasting sandwiches around the globe.

Marinate the pork a few hours or overnight. Stir together in a medium bowl:

**2 tablespoons fish sauce**
**1 small lemongrass stalk, chopped (about ¼ cup)**
**4 garlic cloves, smashed**
**2 teaspoons fresh-ground black pepper**
**1 tablespoon palm sugar (or ½ tablespoon each honey and brown sugar)**
**1 tablespoon sesame oil**
**1 teaspoon salt**

Mix until the sugar and salt are dissolved and add:

**1 pound pork shoulder, sliced thin**

Mix and then refrigerate.

Prepare the pickles. Cut into a medium julienne:

**1 carrot**
**½ daikon**

Mix together:

**½ cup apple cider vinegar**
**¼ cup water**
**1 tablespoon palm sugar**
**2 teaspoons salt**

Stir in the vegetables and let sit until soft, at least 2 hours.

Prepare a mayonnaise (see page 55) with:

**1 egg yolk**
**1 teaspoon fish sauce**
**½ teaspoon water**
**½ cup light olive oil or vegetable oil**

When ready to cook, drain the pork slices and grill over medium-hot coals until crispy and cooked through, about 4 minutes each side.

Slice into four 5-inch long pieces:

**1 sweet baguette (don't use sourdough)**

Slice each piece lengthwise almost all the way through, leaving the halves hinged on one side. Pull a little of the crumb out of each side to make room for all of the ingredients. (Save the bits to make breadcrumbs.) Toast until the crust is crisp. For each sandwich, spread the bread liberally with mayonnaise, and layer in one quarter of the pork. Drain the pickled carrot and daikon and tuck in a generous amount. Finish with:

**A few cilantro sprigs**
**A few slices jalapeño**

VARIATIONS
◆ Add a slice of fine-textured pâté to each sandwich.
◆ Marinate sliced chicken thighs or breast in place of the pork.

## Turnips *(Brassica rapa)*

Fresh tender turnips are a constant on the menus of Chez Panisse in spring, fall, and winter. Small, white *Tokyo* turnips are delicate enough to be eaten raw in a salad or turned into a quick pickle with a sprinkle of salt and a splash of vinegar. Young turnips with their greens still attached are quickly cooked in a touch of water and served with a drizzle of good olive oil. Larger, firmer turnips are delicious in soup, or mashed, or slowly cooked in a bit of butter until caramelized. Whole or sliced, turnips can be fermented like sauerkraut or kimchi.

*Scarlet Ohno* turnips are tender like the white Tokyo and add lots of color with their neon pink skin. I like them sliced into chicory salads or potato gratins. The classic *Purple Top* turnips, white with purple shoulders, are delicious young or mature. Take a bite and peel them if the skin is tough and unpleasant. If they need to be peeled, leave a little of the purple shoulder on for show. Yellow turnips, like *Golden Globe,* are a bit firmer in texture, almost like mini-rutabagas.

Tokyo turnips are ready to harvest in as few as 30 days, and can be planted in spring and fall in just about any climate zone. Succession sowings every few weeks will keep you with fresh turnips for a long time. The other varieties take a few more weeks to mature. Turnips don't store well in the ground and should be harvested when ready. Eat Tokyo-type turnips right away. The more mature and sturdy varieties can be stored in a root cellar or refrigerator for a while.

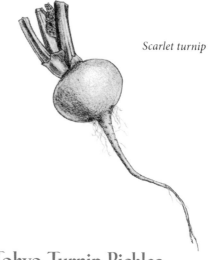

*Scarlet turnip*

## Tokyo Turnip Pickles

Some of my favorite pickles are simple Japanese salt pickles or *asazuke* (shallow pickle), that take just a few minutes to prepare. Pickling accentuates the natural taste and texture, so it's important to use the most vivid, freshly picked vegetables you can. Choose small to medium Tokyo turnips with their tops, or small and tender scarlet turnips and gold turnips.

Trim the tops about ½ inch from the turnip, and wash well to remove any sand or grit hidden between the stems. Use a mandoline or sharp knife and cut the turnips lengthwise from stem to root in ⅛-inch slices. In a bowl, sprinkle the turnips with a few generous pinches of salt and the zest of a lemon. The idea is to add just enough salt to allow the turnips to start softening and releasing water without making them too salty. Place a small plate on top of the turnips, fitted within the bowl, with something heavy (a stone mortar works perfectly) to weigh down the turnips, and let sit for 30 minutes. Squeeze out the water and serve, with a few drops of lemon juice and a drop of soy sauce, if you like. Eat right away, or store the pickles in their liquid for 1 or 2 days.

This is an endlessly adaptable recipe. Substitute a hot chile pepper for the lemon zest and a drop of sesame oil for the soy sauce. Thin slivers of ginger are good, too. For a richer, deeper taste, add a piece of kombu to the turnips when you put them under a weight, a splash of good dashi and a tiny bit of light soy sauce once they've released their water. Pickle slices of radishes or summer squash in the same manner.

# Caramelized Purple Top Turnips

This is a great way to cook mature purple top turnips. The slow cooking and browning makes them very sweet and mild. Prepare ½ to 1 turnip per person depending on their size.

Peel the turnips and cut them in half lengthwise. If they are very large, cut them into quarters. Cut the turnip pieces crosswise into ¼-inch slices. Heat a heavy-bottomed pot over medium heat. Put in a knob of butter per person and when melted, add the turnips and salt to taste. Stir well, lower the heat, and cover tightly. Don't add any water; the turnips will make their own moisture. Cook, stirring now and then, until the turnips are soft and colored with flecks of golden brown, about 15 minutes. They should brown slowly. Adjust the heat if they are browning too quickly. Taste for salt and adjust as needed.

# Scarlet Turnip Risotto with Red Wine

4 SERVINGS

Scarlet turnips and red wine guarantee deep color and flavor. If you have some concentrated and delicious juices remaining from a braise, such as duck legs cooked with red wine, that is the perfect finishing touch for this risotto.

First prepare the turnips to be ready to be added to the rice. Cut off the fresh leafy greens of:

   **4 scarlet turnips**

Cut the greens from the ribs and toss the ribs into the compost bin. Rinse the greens, shake dry, and cut crosswise into wide ribbons. Trim off the stem and root ends of the turnips and peel lightly, leaving as much of the beautiful rose color under the skin as possible. Cut the turnips into medium wedges.

Melt in a heavy-bottomed 2½- to 3-quart saucepan over medium heat:

   **2 tablespoons butter**

Add:

   **1 small onion, diced**
   **1 or 2 thyme sprigs**
   **1 bay leaf**

Cook until the onion is soft and translucent, about 10 minutes. Add:

   **1½ cups risotto rice (Carnaroli, Arborio, or Baldo)**

Cook the rice, stirring now and then, until translucent, about 4 minutes. Do not let it brown.

Meanwhile, in a separate pan, bring to a boil and then turn off:

**5 cups chicken broth**

Pour over the sautéed rice:

**½ cup flavorful red wine**

Cook, stirring fairly often, until all the wine is absorbed. Add 1 cup of the warm chicken stock and cook at a vigorous simmer, stirring occasionally. When the rice starts to get thick, pour in another ½ cup of the broth and add some:

**Salt**

Keep adding broth every time the rice thickens, and don't let it dry out. When the rice is about 10 minutes away from being done (a rice grain bitten in half will have a small raw, white core), stir in the turnips. Add the greens with the next addition of stock. Cook until the rice is tender but still has a firm core, 20 to 30 minutes in all. When the rice is just about done, stir in:

**¼ to ½ cup concentrated duck or other braising juices (optional)**
**1 tablespoon butter**
**⅓ cup grated Parmesan cheese**

Stir vigorously to develop the creamy starch. Taste and add salt as needed. Turn off the heat and let the risotto sit uncovered for a few minutes.

Serve garnished with:

**Freshly grated Parmesan cheese**

VARIATIONS

✦ Substitute farro for the Arborio rice.

✦ Substitute 1 to 2 cups sliced or torn wild mushrooms, such as chanterelle, black trumpet, or hedgehog mushrooms for the turnips.

✦ Add ¼ to ½ cup concentrated duck or other braising juices to the chicken stock when heating it, or stir them in with the butter and Parmesan cheese at the end.

## Beets  (*Beta vulgaris*)

Freshly pulled young beets with their tops still on are sensational. Beets make wonderful winter salads, either grated raw and seasoned with a snappy vinaigrette, or cooked and flavored with a generous splash of your favorite vinegar, a bit of olive oil, and herbs. When you buy or harvest beets with their leaves, don't throw out the leaves. Prep and cook them like chard: they are every bit as tasty—chard and beets are in the same family. Beets come in several different colors. Red beets are the most common and have the earthiest flavor. *Cylindra* (elongated), *Bull's Blood* (with bright red leaves), and *Early Wonder Tall Top* (which makes lots of greens) are all flavorful choices. In containers, try *Baby Ball* (a hybrid). Pink *Chioggia*, yellow *Touchstone Gold*, and white *Blankoma* are lighter-flavored and won't stain what they are being served with. Raw Chioggia beets have beautiful alternating interior hot pink and white stripes. The colors merge when cooked. With a splash of vinegar, golden and Chioggia beets become more brightly colored, almost fluorescent.

Beet seeds have a very tough seed coat. Soak them overnight in tepid water to help speed up germination. Sow seeds or plant seedlings closer than recommended. Thin out the smaller beets as they develop, leaving the others to grow large. The greens may be harvested from growing beets; cut them from the outside in, leaving enough to keep the root going. Keep beets well watered. Of all the roots they like the moistest soil. Mature beets can be stored without their leaves, and unwashed, in a cool moist place for months.

## Chioggia Beet and Carrot Salad

Chioggia beets turn a brilliant pink when tossed with vinegar and are beautiful with orange and yellow carrots. Serve this as one of a group of small salads in an antipasto; on top of a bed of dressed wild rocket or watercress; or in Little Gem leaves as portable hors d'oeuvres when guests gather in the kitchen before dinner.

Select one small beet and carrot for each person. Peel them and grate on the coarse holes of a box grater. Toss with salt and a squeeze of lemon or lime juice. Rice or cider vinegar is good, too. I like to vary the additional seasonings. I recommend adding only 2 or 3 flavors at a time or the tastes will become muddled. A few of my favorite additions are a spoonful of yogurt or crème fraîche; a touch of grated ginger; some coarsely chopped cilantro, dill, chervil, or parsley; a bit of freshly ground, toasted cumin, coriander, cardamom, or caraway seeds; a little finely diced hot pepper; and chopped dried currants, fig, or apricot.

Red beets and purple carrots are pretty in this salad but will bleed their colors onto the other vegetables—so if you want to use them, dress them separately and serve next to the others instead of mixed together.

## Beets Cooked in the Coals

Beets that have a thick skin can be cooked directly in the coals of an open fire. Trim away any leaves leaving a good inch of stem on the root. When the fire has burned long enough to produce a bed of coals and still has a bit of flame, rake out a pile of embers and lay the beets directly on them about 4 or 5 inches away from the flames. Cook the beets until tender, turning them now and then for even cooking. This will take from 30 to 40 minutes depending on the size of the beets. They are done when they are easily pierced with a sharp knife. Remove from the coals and when they are cool enough to handle, cut off the root end, and slip off the burned skins. Cut the peeled beets into wedges or slices and serve warm seasoned with salt and pepper, butter or oil, and herbs. Or toss them with vinegar, salt and pepper, and just a splash of oil. Serve warm or cool.

Artichokes, onions, potatoes, and sweet potatoes can be cooked in the coals as well.

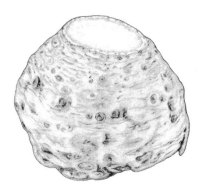

## Celery Root *(Apium graveolens)*

Celery root is an unmistakable knobby brown globe with a few short celery stalks and leaves growing from its top. Peel it and you have a snowy white, dense, sweet-fleshed vegetable ready to go into salads, soups, mashes, or gratins. Its mild flavor marries well with potatoes, either mashed or in a gratin. Chefs love the way it pairs with black truffles. If you have never tried celery root before, start with the soup below and you will quickly become a fan. *Brilliant* is a tasty variety.

Celery root is descended from a marsh plant and is fairly easy to grow in consistently watered soil that has been amended with plenty of compost. Start seeds indoors about ten weeks before planting out after all chance of frost has passed. The seeds are a bit slow to come and will germinate more quickly with an overnight soaking. Too many cold nights will cause the young plants to bolt. In mild climates the roots can overwinter in the ground, but where it gets cold, harvest before freezing weather settles in. The roots sweeten with a bit of frost but cannot tolerate severe cold. Trimmed of

their leaves, the roots will keep for months in a dark, cool, humid environment.

## Celery Root Soup with Celery and Buttered Croutons

MAKES ABOUT 2 QUARTS

This is a silky soup that tastes rich without any cream and with very little butter. The finishing dice of stalk celery adds an unexpected fresh crunch. People are always impressed with the elegance of this soup and it is very simple to prepare—make a lot because you will be happy to eat it again.

Heat a heavy-bottomed pot over medium heat and add:

**3 tablespoons butter**

When melted add:

**1 medium onion, diced**
**1 bay leaf**
**3 thyme sprigs**

Cook until soft, without browning, about 12 minutes.

Meanwhile, wash and slice:

**1 large or 2 small leeks**

Put the slices in water to clean and drain them in a colander. Peel:

**2 medium celery roots (about 1 pound)**

Cut into quarters lengthwise and slice crosswise.

When the onions are soft, add:

**Salt**

Stir well and add the sliced leek and celery root. Cook, stirring now and then, until the celery root begins to soften, about 7 minutes. Add:

**5 cups chicken broth**

Bring to a boil, reduce the heat, and simmer until the celery root is quite soft, about 20 minutes.

While the soup is cooking, wash and trim:

**3 to 4 celery stalks**

Remove the strings with a vegetable peeler. Cut the stalks crosswise into 4-inch pieces, and then lengthwise into thin sticks. Cut across the sticks to make a fine dice. Blanch the diced celery in salted boiling water for 1 to 2 minutes. The celery should be a translucent green color but still have a nice crunch. Remove and spread on a plate to cool.

For the croutons, toss together:

**1 cup bite-size pieces country-style
　　bread (crusts removed)**

**2 teaspoons butter, melted**

Spread on a baking dish and cook in a 350°F oven until crisp and golden brown, about 12 minutes. Stir now and then for even baking.

When the soup is ready, remove the thyme sprigs and bay leaf and purée with a handheld immersion blender or in a conventional blender. A food mill with a fine plate will work, too, but the soup will not be as fine textured. Taste and add salt as needed. If the soup is too thick, thin with chicken stock or water.

Serve in warm bowls with a sprinkling of diced celery and croutons.

VARIATIONS

◆ Substitute 4 parsnips for the celery root and forgo the celery garnish.

◆ Leave the soup brothy (don't purée it) and skip the celery garnish.

◆ Garnish the soup with sautéed black trumpet or chanterelle mushrooms instead of diced celery.

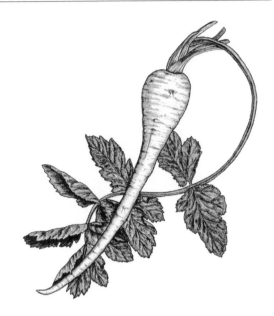

## Parsnip *(Pastinaca sativa)*

A parsnip looks like a large, rough white carrot, but parsnips are definitely not to be eaten raw. Once cooked, their flavor is distinctly perfumed and sweet, with caramel undertones. Parsnips are quite versatile in the kitchen. Cut thin and fried, they make a very addictive and crunchy chip. Roasting, either alone or with other roots, concentrates their sweet flavor. Add them to a roasting chicken, mash them with potatoes or by themselves, layer them into a gratin, or simmer them in a soup. They are also excellent in a pie instead of pumpkin. *Turga*, *Andover*, and *Hollow Crown* are good varieties to grow.

Parsnip seed does not keep for more than a year and takes up to three weeks to germinate. For those reasons, use fresh seed and sow thickly, thinning the plants after they reach a good four inches in height. Parsnips take four months to reach maturity. Plant seeds in midsummer and harvest in the fall all the way through to early spring. Parsnips will sweeten in frost and they winter well underground, as long as they are mulched thickly in freezing weather. The mulch will keep the ground soft enough to harvest and let you know where to look for them under the snow. They lose their sweet flavor once the greens start to grow again in the spring, so be sure to harvest before the weather starts to warm up.

# Parsnip Soup with Sage and Toasted Walnuts

MAKES ABOUT 1 QUART

Crispy fried sage and toasted nuts add richness and flavor to this sweet hearty soup.

Melt in a heavy-bottomed pot over medium heat:

**3 tablespoons butter**

Add:

**4 large shallots, sliced thin**

Cook, stirring occasionally, until the shallots are soft and translucent, about 10 minutes. Stir in:

**1 leek, white part only, sliced, washed, and drained**

**1 sage sprig**

**Salt**

Cook for about 4 minutes and stir in:

**4 large parsnips, trimmed, peeled, and cut into ¼-inch half-moons (about 1¼ pounds)**

Cook for 7 minutes. Pour in:

**3 cups rich chicken broth**

Bring to a boil and then turn down to a simmer. Cook until the parsnips are tender, about 12 minutes.

While the soup is cooking, preheat the oven to 350°F. Spread out on a baking sheet:

**½ cup walnuts**

Toast until golden brown, about 12 minutes. Stir the nuts now and then to ensure even browning. Let the nuts cool and then rub in your hands to remove some of the tannic skins. Chop coarsely.

Heat a small skillet over medium-high heat. Pour in:

**1½ tablespoons olive oil**

Add:

**12 to 15 sage leaves**

Cook until the sage leaves turn translucent. When the sage is done, take the pan off the heat, add the walnuts, and toss with the oil and sage. Season with:

**Salt**

**Fresh-ground black pepper**

Using a mortar and pestle, pound until smooth:

**1 large or 2 small garlic cloves**

Add the nuts and sage with:

**2 tablespoons extra-virgin olive oil**

Pound lightly. Taste for salt and adjust as needed. Set aside.

When the soup is done cooking, remove the sage sprig, taste for salt, and adjust as needed. Serve warm with a spoonful of the sage and walnuts.

VARIATION

◆ For smooth soup, substitute vegetable broth for chicken broth and purée soup with ¼ cup crème fraîche. Finish the sage and walnuts with softened butter instead of olive oil.

## Rutabaga  (*Brassica napo brassica*)

Rutabagas, sometimes called swedes, look like large yellowish turnips, and their flesh when cooked is sweet and delicious. Boiled and then mashed is the classic way to serve rutabagas. Mix them with carrots or potatoes for variety. They are also tasty in slaws, roasted, steamed, finished on the grill, and served with a bit of salsa verde. *Laurentian* and *Marian* are classic, dependable varieties.

Rutabagas are easy to grow, but they do take their time, needing at least four months before they are ready to pull. They are an impressive sight as their roots swell and push up aboveground as they grow. Start them in midsummer for fall and winter harvest. Rutabaga leaves are tasty and you can sneak a few now and then as they are growing. Rutabagas will store in cold ground or in a root cellar for months.

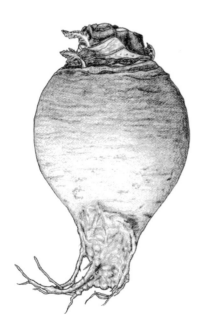

## Rutabaga and Parsnip Gratin

4 SERVINGS

This gratin is an easy and elegant way to serve rutabagas. Translucent creamy orange rutabaga slices are lined up with ivory circles of parsnip, and the onions underneath add richness and loads of flavor. Precooking the rutabagas and parsnips in salted water keeps the gratin succulent and the leftover cooking water is perfect for moistening a pot of rice or for cooking pasta to complete the meal.

Heat a heavy-bottomed pan over medium heat and pour in:
>    **3 tablespoons olive oil or**
>      **1½ tablespoons olive oil and**
>      **1½ tablespoons butter**

When hot, add:
>    **1 onion, sliced thin**

Cook until the onion is soft, about 12 minutes, and add:
>    **1 tablespoon marjoram leaves**
>    **Salt**
>    **Fresh-ground black pepper**
>    **A pinch of Marash pepper (optional)**

Spoon the onion mixture into the bottom of a 6- to 8-inch baking or gratin dish. Preheat the oven to 375°F.

Peel and slice thin:
>    **1 medium rutabaga (about ½ pound)**
>    **2 small parsnips (about ½ pound)**

A mandoline slicer makes this job easier. I like to make the slices about ⅛ inch thick. Cook the rutabaga slices first and then the parsnips in salted boiling water until just tender, no more than 2 minutes. Drain and when the slices are cool, layer them into the baking dish, alternating rows of overlapping slices of each vegetable. When all the slices are in, sprinkle with:

**Salt**

**A drizzle of olive oil**

Cover the gratin with a layer of parchment paper and place in the hot oven. Cook for 15 minutes, remove the paper, and cook for another 10.

VARIATIONS

◆ Other vegetables, such as celery root, parsley root, kohlrabi, potatoes, or turnips, may be used along with (or in place of) the rutabagas and parsnips.

◆ Other herbs and spices can be used instead of marjoram. Try thyme or savory or a mix of ginger, nigella seed, and cilantro. Cardamom is very nice with the sweet flavors of the vegetables.

# Rutabaga à la Grecque

4 SERVINGS

This is a great way to make a fresh salad out of a winter root vegetable that is typically served hot.

Peel:

**1 large or 2 small rutabagas**
**(about 1 pound)**

Cut crosswise into ¼-inch-thick slices. Be careful. If the root is hard to slice, turn it onto one of its ends and cut it in half lengthwise, before cutting crosswise, flat side down, into half-moon slices.

Measure into a medium-size pot:

**3 cups water**

**¾ cup wine vinegar (red or white)**

**¼ cup white wine**

**½ teaspoon black peppercorns**

**1 teaspoon coriander seeds**

**2 large or 4 small garlic cloves,**
**peeled and cut in half**

**2 chile pods**

**4 thyme sprigs**

**4 marjoram sprigs**

**Salt**

Add enough salt so the liquid tastes salty— not inedible, just on the salty side. Bring to a boil and turn down to a simmer. Cook for 3 minutes and then add the rutabaga slices. Cook until tender (not soft), about 15 minutes, depending on the thickness of the slices. Test a corner of one of the slices. Let the slices cool in the liquid. Serve right away as is or drizzled with salsa verde, or store in the liquid for up to a week or so. The rutabaga slices taste even better the next day.

VARIATIONS

◆ Slice sunchokes, kohlrabi, or purple top turnips and cook in the same manner. They will take much less time to cook. Check after 5 minutes.

◆ Use different spices in the cooking liquid. Try ginger, cilantro, and star anise; cumin, fresh turmeric, and nigella; or saffron, cinnamon, and allspice.

## Horseradish (*Armoracia rusticana*)

The dry, rough brown skin of a fresh horseradish root hides the pungent creamy white flesh inside. Cut it open and there is no mistaking what it is. Fresh horseradish is much more pungent than the condiment sold already grated, and it has a much fresher and fuller flavor. I like horseradish with roasted meats, in sandwiches, and with seafood salads. Mix it into lightly whipped cream, crème fraîche, homemade ketchup, or with herbs and olive oil for a fresh salsa.

A root will lose its pungency after sitting a while so it is a good idea to grate the whole thing, mix it with vinegar, and seal it tightly in a glass container. The sharp bite will last for a few weeks. Watch your eyes and nose while you are grating. If you lean too close you may get a very heady whiff, much like taking a big bite of wasabi while eating sushi.

Horseradish is a perennial that grows from root cuttings instead of seed, and any bit of root left in the ground will grow into a new plant. To control its invasive tendencies, it is best to plant it in a deep container. If planting in the ground, sink a barrier, such as an open-bottomed plastic container, around the area you are planting. Nurseries sell root cuttings, or if you find it at the farmers' market it will probably be fresh enough to plant. A two-inch section of root should be enough to start a plant. The pungency of horseradish root is greatly increased by frost. Harvest the roots in fall after the greens have died back, or in spring before the greens have begun to grow again. The young leaves of spring are a tasty and spicy addition to salads and salsas.

## Fresh Horseradish and Tarragon Salsa
MAKES ⅓ CUP

Fresh horseradish and tarragon make a wonderful spring salsa that is delicious paired with hot or cold roast beef. Grated fresh horseradish is quite pungent, so watch your eyes and nose.

Peel and finely grate:

**One 3-inch piece fresh horseradish root**

You should have about 2 tablespoons grated root. Mix with:

**1 tablespoon white wine vinegar**

Stir in:

**2 tablespoons chopped parsley**
**2 teaspoons chopped tarragon**
**Salt**
**¼ cup extra-virgin olive oil**

Taste and adjust salt and acid as needed.

# Tubers and Others:
## Potatoes, Sweet Potatoes, and Sunchokes

## Recipes

New Potatoes with Butter and Thyme 90

Smashed and Fried German Butterball Potatoes 90

Yellow Finn Potato and Black Trumpet Gratin 91

Salt-Roasted Cranberry Red Potatoes with
Crème Fraîche and Chives 92

Fingerling Potatoes Roasted in Duck Fat 92

Straw Sweet Potato Cakes 93

Grilled Sweet Potatoes with Marjoram Sauce 94

Sunchoke and Fennel Soup 95

Sunchoke Chips 95

# Tubers in the Garden

Tubers grow underground, just like roots. Technically, however, tubers are not roots at all; they are thickened or swollen stems. Potatoes, sweet potatoes, sunchokes, and taro are the ones we eat most commonly. Tuberous plants are naturally perennial: when the greens die back in winter, the tubers stay in the ground to resprout in the coming spring. However, we grow them as annual crops, replanting every year; and the plants are not started from seed but from tubers saved from the last harvest. The sprouting eyes of an old potato in the pantry demonstrate just how new potato plants start to grow.

Tubers prefer loose soil. So add lots of compost to your garden soil and they will do fine. Good drainage is important. The plants need moisture, but the tubers will rot if left soaking in soggy soil. The plants need a lot of energy to develop large, energy-filled tubers below ground, so feed them plenty of compost to keep them healthy and thriving. The prime time for harvest is after the plants flower (the blossoms are quite charming, by the way), and leaves begin to turn yellow and droop. Tubers are great fun to harvest because you get to dig for buried treasure!

# Potatoes (*Solanum tuberosum*)

It is easy now to find many varieties of potatoes at the market or the nursery—yellow-, pink-, and purple-fleshed; waxy and floury; baby, fingerling, and new. *Yellow Finn* and *Yukon Gold* are yellow-fleshed varieties, sweet and full of flavor. They both have dense, moist flesh that works well for gratins or mashed potatoes. *Bintje* and *German Butterball* are delicious yellow-fleshed potatoes with a slightly starchier texture that is well-suited for fries, purées, and mashes. *All Blue* and *Peruvian Purple* are eye-catching varieties with indigo-purple flesh and *Mountain Rose* and *Cranberry Red* are super-sweet and magenta inside. Fingerling potatoes such as the *French La Ratte* and *Russian Banana* are firm-fleshed and make great roasted potatoes. There are fingerlings with colorful flesh, too. These are just a few of my favorites; there are many, many more to try.

Standard potatoes are brought to market once they have been "cured": that is, the tubers are harvested after the plant aboveground has died back and the potatoes are left to dry for a week or so to toughen their skins. The toughened skin makes it possible to store potatoes for a long time. New potatoes are young potatoes that are dug up while the green plant above is still alive. They are a gardener's treat. Their skin is delicate, almost nonexistent, and their flesh is sweet and juicy. They must be eaten right away.

Potatoes don't tolerate extremes of either hot and cold or wet and dry. When purchasing potatoes to plant (seed potatoes), read the seasonal planting instructions and choose

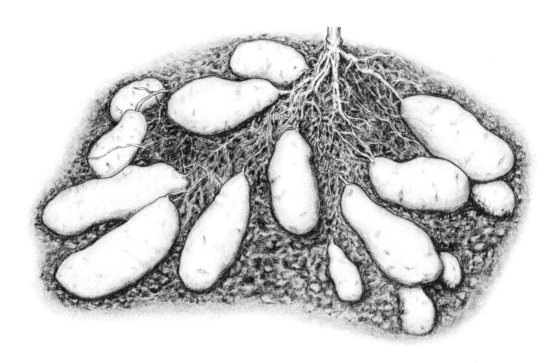

varieties that will do well in your growing area, some of which mature early, others late. Keep in mind that potatoes pass along any problems they encountered where they were grown. Seed potatoes from a nursery or catalog are guaranteed healthy. You can grow potatoes from the farmers' market or your most recent harvest, but be extra sure that they were grown in good, healthy soil.

Plant whole potatoes if they are small, or cut them into pieces that have at least one eye. Tuck them into half-filled containers or trenches and pile up, or "hill," more soil around the plants as they grow, to create a larger harvest and protect the tubers from the sun. Add compost to the hilling soil to keep the potatoes well fed. New potatoes can be harvested as soon as the plants begin to flower. Pull up the whole plant or dig around and harvest as needed. For more mature potatoes, wait until the plants begin to turn yellow and wither. Let the potatoes dry in a cool place for a few days and then store in a cool, dark, dry place. Keep them out of the sun—potatoes begin to develop green skin when exposed to sunlight. If this happens, peel away and discard any green parts before eating.

Inevitably, one or more potatoes get left in the soil at harvest time. In milder climates, if left undisturbed, these will usually grow, producing a new plant and a new crop of potatoes in the early spring; and when you start to work the soil to put in new spring plantings, you will find a bonus crop of new potatoes for a spring dinner.

## New Potatoes with Butter and Thyme

New potatoes are divine on their own. I do very little to them; even the herbs I use with them are the tender mild ones: young thyme with its blossoms, chervil, chives, cilantro, or a little anise hyssop.

Wash the potatoes well and rub off some of the skins if you like. Then steam them until just done and toss with butter, chopped herbs, and a good sprinkle of salt.

VARIATIONS

• If you have a fire going, wrap new potatoes in packages of foil with salt, pepper, butter or oil, and a few herbs. Place the packages in the coals, turning them now and then until the potatoes are done.

• "Stove" them, as the British do (the word comes from *étouver*, the French word for stew): Heat a little butter or olive oil in a heavy-bottomed pan that will hold the potatoes in a single layer. Cast iron works very nicely for this. Add the potatoes and a little salt. Cover the pan tightly and cook over medium-low heat, shaking the pan now and then, until tender—about 12 minutes, more or less, depending on the size of your potatoes. The potatoes should not brown much at all; turn the heat down if they start to brown too quickly. When the potatoes are done, serve them with some fresh butter or olive oil, a sprinkling of chopped tender herbs (if you want), and some fresh-ground black pepper.

## Smashed and Fried German Butterball Potatoes

4 SERVINGS

German Butterball potatoes have a lovely loose, almost floury texture with loads of sweet potato flavor. They make very good mashed potatoes, but I also like to smash them whole and fry them, almost like a little potato pancake.

Wash and gently scrub clean:
> **8 small or 4 medium German Butterball potatoes (about 1 pound)**

Cover with cold water. Bring to a boil and add:
> **Salt, enough to make the water salty**

Cook until tender. Test for doneness with a sharp skewer. Let the potatoes cool. Using a spatula, chef's knife, the back of a skillet, or another flat tool, smash each potato just enough to flatten them.

Heat a heavy-bottomed pan (cast iron works very well) over medium-high heat. Add:
> **2 tablespoons olive oil**
> **2 tablespoons butter**

Place the smashed potatoes carefully in the pan and cook until crisp, about 6 minutes. Turn the potatoes and cook another 6 minutes, or until crisp. Add more oil and butter if the bottom of the pan becomes exposed. Monitor the heat and adjust up or down if the potatoes are not browning or burning. Remove and season with salt.

For a bit of extra flavor sprinkle with:
> **Gremolata (see page 189)**

Or serve with:
> **Garlic Mayonnaise (page 55)**

# Yellow Finn Potato and Black Trumpet Gratin

4 SERVINGS

Yellow Finn potatoes are rich in flavor and have the perfect texture for a gratin. They become soft and luscious without breaking down into a purée. For added color, alternate with rows of a red-fleshed potato such as Cranberry Red. Black trumpet mushrooms (also called black chanterelles or horn-of-plenty mushrooms) can harbor sand. Be sure to rinse them well before cooking.

Gently tear in half lengthwise:

**¼ pound black trumpet mushrooms**

Swish them in a bowl of cool water to clean; drain well. Heat a heavy-bottomed pan over medium heat. Measure in:

**1 teaspoon butter or oil**

Add:

**A pinch of salt**
**1 large thyme sprig**
**Fresh-ground black pepper**

When the butter has melted, add the mushrooms and cook, stirring now and then, until all the water has evaporated and the mushrooms just start to sizzle. Remove from the heat to cool. Taste for salt and add more as needed. Remove the thyme sprig. Peel:

**2 pounds potatoes (Yellow Finn,**
**Cranberry Red, or Yukon Gold)**

Hold in cool water until ready to use to keep them from browning.

Rub a 6-inch by 8-inch baking dish with:

**A peeled garlic clove**

Allow to dry a little and rub the dish with:

**2 teaspoons butter**

Measure:

**⅔ cup crème fraîche**

Pour into a small pot and warm:

**½ cup half-and-half**
**A pinch of salt**

Once all the ingredients are prepared, preheat the oven to 375°F. Slice the potatoes ¼ inch thick. Use a mandoline slicer or a sharp knife to make the slices as consistent as possible. Using one third of the sliced potatoes, make a layer of potato slices on the bottom of the baking dish. Season with:

**Salt**
**Fresh-ground black pepper**

Spoon one third of the crème fraîche over the potatoes, followed by half the mushrooms. Repeat, making another layer with half the remaining potato slices. Add seasoning, half the remaining crème fraîche, and the rest of the mushrooms. For the last layer of potatoes, carefully arrange rows of potato slices overlapped like shingles and completely covering the surface. Dot the surface with the last of the crème fraîche and gently add the half-and-half, pouring down the sides of the baking dish to avoid washing off the crème fraîche and salt. Put the gratin in the oven and bake until tender and golden, about 1 hour. After it has been cooking for 35 minutes, press the top layer of potatoes under the cream with a spatula. Press again after another 15 minutes. This keeps them from drying out. When done, the potatoes should be very soft, the top golden, and the liquid mostly gone. If the potatoes begin to brown too much before being cooked through, loosely cover the top with a bit of foil.

## Salt-Roasted Cranberry Red Potatoes with Crème Fraîche and Chives

4 SERVINGS

Choose small potatoes for this recipe. They will cook faster and make a very pretty hors d'oeuvre or side dish. The bright red flesh of the Cranberry Red potatoes is striking when accented with the green chives and white cream.

Preheat the oven to 375°F. Wash and dry well:

**16 to 20 small Cranberry Red potatoes**
You will need at least:

**4 cups rock salt**
Spread a ½-inch-thick layer of rock salt in a baking or roasting pan large enough to accommodate all of the potatoes in a single layer. Spread out the potatoes, leaving a half inch of space between them. Pour over enough rock salt to barely cover them— you should be able to just see the potatoes. Roast until tender, about 40 minutes. Remove from the salt or keep warm on top of the salt until needed. When ready to serve, cut a cross into the top of each potato with a small sharp knife. Squeeze the potatoes to create an opening. Fill with:

**A small dollop of crème fraîche**
**A pinch of chopped chives**
**A grind of fresh-ground black pepper**
Serve immediately.

## Fingerling Potatoes Roasted in Duck Fat

Fingerling potatoes have fine-textured, dense flesh that is well suited to roasting. Duck fat adds a wonderful savory edge to the sweet flavor of the potatoes. I never peel fingerling potatoes. Their skin is very thin and tasty, and the irregular shape of the potatoes makes it impossible to remove all their skin without losing too much flesh along with it. Instead, soak the potatoes in cool water and scrub them gently with a soft brush. Drain them well. I like to cut them into ¼-inch-thick coins, but you can cut them into wedges or long slices. Toss with salt, fresh-ground black pepper, and a knob of duck fat. Spread them out on a baking sheet or in a roasting pan no more than 2 inches deep and roast at 400°F until golden brown and tender, about 20 minutes. Stir the potatoes now and then to help them brown evenly. When the potatoes are done, toss with a little more coarse salt and a large pinch of chopped parsley. Other oils may be used instead of duck fat, such as olive oil, coconut oil, or fresh lard.

*Cranberry Red potato*

## Sweet Potatoes (*Ipomoea batatas*)

I grew up calling orange sweet potatoes yams, only to discover that they are really sweet potatoes. And orange is not the only color sweet potatoes come in: red-skinned *Beauregard* and brown-skinned *Garnet* have deep orange flesh, but *Okinawan* is a marvel with white skin and deep purple flesh. *O'Henry* and *White Yam* both have white flesh and are less sweet and drier fleshed than orange varieties. Young sweet potato leaves are good to eat, too. Try them sautéed or steamed. Sweet potatoes are not only delicious, they are incredibly good for you, which is probably why they are a mainstay of many diets around the world.

Sweet potatoes are tropical tubers that need a lot of hot sun to flourish, but there are some varieties that have been developed to grow in colder regions. Being relatives of morning glories, most sweet potatoes are vinelike and spread their way through the garden as they grow. Bush, or vineless, varieties will not spread as much and are better suited to small gardens or containers. *Vadaman* and *Puerto Rico* are two good bush types. Sweet potatoes are started with tiny plants called slips instead of seeds. The slips may be purchased or you can make your own with a sweet potato suspended in water, cut side down. Plant and harvest when nighttime temperatures are well above freezing, as sweet potatoes can't withstand any frost. Enrich the soil with lots of compost and some oyster-shell meal, water well, and the vines will quickly grow. Don't store sweet potatoes in the refrigerator; they last much better in a dark place no colder than 50°F.

## Straw Sweet Potato Cakes

4 SERVINGS

I like crisp sweet potato cakes for lunch with a fresh garden salad, and they are very good with all kinds of roasted meat or chicken.

Peel:

**2 medium sweet potatoes**

Grate coarsely using the large holes of a box grater, or cut into a fine julienne with a mandoline slicer.

Measure:

**4 tablespoons clarified butter or olive oil (or a combination of the two)**

Heat a 10-inch cast-iron or nonstick pan over medium heat and pour in half of the butter or oil. Add the sweet potatoes, press them down to a flat layer with a spatula, and season with:

**Salt**

**Fresh-ground black pepper**

Cook for 8 to 10 minutes, pressing down with the spatula occasionally, and loosening the cake so it slides around freely in the pan. When browned on the bottom, flip over the cake using 2 spatulas. Or slide the cake onto a plate, invert it onto another plate, and slide it back into the pan. Add the rest of the butter or oil, pouring it in around the edges of the pan, and cook another 5 minutes or so until the bottom is nicely browned.

Slide the cake out of the pan, cut into wedges, season with salt, and serve.

VARIATIONS

✦ Substitute a small celery root for one of the sweet potatoes. Grate and mix with the sweet potato and proceed as above.

✦ Substitute 2 large russet potatoes for the

sweet potatoes. Soak julienned potatoes in water for 30 minutes to release the starch. Drain and dry well and proceed as above.

• Serve with a dollop of crème fraîche and chopped herbs: cilantro, chives, parsley, marjoram, or a combination.

# Grilled Sweet Potatoes with Marjoram Sauce

Sliced sweet potatoes, white or orange, are wonderful grilled. Scrub them clean and then slice them, with their skins on, into ⅓-inch-thick rounds. Brush with oil and place on a grill over medium-hot coals. Cook for 5 to 6 minutes on each side. If you want to make hatched grill marks, rotate the slices 45 degrees halfway through the grilling on both sides. Sprinkle the cooked potatoes with salt and nap with Marjoram, Garlic, and Marash Pepper Sauce (page 23).

If you aren't grilling, place the oiled slices of potatoes on a baking sheet and cook in a 425°F oven until tender, about 12 to 15 minutes.

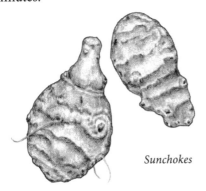

*Sunchokes*

# Sunchokes (*Helianthus tuberosus*)

The knobby, brown-skinned vegetables we call sunchokes are in the same family as sunflowers. They are also called Jerusalem artichokes, although they are native to North America and have nothing to do with artichokes (Jerusalem may be a mispronunciation of *girasole*, the Italian word for sunflower). Sunchokes have a sweet nutty flavor, a crisp texture when raw, and a silky, dense texture when cooked. They make a wonderful soup. When special guests come to Chez Panisse I like to serve a sunchoke soup; its flavor is so unexpected and delightful. Sunchokes are also delicious shaved into salads or roasted, and they make wonderful chips when fried.

Sunchokes resemble other sunflowers and are quite lovely in the garden. They are a tall, hardy perennial and will grow in many different situations and soils. Unlike the other more tender tubers, they can become invasive if not well harvested every year. Many seed companies and nurseries sell the tubers, or you can try growing some that you get from the farmers' market.

Plant the tubers in spring and hill up the stems with soil as they grow to make them stable. Once the plants flower, trim them back to concentrate the growth in the tubers. Frost will increase their sweetness. Except in the very coldest climates, the sunchokes can be kept in the ground for storage. Dig them up before the warm weather comes or they will reproduce and spread. Pull up any unwanted sprouts while they are still young.

## Sunchoke and Fennel Soup

MAKES ABOUT 1 QUART

The trick to this simple soup is to add the fennel at the end so it simmers just long enough to cook through but not lose its fresh taste. Add a knob or two of fresh butter when blending the soup and a few drops of white wine vinegar. You will have a glorious velvety soup.

Heat a heavy-bottomed pot over medium heat. Add:

**1½ tablespoons butter**
**1½ tablespoons olive oil**

When the butter has melted, stir in:

**1 medium onion, sliced thin**

Cook until soft, about 7 minutes. Stir now and then and lower the heat if the onion begins to brown.

Peel:

**6 large or 9 small sunchokes**
**(about 1 pound)**

Cut into same-size chunks and stir into the soft onions. Cook another 5 minutes. Season with:

**Salt**

And pour in 3 cups water. Bring to a boil and then turn down to a simmer. Taste a sunchoke; it should be tender with no hard center. Cook a few more minutes, if necessary. Add:

**1 medium fennel bulb, trimmed and**
**cut into ¼-inch slices**

Cook until the fennel is just tender enough to purée, about 4 minutes. Blend carefully in 2 batches. To each batch, add:

**2 teaspoons cold butter**

When the soup is blended, reheat it, but don't let it boil. Taste for salt and adjust as needed. Finish with:

**A few drops of white wine vinegar**

## Sunchoke Chips

MAKES ABOUT 1½ CUPS

When sliced thin and fried until crisp and golden, sunchokes are mercilessly addictive. Sweet and salty, with a gratifying bite, they are delicious on their own, in a salad, scattered over a soup, or piled next to grilled meat or fish. Sunchoke chips can be made ahead: they will stay crisp for a while. If it is humid or foggy out, let them cool and put them in a tightly sealed container to keep crisp.

Peel:

**3 large or 4 medium sunchokes (about**
**½ pound)**

Slice thin: ⅛ inch thick or less. For even frying, make the slices as uniformly thick as possible. A mandoline makes this job much easier. Put a small, deep heavy-bottomed skillet or pot over medium heat. Pour in:

**Olive or vegetable oil to a depth of**
**1 inch**

When the oil is hot, 350°F on a candy or frying thermometer, add the sunchokes in batches and cook until crisp and golden, 3 or 4 minutes. Remove the chips with a spider or slotted spoon to drain on a plate lined with absorbent paper or a towel. When all the chips are cooked, season with:

**Salt**

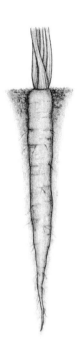

# Crisp Stalks

## Fennel, Celery, Asparagus, Cardoons, and Rhubarb

THESE TALL CRISP STALKS are vegetables of spring that I look forward to every year. The rains stop, the weather warms, and the menu changes. Fresh-cut asparagus spears—cooked whole and bathed in butter, cut up and added to vegetable ragouts, or shaved raw into green salads—are always a welcome sight after the dark days of winter. Celery and fennel cut into shavings make crunchy salads filled with sweet flavor. The magnificent stalks of cardoons are turned into divine gratins, savory salads, and soups. And the ruby stems of rhubarb are a refreshing addition to desserts and salads.

# Recipes

Fennel and Meyer Lemon Relish  102

Roasted Striped Bass with Fennel Fronds  102

Pork Tenderloin with Fresh Fennel Pollen and Seeds  103

Celery and Comice Pear Salad  104

Moroccan Asparagus and Spring Vegetable Ragout  105

Cardoon Salad with Lemon, Anchovy, and Black Olives  106

Cardoons Braised with Olive Oil and Lacinato Kale  107

Cardoon Gratin with Béchamel and Parmesan Cheese  108

Shaved Rhubarb and Chard Crostini  109

Rhubarb Compote  110

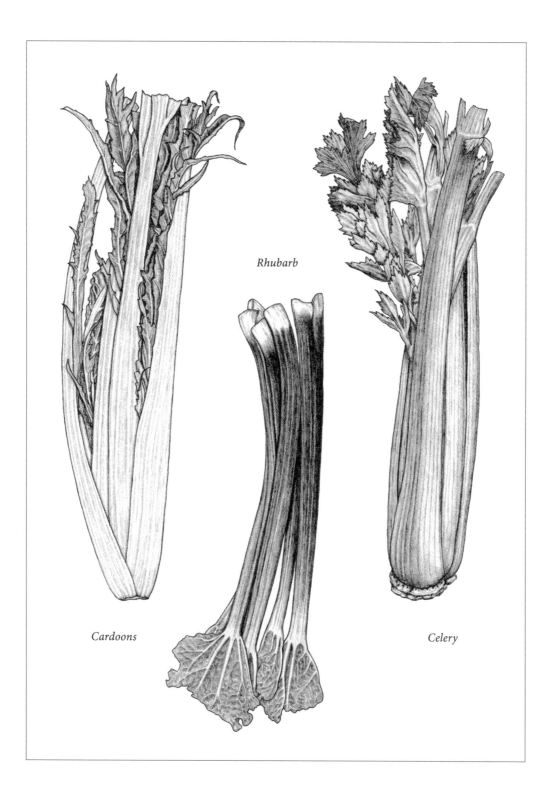

*Rhubarb*

*Cardoons*

*Celery*

# Crisp Stalks in the Garden

Statuesque cardoons and the feathery leaves of asparagus make a bold statement in the garden, as do the tall red stems of rhubarb and the frilly fronds of fennel. For all these vegetables, except asparagus, it is the leaf stems (or petioles) that are harvested and eaten. Asparagus spears are immature shoots that are harvested before they begin to open and leaf out.

While most garden vegetables are annuals that are planted every year, cardoons, asparagus, and rhubarb are all perennials. Perennials will grow for years, and most need at least a couple of years to become established before a harvest is possible. They are not at all difficult to grow, but space is committed for a duration of years instead of months.

The cool weather of spring is the time when these vegetables are usually planted, grown, and harvested. To get the plants started, amend the soil with a generous amount of compost. The best food to feed them as they grow is compost tea. For tender, juicy stems, watering must be consistent. Bouts of drought make the stems tough and stringy. Fennel and celery seeds can also be started indoors and planted in late summer for a fall harvest.

# Fennel  (*Foeniculum vulgare*)

The pale stalks of sweet fennel, sometimes called Florence fennel, swell into a plump bulb just above the ground and then extend into tall, showy dark green fernlike fronds. The bulb is crisp and sweet with a distinctly anise flavor. I love salads made with thinly shaved fennel slices—either by themselves or mixed with greens and other shaved vegetables. Cut in wedges, fennel makes a perfect crudité to serve with a glass of chilled wine. Chopped up and stirred into olive oil with herbs, shallots, and a touch of lemon or vinegar, fennel makes a ravishing salsa for grilled fish. Braised in water or stock, it becomes luscious, soft, and silky. Caramelized in a quick sauté, it makes a lovely savory dish. Substitute fennel for celery in soups and stews for a milder, sweeter taste.

Fennel fronds, flowers, and seeds are also all quite tasty. The feathery leaves can be chopped and sprinkled over a finished dish for color and a hint of anise flavor, as can the flowers, which form large yellow umbrellas that look similar to dill flowers. The seeds are great to cook with, both fresh and dried.

*Zefa Fino* and *Perfection* are common, reliable varieties. You can peruse seed catalogs for other choices.

Though a tender perennial, fennel is grown as an annual. It cannot withstand frost or heat. Start seedlings indoors or sow directly in the garden after all threat of frost has gone. Fennel needs a good amount of water and compost to make a juicy bulb. Hot and dry conditions will cause the plant

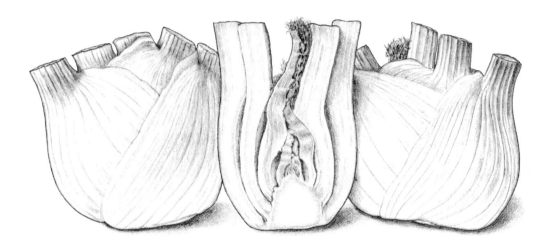

to bolt. If this happens, use the leafy fronds and tough stalks for flavoring. Harvest when the bulb is about three inches in diameter and cut off right at the ground. If bulbs start to elongate, it means they are getting ready to flower, so harvest them right away. In mild climates, the plants may grow back in the spring after a fall harvest.

*Bronze* fennel is an ornamental herb that does not produce a bulb. It is grown for its coppery brown–tinged fronds and yellow flowers. Butterflies and other pollinators love the flowers. It will reseed vigorously.

Wild fennel has a rich heady perfume, much more intense than cultivated fennel. The towering plant does not produce a bulb; it is the fronds, seeds, and pollen that are prized in the kitchen. Originally brought to the United States by Italian immigrants who missed the flavor of home, the wild herb has become an invasive weed that is rampant all over California. I love cooking with it but don't dare plant it. Instead I forage for it from spring through fall.

In early spring, the young fronds make delicious pasta sauce and fritters, when first cooked quickly in salted boiling water. As the fronds mature, use them to stuff whole fish, pork loins, and spit-roasted lamb. Toward the end of summer the flowers open and mature. The pollen and fresh seeds, which can be dried and used all year long, make an incredible marinade or dry rub for meat and fish and a potent seasoning for relishes and sauces. For pollen, cut the flower heads when they are brilliant yellow, then dry them in paper sacks and knock the dried heads to loosen the pollen. For seeds, collect dried flower heads and finish the drying in paper sacks and crumble the seeds loose. Store both seeds and pollen in tightly sealed jars in a cool, dark place.

## Fennel and Meyer Lemon Relish

MAKES ABOUT 1½ CUPS

This is a cross between a relish and a salad. It is perfect as a sauce for grilled fish. Toss it with some butter lettuce or romaine for a crunchy and refreshing salad. Scatter it over a plate of sliced salami for a quick hors d'oeuvre, or spoon it onto a sandwich for extra zest.

Using a sharp, swivel-bladed vegetable peeler, carefully peel the zest from:

**2 Meyer lemons**

Remove any white pith from the strips of zest. It is easily scraped away with the tip of a teaspoon. Cut the pieces of zest crosswise into a very thin julienne. Peel and finely dice:

**1 shallot**

Place the diced shallot in a small bowl with the lemon zest and:

**The juice of 1 Meyer lemon**
**A splash of Champagne vinegar**
**Salt**
**Fresh-ground black pepper**

Mix well and let sit for a few minutes to macerate. Whisk in:

**2 tablespoons extra-virgin olive oil**

Taste for salt and acid and adjust as needed. Trim the fronds and dark green stalks from:

**1 small fennel bulb**

Cut the bulb in half lengthwise and then into a fine dice. Toss with salt to taste and stir into the lemon-shallot mixture. Remove all the remaining peel from the unjuiced lemon and cut half the segments from their membranes. Cut the segments into a me-dium dice and gently stir them into the relish. Let the relish sit for 5 minutes before serving.

VARIATION
◆ If Meyer lemons are not available, use standard lemons and omit the segments.

## Roasted Striped Bass with Fennel Fronds

Whole roast fish is a very easy and tasty dish. A whole fish is much less expensive to purchase than fillets, and the bones add lots of flavor and succulence to the flesh. Fennel fronds richly perfume the fish while it is roasting. When the fish is cooked, nothing more is needed than some good olive oil and a lemon wedge for a sauce—although the Fennel and Meyer Lemon Relish (this page) would be very good, too.

Choose a fresh, bright-eyed fish at your local fishmonger. Figure on a 1-pound fish per person. Ask to have the fish scaled, gutted, and the fins removed, but leave on the head and tail for maximum flavor. If striped bass is not available, look for other small fishes such as rockfish, porgy, or bream.

When you are ready to cook, preheat the oven to 450°F. Rub, or brush, the whole fish with olive oil, inside and out, and season with salt and fresh-ground black pepper. Line the cavity with sliced lemon and a sliced garlic clove, if desired. Stuff the rest of the cavity with wild or cultivated fennel fronds, breaking them into smaller pieces if necessary. Lay the seasoned fish in a baking dish or on a baking sheet. Place in the oven and roast until cooked through but still moist, about 15 minutes. Test with a fork, pulling the flesh away from the backbone. The fish is done when its flesh is opaque and comes away easily from the bones. Serve the fish whole, or remove it from the bones first.

# Pork Tenderloin with Fresh Fennel Pollen and Seeds

4 SERVINGS

The dry rub for this dish is made with fennel blossoms that are just starting to form seeds. The maturing blossoms have a surprising complexity of flavor from their sweet nectar, heady pollen, and soft seeds filled with fresh fennel flavor. Serve the tenderloin hot or room temperature. Add corn on the cob, green beans, and sliced tomatoes for a simple summer meal.

A few hours ahead of time, or the night before, trim any silver skin from:

**1 pork tenderloin (about 1¼ pounds)**

Season with:

**Salt**

**Fresh-ground black pepper**

Cut away the tough stems of:

**6 or more maturing fennel blossoms**

You want to collect the tiny flower heads and seeds only. Crush them using a mortar and pestle to release their juices and aromas. Add:

**A drizzle of olive oil**

Rub the seasoned tenderloin with the crushed flowers and seeds. Refrigerate. Take it out of the refrigerator 20 minutes before cooking.

Prepare a bed of medium coals and push them higher on one side. Put the grill over the fire to get hot. Sear the tenderloin on the hottest part of the grill for 7 minutes, turning every few minutes for even color. Then cook another 5 to 7 minutes on the cooler part of the grill. Let rest for 5 minutes before cutting. Slice across the grain and serve with:

**A drizzle of extra-virgin olive oil**

**A sprinkle of chopped fennel fronds**

VARIATIONS

• If you don't have a grill going, heat a cast-iron pan over medium-high heat. When hot, pour in just enough oil to coat the bottom of the pan, and add the tenderloin. Sear on all sides and then slide into a 375°F oven. Cook for another 10 minutes or until done.

• Make a compound butter: Mix softened butter with crushed fresh fennel pollen and seeds, chopped fennel fronds, a squeeze of lemon juice, a pinch of cayenne, salt, and fresh-ground black pepper. Perfect for beans and corn, too!

## Celery (*Apium graveolens* var. *dulce*)

Celery, like carrots and onions, is a classic element in mirepoix and soffritto, the bases for soups and stews. It also makes a good crunchy addition to salads and is quite tasty braised in flavorful stock. Fresh from the garden, it is filled with clean, sweet flavor. *Red Venture* is a pretty red and green and tastes great. *Tango* and *Conquistador* are tasty green varieties. *Amsterdam* is a leaf celery, grown for its flavorful leaves instead of stalks. Use the leaves tossed in salad, chopped for a sauce, or in soups and stews.

Celery loves water and needs lots of it in order to be crisp and juicy. Transplant seedlings into shallow trenches with plenty of compost to help keep the plants irrigated and moist. Feed every few weeks with compost tea. Celery seedlings can be planted in early spring to harvest before heat sets in or in late summer for an autumn harvest. In areas with dry, hot summers, the later planting is better. Time your planting well and be sure cold nights are over, for celery will bolt if the weather dips below 55°F for an extended period of time. Harvest stalks from the outside in, or cut the whole plant. Celery does fine in containers, provided they are kept watered.

## Celery and Comice Pear Salad

4 SERVINGS

Preheat the oven to 350°F. Spread out on a baking dish or in an ovenproof skillet:

**3 tablespoons walnuts**

Lightly toast in the oven for 7 minutes, stirring once or twice for even coloration. Let the nuts cool and rub them in your hands to remove some of the tannic skins.

Make a simple dressing. Into a small bowl, squeeze the juice of:

**½ lemon**

Add:

**Salt**

**Fresh-ground black pepper**

Whisk in:

**2 tablespoons extra-virgin olive oil**

Taste the dressing and add more salt and lemon juice as needed.

Using a sharp paring knife or vegetable peeler, remove the strings from:

**3 tender inner celery stalks**

Cut into thin slices. With a vegetable peeler, shave into thin slices:

**½ ounce Parmesan cheese**

Collect the slices carefully onto a small plate and set aside.

Peel, core, and slice lengthwise:

**2 small or 1½ large ripe Comice, Anjou, Bosc, or Bartlett pears**

Toss the celery with two thirds of the dressing and turn out onto a serving platter. Arrange the pears on the celery. Spoon the remaining dressing over the pears. Garnish with the sliced cheese and walnuts, crushing the walnuts lightly as you sprinkle them on.

VARIATIONS

• Substitute fennel for the celery. Save 1 or 2 fronds and chop to sprinkle on the salad at the end.

• Use celery root, thinly sliced and julienned, in place of the pear. Chop a few leaves of parsley to toss in with the celeries.

• For part of the lemon juice, substitute sherry or red wine vinegar.

## Asparagus *(Asparagus officinalis)*

The proud, straight green shoots of asparagus are an exciting sight, whether in the garden or at the market. I love the big fat spears, which I think are the sweetest. Snap off their ends, peel them, and they are ready to be cooked—or to be shaved into thin slices with a sharp vegetable peeler and dressed with a vinaigrette. *Purple Passion* is quite sweet and is an extraordinary purple color that turns dark green when cooked. *Mary Washington* is a classic green variety and *Jersey Supreme* is an all-male hybrid that produces more spears. (Female plants produce seeds, which take energy from the plant and reduce its productivity.)

Asparagus is easiest started with crowns, or bare-root plants. If possible, prepare the soil in the fall with a deep layer of compost and plant a cover crop over the site. Asparagus prefers a rich, slightly alkaline soil. Bury the crowns in early spring and keep them consistently moist. Don't harvest any shoots the first year and the next spring harvest sparingly. The third spring and thereafter, harvest any tall shoots that are ½ inch in diameter. In the fall, cut back the plants once the fernlike leaves have yellowed. Spread a thick layer of compost over the area and mulch with straw.

## Moroccan Asparagus and Spring Vegetable Ragout

4 SERVINGS

Serve this Moroccan-style ragout alone or with steamed couscous, *chermoula, harissa,* and lime wedges. Cilantro sprigs are a tasty and festive-looking garnish.

In a heavy-bottomed soup pot, heat:
> **3 tablesoons olive oil**

Add:
> **1 medium onion, diced**
> **1 teaspoon minced green garlic or garlic**
> **Salt**

Cook over medium heat, stirring often. When very soft, but not browned, add:
> **3 cups cooked chickpeas**
> **3 cups chickpea cooking liquid**
> **A pinch of saffron, ground**
> **1 teaspoon cumin seeds, toasted and ground**
> **1 teaspoon coriander seeds, toasted and ground**
> **1 teaspoon paprika**
> **½ cinnamon stick**
> **¼ cup chopped preserved lemon (optional)**

Bring to a simmer and cook for 10 minutes. Adjust seasoning and add:
> **1 cup shelled very fresh sweet peas (about 1 pound unshelled)**
> **½ pound spinach, washed and drained**
> **1 cup snap peas, ends and strings removed, and cut in half lengthwise**

Simmer for 5 minutes. Add more liquid if needed; it should be very juicy.

Meanwhile, cook in salted boiling water until just tender:
> **¾ pound asparagus, trimmed and peeled**

To serve, ladle the vegetable ragout into soup plates and drape whole asparagus spears over.

## Cardoons *(Cynara cardunculus)*

At first glance it may hard to believe that cardoons are related to artichokes. They look more like a giant bunch of celery; and, like celery, it is their stalks that are eaten, and not their flower buds. Cardoons are a bit of work in the kitchen, because they need peeling and parboiling, but what flavor! They are like a juicy, mild artichoke, with the same compelling cross of sweet and bitter flavors. They were made for olive oil and garlic. Serve marinated cardoons in a salad or as an antipasto. Warm, they make fabulous crostini, especially when paired with lacinato kale and *olio nuovo*—new-harvest olive oil. *Gobbo di Nizza* is a large succulent variety of cardoon. Search for other varieties in seed catalogs.

Cardoons are perennials where cool summers and mild winters are the norm. Anywhere it freezes, they must be grown as annuals. They need quite a bit of space in the garden but offer lots of beauty with their towering gray-green stalks and gorgeous purple thistle flowers. Start seedlings indoors. Plant more seeds than you need and be patient, as germination is slow and sporadic. If possible, purchasing seedlings is an easier way to start. Keep the soil moist and mulch well while the small plants are growing.

Cut cardoon stalks from the outside in. Cardoons can be blanched (making them more tender) by tying newspaper around the stalks a couple of weeks before harvest. Cannard Farm, our main supplier at Chez Panisse, doesn't bother, and we like them fine that way. That is how I grow them, too.

Artichokes *(Cynara scolymus)* are grown in exactly the same manner as cardoons. *Violetta* and *Violet de Provence* are small, purple, full-flavored, and chokeless. They make fantastic salads, both raw and cooked, and are delicious stuffed and baked on a bed of lemon-scented onions. *Imperial Star* and *Green Globe* produce large green artichokes good for steaming to eat the leaves one by one dipped in mayonnaise, a garlic and herb salsa, or melted butter. Imperial Star performs well as an annual. Harvest artichokes while they are still buds, firm and tightly closed. As the flowers open, they lose their fine flavor and tender texture.

## Cardoon Salad with Lemon, Anchovy, and Black Olives

4 SERVINGS

Cardoons make delicious salads. Their bittersweet flavor blends well with the pungent flavors of anchovies and olives. A few leaves of Ruby Streak mustard greens or wild rocket make a pretty finishing touch.

Prepare a bowl of acidulated water.
Combine:

**Water**

**Juice of 1 lemon, or 1 tablespoon vinegar**

Remove the leaves and discolored ends from:

**4 large cardoon stalks**

Peel the stalks with a swivel-bladed vegetable peeler to remove the tough strings. Cut into 4-inch pieces. Put the prepared cardoons into the acidulated water to keep them from oxidizing and turning brown. Bring a large pot of salted water to a boil and cook the cardoons about 12 minutes. They should be tender with a little tooth. Cut on the diagonal into ½-inch slices.

Prepare a dressing. Mix together in a small bowl:

> **2 strips of lemon zest (remove with a swivel-bladed peeler)**
> **Juice of 1 lemon, about 2 tablespoons**
> **1 garlic clove, pounded to a purée**
> **Salt**
> **Fresh-ground black pepper**

Whisk in:

> **3 tablespoons extra-virgin olive oil**

Soak and remove the fillets from:

> **2 salt-cured anchovies**

Dry and cut lengthwise into thin strips. Place in a small ramekin and coat with olive oil. Pit:

> **8 dry-cured olives**

Chop coarsely.

Toss the cardoons with the dressing and:

> **1 tablespoon chopped parsley**

Taste for salt and adjust as needed. (Remember that you will be adding salty anchovies and olives.) Arrange the cardoons on a plate, scatter over the olives, and decorate with the strips of anchovy. Wreathe with a few leaves of:

> **Ruby Streaks mustard greens or wild rocket**

VARIATION

◆ Peel, chop, and scatter 1 hard-cooked egg over the cardoons after the anchovies.

# Cardoons Braised with Olive Oil and Lacinato Kale
4 SERVINGS

Cardoons and lacinato kale are a perfect culinary match. The deep green color and robust flavor of the kale set off the pale celadon color and bittersweet overtones of the cardoons. If you have any olio nuovo, use it. The spicy pungency is the perfect seasoning for this delightful dish. Serve as a side dish or on thick slices of grilled garlic toast.

Prepare a bowl of acidulated water. Combine:

> **Water**
> **Juice of 1 lemon, or 1 tablespoon vinegar**

Remove the leaves and discolored ends from:

> **4 large cardoon stalks**

Use a swivel-bladed vegetable peeler to peel each stalk and remove its tough strings. Cut the stalks into 4-inch pieces. Put the prepared cardoons directly into the acidulated water to keep them from oxidizing and turning brown. Bring a large pot of salted water to a boil and cook the cardoons about 12 minutes. They should be tender with a little tooth. Cut on the diagonal into ½-inch slices.

Strip leaves from the tough stems of:

> **½ bunch lacinato kale**

Discard the stems and wash the leaves. Cook in boiling salted water until tender. Drain and cool. Cut into a medium chiffonade.

Place a heavy-bottomed pan over medium heat. Pour in:

¼ cup water
1 tablespoon extra-virgin olive oil
(olio nuovo, if possible)
**Salt**

Add the cardoons and cook at a slow simmer for 4 minutes. Stir in the kale and cook
another 3 minutes. Taste for salt and adjust
as needed. Just before serving pour in:

**1 tablespoon extra-virgin olive oil**
**(olio nuovo, if possible)**

# Cardoon Gratin with Béchamel and Parmesan Cheese

4 SERVINGS

Béchamel, or white sauce as it is called in
English, makes delicious vegetable gratins.
Substituting vegetable cooking liquid for
half the milk gives more flavor and lightness
to the sauce. It is a good trick to remember
for lasagna, soufflés, and other dishes that
call for béchamel.

Prepare a bowl of acidulated water.
Combine:

**Water**
**Juice of 1 lemon, or 1 tablespoon**
**vinegar**

Remove the leaves and discolored ends from:

**4 large cardoon stalks**

Peel the stalks with a swivel-bladed vegetable peeler to remove the tough strings.
Put the peeled cardoons into the acidulated
water to prevent them from turning brown.
Bring a large pot of salted water to a boil and
cook the cardoons about 12 minutes. They

should be tender with a little tooth. Reserve
1 cup of the cooking liquid. Cut the cooked
cardoons into ¾-inch-thick diagonal slices.
Make a thin béchamel. Melt in a small
heavy-bottomed pot over medium heat:

**2 tablespoons butter**

Stir in:

**3 tablespoons unbleached all-purpose**
**flour**

Cook the roux for a few minutes without
browning. Slowly, a little at a time, whisk in:

**½ cup milk**
**½ cup cardoon cooking liquid**

To avoid lumps, whisk in each addition of
liquid completely before adding the next.
Bring slowly to a boil, stirring all the time.
Turn down to a bare simmer (use a flame
tamer if necessary) and cook for 10 minutes,
stirring occasionally to keep the sauce from
sticking. Stir in:

**½ cup grated Parmesan cheese**
**A pinch of cayenne**
**A pinch of grated nutmeg (optional)**

The sauce should be as thin as heavy cream.
If it is too thick, stir in more of the cooking
liquid.

Preheat the oven to 375°F. Liberally coat a
6- to 8-inch gratin or baking dish with:

**Softened butter**

Stir the cooked cardoons into the béchamel
and then spoon or pour into the prepared
dish. Bake for 20 minutes or until the sauce
is bubbling and browned on top.

VARIATION

◆ Chard stems are very good cooked this
way. There is no need to peel or acidulate the
chard stalks.

# Rhubarb (*Rheum rhabarbarum*)

Rhubarb is a harbinger of spring, shooting up in the garden when the mornings are still frosty. Its long ruby stalks are treated as more of a fruit than a vegetable and most rhubarb recipes are for dessert, but it is quite good in savory food, too. Try its puckery sweet flavor with beets in a salsa or shaved into a salad or a mixture of marinated greens. At the end of a meal, I love a rhubarb galette or a simple compote with a dollop of crème fraîche. *Crimson Red* and *Glaskins Perpetual* are lovely red varieties. The heirloom variety *Victoria* is sweet and green, not red. Do not be put off by the apparent lack of color; it is delicious.

In the garden, rhubarb is a tall-growing perennial. Pick a spot at the back of the garden on the south side so it doesn't block the sunlight. The plants will spread out, so give them space. Rhubarb needs cold to break its dormancy and cannot tolerate sun. It thrives in the north, but it can be grown in warmer regions if given the proper exposure. Heat will wilt it quickly. Lots of water and afternoon shade help it thrive.

For best results, start plants as root divisions and crowns. Amend the soil with plenty of compost and water well while the plant is establishing itself. Harvest lightly the first two years. Eat only the stems—the leaves are filled with oxalic acid and are poisonous. To harvest, grasp a stem at the ground and twist it free.

# Shaved Rhubarb and Chard Crostini

4 SERVINGS

The tart vegetable flavor of rhubarb plays well with the earthy tones of chard and kale. *Verjus* (the French spelling of *verjuice*, the juice of unripe green grapes) adds acid and fruit. If you can't find verjus, use a mixture of lemon juice and Champagne vinegar.

Preheat the oven to 350°F.
Remove the leaves from the stems of:
  **1 bunch of chard**
Wash the leaves and cook until tender in boiling salted water. Let the leaves cool, squeeze out most, but not all, of the water and chop them coarsely. Season with:
  **Salt**
  **A splash of olive oil**
Cut 4 slices of:
  **Country-style bread**
Place on a baking sheet and bake until crisp, about 10 minutes. When done drizzle with:
  **Extra-virgin olive oil**
Whisk together a simple dressing of:
  **1 tablespoon verjus**
  **Salt**
  **Fresh-ground black pepper**
  **2 tablespoons extra-virgin olive oil**
Trim off the leaves and tough tail end of:
  **½ rhubarb stalk**
Cut into 3-inch lengths. Using a swivel-bladed vegetable peeler, cutting down the side, shave long thin pieces of rhubarb. Place in a bowl and toss with the dressing and a pinch of salt. Fold in the cooked chard. Taste for salt and acid and adjust as needed. Pile onto the toasted bread and serve.

# Rhubarb Compote

MAKES ABOUT 2 CUPS

A compote is basically fruit cooked with sugar until it softens and makes a kind of sauce. Rhubarb makes a very quick and tasty compote. The only trick is to be sure not to cook it for too long or it will turn into a purée. Rhubarb compote is delicious with crème fraîche or yogurt, on pancakes, next to a simple cake, or over meringues with a little vanilla ice cream.

Trim the leaves and tough root ends from:

**4 rhubarb stalks**

Cut into 1-inch pieces. You should have about 3 cups. Put the cut rhubarb in a heavy-bottomed saucepan with:

**⅔ cup sugar**
**Zest of 1 lemon**
**1 tablespoon lemon juice**

Cook over medium heat, stirring gently until the rhubarb is tender, about 5 minutes. Pour into a bowl to cool.

VARIATIONS

• Use another citrus fruit in place of the lemon. Tangelo, orange, tangerine, blood orange, or grapefruit are all good choices.

• Spice the compote with grated fresh ginger, 1 star anise, a cinnamon stick, black pepper, or a couple of cloves.

• To concentrate the flavor of the compote, strain off the juices, return them to the pan, and reduce to a thickened syrup. Pour the syrup over the cooked rhubarb.

• Add 1 cup of hulled and sliced strawberries to the pan. Increase the sugar by 2 tablespoons.

• The compote can be baked in the oven instead of cooked on the stovetop. Mix the ingredients together in an ovenproof dish, cover tightly, and cook until tender, about 15 minutes in a 350°F oven.

# Fresh and Dried

## Peas, Fava Beans, Green Beans, Shell Beans, and Peanuts

FROM THE MILD DAYS OF SPRING all the way to the last days of summer, markets and gardens offer a marvelous parade of shelling peas, snow peas, sugar snap peas, snap beans, and haricots verts—a parade that ends with a gorgeous array of tasty shell beans. Sharing the task of opening pods and snapping stems can lead to many convivial moments in the kitchen or on the porch. And how I love the dishes that result when peas and beans are cooked! A bowl of tender peas burnished with sweet butter; a plate of fresh pasta topped with a brilliant tangle of sugar snap pods and peas; firm haricots verts tossed with heady garlic and herbs; salads for hot days filled with refreshing green beans; and creamy shell beans cooked into summery soups, gratins, and pastas. Happily, peas and beans are easy and prolific crops to tend, and they are a boon to the soil they grow in.

# Recipes

Sugar Snap Pea Slaw  116

Pea Tops Sautéed with Garlic  116

Fava Greens  118

Roasted Whole Young Favas  118

Squid and Fava Beans with Garlic and Parsley  118

Haricots Verts with Toasted Pecans and Purple Basil  122

Yellow Romano Beans in Tomato Sauce  122

Three-Bean Salad à la Chez Panisse  123

Cranberry Bean and Tomato Salad with
Summer Savory Salsa  126

Cannellini Bean Purée  126

Fresh Flageolet Beans with Spicy Lamb Sausage  127

White Beans with Duck Confit  128

Rio Zape Beans Cooked in the Coals with Garlic and Chiles  129

Chile con Carne  129

Black-Eyed Peas with Sautéed Okra and
Jimmy Nardello Peppers  130

Crowder Pea and Greens Soup  131

Hummus with Preserved Lemon  132

Whole-Wheat Pita Bread  132

Fresh Roasted Peanuts  134

Boiled Peanuts with Star Anise and Soy  134

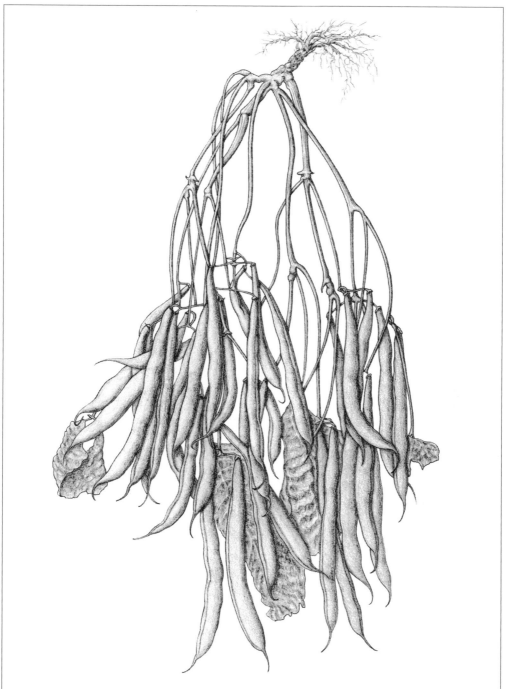

*A flageolet bush bean plant of mature beans ready to shell and cook fresh or to hang and dry*

## Peas in the Garden

Bright green, sweet shelling peas are eaten after being removed from their pods, while slim snow peas (with barely a pea inside) and plump sugar snap peas (sometimes called mangetout peas) are eaten pod and all. They all taste best when harvested young and eaten straightaway. In fact, fresh off the vine and right out of the pod may be the very best way to eat a pea. Children love to shell peas and pop them right in their mouths. Eating vegetables doesn't get any more fun or delicious than this.

Peas are a cool-season crop. Though seeds may be sown directly once the soil is workable, I recommend starting the seeds indoors or waiting until the soil warms up to 50°F. This will ensure a higher rate of germination and a larger yield. A good compromise is to plant seedlings and seeds at the same time once the soil has warmed up; then there will be early peas from the seedlings and a strong harvest from the seeds. A later fall harvest is possible, especially in climates that have a long mild autumn, if peas are planted in midsummer. When planting, amend the soil with a good sprinkling of compost and keep the plants consistently watered. Peas are legumes and, with the aid of soil bacteria, they can pull nitrogen from the air. The plants fix the nitrogen in nodules on their roots, and healthy compost supplies the necessary bacteria for nitrogen fixing.

Pea vines do not grow to be much taller than five feet (with the exception of some tall-growing sugar snap peas) and their fine tendrils need thin wire or twine to climb up. There are a few dwarf pea varieties that don't need trellising, but most varieties need some support. Set the trellis in place and plant the peas close to the supports, on both sides if possible, and guide their tendrils to the trellis as they grow. As the peas start to wind down, other climbing plants such as cucumbers can be planted. Once they have finished producing, the mature pea vines can be cut off at the soil and removed, and the new plants will enjoy the nitrogen fixed into the soil by the pea plants' roots.

Pea tops are the tender and delicious first shoots of pea plants. Harvest them when they are tender and young; once the tendrils have started to establish themselves they can get quite fibrous and chewy. Pea shoots can be grown as a cut-and-come-again crop and will yield lots of fresh young spring greens. Sow beds or containers densely and cut the shoots when they are four inches tall, just above the first set of leaves. Let them grow back, and in three weeks cut again. They should yield three or maybe four cuttings before they start to get tough and bitter.

Once the peas begin to mature, for the tastiest peas and the longest season, keep up on the harvest. To keep the vines going, pick all the mature peas, and when the season is winding down, let them mature on the vine for dried peas (or next year's seeds). When the plants are finished and it's time to remove them—and this goes for beans and other legumes—cut them off at the soil, leaving the roots in place with all their nitrogen nodules attached to enrich the soil for crops to come.

## Peas (*Pisum sativum*)

Sweet tender peas come into season as the weather warms, and they are gone as soon as it gets hot. I make a point of eating as many as I can while they are at the markets and in the garden. Fresh pasta tossed with peas, prosciutto, and a bit of butter; spring vegetable ragouts with shell peas, sugar snaps, and snow peas mixed with baby carrots and asparagus; sugar snap peas chopped into relishes and salads; luxurious purées of shell peas; quickly cooked peas of any type finished with a pat of butter or a drizzle of olive oil and a scattering of chervil and chives. Pea tops are delicious sautéed with ginger and garlic, wilted into a spring vegetable ragout, or stirred into a pasta filling or an omelet.

*Alderman* (*Tall Telephone*), a popular producer in gardens for over a century, is a tall vining shelling pea with large pods filled with lots of sweet peas. *Green Arrow* is a vigorous bush pea that produces loads of peas. *Purple Podded* (*Blauwschokkers*) has gorgeous purple pods with electric green peas inside. They can be eaten whole when small, as a snow pea; or shelled and eaten fresh, as a shelling pea, or dried for winter. *Canoe* is an unusual variety that has few leaves and many tendrils and produces plenty of tasty peas. Snow pea varieties include *Oregon Giant,* with white flowers and very large pods; *Oregon Sugar Pod II*, a very tasty mangetout snow pea with short vines; and *Yellow Sweet,* with beautiful yellow snow-type peas that are best when eaten young. *Carouby de Maussane* is a delicious mangetout-type pea with beautiful purplish flowers. Two reliable sweet sugar snap types are *Cascadia* and tall-growing original *Sugar Snap. Usui* is a snow pea that is frequently grown for pea tops, as is *Dwarf Grey Sugar*, which has purple-red flowers and tender greens.

# Sugar Snap Pea Slaw

4 SERVINGS

Sugar snap peas make a crisp sweet slaw when briefly cooked and finely cut. Radishes provide more bright color and a nice spicy bite. The peas may be cooked and cut ahead, but to preserve their bright green color, wait to dress them until it is time to serve.

Trim:

**¾ pound sugar snap peas**

Snap back the tip of each pea pod and pull it down the side to remove any strings. Cook the peas for less than a minute in boiling salted water. Drain and lay them out on a plate or tray to cool (put the plate in the refrigerator to speed up the cooling). When they are cool, cut them on the diagonal into thin slices about ⅛ inch wide. Set aside.

Wash:

**4 small radishes**

Cut into thin slices. A mandoline makes this job easier. Cut the slices into a fine julienne. Prepare the vinaigrette. Stir together in a small bowl:

**Grated zest of ½ lemon**
**1 tablespoon lemon juice**
**1 teaspoon wine vinegar, red or white**
**Salt**
**Fresh-ground black pepper**

When ready to serve, toss the peas and radishes together with:

**1 tablespoon coarsely chopped chervil**
**or mint**
**1 tablespoon chiffonade of parsley**
**leaves**

Pour in the vinaigrette and toss gently. Taste for salt and acid and adjust as needed.

VARIATIONS

◆ Add 1 scallion cut into thin diagonal slices. Use all the white and half the green leaves.
◆ Cut 1 carrot into thin slices and then into a fine julienne. Blanch briefly in boiling water for 1 minute. Add to the peas and radishes.

# Pea Tops Sautéed with Garlic

4 SERVINGS

I first encountered pea tops in Asian restaurants. I was astonished by how tender and delicious they were. Now pea tops are in farmers' markets every spring, at both Asian and Western stalls. In the garden, cut back the young tops of pea plants, or sow them thickly to thin for the greens only. Once the tendrils have started to grow, the greens become quite tough.

Wash one large handful of pea tops per person and drain. Peel and chop one garlic clove for every two people. Heat a heavy-bottomed pan over medium-high heat. Pour in enough oil to coat the bottom of the pan and add the pea tops with the water clinging to them. Toss in the hot pan until wilted. Clear a hole in the middle of the greens to expose the bottom of the pan. Pour in a drizzle of olive oil and add the chopped garlic. Let the garlic heat through for a few seconds, season everything with salt, and toss the greens and garlic together. If you like, add ¼ teaspoon minced ginger along with each chopped garlic clove.

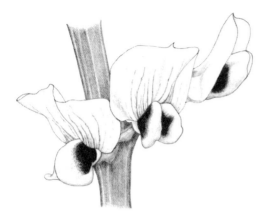

## Fava Beans (*Vicia faba*)

Fava beans, or broad beans as they are sometimes called, are the first beans to come to market. They are a cool weather crop that comes into season right after peas and they are usually finished before the first green beans are ready to harvest. Fava bean vines are quite productive in the garden, supplying delicacies for the kitchen throughout their growth cycle and inoculating the soil with loads of nitrogen all the while. The small new leaves of fava beans offer some of the first fresh greens of the year. While they are still very tiny, the fuzzy young pods are a first-of-the-season treat, whether eaten whole, grilled, or roasted, or cut up and added to a spring vegetable soup. As the pods mature, the beans must be shelled. When they are very young they can be eaten with their skins, but as the season progresses and they grow larger, they should be skinned. Dunk them in boiling water for a few seconds to loosen the skins before putting them in ice water, which cools them. Then the skins can be slipped off easily, revealing the bright lime green beans within, which are a fantastic addition to spring vegetable ragouts and pasta sauces, and which make delicious purée to spread on toasted bread. Both *Aguadulce* and *Windsor* are classic varieties.

Fava beans can be planted in the spring as soon as the soil can be worked. Scatter a good feeding of compost before planting. There is no reason to plant seedlings that have been started indoors, because fava beans grow so easily when directly seeded. In milder climates, fava beans are planted in the fall to get a good start on growth. The plants weather the winter without growing and shoot up once the temperature warms. They can withstand a fair amount of frost: some varieties tolerate temperatures as low as 12°F. Straw mulch helps the roots stay warm. Fava beans do not like warm weather at all.

After flowering (and they are beautiful in flower), the plants begin to set beans. At this point, cut their tops to direct the plants' energy to the beans instead of the leaves. Then bring the tops to the kitchen to cook! Harvest the tiny pods when they are two and a half inches long for eating whole and let the others grow until the beans are plump and fill their pods. Favas taste best when harvested before the beans begin to lighten in color and become starchy. For long production, keep harvesting the beans when they are young. Eat fava beans right away; they don't keep well. Compost the stalks or dry them to use as mulch. Fava beans are a principal nitrogen-fixing cover crop in many parts of the country, grown to nourish and improve soil. To read more about cover crops, go to page 369.

## Fava Greens

Very young fava greens are tasty added to a mixed green salad. Larger greens are very good sautéed or steamed. I like to cut them up and stir them into a juicy vegetable ragout while it is cooking—for example, a mix of cut asparagus, fava beans, and sliced spring onions cooked in an inch of salted water and finished with a pat of butter and chopped chervil or tender lemon thyme. The greens can also be quickly sautéed with a bit of water (the water still clinging to the leaves after washing is usually sufficient) and finished with a chopped garlic clove and a sprinkle of dried chile flakes. With a little grated cheese they make a perfect pasta sauce. Or cool them before seasoning, chop them, and mix with ricotta and seasonings to make a pasta stuffing.

## Roasted Whole Young Favas

Tiny fava pods about 3 inches long are delicious eaten whole. String them, toss them with olive oil and a pinch of salt, and cook in a 450°F oven for 6 minutes until tender and just cooked through. If you have one, a wood-burning oven does a marvelous job of cooking and flavoring them. The oiled and seasoned beans may also be cooked on a hot grill. Put them in a grill basket if the bars of the grill are farther apart than the beans are wide. Serve them as they are, piping hot.

Whole baby fava beans can be cut into pieces and added to a vegetable ragout or pasta sauce. Cook them just as you would green beans.

## Squid and Fava Beans with Garlic and Parsley

4 SERVINGS

This dish is quick and easy to make once the squid is cleaned and the fava beans are shelled—and both can be done in advance. Store the squid over ice in the refrigerator to keep it extra fresh. Serve with toasted crusty bread to soak up the delicious juices, or over a bowl of spaghettini.

Clean:

    **1 pound small squid**

Cut off the tentacles just below the eyes. Gently squeeze at the base of the tentacles to remove the small hard beak at their center. Discard it. Lay the body flat and run the back side of a small knife firmly up the body from the tail end to remove the insides of the squid. Grasp the pointy end of the hard transparent quill poking from the top of the body and pull it free. Cut the cleaned bodies into ¼-inch rings. Refrigerate the rings and tentacles until needed.

Shell:

    **1 pound fava beans (preferably small ones)**

Cook the beans in boiling water for 1 minute or so and cool in ice water. Drain and pop out of their skins.

When ready to cook, season the squid with:

    **Salt**

    **Fresh-ground black pepper**

Heat a heavy-bottomed frying pan over medium-high heat until quite hot. Pour in:

    **Olive oil, enough to cover the bottom of the pan**

Add the squid tentacles and cook until they

begin to contract, about 30 seconds. Add the body pieces. Cook for 3 minutes and then add the fava beans, along with:

**4 garlic cloves, chopped**
**A pinch of dried chile flakes (optional)**
**Salt**

Cook, tossing and stirring for 1 more minute, or until the squid is just cooked through. Turn off the heat and stir in:

**2 tablespoons extra-virgin olive oil**
**1 tablespoon coarsely chopped parsley**
**A squeeze of lemon juice**

Taste for salt and adjust as needed.

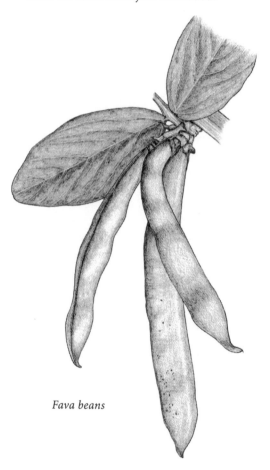

*Fava beans*

## Beans in the Garden

Beans are eaten at three different stages of development, and I adore all three. First come the green beans, or snap beans, the tender immature pods that form after the flowers have set. They are usually green, but there are yellow and purple types as well. These are tastiest when harvested young, before any seeds or fibrous strings have had a chance to develop. When allowed to mature, the pods enlarge and change color, and the seeds within plump up and swell into delectable fresh shell beans. At their last stage, the beans have been dried on the vine and are harvested when the pods are brittle and the seeds inside are shiny, dry, and hard, ready to be stored for winter and spring eating.

Beans are grouped according to their two basic habits of growth: pole and bush. Pole beans, the original form of beans, grow from five to ten feet tall and require some sort of long poles or sturdy trellises to support their twining growth. Pole beans save a lot of room in a small space by growing upward. They take a bit longer to come to harvest, but they do so over a longer period of time, making them more productive than bush beans. Traditionally, Native Americans planted pole beans at the base of corn; this companion planting provided support for the beans and nutrition for the corn. Sunflowers make good supports as well. Let the corn or sunflowers have a head start of a foot or so before planting the quick-growing beans. For planting a tepee of beanpoles, see page 382.

Bush beans grow no taller than two feet

and supply their own support. They mature rapidly, taking about two weeks at the most. For an extended harvest, instead of one large planting, sow plantings successively, every couple of weeks. Bush beans can be planted fairly close together for mutual support and shady mulch.

Beans are very sensitive to cold. Seeds will not germinate and plants will just sit there, not growing, unless the soil temperature is 65°F or higher. Start seeds indoors three weeks before planting, or purchase seedlings to plant out as soon as the weather has stabilized. After that, direct seeding works well. Choose a sunny location that is reasonably well protected from wind. Loosen the soil and amend with compost before planting. Install poles or other support first, or when the beans are planted, to avoid disturbing the growing root system. Keep the plants watered consistently, especially when they are flowering and setting fruit. A drenching or spray of compost tea is a welcome meal after four weeks of growth. Like fava beans and peas, beans supply their own nitrogen by gathering it from the air and storing it on their roots.

Most bean varieties are grown to be harvested at a particular stage, but many of them, especially the older heirloom varieties, can be eaten all through their development. When growing shell beans, always sample a few when they are young and tender to see how they taste as green beans; and if a few of your green bean varieties go too far, let them develop all the way and they may perhaps become a favorite shell bean.

# Green Beans *(Phaseolus vulgaris)*

Green beans come in a variety of sizes and colors. My favorite by far is the tiny, thin, and firm haricot vert, or filet bean. They are heavenly when they are simply boiled in salted water until just done and tossed piping hot with chopped garlic and olive oil. They are equally delicious dressed in a salad, or cut to toss into a quick ragout with corn or other summer vegetables. *Tavera* and *Nickel* are good bush haricots verts. *Emerite* is a high-quality pole variety. Short *Masai* is a good candidate for containers. *Soleil* and *Isar* are yellow, bush filet beans. *Kentucky Wonder* and *Blue Lake* are varieties that bear green beans that are bigger around, and with a slightly softer texture, than filet beans. They can be found as either bush or pole beans. Mature Kentucky Wonders make wonderful plump shell beans.

Yellow wax beans are beautiful in the garden and easy to find when picking. They add color to a bean ragout, and are certainly tasty on their own. *Golden Wax* and *Beurre de Rocquencourt* (*Golden Rocky*), both bush beans, are fine examples. *Dragon Tongue* is an unusual wax bush bean with flat, light-colored pods covered in purple streaks. *Purple Podded* pole bean and the bush *Royal Burgundy* beans are brilliantly colored when raw and turn dark green when cooked.

Long, broad, flat romano beans are remarkably tender with mild sweet flavor. They are delicious cooked until just done and tossed with lots of tender herbs, or stewed with tomatoes or a touch of bacon. *Super Marconi* and *Spanish Musica* (*Smeraldo*) are tasty green types, and *Marvel*

*Haricots verts*

of *Venice* and *Gold of Bacau* are yellow. Romano beans that are allowed to mature make meaty, delicious shell beans. Longer still are the snaky, thin Chinese long beans (*Vigna unguiculata*), which are a different kind of bean, more closely related to black-eyed peas. Green varieties have many interchangeable names: *Chinese Green Noodle* or *Dark Green* long beans are delicious and tender, while *Chinese Red Noodle* produces striking, crisp, burgundy-colored beans. Though they will grow longer, the beans taste best when they are under sixteen inches. (These romano and long bean varieties are all pole beans.)

Runner beans (*Phaseolus coccineus*) are another example of beans that can be eaten at every stage: as fantastic tender green beans (Britain's favorite green bean), as large shell beans, and, finally, as dried beans. They are impressively beautiful plants in the garden with brilliant blooms spilling out along tall dark vines. *Scarlet Emperor* has red blossoms and beans that are mottled black and purple. *Painted Lady* has red and white blossoms with streaked pink and brown beans. *White Emergo* has white flowers and very tasty white beans, while *Sunset* has salmon-pink blossoms with jet black beans. *Gigante*, as the name implies, are runner beans with huge, white, meaty beans. Runner beans tolerate cooler weather better than common beans and will thrive without full sun. In temperate climates they are perennial, producing beans over a number of years. Their splendid blossoms attract both bees and hummingbirds.

I recommend harvesting green beans a little earlier than your seed package advises—they are so much tastier when they are young. Eat them as soon after harvest as possible. A freshly harvested green bean is incomparable. Don't pass up the crisp, juicy, sweet bite of a raw bean just plucked from the vine—the gardener's exclusive reward. To keep the plants in full production, pick the beans as soon as they're ready. Haricots verts especially need to be diligently harvested. Pick them at least every other day so they don't grow big and tough. If quite a few pods have been missed and have started to mature, let them ripen into shell beans.

## Haricots Verts with Toasted Pecans and Purple Basil

4 SERVINGS

When I prepare haricots verts, or any green bean, I only snap off the stem end. I keep on the thin, pointy blossom end: I like the way it looks. (This is the first part that starts to deteriorate when the beans are not fresh, so this is a good tip to know at the market.) I cook green beans until just tender, not crunchy. Otherwise, their flavor is less pronounced.

Preheat the oven to 350°F.
Spread out on a baking sheet:
   **⅓ cup pecans**
Cook until toasted brown on the inside, about 12 minutes. Stir the nuts now and then to ensure even browning. Cool and break into smaller pieces.
Trim the stem end from:
   **1 pound haricots verts**
Remove the leaves from:
   **1 purple basil sprig**
Cut the leaves into a thin chiffonade.
Cook the beans in boiling salted water until tender. Drain well and toss with:
   **Salt**
   **A drizzle of extra-virgin olive oil**
Adjust the salt as needed and then add the pecans and basil and give a final toss.

VARIATIONS
◆ Wax beans, purple beans, yellow beans, or green beans would work as well as haricots verts, together or separately.
◆ Walnuts, hazelnuts, almonds, or pine nuts could be used instead of pecans.

◆ Try other herbs instead of basil: summer savory, marjoram, cilantro, shiso, or anise hyssop, to name a few.

## Yellow Romano Beans in Tomato Sauce

4 SERVINGS

Bring a large pot of salted water to a boil. Meanwhile, make a quick tomato sauce. Core and cut into large dice:
   **¾ pound ripe tomatoes**
Peel and coarsely chop:
   **4 garlic cloves**
Heat a heavy-bottomed pan over medium-high heat and pour in:
   **3 tablespoons olive oil**
Add the garlic and let sizzle until soft (do not let brown), about 30 seconds. Add the tomatoes and:
   **Salt**
   **8 basil leaves, cut into chiffonade**
   **A pinch of dried chile flakes (optional)**
Cook for 2 to 3 minutes until the tomatoes have softened and released their juices. Turn off the heat.
Trim the stem ends and slice diagonally into ½-inch pieces:
   **½ pound yellow romano beans**
Cook the beans in the boiling water until just tender. Drain, season with a bit of salt, and add to the warm tomato sauce. Turn on the heat and simmer for 4 to 5 minutes to marry the flavors. Taste for salt and adjust as needed. Finish with a drizzle of:
   **Extra-virgin olive oil**

# Three-Bean Salad à la Chez Panisse

4 SERVINGS

This is a recipe for the classic, all-American summer dish. When made with fresh ingredients from the garden and a simple herb vinaigrette it is great fare for a cool main dish or a picnic lunch. Don't stop at 3 types of beans—the more the merrier!

Shell:

**½ pound fresh cannellini shell beans (yields 1 cup shelled beans)**

Put the beans in a heavy-bottomed pan and cover by 1 inch with water. Add salt to taste. Bring to a boil and turn down to a simmer. Cook until tender, about 25 minutes; start checking after 15 minutes. When the beans are creamy and tender, turn off the heat and let them cool. Bring a large pot of salted water to a boil.

Trim the stem ends and cut into thirds:

**¼ pound yellow filet beans or wax beans**

Trim the stem ends and slice diagonally into ½-inch pieces:

**¼ pound romano beans**

Cook the beans separately in the boiling water until tender, yellow beans first. When done, drain the beans and lay out on a plate to cool. Sprinkle with a bit of salt and toss. Prepare a vinaigrette. In a small bowl, mix:

**1½ tablespoons red wine vinegar**
**Salt**
**Fresh-ground black pepper**
**1 teaspoon chopped marjoram**

Add to the vinegar mixture:

**1 shallot, halved and sliced thin**
**1 garlic clove, peeled and pounded to a purée**

Let sit for at least 5 minutes and then whisk in:

**¼ cup extra-virgin olive oil**

Taste and adjust the vinegar and salt. Drain the cannellini beans and toss all the beans with the vinaigrette. Let marinate for 30 minutes. Right before serving toss with:

**1 teaspoon chopped marjoram**
**2 teaspoons chopped parsley**

VARIATIONS

• Add other shell beans; garbanzo beans, flageolet beans, and black-eyed peas would all be good additions.

• Substitute other herbs for the marjoram and parsley, such as summer savory, basil, cilantro, or chives.

• Use Kentucky Wonder or Blue Lake beans in place of the romano beans.

• Fold in a few halved cherry tomatoes with the herbs.

• Garnish with a few strips of marinated roasted peppers. Roast and peel the peppers, season with salt, and toss with a spoonful of vinaigrette.

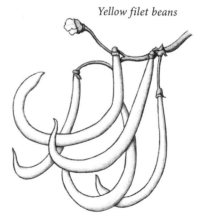

*Yellow filet beans*

## Shell Beans (*Phaseolus vulgaris*)

Farmers' market shoppers and gardeners have the greatest opportunity to try an assortment of fresh shelling beans. I cannot say enough how utterly delicious they are. If you haven't already tried them, please do! The beans are tastiest and easiest to shell after the pod has changed color and is no longer green but still pliable, and the beans within are fully formed and fresh looking. Many are stunningly beautiful, with vivid colors striped and splashed in remarkable designs over shiny firm surfaces. Shell beans are extremely versatile in the kitchen. They cook up more quickly than their dried counterparts, and they are more delicate-tasting. Try them straight out of the pot, flavored with sautéed onions and herbs; in a ragout with green beans; cooled and tossed in a summery salad; or mashed to a purée and spread on toasted garlic croutons. Shell beans are a nutritional powerhouse as well, packed with protein, fiber, minerals, and vitamins. Any shell bean may be eaten fresh or dried, though fresh dried beans have more flavor and cook faster than old ones. Look for beans from the latest harvest (no more than one year old); it really does make a difference. Shelled and stored in glass jars, dried beans make a lovely still life in the pantry, and a most welcome ingredient.

Creamy textured white *cannellini* beans are mild-flavored and make a beautiful clear broth. *Cranberry* and *French Horticultural* beans are ivory when ripe, splashed with a vivid mottling of red; they turn a tasty light brown when cooked. Sleek, plump black *Coco Nero* and shiny white *Coco Bianco* are hearty with full flavor whether added to a soup, ragout, or gratin. The elegant light green *flageolet* has a distinctive green bean flavor that I love with lamb and duck. These are the shell beans I cook most often and are the easiest to find in the markets where I live. They are also the most common varieties used in the cooking of France and Italy; but there are many, many more to try. Look over the offerings of seed catalogs and seed banks to get a feeling for the wide selection that is available. Try to plant some of your favorite organic dried beans from your pantry; they very well may grow. Many varieties of shell beans come as either pole or bush.

If you think you aren't a fan of lima beans (*Phaseolus limensis* and *Phaseolus lunatus*), you must try them fresh; they are seriously good. They come as both bush and pole plants: *Christmas* pole limas are large creamy, burgundy-splashed beans with a deep nutty flavor. *Jackson Wonder* bush is a smaller speckled lima bean. *Henderson's* bush is a small variety and *King of the Garden* is a large one; both are tender and pale green. Limas prefer a warm climate with a long growing season.

Black-eyed peas, cowpeas, crowder peas, and field peas (*Vigna unguiculata*) come in varied hues, some with eyes of a different color. The slender pods of these beans are crowded with calcium-rich, small round "peas." Try them as green beans when they are young and tender and as fresh or dried shelling beans. Fresh black-eyed peas are amazingly delicious. *California Blackeye* and *Purple Hull Pink Eye* are the two varieties I cook and find most often at the farmers' market. Most black-eyed peas are

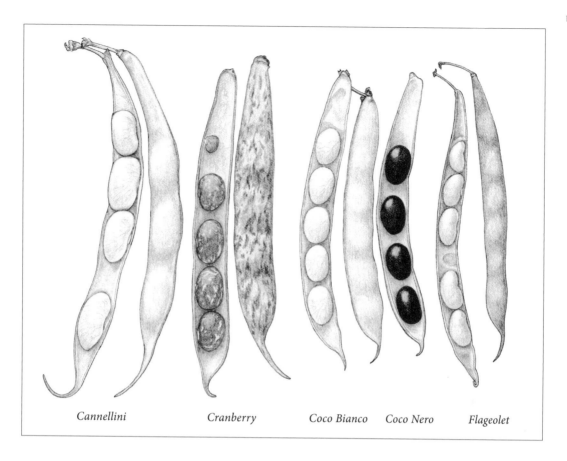

*Cannellini*        *Cranberry*        *Coco Bianco*    *Coco Nero*    *Flageolet*

low-growing bush types; all are easy to grow.

Fresh soybeans (*Glycine max*) boiled in their pods until just tender are a great hors d'oeuvre. (They are called *edamame* in Japanese.) Kids love them, and they are a healthy and fun-to-eat snack. *Envy* is a tasty choice, and *Black Jet* has unusual, highly regarded black beans. Fresh garbanzo beans (*Cicer arietinum*) are a delicacy. Each pod contains two tender beans, and when fresh and young they need just a moment in boiling water to cook. They are elegant tossed in salads or used as a garnish for hummus or other chickpea dishes. *Black Kabouli* plants are striking with purple flowers and black beans.

Harvest fresh shell beans when the pods are brightly colored and the beans will be plump and easy to shell. Picking the pods when they are immature compromises the flavor of the beans; they are also much harder to shell. Dried beans taste best when allowed to dry on the bush or vine. Wait until the pods are brittle and the beans inside rattle but not so long that the pods split open and spill their beans. If rain or frost is threatening, the beans may be harvested before fully ready, stripped from the plant and dried in a cool dry attic, garage, or other convenient place. Bush types may be pulled as a plant and hung inverted to dry. Once fully dry, shelling the beans by hand is easiest for small quantities.

# Cranberry Bean and Tomato Salad with Summer Savory Salsa

4 SERVINGS

Shell beans and tomatoes are at their prime in late summer. I love them together in all sorts of hot dishes, and they make a marvelous salad as well. Serve this salad with grilled or roasted meats, or make it the center of a light and refreshing dinner.

Shell:

**1 pound fresh cranberry beans**

Simmer in lightly salted boiling water until tender and creamy. Start checking after 20 minutes. Add water as needed to keep the beans submerged. When they are done, let the beans cool in their cooking liquid. The beans can be cooked 1 day ahead.

Prepare the salsa. Peel and dice fine:

**1 large shallot or 1 small fresh onion**

Season with:

**Salt**

**2 tablespoons wine vinegar, Banyuls or red**

Let the shallots and vinegar sit to macerate while preparing the rest of the ingredients. Stir together:

**1 tablespoon chopped summer savory**

**1 tablespoon chopped parsley**

**2 garlic cloves, pounded to a purée**

**Salt**

**Fresh-ground black pepper**

**A pinch of Marash or other pepper (optional)**

**¼ cup extra-virgin olive oil**

Taste and adjust the salt as needed.

Remove the core from:

**4 ripe tomatoes, assorted types and colors**

Cut in slices and wedges for an assortment of shapes. Drain the cooled beans, reserving the cooking liquid for another use.

When ready to serve, arrange the tomatoes on a platter and season with:

**Salt**

Using a slotted spoon or fork, lift the shallots from the vinegar and stir into the savory salsa. Sprinkle some of the vinegar over the tomatoes and reserve the rest for another dish. Toss the beans with half the salsa. Spoon the rest of the salsa over the tomatoes and scatter the beans over the tomatoes.

# Cannellini Bean Purée

MAKES ABOUT 2 CUPS

Bean purée makes a great crouton topper for an appetizer or light meal and it is a good side dish (and a much healthier one than mashed potatoes). Cannellini beans have a light texture and a mild flavor that goes very well with sage.

Shell:

**2 pounds fresh cannellini beans**

Put them in a pot and cover by 1 inch with water. Add:

**1 sage sprig**

**Salt**

Simmer until just starting to fall apart, about 35 to 40 minutes. Let cool. Drain the beans, reserving the cooking liquid. Remove the sage sprig and purée the beans with a food mill or a bean or potato masher, adding just enough cooking liquid to make a thick texture. Measure into a small heavy-bottomed pot:

**1 tablespoon extra-virgin olive oil**
**1 tablespoon chopped sage**

Heat over medium heat until the sage just starts to sizzle on the edges. Turn off the heat and let the sage warm through for another minute. Pour into the bean purée and stir in:

**2 garlic cloves, pounded to a purée**
**2 tablespoons extra-virgin olive oil**

Taste for salt and adjust as needed. Finish with:

**A spritz of lemon juice**

If you prefer a thinner purée, stir in enough bean cooking liquid to reach the desired consistency.

VARIATIONS
◆ Use rosemary instead of sage.
◆ Try fava beans or other shell beans, fresh or dried, instead of cannellini beans.
◆ Garnish bean purée croutons with Sungold Cherry Tomato Salsa (page 165).

# Fresh Flageolet Beans with Spicy Lamb Sausage

4 SERVINGS

Fresh sausage is very easy to assemble at home and well worth the effort. This sausage is based on Moroccan *merguez* and has a nice balance of acid and spice that is well matched by the distinctive flavor of the fresh beans. Dried flageolet beans will work nicely, too, but look for fresh ones, as they are a very special treat.

Measure into a large bowl:

**1 pound ground lamb**
**1 teaspoon salt**
**¼ teaspoon fresh-ground black pepper**
**2 tablespoons dry red wine**
**2 teaspoons red wine vinegar**
**2 garlic cloves, pounded to a purée**
**2 teaspoons chopped parsley**
**1 teaspoon sweet paprika**
**¼ teaspoon cayenne (more for a spicier sausage)**
**1 teaspoon cumin seeds, toasted and pounded**
**1 teaspoon coriander seeds, toasted and pounded**
**½ teaspoon fennel seeds, toasted and pounded**
**A pinch of dried chile flakes**

Mix gently, using stiff open fingers like a comb, until the ingredients are well combined. Take a small ball of the mixture and pat into a thin patty. Heat a small heavy-bottomed pan over medium-high heat. Add the patty and cook until done, about 3 minutes on each side. Taste for salt and spices, and adjust as desired. (Sprinkle a grain or two of salt on a piece of the patty to see if it tastes better with more salt.) Roll the mixture into small meatballs or form into small patties. Refrigerate until needed.
Shell:

**2 pounds fresh flageolets**

Submerge in lightly salted boiling water and cook until tender. Check after 20 minutes. Let the beans cool in their cooking liquid. When ready to cook, heat a cast-iron or other heavy-bottomed pan over medium-high heat. When hot, pour in:

**Olive oil, enough to coat the bottom
of the pan**

Add the meatballs or patties in a single layer; just enough to comfortably cover the bottom of the pan. Cook in batches if necessary. When the meat is well browned on all sides, carefully pour off most of the fat and add the beans, along with enough of their cooking liquid to come ¼ inch up the sides of the pan. Gently stir in:

**3 garlic cloves, chopped
1 tablespoon marjoram leaves**

Simmer for a few minutes to finish cooking the meat and to marry the flavors. If the pan becomes dry, add more cooking liquid. When done, turn off the heat and stir in:

**1 tablespoon chopped parsley**

Taste for salt and adjust as needed.

# White Beans
# with Duck Confit

4 SERVINGS

The luscious texture and taste of duck confit is perfectly matched with creamy mild beans. Take the time to carefully crisp the skin. It adds a delectable crunchy caramelized bite that really makes this dish.

Shell:

**1½ pounds fresh cannellini shelling
beans (3 cups shelled beans)**

Put the beans in a heavy-bottomed pan and cover with water by 1 inch. Add:

**Salt**

Simmer until tender, about 25 minutes (start checking after 15 minutes). Add water, if needed to keep the beans submerged while cooking. When done, drain off and reserve the cooking liquid, leaving just enough to cover the beans. While the beans are cooking, heat in a heavy-bottomed pan:

**3 tablespoons duck fat or olive oil**

Add:

**3 shallots, diced (about ⅓ cup)
3 thyme sprigs, leaves only**

Cook until soft over medium heat, stirring occasionally, about 8 minutes. Add:

**4 garlic cloves, finely chopped
Fresh-ground black pepper
Salt**

Cook another few minutes and then stir into the cooked beans.

Chop together to mix:

**2 tablespoons coarsely chopped
parsley
1 garlic clove, chopped fine**

Set aside.

Remove from their fat:

**4 legs of duck confit**

Heat a heavy-bottomed skillet large enough to hold the 4 legs in a single layer over medium heat. Cast iron works well. When hot, place the legs in the pan skin side down. Cook until the skin is brown and crispy, about 6 minutes. Keep an eye on the heat and turn it down if the skin begins to brown too quickly. Turn and cook another 3 or 4 minutes. Place on a rack or absorbent paper to drain for a moment.

While the duck is browning, heat the beans and taste for salt. Adjust as needed. Plate the beans and then arrange the duck legs on the beans and sprinkle parsley and garlic over the top.

# Rio Zape Beans Cooked in the Coals with Garlic and Chiles

4 SERVINGS

This is a great way to cook beans if you have a fire going in your grill or hearth. The beans soak up a little smoke to add to their natural seasoning. A ceramic bean pot does the best job, but any ovenproof pan will work. Rio Zape beans are indigenous to the American Southwest and are meaty-tasting beautiful brown beans striped and speckled with black. Serve with grilled or roasted meats and vegetables.

Soak for 8 hours or overnight:
> **1 cup dried Rio Zape beans**

Drain and put in a ceramic bean pot or other ovenproof pot, cover with fresh water by 2 inches. Add:
> **2 dried chiles (ancho, guajillo, New Mexico, or other variety)**
>
> **4 garlic cloves, peeled and coarsely chopped**

Put the pot over medium heat, bring to a boil, and remove the pot to the side of a fire or to a bed of coals. If you are using a round-bottomed bean pot, rake or scoop out some ash so the pot will be propped up by the ashes around it and not tip over. Move the pot nearer to or farther from the fire to keep it at a low simmer, rotating the pot occasionally if need be. The beans should be submerged at all times, so add water if needed. Cook until the beans are tender, about 1 hour. Season with salt and let cook a few more minutes.

VARIATIONS
- Cut 2 slices pancetta or bacon into bite-size pieces and add them to the beans with the chiles and garlic.
- Any dried or fresh shell bean is delicious cooked like this. Cook fresh shell beans a shorter time, 25 to 45 minutes, depending on the bean used.

# Chile con Carne

4 SERVINGS

Cut into 1-inch pieces:
> **1 pound pork shoulder**

Season well with:
> **Salt**
>
> **Fresh-ground black pepper**

Shell:
> **1 pound fresh cranberry shell beans (about 2 cups shelled beans)**

Put the beans in a heavy-bottomed pan and cover by 1 inch with water. Add salt to taste. Bring to a boil and turn down to a simmer. Cook until tender, about 25 minutes. (Start checking after 15 minutes.) Add water if needed to keep the beans submerged while cooking. When the beans are creamy and tender, turn off the heat. Meanwhile, heat a pot of water to a boil. Core:
> **3 medium tomatoes**

Dip the tomatoes in the water for 30 seconds or so to loosen the skins. Remove and submerge in cold water to stop the cooking. Peel the tomatoes and cut in half horizontally. Gently remove the seeds and pulp into a strainer and bowl to catch all the juices. Rub the seeds in the strainer to strain out the rest of the juice. Discard the seeds. Chop the tomatoes and combine with the juice. Heat a heavy-bottomed pot over medium-high heat. When hot, add:

**2 tablespoons olive oil**

Carefully add the pork and brown well on all sides. This may take some time, especially if the pork gives off some water. It is worth being patient in order to achieve a nice brown caramel color. Turn down the heat if the meat is browning too quickly. When done, remove the meat with a slotted spoon. Pour off half the fat and add:

**1 onion, diced**

**1½ teaspoons ground ancho chile**

**1½ teaspoons ground New Mexico or smoky chipotle chile**

**½ teaspoon cayenne (optional)**

Cook over medium heat, stirring occasionally, until soft, about 5 minutes. Stir in:

**5 garlic cloves, peeled and coarsely chopped**

**Salt**

Cook for 2 minutes. Stir in the tomatoes and pork and cook for 6 minutes. Add 1 cup water and 1 cup of the bean liquid and cook for 30 minutes. Taste for salt and adjust as needed. Drain and add the beans and cook for another 30 minutes. If the chile gets too thick, add water to thin. Serve garnished with:

**Crème fraîche**

**Chopped cilantro**

VARIATIONS

◆ Use 2 cups cooked dried beans instead of fresh shell beans.

◆ Substitute 1 cup canned tomatoes with their juice for the fresh tomatoes.

◆ Use beef chuck or turkey leg instead of pork.

# Black-Eyed Peas with Sautéed Okra and Jimmy Nardello Peppers

4 SERVINGS

The glossy red peppers, green okra, and ivory black-spotted peas make a beautiful dish. I love all the flavors mixed together: sweet peppers, earthy beans, and tender mild okra. Serve it with crispy chicken cooked under a brick (chicken al mattone) or crumbly pieces of cornbread.

Shell:

**1 pound fresh black-eyed peas (yields 2 cups shelled beans)**

Cook in ample lightly salted water until tender, about 25 minutes. Let cool in their cooking liquid. Meanwhile, cut in half:

**4 Jimmy Nardello peppers**

Cut off the stems and clean out the seeds. Slice the halves into 4 or 5 pieces at an acute diagonal. Trim the stem end and cut in half lengthwise:

**½ pound okra (choose smaller pods)**

Heat a cast-iron or other heavy pan over medium-high heat. When hot, pour in:

**Olive oil, enough to coat the bottom of the pan**

Add the peppers and okra and:

**Salt**

Cook, stirring and tossing, until nicely browned, about 6 minutes. Add the black-eyed peas with a spoonful or two of their cooking liquid. Cook just until the okra is tender, about 3 or 4 minutes. Serve garnished with:

**1 tablespoon chopped parsley**

**A drizzle of extra-virgin olive oil**

# Crowder Pea and Greens Soup

MAKES ABOUT 1½ QUARTS

Peas and greens are a natural pairing. I like them in soup: think of minestrone and soupe au pistou. This is a simpler soup, with crowder peas (I use Purple Hull variety) and spicy mustard greens.

Shell:

**2 pounds fresh crowder peas (about 2 cups shelled beans)**

Cook in an ample quantity of boiling salted water. Simmer until tender, about 30 minutes.

While the beans are cooking, remove the stems from:

**1 large bunch of mustard greens**

Wash, drain, and chop coarsely.

Heat in a heavy-bottomed pot:

**3 tablespoons olive oil**

Add:

**1 onion, diced**
**2 savory sprigs**
**2 thyme sprigs**
**1 bay leaf**

Cook over medium heat until soft, stirring occasionally, about 10 minutes. Add:

**4 garlic cloves, coarsely chopped**
**1 mild pepper (Anaheim, poblano, Corno di Toro, etc.)**
**1 pinch dried chile flakes (optional)**
**Salt**

Cook for 4 minutes, then add:

**1 large or 2 medium tomatoes, seeded and diced (about ½ pound)**

Cook another few minutes and add the cooked beans and their liquid. Bring to a simmer and add the mustard greens. Cook for 10 minutes or until the mustard greens are tender. If the soup is too thick, thin with water to the consistency you want. Taste for salt and adjust as needed. Serve garnished with:

**A drizzle of extra-virgin olive oil**

VARIATIONS

• Serve individual portions of soup over toasted crusty bread rubbed with garlic and brushed with olive oil.

• Cut 2 slices of bacon into ½-inch pieces. Cook in the olive oil until slightly crisp, remove from the pot, add the onions, and proceed as above. Sprinkle the bacon over the finished soup with the olive oil.

• Use collard greens instead of mustard greens. Cook another 5 minutes or until tender.

• Instead of crowder peas, use other beans such as black-eyed peas, cannellini beans, flageolets, or cranberry beans.

• Use 1 cup dried beans instead of fresh shelling beans. Increase the cooking time to 1 hour or so.

# Hummus with Preserved Lemon

4 SERVINGS

I have always preferred a savory breakfast. I eat this hummus many mornings with Whole-Wheat Pita Bread (this page) and a spoonful of Cucumber and Yogurt Raita (page 140) along with a cup of pu-ehr tea. I love the sweet and savory punch the preserved lemon adds to the hummus.

Soak for 8 hours, or overnight:
   **¾ cup chickpeas**
Drain and cook in plenty of water until quite tender, 1 to 2 hours. Check the water level and add more as needed. Drain the cooked beans, reserving ¼ cup of the cooking liquid. Purée with a food mill or in a food processor or blender.
Stir in:
   **2 garlic cloves, peeled and pounded to
      a purée**
   **¼ cup tahini (sesame seed paste)**
   **2 tablespoons extra-virgin olive oil**
   **3 tablespoons lemon juice**
   **¼ preserved lemon, rind only,
      chopped fine**
   **Salt**
   **¼ teaspoon toasted ground cumin**
   **A large pinch of cayenne**
Mix until smooth, adding some of the cooking liquid if needed. Taste and add more salt and spice as desired. Arrange in a bowl and, if you want, garnish with:
   **A drizzle of extra-virgin olive oil**
   **A pinch of ground cumin**
   **A pinch of cayenne**

# Whole-Wheat Pita Bread

MAKES 8 BREADS

Homemade pita is well worth making. It is one of the quickest breads to make and bake. It's also easy enough that kids can help; they often love the process of making bread. Another plus is that when the dough is ready, you can bake a few breads and put the rest of the dough into the refrigerator to use later. It will last up to a week.

As well as eating warm pita bread with raita, hummus, or a scrambled egg for breakfast, I like to serve the pita for dinner and use them to soak up extra juices of a braise or stew. Pita can also be dried out and crisped and used for crackers, croutons, or Tomato and Toasted Pita Bread Salad (page 164).

Measure into a medium bowl:
   **1¼ cups lukewarm water**
Sprinkle over:
   **1½ teaspoons active dry yeast**
Let sit for 1 minute and then stir to dissolve. Add
   **1½ cups whole-wheat flour**
Mix well to combine, and keep mixing for 1 minute to make a sponge. Let the sponge sit for 10 minutes or so (you can leave it for a few hours if necessary).
Stir in:
   **1 teaspoon salt**
   **1 teaspoon olive oil**
Then start gradually mixing in:
   **1½ cups whole-wheat flour**
Keep adding flour until the dough is soft but not tacky. (I usually stir in 1 cup and then knead in the rest. The amount used depends on the flour—sometimes I use it all, some-

times not quite all.) Turn the dough onto a floured board or countertop and knead for 8 to 10 minutes, or until smooth and elastic. Clean and lightly oil the mixing bowl, put in the dough, and cover. Let the dough rise until double in size, about 1½ hours.

When ready to bake, remove the upper rack from the oven, put the lower rack in the lowest position, and, if you have one, put a pizza or baking stone on it. Preheat the oven to 500°F. Gently punch down the dough and divide it into 8 pieces. Flatten each piece into a disk, put it on a floured surface, and cover with a towel. One by one, roll out the disks into 8-inch circles about ¼ inch thick. Set them aside, covered, until ready to bake. Don't stack the rolled-out breads: they will stick together.

Bake each pita individually for 3 minutes directly on the baking stone (or on a baking sheet). The dough should puff up like a balloon. Let them cool and wrap them in a kitchen towel to stay warm and soft (pita hardens very quickly). Or put the extra dough into an airtight container or plastic bag. Take out of the refrigerator to come to room temperature before rolling and baking.

VARIATION
♦ Make smaller breads by dividing up the dough into more pieces and rolling into smaller disks.

## Peanuts (*Arachis hypogaea*)

Peanuts are a legume, like beans, and not a nut. Even if you don't grow your own, you can frequently find fresh raw peanuts at farmers' markets or in the bulk section of the grocery. (Make sure they're raw.) They are especially tasty when freshly roasted or boiled. I never really thought about peanuts until a friend, farmer-gastronome Andy Griffin of Mariquita Farm, sent me a big bag of peanuts he had grown down in Watsonville, California. I roasted them and was taken by surprise by how tasty they were.

Peanuts are unique in the way they grow. Once the petals have fallen from the flowers the stems drop down to the ground and burrow into the soil where the peanuts form, underground. The burrowing stems are called pegs.

There are a few varieties to choose from, some with longer growing-season requirements and others with shorter ones. Look for seeds in catalogs, or save your favorite raw peanuts from the market and try growing them. Peanuts do best in loose soil with lots of compost, but they can be grown in heavier soils if they are planted in trenches and hilled up with loose soil as they grow.

## Fresh Roasted Peanuts

Moisten fresh peanuts with salt water before roasting and the salt will penetrate the shells and flavor the peanuts. They take a bit longer to cook than you might expect, but the results are delicious.

Preheat the oven to 350°F. Put in a large bowl:

> **1 pound fresh, raw, washed peanuts in the shell**

Dissolve:

> **1 teaspoon of salt**

in:

> **2 teaspoons water**

Pour the salty water over the peanuts and toss well. Lay out the peanuts on a baking tray and roast for 30 to 40 minutes. After the first 15 minutes stir the nuts. Then, for even roasting, stir every 5 minutes until done. Taste a peanut after 25 minutes. Cook until the shells are evenly golden brown. The peanuts inside will crisp up after they cool down.

## Boiled Peanuts with Star Anise and Soy

Boiled peanuts have a texture and flavor reminiscent of soft shell beans. Green, freshly harvested peanuts are the best to boil, but any fresh raw peanuts, shelled or whole, are fine, as long as they haven't been dried.

Put washed peanuts in a heavy-bottomed pot and cover with water by 1 inch. Add enough salt to make the water taste pleasantly salty, and 1 small piece of cassia, 2 star anise pods, and a large splash of soy sauce. Bring to a boil, turn down to a simmer, and cook for 1½ hours, or until cooked through. Bite into a peanut: there should be no white core. If the peanuts are not eaten up right away, refrigerate them for up to one week.

Try other spice combinations: for example, a handful of cumin seeds, a head of garlic, and a few dried chiles; or a ham hock, a good glug of beer, and coriander seeds.

# Meandering Vines

## Cucumbers, Melons, Summer Squash, and Winter Squash

CRISP CUCUMBERS, LUSCIOUS MELONS, tender zucchini, sturdy pumpkins, and sweet winter squash grow on vines that wind through fields and gardens in summer. As the weather warms, the markets fill with the bounty, beauty, and variety of these plants—cucumbers for salads, drinks, or pickles; melons to eat right away or chill into refreshing salads and desserts; summer squash to grill, stuff, or cook into flavorful vegetable braises. The winter squashes conveniently grow a hard skin that allows them to keep all winter long, for making smooth purées, ravioli, soups, and pies.

# Recipes

Cucumber and Yogurt Raita 140

Lemon Cucumber, Purslane, and Cherry Tomato Salad 141

Cucumber Agua Fresca 141

Sliced Crenshaw Melon with Salt, Chile, and Lime 143

Chilled Melon Soup with Mint 144

Watermelon Granita 145

Zucchini Ribbons with Lemon and Basil 146

Summer Squash Pizza with Marjoram and Fresh Ricotta 147

Pizza Dough 147

Grilled Crookneck Squash Fans with Basil Vinaigrette 148

Squash Blossom Quesadillas 149

Whole-Wheat Tortillas 149

Stuffed and Fried Squash Blossoms 150

Winter Squash Antipasto 152

Roasted Delicata Squash Salad with Scallions and Rocket 152

Red Kuri Squash Soup 154

Toasted Squash Seeds 155

Butternut Squash and Celery Root Gratin 155

# Vines in the Garden

The long vines and broad bushes of cucumbers, melons, and squash make a pretty show with their green leaves, jaunty bright orange blossoms, and bright splashes of ripening fruits. They are all garden ramblers that need plenty of room. Cucurbit is the family name and it holds an enormous range of varieties, from tiny cornichon cucumbers no bigger than your little finger to pumpkins large enough to sit in. The entire family is tender and quite sensitive to cold. Wait a full week past the frost date to plant outdoors. To get a jump on the season, especially for long-season varieties, start seeds indoors in a warm sunny area. Sow in individual four-inch pots, as they grow large very quickly. Don't start too early (no more than four weeks before the last frost) or the plants will grow quite large and won't transplant well.

Choose a site in full sun with rich soil and good drainage. A raised bed or a large hill will warm more quickly and drain better than a flat bed. Feed with a good amount of compost and water well. Continue to feed the plants throughout the season with a monthly drenching or foliar feeding of compost tea. These are thirsty plants and require frequent watering. Wilting leaves will let you know you are not keeping up with their needs. Apply water at the base of the plants to avoid wetting the leaves, which are susceptible to mildew when damp. Mulch will help keep weeds down and the soil moist, and prevent ripening fruit from sitting on the damp ground.

To save space, train the trailing vines into neat spirals or plant them as a ground cover, or plant them on the outside edges of the garden. Good places for vines to stretch out can be found alongside fences, driveways, or even sidewalks. Cucumbers, small winter squash, and melons can be trained up sturdy trellises, which saves space and keeps the fruits neat and tidy, too. Most summer squash grow in broad bushes that tend to spread evenly rather than snake, but many of them just keep spreading, so be sure to give them adequate space. Small varieties will do well in containers.

Melon and winter squash seeds are very easily saved. The seeds are mature when the fruits are ready to eat. Dry the seeds and save them to plant the next year. (Plants in the same species will crossbreed, so keep them separate when growing different varieties simultaneously.)

# Cucumbers  (*Cucumis sativus*)

Juicy, crisp, and refreshing, cucumbers are a happy addition to the summer table. They are delightful straight from the garden with a chilled glass of rosé. Pack them in a lunch, toss them in a salad, or add them to seasoned yogurt to make a raita to eat with flatbread or tortillas. In southern Italy, cucumbers are eaten at the end of the meal, along with grapes, melons, and other fruits, as a dessert. I love the idea. Pickles—dill pickles, cornichons, half-sours, to name just a few—are a great way to preserve the harvest. Serve them with cured and braised meats or use them to spice up sandwiches and sauces. Cooking cucumbers is less well known but well worth trying: sauté slices in butter with a squeeze of lemon for a beautiful side dish to accompany grilled fish or roast lamb.

My favorite cucumbers are found under the heading of "specialty varieties." They are all thin-skinned and never bitter. Round, pale yellow *Lemon* cucumbers are a sweet and juicy old variety that performs well even today. The seeds within are quite tender and edible. Light green, ribbed *Armenian* cucumbers (*Cucumis melo*) are technically long thin melons. Their flesh is dense and

sweet. Another Armenian type is the curly, twisting *Painted Serpent*, beautifully striped in light and dark green. It is as tasty as it is beautiful. *Persian*, or *Beit Alpha*, is practically seedless, with bright green, sweet, crisp flesh. These cukes are fantastic eaten right out of hand. *Little Fingers* is perfect for a container. Japanese cucumbers are slender, dark green, and slightly knobby, with thin skin and sweet flesh. *Sooyow Nishiki* (*Suhyo Long*) is a hardy and good-flavored variety.

Pickling cucumbers are considered to be the closest to the ancient form of the plant with smaller, stockier, blunt-ended fruits covered with warty bumps that have black or white spines. The warts help the pickling brine penetrate more easily. Most pickling cucumbers are good to eat raw, once peeled. Tiny *Cornichon* makes the classic small French pickle that I especially like, and *Boston Pickling* is reliable and good. Slicing cucumbers are garden variety green in color, long and smooth, and with fairly thick skin that requires peeling. They are occasionally bitter, especially at their ends. Taste the ends before cutting them up and trim off any bitterness. *Marketmore* is a well known heirloom variety.

Cucumber roots are delicate and do not grow well when disturbed, so keep the root ball as intact as possible while transplanting, and be careful when cultivating and weeding around the plants. Keep the plants evenly watered and well fed with compost or compost tea, especially when they are producing fruit.

Like squash and melons, cucumbers are monoecious: each individual develops

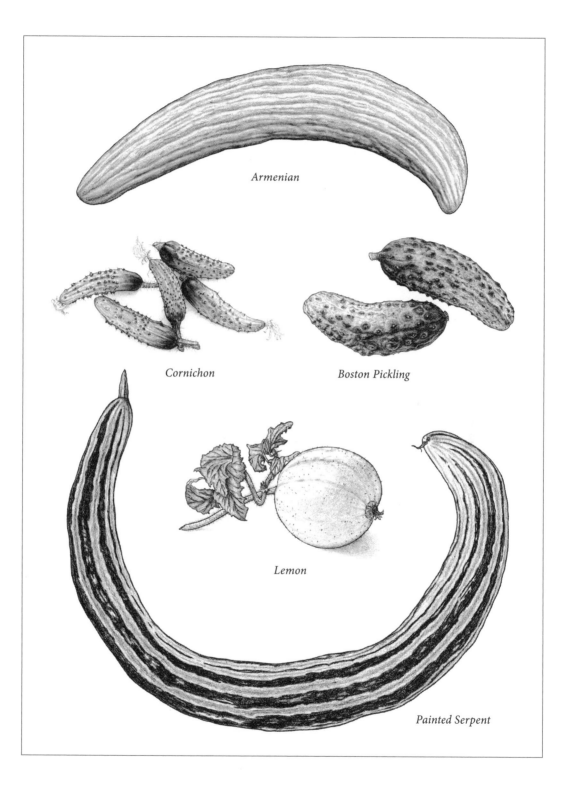

*Armenian*

*Cornichon*

*Boston Pickling*

*Lemon*

*Painted Serpent*

both male and female flowers, and the male pollinates the female, which produces the cucumber. Through breeding, other types of reproduction have been developed for the plants. There are parthenocarpic plants that only produce self-pollinating female blossoms. Most of these are hybrids, though some open-pollinated varieties do exist, such as Beit Alpha. Other hybrids are gynoecious; that is, they have been bred to produce only female blossoms that do not self-pollinate. These require a male plant to be sown among them to propagate the fruit. Be sure to read the seed package for the requirements of what you are planting.

Harvest cucumbers before the seeds have a chance to develop. This is frequently much sooner than the seed packet suggests. Try them as they grow to decide when you think they taste best. Cut—don't pull—the fruits off the vines. Keep up with the harvest: picking them while the cucumbers are still small encourages the plants to keep up production. Search well for the maturing fruit, as they can be easy to miss hiding under the leaves, especially when growing on the ground.

Choose small varieties for containers and provide a trellis or other structure for the vines to climb up.

# Cucumber and Yogurt Raita
MAKES ABOUT 1 CUP

Raita is the Indian mixture of fruit or vegetables, yogurt, and spices. I especially like to make it with cucumbers. The sour tang of yogurt is complemented by the refreshing sweet crunch of cucumbers. It is superb with spicy vegetable braises, grilled meats and fish, and saffron rice, or as a condiment for stuffed sandwiches and other wraps. With the addition of more yogurt, it can even become a cold soup. To see another recipe for raita, go to Spiced Carrot Raita (page 73).

Peel and dice, or grate:
> **1 small or ½ medium cucumber (Lemon, Armenian, or Persian are good choices)**

You should have about ½ cup. Season with:
> **A pinch of salt**

Set aside.

Heat in a small heavy-bottomed skillet:
> **⅛ teaspoon cumin seeds**
> **¼ teaspoon coriander seeds**
> **⅛ teaspoon nigella seeds**

When warmed and slightly toasted, use a mortar and pestle to pound the spices to a coarse powder. Stir the spices into:
> **½ cup Yogurt (page 183)**

Drain any liquid off the cucumbers and add them to the yogurt with:
> **2 teaspoons chopped mint**
> **Salt**
> **A small pinch of cayenne or dried chile flakes (optional)**

Stir together and taste. Adjust as needed.

VARIATIONS
- Use cilantro, dill, or chervil instead of mint.
- Use black mustard seeds or fennel seeds in place of the nigella or cumin.
- For a creamier sauce, drain the yogurt before using. Put it in a strainer over a bowl for a few hours or overnight to allow its liquid, or whey, to drain off.

## Lemon Cucumber, Purslane, and Cherry Tomato Salad

4 SERVINGS

Lemon cucumbers make a beautiful salad when cut into juicy, sweet wedges and complemented by the sweetness and acidity of cherry tomatoes. Purslane is often found growing unbidden in the garden. It is quite tasty and full of nutrition. Pull it from the garden when it is young and tender for a wonderful salad green, or sauté it when it is more mature. Purslane is sold at many farmers' markets, and in Latin markets under its Spanish name, *verdolaga*.

Make a dressing. In a small bowl, stir together:

**1 small shallot, finely diced**
**1 tablespoon red wine vinegar**
**Salt**
**Fresh-ground black pepper**

Let sit for 10 minutes to macerate. Whisk in:

**3 tablespoons extra-virgin olive oil**

Taste for salt and acid and adjust as needed. Meanwhile, remove the large stems from:

**2 handfuls of purslane**

Wash, drain, and spin dry. Remove the stems, wash, and cut in half:

**A large handful of cherry tomatoes
    (a mix of Sungold and Sweet 100s,
    if possible)**

Peel:

**4 small or 3 medium lemon cucumbers**

Cut in half lengthwise and cut the halves into ⅓-inch wedges. Toss the purslane and cherry tomatoes with two thirds of the dressing and:

**A pinch of salt**
**10 to 12 basil leaves, torn**

Arrange on a plate. Put the cucumbers in the same bowl you dressed the purslane and tomatoes in. Sprinkle with:

**Salt**

Pour over the rest of the dressing and gently fold to coat well. Arrange the dressed cucumbers on the salad.

VARIATION

◆ Add ¼ cup crumbled feta to the cucumbers along with the dressing.

*Persian cucumber*

## Cucumber Agua Fresca

4 SERVINGS

Cucumbers make a very refreshing drink. Sweet, fine-fleshed cucumbers such as Japanese, Persian, English, and Armenian are good choices. The simple syrup may be made ahead. It will keep for weeks in the refrigerator and is a great ingredient to have on hand for other drinks and cocktails.

First make the simple syrup. Measure into a small pot:

**1 cup water**
**1 cup sugar**

Bring to a boil, stirring to dissolve the sugar. Boil for 30 seconds. Pour into a heatproof bowl and set aside to cool.

Peel and cut in half lengthwise:

**2 medium cucumbers**

If the cucumber has large seeds scrape them out with a small spoon. Coarsely chop the cucumber and stir in:

**A pinch of salt**

Cut in half and squeeze:

**3 limes**

You should have about ¼ cup juice. Measure into the jar of a blender:

**1 cup water**

Add the cucumbers and purée well, about 1 minute. Pour through a strainer, pushing the pulp with a spoon to extract as much liquid as possible. Add the lime juice along with ¼ cup simple syrup. Taste and add more syrup and lime juice as desired. Add more water if a lighter drink is desired. Serve over ice and garnish with:

**A slice of cucumber**

**A slice of lime**

VARIATIONS

❖ For a greener drink, leave the skin on thin-skinned cucumbers (Persian, Armenian, or Japanese).

❖ Flavor the simple syrup with any of the following: 2 jalapeños or serrano chiles cut in half (remove the seeds for less spice); a 1-inch piece of ginger thinly sliced; or a large lemon verbena sprig. Garnish the drinks with a slice of chile or ginger or a leaf of lemon verbena along with the cucumber slice.

❖ Add a handful of spearmint leaves to the blender and garnish with a mint leaf.

❖ Substitute watermelon for half the cucumber.

❖ For a thicker drink, don't strain the cucumbers, and for a slushy *agua fresca*, add ice cubes while blending.

# Melons  (*Cucumis melo*)
# Watermelon  (*Cucumis lanatus*)

The pastel colors of lush and aromatic melons are as alluring as their flavors. From juicy giant watermelons to tiny fine-fleshed French cantaloupes, there is such a range to choose from. A slice of melon is a refreshing bite on its own, or try dressing it up with a velvety slice of prosciutto or sprinkling it with a mixture of lime zest, crushed chile, and salt. Puréed, melons make a sublime soup decorated with assorted jewel-like melon balls or frozen into an icy granita. Season melons with a light touch: a bit of herb or spice, or a splash of sweet wine.

The melon family is large and complicated, even for experts. Apart from watermelons I am going to sidestep groupings and list some of my favorites. Each of them has its own merits in aroma, texture, and flavor. Many melons are hard to ship and are not grown commercially. Your local farmers' market and gardens are the best places to look for interesting, highly flavored varieties. Small, striped, and smooth-skinned *Charentais* has fine orange flesh and a highly perfumed aroma and flavor. *Crenshaw* is a large, smooth, yellow to green elongated melon with sweet juicy, peachy pink flesh. It is a personal favorite of mine. *Eden's Gem* (or *Rocky Ford Green Fleshed*) is a netted muskmelon with delicious light green flesh inside. *Ha'Ogen* has smooth yellow skin with green stripes and juicy, sweet green flesh. *Piel de Sapo* (toad skin in Spanish) has knobby green skin and very sweet, fine white flesh. *Orange-Fleshed Honeydew* has light green skin with brilliant and delicious orange flesh. There are many, many more to discover.

Watermelon has a grainier flesh that makes it particularly juicy and refreshing. There is an incredible number of available varieties. There are watermelons with striped rinds, dark green rinds, light green rinds, yellow rinds, green rinds speckled with constellations of yellow spots, and more. The melon inside comes in a range of colors, too: red, pink, yellow, orange, and even white. Fruits range in size from giant to small. The smaller fruits are referred to as icebox melons. I invite you to grow open-pollinated melons: they will have beautiful seeds within. Seedless watermelons are modern hybrids, and they are pushing some of the delicious older heirloom varieties to the brink of disappearance. Some of my favorite watermelons are: pink-fleshed *Moon and Stars*, bright red *Crimson Sweet*, small red-fleshed *Sugar Baby*, deep orange-fleshed *Orangeglo*, and small *Yellow Doll*.

Melons need lots of heat to produce sugar and plenty of long sunny days to ripen. And like all the other vines, they are thirsty for water, especially during fruit production. Melons in particular need well-draining soil. They don't thrive with their roots sitting in soggy soil. A raised bed is a good idea if your soil is dense or clayey. Some people have good luck growing melons in their compost pile in cooler climates. The pile has good drainage, and the heat generated by decomposition helps the melons ripen and develop flavor. Smaller or mini melons do fine in containers. Train them on a sturdy trellis rather than letting them roam over the ground.

Melons taste the very best when picked at the perfect point of ripeness. Follow the instructions on the seed packet for harvest. Each type of melon has its own specific culture. It is good to know (both at the market and in the garden) that the more netted the rind, the sweeter the melon; and with most kinds of melon, aroma is a dead giveaway for ripeness.

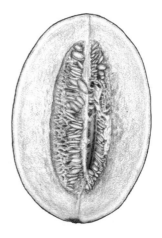

## Sliced Crenshaw Melon with Salt, Chile, and Lime

I first tasted melon served this way in the open markets of Mexico. The salt brings out the taste of the melon while the chile and lime get your juices moving. It is amazingly delicious and refreshing. The chile mixture is good both freshly made and aged. As it ages, the lime zest dries in the salt and adds a wonderful depth of flavor. If you have any flaky salt such as Maldon or fleur de sel, this would be a good place to use it. Look for freshly ground chile if possible, or roast and grind your own. Choose as spicy or as sweet a chile as you like.

Measure into a small bowl:

**2 tablespoons flaky sea salt or other
sea salt**

**2 teaspoons crushed dried chiles (ñora,
Marash, or ancho are good choices)**

**Grated zest from 2 or 3 limes,
depending on their size**

Massage the zest and chiles into the salt to marry the flavors.

Cut in half lengthwise:

**1 Crenshaw melon**

Cut into slices and arrange on a plate. Sprinkle with the chile-lime salt and serve.

VARIATIONS

◆ Use other melons such as watermelon, Orange Honeydew, or Charentais. I like to serve watermelon stone cold and the others at room temperature.

◆ Remove the rind from the melon and cut into bite-size chunks. Toss with the salt and serve in a bowl or cup.

# Chilled Melon Soup with Mint

4 SERVINGS

This is the recipe for melon season—the soup looks and tastes the best when a few different melons are used. So this is a great excuse to buy all those fragrant, perfectly ripe melons tempting you at the farmers' market! Serve as a refreshing breakfast, light appetizer, or elegant dessert (adjusting the seasonings appropriately). The mint can be added to the soup itself or sprinkled over as a garnish. Try it both ways.

Gather together:

**3 ripe melons of different varieties**

From one of the melons, cut and measure:

**3 cups cubed melon**

Purée in a food mill, blender, or food processor with:

**A pinch of salt**

**A handful of mint leaves (optional)**

If thick, thin with water to a desirable soup consistency; then chill.

Make an assortment of melon balls of different sizes from all three varieties of melons, about 6 balls per person. Toss the balls with:

**A pinch of salt**

**2 mint sprigs, leaves only, cut into a
thin chiffonade**

**A splash of sweet wine, such as
Beaumes-de-Venise or Moscato
d'Asti (optional)**

**A pinch of cayenne**

When ready to serve, ladle the soup into chilled bowls or compote dishes. Garnish with the melon balls and sprinkle with:

**A few more mint leaves, freshly cut
into a chiffonade**

**A julienne of prosciutto (optional)**

VARIATIONS

◆ Add ½ cup sweet wine or Vin d'Orange (page 352) to the soup.

◆ If using prosciutto, sprinkle with crushed Marash or ñora pepper.

◆ Add ½ cup yogurt or crème fraîche along with 2 tablespoons simple syrup (see page 141) to the blender when puréeing the melon.

◆ Flavor the melon balls with a splash of Pernod instead of sweet wine.

◆ Garnish with basil instead of mint.

# Watermelon Granita

MAKES 4 CUPS

Cut the rind from:

**A 2-pound wedge of watermelon**

Put the rind in the compost bin and cut the flesh into small cubes. Remove and discard the seeds as you go. Place in batches in a blender and purée. Stir in:

**½ cup sugar**
**Juice of 1 lime, about 1 tablespoon**
**A pinch of salt**

Stir to dissolve the sugar. Pour into an 8-inch glass baking dish or other low-sided container and place in the freezer. Stir after 1 hour and then allow to freeze solid. Scrape with a fork until light and fluffy. Spoon into cold glasses or bowls and serve immediately.

VARIATIONS

• Garnish with a wedge of watermelon, chopped mint, or grated lime zest.
• Blend and freeze different colors of watermelon separately. Serve together.
• Make a simple syrup and use it instead of the sugar in the recipe. Combine ½ cup sugar, ½ cup water, and the grated zest from 1 lime in a small pot. Bring to a boil, stirring to dissolve the sugar. Boil for 30 seconds and then turn off the heat. Strain when cool.

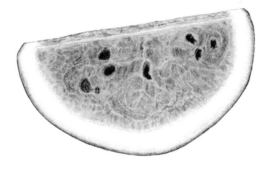

# Summer Squash  (*Cucumis pepe*)

Quick growing and highly productive, summer squash are available from late spring through early fall. Choose small squash for the best flavor. I like them sliced thin and served raw as a salad with lemon and basil, grilled over the coals, cooked into a gratin, and combined with eggplant, tomatoes, and peppers for ratatouille and other vegetable stews. Quickly sautéed with a few capers and garlic, they make a perfect pasta sauce. A favorite summer pizza at the Chez Panisse café is topped with summer squash and ricotta. Summer squash produces loads of bright orange blossoms to fry, bake, poach, or shred. (The male flowers don't produce squash.) They are the perfect mix of sweet and savory.

There are many varieties of summer squash to choose from, and I have to admit that the ubiquitous green zucchini is not my favorite. *Costata Romanesca* is. It's ribbed with dark and light green stripes. Its fine dense flesh is never bitter and never gets pulpy when cooked. *Cocozelle*, smooth and striped, is good, too. *Ronde de Nice* is round and dark green with good flavor. *Gold Rush* is a fine yellow zucchini. *Lebanese White* is light green, short and slightly stubby, sweet, and fine textured. Flying saucer–shaped scallop or pattypan squash, called cymlings in Thomas Jefferson's time, are mild and densely textured. Try light green *Bennings Green Tint*, *White Scallop*, or *Patisson Golden Marbre*. *Yellow Crookneck* is pretty, especially when cut in a fan and grilled.

Summer squash are prolific. One plant will easily keep a family of two in squash.

Stagger plantings about a month apart to enjoy different varieties and a longer season. The squash themselves grow at breakneck speed, and require harvesting almost every day. Pick them while they are young and tender, for best flavor and long, continual production. Cut male blossoms to eat the same day they bloom, preferably in the cool of morning or evening. Leave a few to pollinate the female flowers. Or use a small paintbrush to collect pollen from the male flowers and brush into the center of the female flower to guarantee pollination. The longer male flower is distinguished by its long stem, which sends the flower higher, beckoning bees and other pollinators to come hither. Female flowers are on shorter stems and have a bump behind the flower, the tiny beginning of the squash to be. When your kitchen is running over with squash, the female flowers can be picked and eaten, too.

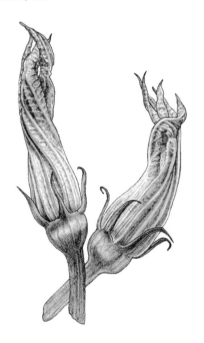

# Zucchini Ribbons with Lemon and Basil

4 SERVINGS

This is a wonderful way to serve summer squash. Raw squash have a dense texture and a sweet flavor that is set off by the fresh herb and lemon juice.

Wipe clean with a damp cloth and remove the ends from:

**2 to 3 small zucchini (a mix of colors makes a pretty dish)**

Slice lengthwise into thin strips, about ⅛ inch thick. A mandoline makes this job easier. Prepare the rest of the ingredients. Remove the leaves from:

**¼ bunch of basil**

Stack the leaves and cut them thinly crosswise. Squeeze the juice from:

**1 lemon**

Have ready:

**Salt**

**Fresh-ground black pepper**

**Extra-virgin olive oil**

Layer the squash slices into a shallow dish (use a pretty one if you are going to serve the ribbons in it). Sprinkle each layer with salt, pepper, basil, lemon juice, and olive oil. Let sit for at least 10 minutes and serve.

VARIATIONS

• Other tender herbs will work well with the basil or by themselves: try mint, cilantro, shiso, or chervil.

• A mixture of summer squash is good in this dish: crookneck, Lebanese, Ronde de Nice, pattypan, and so on. The more shapes and colors used, the prettier and tastier it will be.

# Summer Squash Pizza with Marjoram and Fresh Ricotta

MAKES ONE 10- TO 12-INCH PIZZA

Preheat the oven to 500°F. If you have one, place a baking stone on the lower rack and heat for 30 minutes before baking the pizza. Mix together in a small bowl:

**1 garlic clove, chopped fine**
**1 tablespoon olive oil**

Slice thinly:

**2 small summer squash (mixed colors, if possible)**
**1 Torpedo onion**

Place the squash in a bowl and toss with:

**A squeeze of lemon**
**Salt**
**Fresh-ground black pepper**
**A splash of olive oil**

Stretch out:

**One 6-ounce ball Pizza Dough (this page )**

Place on a floured peel and brush the garlic oil over the dough, leaving the edge bare. Sprinkle the onions over the dough, followed by:

**⅓ cup grated mozzarella cheese**

Lay out the sliced squash over the cheese and onions. (It is okay if the slices overlap a bit, but they shouldn't be piled on each other.) Dot the top with large spoonfuls of:

**⅓ cup fresh ricotta**

Slide the pizza onto the stone and bake until puffed and browned, 5 to 8 minutes. If you don't have a stone, place the pizza on a pizza pan and bake. Remove from the oven and sprinkle with:

**2 tablespoons chopped parsley**
**1 tablespoon chopped marjoram**

# Pizza Dough

MAKES FOUR 6-OUNCE BALLS FOR FOUR 10-INCH PIZZAS

This dough makes a light bubbly crisp-crusted pizza. It is a wet sticky dough so when you handle it be sure that the dough, all work surfaces, and your hands are generously floured. A very soft, moist dough makes the best pizza.

Stir together:

**2 teaspoons active dry yeast**
**¾ cup lukewarm water**

Add and mix well:

**½ cup unbleached bread flour**
**¼ cup rye flour**

Allow this mixture to sit until quite bubbly, about 30 minutes.

Stir together in another bowl:

**2⅔ cups unbleached bread flour**
**2 teaspoons salt**

Stir this into the yeast and flour mixture with:

**¾ cup cold water**
**¼ cup olive oil**

Mix thoroughly by hand or in an electric stand mixer. If working by hand, turn the dough out onto a well-floured board and knead for 5 minutes. Or use the mixer, fitted with the dough hook, and knead for about 5 minutes. The dough is the right texture when it pulls away from the sides of the bowl of the mixer, but still adheres to the bottom.

Turn the dough out onto a generously floured board. Cut into 4 pieces and, with floured hands, roll each piece into a ball. Place on a parchment-paper-lined and floured sheet pan. Sprinkle the balls with flour and cover with plastic wrap or a plastic bag. Let rest overnight in the refrigerator. (If you are in a hurry, let rest at room temperature for 2 hours.) The dough will keep in the refrigerator for up to 3 days.

Take the dough out of the refrigerator 2 hours before baking. Preheat the oven to 500°F (or higher if your oven goes higher). If you have one, place a baking stone on the lower rack and let it heat for 30 minutes before baking the pizza.

Flour your hands well and gently stretch a ball of dough into a 10- to 12-inch circle. Use the back of your hands and knuckles, as they are less likely to poke a hole in the dough. Place the shaped dough on a floured peel or the back of a sheet pan. Put whatever topping you are using on the dough and slide it into the oven right onto the pizza stone. Bake for 5 to 8 minutes, until puffed and browned. If you don't have a stone, place the dough on a pizza pan and bake on the pan.

# Grilled Crookneck Squash Fans with Basil Vinaigrette

4 SERVINGS

Prepare a medium-hot fire and place a grill over it to preheat. When the fire is ready, clean the grill well and oil it using a cloth or paper towels.

Wipe clean with a damp cloth:

**4 medium crookneck squash**

Make lengthwise cuts from the top of the bulbing part of the squash through to the blossom end making a fan of squash slices held together by the swanlike neck. Gently open the slices and season with:

**Salt**

**Fresh-ground black pepper**

Mix together in a small bowl:

**1 shallot, diced fine**

**1 large purple basil sprig**

**1 tablespoon vinegar**

**Salt**

**Fresh-ground black pepper**

Let sit for 10 minutes or so to macerate. Whisk in:

**3½ tablespoons extra-virgin olive oil**

Taste for salt and acid and adjust as needed. Remove the basil sprig before serving.

When ready to cook, brush the squash lightly with oil and place them on the grill. As the squash are cooking, gently flatten them onto the grill so that the slices open and fan out. Cook for 4 minutes and then turn and cook until tender, another 3 or 4 minutes. Arrange on a plate and spoon over the vinaigrette. Sprinkle over:

**5 large or 8 medium purple basil leaves, cut into a fine chiffonade**

## Squash Blossom Quesadillas
4 SERVINGS

Squash blossoms are a classic addition to quesadillas in Mexico. The blossoms add a sweet squash flavor to the creamy cheese filling. Serve with Sungold Cherry Tomato Salsa (page 165) or Roasted Tomatillo Salsa (page 168). Happily, it is now easy to find good-quality organic Monterey Jack cheese.

Break off the fibrous green mini-petals, or sepals as they are called, around the bases of:
**6 squash blossoms**
Gently open the petals and remove the pointy center (the anther in the male blossom, the pistil in the female), which can be bitter. Cut or tear the flowers into quarters. Gather:
**4 Whole-Wheat Tortillas (this page)**
**1¼ cups grated Monterey Jack (or other mild melting cheese)**
Sprinkle the cheese over half of each tortilla. Then lay the blossoms over the cheese. Fold the empty half of each tortilla over the cheese and blossoms. Heat a griddle or heavy-bottomed pan over medium-high heat. When hot, add:
**2 teaspoons butter**
Lay the tortillas on the griddle (or in the pan) and brown on one side. Turn and brown the other side. Sprinkle with salt and serve.

VARIATIONS
• Add 1 or 2 torn leaves of epazote to each quesadilla.
• Sauté a diced red onion in olive oil until soft and stir in the kernels from an ear of corn. Season with salt and cook for a minute or two. Divide among the 4 quesadillas.

• Roast, peel, and seed 2 ancho or poblano peppers. Cut into strips and season with salt. Divide the chile strips, or *rajas* as they are called in Spanish, among the 4 quesadillas.
• Use corn or flour tortillas instead of whole wheat.

## Whole-Wheat Tortillas
MAKES EIGHT 8-INCH TORTILLAS

Every time I make tortillas I am amazed at how easy it is. I am reminded of the diversity and range one can achieve by mixing flour with water. Whole-wheat tortillas are my new favorite breakfast. I heat one up directly over the flames of a burner and eat it with a bit of hummus sprinkled with za'atar or a mix of ground peppers or topped with a spoonful of yogurt flavored with a touch of garlic and olive oil; or I melt some cheese on top and roll the tortilla around a few bites of dressed lettuce and rocket.

In a medium mixing bowl, stir together:
**2 cups whole-wheat flour**
**½ teaspoon salt**
Add and mix well:
**2 tablespoons olive oil or fresh lard**
Measure:
**¾ cup warm water**
Gradually pour ½ cup of the water into the flour mixture, stirring constantly with a fork. The mixture should gather into a ball. Add more water as needed, a tablespoon at a time, though take care not to make it too wet. Turn the dough out onto a work surface and knead briefly. The dough should be neither wet nor dry and should be kneadable

without any additional flour. Divide into 8 pieces. Flatten each piece into a disk and lay them out in a single layer and cover with plastic wrap or a towel. Let rest for ½ hour or so.

Heat a comal, griddle, or cast-iron pan over medium-high heat. Roll out each disk to an 8- to 9-inch circle. Turn the tortilla over now and then to keep it from sticking (you shouldn't need flour). Place the tortilla on the hot pan and cook for 30 to 45 seconds, as it puffs and browns in places. Turn and cook for another 30 seconds or so. Then cover the cooked tortillas with a clean kitchen towel to keep them warm and soft. Cooled tortillas may be stored in a plastic bag or airtight container in the refrigerator for up to 1 week. Reheat on a hot pan or over the open flame of a burner.

# Stuffed and Fried Squash Blossoms
4 SERVINGS

Cut and remove the crust from:

**2 slices day-old crusty country-style bread**

Tear or cut into smaller pieces and process in a blender or food processor until the crumbs are medium fine. You should have about ½ cup crumbs. Toss with:

**A pinch of salt**
**2 teaspoons extra-virgin olive oil**

Spread the crumbs on a baking sheet in a thin layer. Bake in a 350°F oven until golden brown, stirring the crumbs every few minutes for even browning. Let cool.

Mix the cooled crumbs with:

**2 tablespoons cubed fresh mozzarella**
**4 salt-cured anchovy fillets, chopped**
**2 tablespoons chopped parsley**
**1 garlic clove, chopped fine**
**2 teaspoons extra-virgin olive oil**
**Salt**
**Fresh-ground black pepper**
**A pinch of dried chile flakes (optional)**

Break off the fibrous green mini-petals, or sepals as they are called, around the bases of:

**8 squash blossoms**

Gently open the petals and remove the pointy center (the anther in the male blossom, the pistil in the female), which can be bitter. Fill each blossom with a spoonful of stuffing and close the petals over the stuffing. Pour into a heavy-bottomed pot and heat to 350°F:

**3 inches of olive or vegetable oil**

Make a quick batter while the oil is heating. Measure:

**1 cup all-purpose flour**

Whisk in about:

**1 cup cold sparkling water or beer**

Add just enough sparkling water to make a fairly liquid batter, about the consistency of cream. Whisk just until mixed; a few lumps are okay. When the oil is hot, hold each blossom by its stem, dip in the batter, let the excess run off, and then carefully slip it into the hot oil. Cook until golden on both sides and remove to a plate lined with absorbent paper or a towel. Cook in batches if necessary. Serve immediately, seasoned with salt.

VARIATIONS
◆ Stuff the blossoms with seasoned ricotta.

◆ Don't batter the blossoms; bake them on an oiled baking sheet in a 375°F oven until warmed through, about 12 minutes.

◆ Instead of the batter, dip the blossoms in beaten egg and dredge in cornmeal or fine breadcrumbs. Fry as above.

◆ Sprinkle with gremolata (see page 189) before serving.

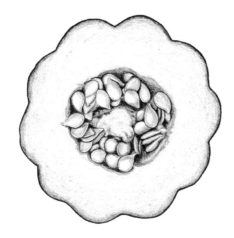

## Winter Squash

*(Cucurbita moschata, Cucurbita maxima, Cucurbita mixta,* and *Cucurbita pepo)*

Annabelle Lenderink, a bright-eyed, incredibly hard working local farmer-gastronome, has opened my eyes to the world of winter squash. Her Marin County farm, La Tercera, specializes in rare European cultivars. I am amazed each fall by the sheer beauty and diversity of the squash piled up around her stand. They are fantastic to eat and bring long-lasting color and texture to my countertops and table at the moment when flowers from the garden are hard to come by. Winter squash are divided into four different species and each has its own particular culinary attributes.

*Cucurbita moschata* has hard, spiny, round stems that are thicker right where they are attached to the squash. Its fine, sweet flesh does not fall apart when cooked, making it a great choice for brothy soups, risottos, and marinated antipasti. *Butternut* is the workhorse of the fall and winter kitchen. *Amish Neck* pumpkins, *Rugosa Violina, Sucrine du Berry,* and *Dickinson* field pumpkins (which, although little known to most of us, is the squash used in commercial purée) are other tasty large butternut look-alikes. *Long Island Cheese* pumpkins and *Musquée de Provence* are large, tan, and scalloped, with bright orange flesh. A Southern favorite is the Native American heirloom *Seminole* pumpkin.

*Cucurbita pepo* (the same family as most summer squash) has deeply furrowed stems and is usually a bit thinner-skinned than other winter squash. The tastiest varieties are small, oblong *Delicata* and round squat *Sweet Dumpling*. Both are light colored, with green stripes, and are perfect for stuffing or roasting for a single serving. Though most large orange pumpkins are wonderful to carve and the seeds are good for roasting, the flesh is watery and fibrous and fairly useless for cooking. For pie, I highly recommend *New England Sugar Pie* pumpkin and *Long Pie* pumpkin. They are not good carving material but do make sweet, creamy purée for splendid pies. *Table Gold Acorn* is delicious both as a tender summer squash and as a hard-skinned winter squash.

*Cucurbita maxima* is recognized by its corky, fat stems and has brightly colored, dry, fluffy, almost starchy flesh. All of its varieties make delicious purée that is especially good for soup, gnocchi, and ravioli stuffing. Some of my favorites are dark green *Marina di Chioggia*; slate blue tricornered *Triamble*; pink—and amazingly warty—*Galeux d'Eysines*; long pink *Banana*; teardrop-shaped *Blue Hubbard*; and small orange *Gold Nugget*.

*Cucurbita mixta*, a lesser-known species that traces its history right to our southern states, grows well in long hot summer weather. *Cushaw*, a light gourdlike squash with green stripes, is revered for its purée, which is used for custards and pies.

Winter squash is insipid in flavor when immature. Harvest fruit when the stems have hardened, the squash feels dense and heavy, and the skin is deep in color and hard enough that you can't dent it with your fingernail. Cut (don't pull) the squash from the vine, leaving one to two inches of stem on the fruit to prevent damaging the skin. The flavor of most squash, with the exception of the smaller *Cucurbita pepo* varieties (Delicata, Dumpling, Acorn, etc.), benefits from a week or two of "curing." This involves nothing more than leaving the fruit to sit after harvest, either in the garden or indoors at room temperature. Squash keeps very well: six months or more for the thicker-skinned varieties, three months for the thinner-skinned ones. Store outside of the refrigerator and away from the damp—a dry place that's over 50°F is the best and a kitchen cupboard or a shelf out of direct sun will do fine. Once cut, refrigerate the squash.

## Winter Squash Antipasto

Use squash that will keep their shape when cooked, such as Delicata or Sweet Dumpling, or any *Cucurbita moschata*.

Wash the squash. Leave the skin on: it helps the squash keep its shape after cooking; the peel softens in the oven and is tender enough to eat. Cut into ¼- to ⅓-inch-thick slices. Remove the seeds and strings. Season the slices with salt, drizzle with olive oil, and spread them out on a baking sheet. Roast at 400°F until the flesh is soft and marked with a few specks of caramelization. Sprinkle with vinegar, salt, black pepper, chopped herbs, and extra-virgin olive oil. Serve at room temperature with sliced salume, olives, and other marinated or pickled vegetables. I love this served on crostini with sherry vinegar, loads of chopped marjoram, and burrata or ricotta cheese.

## Roasted Delicata Squash Salad with Scallions and Rocket

4 SERVINGS

This recipe calls for a squash that keeps its shape after cooking. Good choices are butternut, Delicata, Sweet Dumpling, Rugosa Violina, Sucrine du Berry, or Long Island Cheese. If using the small Delicata or Sweet Dumpling, don't bother to peel the squash. Just cut in half, remove the seeds, and cut into chunks or slices. The skin will be just fine in the salad. Serve this salad as part of a picnic, light lunch, or as a side dish with roasted or grilled meats.

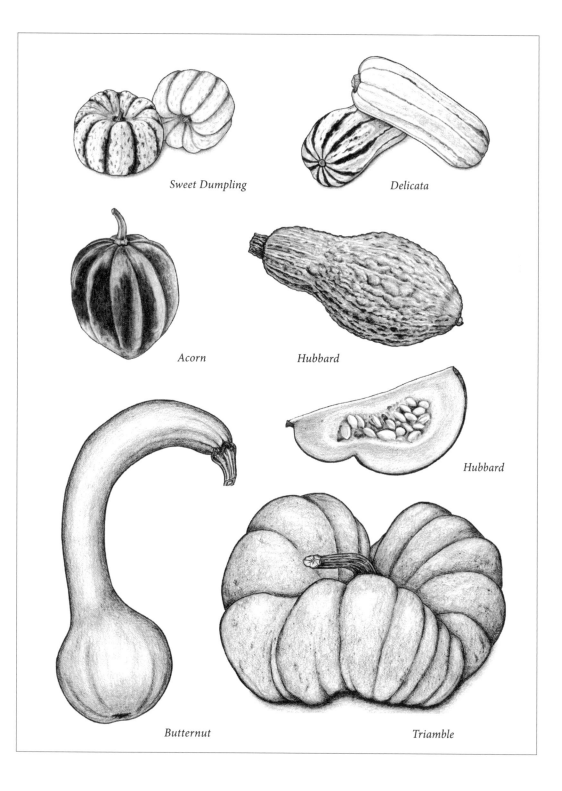

Sweet Dumpling

Delicata

Acorn

Hubbard

Hubbard

Butternut

Triamble

Preheat the oven to 400°F. Cut in half lengthwise:

**2 or 3 small Delicata squash**

Scoop out the seeds and strings. Save the seeds to toast if desired. Cut the squash into 1-inch-thick slices, cut the slices into 1-inch-wide sticks, and then cut the sticks crosswise to make 1-inch cubes. (Or be creative and cut any shape you would like. Just be sure to cut the pieces more or less the same size so they cook evenly.) Place the cut squash into a bowl and toss with:

**Olive oil**

**Salt**

Spread on a baking sheet and roast until tender, about 20 minutes. When done, remove from the oven and let cool. Meanwhile, make a vinaigrette. Combine in a small bowl:

**1 tablespoon wine vinegar (Banyuls, sherry, or red wine)**

**Salt**

**Fresh-ground black pepper**

Stir to dissolve the salt. Remove the leaves from:

**2 large marjoram sprigs**

Chop the leaves coarsely and add to the vinegar. Whisk in:

**3 tablespoons extra-virgin olive oil**

Taste for salt and acid and adjust as needed. Remove the roots and tips of:

**2 or 3 scallions**

Pull off the outer layer. Slice thin, using the green and white parts. Wash and dry well:

**2 large handfuls of rocket or wild rocket**

Put the rocket and scallions in a large bowl, add the vinaigrette, and toss well. Fold in the roasted squash. Taste for salt, acid, and olive oil and adjust as needed.

VARIATIONS

• Substitute 1 large or 2 medium shallots for the scallions. Peel, cut in half, and slice into thin wedges. Toss with olive oil and salt and roast until tender and slightly caramelized. Fold in with the squash.

• Increase the quantity of the vinaigrette by adding 1 teaspoon vinegar and 1 tablespoon oil. Toss 2 cups cooked farro or spelt with the vinaigrette, then add the rest of the ingredients.

• Make more vinaigrette, as in the second variation, toss with ½ cup cooked green lentils and 1½ cups cooked spelt.

• Substitute basil for the marjoram.

• Use sweet potatoes in place of the squash.

# Red Kuri Squash Soup

MAKES ABOUT 1 QUART

Red Kuri squash has a brilliant orange flesh with a sweet chestnut flavor. By varying the type of squash and the garnish you use, this simple recipe can make many different soups. Sage, marjoram, ginger, and toasted nuts are some of the flavorings that go well with squash, and I especially like it seasoned with Indian spices.

Pour into a large heavy-bottomed pot:

**3 cups water**

Bring to a boil and add:

**½ onion, or 1 medium leek, diced coarsely**

**Salt**

**1 bay leaf**

**3 cups cubed squash**

Return the water to a boil, reduce to a sim-mer, and cook until the vegetables are quite tender. Remove the bay leaf and purée until smooth in a blender (or use an immersion blender or a food mill fitted with a fine plate). Taste and add salt to taste.

VARIATIONS

• Cook the leek and onion until tender, stir in 2 cups of squash purée, and proceed as above.
• Use 2½ cups water and finish the puréed soup with ½ cup milk or half-and-half.
• Stir in 1 cup of diced roasted fennel and garnish with a drizzle of extra-virgin olive oil and chopped fennel fronds.
• Stir in a pat of sweet butter and a splash of dry sherry. Garnish with a twist of black pepper.
• Chop toasted pecans and mix them with extra-virgin olive oil, black pepper, and chopped marjoram—add a spoonful to each bowl as a garnish.
• Use butternut squash for a fine-textured sweet soup.
• Add 1 tablespoon chopped fresh ginger to the water along with the leek and onion.
• Fry *pepitas* (squash seeds) in butter with chopped sage over medium heat until golden brown. Finish with a pinch of salt and cay-enne (or another chile powder). Garnish each bowl with a spoonful of the spicy seeds.

## Toasted Squash Seeds

Rinse the squash seeds in a colander to remove all the strings and pulp. Spread out the seeds on a kitchen towel to dry. Pre-heat the oven to 325°F. Spread the seeds on a baking sheet and toast until they start to pop and turn golden brown, about 10 to 15 minutes. Toss with salt and butter, and coconut oil or olive oil. Add chopped herbs and freshly pounded spices for variety. I love using a little cayenne and ajwain seed, an Indian spice with an intense thymelike flavor.

There are squash that yield hull-less, or naked, seeds; these are particularly deli-cious. Kakai and Lady Godiva (both *Cucur-bita pepo*) are good examples. If using, clean the seeds as above and cook for 5 to 8 minutes.

## Butternut Squash and Celery Root Gratin
6 SERVINGS

Celery root adds complexity to the sweet-ness of butternut squash. The gratin can be made ahead and reheated. It is fine to leave it out at room temperature for a few hours—it tastes better and is easier to reheat if it has not been chilled completely. Pack it in a sack lunch or as a picnic treat, to be served at room temperature.

Preheat the oven to 375°F. Trim the ends from and peel (a vegetable peeler works well):

**1 medium butternut squash**
**1 medium celery root**

Cut them both in half lengthwise. Scoop out the seeds from the squash. Compost the peels and seeds. Using a sharp knife or mandoline slicer, cut both the squash and celery root crosswise into thin slices. (A mandoline makes this job much easier, but it is certainly not essential.) Strip the leaves from:

**3 marjoram or sage sprigs**

Chop coarsely; you should have about 2 teaspoons. In a gratin dish or a low-sided baking dish, lay out a single layer of squash, packing the slices tightly and leaving as little exposed dish as possible. Sprinkle the layer with one quarter of the herbs, and:

**Salt**

In the same way, lay out celery root in a single layer on top of the squash and sprinkle with salt and herbs. Continue until you have 3 layers of squash and 2 of celery root. The top layer gets salt only.

Mix together in a small heavy-bottomed pot:

**1 cup half-and-half**
**1 cup cream**
**Salt to taste**
**A pinch of cayenne**

Heat until warm. Pour over the vegetables; the level of the liquid should just reach the top layer of vegetables. Press down on the vegetables; they should be fully submerged when pressed. Place in the middle of the oven to bake. After the gratin has been cooking for 35 minutes, take a spatula and press the top layer of squash under the cream. This keeps the top layer from drying out. Bake until the liquid is absorbed, the top is browned, and the vegetables are tender (test by probing them with the point of a paring knife), about 1 hour of cooking in all. If the gratin begins to brown too much before it is cooked through, loosely cover the top with a piece of foil.

VARIATIONS

◆ Substitute sautéed leeks for the celery root.
◆ Make the gratin with other kinds of squash such as Seminole, Amish Neck pumpkin, or Musquée de Provence.
◆ Use stock in place of the cream, adding a drizzle of olive oil on every layer.
◆ Lightly sprinkle grated cheese, such as Parmesan or Gruyère, on each layer.

# The Height of Summer

## Tomatoes, Eggplant, Peppers, Corn, and Okra

THE LONG HOT DAYS OF SUMMER bring juicy tomatoes and tomatillos, glossy egg-plants, brightly colored peppers, sweet corn, and tender okra. The first tiny cherry tomatoes are the harbingers of the incredible variety to come: sweet and tangy heirloom tomatoes in a rainbow of hues; sweet and sour tomatillos; peppers, crisp and shiny, in a panoply of red, orange, yellow, and green; eggplants, from deep purple giants to light purple fingers to violet and white striped globes; ears of corn in all their multicolored sweetness; and peerless pods of okra, green and burgundy. These are the vegetables that make up the heart of the Mediterranean-inspired food I love to cook and eat: beautiful salads; deeply flavored savory braises and stews; quick colorful summertime pastas; soups; and grilled vegetables seasoned with garlic, herbs, and olive oil. Summer cooking has begun.

# Recipes

Fried Green Tomatoes  163

Tomato and Toasted Pita Bread Salad  164

Golden Jubilee Tomato Soup with Spiced Yogurt  164

Sungold Cherry Tomato Salsa  165

Chicken Braised with Tomatoes and Vinegar  166

Eggs Baked in Spicy Tomato Sauce  166

Crostini with Dried Roma Tomatoes, Anchovies,
and Capers  167

Roasted Tomatillo Salsa  168

Eggplant Canapés  169

Roasted Rosa Bianca Eggplant with Feta and Mint  171

Simple Eggplant Parmesan  171

Moroccan Braised Eggplant  172

Julienned Gypsy Pepper Salad  176

Bulgur Salad with Roasted Sheepnose Pimientos
and Cilantro  176

Sautéed Salted Fish and Peppers  177

Sweet and Spicy Peppers Pizza  178

Grilled Jimmy Nardello and Padrón Peppers  179

Padrón Peppers Stuffed with Corn and Queso Fresco  179

Paella with Pimientos and Chorizo  180

Chile Verde  181

Grilled Pork Shoulder with Ancho Chiles  182

Yogurt-Spiced Chicken Skewers  183

Yogurt  183

Pickled Jalapeños and Carrots  185

Corn and Summer Squash Soup  186

Basil-Squash Blossom Butter  187

Fresh Corn Tamales  187

Creamed Corn  188

Cornmeal-Fried Okra  189

Sautéed Spiced Okra with Tomatoes  189

## Tomatoes, Eggplant, and Peppers in the Garden

All the summer nightshades (as these vegetables are called) add color to the garden. As the days grow longer and hotter, the colors become bolder and the flavors stronger. Soon it will be time to harvest perfectly ripe tomatoes, incredibly flavored peppers, sweet firm eggplant. Each year as I watch the tomatoes ripen, I feel the same anticipation I did as a child waiting for Christmas. The eggplants with their cheerful flowers and the bright pepper plants all look as if they have been decorated. These are the gifts of summer—exciting and delicious.

Tomatoes, peppers, and eggplants are originally from climates with subtropical warmth and long sunny growing seasons, and the closer you can come to replicating those conditions, the better the nightshades will grow. Start with seedlings, or sow seeds indoors about eight weeks before the last frost to give plenty of time for the fruit to ripen. Start the seeds in larger pots so the roots will have lots of room. A heat mat may be necessary to keep the soil warm enough for germination. Don't plant seedlings until the evenings are consistently above 60°F. Choose a site that is in full sun and protected from the wind. Black mulch and a heat-reflecting wall are helpful in colder climates. In very hot climates a little afternoon shade will help protect the fruit from sunburn. It is also helpful to know that most tomato plants will not set fruit at temperatures over 90°F. Be patient and keep the plants watered through heat waves and they will start producing once temperatures drop. Smaller varieties of all these plants do well in containers. In colder climates they sometimes perform better in containers because the soil warms up more quickly and stays warm longer.

All these plants have big appetites and like a lot of compost and minerals. However, be aware that nitrogen will increase leaf growth but discourage fruiting, so avoid heavy feedings of manure and other foods high in nitrogen. Amend the soil with compost when planting and monthly after that. Keep the plants consistently watered; dry spells can stress the plants and cause them to drop blossoms. The plants are self-pollinating.

The stems of tomatoes, eggplants, and peppers are brittle and easily broken. Provide support as they grow, especially when their fruit begins to grow heavy and hang from the branches. When harvesting, to avoid breaking branches, cut, don't pull, the fruit.

## Tomatoes (Solanum lycopersicum)

A vine-ripened tomato is a revelation, whether sliced in a salad; chopped and tossed with some hot noodles, garlic, basil, and oil; puréed into a cold soup; or made into the most delicious tomato juice you have ever had. As the summer abundance piles up, be sure to preserve some of the bounty for winter cooking—canned, frozen, or dried. Your own preserves will outshine any fresh tomato sold out of season. With a garden you can enjoy green tomatoes, too, either fried, pickled, or cut into a salsa for a bit of sweet-and-sour pucker.

Tomatoes come in an astonishing range

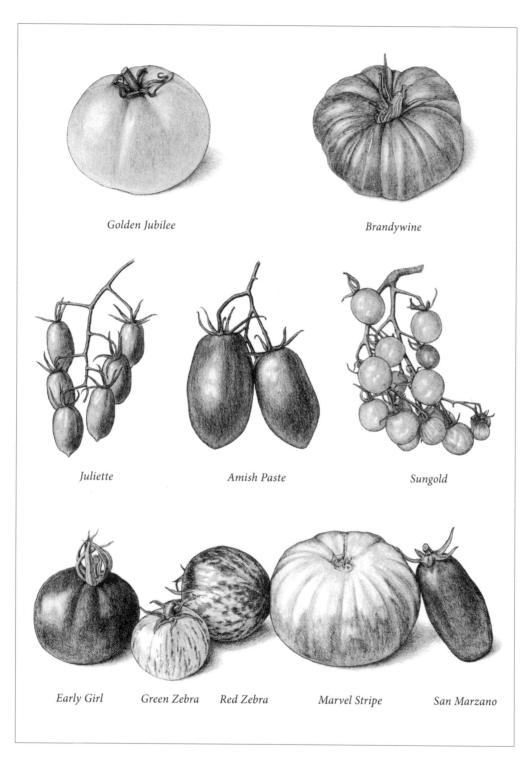

Golden Jubilee

Brandywine

Juliette

Amish Paste

Sungold

Early Girl

Green Zebra

Red Zebra

Marvel Stripe

San Marzano

of colors: reds, oranges, yellows, greens, purples, and dusky browns. A colorful variety of sliced tomatoes not only looks gorgeous, but it also provides an interesting interplay of flavors. Yellow and gold tomatoes tend to be lower in acid, and the red, purple, and brown varieties usually have more tang. *Lemon Boy* tomatoes are small and bright yellow. *Golden Jubilee* is large, golden, and sweet. *Marvel Stripe* and *Pineapple* are very tasty, a marbled mix of golden and yellow. *Cherokee Purple* is a smaller purple-brown with delicious flavor. *Green Zebra* is light green with darker green stripes when ripe— I especially love its sweet taste and lively look. Little golden *Sungold* is my favorite cherry tomato of all; it is almost as sweet as candy. *Early Girl* is early ripening and red, with good flavor and acid balance, making it a great choice for cooking. Oval plum, or paste, tomatoes have meatier flesh, and fewer seeds, and make rich sauce (they are not as good raw); try *San Marzano* or *Amish Paste*. This is really just the tip of the iceberg: thousands of varieties are available. Take note of your favorites at the market and try new ones from the nursery or seed catalog.

I fear that the word *heirloom* when used for tomatoes has frequently been co-opted as a marketing term that does not guarantee great flavor. Good growing practices, healthy fertile soil, and vine ripening are more important than any name. The most delicious tomatoes, whatever the variety, are vine-ripened from small organic farms or your own kitchen garden.

Harvesting a ripe tomato warm from the sun in your own garden is a supreme pleasure. To ensure a delicious harvest, be sure to take your local microclimate into consideration. In my garden, I can grow quick-ripening small cherry tomatoes with great success, and occasionally have luck with smaller tomatoes like *Cherokee Purple*, but the coastal fog that comes to my garden every summer makes it hard for the larger heirloom varieties to ripen. For those, I depend on the sun-drenched inland farms nearby.

There is an important distinction to note about tomatoes: there are two basic kinds of plants, determinate and indeterminate. Vining indeterminate plants will grow up to eight feet tall, and produce fruit up to the first frost or cold rains. (The majority of heirloom tomatoes are indeterminate.) Bushy determinate plants grow no taller than three feet and produce all their fruit at one time. Indeterminate plants are much more productive and can be trained up a sturdy trellis or cage to save room. Determinate plants work well in containers. Cherry tomatoes are also a good choice for container growing.

When transplanting tomatoes, dig a deep hole, as they do best when half their growing stem is buried below the soil. Before planting, add a shovelful of compost and some organic eggshells (for calcium) to the bottom of the hole, and pinch off the lower leaves that will be buried below the soil line. Roots will grow from these nodes strengthening the plant's root system. Set cages or stakes for support right away so the root systems are not damaged later on. Feed the growing plants with compost or compost tea monthly. Once the tomatoes are starting to color, diminish the amount of water to the bare minimum. Overwatered tomatoes are dilute in flavor and risk splitting.

## To Peel and Seed Tomatoes

Wash the tomatoes and cut out a cone at the stem end to remove the core. Plunge them into rapidly boiling water and remove them once the skin is loosened, which will take roughly between 15 and 60 seconds (check the tomatoes often to know when to pull them out). Cool the tomatoes quickly in ice-cold water and slip off the skins. To seed a tomato, cut it in half crosswise and gently squeeze each half, coaxing the seeds out of each little cavity with your fingers. The juice can be strained to use in cooking or to drink.

## Fried Green Tomatoes

4 SERVINGS

Green tomatoes have a wonderful sour edge to them that is delicious fried in a crispy crust. Serve these with a garden lettuce salad and Basil Mayonnaise (page 13).

Remove the core from:

**4 medium green tomatoes
(about 1 pound)**

Cut into ⅓-inch slices. Season with:

**Salt**

Lay out the slices to drain in a single layer on a cooling rack or in a large colander.

Cut the crusts from:

**½ loaf firm white, buttery type bread
(pain de mie)**

Tear into pieces and process into crumbs in a food processor or blender. You should have about 2 cups. Pour them into a low-sided dish.

Crack into a low-sided bowl:

**2 eggs**

Pour in:

**1 tablespoon water**

Beat well. Measure into another low-sided dish:

**1 cup flour**

When ready to fry, pat the tomatoes dry. Heat a low-sided heavy skillet over medium heat, and pour in to a depth of 1 inch:

**Vegetable oil**

Bread the tomato slices: Line up the flour, egg, and breadcrumb dishes side by side. Dredge 1 tomato slice in the flour and shake off the excess; dip it into the egg to coat well; and then coat with breadcrumbs, patting them gently to help them stick. Set on a plate and bread the rest of the slices. When the oil is hot (a few crumbs will sizzle up when added to the pan), add as many slices as will comfortably fit in one layer. Cook in batches if necessary. Fry the tomatoes until golden on 1 side, about 3 minutes. Then turn and finish cooking on the other side. Monitor the heat, turning it up or down as needed to fry the tomatoes so they have a crisp golden crust on each side. Drain the fried tomatoes on a rack or absorbent paper.

Sprinkle with:

**Salt**

Serve warm.

## Tomato and Toasted Pita Bread Salad

4 SERVINGS

Dead ripe tomatoes, Mediterranean cucumbers, parsley, and toasted pieces of day-old Whole-Wheat Pita Bread (page 132) are the base of this exquisite salad, called *fattoush* in the Middle East. Use curly parsley if possible; I prefer its flavor in Middle Eastern salads. The sumac in the dressing adds color and a tart flavor. It is made from the ground berries of the sumac bush, *Rhus coriaria*. When shopping for sumac, look for a deep, bright burgundy color. Older sumac loses its color as well as its flavor.

Preheat the oven to 350°F. Cut in half:

**2 day-old pita breads**

Cut the halves into quarters. Separate or split the pita wedges in 2 pieces and spread out in a single layer on a baking sheet. Brush lightly with:

**Olive oil**

Toast for 7 to 10 minutes, until crisp and slightly golden. Remove from the oven and let cool. They will crisp up as they cool. (Fresh pita is fine to use, it will just take longer to toast.)

Mix together in a medium bowl:

**2 ripe tomatoes, cored and diced**
**1 cup purslane leaves**
**1 medium cucumber, peeled, quartered, and sliced**
**½ cup chopped parsley**
**½ cup chopped scallions, green tops included (about 6 scallions)**
**¼ cup mint leaves, coarsely chopped**

Sprinkle with:

**Salt**

Mix gently. Prepare the dressing. In a small bowl mix:

**¼ cup lemon juice**
**2 teaspoons sumac (if unavailable, use 1 teaspoon red wine vinegar)**
**Salt**
**Fresh-ground black pepper**

Whisk in:

**¼ cup extra-virgin olive oil**

Taste for salt and acid and add lemon juice, sumac, and salt as needed. Pour over the vegetables and mix gently. Let sit for 10 minutes or more to allow the flavors to marry. Break the toasted pita into smaller pieces and fold into the salad. Serve.

VARIATIONS

‣ Add a teaspoon of pomegranate molasses to the vinaigrette. Or in the fall, sprinkle the salad with fresh pomegranate seeds.

## Golden Jubilee Tomato Soup with Spiced Yogurt

MAKES ABOUT 1½ QUARTS; 4 TO 6 SERVINGS

This golden yellow soup is beautiful garnished with yogurt spiked with golden turmeric. The chile in the soup base is a mild one, but use a spicier chile if you like.

Heat a heavy-bottomed pot over medium heat and pour in:

**2 tablespoons olive oil**

Add:

**1 white onion, diced**

Cook about 6 minutes, until the onion is soft, but not brown. Add:

**1 light green mild chile (such as Anaheim), seeded and chopped**
**1 cilantro branch**
**2 garlic cloves, chopped**
**Salt**

Cook another 5 minutes to wilt the chile. Add:

**2 pounds Golden Jubilee tomatoes, cored and chopped**

Cook, stirring occasionally, until the tomatoes are juicy and heated through, about 6 minutes. Add:

**1 cup water**

Bring to a boil, reduce to a simmer, and cook for another 10 minutes. Allow the soup to cool slightly and then purée in a blender and strain. (Take care when blending hot soup to leave a vent for the steam to escape.) Return the soup to the pan. Taste for salt and adjust as needed. If the soup is too thick, thin with water.

For the garnish, mix together:

**⅓ cup Yogurt (page 183)**
**1 tablespoon extra-virgin olive oil**
**¼ teaspoon ground turmeric**
**½ teaspoon cumin seeds, toasted and pounded in a mortar**
**A few cardamom seeds, toasted and pounded in a mortar**
**A pinch of cayenne**
**2 tablespoons chopped cilantro**
**Juice of ½ lime**
**Salt**
**Fresh-ground black pepper**

Taste for salt and adjust as needed. Serve the soup with a spoonful of the yogurt garnish and more:

**Chopped cilantro**

VARIATIONS

◆ Make 2 soups, 1 red and 1 yellow. Ladle them together at the same time into the same bowl yin-yang style.
◆ Use crème fraîche instead of yogurt for a richer soup.
◆ Peel, seed, and dice the tomatoes before adding and don't purée the soup.

# Sungold Cherry Tomato Salsa
MAKES ABOUT 2 CUPS

Sungold cherry tomatoes make a delightful sweet salsa for just about anything coming off the grill: fish, fowl, meat, or vegetable.

Wash, dry, and stem:

**2 cups Sungold cherry tomatoes**

Cut the small tomatoes in half and larger ones in quarters. Put in a bowl and mix with:

**A splash of red wine vinegar**
**Salt**
**2 tablespoons basil chiffonade (or Fino Verde basil leaves)**
**2 tablespoons finely diced fresh red onion or scallions**

Taste for salt and acid and adjust as needed. (Some tomatoes will be much more acidic than others.) Let the salsa sit for 5 minutes to allow the flavors to marry.

VARIATIONS

◆ Use different colors of cherry tomatoes for a colorful mix of flavors.
◆ Add a pinch of cayenne for a touch of heat.
◆ Roast a poblano pepper and dice. Mix with the tomatoes and use lime juice, coarsely chopped cilantro, and white onion instead of vinegar, basil, and red onion.

# Chicken Braised with Tomatoes and Vinegar

4 SERVINGS

This sounds like an unlikely dish, but the acidity of the vinegar smooths out during the cooking and adds a wonderful fruity quality to the braising juices and chicken. Serve alongside a tangle of buttered fresh pasta and sautéed spinach.

An hour ahead, or the night before if possible, season:

**8 bone-in chicken thighs**

with:

**Salt**

**Fresh-ground black pepper**

Peel, seed, and dice:

**2 garden-ripe tomatoes**

Heat a heavy-bottomed braising pot or cast-iron skillet over medium-high heat. When hot, measure in:

**2 tablespoons butter**

**1 tablespoon olive oil**

When the butter is melted, add the chicken thighs, skin side down. Don't crowd the pan; brown the chicken in batches, if necessary. Cook until the skin is nicely browned. This will take a while, 10 minutes or so. Don't skimp on time: the skin needs to be quite brown; otherwise the color will wash off as the chicken braises. When the skin is brown, turn the thighs, cook for another 2 minutes, and remove them from the pan. Pour off most of the fat and add:

**4 shallots, peeled and sliced thick**

Cook for a couple minutes to soften the shallots. Add the tomatoes and a little salt, to taste. Cook for a few minutes more and add:

**⅔ cup red wine vinegar**

Bring to a boil and cook until the vinegar is reduced by half. Return the chicken to the pan, skin side up, and pour in:

**¾ to 1 cup chicken stock**

Add enough stock to come halfway up the chicken. Bring to a simmer and cook, uncovered, for 10 minutes, or until the thighs are cooked through. Remove the thighs, skim the sauce, taste, and add salt as needed. Bring to a boil and swirl in:

**1 tablespoon cold butter**

Return the thighs to the pan and serve.

VARIATIONS

◆ Instead of thighs, use a whole chicken cut into 8 pieces.

◆ Crème fraîche can be substituted for the final butter.

◆ Use Banyuls, sherry, or white wine vinegar in place of the red wine vinegar.

◆ Use 3 canned tomatoes instead of the fresh tomatoes.

# Eggs Baked in Spicy Tomato Sauce

4 SERVINGS

This makes a wonderful light lunch, especially served with Parsley and Herb Salad (page 11). Dead-ripe tomatoes are the secret to this dish, either fresh or Canned Tomatoes (page 328). The sauce can be made ahead.

Peel, seed, and dice (saving all the juice):

**1½ pounds ripe tomatoes**

You should have about 3 cups of tomatoes and juice. Trim the stem from:

**1 fresh cayenne or other hot chile**

Cut in it half lengthwise, seed it (if you want it really hot, leave the seeds in), and chop fine. Be sure to wash your hands afterward; they will have spice all over them.
Peel:

**4 large garlic cloves**

Smash and chop them coarsely.
Heat a heavy-bottomed pan over medium-high heat and pour in:

**¼ cup extra-virgin olive oil**

Add the garlic and let it sizzle, add the hot pepper and cook for a few moments, and then add the tomatoes and:

**Salt**

Cook at a simmer for 10 to 15 minutes until slightly thickened. Taste and add salt as needed.

Preheat the oven to 400°F.
Heat the tomato sauce to a simmer in an ovenproof pan, or pour it, hot, into a low-sided baking or gratin dish. Stir in:

**1 tablespoon marjoram leaves, basil
chiffonade, or oregano leaves**

Carefully crack into the tomato sauce:

**4 eggs**

Season with:

**Salt**
**Fresh-ground black pepper**
**A pinch of dried chile flakes
(optional)**

Bake until the eggs are opaque on top and the white is cooked through (the yolks should still be soft), about 20 minutes.

VARIATIONS

◆ Add 1 or 2 tablespoons of chopped herbs such as savory, marjoram, or basil to the sauce while it is cooking. Garnish the finished eggs with more chopped herbs or parsley.
◆ Bake 8 eggs instead of 4 for a more substantial meal.
◆ Use a 1-quart jar of canned tomatoes instead of fresh tomatoes.

# Crostini with Dried Roma Tomatoes, Anchovies, and Capers

Sweet, dense Roma or plum tomatoes are good for sauces and canning, and they make excellent Dried Tomatoes (page 329). I like to pack the dried tomatoes in jars of olive oil, and then, in the winter months, make bright tasty crostini that bring back the flavor of summer tomatoes.

Exact proportions of the mixture are not important; I make it differently every time. As a general guide, use ½ cup dried tomatoes; 2 salt-cured anchovies, rinsed and filleted; and 1 tablespoon salt-cured capers, rinsed and drained. Chop the tomatoes, anchovy, and capers together to make a rough paste. Moisten with olive oil and season with fresh-ground black pepper. If you like, add crushed dried chile flakes or Marash pepper for a spicy note. Spread on thin toasted slices of crusty bread and finish with chopped parsley, marjoram, or your own dried marjoram.

# Tomatillos  (*Physalis ixocarpa*)

Tomatillos grow in a paper husk. When it is peeled away, they look like small green or purple tomatoes. They have a sweet sharp flavor that is familiar from the green sauce for chicken enchiladas and fresh green salsa for tortilla chips and tacos. The tiny fruit of *Purple de Milpa* is a beautiful mottled purple and green; *Verde Puebla* bears shiny green medium-size fruit. Tomatillos are very easy to grow and bear fruit all summer long. No staking is required, as the bushy plants don't reach much higher than three feet. Keep the husk on the fruit until ready to use. The plants will very readily reseed all through the garden.

# Roasted Tomatillo Salsa

MAKES ABOUT 2½ CUPS

This is a classic fresh sauce for dipping tortilla chips or garnishing grilled meat, tamales, and enchiladas. I like to add it to the pan with a fried egg after the egg has been flipped.

Remove the outer husk of:

    **1 pound tomatillos**

Heat a cast-iron or other heavy skillet (or a comal if you have one) over medium-high heat. Add:

    **3 whole jalapeño or serrano chiles**
    **4 garlic cloves, unpeeled**

Cook, turning now and then, until blistered and blackened here and there, about 4 minutes. Remove and set aside. Add the tomatillos to the hot pan and cook until soft and blistered, about 6 minutes.

Peel the garlic when it has cooled. Cut the stems off the peppers, remove the seeds if desired, and coarsely chop. Pound the chiles and garlic using a mortar and pestle (or *molcajete*). Add the tomatillos a few at a time until they are all pounded to a purée. Or put the garlic, peppers, and tomatillos in the jar of a blender and blend to the desired consistency (sometimes I make it chunky and sometimes very smooth). Pour into a nonreactive bowl and stir in:

    **¼ cup diced white onion**
    **⅓ cup chopped cilantro, stems and**
      **leaves**
    **1 tablespoon lime juice**
    **Salt**

Taste for salt and acid and adjust as needed.

VARIATIONS

◆ Stir in 1 diced avocado.

◆ Use hotter chiles for a spicier salsa.

◆ Instead of roasting them in a pan, boil the tomatillos and peppers until tender in just enough water to cover. Use the garlic raw.

◆ For a cooked sauce to use for enchiladas or other cooked dishes, heat a heavy-bottomed skillet and measure in 2 tablespoons lard or olive oil. When the fat is hot, add the sauce and sauté for 10 minutes, or until it is thick enough to coat the back of a spoon.

## Eggplant (*Solanum melongena*)

Once it was hard to find any other eggplants than large purple globes. Now the market is full of all kinds of eggplant, from many parts of the world. The smaller Asian varieties have thinner skin and fewer seeds. They are fantastic to grill and when sliced partway through, make beautiful fans to braise on a bed of onions. Large globe eggplants are good roasted or charred whole to cook into a soft purée to season for a dip or sauce. The mild flavor of eggplant is well suited to herbs and spices. I especially like to use garlic, parsley, basil, lemon, and coriander seeds. Eggplant is an integral part of ratatouille, caponata, and other vegetable braises. Thai curries, Chinese stir fries, and Japanese salads are some of the delicious non-Mediterranean ways to eat eggplant.

When overly mature or old, eggplant can be filled with seeds and taste bitter. The flesh soaks up an inordinate amount of oil, too. So look for young, firm, freshly harvested eggplant with taut glossy skin and a fresh-looking cap. When picked like this, eggplant is almost sweet enough to eat raw.

*Black Beauty* is a classic large, dark purple globe; long, thin, light purple *Ping Tung Long* is sweet and tender; *Rosa Bianca* is a bicolored violet and white, plump ribbed globe; *Listada di Gandia*—a smaller white oval fruit with bright purple stripes—is a real beauty, with great taste; and *Long Purple* is a small, tasty, dark purple Japanese eggplant. There are many others to look for and try. Look for very small round Thai eggplant; they are delicious and fun to cook with.

Eggplants are particularly susceptible to cold. Start seeds indoors in a warm place and don't plant out the seedlings until the soil has warmed and nighttime temperatures have stabilized. The short bushy plants are quite pretty in the garden with lavender blossoms and shiny fruit. They do very well in containers, especially the smaller fruiting varieties.

Harvest eggplant while still young and firm. Keep the plants regularly harvested for maximum production. Eggplant tastes the best when fresh. It does not store well at all.

## Eggplant Canapés

Slices of roasted eggplant offer a pretty and tasty hors d'oeuvres alternative (gluten-free!) to bread and croutons. Slender Japanese eggplant are good for size and texture. Cut them crosswise into round slices about ½ inch thick. Brush the slices on both sides with olive oil and lay them on a baking sheet lined with parchment paper. Bake at 400°F until soft and browned on the bottom, about 15 minutes. Carefully turn them over with a spatula and cook another 5 minutes or so until lightly browned on the other side. Cool on the pan.

Top the eggplant slices with whatever suits your fancy: slices of fresh mozzarella or burrata with olive oil and herbs; ricotta with cherry tomato salsa; basil or rocket pesto; slices of tomato with capers or herbs; tapenade; greens wilted with garlic and Indian spices; spicy chutney… Keep the toppings light so they can be picked up and eaten easily.

Roasted (or grilled) eggplant slices are

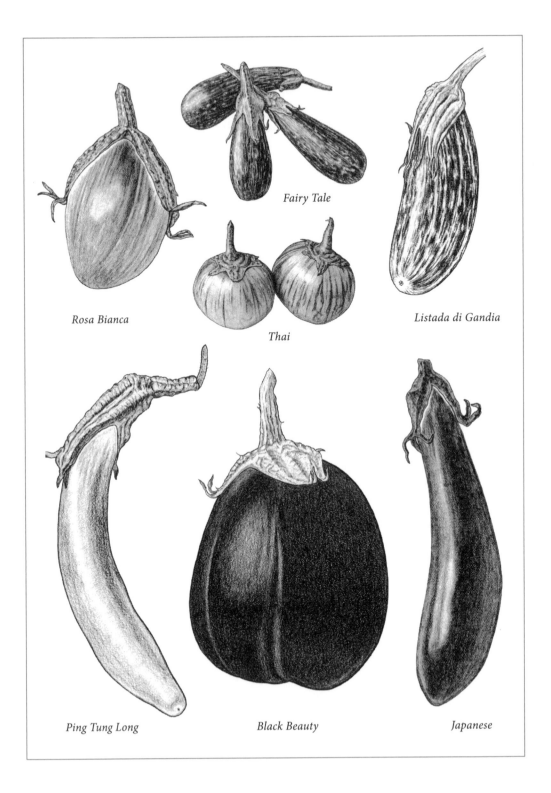

Fairy Tale

Rosa Bianca

Thai

Listada di Gandia

Ping Tung Long

Black Beauty

Japanese

very good on their own served as a side dish. Macerate a diced shallot in red wine vinegar and a bit of salt for 15 to 30 minutes. When the eggplant is warm from the oven or grill, sprinkle with the shallots, some chopped parsley, and salt, and serve.

# Roasted Rosa Bianca Eggplant with Feta and Mint

4 SERVINGS

Preheat the oven to 400°F.
Trim the stem end from:

**2 medium Rosa Bianca eggplants**

Cut them in half lengthwise and cut each half into 4 long wedges. Season the wedges with:

**Salt**

Pour into a small ramekin or dish:

**1 tablespoon olive oil**

Brush the wedges on both sides with olive oil and lay them flat on a baking sheet lined with parchment paper. Bake until soft and browned on the underside, about 20 minutes. Turn them over with a spatula and cook another 5 minutes or so, until lightly browned on the other side. Cool on the pan. While the eggplant is roasting make the dressing. In a small bowl, stir together:

**1 tablespoon red wine vinegar**
**Salt**
**Fresh-ground black pepper**
**1 mint sprig**

When the salt has dissolved, whisk in:

**3 tablespoons extra-virgin olive oil**

Taste and adjust the acid and salt as needed. Spoon half the vinaigrette over the eggplant wedges as they are cooling. When ready to serve, trim away the root ends and any blemished outer leaves from:

**3 large or 4 medium scallions**

Slice thinly, at a slight angle, all the white base and half the green leaves. Remove the mint sprig from the rest of the vinaigrette and toss the scallions in it, along with:

**8 mint leaves, sliced thin**
**A large pinch of Marash pepper**
**A small pinch of cayenne**

Arrange the eggplant wedges on a plate, spoon over the vinaigrette, and garnish with:

**4 ounces sheep's-milk feta, crumbled**
**4 mint leaves, sliced thin**

If desired, serve with:

**Toasted bread**

VARIATIONS

◆ The eggplant wedges can be grilled instead of roasted.
◆ Sprinkle the salad with the seeds from half a pomegranate.
◆ Use basil, summer savory, or marjoram instead of mint.
◆ In place of the feta, soak and chop a spoonful of salt-cured capers, and add them to the vinaigrette with the scallions and herbs.

# Simple Eggplant Parmesan

4 SERVINGS

These small individual servings of eggplant Parmesan are lighter than the classic casserole. They can be made ahead and baked when ready to serve. Make extras for delicious leftovers the next day. They make a great sandwich on crusty bread.

Preheat the oven to 425°F. Trim the stem ends from:

**2 globe eggplants, about 1 pound each**

Cut, crosswise, into ¾-inch slices. Season well with:

**Salt**

Pour into a small ramekin or dish:

**1 tablespoon olive oil**

Brush the slices on both sides with olive oil and lay them flat on a baking sheet lined with parchment paper. Bake until soft and browned on the underside, about 20 minutes. Turn them over with a spatula and cook another 5 minutes or so, until lightly browned on the other side. Turn the oven down to 375°F.

While the eggplants are cooking, prepare:

**About 1½ cups spicy tomato sauce (about half the recipe on page 166)**

(Leave out the hot peppers if you don't want it to be spicy.)

Cut into ¼-inch slices:

**½ pound fresh mozzarella**

Grate on the small holes of a box grater:

**2 ounces Parmesan cheese (about ½ cup grated)**

Remove the leaves from:

**2 large basil sprigs (about ¼ cup packed)**

Brush a 12-inch-square baking dish (or another baking dish large enough to hold 4 stacks of eggplant slices) with:

**Olive oil**

Spoon 4 small spoonfuls of tomato sauce near the 4 corners of the dish. Place 4 large eggplant slices on the tomato sauce. Place half the mozzarella slices over the 4 eggplant slices. Lay half the basil leaves over the mozzarella. Spoon one third of the to-mato sauce over the mozzarella and sprinkle with one third of the Parmesan cheese. Place another large slice of eggplant on top and repeat with the other ingredients. Place a final layer of eggplant, using more than 1 slice, if necessary, and top with a spoonful of tomato sauce and the last of the Parmesan. Bake until hot and bubbling, about 15 to 20 minutes. Serve warm or at room temperature.

VARIATIONS

◆ Cut summer squash into ½-inch slices and roast. Instead of eggplant, make stacks of a few squash slices for each layer.

# Moroccan Braised Eggplant

4 SERVINGS

This is a delicious braise reminiscent of ratatouille. Double the amounts if you like; it tastes great the next day.

Grate on the coarse holes of a box grater:

**1 medium onion, peeled**

Trim off the stem ends of:

**½ large bunch of cilantro**

Cut the leaves away from the stems and set aside. Cut the stems finely.

In a heavy-bottomed pot, heat:

**1 tablespoon oil (or enough to cover the bottom)**

Add the grated onion and cook for 3 minutes over medium heat. Stir in the cilantro stems and:

**One 1-inch piece of ginger, peeled and minced**

**A large pinch of saffron**

**¼ teaspoon cayenne**

1 teaspoon cumin seeds, crushed
Salt

Cook for 5 minutes. Stir in:

4 Japanese or other small eggplants,
trimmed and cut into 1½-inch
chunks

3 medium tomatoes, cored and cut
into 1½-inch chunks

Continue cooking at a simmer until the vegetables are soft, about 15 to 20 minutes. Check for salt and add more if necessary. Chop the cilantro leaves coarsely, add half to the vegetables, and cook for 2 minutes. Serve garnished with the rest of the chopped cilantro.

VARIATION

◆ Add 3 medium summer squash cut into 1½-inch chunks with the eggplant and tomatoes.

# Peppers *(Capsicum annuum)*

Peppers add a delightful splash of color and loads of flavor to so many dishes. Before Columbus left Spain to find a new spice route, peppers were unknown except in the Americas. They quickly spread around the globe, gratefully incorporated into many sixteenth-century cuisines for their color, flavor—and vitamins. (Peppers, especially red ones, contain large amounts of vitamins A and C.) Sweet, hot, fresh, and dried—peppers are amazingly versatile. I love sweet peppers sliced thin and tossed into a salad or on a pizza before it goes into the oven. They are luscious roasted and marinated for an antipasto or a flavorful sandwich.

They keep their bright color whether they are sautéed for a pasta sauce or a side dish or long-cooked in a vegetable stew. And hot peppers add spice and depth to stews, soups, and sauces.

*Corno di Toro,* or *Bull's Horn,* is a sweet pepper with a pungent depth of flavor that is more complex than that of sweet bell peppers. Italian and Spanish recipes are especially delicious when you use them. I find that their skins and flesh are too thin to peel easily when roasted, so for roasted peppers I use different-colored sweet thick-walled bell peppers: *Quadrato d'Asti Giallo, Rosso,* and *Orange Sun* are, respectively, yellow, red, and brilliant orange; the more unusual *Chocolate Beauty* is purplish brown. *Sheepnose* pimientos are small and very fleshy, with a deep rich sweet flavor. I am especially fond of them. I don't know why they are not as easy to find as bell peppers. I like to serve a purée of pimiento soup with fried polenta sticks. *Padrón* and *Jimmy Nardello* are two varieties of frying peppers. They are easy to cook quickly over a hot flame, and are incomparable in flavor. *Lipstick, Hungarian Wax,* and *Gypsy* are some other favorite flavorful sweet peppers. *Cayenne* and *Chile de Árbol* are hot peppers that are easy to grow and great to have dried in the kitchen. I don't even bother to string them up but dry them as a beautiful bouquet. I pinch off a pepper when needed to toss into some pickles, a braise, a soup, or a sauce. *Jalapeños, Serranos,* and *Hungarian Banana* are some of the medium-hot peppers I use. There are many, many more, from blazing hot to warm. *Thai, Bird,* and *Habanero* are HOT.

Capsaicin is the component that gives a

hot pepper its kick. It is located in the central white core (referred to as the placenta) that the seeds are attached to. (Interestingly, capsaicin is a dominant trait in peppers and sweetness is a recessive quality.) Remember that capsaicin will get on your fingers when cooking or harvesting spicy peppers. So be sure to wash your hands well after working with them, or use rubber gloves. You don't want to inadvertently burn your eyes or other delicate parts of your body.

Peppers are gorgeous in the garden with their dark green leaves and colorful fruit. They definitely like sun, heat, and consistent water. Start seeds indoors in a warm place (a heat mat is useful) and don't plant seedlings until the weather has truly warmed up. Hot chiles tend to be the most susceptible to cold soil and air temperatures, while sweet peppers can tolerate wider swings. Smaller peppers fruit earlier and are frequently more vigorous. They do very well in containers. Peppers, even small ones, will benefit from a little support, as wind or an inadvertent knock can easily break their delicate branches. Be sure to cut the fruit and not pull them when harvesting. Peppers to be dried should be harvested when fully ripe.

## Dried Peppers and Chile Flakes

Dried peppers are filled with deep rich flavor. They can be used whole to add flavor to long-cooked dishes. I often toss a dried cayenne into a pickle brine, soup, stew, or pasta sauce. If it is not cut open it adds a mere hint of spice; when opened up, the flavor it adds is much more spicy. A pot of beans is delicious with a dried chile or two tossed in. Choose what kind of pepper according to how spicy you would like it to be.

Dried peppers can be roasted and rehydrated with hot water to pureé into a sauce or paste to use for flavor: for example, rouille, harissa, and many Mexican salsas. Or they can be ground into flakes, with or without their seeds, to sprinkle like a spice into a dish while it is cooking, or over the top as a colorful and pungent garnish.

Different cuisines use varieties that make the flavor of their food distinctive. These are the dried chile flakes and powders I use the most: Hungarian paprika, which has a delicious sweet flavor; Mexican chipotle, which adds a smoky flavor along with spicy heat; Spanish *ñora*, with a rich sweet flavor and relatively little spice; Spanish *pimentón*, which contributes a deep smoky richness to a dish; Turkish Aleppo, with its deep intensity; and Turkish Marash—probably the pepper flake I reach for most often—which has a sultry heat that is not truly spicy and loads of rich flavor. Last, but certainly not least, is the common generic dried chile flakes and cayenne powder. Both are a great way to add a touch of heat during cooking or after the dish is done.

Dried peppers, especially when crushed or ground, lose their vibrancy as they age. Keep them out of direct sunlight and replace them every year or so. When buying them, look for bright color and a fresh, almost fleshy appearance.

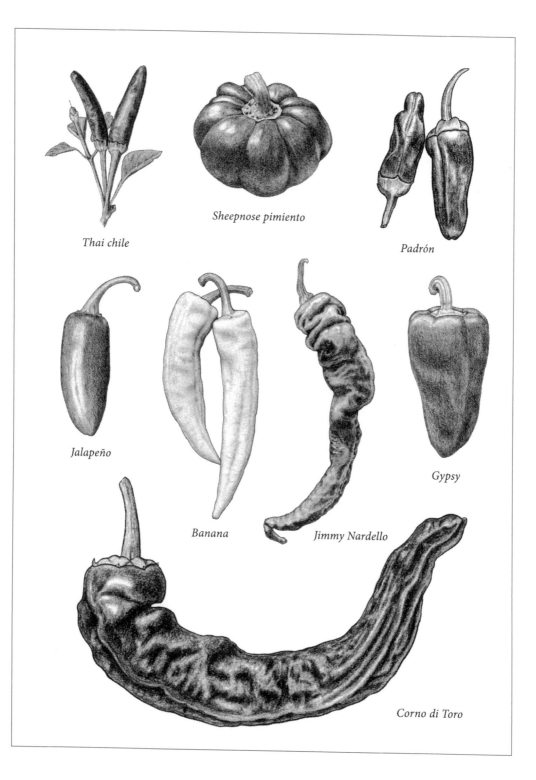

Thai chile

Sheepnose pimiento

Padrón

Jalapeño

Banana

Jimmy Nardello

Gypsy

Corno di Toro

# Julienned Gypsy Pepper Salad

4 SERVINGS

Look for different colors of Gypsy peppers—yellow, orange, and red—to make a colorful salad. I love the crisp clean flavor of Gypsy peppers; they are not spicy, but they have a livelier flavor than a classic sweet bell pepper.

Trim away the stem end of:

**4 Gypsy peppers**

Cut in half lengthwise, remove the seeds, and cut away any veins. Turn the halves cut side up and slice lengthwise as thin as possible to make a julienne. Set aside under a damp towel.

Prepare the dressing. Mix together in a small bowl:

**1 tablespoon red wine vinegar**
**2 garlic cloves, pounded to a purée**
**1 marjoram sprig, leaves only**
**2 basil leaves, chopped**
**Salt**
**Fresh-ground black pepper**

Stir to dissolve the salt and let sit to macerate for 10 minutes. Whisk in:

**3½ tablespoons extra-virgin olive oil**

Taste for salt and acid and adjust as needed. When ready to serve, toss the julienned peppers with:

**Salt**

Add three quarters of the vinaigrette and toss. Tear or cut into large pieces:

**8 basil leaves**

Remove the leaves from:

**1 small marjoram sprig**

Add the herbs to the peppers and toss. Taste for salt and adjust as needed. Add:

**1 large handful of rocket or wild rocket**

Gently toss and plate. Spoon the rest of the vinaigrette over the salad and serve.

VARIATIONS
◆ Use sherry vinegar in the dressing and toss chopped toasted almonds and parsley in the salad instead of marjoram and basil. Garnish with fried sage leaves.
◆ Slice a shallot or small red onion and toss with the peppers.

# To Roast and Peel Peppers

Place the peppers, whole, on a hot grill, directly in the open flame of a gas stove, or under a hot broiler. Cook them, turning frequently, until all of their skin is blackened. As the peppers are done, put them in a paper bag or a pot with a lid. Close the bag or cover the pot and let them steam for a few minutes.

Take a pepper and cut off and discard the stem end. Slice it open lengthwise and spread it out flat. With the back of a small knife scrape away the seeds and veins. Turn the pepper over and, still with the back of the knife, scrape away all the blackened skin. Wipe the board clean before continuing on to the next pepper. Cut and season as required.

# Bulgur Salad with Roasted Sheepnose Pimientos and Cilantro

4 SERVINGS

Sweet roasted pimientos are complemented by cilantro, basil, and mint and tossed with bulgur for a satisfying and colorful salad. This is a perfect dish for a picnic or to serve with a summer meal off the grill.

Preheat the oven to 375°F.
Cut in half:

**4 Sheepnose pimientos**

Remove the seeds and veins, and snap out the stem. Place the halves on a baking sheet, cut side down, and bake until the peppers are soft and the skin blistery and loose, about 15 minutes. Let them cool, peel them, and cut into ¼-inch strips. Cut the strips into 1-inch pieces. You should have about 1 cup of cut peppers. Season with:

**Salt**

**A splash of red wine vinegar**

While the peppers are cooking, cover with cold water by 1 inch:

**½ cup medium bulgur**

Soak for 20 minutes to plump the grains and then place in a sieve to drain. Meanwhile prepare the other ingredients.
Chop:

**⅔ bunch of cilantro, leaves and stems (about ½ cup)**

**½ bunch of mint, leaves only (about ¼ cup)**

**1 small bunch of basil, leaves only (about ⅓ cup)**

To make the dressing, measure into a small bowl:

**2 teaspoons red wine vinegar**

**2 teaspoons lemon juice**

**Salt**

**Fresh-ground black pepper**

**1 large or 2 small shallots, peeled and sliced thin**

Stir to dissolve the salt and let sit for 10 minutes. Whisk in:

**¼ cup extra-virgin olive oil**

Taste for salt and acid and adjust as needed.

Squeeze the bulgur to remove as much water as possible and mix with the seasoned peppers, herbs, and dressing. Let sit 15 minutes to allow the flavors to marry. Taste one last time for salt and acid and adjust if needed.

VARIATIONS

* Fold in a few handfuls of rocket or purslane just before serving the salad.
* Add ⅔ cup halved cherry tomatoes when mixing the salad together.
* Add ½ cup diced or sliced Persian or Armenian cucumbers to the bulgur.

# Sautéed Salted Fish and Peppers

4 SERVINGS

This is a classic Roman dish. The peppers and tomatoes make a sweet and savory sauce for salted fish, either freshly salted or soaked.

Rinse well:

**1 pound soaked salt cod (or other fish)**

Cut into 4 portions and set aside.
Remove the stem end from:

**2 large or 4 small Gypsy or Corno di Toro peppers, mixed colors**

Cut the peppers in half lengthwise and remove the veins and seeds. Cut into ⅓-inch strips.

Heat a heavy-bottomed pan over medium heat and pour in:

**Olive oil, enough to cover the bottom**

Add:

**1 onion, diced medium**

Cook over medium heat until soft, stirring occasionally. Do not let the onions brown; turn down the heat if necessary. Once the onions begin to soften, after 7 minutes or so, add the peppers and cook until the peppers begin to soften, about another 4 minutes. Add:

**Salt**

**4 garlic cloves, sliced thin**

Cook 1 or 2 minutes and then add:

**3 ripe red tomatoes, seeded and chopped**

Cook until the tomatoes begin to fall apart, about 8 minutes. Taste for salt and adjust as needed. While the vegetables are cooking, pat the salt cod dry, and dredge it in:

**Flour**

Heat a heavy-bottomed frying pan over medium-high heat and add:

**Olive oil, ¼-inch deep**

Add the floured salt cod and cook until golden brown. Turn the fish and cook until golden brown on the other side. Add the fried cod to the peppers and tomatoes and cook together for a few minutes. Serve hot garnished with:

**1 tablespoon or more chopped parsley**

VARIATIONS

◆ Instead of frying the salt cod, add it to the pan after the tomatoes have cooked a few minutes and cook with the vegetables for 6 minutes, turning the fish after the first 4 minutes.

◆ Add a splash of white wine to the onions and peppers before adding the tomatoes. Let it cook a couple of minutes, then continue with the recipe.

# Sweet and Spicy Peppers Pizza

MAKES ONE 10- TO 12-INCH PIZZA

This is my favorite pizza. I love the bright colors and flavors of the peppers and basil and the surprise bite of hot pepper here and there.

Preheat the oven to 500°F. If you have one, place a baking stone on the lower rack and heat for 30 minutes before baking the pizza. Mix together in a small bowl:

**1 garlic clove, chopped fine**

**1 tablespoon olive oil**

Trim off the stems ends and cut in half lengthwise:

**2 Gypsy or other sweet peppers, mixed colors if possible**

**1 jalapeño**

Remove the seeds and veins and slice thinly. Place in a bowl and toss with:

**1 small red onion, sliced thin**

**A splash of red wine vinegar**

**2 tablespoons chopped basil**

**Salt**

**Fresh-ground black pepper**

**A splash of olive oil**

Stretch out:

**One 6-ounce ball Pizza Dough (page 147)**

Place on a floured peel and brush the garlic oil over the dough, leaving the edge bare. Sprinkle on:

**⅓ cup grated mozzarella cheese**

Spread the peppers over the cheese. Slide the pizza onto the stone and bake until puffed and browned, 5 to 8 minutes. If you don't have a stone, place the pizza on a pizza pan and bake. Remove from the oven and sprinkle with:

**2 tablespoons chopped basil**

# Grilled Jimmy Nardello and Padrón Peppers

Jimmy Nardello and Padrón peppers are small peppers that can be eaten whole. The bite-size Padrón is a thin-walled pepper picked while still young and green. They are full of lively flavor, but—and this is where the excitement lies—one out of every dozen or so is hot and spicy. Eating them is a bit of a game; will you get a spicy one or not? Jimmy Nardello peppers are thin as a pencil and fairly long. They are a bright shiny red when ripe and sweet as candy. Both peppers are divine when cooked quickly and seasoned with nothing more than a sprinkle of salt. Grilled, they are by far one of my most favorite summer appetizers to eat standing around the fire while the rest of the meal is cooking. And they are elegant enough in their natural beauty and impeccable flavor for a more formal moment as well.

Have ready a medium-hot bed of coals and a hot, clean, oiled grill. If the grates of your grill are far apart, use a grill basket to hold the peppers or skewers to thread the peppers. Toss the peppers with oil and lay them on the hot grill. Cook, turning now and then, until soft, about 5 minutes. Plate and sprinkle with salt. If a grill is not handy, heat a cast-iron or other heavy skillet until quite hot, lower the heat to medium-high, add just enough oil to cover the bottom of the pan, and add the peppers right away. Cook, tossing now and then, until done. Or, heat a cast-iron pan in a 500°F oven. When hot, add a splash of oil and the peppers. Return the pan to the oven and cook until done, about 4 minutes, tossing once.

# Padrón Peppers Stuffed with Corn and Queso Fresco

4 to 6 servings

Small bite-size Padrón peppers are fabulous quickly fried and served with flaky salt. Peppers that are a bit larger are great for stuffing and roasting. Serve as a dish on its own, with rice and beans, or with grilled steak or fish.

Preheat the oven to 375°F.
Slice off the stem ends of:

**1 pound Padrón peppers**

Use a small spoon or knife to remove the seeds and membranes inside, but keep the peppers whole.
Shuck:

**2 ears sweet corn**

Cut the kernels off the cobs. Heat a sauté pan over medium-high heat, and put in the corn kernels along with:

**2 tablespoons butter**

Cook about 5 minutes, until the corn is just done (if the corn looks dry, add a splash of water). Transfer to a bowl and season with:

**Salt**

**Juice of 1 small lime**

**2 tablespoons chopped marjoram, cilantro, parsley, or basil**

Grate:

**½ pound queso fresco, Monterey Jack, or another melting cheese**

Stuff each pepper with a good pinch of cheese and fill with corn. Pack the stuffed peppers tightly in a single layer in an earthenware dish and drizzle with:

**Olive oil or vegetable oil**

**Salt**

Bake for 15 to 20 minutes, until the peppers are wilted and tender. Serve hot.

## Paella with Pimientos and Chorizo

10 SERVINGS

Cooking a paella outdoors over a bed of wood coals is a magical, festive experience for a gathering of friends. Everyone is irresistibly drawn to the fire by the aromas and the sight of the generous pan of rice—the anticipation is the secret ingredient. I've made paella at all times of year, but the best might be in the fall when there's a chill in the air. The magic starts with the pleasure of building and tending a wood fire, usually two hours or so before cooking. I build the fire on the firebrick surface where I usually grill, but a fire pit or a safe spot directly on the ground works, too. Before lighting the fire, make two stacks of fireproof bricks of equal height and the right distance apart so the handles of the paella pan (18 inches in diameter) will rest on them. The pan should be a few inches over the coals, which will be a few inches deep.

Cooking a paella is simple, like making a risotto. While the fire is burning down, prepare all the ingredients—the *mise en place*—and have them at hand when the coals are ready and it is time to begin. I like to use two kinds of chorizo and to bone chicken thighs and marinate them for extra flavor.

It is fun to serve the paella in its pan in the middle of the table, with bottles of cold rosé and slices of lemon, and let everyone help themselves. The meal doesn't end until the last bits of crust have been scraped from the pan.

Put in a bowl, the day before cooking, if possible:

**10 chicken thighs, boned**

Season the chicken with:

**Zest of 2 lemons**

**3 garlic cloves, chopped fine**

**1 tablespoon chopped marjoram**

**1 tablespoon pimentón dulce**

**Salt**

Let marinate several hours or overnight. Before cooking, re-form the thighs and secure them with toothpicks.

When ready to cook, heat to simmering:

**4 quarts flavorful chicken broth**

Season the stock with:

**A pinch of saffron threads**

**Salt (enough to flavor all the rice)**

Spread the coals and place the pan over them. (Let the coals burn and cool down a bit if they are too hot. The ideal is to have even, medium-high heat for 30 to 40 minutes.) Pour into the hot pan:

**½ cup olive oil**

Brown the chicken thighs, skin side down, for 5 minutes or so. Turn them over and add:

**2 onions (white or yellow), diced**

**6 sweet pimientos (or other meaty sweet red pepper), cored, seeded, and cut in wide strips**

**1 pound fresh Mexican chorizo, pulled apart in hunks**

Cook, stirring frequently, about 5 minutes, until the vegetables have softened and browned lightly. Add:

**1 pound Spanish chorizo, sliced ¼ inch thick**

**2 garlic cloves, chopped**

**3 tablespoons smoked sweet paprika**

**1 cup chopped parsley**

Cook, stirring, for 1 minute. Add:

**4 cups Bomba or Valencia rice**

Cook the rice, stirring, for another minute. Add the hot stock. Gently stir to evenly distribute the rice, meat, and vegetables. Tend the coals, arranging them so that the paella bubbles and cooks as evenly as possible. Do not stir the paella again. After 5 minutes or so, add and gently submerge throughout the paella:

**3 pounds Manila clams**

After another 15 to 20 minutes, the rice will have absorbed the stock and be nearly cooked through. This is the time to watch closely for the formation of the *socarrat*—the delicious brown crust on the bottom of the pan. It is easy to go from browned to burned, so check different areas and keep a watchful eye. Remove from the fire when the bottom is just browned. Cover the paella with a clean towel and let rest for 10 to 15 minutes to steam and mellow.

VARIATIONS

• Cook on a grill or over a gas burner instead of an open fire.

• Use shrimp or mussels in place of the clams, or a combination of shellfish.

• In place of two kinds of chorizo, use only Spanish.

# Chile Verde

4 SERVINGS

*Chile verde* is a saucy pork stew of the Southwest. It is a delicious way to use the chiles in your garden. Anaheim are the classic peppers used, but any large green chile, hot or not, will work. Anaheims are usually mild, with an occasional hot one sneaking in here and there, but as with all chiles, it really depends on where they were grown and how hot the weather is. When I make this stew I always double the recipe, because like most stews it tastes even better 1 or 2 days later. Serve it with rice, beans, and tortillas.

The white onion and dried Mexican oregano give this dish its authentic taste.

Season generously, a day ahead, if possible (or even a few hours):

**3 pounds pork shoulder, cut into
1-inch cubes**

with:

**Salt**

**Fresh-ground black pepper**

Roast, peel, and seed:

**12 Anaheim chiles**

Cut the chiles into 1-inch squares and season with:

**Salt**

Toss the pork with:

**1 tablespoon flour**

Heat a cast-iron or heavy-bottomed skillet over medium-high heat. When the pan is hot, measure in:

**2 tablespoons olive oil or fresh lard**

Add the pork—but only add as much as will loosely cover the bottom of the pan. Cook it in batches if necessary. Brown the meat well on all sides. Put the browned meat into a heavy pot. Turn down the heat to medium, pour off most of the fat, and add:

**1 white onion, diced**

**4 to 5 garlic cloves, chopped**

Cook until soft, stirring up all the brown bits from the pan, about 5 minutes. Add:

**Salt**

**2 diced tomatoes (fresh or canned)**

**A large pinch of dried Mexican oregano**

Stir together and cook for a few minutes more. Add the chiles, pork, and any resting juices. Stir together and pour over:

**2 cups chicken stock**

The stock should come just to the top of the meat; add more if needed. Bring to a boil, reduce to a simmer, cover the pot, and cook until the pork is soft, about 45 minutes. Check now and then to be sure it is barely simmering and that there is enough liquid. Taste a piece of meat to see if it is tender and continue cooking if necessary. If the meat has given off a lot of liquid while cooking, take the lid off halfway through to allow the sauce to reduce. When the stew is done, taste for salt, and adjust as needed.

VARIATION

◆ Use chicken thighs instead of pork.

# Grilled Pork Shoulder with Ancho Chiles

6 SERVINGS

This is a great dish for a leisurely evening. The pork is long-cooked ahead of time and then finished on the grill for smoky flavor and a crispy seared finish. The braising liq-uids could be used to cook a pot of beans or make a soup to start.  Serve the pork with Pickled Jalapeños and Carrots (page 185).

The day before you grill the pork, season generously:

**One 4-pound pork shoulder roast**

with:

**Salt**

**Fresh-ground black pepper**

Refrigerate overnight. Bring the pork to room temperature before putting it in a pot with:

**Water to cover by 2 inches**

**1 tablespoon cumin seeds**

**1 tablespoon coriander seeds**

**2 whole dried ancho chiles**

**1 yellow onion, peeled and halved**

**4 garlic cloves**

**2 bay leaves**

**1 oregano sprig**

Bring to a simmer, skim any foam that rises, and cook at low heat for 3 to 4 hours, until tender but not quite falling apart. A knife inserted into the meat should pull out eas-ily. Carefully lift the pork out of the liquid and allow both to cool. Place the pork in a large bowl and pour the cooled liquid over to cover. Refrigerate until cold. Remove the pork from the bowl, wipe away any fat or gelled liquid, and cut the meat into 1-inch-thick slices or chunks. Reheat 1 or 2 cups of the cooking liquid. Grill the pork over a bed of hot coals (or brown under the broiler). The meat is already fully cooked, so you are only looking to brown the surface well and heat through. Serve hot, moistened with a little of the hot cooking liquid. Save the re-maining liquid to make soup.

VARIATIONS

* Shred the cooked pork, cook it in a skillet until hot and lightly crisped, and you have carnitas. Spoon in some of the cooking liquid if the meat is getting dry. Bring on the salsa and tortillas.
* Leave any uneaten meat in the cooking liquid to keep it moist. It will keep for several days in the refrigerator.
* Cook beans in the pork liquid. (Remember that it is already seasoned, so you probably won't need to add any more salt.)

# Yogurt–Spiced Chicken Skewers

4 SERVINGS

These chicken skewers are easy to make and are quite delicious. Children love them, too. The crushed chile for this dish is the chile powder sold in Indian spice stores; it is quite spicy. Use Marash, ñora, or even New Mexico pepper for a milder version.

Remove the skin and bones from:

**4 chicken thighs or 2 whole chicken legs**

Cut into strips and season with:

**Salt**

Set aside.

Measure into a small heavy-bottomed skillet:

**¼ teaspoon cumin seeds**
**½ teaspoon coriander (if you are using green coriander seeds, don't toast them)**
**2 cloves**
**½ teaspoon fenugreek**
**¼ teaspoon black peppercorns**

Toast the spices over medium heat until fragrant. Pour into a spice grinder, or use a mortar and pestle, and grind to a fine powder.

Measure into a small bowl:

**¾ cup Yogurt (below)**
**½ teaspoon turmeric**
**2 garlic cloves, pounded to a paste**
**¼ teaspoon dried chile flakes (more for a spicier version)**
**A pinch of cayenne**
**Salt**
**1 tablespoon olive oil**

Add half (1 teaspoon) of the ground spice mixture (save the other half for next time) and stir to combine. Add the chicken and let sit for ½ hour. This can be done a few hours ahead of time and stored in the refrigerator. Prepare a bed of medium-hot coals. Thread the chicken onto 12 skewers and grill until done, about 4 minutes a side.

# Yogurt

MAKES ABOUT 4 CUPS

Fresh homemade yogurt has a soft delicate texture and wonderful flavor, and it is very simple to make. Choose your favorite commercial plain yogurt for the starter of your first batch. Whatever cultures that yogurt has will be the ones that grow and flavor your own. Once you have made yogurt it will be hard to go back to store-bought. Whole milk makes a thicker, creamier yogurt, and nonhomogenized milk will make yogurt with a cream cap on top. Experiment with different milks, but always use the freshest organic milk available.

When making yogurt, the initial heating of the milk denatures the proteins in the milk to make a smooth thick yogurt. After being heated the milk is cooled to about 105°F. The yogurt cultures are stirred in, and it is held warm until the milk is cultured. It is important to keep the temperature stable during this time. The beneficial bacteria (frequently called probiotics) that ferment milk into yogurt are alive, and when the milk is too cold or too hot they become dormant or die. There are yogurt machines available that keep the mixture warm, but an oven with a pilot light or a small insulated cooler will work well, too. Warm the cooler with a jar or two of hot water, and keep them in the cooler while the yogurt ferments.

Pour into a clean heavy-bottomed nonreactive pot:

**4 cups (1 quart) milk**

Heat to 180°F. Stir now and then to make sure the milk does not scorch on the bottom of the pan. Take off the heat and let cool to 105°F. To speed up the cooling process, place the pot in cold water in a sink or larger pot. I pour the milk into warmed Mason jars (leaving a couple inches of head space in each jar) and place those in cold water. Be sure to use jars that are made with heat-tempered glass. Once the milk is at the proper temperature, stir in:

**2 tablespoons yogurt**

Cap the jars and place in the preheated cooler, a low oven (100°F), or a yogurt maker. Let the yogurt sit, undisturbed, for 4 to 8 hours. The longer the yogurt ferments, the thicker and more sour it will become. Cool the yogurt for a few hours to thicken before eating. Remember to save a few spoonfuls of yogurt for the next batch. You will never have to buy yogurt again.

NOTES

◆ If the yogurt does not set, the temperature may have been incorrect, either too hot or too cold. Try raising the temperature (more hot water in the jars in the cooler) and waiting a few more hours. If the temperature was too hot when you started, you will need to start over.

◆ Sometimes the yogurt won't set because there is not enough starter culture, or it was not alive to begin with. Read the ingredients and be sure to use yogurt that says on the label that it has live cultures. If the culture is live, try stirring in a bit more. Wait and see.

VARIATIONS

◆ To make Greek-style, or thickened yogurt, place the yogurt in a strainer lined with cheesecloth and let it drain (refrigerated) for a few hours.

◆ To make *labneh*, or yogurt cheese, drain overnight. Season with olive oil and salt. Add pounded garlic and chopped herbs, if desired.

◆ For flavored yogurt, put a layer of warm (105°F) fruit preserves on the bottom of the Mason jars before pouring in the warm cultured milk.

## Pickled Jalapeños and Carrots

MAKES ABOUT 1 PINT

Unlike many quick-pickle recipes, this one starts not with a liquid brine, but a sauté, with the brine ingredients added to the pan. These pickles will be familiar from taco trucks and other Mexican eateries. They keep well for a week in the refrigerator.

Slice into ¼-inch slices:

**½ pound jalapeños**

Put in a colander and rinse under hot tap water, swirling and tossing the slices for 1 or 2 minutes to take some of the heat out of the chiles. Peel:

**½ pound carrots (2 large carrots)**
**1 yellow onion**

Slice the carrots into ¼-inch-thick coins and the onions into slender wedges. Heat a large skillet and pour in:

**2 tablespoons olive oil**

Add the jalapeños, carrots, and onion and:

**1½ teaspoons salt**

Cook over medium-high heat, stirring occasionally, for 5 minutes. Add:

**1 cup apple cider vinegar**
**½ cup water**
**1 tablespoon sugar**
**2 bay leaves**

Bring to a simmer and cook until the peppers are beginning to get tender but are still quite crisp, about 10 minutes. Pour into a nonreactive bowl and cool before serving.

VARIATIONS

◆ Omit the sugar and add 1 peeled and thinly sliced apple with the vegetables for sweetness.

◆ Add a pinch of Mexican oregano, toasted cumin seeds, or crushed coriander seeds when you add the vinegar.

◆ For a more fiery pickle, proceed without rinsing the jalapeños.

## Corn *(Zea mays)*

A steaming ear of sweet corn on the cob slathered with butter is an emblem of summer and local farms. Fresh corn just picked from the farm or garden is unbeatable. Grilled or boiled on the cob, it tastes divine and is fun to eat. Flavor the butter with lime and chile, herbs, or roasted pepper for even more flavor. Or cut the kernels off the cobs to make into salad, a quick sauté, soup, or a stuffing.

Corn has been hybridized and changed genetically more than almost any other crop. I strongly urge you to shop for corn at farmers' markets and other places that support small local organic farmers. *Golden Bantam Sweet* is a sweet heirloom yellow corn filled with deep corn flavor; tender sweet *Country Gentleman* is charming with small white "shoe peg" kernels that zigzag along the cob instead of lining up in orderly rows. *Double Standard* is bicolored with white and yellow kernels on the same cob. Unlike regular corn, hybrid corns stay sweet for days instead of having their sugars quickly turn to starch once picked; but some deep corn flavor has been sacrificed for long-lasting sweetness. *White Silver Queen* is a hybrid that is sweet, but not overly so.

Field corn is starchy and grown to be dried for hominy, cornmeal, polenta, popcorn, and animal feed. There are some beautiful varieties: with green kernels (*Oaxacan Green Dent*), blue (*Blue Jade*), and multi-colored burgundy and orange (*Mandan Bride*). There are more and more local mills and farms selling fresh-ground heirloom cornmeal and polenta. Look for them at the farmers' market and online.

Corn needs heat and sun to grow well. Start seeds indoors where the growing season is short. Corn is a grass, or monocotyledon, so only one leaf will come up as the seedling sprouts. Plant corn with plenty of compost and keep it watered well. Feed monthly with more compost or compost tea. Corn requires pollination and does best planted in blocks instead of long rows. A minimum of a two-foot-square block is suggested for good ear production. Plant blocks in two successions for a longer harvest. Each corn stalk produces one or two ears of corn, though some may produce more. Corn is ready to harvest when the ear is full and round and the kernels are plump and filled with milky liquid. Pull back a bit of husk and pierce a kernel with a fingernail to judge ripeness. Allow field corn to dry on the stalk.

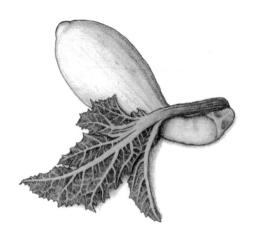

# Corn and Summer Squash Soup
MAKES ABOUT 2 QUARTS

Yellow summer squash gives this soup a beautiful golden color.

Shuck and slice the kernels from:

**4 ears corn**

Set aside the kernels. Put the cobs in a pot and cover with 2 quarts water. Bring to a boil, reduce the heat to a simmer, and cook for 20 minutes. Remove and discard the cobs. While the cob stock is simmering, heat in a heavy-bottomed soup pot:

**1 tablespoon olive oil**
**1 tablespoon butter**

Add:

**1 onion, sliced**

Cook until soft, without browning, about 10 minutes. Add:

**Salt**
**3 garlic cloves, sliced thin**
**3 basil sprigs, tied together with string**

Cook another 3 minutes and add:

**2½ cups diced yellow summer squash (5 squash or about ¾ pound)**

Cook for 5 minutes and pour in 1 quart cob stock. Bring to a boil, add the corn, and simmer until the corn is tender, about 5 minutes. Let cool slightly, remove the basil bouquet, and purée in small batches in a blender. Strain the soup through a medium-mesh strainer, pushing down on the skins to remove all the liquid. Taste and adjust for salt as needed. Serve garnished with:

**A spoonful of Basil–Squash Blossom Butter (page 187)**
**A squeeze of lime**

## Basil–Squash Blossom Butter

MAKES 6 TABLESPOONS

Break off the fibrous green mini-petals, or sepals, around the bases of:

**3 squash blossoms**

Gently open the petals and remove the pointy center (the anther in the male blossom, the pistil in the female), which can be bitter. Chop coarsely.

Mix together:

**4 tablespoons butter, softened**
**Salt**
**Fresh-ground black pepper**
**A pinch of cayenne**
**1 teaspoon lemon or lime juice**

Stir in the squash blossoms and:

**1½ tablespoons chopped basil**

Taste for salt and acid and adjust as needed.

## Fresh Corn Tamales

MAKES ABOUT 15 SMALL TAMALES

These delicately textured sweet tamales are a special seasonal treat. The batter is made with fresh corn as opposed to the usual masa made from dried corn. Serve the tamales with a spoonful of crème fraîche and Roasted Tomatillo Salsa (page 168).

Carefully cut the stem end off:

**6 ears corn**

Unroll the husks off the ears as carefully as possible. Save for wrapping the tamales. Clean the ears of silk and cut the kernels off the cobs. Set aside the kernels from one cob and purée the rest in a food processor until smooth. Add:

**Salt**
**2 tablespoons butter, softened**

Put the puréed kernel mixture in a nonreactive bowl and refrigerate.

Melt in a small heavy-bottomed pan over medium heat:

**2 teaspoons butter**

Add the reserved corn kernels and:

**⅓ cup finely diced summer squash (about 1 very small squash)**
**Salt**

Cook until tender. Taste for salt and adjust as needed. Set aside to cool.

To assemble the tamales, take a corn husk, and holding the tapered end toward you, spread about 2 tablespoons corn purée over the middle of the leaf. (If the corn purée is separating, whisk it back together.) Leave bare a good 2 inches at the pointy end of the leaf and ¾ inch along the other edges. Spread a small spoonful of the corn and squash mixture down the middle of the corn purée. Fold (almost rolling) the long edges over each other and then fold the pointy end of the leaf up and over the seam. Stack them into the basket of a steamer, top side up so they don't leak.

When all the tamales are formed and stacked, cover them with a few more corn husks and steam for at least 1 hour and up to 2 (depends on how juicy the corn and how liquid the mixture). Keep an eye on the water level in the steamer and don't let it boil dry. An old trick is to put a penny in the water: you can hear it jangling away in the simmering water. If it stops making noise, add more water right away. The tamales are done when they have firmed up and are beginning to separate from the leaf. (If the purée is very wet, this can take up to 2 hours.) Serve warm. If made ahead, the tamales can be reheated in the steamer.

# Creamed Corn

4 SERVINGS

The juicy creaminess of this dish comes from the fresh corn itself. After taking off the kernels, the corn milk is scraped from the cob to get all the delicious corn essence into the dish.

Husk and remove all the silk from:

**4 ears corn, fresh white or bicolor varieties are best**

Grate the kernels from one of the ears of corn into a bowl using the large holes on a box grater. Slice the kernels from the other 3 ears. Take the back of a knife and scrape down all 4 cobs to collect all the juicy milk and bits of corn out of the cob.

Melt in a heavy-bottomed pan over medium heat:

**4 tablespoons butter**

Add:

**⅓ cup diced onion**

Cook until soft, about 5 minutes. Add the corn and milky juices along with:

**Salt**

**2 teaspoons chopped summer savory**

Cook, stirring now and then, until the corn is soft and the liquid has thickened, about 5 minutes. Taste for salt and adjust as desired.

VARIATIONS

✦ Use another herb such as basil, marjoram, or thyme instead of summer savory.

✦ Add ¼ cup of heavy cream for a richer dish.

# Okra  (*Abelmoschus esculentus*)

People seem to love or hate okra. I like it very much. I like it fried or quickly sautéed at high heat, or long cooked in a soup or stew. Perhaps the okra haters have simply had a bad encounter with it. Okra will indeed get slippery if stewed for a short time, but when quickly sautéed at high heat or cooked for a long time in liquid that texture is a nonissue. Southern dishes that use okra abound, as do Indian okra dishes: okra in soup and gumbo, and okra fried, grilled, pickled, curried, spiced, and sautéed. Look for freshly picked young pods; more mature okra is tough and fibrous. *Cajun Jewel* produces small green pods, and *Red Burgundy* has striking long red pods. Both are well-adapted to colder climes.

Okra is a relative of hibiscus and it has pretty yellow blossoms. Although there are early-ripening varieties that do well in colder climates, okra still needs a good amount of heat to thrive. Start plants indoors to lengthen the growing season, but plant the seedlings outside before the roots have a chance to crowd. Choose a spot in full sun and amend the soil with plenty of compost when planting. Feed monthly after that, with compost or compost tea. Harvest pods when young and tender. Harvest regularly or the plants will stop producing.

# Cornmeal-Fried Okra

4 SERVINGS

Crispy fried okra is delicious. It is the most common way it is served in the South, and for good reason!

Trim the tops off:

**1 pound okra**

Cut the pods in half lengthwise or, if very large, in quarters. Season with:

**Salt**

**Fresh-ground black pepper**

**¼ teaspoon cayenne**

Pour over:

**¾ cup buttermilk**

This can be done a few hours ahead. Refrigerate until ready to use.

Measure into a bowl:

**1 cup cornmeal**

**½ cup flour**

Put the okra in a colander to drain. Heat a heavy-bottomed frying pan over medium heat. Fill the pan to a depth of 1 inch with:

**Fresh lard, melted, or vegetable oil**

Toss the okra in the cornmeal and flour until well coated. Shake off the excess cornmeal and carefully add the okra to the pan when the oil is hot. (Shake a piece of okra over the pan; if the cornmeal sizzles up the oil is ready.) Fry until crisp and golden, turning the okra as needed. Remove with a slotted spoon and drain on a rack, or on absorbent paper. Serve hot sprinkled with salt.

VARIATIONS

◆ Cut the okra into ½-inch slices. Toss in corn flour instead of cornmeal.

◆ Sprinkle with gremolata: Mix together 1 tablespoon chopped parsley, 1 garlic clove chopped fine, and the finely chopped zest of 1 lemon.

# Sautéed Spiced Okra with Tomatoes

4 SERVINGS

The mild taste of okra goes well with the bold spices of Indian cuisine. A quick sauté to brown the okra makes the flavor more robust. Serve this with basmati rice, Yogurt-Spiced Chicken Skewers (page 183), and Spiced Carrot Raita (page 73).

Trim the stem end from:

**½ pound okra (choose smaller pods)**

Slice diagonally into ⅓-inch-thick slices. Season with:

**Salt**

Make the spice mixture. Toast in a small skillet until fragrant but not brown:

**½ teaspoon fenugreek seeds**

**½ teaspoon coriander seeds**

**¼ teaspoon cumin seeds**

Pound or grind the spices into a powder. Heat a cast-iron frying pan or another heavy-bottomed pan over medium-high heat. Pour in:

**1 tablespoon coconut or olive oil**

Add the okra and cook until browned, stirring and tossing now and then, about 5 minutes. Stir in the spices and:

**1½ cups spicy tomato sauce (see page 166)**

Simmer over low heat until the okra are tender. Taste for salt and adjust as needed. Serve garnished with:

**Chopped cilantro**

# Colorful Chicories

## Frisée, Escarole, Radicchio, Belgian Endive, and Puntarelle

CHICORY SALADS are the highlight of winter for me. Their bracing flavor and vibrant colors brighten dark cold days. Frilly green puffs, flouncy lime green heads speckled with magenta, smooth ruby and white streaked balls, and long, pointy light green, almost white heads all bear sturdy leaves. Toss them with winter fruit, tangy cheeses, toasted nuts, citrus, or pungent garlic and anchovy. You can also roast or grill them to serve on their own, stir them into a risotto, or use them atop a pizza. Poach them in rich broth for a satisfying soup, wilt the leaves with beans and olive oil, or sauté them for pasta or for an excellent side dish, or a tasty lunch.

## Recipes

Frisée Salad with Roasted Figs and Pancetta Croutons  195

Warm Frisée Salad  196

Escarole Salad with Hazelnut Vinaigrette  196

Escarole Soup with Poached Egg  197

Castelfranco Chicory Salad with Celery Root,
Apples, and Walnuts  199

Tardivo Radicchio and Farro Salad with Dried Persimmons  200

Treviso Radicchio, Merguez Sausage, and
Whole-Wheat Spaghetti  200

Roasted Radicchio Pizza with Pancetta and Fried Rosemary  201

Chopped Pan di Zucchero Chicory Salad  202

Belgian Endive Leaf Hors d'Oeuvres  202

Puntarelle Chicory with Lemon, Garlic, and Anchovies  203

Puntarelle Chicory Soup with Chicken Meatballs  204

Treviso radicchio

Tardivo radicchio

Escarole

Chioggia radicchio

Castelfranco chicory

# Chicories in the Garden

The chicory family is quite large, including everything from frisée to *puntarelle* with many kinds of chicories and radicchio in between. Some are so beautiful I am hard-pressed as to whether to use them as a decorative arrangement or cook them. American kitchen gardeners are catching on to the wonders of chicories. In Europe, they have been grown and loved for centuries. Italians have festivals devoted to radicchios of all kinds. Many varieties have French and Italian names and France and Italy are where the recipes I love come from, too. I can't stop saying how passionate I am about eating and growing chicories.

Cool weather is the season for chicories—the heat makes them tough and inedibly bitter. Loose-leaf varieties such as frisée, escarole, and Catalogna can be planted in spring or late summer. The slower growing, heading types are better planted in late summer for fall and winter harvest. In spring, the weather warms up too quickly for them to mature. Many varieties may be grown in spring or fall as a small-leaf cut-and-come-again crop.

Chicories grow well in most soils with a good addition of compost. Once established, they are hardy, self-sufficient, and require little attention beyond consistent watering. (Dry spells can cause them to become bitter.) Cold weather sweetens the greens, and many will survive frosty cold. In balmy Berkeley, I can grow them all winter. If you have mild winters, stagger plantings for harvest through winter into spring. In other zones, a cold frame will keep them going in all but the very coldest climates. A layer of burlap or straw will protect the plants from a severe cold snap.

# Frisée and Escarole
*(Cichorium endiva)*

Curly, frilly-leaf frisée, sometimes called curly endive, and flat-leaf escarole are the two endives we eat. (Despite its name, Belgian endive is not a true endive and is discussed on page 198 in the chicory section.) I love both these salad greens. The crisp texture and slightly bitter flavor of the leaves give loft and intensity to salads. The best specimens have light, creamy-colored hearts. The pale hearts are created through a process called blanching: formerly a cloche, flowerpot, or opaque plastic dome was placed over the plant to block the sunlight and prevent the leaves from producing green-pigmented chlorophyll. The light leaves are more tender and sweeter than the darker, outer leaves. Many varieties today are self-blanching and don't require the extra work. Both *Très Fine Maraîchère* and its cousin *Rhodos* have thin frilly leaves. *Natacha* is a large bountiful self-blanching escarole. *Broad Leaf Batavian* is another popular escarole. Italian seed catalogs have many more varieties to choose from.

Escarole and frisée are both loose leaf and don't form tight heads. Their growing habit and needs are much the same as lettuce, but they require more time to come to maturity. Direct seed in the spring or fall or start seedlings indoors in the spring to add a few weeks to their growing season before very hot weather sets in. Add a generous amount of compost to the soil when planting and water with compost tea after five weeks. Both frisée and escarole respond well to cut-and-come-again cultivation.

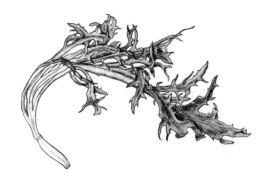

# Frisée Salad with Roasted Figs and Pancetta Croutons

4 SERVINGS

This is a perfect salad for fall with the sweet taste of figs, salty pancetta, and the bitter crunch of frisée. I like to mix red wine vinegar and balsamic together. (I find balsamic vinegar a bit too sweet on its own.)

Tear off and discard the tough dark outer leaves from:

**3 small heads of frisée**

Remove and discard the root ends of each head, separate the individual leaves, and wash and dry well.

Preheat the oven to 375°F.

Cut in halves lengthwise and arrange in a baking dish cut side up:

**6 ripe figs**

Sprinkle with:

**1 teaspoon balsamic vinegar**
**1 teaspoon red wine vinegar**
**Salt**
**Fresh-ground black pepper**
**1 teaspoon olive oil**

Bake for 7 to 10 minutes, or until soft and puffed. Leave the oven on.

Prepare the vinaigrette. Mix together in a small bowl:

**1 small shallot, diced**
**2 teaspoons balsamic vinegar**
**2 teaspoons red wine vinegar**
**Salt**
**Fresh-ground black pepper**

Let the mixture sit to marry for 10 minutes or so. Whisk in:

**4 tablespoons extra-virgin olive oil**

Taste and add more vinegar, oil, or salt. If there are any roasting juices from the figs, stir them into the finished vinaigrette.

Prepare the croutons. Cut off and discard the crusts from:

**3 slices country-style levain bread,**
**  sliced ¾ inch thick**

Cut the slices lengthwise into 2 or 3 long ¾-inch-wide sticks. You should end up with 8 sticks. Brush the sticks with:

**Olive oil**

Take out of the refrigerator and separate:

**8 thin slices pancetta**

Wrap each stick of bread with a slice of pancetta like a candy cane. Place the wrapped bread sticks on a baking sheet and bake for 10 minutes, or until the pancetta begins to crisp. These can be kept warm for a few minutes until serving.

Toss the frisée with the vinaigrette. Arrange the figs and pancetta croutons on the greens. Serve immediately.

# Warm Frisée Salad

4 SERVINGS

Frisée's frilly leaves stand up well to a warm vinaigrette and the duck fat in this salad tames its bitter nuances in a most delectable way. Crunchy garlic croutons add a delightful textural contrast.

Preheat the oven to 375°F. Cut:

**2 thick slices country-style bread**

Cut the slices into cubes and toss them with:

**A drizzle of duck fat or olive oil**
**Salt**
**Fresh-ground black pepper**

Spread out the seasoned cubes on a baking sheet and bake, stirring now and then, until golden and crisp. While still hot, tip them into a bowl and toss with:

**2 garlic cloves, finely minced**

Set aside.

Meanwhile, tear off and discard the tough dark outer leaves from:

**3 small heads of frisée**

Remove and discard the root ends of each head, separate the individual leaves, and wash and dry them well.

Mix together the dressing in a heat-proof bowl large enough to easily hold all the frisée:

**1 tablespoon red wine vinegar**
**2 teaspoons Dijon mustard**
**Salt**
**Fresh-ground black pepper**
**Leaves from 1 thyme sprig, chopped**

Stir until the salt is dissolved and then slowly whisk in:

**3 tablespoons olive oil**
**1 tablespoon duck fat**

Taste for salt and acid and adjust as needed.

A warm vinaigrette should be a little acidic, as the acetic acid burns off as it is heated.

When ready to serve, choose a pot that the bowl will fit on snugly and fill it with 3 inches of water. Bring to a boil and place the bowl with the vinaigrette over the boiling water. Add the frisée and toss everything together in the warm vinaigrette. Don't leave the bowl over the boiling water for too long. The salad should be warmed but not wilted or cooked. Arrange the salad on warm plates. Add the croutons to the tossing bowl and toss them to gather up any extra vinaigrette. Scatter them over the salad and finish with a grind of black pepper. Serve immediately.

VARIATIONS

◆ Serve the salad with 1 poached egg for each diner.
◆ Before tossing the frisée with the warm vinaigrette, add some torn pieces of duck confit, sliced confited duck gizzards, or crispy bacon lardons.
◆ Toss the warm croutons with garlic and chopped thyme and parsley.
◆ Other greens (either separately or mixed) work well in this salad: escarole, radicchio, or dandelion greens.

# Escarole Salad with Hazelnut Vinaigrette

4 SERVINGS

Use the lighter-colored leaves from the heart for this salad. Save the darker outer leaves for a pasta sauce or the Escarole Soup with Poached Egg (page 197).

Preheat the oven to 350°F. Spread on a baking sheet:

**¼ cup hazelnuts**

Toast until golden, about 15 minutes. When the nuts have cooled, roll them in your hands to remove the nuts' skins. Chop coarsely.

Remove the dark green outer leaves from:

**1 medium head of escarole**

Cut off and discard the root end of the head, separate the leaves, wash them, and dry well. Prepare the dressing. Mix together:

**1 garlic clove, peeled and slightly smashed**

**½ tablespoon sherry vinegar**

**1 tablespoon red wine vinegar**

**Salt**

**Fresh-ground black pepper**

Stir to dissolve. Whisk in:

**3 tablespoons extra-virgin olive oil**

**2 tablespoons hazelnut oil**

Taste and add more vinegar and salt as needed. Using a vegetable peeler, shave thin slices of:

**1½ ounces firm sheep's-milk cheese, like Pecorino Toscano, Ossau-Iraty, or P'tit Basque**

Collect the slices on a small plate.

When ready to serve, remove the garlic clove from the vinaigrette and toss the escarole with the dressing and half the hazelnuts. Top the salad with the cheese and the rest of the nuts.

VARIATIONS

◆ Add slices of apple, pear, or persimmon to the leaves as they are being dressed.

◆ Use a mix of radicchio, escarole, and frisée.

◆ Use all olive oil in place of the hazelnut oil.

# Escarole Soup with Poached Egg

4 SERVINGS

This easy and revitalizing soup is full of flavor, comfort, and nutrition. If you have a batch of homemade chicken stock on hand, this soup will be ready in 10 minutes or less. The eggs can be poached right in the soup itself, but I like to poach them in a separate pot of water to keep the broth clear.

Wash and drain:

**A large handful of outer escarole leaves**

Cut or tear the leaves into bite-size pieces. Toast:

**4 slices country-style bread**

Rub the bread with:

**1 or 2 garlic cloves, peeled**

In a heavy-bottomed soup pot, heat:

**1 quart chicken stock (preferably homemade)**

While the stock is heating, fill another pot with 4 inches of water and bring to a bare simmer.

Once the chicken stock has come to a boil, turn down to a simmer, and add the escarole along with:

**Salt**

**2 garlic cloves, sliced**

Cook for 4 minutes. Turn off the heat.

One at a time, crack into a ramekin and gently slide into the simmering water:

**4 eggs**

Poach gently until the whites are firm, about 4 minutes.

Warm 4 soup bowls. While the eggs are cooking, put a piece of toast into each bowl.

Ladle in the soup and add a poached egg. Garnish with:

**A drizzle of extra-virgin olive oil**
**A grating of Parmesan cheese**

VARIATIONS

⁕ For a more substantial soup, add 1 cup cooked white beans to the broth and return to a simmer before adding the escarole.
⁕ Add 4 sage leaves with the garlic.

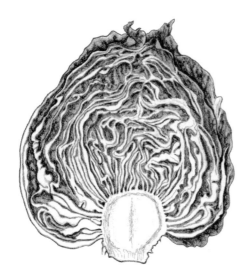

*Chioggia radicchio*

# Chicory and Radicchio
*(Cichorium intybus)*

The chicory family includes red radicchios and all the other green and speckled varieties. Many have names from the regions where they were developed in Italy. My favorite of all is *Castelfranco* chicory, which is a loose head of magenta-speckled light green leaves. Its flavor is less bitter than some of the darker colored ones. *Pan di Zucchero* or *Sugar Loaf* chicory makes a huge elongated head of tender bittersweet leaves that I love chopped into salads. *Chioggia* radicchio and *Verona* radicchio are both red round heads with dense white stems. Chioggia is lighter in color while Verona is deep red. *Treviso* radicchio makes a compact, pointy head with deep red leaves filled with a white stem. Treviso is good roasted and in salads. It can be quite bitter, so give a leaf a little taste before committing. Cooking will greatly reduce the bitter quality of the leaves. Try all the radicchios in salads, roasted, grilled, or sautéed.

Other chicories include the elegant, smooth, and pointy-headed *Belgian* endive, which is tender and sweet from its rebirth in the dark. The heads are excellent roasted and braised, and the individual leaves make perfect boats for passed hors d'oeuvres and salads. *Puntarelle*, sometimes called asparagus chicory, is quite a sight with thin green leaves making a halo around a fat heart of pointy green spears. It is divine in salad and makes a delicious soup. Robust *Catalogna* chicory is sometimes called Italian dandelion (because the leaves resemble dandelion greens). The leaves add depth to hearty soups and stews, while the white stems make good salads. *Grumolo Verde* and *Rosso* chicories make very cute little rosettes for salads and soups.

Heading chicories can be a bit of a challenge in the garden, but even if they don't make a perfect tight head they are still delicious. Plant them in the late summer for fall and winter harvest—spring plantings rarely form good heads. Be patient; it takes some time, up to three and a half months, to fully mature. You will see that cold weather makes red radicchio and chicory deeper and brighter in color. Puntarelle are as easy to grow as most of the other chicories. Grumolo Verde and Rosso will overwinter and resprout with lovely little heads. Belgian endive is grown, cut away, and then the roots are taken into the dark to sprout again. It is a long procedure, but not impossible for gardeners eager for a challenge.

Chicories and radicchios are also good to grow and cut as young leaves (cut-and-come-again style) for two or three successive harvests. Many companies sell mixes of chicories and radicchio for such plantings. They make lovely tender salads.

# Castelfranco Chicory Salad with Celery Root, Apples, and Walnuts

4 SERVINGS

The flavors and textures of this salad are refreshing and compelling—buttery walnuts, bittersweet greens, and crunchy, sweet apples. Each bite is as tasty as it is beautiful. The verjus in the vinaigrette amplifies the fruity flavors.

Preheat the oven to 375°F. Spread out on a baking sheet and toast until golden, about 8 minutes:

**¼ cup walnuts**

When cool, rub the nuts in your hands to remove their tannic skins. Crush or chop coarsely.

Tear off and discard any tough, blemished leaves from:

**1 medium or 2 small heads of Castelfranco chicory**

Cut the root ends off and separate the leaves. Wash and dry well.

Stir together in a small bowl:

**3 tablespoons verjus**
**Salt**
**Fresh-ground black pepper**

When the salt is dissolved, whisk in:

**3 tablespoons extra-virgin olive oil**

Taste for salt and acid and adjust as needed. (If the verjus tastes too sweet, add a dash of white wine or Champagne vinegar.) Peel:

**1 small or ½ medium celery root**

Cut into quarters and remove the core of:

**2 small apples or 1 large apple (any crisp tasty variety)**

Just before serving, cut the celery root into thin slices. (If you cut the celery root and apple ahead of time they will oxidize and turn brown.) Cut the celery root slices into a thin julienne. Add the celery root to the vinaigrette, and let marinate while you cut the apple into thin lengthwise slices. Add the Castelfranco and walnuts to the vinaigrette and toss. Add the apples and give a last toss. Arrange prettily on a plate and serve.

VARIATIONS

◆ Use a mix of chicories instead of only Castelfranco.

◆ Pears, Asian pears, or persimmons can be substituted for or added to the apples.

◆ Other nuts can replace the walnuts.

◆ A few shavings of a richly flavored cheese such as cheddar, Gruyère, or a sheep's-milk or goat cheese are delicious on this salad.

# Tardivo Radicchio and Farro Salad with Dried Persimmons

4 SERVINGS

Tardivo radicchio has a mysterious look. It reminds me of a clump of witch's fingers—long, thin bone white stems topped with curling, deep burgundy tips. It is gorgeous and delicious. The preponderance of white stem makes it sweeter than many radicchios.

Cut in half:

**6 slices dried persimmon**

Cut each half into quarters. Toss the cut persimmon with:

**1 teaspoon sherry vinegar**

**1 tablespoon hot water**

**A pinch of Marash pepper**

Set aside to plump. Bring a large pot of salted water to a boil. Stir in:

**¾ cup farro**

Cook at a simmer until tender, about 20 minutes or so. Drain and transfer to a bowl. Trim the root end from:

**3 small heads of Tardivo radicchio**

Separate into individual leaves and wash and dry well.

Make a dressing. Mix together:

**2 teaspoons sherry or Banyuls vinegar**

**Salt**

**Fresh-ground black pepper**

**1 mint sprig**

Stir to dissolve the salt. Whisk in:

**3 tablespoons extra-virgin olive oil**

Taste for salt and acid and adjust as needed. Toss the farro with two thirds of the dressing; remove the mint sprig. Stir in the plumped persimmons and:

**12 mint leaves, cut into a fine chiffonade**

**3 scallions, trimmed and sliced thin**

**¼ teaspoon Marash pepper**

**1 tablespoon chopped parsley**

Toss the radicchio leaves with the rest of the dressing and fold into the farro.

VARIATION

◆ Instead of tossing the radicchio leaves with the farro, brush them with vinaigrette and put a spoonful of the farro salad in the tip for a passed appetizer.

# Treviso Radicchio, Merguez Sausage, and Whole-Wheat Spaghetti

4 SERVINGS

Merguez, a small North African–style spicy lamb sausage, is particularly good with the strong flavor of fall chicories. Sweet vinegar added at the end tempers the bitterness in a delicious way. I prefer an *agrodolce* (sweet-and-sour) Zinfandel or Cabernet red wine vinegar with good flavor to an overly sweet generic balsamic.

Trim and cut crosswise into wide ribbons:

**2 large or three medium heads of Treviso radicchio**

Rinse in a colander and let drain.

Heat a large sauté pan over medium heat, and add:

**2 teaspoons olive oil**

**8 merguez sausages, or 4 spicy pork sausages**

Cook the sausages until browned and just cooked through. Prick the sausages to release some of the juices, then remove them from the pan and set aside to keep warm. Bring a pot of salted water to a boil. Add:

**¾ pound whole-wheat spaghetti**

While the pasta cooks, wilt the radicchio in the sausage juices in the sauté pan over medium heat. Just before the pasta is cooked al dente, make a well in the radicchio in the pan, and add:

**1 tablespoon olive oil**

**2 garlic cloves, chopped**

Let the garlic soften, then stir into the wilted radicchio. Add, to taste:

**Salt**

**Fresh-ground black pepper**

**2 to 3 teaspoons sweet red wine vinegar**

When the pasta is cooked, drain it in a colander, reserving some of the cooking liquid. Add the drained pasta to the pan, toss everything together, and add a splash of the pasta water to keep it loose. Taste and adjust for salt and vinegar, if needed. Serve on warm plates with the sausages.

## Roasted Radicchio Pizza with Pancetta and Fried Rosemary

MAKES ONE 10- TO 12-INCH PIZZA

Preheat the oven to 500°F. If you have one, place a baking stone on the lower rack and heat it for 30 minutes before baking the pizza. Wash and dry well:

**Leaves from 1 small head of radicchio or chicory (about ¼ pound)**

Toss the leaves with:

**A splash of white wine**

**A splash of white wine vinegar**

**A splash of olive oil**

**Salt**

**Fresh-ground black pepper**

Spread on a parchment-paper-lined baking sheet and roast until wilted and slightly browned, about 12 minutes.

Cut into ¼-inch sticks:

**Two ¼-inch-thick slices pancetta**

Heat a small heavy-bottomed pan over medium-high heat. Pour in:

**2 teaspoons olive oil**

Add the pancetta and cook, stirring occasionally, until lightly colored. Remove from the pan and add:

**½ onion, diced**

Cook until soft, about 10 minutes.

Mix together in a small bowl:

**1 garlic clove, chopped fine**

**1 tablespoon olive oil**

Stretch out:

**One 6-ounce ball Pizza Dough (page 147)**

Place on a floured peel and brush the garlic oil over the dough, leaving the edge bare. Sprinkle on:

**⅓ cup grated mozzarella cheese**

Spread the radicchio over the cheese and sprinkle the pancetta lardons over the radicchio. Slide the pizza onto the stone and bake until puffed and browned, 5 to 8 minutes. If you don't have a stone, place the pizza on a pizza pan and bake. Remove from the oven and sprinkle with:

**2 tablespoons Fried Rosemary (page 27)**

Cut and serve.

VARIATION

◆ Crack an egg into a coffee cup. When the pizza is in the oven carefully tip the egg onto the center of the pizza.

## Chopped Pan di Zucchero Chicory Salad

4 SERVINGS

Cut in half lengthwise:

**1 head of Pan di Zucchero**

Wrap up one of the halves and store in the refrigerator for later. Cut the other half into crosswise ribbons. Wash and dry well.

Make the dressing. Mix together in a small bowl:

**2 teaspoons lemon juice**

**1 teaspoon red wine vinegar**

**1 garlic clove, smashed to a fine purée**

**Grated zest of 1 lemon**

**Salt**

Whisk in:

**1½ tablespoons olive oil**

**2½ tablespoons crème fraîche**

Taste for salt and acid and adjust as needed.

Trim the root end from:

**2 radishes**

**1 scarlet turnip**

Peel:

**2 sunchokes**

**1 carrot, any color**

Slice all the vegetables thinly; a mandoline makes this job easy. Put the Pan di Zucchero in a large bowl with the dressing, sliced vegetables, and:

**1 tablespoon chopped chives**

**1 teaspoon chopped parsley**

Toss well and plate. Garnish with:

**1 hard-cooked egg, peeled and chopped**

## Belgian Endive Leaf Hors d'Oeuvres

Raw Belgian endive leaves make perfect flavorful little boats to fill with a little something and serve as passed appetizers and hors d'oeuvres. Season the leaves with a touch of salt or brush them with a little vinaigrette before spooning in the filling. Here are a few ideas for fillings:

◆ Halibut Ceviche with Lime (page 315).

◆ Smoked trout with chervil and crème fraîche.

◆ Fish Tartare with Pickled Buddha's Hand (page 324).

◆ Fresh salmon roe with chives and crème fraîche.

◆ Tardivo Radicchio and Farro Salad with Dried Persimmons (page 200).

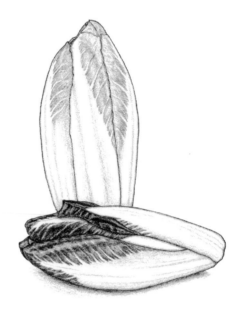

# Puntarelle Chicory with Lemon, Garlic, and Anchovies

4 SERVINGS

The first time I saw puntarelle in the markets of Rome I was amazed. What is that? I asked. The large green leaves surrounding the spiky heart seemed perfectly alien. Later, after having the classic Roman salad with this pungent dressing, I was in love. Anchovies, lemon, and garlic are a perfect match for the bittersweet flavor of all chicories, and puntarelle is no exception.

When dressing the salad, don't be shy; I really don't think it can be overdressed. Add a hard-cooked egg and this salad makes a lovely lunch.

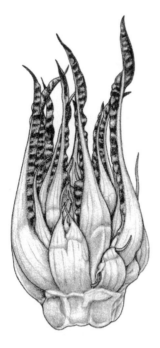

Remove all the leaves from:

**1 head of puntarelle**

Save the white, crisp stems of the leaves and compost the dark green ones. Trim the bottom root end from the heart and cut the heart in half lengthwise. Separate each spike, or *puntarella*, from the heart, cut each in half lengthwise, and then cut them into long, thin strips. Soak the cut puntarelle in ice water to crisp and curl.

Prepare the dressing. Mix together:

**1 tablespoon lemon juice**
**1 teaspoon red wine vinegar**
**Salt**
**Fresh-ground black pepper**
**1 garlic clove, pounded to a purée**
**4 salt-cured anchovy fillets, chopped**

Stir to dissolve the salt and whisk in:

**¼ cup extra-virgin olive oil**

Taste for salt and acid and adjust as needed. When ready to serve, drain the puntarelle, spin-dry, and toss with the dressing.

VARIATIONS

• Garnish with a dusting of grated Parmesan cheese.

• Add the grated zest of 1 lemon to the lemon juice when making the vinaigrette.

• Add thin slices of sunchokes or scarlet turnips.

• Toss 1 tablespoon of parsley leaves with the puntarelle.

• Substitute 2 tablespoons of cream for 2 tablespoons of the olive oil.

# Puntarelle Chicory Soup with Chicken Meatballs

MAKES ABOUT 1 QUART

Broths with greens make some of the most satisfying winter soups. Use the tender small leaves and white stems of the larger leaves as well as the interior pointy spikes. Beans and tender chicken meatballs turn this soup into a festive meal.

Cut away all the leaves of:

**1 large head of puntarelle**

Save the tender inner leaves and the white stems of the larger leaves. Trim the bottom root end from the puntarelle and cut in half lengthwise. Separate the individual spikes or puntarelle, cut them in half lengthwise, and then diagonally into thin slices. Try to keep the slices bite-size. Cut the stems and leaves into bite-size pieces. Toss the cut puntarelle with salt.

Prepare the meatballs. Cut the crusts from:

**2 thick slices day-old country-style bread**

Cut the slices into cubes; you should have about 1 cup. Put them in a bowl and cover with water.

Put in a large bowl:

**1 pound ground chicken, dark meat**
**1 teaspoon salt**

**1 tablespoon red wine**
**Fresh-ground black pepper**
**1 egg**
**2 garlic cloves, pounded to a rough paste**
**¼ cup freshly grated Parmesan cheese**
**1 teaspoon chopped marjoram**
**2 teaspoons chopped parsley**
**A pinch of dried chile flakes (optional)**

Drain the bread, squeezing out the water. Crumble the bread into the bowl with the other ingredients. Using stiff open fingers like a comb, mix gently until the ingredients are well combined. Take a small ball of the mixture and poach it in boiling salted water. Taste for salt and spices and adjust as needed. Roll the mixture into small meatballs. Refrigerate until needed.

Pour into a large pot:

**3 cups chicken stock (preferably homemade)**

Season with:

**Salt**

Bring to a boil and add the puntarelle. Cook for 5 minutes. Add the meatballs and:

**1 cup cooked cannellini beans**

Cook until the meatballs are done, about 6 minutes. Taste the soup for salt and season as needed. Serve garnished with:

**Freshly grated Parmesan cheese**
**A drizzle of good olive oil**

# Essential Greens

## Kale, Collard Greens, Broccoli Rabe, Chard, Spinach, Amaranth, and Asian Greens

GREENS ARE INDISPENSABLE in my kitchen, but they weren't always. When I was young, the only green we ate was spinach. All the others had a bad reputation for flavor—their only redeeming quality was that they were good for you. I have to admit I resisted them just for that reason. The idea of eating them for breakfast, lunch, or dinner (as I do now!) was unimaginable. Only when I traveled to Italy did I discover how delicious greens really are. The markets there were filled with them: kale, chard, broccoli rabe, beet greens, and turnip tops, along with all sorts of wild greens I had never seen before. I ate mounds of garlicky greens—in antipastos, on grilled bread, in soups, cooked with eggs, on pizza, with roasted meat and earthy beans. Now I crave the bitter-savory flavors of greens and love them as much as I do salad. With fresh greens in the kitchen and growing in the garden, I always have the makings of a quick and satisfying meal.

# Recipes

Garden Greens and Goat Cheese Pasta  209

Green Polenta with Red Russian Kale  210

Lacinato Kale Salad with Salt-Preserved Kumquats
and Parmesan  210

Collard Greens with Cumin and Black Mustard Seeds  211

Broccoli Rabe and Ricotta Pancakes with
Lemon-Coriander Butter  213

Lemon-Coriander Butter  213

Chickpea and Broccoli Rabe Soup  214

Golden Chard and Bulgur Pilaf  215

Bloomsdale Spinach Sformato  216

Spinach and Pork Crépinettes  217

Spiced Spinach with Fried Paneer Cheese  218

Paneer Cheese  219

Ricotta and Amaranth Cannelloni  220

Bok Choy Sautéed with Ginger and Garlic  221

Salumi with Mustard Flowers  221

Red Mustard Salad with Asian Pears and Pecans  222

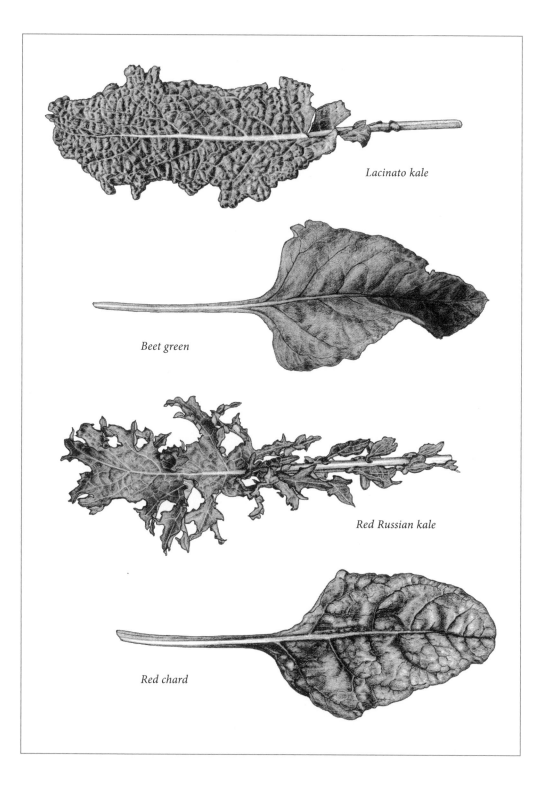

Lacinato kale

Beet green

Red Russian kale

Red chard

# Leafy Greens in the Garden

If you have never grown leafy greens, you must try. They are an easy and generous addition to the kitchen garden. The crinkled and frilly leaves of the different kales and the cool gray-green colors of collards are beautiful. Chard makes a striking sight with colorful stems holding up shiny dark green leaves. Recently I wanted more purple and red in the garden, so I started growing purple kale and an amazing lacy-leaf red mustard that I bought simply because I liked the way it looked. Now I love the way it tastes as well. I am also growing more and more varieties of Asian greens, which are all gorgeous and tasty. I am not surprised to hear from farmers that they are growing more and more greens, and different varieties, to meet their customers' demand. Our farmers' markets are almost as full of greens as those Italian markets that got me started eating greens in the first place.

Whether planted in the ground or in containers, greens are quick-growing and produce lots of leaves to harvest over an extended period of time. Feed them compost as you plant them and water them regularly and you will have plenty of greens for the kitchen. As a general rule, greens prefer cool weather, thriving in spring and fall. That said, there are varieties that can withstand heat or cold and climates where greens can be harvested all winter and all summer.

When harvesting greens, cut away the outer leaves and leave the central heart intact so it will keep sprouting new leaves. Some greens, such as broccoli rabe, tatsoi, and mustards, can be cut off an inch above the ground, cut-and-come-again style, to grow back at least once for another harvest and sometimes up to three times.

# Kale (*Brassica oleracea*)
# Collard Greens (*Brassica napus*)

*Lacinato* kale, also called Tuscan flat black cabbage, looks formidable, with long, dark, puckered leaves; but it is actually quite tender when in season and, to my mind, the tastiest member of the kale family. *Red Russian* kale is sweet and pretty with red-tinged deeply cut leaves. *Siberian* kale has amazingly frilly blue-green leaves. *Portuguese* kale has rounded, flat, blue-green leaves similar to collard greens. *Champion* collard greens are tasty and hardy in the cold, while *Vates* will do well in the heat.

The young leaves of lacinato and Red Russian kale are good raw in a salad as well as steamed or sautéed. More mature kale and collard greens have sturdy leaves that benefit from being precooked in salted boiling water before sautéing, unless they are going directly into a hearty soup or pilaf. When you grow kale and collards, you can take advantage of the tender flowering stalks and brilliant yellow flowers that come as the plants mature. Steam the flower stalks and then sauté them with a bit of garlic for a special treat. No need to cook the flowers— just sprinkle them over pastas and salads.

Kale and collards need little care beyond a good amount of compost and consistent watering. For the most part, kale is a cool-weather crop. Heat will cause its leaves to become tough and bitter, while cold weather and frost turns them tender and sweet. Siberian kale can survive snow and freezing temperatures. Lacinato kale grows tall, resembling a miniature palm tree in the garden. Red Russian kale can be sowed and harvested as a cut-and-come-again crop; if you let it go to flower, the plants will reseed themselves easily. When they come up the next season, just pull out the ones that are growing where you don't want them to. Their leaves are quite distinct and easy to spot. Toss the thinnings into a salad.

Collard greens will survive both the hottest days of summer and the dead of winter. There are perennial tree collards, which grow for years in mild climates. They are started with cuttings instead of seeds.

# Garden Greens and Goat Cheese Pasta

4 SERVINGS

This pasta is tasty made with kale, collards, or any other greens you have growing in the garden. I will go and cut whatever is ready or use what I brought home from the farmers' market. I like to include something that has a bit of spice, such as broccoli rabe, red mustards, or mature rocket. Many times I will cook more greens than I need and put them in the refrigerator to make a quick pasta another time. (Add the garlic and goat cheese at the time you are going to toss them with the pasta.) This is perfect for those days when dinnertime shows up before you know it.

Pull the tough stems away from the leaves of:

**1 bunch of kale (lacinato, Red Russian, or Siberian)**

Put the stems into the compost bucket and wash the leaves in cool water. Drain. Cook the leaves until tender in boiling salted water. Remove from the water and let cool. Bring the water back to a boil and add:

**1 pound whole-wheat spaghetti**

While the pasta is cooking, heat a heavy-bottomed skillet over medium-high heat and pour in:

**2 tablespoons extra-virgin olive oil**

Stir in the greens and heat through. Move the greens from the center of the pan and add:

**2 garlic cloves, finely chopped**

Allow to cook for a minute and stir into the greens. Taste for salt and add as needed. When the pasta is cooked, drain it in a colander, reserving some of the cooking liquid. Add the drained pasta to the greens with:

**⅓ cup crumbled fresh goat cheese**
**A pinch of dried chile flakes**
**A drizzle of extra-virgin olive oil**

Stir the greens, pasta, and goat cheese together. The cheese will melt, making a creamy sauce. Add cooking water as needed to loosen. Taste for salt one last time before serving.

VARIATION

◆ Depending on how sharp the cheese is, sometimes I add a splash of vinegar to the finished greens.

# Green Polenta with Red Russian Kale

4 SERVINGS

This is a beautiful dish: the puréed kale turns the polenta a bright green color and gives it a fresh taste. I have suggested the red-tinged, deeply cut leaves of Red Russian kale for this recipe, but lacinato kale or curly Siberian kale would be delicious, too. For a creamier polenta, ladle a dollop of mascarpone cheese on top.

Whole-grain polenta is becoming easier to find. There are many heritage and heirloom varieties of corn being grown that make polenta with a richer and deeper flavor than the common polished variety. As with wheat and other whole grains, being freshly milled makes a big difference. Find out if there is a mill near you or a farmer who is bringing fresh grain to market. If not, there are numerous small mills that will ship it to you. Be sure to store whole-grain polenta in the refrigerator, as it will quickly spoil and go rancid when exposed to light and heat.

Bring 3 cups of water to a boil in a heavy-bottomed pot. When the water is boiling, slowly whisk in:

**1 teaspoon salt**
**1 cup whole-grain polenta**

Keep whisking until the polenta is suspended in the water and no longer sinking to the bottom of the pot. Turn down the heat and cook for 1 hour at a bare simmer, stirring now and then. If the polenta gets very thick, add water as needed, but keep it fairly thick, as the greens will loosen it when they are added later.

Meanwhile, pull the tough stems away from the leaves of:

**1 bunch of Red Russian kale**

Wash the leaves and drain. Cook until tender in boiling salted water. Drain well, reserving 1 cup or so of the cooking liquid, and let cool. Place the cooked greens in a blender or food processor and purée with:

**2 teaspoons butter or olive oil**
**Salt**

Add a splash of the cooking liquid if needed to get it to purée. Or chop the kale very fine and stir in the salt and fat. You should have about 1 cup of purée.

When the polenta is done cooking, add the kale purée along with:

**¼ cup grated Parmesan cheese**
**1 tablespoon butter or olive oil**

# Lacinato Kale Salad with Salt-Preserved Kumquats and Parmesan

4 SERVINGS

Younger tender kale leaves are best for this salad. The sweet and salty kumquats accent the deep green flavor of the kale, while the crisp nuts and cheese add a rich flavor and texture. Much like coleslaw, kale salad is better when it has had a chance to sit after it is dressed. The vinaigrette softens and flavors the leaves. Kale salad is perfect for a picnic or buffet lunch or dinner.

Preheat the oven to 350°F. Toast until deep golden brown:

**¼ cup hazelnuts**

When the nuts are cool, roll them in your hands to remove the skins.

Strip the stems from:

**1 small bunch of young lacinato kale**

Wash and dry thoroughly. Stack the leaves and cut them crosswise into thin ribbons. Whisk together in a small bowl:

**1 tablespoon lemon or Meyer lemon juice**

**1 teaspoon white wine vinegar**

**Salt**

**Fresh-ground black pepper**

**1 tablespoon chopped Salt-Preserved Kumquats (page 352)**

Whisk in:

**⅓ cup extra-virgin olive oil**

Taste for salt and acid, and adjust as needed. Toss the kale with the dressing and let sit for 10 minutes or so. Chop the hazelnuts coarsely, and with a sharp vegetable peeler shave:

**1 ounce Parmesan cheese**

When ready to serve, toss the salad with the nuts and cheese.

VARIATIONS

• Add some Ruby Streak mustard leaves for color and flavor.

• Thinly slice a few stalks of celery and add them to the kale with the dressing.

• Use preserved lemon or Meyer lemon in the dressing instead of kumquats, and add 1 garlic clove pounded to a purée.

• Substitute thinly sliced Brussels sprouts for half of the kale.

• Use fresh pecorino or another sheep's-milk cheese in place of the Parmesan.

# Collard Greens with Cumin and Black Mustard Seeds

4 SERVINGS

Collard greens are very popular in India. The sweet and bitter flavors of the cooked leaves go very well with the pungent spices used in the local cuisine. Serve these greens with saffron rice and raita for a light lunch. Yogurt-Spiced Chicken Skewers (page 183) are delicious with them, too.

Remove the stems from:

**1 bunch of collard greens**

Wash and drain the leaves, and cook until tender in boiling salted water. Drain and let cool. Cut the leaves crosswise into a fine chiffonade. Put a heavy-bottomed pan over medium heat and pour in:

**1 tablespoon coconut oil or olive oil**

When hot, add:

**½ teaspoon cumin seeds**

**¼ teaspoon black mustard seeds**

Let the spices sizzle for 30 seconds and add:

**1 onion, sliced thin**

Cook over medium heat until soft, about 5 minutes. Add the collard greens and season with:

**Salt**

Cook partly covered for another 4 minutes, stirring occasionally. Taste for salt and adjust as needed.

VARIATION

• Use kale, chard, or spigarello broccoli (see page 231) instead of collard greens.

## Broccoli Rabe (*Brassica rapa*)

Broccoli rabe has a nutty spicy flavor that I love. Don't overlook the stems; they are the sweetest part of the plant. I trim any woody ends from the stalks and cook the rest. Broccoli rabe is tender enough to need no precooking, although some recipes call for it. I usually cook it in a bit of oil, with the water from washing still clinging to the leaves, and finish it with plenty of garlic and dried chile flakes to use as a pasta sauce or a side dish. I could eat it every day. Or I let the greens cool and then toss them with a vinaigrette for an antipasto or to eat in a sandwich with a bit of fresh ricotta. Delicious.

Broccoli rabe grows easily in the garden, but it is particularly sensitive to heat and will run to flower and develop woody stems as temperatures rise. I like to plant it densely and harvest it as a cut-and-come-again crop when it is still fairly small. Some varieties make large florets. Be sure to harvest the plants as soon as the florets are formed, for they will soon flower. Look for a variety that grows best in the season you are planting in. You will also find it listed in catalogs as rapini, *cima di rapa*, and raab.

# Broccoli Rabe and Ricotta Pancakes with Lemon-Coriander Butter

4 SERVINGS

Serve these pancakes with a green salad as a light meal, or as a side dish to a roast or a bowl of savory beans. They make a wonderful passed hors d'oeuvre or appetizer.

Trim the tough ends from:

**¾ bunch of broccoli rabe**

Chop coarsely and wash thoroughly. Drain. Heat a heavy-bottomed pan over medium-high heat. Put the broccoli rabe in the pan and cook until wilted and soft. Spread out on a plate to cool. When cool, squeeze out the excess water and reserve ¼ cup. You should have about 1 cup cooked, squeezed broccoli rabe.

While the greens cool, measure into a bowl:

**¾ cup unbleached all-purpose flour**

**1 tablespoon baking powder**

**1 teaspoon salt**

**A pinch of cayenne pepper**

Measure:

**⅔ cup milk**

Separate:

**1 egg**

Set aside the egg white and stir the yolk into the milk along with the reserved ¼ cup of cooking water. Pour the milk mixture into the flour and mix lightly with a fork. If the batter is very thick, add a splash more milk or water.

Add:

**2 tablespoons butter, melted**

**3 scallions, sliced fine**

Fold in the broccoli rabe along with:

**2 teaspoons marjoram, chopped fine**

**2 tablespoons parsley, chopped fine**

**1 cup ricotta cheese**

**½ cup grated Parmesan cheese**

Whisk the egg white until it forms soft peaks and fold it into the batter. Heat a cast-iron pan or griddle over medium heat. When hot, wipe with a paper towel moistened with olive oil. Spoon the batter onto the hot pan. Smaller cakes—about 3 inches across—work better than larger ones. Turn after 2 minutes or so, or when the underside is brown and the cake has set a little. Cook until set all the way through, about 2 minutes more. Oil the pan between each batch. Serve the pancakes with a dab of:

**Lemon-Coriander Butter (recipe follows)**

VARIATIONS

• Any green can be used in place of the broccoli rabe: spinach, chard, collards, kale, borage, beet greens, and so on.

• Substitute other herbs, such as mint, chervil, cilantro, anise hyssop, or chives, for all or part of the marjoram.

# Lemon-Coriander Butter

MAKES 3 TABLESPOONS

This is a compound butter—butter softened and flavored with different herbs and spices. It is served soft, to gently melt from the heat of the pancakes. Compound butters are also a delicious way to add fresh herb flavors to grilled, roasted, or sautéed meats and vegetables at the moment of serving. Compound butters will keep for a few days in the refrigerator and 1 to 2 months in the freezer.

Stir together until well mixed:

**3 tablespoons butter, softened**

**¼ teaspoon salt**

**Grated zest of 1 lemon**

**Juice of ½ lemon**

**1 teaspoon coriander seeds, toasted and coarsely crushed**

**2 cilantro sprigs, coarsely chopped**

Taste for salt and add more if needed.

## Chickpea and Broccoli Rabe Soup

MAKES ABOUT 2 QUARTS

Heat a heavy-bottomed pot over medium heat. Add:

**2 teaspoons olive oil**

**2 slices pancetta, chopped fine**

Cook for 3 minutes and then add:

**1 large or 2 small carrots, peeled and diced**

**2 celery stalks, diced**

**1 onion, diced**

**4 oregano sprigs**

**A pinch of dried chile flakes (optional)**

Cook, stirring now and then, until soft and lightly browned, about 12 minutes. Turn down the heat if the vegetables start to brown too quickly. When the vegetables are cooked, add:

**Salt**

**4 garlic cloves, chopped**

**2 cups cooked chickpeas**

Cook for a few minutes and pour in:

**2 cups chickpea cooking liquid**

**2 cups chicken stock**

Bring to a boil and reduce to a simmer. Cook for 10 minutes.

Meanwhile, trim off and discard the woody stems from:

**1 bunch of broccoli rabe**

Wash and drain, chop coarsely, and add to the soup. Cook for another 10 minutes. Test a large rabe stem. If it is not tender, cook the soup a few more minutes. Taste for salt and adjust as needed. Serve garnished with:

**A drizzle of extra-virgin olive oil**

VARIATIONS

◆ Use 1 small bulb of fennel in place of the celery.

◆ Use cannellini or borlotti (cranberry) beans instead of chickpeas.

## Chard  (*Beta vulgaris*)

Chard is easy to grow in both flower beds and containers, and it yields a long and prolific harvest with very little effort. *Bright Lights* and *Rainbow* chard, with their neon-colored stems and leaves that range from dark green to bronze, taste great and are beautiful. *Erbette* chard, also called *Verde da Taglio*, is very tender, with small stems. It responds well to being harvested cut-and-come-again style, cooks quickly, and tastes like a cross between chard and spinach (and is much easier to grow than spinach).

Use chard for any recipe calling for leafy greens. I love it sautéed, cooled, and then mixed with a bit of vinegar and wrapped in a slice of prosciutto or watermelon radish. Or serve it hot with a generous blast of minced garlic and dried chile flakes. Try it cooked in minestrone or another vegetable soup. A frittata with chard, caramelized onions, and feta cheese gets rave reviews every time I make it. To cook chard evenly, separate the stems from the leaves, slice the stems, and add them to the pan a few minutes before the leaves.

In the garden, chard needs a good amount of sunshine and soil with good drainage. When planting, add a dash of compost, sow the seeds thickly, and water consistently. Pull the thinnings as young plants until there are a few well-spaced plants left. As these mature, harvest the outer leaves and enjoy steady production for months to come.

# Golden Chard and Bulgur Pilaf

4 SERVINGS

Bulgur is a common ingredient in Middle Eastern and Turkish food. It is the grain you find in tabbouleh salad. Bulgur is made from wheat berries that are parboiled until soft and then air-dried and crushed. The precooking makes bulgur a quick-cooking shelf-stable whole grain. Bulgur comes in different grades based on how coarsely or finely it is crushed—number one is the finest. A little hot red pepper paste adds flavor and gentle heat to the pilaf, as do the Aleppo and Marash peppers, which are only slightly spicy and have loads of sweet flavor. Both peppers are sold in Middle Eastern stores

and by spice purveyors and are versatile additions to your spice cabinet. (Note that if you use red chard, the pilaf will turn red.)

Wash and drain:

**1 bunch of golden chard**

Remove the stems and slice thinly. Stack the leaves and cut into ½-inch-wide strips. Put the sliced stems and leaves into a large, heavy-bottomed pot with:

**2 medium onions, diced**

**1 head of garlic, broken into cloves, peeled, and coarsely chopped**

**1 cup coarse-grained bulgur (#3)**

**¼ cup extra-virgin olive oil**

**1 tablespoon hot red pepper paste**

**½ teaspoon Aleppo or Marash pepper**

**Salt**

**Fresh-ground black pepper**

**1 cup water**

Cover the pan tightly and cook over low heat for half an hour, stirring occasionally. The bulgur should be chewy and tender. Turn off the heat, cover, and let sit for 15 minutes to allow the bulgur to absorb the steam. Serve garnished with:

**3 scallions, sliced thin**

*Dried chile flakes*

## Spinach (*Spinacia oleracea*)

*Bloomsdale* spinach's dark green crinkled leaves are full of rich, sweet flavor. Try them cooked or raw. Purée them to make green pasta or mix them with ricotta to make a filling for cannelloni and ravioli. Make a spinach soup with onions and garlic and purée it for an amazing green potage. Or cook spinach leaves with a knob of butter for a dish of delicious simplicity. I like tiny spinach leaves in salads, and larger leaves are good in warm salads with bacon and croutons.

I have found spinach to be a little particular in my garden and instead I grow other easier-to-cultivate greens. But try growing it anyway, especially if you love spinach. Eliot Coleman, renowned organic greenhouse gardener in Maine, says that spinach is his most productive leafy crop all winter long. Spinach prefers cool weather, moist soil, and a good dash of compost to start. It is very cold hardy and can winter over in many climates. Plant densely to harvest as a cut-and-come-again crop, or allow it to mature and harvest only the outer leaves, leaving the heart intact to continue producing.

## Bloomsdale Spinach Sformato

4 SERVINGS

*Sformato* means "unmolded" in Italian, which is a very accurate way of describing this dish. It's not really a soufflé, because it doesn't use stiffly beaten egg whites to make it light and airy. Instead, it is luscious and dense and filled with sweet spinach flavor.

Italian chef Benedetta Vitali inspired me to use ricotta instead of béchamel sauce.

Wash and drain:
  **2 pounds spinach, stems removed**
Heat a heavy-bottomed pan over medium-high heat and add:
  **1 teaspoon olive oil**
  **A large pinch of salt**
Add the spinach and cook, stirring now and then, until it is wilted and cooked through. Spread out on a plate and when cool, squeeze out the excess liquid. Return the liquid to the pan and reduce to a few tablespoons. Preheat the oven to 350°F. Finely chop the spinach and return to the pan. (For a uniformly green color, blend the mixture with a hand blender or purée in a food processor.) Stir into the pan with the spinach, mixing thoroughly:
  **½ pound ricotta cheese (about 1 cup)**
  **⅓ cup grated Parmesan cheese**
  **2 eggs, beaten**
  **3 tablespoons olive oil**
  **Salt**
  **Fresh-ground black pepper**
  **A small pinch of cayenne pepper**
Butter a 6-inch-square baking dish. Pour in the spinach mixture and place the dish in a slightly larger ovenproof pan. Pour in enough warm water to come two thirds of the way up the sides of the sformato dish. Bake until just set in the middle, about 35 minutes. Serve warm or cool.

VARIATIONS
✦ Bake in 4 individual ramekins.
✦ Substitute other greens for part or all of the spinach. Nettles, lamb's-quarters, borage, and other tender greens are good choices.

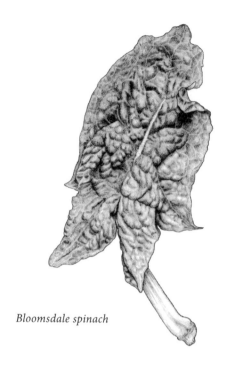

*Bloomsdale spinach*

# Spinach and Pork Crépinettes

MAKES 4 LARGE OR 8 SMALL CRÉPINETTES

*Crépinettes*—flat, round sausages—are named after the thin lacy caul fat, or *crépine*, that they are wrapped in. Crépinettes are easy to make at home, unlike traditional sausages, because they can be stuffed without any special equipment. Be sure to buy caul fat from the same sustainable producers that your pork comes from. Caul fat browns beautifully when cooked and makes juicy, tender sausages.

Wash and drain:

**1 pound spinach, stems removed**

Heat a heavy-bottomed pan over medium-high heat and add:

**1 teaspoon olive oil**

**A large pinch of salt**

Add the spinach and cook, stirring now and then, until it is wilted and cooked through. Spread out on a plate to cool. When it is cool enough to handle, squeeze out the excess liquid from the spinach and chop. Put the spinach in a medium-size bowl and add:

**¾ pound ground pork**

**1 teaspoon salt**

**¼ teaspoon fresh-ground black pepper**

**4 garlic cloves, chopped fine**

**1 tablespoon red wine or ½ teaspoon red wine vinegar**

**A pinch of cayenne pepper**

**2 thyme sprigs, leaves only, chopped**

Mix gently, using your rigid fingers as combs to blend the ingredients lightly and evenly without warming, or smearing, the meat. To taste for seasoning, fry a small flat patty of the mixture. (Keep the mix refrigerated while cooking the tester.) Add more salt to the mixture as needed. Wine brightens the other flavors and brings them forward, so add more if you feel it is needed. Put a small drop of wine on your taster patty and see if tastes better with a touch more.

Rinse and drain:

**¼ pound caul fat**

Spread out the caul fat on a cutting board. Put a spoonful of sausage in a corner of the caul fat and cut around it so there is a 1½-inch border of fat surrounding the sausage. Fold the caul fat around the meat and gently flatten the patty. The fat should completely encase the meat. If it doesn't, unwrap and try again with a larger piece of caul fat. Wrap up all the crépinettes and refrigerate until ready to cook.

Heat a heavy-bottomed pan (cast iron is

perfect) over medium-high heat. When the pan is hot, add:

> **Oil (just enough to coat the bottom of the pan)**

Add the crépinettes, without crowding them, and cook until well browned, about 5 minutes. Lower the heat if they are browning too quickly. Turn and cook until done, another 5 minutes or so.

# Spiced Spinach with Fried Paneer Cheese

4 SERVINGS

This recipe is based on the Indian dish *saag paneer*. When fried, paneer cheese turns a delicious crispy brown; and its flavor perfectly complements and tempers spicy spinach.

Wash, dry well, and chop coarsely:

> **¾ pound baby spinach, or 2 large bunches of mature spinach, stems removed**

Pound fine using a mortar and pestle (or grind in a spice grinder):

> **2 cloves**
> **¼ teaspoon coriander seeds**
> **Half the seeds of 1 cardamom pod**
> **A pinch of black mustard seeds**

Heat a heavy-bottomed pan over medium-high heat and add:

> **1 tablespoon olive oil or ghee**

When the pan is hot, add:

> **6 ounces Paneer Cheese (recipe follows), cut into 1-inch cubes (about 1½ cups)**

Cook the paneer, turning now and then until the cubes are browned on at least 2 sides, about 7 minutes. Remove the cheese from the pan and add:

> **1 teaspoon olive oil or ghee**
> **4 garlic cloves, finely chopped**
> **1 teaspoon minced fresh ginger**
> **1 green serrano chile, minced**
> **¼ teaspoon cumin seeds**

Cook for 1 minute, stirring now and then. Add:

> **1 onion, diced**

Cook, stirring occasionally, until the onion is soft and translucent, about 7 minutes. Turn down the heat if the onion starts to brown. When the onions are done, stir in the ground spices along with:

> **Salt**
> **¼ teaspoon turmeric**
> **A pinch of dried chile flakes**

Cook for 1 or 2 minutes. Add the spinach and cook until it is wilted, about 4 minutes. Stir in the browned paneer and:

> **¼ cup plain yogurt**

Cook for another 1 or 2 minutes. Taste for salt and adjust as needed. If desired, finish the dish with:

> **A squeeze of lemon or lime juice**

VARIATIONS

◆ For half the spinach, substitute ½ pound chard leaves, beet greens, or fresh fenugreek leaves. (If using chard or beet greens, cook them for a few minutes before adding the spinach.)

◆ For a richer dish, add a splash of heavy cream along with the yogurt.

◆ For a spicier version, add more green chiles or a pinch of cayenne pepper.

# Paneer Cheese

MAKES 6 OUNCES CHEESE

Paneer, also spelled *panir*, is a fresh cheese used in Indian cooking. I use buttermilk to make paneer, because I like the underlying rich tang it gives to the cheese. Use fresh organic milk; do not use ultra-pasturized milk, as it will not form curds.

Pour into a heavy-bottomed pot:

**6 cups (1½ quarts) whole milk**

Measure and set aside:

**3 cups buttermilk**

Heat the milk over medium heat, stirring now and then to keep it from scorching, to 190°F. Pour in the buttermilk and stir briefly. Bring the temperature back to 190°F. The milk and buttermilk will coagulate and separate into white curds and a lighter, yellowish-colored whey. Turn off the heat and let it sit undisturbed for 10 minutes. Place a strainer over a large bowl and line with damp butter muslin or cheesecloth. Gently ladle the curds from the pot with a slotted spoon into the cloth-lined strainer. Gently stir in:

**1½ teaspoons salt**

Let drain until cool enough to touch. Fold the cheesecloth around the cheese and remove it from the strainer. Press on the cheese to remove more whey. Put the cheese on a plate with another plate or a small cutting board on top and weigh it down with a weight such as a small canister or jar filled with water. Refrigerate and let drain for 2 hours. Unwrap and store for up to 2 days—however, paneer tastes the very best the day it is made.

# Amaranth (*Amaranthus caudatus*)

I discovered amaranth about thirty years ago at my farmers' market, but it has been an important food around the world for millennia. There are both green- and red-leaf varieties. The tender young leaves are delicious raw in salad and the larger leaves, still tender, cook much like spinach, but with a richer, nuttier flavor. Amaranth is even more nutritious than spinach with loads of vitamin C, calcium, and even some protein. The seeds are edible as well, though I have only cooked the leaves.

Amaranth is a heat-loving plant and will do well in drought situations. It is easy to grow and the colorful plants are quite ornamental, making them a perfect edible addition to the flower garden. Plant it after any threat of frost in full to partial sun. Amaranth is a great hot weather stand-in for spinach. The many edible varieties are often divided into two categories: vegetable amaranths, grown for their leaves, and grain amaranths, grown for their seeds (though their leaves are perfectly good to eat, too). *Red Leaf*, or *Red Callaloo* (what amaranth is called in the Caribbean), has beautiful red- and green-tinged leaves. *All Red* is a brilliant red and *White Leaf* (sometimes called Chinese spinach) has light green leaves. Amaranth greens may be harvested young as a cut-and-come-again crop or grown to maturity. Harvesting the young leaves and tops will encourage side growth.

# Ricotta and Amaranth Cannelloni

4 SERVINGS

Ricotta stuffing is a perfect destination for tender and wild greens. Amaranth tastes wonderful on its own, or you can mix it up with young borage leaves, chickweed, lamb's-quarters, nettles, or spinach. The all-red varieties of amaranth will make the stuffing red.

Prepare:

**1 recipe Farro Tagliatelle (page 313)**

Remove and discard the stems and wash well:

**1 bunch of amaranth (about 2 cups leaves)**

Drain in a colander. Heat a heavy-bottomed pan over medium-high heat and add the amaranth. Season with:

**Salt**

Cook until wilted, about 3 minutes. Remove to a plate to cool. When cool enough to handle, squeeze all the excess water from the leaves and chop them coarsely. You should have about ½ cup. Put the cooked amaranth in a mixing bowl with:

**¾ cup ricotta cheese**
**1 garlic clove, pounded to a purée or chopped fine**
**⅓ cup grated Parmesan cheese**
**1 thyme sprig, leaves removed and chopped**
**1 egg, beaten**
**Salt**
**Fresh-ground black pepper**

Mix well. Taste and add salt as needed.

Preheat the oven to 400°F. To assemble the cannelloni, roll out the pasta and cut the sheets into rectangles about 3 × 4 inches. Cook al dente, about 2 minutes, in abundant salted boiling water. Cool in a large bowl of cold water and lay out the rectangles on a cloth. Avoid stacking them; they will stick together unless you brush them first with olive oil or melted butter.

Pipe or spoon a bit of filling along one third of the length of a piece of pasta. Gently roll the pasta to form a large straw. Place the cannelloni seam side down in a buttered ovenproof pan. Top with:

**Tomato sauce, stock, or melted butter**
**Grated Parmesan cheese**

Bake for 20 minutes.

# Asian Greens

(*Brassica rapa* and *Brassica juncea*)

Once thought of as exotic, Asian greens are more readily available as Asian farmers (Vietnamese, Hmong, Thai, and others) bring their ethnic produce to local farmers' markets. Their stands are a delight to walk through, a living encyclopedia of new tastes for the uninitiated to learn about, and a joy for those looking for traditional ingredients. Most Asian greens are delicate and quick cooking. Leafy, white-stemmed *bok choy* forms small, tender heads and its very close relative, *Shanghai bok choy*, has celadon-green stems. Their flavor is well suited to cilantro, garlic, ginger, and hot pepper. I cook mature mustard greens, alone or mixed in with others. I love the spicy bite they add. When young, they are good raw and make a spectacular salad with Asian pears and

Parmesan. *Ruby Streak* mustards are delightfully lacy and red. Delicate, dark green *tatsoi* is interchangeable with spinach in the kitchen. *Mizuna* has the flavor of a very mild mustard. I like to grow it as a salad green and cut it when it is quite young and small.

Asian greens are particularly quick to grow. The can be harvested at many stages: as young baby leaves for salad, as tender small plants for a quick stir-fry, or as larger plants. Sow them densely for younger harvests. Asian greens are all relatively cool-weather plants. When growing large mature plants, plant in late summer for fall harvests. There are new varieties being developed every year, many of them bred to withstand heat.

*Bok choy*

# Bok Choy Sautéed with Ginger and Garlic
4 SERVINGS

Bok choy are beautiful cooked whole, but be sure to soak the greens well so any grit that might be hiding in the hearts gets dislodged. This dish can be garnished with Crispy Fried Shallots (page 65) or ginger. Just about any Asian greens can be cooked this way, as can chard, kale, and other leafy greens.

Remove any blemished outer leaves from:
   **1 bunch of bok choy**
If small, leave plants whole; larger ones can be halved or quartered, or sliced. Wash well and drain.
Heat a wok or heavy-bottomed skillet over medium-high heat. When hot add:
   **2 teaspoons olive, coconut, or other vegetable oil**
   **4 garlic cloves, smashed**
   **2 slices ginger, peeled and smashed**
Cook until the garlic just starts to color and then add the greens. Cook until tender, stirring and tossing. Season with:
   **Salt**
   **A splash of soy sauce or fish sauce**

# Salumi with Mustard Flowers

Mustard flowers are bright yellow and bursting with spicy sweet flavor. Arrange sliced salumi (salami, *coppa*, *sopressata*, prosciutto, or other cured meats) on a plate and strew freshly picked mustard flowers across the top. The richness of the meat is spiked by the lively flavor of the flowers.

# Red Mustard Salad with Asian Pears and Pecans

4 SERVINGS

The tangy, peppery flavor of mustard greens is perfectly complemented by the buttery sweet flavors of pears and pecans in this salad. If you can find the lacy Ruby Streak mustards, they make a very striking salad indeed.

Preheat the oven to 350°F. On a small baking sheet or in an ovenproof skillet, spread out:

**¼ cup pecans**

Toast until golden, about 10 minutes. Let cool.

Meanwhile, wash, drain, and dry well:

**4 handfuls of tender young red
    mustard greens**

Prepare the dressing. Mix together in a small bowl:

**1 tablespoon rice wine vinegar
½ shallot, diced fine
Salt
Fresh-ground black pepper
1 slice ginger, peeled and smashed**

Let sit for 10 minutes or so. Whisk in:

**3 tablespoons olive oil**

Taste for acid and salt and adjust as needed. Peel:

**1 large or 2 smaller ripe Asian pears
    (Hosui, Shinko, Kikusui)**

When ready to serve, remove the ginger and toss the greens (or reds!) with two thirds of the vinaigrette. Top with the pecans. Cut the pear in quarters, core, and slice lengthwise. Arrange the slices in the salad and spoon the rest of the vinaigrette over them.

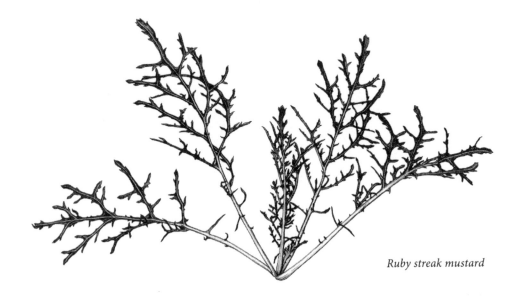

*Ruby streak mustard*

# Heading into Winter

## Cabbage, Broccoli, Cauliflower, Kohlrabi, and Brussels Sprouts

THE MANY MEMBERS of the cabbage family are far from bland and uniform. Instead they bring welcome versatility to winter menus, served both raw and cooked, cold and hot, and complemented with such sweet and savory seasonings as chestnuts, apples, bacon, carrots, citrus, wine, and vinegar. I look forward to the slaws of cabbage and kohlrabi, to roasted cauliflower, to sautéed Brussels sprouts with homemade pancetta, and to sprouting broccoli tossed with garlic and oil. And cabbages lend themselves to pickling and fermentation: I like making and eating all sorts of sauerkrauts and kimchi. A complexly flavored sauerkraut can turn an ordinary grilled cheese sandwich into an even tastier lunch.

## Recipes

Red Cabbage Salad with Medjool Dates and Kumquats  227

Spicy Napa Cabbage Slaw  228

Sweet and Hot Green Cabbage  228

Spicy Korean Pork Stew with Kimchi  229

Sauerkraut Sautéed with Parsnips and Juniper  230

Sprouting Broccoli with Anchovies and Garlic  231

Calabrese Broccoli and Green Garlic Frittata  232

Sautéed Spigarello Broccoli with Bacon  232

Whole Roasted Cauliflower  234

Almond, Marjoram, and Red Wine Vinegar Sauce  235

Parsley and Anchovy Sauce  235

Deep-Fried Romanesco Cauliflower  235

Spicy Indian Cauliflower Stems  236

Orange Cauliflower Salad with Fried Capers and Rocket  237

Kohlrabi, Carrot, and Apple Slaw  238

Kohlrabi and Red Lentil Dal  239

Sautéed Brussels Sprouts with Sherry Vinegar  240

Roasted Brussels Sprouts with Sesame Seeds and Ginger  241

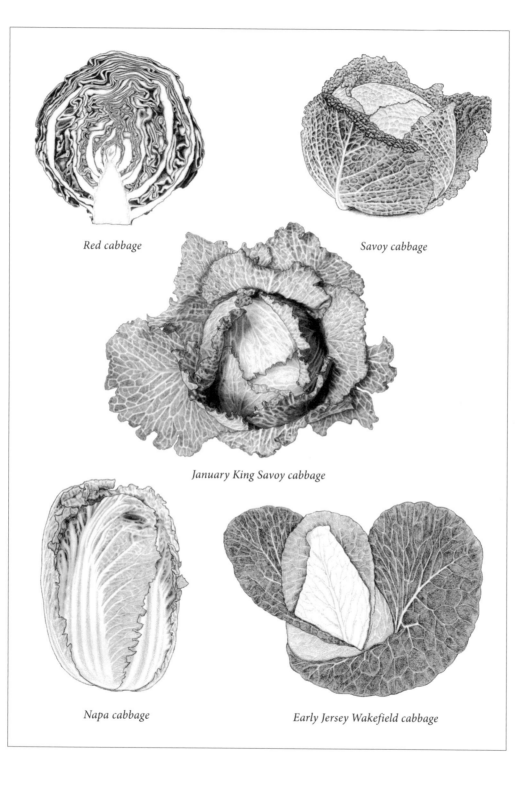

Red cabbage

Savoy cabbage

January King Savoy cabbage

Napa cabbage

Early Jersey Wakefield cabbage

# The Heading Cabbage Family in the Garden

Heading cabbage plants are beautiful—just about every photo of an edible landscape has a stately blue-green cabbage in it—but they take up quite a bit of room in the garden. Local farms grow all my favorite varieties, so I don't grow large cabbage and cauliflower in my small garden. But if you have the space, then I suggest planting some cabbage family members. The easiest one to grow is kohlrabi, followed by sprouting broccoli. Like other leafy greens, these can be harvested over an extended period of time. They are both ornamental, delicious, and well worth a try. Cabbages are the next easiest to grow, and there are smaller varieties to choose from that grow well in either containers or small garden plots. Cauliflower and enchanting towers of Brussels sprouts are a bit more difficult.

The cabbage family tree has many branches: besides cabbage, broccoli, cauliflower, kohlrabi, and Brussels sprouts, other close relatives are collards, kale, radishes, turnips, rutabaga, rocket, mustards, and various Asian greens, including bok choy. All these vegetables have similar nutrient needs and growing requirements.

The entire cabbage family prefers cool weather and needs rich soil and consistent water. They do well when they are planted where onions and garlic just grew. Plant cabbages in spring, and harvest them before hot weather begins; or plant in mid- to late summer, so they mature in the fall. Some cabbages, particularly savoy types, will sur-

vive chilly weather, withstanding even frost and snow; and all cabbages are sweeter after a morning frost. Hot weather will cause most varieties to flower and become tough and bitter, but some seasonal varieties have been developed for growing throughout the year. Look for those that can withstand cold or heat, and plant different varietals for an extended harvest.

## Cabbage (*Brassica oleracea*)

My favorite type of cabbage to eat and cook is savoy cabbage. The leaves are more pliable than smooth cabbage, which makes them easier to separate to stuff and wrap; and the flavor is sweet and mild. *January King* has beautiful green crinkled leaves tinged with a touch of purple and *Alcosa* is a tasty small variety. I like savoy cabbage braised with herbs and spices, roasted, cooked into soups, or simply steamed with a bit of butter or olive oil. At Chez Panisse we make *garbure*, a hearty cabbage soup cooked in the fireplace. I love the way the smoky flavors combine with the sweet cabbage. Savoy cabbage makes good sauerkraut, too.

I prefer smooth-leaf cabbages for coleslaw. And they do make good sauerkraut. Because their heads are more compact, they are especially useful for making large amounts. *Early Jersey Wakefield*, a smaller heirloom cabbage with a whimsical conical shape, is tasty and easy to grow. *Gonzales* is a round mini-cabbage that is perfect for containers and small gardens. For bright color in the kitchen and the garden, choose

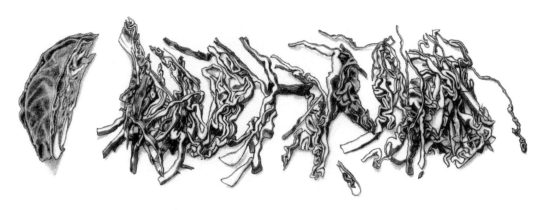

*Red Express.* Cook red cabbage with a bit of vinegar to keep the color; otherwise it will turn gray. Cider vinegar is particularly tasty with cabbage.

Chinese, or napa, cabbage is long, light in color, extra tender, and mild-flavored. It makes wonderful salads and stir-fries. Kimchi, Korean pickled cabbage, is classically made with napa cabbage. There are many varieties to choose from. *Wong Bok* is open-pollinated and *Little Jade* is a mini-hybrid.

With their large colorful outer leaves, cabbages are quite beautiful in the garden. They are slow growing and may be interplanted when young with lettuces or with other quick-growing brassicas, such as kohlrabi, radishes, or turnips. Red cabbages are less susceptible to some bugs. The mature size of a cabbage can be controlled by spacing. Plant them densely for smaller heads.

Cabbages can be harvested cut-and-come-again style. Cut the mature head from the stalk, leaving the stem and outer leaves in place. If the weather is conducive, in a few weeks another cabbage—or a number of little ones—will sprout. Some cabbage varieties keep longer than others, but all will last at least a few weeks in the refrigerator.

# Red Cabbage Salad with Medjool Dates and Kumquats

4 SERVINGS

This salad marries the sweet and sour flavors of kumquats, sorrel, dates, and cabbage in a creamy dressing. It is gorgeous on its own or served with a grilled steak or chop.

To prepare the dressing, mix together:

**1 tablespoon red vinegar**
**1 tablespoon lemon juice**
**Salt**
**Fresh-ground black pepper**

Stir to dissolve. Whisk in:

**4 tablespoons olive oil**
**2 tablespoons crème fraîche or heavy cream**

Taste and adjust the acid and salt as desired. Tear off and discard the tough outer leaves of:

**1 small red cabbage**

Cut into quarters lengthwise and remove the core. Turn the quarters cut side down and slice crosswise into fine shreds. Remove stem ends from:

**4 Medjool dates**

Slice the dates lengthwise to remove the pits and then slice crosswise into thin circles.

Slice thinly:

**4 kumquats**

Remove the stems from:

**½ bunch of sorrel**

Cut the leaves in half lengthwise and slice crosswise into a thin chiffonade. Toss the cabbage with a pinch of salt and the dressing. Taste and adjust as needed. Fold in the fruit and sorrel and:

**1 small handful of chervil, chopped coarse**

Let sit 5 minutes before serving.

## Spicy Napa Cabbage Slaw

4 SERVINGS

Tender napa cabbage makes a refreshing slaw. For a great sandwich, slip it, along with a few slices of roast chicken or lamb, into pita bread or between slices of crusty bread.

Preheat the oven to 375°F.

First prepare the dressing. Mix together:

**2 tablespoons rice wine vinegar**
**Salt**
**Fresh-ground black pepper**

Stir to dissolve. Whisk in:

**3 tablespoons olive oil**

Taste and adjust the acid and salt as desired. Spread out on a small baking pan:

**¼ cup raw peanuts**

Toast for 8 to 10 minutes, or until golden brown. Put the warm nuts in a small bowl and toss with a touch of olive oil. Tear off and discard the tough outer leaves of:

**1 small napa cabbage**

Cut in half lengthwise and remove the core. Turn the halves cut side down, and slice crosswise into fine shreds.

Peel and slice thin:

**½ red onion**

Remove the stems ends and chop coarse:

**½ bunch of cilantro**

Remove the stem end and scoop out the seeds and veins of:

**1 jalapeño or other hot chile**

Slice crosswise into thin circles. Toss the cabbage with a pinch of salt and the dressing. Taste and adjust as needed. Fold in the pepper slices, onions, cilantro, and peanuts. Let sit 5 minutes before serving.

VARIATIONS

✦ Omit the peanuts if needed.

✦ Instead of napa cabbage, use savoy or red cabbage, or shaved Brussels sprouts.

✦ Grate some peeled ginger into the dressing.

✦ Lightly steam the cabbage, onion, and jalapeño together and serve warm with the dressing and peanuts.

## Sweet and Hot Green Cabbage

4 SERVINGS

The year Chez Panisse turned forty, we decided to base the menus in the café on a different chef's cookbook each week. We had a lot of fun rereading cookbooks written by our dear friends and mentors. This recipe was inspired by one of Cecilia Chiang's dishes. It is surprisingly simple and delicious. Serve it with duck or pork, or with rice and a fried egg. I have changed her napa cabbage to regular green cabbage, which I find sweeter, requiring less sugar. Napa or savoy cabbage will work, of course, as will red cabbage—or a mixture of different kinds. The cabbage will keep well for several days in the refrigerator.

Cut in half lengthwise:

**1 green cabbage (about 3 pounds)**

Cut each half into thirds lengthwise, so you have 6 wedges. Remove the core from each wedge and cut crosswise into ½-inch-thick slices. Place the cut cabbage in a large mixing bowl and add:

**1 tablespoon salt**

Toss well and put in a colander to drain for 30 minutes or so. In a small bowl, stir together:

**3 tablespoons sugar**

**¼ cup vinegar (white wine, rice, or cider)**

Heat a large heavy-bottomed skillet over high heat and add:

**2 tablespoons light olive oil or vegetable oil**

Immediately add half the cabbage and sauté, stirring occasionally, for about 4 minutes, until the cabbage is wilted but still crunchy and not browned. Add:

**½ teaspoon dried chile flakes**

Stir and add half the vinegar mixture and a couple of tablespoons of water. Cook for 2 minutes more and turn out into a dish large enough to hold all the cabbage. Repeat with the remaining cabbage. Stir the 2 batches together and taste for salt, sweet, sour, and heat and correct to your preference. Serve warm or cool.

VARIATION

✦ Add other spices with the chile flakes, such as mustard seeds, cumin, or coriander.

# Spicy Korean Pork Stew with Kimchi

4 SERVINGS

A *jjigae* is a traditional Korean stew, and this jjigae is made with pork and full-flavored kimchi that has had a chance to ferment for a couple of weeks. It is the perfect way to use up your older kimchi while a new batch is fermenting.

Jjigae are classically cooked, and served, in a heat-proof ceramic pot called a *dol sot*. So if you have one, you could put it to good use here. Serve this stew with a bowl of rice and some quick pickles for a warming winter meal.

Cut into small slices or dice:

**¼ pound pork belly or shoulder**

Season with:

**Salt**

Heat a heat-proof ceramic pot or heavy-bottomed pot over medium heat. When hot add:

**2 teaspoons sesame oil**

Add the pork and cook about 4 minutes until it has changed color and is slightly brown. Stir in:

**1 large garlic clove, minced**

**½ onion, coarsely chopped**

Cook for a few minutes to soften the onion. Add:

**2 cups Kimchi (page 338), preferably at least 2 weeks old**

**2 tablespoons kimchi liquid**

Cook for 5 minutes. Add enough water to cover the vegetables and meat, about 1¼ cups. Bring to a boil and then turn down to a simmer. Cover and cook for 15 minutes.

Then gently stir in:

**4 slices medium-firm tofu**

**2 green onions, sliced thin**

**3 salt-cured anchovy fillets, chopped**

Cook for another 15 minutes, or until the pork is tender. If the stew gets too dry, add more water. Taste for salt and adjust as needed. Serve very hot garnished with:

**Sliced green onions**

VARIATION

◆ Tuna confit can be used in place of the pork. Start the recipe with the onions and add the tuna with the tofu.

# Sauerkraut Sautéed with Parsnips and Juniper

4 SERVINGS

Sauerkraut is a very tasty condiment on its own, but it is also delicious sautéed and served with sausages, pork chops, or a root vegetable gratin. This recipe pairs the kraut with sweet parsnips—apples, kohlrabi, parsley root, or rutabagas would be good, too. The bacon is traditional but optional.

Heat a heavy-bottomed pan over medium-high heat. When hot add:

**2 teaspoons olive oil, duck fat, or lard**

**1½ slices bacon, cut into ½-inch pieces**

Cook until the bacon is rendered and just beginning to brown (turn down the heat if the bacon browns too quickly or the fat starts to smoke). Remove the bacon and add:

**1 small onion, sliced thin**

**5 juniper berries, crushed**

**1 bay leaf**

Cook until the onions are soft, about 10 minutes. Add:

**2 parsnips, sliced or diced ¼ inch thick**

**Salt**

**Fresh-ground black pepper**

Cook for a few minutes and pour in:

**¼ cup white wine (Riesling or other fruity wine)**

Bring to a boil and reduce for 1 to 2 minutes. Add:

**1½ cups plain sauerkraut, with its brine (see page 338)**

Stir, cover, and cook at a bare simmer until the parsnips are tender, about 20 minutes. When done, taste for salt and add as needed. Stir in the bacon.

VARIATIONS

◆ If omitting the bacon, increase the amount of oil to 1 tablespoon and garnish with a drizzle of sesame or pumpkin seed oil.

◆ Other spices can be used instead of (or in addition to) the juniper, such as mustard seed, coriander, and caraway. Or omit the juniper and be untraditional with a bit of cardamom seed, ginger, cinnamon, or nigella seed.

*Juniper berries*

## Broccoli  (*Brassica oleracea*)

Classic broccoli with a large central head has been edged out at Chez Panisse by tastier sprouting varieties—*Broccoli di Cicco* and *Calabrese*. Instead of producing a single head sold with its leaves, these varieties send out smaller shoots and leaves. Sprouting broccoli needs no other preparation than a trim of its stems if they look dry. Keep the leaves on; they are every bit as tasty as the florets. My favorite way to eat sprouting broccoli is roasted, which concentrates its sweet flavors. Try it in a wood-burning oven if you have one. It's also delicious simply steamed and served with a drizzle of good olive oil or dressed with a pungent sauce of lemon, garlic, and anchovies.

Standard broccoli needs lots of space and can be a bit temperamental in the garden. Sprouting varieties, on the other hand, flourish in the land or in containers. To encourage sprouting, cut the first main head when it is between two and three inches around (and before it has started to flower), cutting it off at an angle and leaving a few inches of stem. Side sprouts, or shoots, will start to grow and can be harvested for up to six weeks. Keep cutting them: if the sprouts flower all production will stop.

Curly *spigarello* looks like a crazy spiral-leaf kale, but it is technically in the broccoli family. As it grows, spigarello forms small florets, but it is the leaves that are most abundant. Grow, harvest, and cook it just as you would kale (see page 208). Like other leafy greens, spigarello can be harvested over a long period of time if you keep the florets trimmed so they don't bloom.

*Broccoli di Cicco*

## Sprouting Broccoli with Anchovies and Garlic
4 SERVINGS

Trim off the stem ends and wash:
> **1 pound sprouting broccoli**

Set aside to drain.

Mix together in a small heavy-bottomed pot:
> **4 garlic cloves, peeled and sliced**
> **1 large pinch dried chile flakes**
> **3 salt-cured anchovy fillets, chopped**
> **3 tablespoons extra-virgin olive oil**
> **Salt**

Set the pot over low heat to warm. Place the broccoli in a steamer and cook until just soft. Remove and place in a warm bowl.

Swirl the oil to mix the ingredients and squeeze in:

**Juice of ½ small lemon**

Taste and add salt as needed. Pour over the warm broccoli and serve.

VARIATION

• Roast the broccoli in a 450°F oven until done, about 12 minutes.

# Calabrese Broccoli and Green Garlic Frittata

4 SERVINGS

Trim the ends from:

**1 pound Calabrese or other sprouting broccoli**

Wash well, drain, and chop coarsely.

In a large bowl, mix the broccoli together with:

**1 medium onion, peeled and diced**
**4 large eggs, lightly beaten**
**¼ cup grated Parmesan cheese**
**1 stalk green garlic, trimmed and sliced thin**
**2 tablespoons chopped parsley**
**2 tablespoons olive oil**
**Salt**
**Fresh-ground black pepper**

Heat a 10-inch cast-iron or nonstick pan over medium-low heat and pour in:

**2 tablespoons olive oil**

Tilt the pan to coat with the oil and pour in the egg mixture. With a wooden spoon, push around the broccoli-egg mixture so that it forms an even layer. Cook gently until the eggs are nearly set. Turn the frittata: First slide the frittata out of the pan and onto a plate. Next turn the pan over and cover the plate and frittata with it. Then, while holding them together, flip over the pan and plate and remove the plate. Return the pan to the heat and drizzle a bit more olive oil around the sides of the pan. Cook for 3 or 4 minutes more and slide the frittata onto a plate. Serve warm or at room temperature.

VARIATIONS

• Use broccoli rabe or Romanesco, or another cauliflower in place of the broccoli.
• Slowly cook a sliced onion in olive oil until well browned and caramelized, about 15 minutes. Stir into the eggs with the broccoli.
• Add a large pinch of dried chile flakes for a bit of spice.
• Stir ¾ cup crumbled feta or fresh goat cheese into the eggs with the broccoli.

# Sautéed Spigarello Broccoli with Bacon

4 SERVINGS

Spigarello has the flavors of both kale and broccoli. It is fairly tender and does not need any precooking when sautéed. The smoky bacon in this recipe adds a southern touch to a very Italian dish. Serve it as a side dish, as a pasta sauce, or let it cool and toss it with a little vinegar for an antipasto.

Trim away any tough stems from:

**1 bunch of spigarello**

Cut coarsely crosswise, wash well, and set aside to drain.

Heat a heavy-bottomed pan over medium-high heat. Add:

1 tablespoon olive oil

**2 slices bacon, cut into ¼-inch lardons**

Cook the bacon until it is partially rendered and just starting to brown. Remove with a slotted spoon and add:

**1 small red onion, peeled and sliced thin**

Toss the onion with the fat in the pan and cook for 5 minutes or until soft and wilted. Add:

**Salt**

Stir and cook for 1 minute. Add the spigarello with the water still clinging to its leaves. Cook until tender, tossing with the onion as it wilts. There should be enough water, but add a bit if the pan is getting dry. A couple of minutes before the spigarello is done cooking, stir in the bacon. When the leaves are tender, taste and add salt as needed. If desired, top with:

**A drizzle of extra-virgin olive oil**

**A grating of pecorino or Parmesan cheese**

VARIATIONS

• When using as a pasta sauce, save some of the pasta water to toss with the noodles and spigarello.

• Sprouting broccoli, broccoli rabe, chard, lacinato kale, or collard greens may be used in place of the spigarello. Precook the kale and collard greens in salted boiling water before starting.

• Add a couple of spoonfuls of spicy tomato sauce (see page 166) to the greens with the bacon.

• Use pancetta in place of the bacon.

• Omit the bacon and when the greens are close to being done, clear a spot in the middle of the pan, pour in a nice drizzle of olive oil, add 2 or more sliced or minced garlic cloves, and add a healthy pinch of dried chile flakes. Let the garlic and chile cook for a moment and then stir all together.

*Spigarello broccoli*

## Cauliflower *(Brassica oleracea)*

Just like broccoli, cauliflower was developed from the cabbage plant and new varieties are being developed all the time. My favorite variety of cauliflower, *Romanesco*, is frequently identified as a kind of broccoli. It is a crazy, brilliant chartreuse color, with a spiraling pointed head that is a wonder to look at and fun to cook. *Purple Graffiti* and orange *Cheddar* are other brightly colored, tasty varieties of cauliflower. I like cauliflower roasted and dressed with capers, marjoram, and lemon or served chilled in a vinaigrette with a few anchovies. Sauté it and add it to a pasta sauce, or try it dipped in yogurt and deep-fried.

Cauliflower is grown for its flowering head. It is a bit fussy and needs consistent water and food or it will quickly button (produce small heads). Although they prefer cool temperatures, seedlings will bolt if temperatures drop too low. A thick mulch will help buffer any weather fluctuations, drought, or other stressors. Harvest your cauliflower when the heads are developed; otherwise they will quickly go to flower and lose their fine flavor.

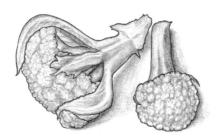

## Whole Roasted Cauliflower

Whatever its color, cauliflower makes an impressive sight when brought to the table cooked whole. Keep on the leaves as they add to the beauty and are quite tasty, too. First, wash it well and drain. To roast, place the cauliflower in an oiled baking dish that just holds it comfortably. Sprinkle with salt and drizzle with olive oil. Bake at 425°F until golden and tender, about 1 hour, depending on the size of the head. It is done when it can easily be pierced by a sharp knife. To steam, sprinkle with salt and oil and cook in a steamer until tender, about 20 minutes. Serve hot or cold with a sauce either spooned over it or served in a ramekin to use for dipping. A whole roasted cauliflower makes a great hors d'oeuvre at a cocktail party; people can break off a floret and dip in a sauce while standing around chatting.

Try it with the versatile sauces that follow; they are delicious with other vegetables, fish, and meat.

# Almond, Marjoram, and Red Wine Vinegar Sauce

Mix together:

**1 tablespoon red wine vinegar or sherry vinegar**
**Salt**
**Fresh-ground black pepper**

Whisk in:

**3 tablespoons extra-virgin olive oil**

Add:

**2 tablespoons toasted sliced almonds**
**2 teaspoons chopped marjoram or parsley**

Taste and adjust the salt and acid as needed.

VARIATION

◆ Add a large pinch of ground cumin or fennel to the vinegar.

# Parsley and Anchovy Sauce

Pound to a purée using a mortar and pestle:

**1 garlic clove**

Add and continue to pound:

**3 salt-cured anchovy fillets**

Once puréed, add:

**Juice of ½ lemon**
**Salt**
**Fresh-ground black pepper**

Stir to dissolve the salt and whisk in:

**3 tablespoons extra-virgin olive oil**

Stir in:

**2 teaspoons chopped parsley**

VARIATIONS

◆ Add 1 teaspoon capers and a pinch of dried chile flakes.
◆ Add the grated zest of 1 lemon.

# Deep-Fried Romanesco Cauliflower

One of the simplest and best ways to fry vegetables, or nearly anything else, is to dip them in yogurt, flour, and then into hot oil. The yogurt clings well to the vegetables and gives a sweet and slightly tangy flavor. The nature of the item you are frying will determine how thick or thin the yogurt should be. Thin the yogurt with water or milk to make a lighter coating for delicate shapes such as onion rings or asparagus spears. For a somewhat thicker coating for chunkier vegetables like cauliflower or whole spring onions, or for pieces of fish or chicken, thin the yogurt only slightly, if at all. Unlike some batter and breading preparations for deep-frying, this yogurt-flour combination does not need to rest or set up, so heat the oil before starting to dip the vegetables. Most of the time, I fry in rice bran oil, but safflower and grapeseed oils work well, too. Fry a test piece to judge the thickness of the yogurt and thin it a bit if the coating seems stodgy.

I like serving fried Romanesco cauliflower florets hot from the pan while friends are helping and talking in the kitchen, so I fry small batches in a cast-iron skillet. Use a deeper pot for frying larger batches. To get the temperature right, heat the oil slowly over a moderate flame. To test the temperature of the oil, dip a finger into the yogurt and then into the flour, roll up a little ball of batter, and drop it into the oil. If it sinks and sends up no bubbles, or only a lazy line of them, it is too cool. If the batter bubbles ferociously and breaks up into brown bits, the oil is too hot and must be left to cool for

10 minutes or so. Cut the cauliflower into thick slices or break into thumb-size florets. In batches, drop them into a bowl of yogurt and toss them with your finger to coat completely. Lift the cauliflower out of the yogurt and drop into a wide bowl of flour, shaking to coat thoroughly. Lift the cauliflower from the bowl, shake off the excess flour, and carefully drop into the hot oil. When the coating is golden brown, scoop the cauliflower from the oil, drain, sprinkle with salt, and serve immediately.

VARIATIONS

◆ When frying in a large pot, heat the oil to 360°F, using a candy or deep-fry thermometer to monitor the heat.

◆ Use the same method to fry other vegetables such as onion rings, scallions, bell pepper slices, Belgian endive wedges, fennel wedges, and green beans.

◆ Yogurt-frying is ideal for fish fillets and boneless chicken breasts or legs (skin on). Leave the chicken in the yogurt for up to 2 hours (refrigerated) to tenderize the meat.

◆ Add ground spices such as cumin, turmeric, or coriander to the flour.

◆ Serve with dipping sauces, such as Almond, Marjoram, and Red Wine Vinegar Sauce (page 235), Parsley and Anchovy Sauce (page 235), or Spiced Carrot Raita (page 73).

# Spicy Indian Cauliflower Stems

4 SERVINGS

My office is filled with wonderful interns and assistants who make it possible for me to accomplish all that I do. Although they are not all cooks, food is a frequent topic of their conversation. When we talked about this book, many ideas were tossed around, including this recipe, a northern Indian way of cooking the core and stem of cauliflower—parts that I used to relegate to the compost bucket. Not anymore!

Put in a heavy-bottomed skillet:
> ½ teaspoon black peppercorns
> Seeds from 1 brown cardamom pod (badi elaichi)
> One 2-inch piece cassia
> 3 cloves

Place the pan over medium-high heat and cook, tossing the spices in the pan now and then, until fragrant. Take care not to burn the spices. Let cool and grind to a powder in a spice grinder or using a mortar and pestle. Peel the outer woody parts from:
> 2 large cauliflower cores and stems

Cut into large dice or into thick slices. Put a skillet large enough to accommodate the stems over medium-high heat. When hot, add:
> 2 teaspoons olive, coconut, or vegetable oil
> 1 teaspoon cumin seeds

Cook until the cumin starts to crackle and then add the stems. Season with:
> Salt

Toss, and turn down the heat to low. Cover tightly and cook until tender. Check and stir, letting all the condensation on the bottom of the lid run back back into the pan. If the cauliflower is starting to brown too quickly, turn down the heat (or use a flame tamer). As the cauliflower turns tender, season with the ground spice mixture, and:

> **1 teaspoon dried mango powder (amchoor)**

Stir to coat evenly. When the cauliflower is tender, taste for salt, and adjust as needed.

VARIATIONS

• Substitute kohlrabi or broccoli stems for the cauliflower stems.
• If mango powder is unavailable, finish with the juice of a half lemon.

# Orange Cauliflower Salad with Fried Capers and Rocket

4 SERVINGS

Red quinoa (I much prefer it to the white) has a wonderful nutty flavor and crisp texture—a perfect match to the sweet tender orange cauliflower. Rocket adds spice and the fried capers add a final briny crunchy touch. You may find yourself roasting extra cauliflower to have on hand for this delicious, easy-to-make salad.

Preheat the oven to 425°F.
Soak in a bowl of cold water for 15 minutes:

> **2 tablespoons salt-cured capers**

Remove the outer leaves from:

> **1 head of orange cauliflower**

Cut in half, remove the core, and separate into florets. Place in a bowl and toss with:

> **1 tablespoon olive oil**
> **Salt**

Spread on a baking sheet and roast until soft and caramelized, about 15 minutes. Set aside to cool.
Make the dressing. Mix together:

> **1 medium shallot, diced fine**
> **2 tablespoons red wine vinegar**
> **Salt**
> **Fresh-ground black pepper**

Let sit for 10 minutes to allow the flavors to marry. Whisk in:

> **⅓ cup extra-virgin olive oil**

Taste for salt and acid and adjust as needed. Drain the capers and squeeze dry. Heat a small heavy-bottomed pan over medium-high heat. Pour in:

> **½ inch of olive oil**

When the oil is hot, add the capers and fry until the buds have opened. Remove with a slotted spoon to absorbent paper. In a large bowl, mix together the cauliflower and:

> **1½ cups cooked red quinoa**
> **2 handfuls of rocket**
> **Salt**
> **A pinch of Marash or Aleppo pepper**

Pour in the vinaigrette and mix carefully. Arrange on a large plate and sprinkle the fried capers over the top.

VARIATIONS

• Garnish with Crispy Fried Shallots (page 65).
• Serve on a bed of dressed Little Gem leaves.
• Serve warm without the rocket and with a generous pinch of marjoram.

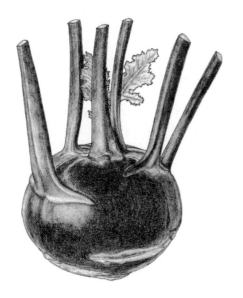

*Early Purple Vienna kohlrabi*

## Kohlrabi (*Brassica oleracea*)

As kohlrabi grows, the stem swells into a round ball, with thin stems of the leaves protruding from the squat bulb. In the garden, or at the market, it looks like a pretty space alien. Like cabbage, kohlrabi is delicious raw in salads or cooked. The flavor is sweet and mild with a crisp and juicy texture. The Chez Panisse café makes tasty slaws with it all winter long. Try *Early White Vienna* and *Early Purple Vienna* roasted, steamed, or pickled. When fresh, the leaves are good to eat, too. Choose smaller kohlrabi for cooking, as the larger ones tend to be woody.

Kohlrabi is an easy, quick-growing plant. It can be interplanted among slow-growing cabbages and rutabagas. For tender texture and the best flavor, harvest when it is no larger than three inches in diameter. Plant every few weeks for an extended harvest.

## Kohlrabi, Carrot, and Apple Slaw
4 SERVINGS

Kohlrabi makes a wonderful slaw. This one is with carrots, but don't hesitate to mix different root vegetables. They all make lovely winter salads to serve alongside a bit of salami or prosciutto, some fried vegetables, or a spicy baked Dungeness crab.

Peel the outer woody skin from:
**1 medium or 2 small kohlrabi bulbs**
Using a sharp knife or a mandoline, cut the kohlrabi into thin slices. Then cut the slices into matchstick pieces.
Peel and trim:
**1 red, orange, or yellow carrot**
Cut into slices and then into a matchstick julienne as above.
Cut in quarters and core:
**½ apple (such as Cox's Orange Pippin, Pink Pearl, or Braeburn)**
Cut the quarters into slices and then into matchsticks.
Toss the sliced fruit and vegetables with:
**1½ teaspoons cider vinegar**
**1 teaspoon coarsely chopped parsley**
**Salt**
**Fresh-ground black pepper**
**1 teaspoon olive oil**
Taste for salt and acid and adjust as needed.

VARIATIONS
◆ Omit the apple, use lemon or lime juice instead of cider vinegar, and cilantro instead of parsley. In a dry pan, heat ½ teaspoon nigella and ½ teaspoon black mustard seeds until they pop. Stir them into the slaw.

⬩ In addition to (or instead of) the kohlrabi, use other root vegetables, such as radishes, turnips, rutabagas, beets, or celery root. Fennel is also a great addition.

# Kohlrabi and Red Lentil Dal

4 SERVINGS

Kohlrabi is used frequently in Indian cooking, and fragrant spices complement its sweet, mild flavor. A sizzling garnish of oil and spices provides the traditional and tasty flair. Split red lentils, called *masoor dal*, are easy to find sold in bulk in Indian and Middle Eastern grocery stores. Serve the dal with some steamed basmati rice and Spiced Carrot Raita (page 73).

Measure into a strainer and rinse well under cold water:

**1 cup split red lentils (masoor dal)**

Set aside to drain. Into a heavy-bottomed pot, over medium-high heat, put:

**2 teaspoons coconut oil or olive oil**
**1 onion, diced**

Cook for 5 minutes, stirring now and then. Add the lentils and 3½ cups water. Bring to a boil and lower to a simmer. Skim away any foam that comes to the top. Once the foam has stopped forming, add:

**½ teaspoon turmeric**
**1 medium or 2 small kohlrabi bulbs, peeled and diced (about 2 cups)**
**1 hot pepper (such as jalapeño or serrano), seeded and sliced (optional)**

Cook until the lentils are tender, about 20 to 30 minutes, depending on how fresh the lentils are.

Season to taste with:

**Salt**

Just before serving, prepare the sizzle, or temper, as it is called in Indian cooking. Put a small heavy-bottomed pan over medium-high heat. When it is hot, add:

**1 tablespoon ghee, coconut oil, or olive oil**
**2 large or 4 small garlic cloves, minced**
**½ teaspoon cumin seeds**
**¼ teaspoon black mustard seeds**

Cook until the garlic just begins to color and the seeds begin to crackle. Pour over the soup.

VARIATIONS

⬩ Add a few curry leaves (*Murraya koenigii*) to the sizzle, offering wonderful aromatic flavor. Some farmers' markets carry them, or look in the produce section of Indian and Asian stores. It is a very tender plant; keep it in a pot to bring inside in most zones.

⬩ Use butternut squash instead of kohlrabi.

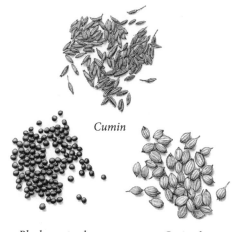

*Cumin*

*Black mustard*          *Coriander*

## Brussels Sprouts *(Brassica oleracea)*

Brussels sprouts are the quintessential winter vegetable. They always taste better after cold weather and frost have come. Slice them thin to make a sophisticated salad or a flavorful sauté. A little bacon or pancetta suits Brussels sprouts. They roast nicely, and make a great gratin when steamed. I also like to separate the sprouts into individual leaves (cut out the core of the sprouts with a sharp paring knife and carefully pull them apart) and cook them gently to keep the delicate leaves intact. Brussels sprouts are sometimes sold at markets still on their three-foot stalks—an arresting sight.

In the garden, topped with blue-green floppy leaves, Brussels sprouts look like palm trees, with bumpy sprouts all down their stalks. *Faustus*, a red variety, puts on an even more dramatic show. For sweet sprouts, farmers in northern California grow *Gustus*. Most varieties are a bit sensitive and need well-amended soil and plenty of water. Feed or spray with compost tea every few weeks to keep the plants thriving. In cold climates, about a month before freezing weather, cut the top off each plant. This will stop new growth and allow the plants to concentrate on ripening the existing sprouts. Don't discard the tops; they are quite edible, like sweet, mild, loose-leaf cabbages.

## Sautéed Brussels Sprouts with Sherry Vinegar

4 SERVINGS

I think Brussels sprouts are at their best when cut thin and quickly sautéed. The edges are caramelized to a crispy golden brown while the rest is fresh and sweet. A generous splash of sherry vinegar heightens the flavors and adds a tangy zip.

Trim the outer leaves and stems from:

**1 pound Brussels sprouts**

Cut them lengthwise into thin slices. Heat a heavy-bottomed skillet or sauté pan over medium-high heat. Pour in:

**2 tablespoons olive oil**

Add the sliced Brussels sprouts and toss in the oil. Season with:

**Salt**

**Fresh-ground black pepper**

Cook, stirring often, until the sprouts soften and brown. If they are browning too quickly, turn down the heat. Add:

**1½ teaspoons sherry vinegar**

**1 tablespoon chopped parsley**

Toss or stir and turn off the heat. Taste for salt and acid (don't be shy with the vinegar) and add as needed.

VARIATIONS

✦ Cut 2 slices pancetta into small pieces, cook in the oil until they begin to brown, then add the sprouts and sauté as above.

✦ Before sautéing the sprouts, cook a diced shallot or a small sliced onion in the oil for about 1 minute. Add the sprouts and continue as above.

✦ Replace the parsley with sweet marjoram.

# Roasted Brussels Sprouts with Sesame Seeds and Ginger

4 SERVINGS

Preheat the oven to 400°F.
Remove any blemished outer leaves from:

**1 pound Brussels sprouts**

Cut in half (or, if very large, in quarters) and toss in a bowl with:

**1 tablespoon olive oil**
**Salt**
**Fresh-ground black pepper**

Scrape off the skin from:

**½-inch piece of ginger**

Cut into thin slices and cut the slices into a fine julienne. Toss the ginger with the sprouts and lay them out on a baking sheet or baking dish. Roast until tender and golden, about 35 to 40 minutes. Stir the sprouts now and then for even cooking. When the sprouts are almost done, heat a small heavy-bottomed skillet over medium heat. When hot, measure into the skillet:

**2 teaspoons sesame seeds**

While stirring constantly, cook until toasted, about 5 minutes. Put in a mortar with:

**A large pinch of salt**
**2 teaspoons chopped parsley or cilantro**

Grind coarsely. When the sprouts are done, put them in a bowl and toss with the sesame seeds. Serve with:

**Lemon wedges**

VARIATIONS

• After oiling and seasoning the halved sprouts, thread them onto skewers, and grill them over a hot fire.

• Omit the ginger and sesame seeds, and instead make a pungent salsa verde with thyme, parsley, and a touch of rosemary to spoon over the cooked sprouts.

# Ripe Summer Fruit

## Cherries, Apricots, Plums, Peaches, and Nectarines

JUICY, YIELDING, AND BRILLIANT-COLORED with intoxicating aroma and sweet flavor: apricots, cherries, peaches, nectarines, and plums are the "stone" fruits of spring and summer. They have a hard pit containing a single seed in the center of the fleshy fruit. Eaten out of hand and out of doors, a perfectly ripe peach or bowl of cherries is my ideal dessert. Stone fruit, alone or with other fruit, also make delectable galettes, tarts and pies, crisps, compotes, and ice creams. Market stands and trees full of ripe fruit offer the abundance of summer to preserve for the rest of the year by canning, drying, or making jam. Don't neglect the kernel inside the stones, called the *noyau* in French. The *noyaux* of apricots, especially, with their subtle flavor of bitter almond, add a haunting complexity when infused into ice cream and custard.

# Recipes

Galette Dough  246

Frangipane  247

Pie Dough  248

Sweet Tart Dough  248

Bing Cherries Roasted with Lemon Verbena  250

Black Cherry Galette  250

Sour Cherry Pie  251

Apricot Galette  254

Royal Blenheim Apricot Sorbet  254

Apricot Almond-Custard Tart  255

Apricot Aperitif  256

Pluot and Raspberry Galette  257

Santa Rosa Plum Cake  258

Wild Plum Jam Turnovers  259

Roasted Italian Prune Plums and Rosemary  260

Peach Leaf Ice Cream  261

Grilled Rio Oso Peaches  262

Nectarine and Blackberry Galette  262

# Stone Fruits in the Garden

Stone fruit trees are a beautiful addition to an edible landscape, bringing bright flowers in spring, brilliant green leaves, welcome shade, and colorful accents of ripe fruit in summer, and glorious yellow and orange leaves in fall. The fruit begins to ripen in late spring with the earliest cherries and apricots. My favorite time is midsummer, with its virtual avalanche of peaches, nectarines, and plums. Late-ripening Last Chance peaches and the prune plums sweeten the end of summer. Growing your own fruit will supply you with luscious just-ripe fruit that is close to impossible to find outside of the best farmers' market stalls. And even those farmers don't always grow the tastiest varieties, as they are often the most difficult to bring to market owing to their tender quality and sometimes imperfect appearance.

Mas Masumoto, renowned peach farmer, has solved that problem in his orchards. He does not bring his remarkable Elberta peaches to market, but offers fruit trees for adoption instead. He cares for the trees and fruit throughout the year, but when it is time to harvest, the adopters are called to come and pick the fruit from their tree (an astounding three-hundred-plus pounds).

There are a few things to consider when choosing a tree to grow. Be empowered, not overwhelmed, with all this information—it will save you time and trouble in the end. I planted a cherry tree and kept wondering, year after year, why I never got any cherries. I did not realize that I needed another cherry nearby for it to make fruit. Now I know!

All stone fruits require a period of winter chill to keep the trees healthy and to produce winter crops. The number of chill hours varies according to variety. Also, some stone fruit flowers are self-fruitful, while others need to be pollinated by a different variety of the same species in order to set fruit. Fruit trees are perennials that will remain in the same spot for decades. Some can grow quite large, and all will cast a certain amount of shade. Talk to farmers or visit a nearby nursery or Cooperative Extension office to help you find the tastiest varieties suited to your location.

Once you have decided what to grow, choose a location where the trees can grow undisturbed, with loose, well-drained soil and a sunny exposure. Think about the path of the sun and pick a spot that won't cast too much shade on your vegetable-growing areas. (You can move your tree in the first few years if you find the first spot was not as ideal as you thought.) Feed trees compost throughout the year to keep them in top form and so they are better able to ward off pests and disease. Young fruit trees will need to be shaped each year, and afterward some yearly pruning is required to keep the trees healthy and the harvest plentiful.

Most stone fruits begin bearing one or two years after planting (depending on the age of the tree you plant), with maximum production coming a few years later. As fruit develops, thin young fruit and prop sagging limbs to avoid the heartbreak of broken branches and tiny fruit. Pick your fruit at the peak of ripeness and enjoy the delectable harvest.

# Stone Fruit Galettes

Most often I end a meal with a piece of ripe fruit, but when dessert is in order, a fruit galette is what I want. It is by far my favorite—a thin round of crisp golden pastry topped with richly concentrated ripe fruit— a crunchy sweet taste and texture sensation. As with anything simple, the quality of each part is important. A delicately made, flaky dough and ripe delicious fruit are essential.

Cherries, apricots, plums, nectarines, and peaches are each cut in a different way and require different amounts of sugar. The fruit is quite juicy and I like to spread a thin layer of frangipane—a mixture of almond paste, butter, and egg—to help seal the dough and keep the juices from leaking and to enhance the flavor of the stone fruit. If you are baking without nuts, sprinkle a mix of flour sweetened with a touch of sugar to help soak up and thicken any juice threatening to leak.

The recipe for galette dough follows, as does the frangipane. Free-form fruit galettes are simple to make. Roll the dough out quite thin, spread it with frangipane, arrange the fruit leaving a border of dough uncovered, sprinkle with sugar, and turn the edge of the dough back over the fruit to hold in the juices of the baking fruit. Carefully arranging the fruit is not necessary, but it makes a prettier tart, and the fruit can be tightly packed, as it shrinks while cooking. Bake the galette until it is a rich golden brown on the bottom. If taken out too soon, the pastry will be soggy instead of crisp and flaky.

# Galette Dough

MAKES TWO 10-OUNCE DISKS, ENOUGH FOR TWO
12-INCH GALETTES OR 12 TURNOVERS

This is the most versatile and widely used dough at Chez Panisse. Every day, it is rolled out for fruit or savory galettes. The recipe has been included in all of our cookbooks so far, but like many recipes, over time and with new cooks and chefs, the method has been tweaked and modified. This is our current updated version. It makes a wonderfully flaky and crisp pastry. Keep in mind when making the dough that the moisture content of both flour and butter varies from day to day, so the amount of water added to the dough will vary as well.

Combine in a mixing bowl:
    **2 cups unbleached all-purpose flour**
    **¾ teaspoon sugar**
    **¼ teaspoon salt**
Measure:
    **½ cup ice-cold water**
Cut into ½-inch pieces:
    **10 tablespoons (1¼ sticks) cold
      unsalted butter**
Let the cold butter soften slightly. Before mixing into flour mixture, test by pressing your finger on one of the pieces. It should press easily but remain cold and not leave butter on your finger. If it has become too soft, put it back into the refrigerator for a few minutes.

Add the butter to the flour mixture and toss to coat. Press the pieces of butter with your thumb and forefinger one by one to flatten them. When all the pieces of butter are flattened, drizzle in half the water, mixing all the while with your fingers spread and curved slightly, raking the dry mix from the bottom to the top to evenly incorporate the water. Continue mixing until the dough starts to come together, breaking apart any large clumps as you go. Resist the urge to squeeze or press the dough together, as this will activate the gluten in the flour and can make the dough tough. After the water is incorporated, if there is unincorporated flour, drizzle water over, 1 tablespoon at a time. Keep drizzling and raking until the dough looks moist and ropy with very little dry flour. Give the dough a final rake to break apart any large clumps.

Divide the dough in half, roll each part gently into a rough ball, and wrap each ball in plastic wrap or a plastic bag. Compress each ball, and then flatten and smooth them into disks. Press in any outstanding dry areas or butter into the dough, as they may create a hole in the galette as it bakes. Let the dough rest refrigerated for 1 hour or longer.

When rolling the dough, it should be malleable, but still cold. Lightly flour the countertop, unwrap the dough, and dust lightly with flour. Roll the disk out into a 14-inch circle about ⅛ inch thick. Dust off any excess flour from both sides of dough with a dry pastry brush and place the rolled dough on a baking sheet lined with parchment paper. Chill for 30 minutes before assembling your galette.

Dough may be stored in the refrigerator for 2 days or in the freezer for a month or two. Thaw frozen dough overnight in the refrigerator before using.

# Frangipane

MAKES ABOUT 1 CUP, ENOUGH FOR 8 GALETTES

When making galettes with the juicy stone fruits of spring and summer, spread a little bit of frangipane on the dough underneath the fruit to help prevent leaks and give the fruit a greater depth of flavor.

Measure into the mixing bowl of a stand mixer:

**4 ounces almond paste**
**4 tablespoons (½ stick) unsalted**
   **butter at room temperature**

Using the paddle attachment, mix the almond paste and butter together on medium speed until smooth. Reduce the speed to low and add in this order:

**⅛ cup beaten egg (about ½ egg)**
**1 tablespoon sugar**
**1½ teaspoons unbleached all-purpose**
   **flour**

Increase the speed to medium and mix until well combined. Place in an airtight container. Frangipane will keep in the refrigerator for up to 2 weeks or in the freezer for up to 3 months.

# Pie Dough

MAKES TWO 10-OUNCE BALLS OF DOUGH, ENOUGH
FOR 1 DOUBLE-CRUSTED PIE OR 2 SINGLE PIE SHELLS

I like the flavor of pie dough made with butter, but I sometimes like to include a few tablespoons of lard in the dough. The butter gives a lovely rich flavor and tenderness and the lard makes the dough crisper and flakier, and easier to handle. If you don't have good, fresh lard on hand, organic vegetable shortening will accomplish the same result. The butter and lard are cut and worked into smaller pieces in this dough creating a more tender pastry than the crisp gallette dough.

Have ready in a measuring cup:

**6 tablespoons ice-cold water**

Mix together:

**2 cups unbleached all-purpose flour**
**½ teaspoon salt**
**A pinch of sugar**

Add:

**12 tablespoons (1½ sticks) chilled unsalted butter, cut into ¼-inch cubes**
**3 tablespoons chilled lard**

Using a pastry blender or your fingertips, quickly work the butter and lard into the flour mixture until most of the fat has been broken into small pieces but there are still a few large flakes. Don't try to make the mixture look uniform.

Dribble in the tablespoons of ice water, mixing and tossing the dough with a fork. Don't try to force the dough into a ball, just keep adding water until it starts to cling together in clumps. After all the water has been added, check for dry dough mixture in the bowl and add drops of water to moisten.

Collect the dough and press it together into two balls. Shape the balls into plump cakes, making the edges as smooth as possible, and wrap in plastic. Press down on the plastic lightly to compress the dough. Refrigerate the dough for several hours before using to allow the gluten to relax and the flour to fully absorb the water. Dough may be stored in the refrigerator for 2 days or in the freezer for 1 or 2 months. Thaw frozen dough overnight in the refrigerator before using.

# Sweet Tart Dough

MAKES 11 OUNCES OF DOUGH, ENOUGH FOR ONE 11-
INCH TART, SIX 4-INCH TARTLETS, OR 30 COOKIES

This dough is soft and tender, very similar to a sugar cookie, and yields a finished pastry that is short and crumbly instead of crisp and flaky, perfect for soft and creamy fillings. The rolled dough is usually pressed into tart pans or small tartlet tins and often prebaked so that it stays firm when baked with liquid fillings. Besides making tart shells, the dough can be rolled into little cookies to fill with jam. See Yuzu Marmalade Thumbprint Cookies (page 323).

Beat together until creamy:

**8 tablespoons (1 stick) unsalted butter at room temperature**
**⅓ cup sugar**

Add and mix until completely combined:

**¼ teaspoon salt**
**¼ teaspoon vanilla extract**
**1 egg yolk**

Add:

**1¼ cups unbleached all-purpose flour**

*Royal Anne cherries*

Mix well, stirring and folding, until there are no dry patches. Chill for at least 4 hours or overnight until firm.

Sweet tart dough is soft and sticky by nature so roll it out between 2 sheets of parchment or waxed paper. Flour the bottom piece of paper and center the unwrapped dough on it. Dust the top of the dough with flour and place the other sheet of paper on top. Roll the dough, from the center out, into a 12-inch circle. If the dough sticks to the paper, peel back the paper and dust the dough with a bit more flour. If the dough gets too soft while rolling, chill it in the freezer for a few minutes to firm it up.

# Sweet Cherries *(Prunus avium)*
# Sour Cherries *(Prunus cerasus)*

Sweet cherries are among the first stone fruits of the year, with the first harvest starting in late spring. Eat them out of hand right off the tree or refreshingly chilled from the refrigerator. Roast them quickly for a juicy compote to spoon over lemon verbena ice cream (see page 32) or cook them into a galette or pie. The first fruits to come are good, but I adore the midseason varieties like the dark red *Bing*, which is big, crisp, juicy, and full of flavor. *Lambert*, deep red *Black*

*Tartarian*, and *Stella* are other favorites. There are white varieties, too. *Royal Anne*, a very old French heirloom, has beautiful pale yellow skin with a blush of rose pink on its cheeks and a rich balance of sweet and tart. It doesn't ship well and is almost never seen in the market. There are many more varieties to taste and choose from.

Sour cherries are too tart to eat out of hand, but they are fantastic in pies and preserves where additional sugar improves flavor balance. Because they are softer and more perishable than sweet cherries, sour cherries are difficult to find fresh in the market—all the more reason to have a tree of your own. *Montmorency* is a fine old French variety; *Meteor*, *North Star*, and *Morello* are good, too.

Cherries should be allowed to ripen completely on the tree, as their quality will not improve after harvesting. Pick one or two to taste when they are fully colored to make sure you don't harvest too early. Twist the cherries from the trees with their stems on for greater longevity. Keep an eye out for birds as your crop begins to ripen: they have a voracious appetite for fruit and an uncanny ability to know when it is ready for picking. If needed, cover the tree with bird netting to help protect the ripening fruit. Once harvested, store cherries in the refrigerator. They will last a few days at most.

All cherries need a considerable amount of winter chill. Sour cherries are especially cold hardy. Almost all sweet cherries need pollination by a different, and sometimes specific, variety in order to ensure a good crop. Black Tartarian and Stella are good pollenizers (as the variety supplying the pollen is called) and will pollinate a large variety of cherries; Stella is self-fruitful. Most sour cherries are self-fruitful. Once established, cherries need the least amount of pruning and fruit thinning of all the stone fruits.

# Bing Cherries Roasted with Lemon Verbena

4 SERVINGS

When roasted whole, cherries become perfumed with the bitter almond flavor of the pit—a heavenly combination. Lemon verbena adds to the symphony. Serve the cherries with whipped cream or Lemon Verbena Ice Cream (page 32).

Preheat the oven to 450°F.
Destem, wash, and dry:
   **1 pound Bing or other sweet cherries**
Spread out in a baking dish that just holds the cherries in a single layer. Sprinkle with:
   **2 tablespoons sugar**
   **A splash of kirsch or brandy (optional)**
Roll the cherries around to coat with sugar. Remove the leaves and discard the stem from:
   **1 lemon verbena sprig**
Tuck the leaves among the cherries. Roast until the cherries are puffed and soft, about 8 minutes. Serve warm or room temperature.

# Black Cherry Galette

MAKES ONE 12-INCH GALETTE, ABOUT 8 SERVINGS

Brooks, Burlat, Bing, or Stella cherries are the black cherries I use most. When I can find them, I like to add a few sour cherries to the mix. Serve the galette with sweetened whipped cream, crème fraîche, or à la mode.

Preheat the oven to 400°F.
Roll out into a 14-inch circle approximately ⅛ inch thick:
   **1 disk Galette Dough (page 246)**
Brush off any excess flour and transfer the dough to a baking sheet lined with parchment paper and refrigerate for 10 minutes or so to firm up.
Combine in a mixing bowl:
   **5½ cups cherries (pitted)**
   **¼ to ½ cup sugar (depending on the sweetness of the cherries; start with ¼ cup, taste halfway through baking, then add more as needed)**
   **Grated zest and juice from ½ lemon**
   **A splash of kirsch (optional)**
Toss all the ingredients together and set the bowl aside.
Take the dough from the refrigerator and spread, in a thin layer over the center of the dough, leaving a bare 1½-inch border:
   **2 tablespoons Frangipane (page 247)**
This will add some extra protection from the juicy fruit that might leak through.
Remove about 10 or so cherries from the bowl and cut them in half. Place the cherry halves in a ring around the edge of the frangipane to form a border (cut additional cherries as needed). Place the remaining cherry mixture in the center of the dough and

spread them out in a single layer. For a rustic look, fold the edges of the dough over the cherry halves toward the center. For a more composed look, twist the dough edge over itself toward the center, creating a rope pattern, pinching together the beginning turn and the final turn. Brush the crust with:

**1 tablespoon melted butter**

Sprinkle the crust with:

**1½ tablespoons sugar**

The butter and sugar will caramelize as the galette bakes, giving the crust a nice sweet crunch. If the dough is soft, return the galette to the refrigerator or freezer to firm up. Bake on the bottom rack of the oven for 45 to 50 minutes, until the crust is golden brown on the bottom. Slide off the pan and cool on a rack.

# Sour Cherry Pie

MAKES ONE 9-INCH PIE

Sour cherries make the best cherry pie. Their tart flavor works beautifully with sugar and buttery pie dough. The cherries are very perishable though, and should be used within a day or two of harvest. Keep a couple of disks of pie dough in your freezer and you will be ready when the cherries are.

Soften at room temperature for 20 minutes:

**Two 10-ounce disks Pie Dough
    (page 248)**

Roll 1 disk of dough on a cool, lightly floured surface into a 12-inch round, about ⅛ inch thick. Line a 9-inch pie pan with the dough. Trim the edges to leave about ½-inch overhang. Roll the other disk of dough into a 12-inch round and transfer to a parchment-lined baking sheet. Refrigerate the lined pie pan and the round of dough while preparing the fruit.

Position a rack in the lower third of the oven. Preheat the oven to 400°F in time to bake the pie.

Stem and wash:

**2 pounds sour cherries
    (about 4½ cups pitted)**

Pit the cherries using a cherry pitter or squeezing out the pits gently with your fingers. Toss the pitted cherries in a bowl with:

**1 cup sugar**

**¼ cup unbleached all-purpose flour**

Season the fruit mixture with:

**3 drops of almond extract**

Let stand until the juice from the cherries has moistened the mixture, about 5 minutes. Turn the fruit mixture into the prepared pie shell. Cut into small cubes and sprinkle over the berries:

**2 tablespoons butter**

Brush the edges of the bottom crust with water and cover the pie with the top crust. Trim the edges of the top crust to leave a ½-inch overhang. Fold the edge of the top crust under the edge of the bottom crust and pinch together all around. Crimp the edge using your thumb and forefinger to make a pretty border. If you like, you can decorate the top of the pie by making a few swirling cuts 1/16 inch deep with a paring knife, being careful not to cut all the way through the crust. Cut 4 or 5 small steam vents all the way through the top crust.

Brush the top of the pie with water and sprinkle with:

**1 tablespoon sugar**

Bake the pie for about 1 hour. The pie is done when the juices bubble thickly out of the steam vents and the crust is brown. If the edges start to brown too quickly, cover them with strips of foil. Let the pie cool for several hours. Serve with whipped cream or vanilla ice cream.

VARIATIONS

◆ Substitute 1 teaspoon or more maraschino or kirsch eau-de-vie for the almond extract.
◆ Use sweet cherries, with only ⅔ cup sugar and 2½ tablespoons flour in the filling.
◆ Use half sweet and half sour cherries, with only ¾ cup sugar and 2½ tablespoons flour in the filling.

## Apricots *(Prunus armeniaca)*

The heart of the fleeting apricot season comes in early summer, bringing back apricot tarts, galettes, sorbet, and soufflés. Apricots are divine made into jam or canned in a light syrup, preserving their fantastic golden color and fragrant flavor for chilly winter days. My favorite—the small, firm, juicy, aromatic *Blenheim* (*Royal Blenheim*)—is blushed with deep rose, and packed with flavor. I love to eat them just like that, right off the tree or at the farm stand. *Moorpark* has an abundance of large, pale pink flowers and big, rich-tasting fruit. The fruit has green shoulders so commercial farmers have stopped growing them. Both Blenheim and Moorpark are not favored by commercial growers and are becoming increasingly hard to find at the market. Plant a tree for yourself and help keep these wonderful fruits from disappearing. *Autumn Glo* is another very tasty apricot, and *Red Cloud* and *Tilton* are good varieties for cooking and preserving.

Apricots have the most specific growing requirements of all stone fruits. They need a moderate amount of winter chill, yet they bloom early and are susceptible to late frost. They also need relatively dry spring weather, and a period of dry heat when ripening to avoid problems with diseases. But if all goes well, what a magnificent reward—a handsome tree with scalloped heart-shaped leaves and rosy stems that gives shade in the heat of summer, and some of the most mouthwatering fruit you will ever have.

Apricots are ready to harvest when they are fully colored and begin to give slightly to a gentle squeeze. After harvest, spread them out on paper for a couple of days to finish ripening. They are easy to prepare for cooking; just run a small knife along the natural seam of the fruit and gently twist apart.

The pits can be dried in a low temperature oven and cracked open with a hammer to extract the kernel inside. The kernels (called noyaux) have a lovely bitter almond flavor. They can be used to flavor custards, ice cream, fruit compotes, and preserves and jams. Place the kernels in an airtight container; they will keep in the freezer for up to 1 year.

*Royal Blenheim apricots*

*Italian prunes*

*Flavor King pluot*

*Arctic Glo nectarine*

*O'Henry peaches*

# Apricot Galette

MAKES ONE 12-INCH GALETTE, ABOUT 8 SERVINGS

Use different apricots throughout the season as they become available—Honey Rich, Robada, Orange Red, Golden Sweet, Blenheim, and Red Cloud.

Prepare the dough as for Black Cherry Galette (page 250). Cut about 20 apricots into quarters and make a border of fruit along the edge of the frangipane. Place the remaining wedges skin side down with the tips pointing up in a circular pattern around the dough. Fold the edge of the dough over the fruit as desired. Sprinkle the fruit with ¼ cup of sugar. (Depending on the sweetness and variety of the apricot, you may need to adjust the sugar quantity. It is best to start with ¼ cup and then taste a piece of fruit from the galette halfway through baking and add more sugar if needed.) Brush the crust and bake as for Black Cherry Galette.

# Royal Blenheim Apricot Sorbet

MAKES 1 GENEROUS QUART

This sorbet concentrates the flavor of really good apricots. The finished mix can be stored in the freezer for several weeks to extend your apricot season. Just defrost the mixture in the refrigerator for a day or so and spin it in your ice-cream maker when you are ready for a smooth, fresh tasting sorbet. I like to serve it alone, or with fresh berries or sliced fruit, and a little bit of whipped cream. Use any extra sorbet mixture that doesn't fit in your ice-cream maker as a bright sauce for other fruits or with vanilla ice cream.

Cut in half and reserve the pits of:

**2¼ pounds ripe Royal Blenheim
    apricots**

Cut the fruit into rough pieces and place in a heavy-bottomed, nonreactive saucepan with about ¼ cup water. Crack 1 or 2 of the pits and add the noyau kernels inside. (Freeze the remaining pits for another noyau project.) Bring the apricots to a simmer, cover the pan, and cook gently stirring once or twice, until the fruit is very tender, about 10 minutes. Remove from the heat and let cool briefly. Remove the noyau and purée the apricots through the fine blade of a food mill or in a food processor. Pass the purée through a fine sieve if it seems fibrous. You should have about 3 cups. Cool the purée to room temperature.

Make a syrup by heating:

**1 cup water**

**1 cup sugar**

in a small saucepan until the sugar is dissolved. Cool the syrup. Add to the apricot puree until it tastes overly sweet. The impression of sweetness will be less after freezing. Depending on the sweetness of the fruit, you may not need to use all of the syrup. Add to enhance the apricot flavor:

**1 to 2 teaspoons lemon juice**

Chill the mixture in the refrigerator, then freeze in an ice-cream maker, following the manufacturer's instructions. Transfer the frozen sorbet into a clean dry container, cover, and store in the freezer for several hours to firm up before serving.

VARIATION

⬩ Add a teaspoon of kirsch or ¼ teaspoon of vanilla extract to the sorbet before freezing.

# Apricot Almond–Custard Tart

MAKES ONE 10-INCH TART, ABOUT 8 SERVINGS

This versatile tart is packed with fruit and a soft custard that bakes to a tender golden brown. The sweet dough combined with the custard filling renders it very stable, making it a perfect dessert to make ahead for a picnic or potluck. It actually tastes better after it has had a chance to sit a few hours for the flavors to marry.

Preheat your oven to 350°F.
In a small pot, melt:

**1 tablespoon unsalted butter**

With a small brush, butter a 10-inch fluted tart ring with a removable bottom.
Roll out into a 12-inch circle:

**1 disk Sweet Tart Dough (page 248)**

Gently press the dough into the prepared tart pan. Cut off the excess dough by rubbing your thumb across the top edge of the pan. Any cracks can be pressed back together and holes repaired with excess dough. Prick the bottom of the dough lightly with a fork. Place in the freezer for 10 minutes to chill before baking.

Prebake the tart shell until it is lightly golden (about 15 to 20 minutes). Remove from the oven and set aside to cool.
To make the almond custard, sift together and set aside:

**9 tablespoons almond flour**
**3 tablespoons unbleached all-purpose flour**
**¼ teaspoon salt**

Whisk together in a separate bowl:

**3 eggs, room temperature**
**1 tablespoon kirsch (optional)**

Measure into the bowl of a stand mixer fitted with the paddle attachment:

**7 tablespoons unsalted butter at room temperature**
**6 tablespoons sugar**

Cream together until light and fluffy. Turn off the mixer, scrape down the sides of the bowl and add:

**Grated zest of 1 lemon or ½ orange (optional)**

Turn the mixer to the low setting, and add the flour mixture alternately with the eggs, starting and ending with one third of the flour. Mix until all the ingredients are well incorporated.
Cut into quarters:

**8 to 10 apricots**

Set 8 quarters aside. Arrange the rest of the fruit over the bottom of the pan in a circular pattern in a single layer with the tips pointing up. Sprinkle the fruit with:

**3 tablespoons sugar**

Spread the custard over the fruit, then arrange the reserved fruit on top of the tart, pressing down slightly into the custard. Place the tart on a baking sheet and bake until the custard is golden brown, about 30 to 35 minutes. Cool before removing the tart from the ring. Serve each slice with:

**A spoonful of lightly sweetened whipped cream or crème fraîche**

VARIATIONS

• Cherry Almond-Custard Tart: Pit and slice in half 2 cups Bing cherries. Toss with 3 tablespoons sugar. Arrange the fruit cut side down.

• Berry Almond-Custard Tart: Use 3 cups blueberries, blackberries, raspberries, or boysenberries. Toss gently with 2 to 3 tablespoons sugar. Arrange the fruit as desired.

• Pear Almond-Custard Tart: Peel, core, and slice 4 or 5 ripe Comice or Bosc pears. Brush the arranged pears with a bit of melted butter and a light sprinkle of sugar.

• Fig Almond-Custard Tart: Slice 10 to 12 figs into quarters; set aside 8 pieces. Arrange the rest over the bottom of the shell in a single layer in a circular pattern with tips pointing up. Sprinkle with 1 to 2 tablespoons sugar. Cover with the custard; arrange the remaining fig quarters on top; sprinkle with 1 teaspoon more sugar.

• Apple Almond-Custard Tart: Peel, core, and slice 4 or 5 Gravenstein, Pink Lady, or other good baking apples. Brush the arranged apples with a bit of melted butter and a light sprinkle of sugar.

• Dried Cherry Almond-Custard Tart: Pour 1½ cups boiling water over 3 cups dried cherries and add a splash of kirsch or Cognac. Cover and let cool. Drain off the liquid; arrange the fruit as desired.

• Marsala and Dried Fig Almond-Custard Tart: Combine 2 cups dried figs with 1½ cups Marsala wine and bring to a boil. Remove from heat, cover, and let cool. Drain off the liquid; slice the figs in half; arrange the fruit as desired.

• Armagnac and Prune Almond-Custard Tart: Combine 1 cup Armagnac, ½ cup white wine, and 2 tablespoons sugar and bring to a boil to dissolve the sugar. Remove from the heat, add 2 cups pitted prunes, cover, and let cool. Drain off the liquid (save for another use); slice the prunes in half; arrange the fruit as desired.

• Dried Apricot Almond-Custard Tart: Combine 1½ cups sweet white wine, one 2-inch piece vanilla bean (cut in half and scraped), and 1 tablespoon sugar and bring to a boil to dissolve the sugar. Remove from the heat, add 2 cups dried apricots, cover, and let cool. Drain off the liquid; remove the vanilla bean; slice or split the apricots in half; arrange the fruit as desired.

## Apricot Aperitif
MAKES 4 DRINKS

Chill 4 small glasses in the freezer.
Measure into a pitcher or cocktail shaker:

**6 ounces Apricot Liqueur (page 354)**
**6 ounces Vin d'Orange (page 352)**
**6 ice cubes**

Stir until well chilled. Strain into the chilled glasses. Top with:

**A splash or two of sparkling wine or water**

Stir and serve.

VARIATIONS

• Use *soju* (a rather sweet Korean liquor) instead of vin d'orange.
• Use sparkling wine (Prosecco or Cava) instead of vin d'orange.

# Japanese Plums (*Prunus salicina*)
# European Plums (*Prunus domestica*)
# and Pluots

There is an enormous variety of plums, brilliant red, yellow, and purple on the outside, yellow, green, deep red on the inside. Plums are divided into two major categories. Each has its own flavor nuances and growing practices. I like them all.

Japanese plums are juicy and have tart flesh near the pit and skin. They ripen earlier than European varieties and are good for eating fresh, making jam, and slicing into open-faced galettes. Because of their sweet-sour nature, they are perfect for desserts with added sugar, like ice cream and sorbet. Some of my favorites are tart and sweet *Santa Rosa* with purple skin and yellow flesh; distinctive yellow *Howard Miracle* with a slightly spicy note; large heart-shaped *Elephant Heart* with richly sweet plum red flesh; and deep red *Satsuma* with its sweet and mild flavor.

European plums are naturally very sweet and less juicy. They dry well and are the plums that are used to make prunes. Try them with a tiny sprinkle of sugar, roasted or grilled, or as a topping baked into a cake. Use them for savory cooking, too, in chutneys and other spiced compotes to serve with roasted meats and poultry, or cooked down into dense fruit cheeses. Roast or grill them wrapped in a piece of bacon for a fantastic appetizer. *Italian* and *Stanley Prune* plums are purple with sweet yellow-green flesh; I like to eat them out of hand like candy. They are frequently used to make prunes. *Green*

*Gage* (*Reine Claudes*) are pale green with sweet yellow flesh. Dark purple and almost black *Damson* have dense, tasty yellow flesh.

Pluots, a hybrid between plums and apricots, can be used like either type of plum. They are wonderfully refreshing as a snack or on an after-dinner fruit plate with a few berries. They are great in open-face tarts or sorbet. *Flavor King*, a favorite at Chez Panisse, carries flavor reminders of its parents, winey Santa Rosa plum and luscious apricot.

When you are thinking about varieties to plant, remember that European plums do well in cold climates where they get enough winter chill. They bloom later in the spring and many are self-pollinating. Japanese plums don't need much winter chill and are adapted to warmer climates. They bloom quite early, sometimes before frost and snow have left colder climates. Many varieties require a pollenizer. Pluots, like Japanese plums, require a pollenizer and some winter chill. There are hybrids of Japanese and native American plums that can withstand the cold as far north as southern Canada.

# Pluot and Raspberry Galette
MAKES ONE 12-INCH GALETTE, ABOUT 8 SERVINGS

Flavor King, Dapple Dandy, and Flavor Treat pluots are the main varieties that I use, but there are many varieties available throughout the season.

Prepare the dough as for Black Cherry Galette (page 250). Slice 12 to 15 pluots into ¼-inch wedges. Make a border of fruit along the edge of the frangipane. Arrange the wedges on their sides slightly overlapping in a circular pattern. Fold the edge of the dough over the fruit as desired. Sprinkle the fruit with ⅓ cup of sugar. (Depending on the sweetness and variety of the pluot, you may need to adjust the sugar quantity. It is best to start with ⅓ cup and then taste a piece of fruit from the galette halfway through baking and add more sugar if needed.) Brush the crust and bake as for Black Cherry Galette. About 10 minutes before the galette is finished baking, toss 1 cup of raspberries in a tablespoon of sugar and sprinkle them over the surface of the pluots. Return to the oven to finish baking.

## Santa Rosa Plum Cake

MAKES ONE 9-INCH CAKE

The inspiration for this recipe comes from the German Pflaumenküchen, a light yeast dough covered with plum slices. It is good with breakfast or coffee anytime, and the recipe is easily doubled for a crowd at brunch. It is also good for dessert with whipped cream or Peach Leaf Ice Cream (page 261).

In a small bowl, stir together:

**¼ cup warm water**
**2¼ teaspoons active dry yeast**

In a small saucepan, heat until just warm:

**½ cup milk**
**¼ cup sugar**
**1 teaspoon salt**

Pour the sugar and milk mixture into a bowl and whisk in:

**2 eggs**
**1½ teaspoons vanilla extract**
**Grated zest of ½ orange**

Stir in the yeast mixture and:

**2 cups unbleached all-purpose flour**

Continue stirring until all the flour is incorporated. Beat in:

**4 tablespoons (½ stick) butter, very soft**

Stir vigorously until smooth, about 2 minutes. Cover loosely with plastic wrap and set in a warm place to rise until doubled, about 1 hour.

Cut into ¼-inch-thick slices:

**1¼ pounds Santa Rosa plums**

Melt:

**2 tablespoons butter**

Butter a 9-inch pie plate or round cake pan with a pastry brush and some of the melted butter. Pour the risen dough into the prepared pan. Press one third of the plum slices evenly into the dough around the whole cake, completely submerging them. Arrange the remaining plum slices in concentric circles around the top of the cake, pressing them in gently. Let the cake rest for 15 minutes. Preheat the oven to 375°F.

Mix together:

**1½ tablespoons brown sugar**
**1 tablespoon granulated sugar**
**⅛ teaspoon cinnamon (optional)**
**¼ teaspoon freshly grated nutmeg (optional)**

Gently brush the top of the cake with the remaining melted butter and sprinkle with the sugar mixture. Bake the cake on the middle shelf of the oven for 20 minutes or until dark golden.

VARIATION

◆ Use any other stone fruit (sliced peeled peaches or nectarines, apricots, pitted cherries, or pluots) instead of plums.

# Wild Plum Jam Turnovers

MAKES ABOUT 24 RAVIOLI

I call these small pastries "ravioli" as they are filled and folded the same way pasta dough is filled and folded for ravioli. They are a great little sweet that goes perfectly with an afternoon cup of tea, a picnic, or a simple dinner. I use a galette dough made with half whole-wheat flour. The flavors of wild plum are perfect with the whole-grain crust, but any other jam, conserve, or chutney will do.

To make the dough, cut into cubes the size of dice:

**6 tablespoons (¾ stick) unsalted
cold butter**

Set aside.

Measure:

**¼ cup ice-cold water**

In a large mixing bowl, stir together:

**½ cup whole-wheat flour**
**½ cup unbleached all-purpose flour**
**½ teaspoon sugar**
**¼ teaspoon salt**

Toss the butter with the dry ingredients and press the pieces of butter with your thumb and forefinger one by one to flatten them. Dribble three quarters of the water over the dry mixture and toss together gently to moisten. Continue adding water, tossing and lifting the mixture until it is evenly moist. Don't squeeze the dough into balls or knead it while doing this; it should be loose and shaggy. When it is uniformly moist, form it into a ball and wrap in plastic. Flatten the ball and form into a rectangle. Check the edges for cracks in the dough and smooth them out by pinching through the plastic to make sure all the edges are smooth. Chill for at least 1 hour or overnight.

Preheat the oven to 400°F.

Measure:

**¾ cup Wild Plum Jam (page 342)
(remove any pits)**

Take the dough from the refrigerator and cut it in half lengthwise. Lightly flour a rolling surface, and roll out one of the halves into a narrow rectangle about ¼ inch thick and 5½ inches wide. Spoon about 1 teaspoon of jam per "ravioli" along the lower half of the rectangle of dough, leaving enough room between jam dollops for sealing and cutting each one (about 2 inches). Using a pastry brush dipped in water, moisten the space between the jam dollops and all along the lower edge. Fold the upper half of the dough over so the edges meet along the bottom. With your finger, gently press the areas between the jam dollops and all along the bottom edge to seal. Using a fluted pastry cutter, trim the bottom edge and the two ends. Brush the dough with:

**Melted butter**

Sprinkle generously with:

**Sugar**

Cut between the ravioli, separating them, and place them on a sheet pan lined with parchment paper. Put the ravioli in the refrigerator while you roll out and cut the second piece of dough. Bake the ravioli until golden brown, 20 to 30 minutes.

# Roasted Italian Prune Plums and Rosemary

4 SERVINGS

I especially like Italian prune plums paired with rosemary. Roasted plums can be served either sweet or savory: as a simple dessert with whipped cream, ice cream, or crème anglaise or as a side dish to roasted, grilled, or braised pork or lamb.

Preheat the oven to 400°F.
Cut in half and remove the pits from:
> **12 to 16 Italian prune plums**

Toss the cut plums with:
> **2 tablespoons to ⅓ cup honey or brown sugar (use less sugar for a savory dish)**
> **1 small rosemary sprig, leaves only**
> **½ teaspoon crushed fennel seeds (optional)**

Arrange the plums, cut side down, in a baking dish or low-sided ovenproof pan that will just hold them in a single layer. Sprinkle over:
> **¼ cup red wine**
> **1 tablespoon red wine vinegar**
> **Fresh-ground black pepper**
> **1 tablespoon olive oil or melted butter**

Roast for 12 minutes. Turn over the plums and spoon some of the roasting juices over them. Return them to the oven and cook another 5 minutes or until soft and juicy. If the juices dry out in the oven add 1 or 2 spoonfuls of water.

# Peaches (*Prunus persica*)
# Nectarines
(*Prunus persica* var. *nectarina*)

For me, the highlight of the fruit year is midsummer, when first nectarines, and then peaches are at their best. A perfectly ripe peach is utterly divine on its own, and nectarines are not far behind. In the kitchen, peaches and nectarines can be used in many of the same kinds of desserts. Cut them in half and grill or bake them with a touch of honey or sprinkle of sugar. Turn them into delicious pies and crisps, alone or with mixed berries. Use them for the base of a summer fruit compote or a garnish in a berry soup. Peach or nectarine ice cream is one of the glories of the summer kitchen. Early in the season, peach leaves add a lovely almond flavor to custards and ice cream.

One of the first peaches and nectarines to ripen is *Arctic Glo*, a white-fleshed nectarine with streaks of red near the pit. It makes a gorgeous pink sorbet. About the same time come the first delicious yellow-fleshed peaches, *Flavorcrest* and *Red Haven*. Two white peaches that ripen a little later, *Nectar White* and *Silver Logan*, have the right balance of sweet and acid character to be used fresh or cooked. Beware of white peaches that are labeled "sub-acid," a sure indication they will be flat tasting when fully ripe, for it is the acid that gives the fruit its lively taste.

The hottest part of the summer brings perfectly ripened *Elberta*, *O'Henry*, and *Suncrest* peaches. They are ideal varieties to grow in a home garden, as they must be picked ripe in order to show their remarkable flavor. As the season winds down, yellow nectarines *Flavortop* and *Fantasia* start to ripen, followed by *Heavenly White* in early August. Another favorite peach is *Rio Oso Gem*. It is not a beauty, making it unlikely to be found at a supermarket, but with its true peach flavor and texture, it is the best peach to end the season. *Last Chance* is another delicious late-ripening peach that is worth seeking out.

Peaches and nectarines should remain on the tree until there is no green showing anywhere on the skin. At this stage, they bruise easily, and should be twisted carefully from the twig and brought indoors for a few days to soften before using. Peaches and nectarines when ready to eat should just give to gentle pressure at the shoulder. Peaches and nectarines are either freestone or clingstone. The flesh of a freestone fruit is not connected to the pit inside making it easy to remove the pit. The flesh of a clingstone fruit literally clings to its pit making it necessary to cut the fruit away. Clingstone fruit is generally juicier than freestone fruit.

To peel peaches for cooking or slicing, use a sharp paring knife or vegetable peeler, using a side-to-side sawing motion if necessary. Or immerse the peaches for a few seconds or so in boiling water and the skins will slip off easily. (The timing depends on the ripeness of the peach.) The thin skin of nectarines doesn't need peeling. To slice, cut into the fruit at the stem end, all the way around and up the other side. If the fruit is freestone, you can gently twist the two sides off the pit and proceed. If it is a variety that clings to the pit, cut slices into and then away from the pit.

# Peach Leaf Ice Cream
MAKES 1 QUART

Collect a big handful of tender young leaves from your peach trees in late spring or early summer. Crush several with your fingertips; they should exude a sweet scent of almond. (If they smell bitter, don't use them.) An infusion of the roughly crushed leaves, milk, and cream forms the base for this ice cream. Be careful to steep the leaves for only a few minutes; any longer and you will find unpleasant bitterness. Peach leaf ice cream goes beautifully with berries or any stone fruit.

Separate:

**6 eggs**

Refrigerate the whites for another use. Beat the yolks lightly, but don't let them get foamy. Pour into a heavy-bottomed saucepan:

**1½ cups half-and-half**

**⅔ cup sugar**

Warm over medium heat until steaming. Crush and coarsely tear in your hands:

**1 cup loosely packed peach leaves**

Add the crushed leaves to the hot mixture and reduce heat to low. Let steep for 4 minutes below the simmer, stirring occasionally; then start tasting. When the half-and-half mixture has a mildly herbaceous, almond flavor, remove the leaves with a slotted spoon. Whisk a little of the hot mixture into the egg yolks to temper them, then whisk the warmed yolks back into the remaining half-and-half mixture. Cook over medium heat, stirring constantly with a heat-proof spatula until the mixture thickens slightly and coats the back of a spoon

(168°F). Immediately remove from heat and strain into a bowl set in ice. Stir in:

**1½ cups heavy cream**

When cool, cover and refrigerate until thoroughly chilled. Freeze in an ice-cream maker, following the manufacturer's instructions. Transfer the frozen ice cream into a clean dry container, cover, and freeze for several hours to firm up before serving.

VARIATION

◆ For noyau ice cream, infuse ¼ cup smashed apricot kernels instead of peach leaves. When the half-and-half is hot, turn off the heat and leave to infuse for 20 minutes.

## Grilled Rio Oso Peaches

Grilled peaches are delicious sliced into a salad or sweetened and served for dessert. As the fruit heats over the smoky fire, the flesh softens and the flavors sweeten. Don't peel the peaches, as the skin holds the flesh and juices intact while they cook.

Count on ½ to 1 peach per person, depending on their size. Cut the peaches in half. Have ready a fire with medium-hot embers. Make sure the grill is preheated, cleaned, and oiled. Place the peaches on the grill cut side down. Cook for 3 to 4 minutes. The flesh should be well marked by the hot grill. Turn the peaches and cook another few minutes, until the peaches are softened and heated all the way through.

For a sweet version, mix 1 teaspoon of honey and a squeeze of lemon juice per peach (heat just to melt if needed). Brush the tops of the peaches with the honey mixture and grill as above. When the peaches are turned, pour the remaining honey into the well of each peach half.

## Nectarine and Blackberry Galette

MAKES ONE 12-INCH GALETTE, ABOUT 8 SERVINGS

I like to use yellow nectarines for a galette; they tend to have a little more acidity and balanced flavor. I also tend to wait for the freestone varieties that come later in the season since they are much easier to slice, but cling varieties are also delicious. Choose fruit that is fragrant and ripe but still firm to the touch. The varieties I typically choose include *May Grand, Ruby Grand, Fantasia, Summer Fire,* and *August Red.*

Prepare the dough as for Black Cherry Galette (page 250). Slice 6 to 8 nectarines into ½-inch wedges. Make a border of fruit along the edge of the frangipane. Arrange the wedges on their sides, slightly overlapping in a circular pattern. Fold the edge of the dough over the fruit as desired. Sprinkle the fruit with 2 tablespoons sugar. (Depending on the sweetness and variety of the fruit, you may need to adjust the sugar quantity. It's best to start with 2 tablespoons and then taste a piece of fruit from the galette halfway through baking and add more sugar if needed.) Brush the crust and bake as for Black Cherry Galette. About 10 minutes before the galette is finished baking, toss 1 cup blackberries in 1 tablespoon sugar and sprinkle over the surface of the nectarines. Return to the oven and finish baking.

# Just-Picked Berries

## Strawberries, Raspberries, Blackberries, Blueberries, Huckleberries, Mulberries, and Red Currants

IS THERE ANYTHING MORE compelling than a ripe berry? Whether it is a soft red raspberry, a plump, juicy blackberry, a round, frosty blueberry, a tender mulberry, or a jewel-like red currant, they all ask—no demand—to be eaten, and right away. Thank goodness for farmers' markets and kitchen gardens, to provide us with these delicate luxuries exploding with flavor. When we have had our fill of eating them out of hand, there are plenty of delicious dishes to cook them into: cobblers, jams, soufflés, shortcake, trifles, and summer puddings. And then maybe just a few more to pop into our mouth while they are here.

# Recipes

Strawberry Jus  266

Alpine Strawberry Tartlets with Crab Apple Glaze  267

Strawberries Roasted with Lemon Thyme  267

Golden and Red Raspberry Fool  268

Raspberry Turnovers  269

Raspberry and Peach Trifle  270

Sponge Cake  271

Noyau Crème Anglaise  271

Blackberry and Honey Compote with Tarragon  273

Blackberry Coulis  273

Blackberry Soufflé  274

Blueberry and Poppyseed Butter Cake  276

Almond Ice Milk with Huckleberry Sauce  276

Mulberry Ice Cream  278

Red Currant Granita  279

Summer Pudding  280

## Small Fruits in the Garden

Being able to pick a fresh berry is an incredible luxury yet one that is quite within reach. Small fruits, especially the rambling ones, provide abundant harvests from a small footprint, and are, for the most part, easy to grow. Many thrive in containers, and they offer not only exquisite flavor but beauty, too: glossy green leaves, colorful berries, rambling vines, compact plants, pretty little flowers, and then crimson and orange leaves in the fall. When well tended, they are prolific as well, offering a harvest to pluck daily and enjoy with pride. Any abundance can be made into jam and other preserves or frozen to enjoy when winter months have no berries on offer. Besides fruit, these plants can be quite useful in the landscape. Blueberries and huckleberries grown as hedges or screens can quickly hide a problematic view. Blackberries and other thorny brambles make impenetrable screens, while providing welcoming shelter and food for birds and other small animals. A tall mulberry tree will provide shade and bear the most delicate fruit for the best ice cream imaginable.

Once you have decided what kind of berry you want, do a little research before planting. Look for varieties that will do well in your location, and get to know the habit of your chosen varieties. They all need well-draining soil and lots of sunshine. Raspberries and blackberries have canes that need support and annual pruning. Keep an eye out for birds; they love berries, too. Depending on where you live, you may need to protect your fruit with netting to keep your harvest intact.

Mulberries are in this section not by mistake. Though the trees can reach thirty feet high and wide, the fruits look like blackberries on a tree, and they can be used much the same way as other berries. Avoid planting the trees near pavement, where fallen fruit can make an indelible stain.

*Alpine strawberries*

## Strawberries *(Fragaria × ananassa)*

Strawberries' bright red color and supreme juicy sweetness make them impossible to resist. The first berries to ripen are for eating straight from the market or the garden. Then come shortcakes, tarts, sorbet, ice cream, and jam. I adore the little wild alpine berries (also called *fraises des bois* or wild strawberries), too. They are not nearly as juicy and have a highly fragrant flavor. The plants are not very productive and the fruit is very fragile, which makes them hard to find outside of the kitchen garden.

*Seascape*, *Chandler*, and *Albion* strawberries all come to markets here in northern California, and they are all tasty. I vacillate from week to week about which is my all-time favorite. *Ali Baba*, *Alexandria*, and *Mignonette* are tasty red alpine varieties. *Yellow Wonder* is a yellow alpine and *Alpine White* is quite good, too. There are strawberry varieties that are suitable for every climate zone. Ask around to see what your locally grown favorites are and how they perform. It is illuminating to start critically tasting strawberry varieties to learn the differences in size, flavor, and texture. Berries tend to be smaller their first year.

There are three types of strawberries: day neutral, June-bearing, and ever-bearing. Day-neutral types bear fruit starting in late spring in mild climates and continue through the fall. June-bearing types set a lot of fruit all at once to be harvested in early summer, and ever-bearing types set two crops: one in early summer, the other in fall.

Strawberry plants are propagated by runners, not seed, and they need plenty of room to stretch out, with the exception of alpine berries, which grow in well-behaved clumps that can be used as groundcover or flower bed edging. All strawberries need good well-draining soil and plenty of sun (although alpine varieties will grow in partial shade). Keep the plants consistently watered and fed with compost. Mulch with straw to keep the soil moist and the berries clean, and protect them during winter cold. When well tended, strawberry plants will remain healthy and productive in the same bed for up to five years. Start a new bed in a different location every four or five years. All strawberries do very well in containers.

# Strawberry Jus
MAKES ABOUT 1 CUP

This is a simple way to extract a crystal-clear deeply flavorful berry juice. Use the juice to make sparkling strawberry drinks or cocktails, to flavor yogurt, or as a sauce.

Fill a 1-quart canning jar with:
**1 pint cleaned and hulled strawberries**
Cut off and discard any blemished bits as you add them to the jar. Sprinkle the berries with:
**2 tablespoons sugar**
Cover the jar loosely with the lid.
Fill a medium pot with enough water to come two thirds of the way up the sides of the jar. Put the jar in the water, bring to a boil, and reduce the heat to a simmer. Cook for about 30 minutes. Keep an eye on the water, adding more as needed. Most of the juice from the berries will have been released and settled in the bottom of the jar. Tighten the lid and simmer another 15 minutes, or until the berries look pale and shriveled.

Remove the jar from the pot and let it cool slightly. Carefully remove the lid with a towel and pour the contents into a cheesecloth-lined strainer or chinoise, and drain for 2 hours, pressing gently on the berries so they release all their juice. Use the juice immediately or store in the refrigerator for a week or in the freezer for up to 3 months.

VARIATIONS
♦ Raspberry, blackberry, boysenberry, or mulberry jus is made the same way. The yield may vary depending on the moisture content of the berries.

*Seascape strawberries*      *Albion strawberries*

# Alpine Strawberry Tartlets with Crab Apple Glaze

The bright aromatic flavor of alpine strawberries is remarkable. The berries are quite fragile and it is rare to have a large quantity of them, but when I have enough, I like to make these beautiful tiny tartlets—perfect little bites.

Press a thin layer of softened Sweet Tart Dough (page 248) into small tartlet tins (no need to roll it out). Small tartlet tins come in a variety of shapes: fluted diamonds, ovals, and circles. An 11-ounce ball of dough is more than enough for 24 tartlets; how many you make will depend on the occasion and your supply of strawberries. (You can freeze any extra dough as a ball, or pressed into the tins, and save it for another time.) Refrigerate the dough in the tins for 20 minutes to firm it up, or freeze it for 5 minutes. Preheat the oven to 375F°. When ready to bake, poke the bottom of each tartlet with the tines of a fork, place the tartlets on a baking sheet, and bake until they are a light golden brown, 10 to 12 minutes.

When they have cooled, tip the tart shells out of the tins and fill them with alpine strawberries. A mix of red and white berries is very pretty. Warm some Crab Apple Jelly (page 344) until just melted and use a pastry brush to gently glaze the berries. Arrange on a pretty plate and serve. Red and gold raspberries make excellent tartlets, too, alone or combined with the strawberries.

# Strawberries Roasted with Lemon Thyme

Roasting strawberries softens them and concentrates their flavor. The perfume of lemon thyme complements the berries' floral aroma. Spoon the roasted berries over ice cream, yogurt, or a simple cake.

Preheat the oven to 400°F. Toss 1 pound hulled strawberries with 1 tablespoon sugar and 4 lemon thyme sprigs. Lay them out in a low-sided baking dish and bake for 7 minutes (only 5 minutes if using a metal pan). Toss the berries and cook for 2 or 3 more minutes. The berries should be warm all the way through and just starting to give off juice. Let them rest in the warm pan for a couple of minutes before serving. Just about any berry can be roasted like this, except raspberries: they are too soft and juicy.

## Raspberries *(Rubus idaeus)*

A just-picked raspberry is divine. I have a bed of raspberries in my backyard. On summer mornings, I go out and eat the ripe berries right off the plant. Of course, some make it into the house, but I love that morning ritual. The soft and delicate berries are easily turned into a purée for saucing fresh peaches and ice cream for peach Melba, for folding with whipped cream into a fool, or for making a pretty apéritif. Sprinkle raspberries with sugar and they soften and yield their juices to mix into a summer pudding, fold into a crispy turnover, or bake into a soufflé. And raspberry jam is pure indulgence.

Red and golden raspberries have a similar texture, although golden raspberries are milder in flavor. Black raspberries (*Rubus occidentalis*) are firmer and less juicy, with a deeper berry flavor and more pronounced seeds. Eating the three together is a real treat. There are many varieties of each and it is important to choose one that does well in your area.

Red and gold varieties are either summer-bearing, producing one large crop in the summer, or ever-bearing, with two smaller crops, one in summer and one in fall. Raspberry plants grow on canes that reproduce by runners and will expand throughout the yard if left unattended, but they are easy to keep in place by cutting out runners. Water deeply and feed with compost every month in the early months of the growing season. Different types are pruned differently.

Pick raspberries when they are fully colored and come off the stem with a gentle tug. The core will stay on the plant. Don't let the fruit pile up in the picking container, or they will be crushed by their own weight. Try to use them the same day without refrigerating. Don't wash raspberries or other soft berries unless you feel you have to, and then with only a quick rinse with cold water. If you must store them, spread out the berries on a paper-lined baking sheet and refrigerate for no more than a day or two. For longer storage, freeze them in a single layer on an unlined baking sheet and then transfer to an airtight container. They will be a wonderful treat in the middle of winter.

## Golden and Red Raspberry Fool

4 SERVINGS

Fools are very easy to make—they are simply crushed berries folded into whipped cream. They are delicious and look beautiful when made and displayed in a glass serving dish.

Purée with a food mill or in a food processor:
> **1½ cups red raspberries**
> **2 tablespoons sugar**

Look for and discard any moldy or blemished berries as you put them in the food mill or processor bowl. Strain the purée through a fine-mesh nonreactive sieve. Push on the seeds with a rubber spatula or wooden spoon to extract as much of the fruit as possible. Taste and add more sugar as needed. Finish with:
> **A few drops of lemon juice**

Measure into a mixing bowl:
> **¾ cup heavy cream**
> **2 teaspoons sugar**

Whisk the cream and sugar until they start to form stiff peaks. Toss together:

**¾ cup whole golden raspberries**
**1 tablespoon sugar**

Fold the raspberry purée and golden raspberries into the whipped cream.

Spoon the cream into a large glass serving bowl or 4 individual glasses. Top with:

**¼ cup golden raspberries**
**¼ cup red raspberries**

Serve immediately or cover and refrigerate until ready to serve.

VARIATIONS

• Barely fold the raspberry purée and whipped cream together for a layered or striped effect.

• Use any other soft berries instead of raspberries: blackberries, boysenberries, loganberries, mulberries, and so on.

# Raspberry Turnovers

MAKES 12 TURNOVERS

The trick to a turnover is getting as much fruit inside as possible without overstuffing the pastry. Soft raspberries are some of the easiest and tastiest fruits to pack inside. Turnovers are great for a party or picnic where there is only finger food.

Preheat the oven to 400°F.

On a lightly floured surface, roll out into a 12- × 16-inch rectangle about ⅛ inch thick:

**One 10-ounce disk Galette Dough**
**(page 246)**

Brush off any excess flour and cut into twelve 4-inch squares. Place on a parchment-paper-lined pan and cover with another sheet of parchment. Chill to firm up.

Measure:

**¼ cup Frangipane (page 247)**

Discard any moldy or blemished berries from:

**1 pint raspberries**

Melt:

**1 tablepoon butter**

Spread 1 teaspoon frangipane in a thin layer at the center of each square of dough. Place 10 to 15 raspberries (depending on their size) just off center in a small pile on each square. Sprinkle the fruit with:

**½ to ¾ teaspoon sugar**

Keep the edges of the dough clear of frangipane and sugar. Using a pastry brush or your finger, spread a small amount of water around the edge of the dough. Fold the dough over the fruit, making a triangle, and press the edges together to close. Use the tines of a fork to seal the dough shut.

Brush the tops of the turnovers with melted butter and sprinkle with sugar—this will caramelize as the turnovers bake and give the crust a nice sweet crunch. Return to the refrigerator to chill for 20 minutes or put in the freezer for 5 minutes.

Bake on a parchment-paper-lined baking sheet until the crust on the edges and bottom is baked through and golden, about 15 to 20 minutes. Cool on a rack. Serve warm or at room temperature.

VARIATION

• Boysenberries and blackberries make good turnovers, too, or try a mixture of all three.

# Raspberry and Peach Trifle

6 SERVINGS

This is a lighter version of the classic dessert, with layers of sponge cake, fruit, and crème anglaise. It is a wonderful way to enjoy seasonal fruit. It's fresh, simple, and delicious. Layer the dessert into a large glass bowl or make individual portions in dessert glasses. For a more casual look, use wide-mouth, one-pint Mason jars. Perfect for a picnic or party—easy to transport, easy to eat.

Measure the inner diameter of the 6 cups or jars you are using. Cut 18 circles from:

**⅓ sheet Sponge Cake (page 271)**

If using 1 large bowl, cut 2 circles. Combine in a nonreactive bowl:

**2½ cups raspberries**

**1 to 2 tablespoons sugar**

Look for and discard any moldy or blemished berries as you put them in the bowl. Let the berries and sugar sit for 10 minutes or so to macerate.

Peel and cut into ½-inch dice:

**3 ripe peaches**

Gently toss with:

**1 to 2 tablespoons sugar**

Measure:

**2¼ cups Noyau Crème Anglaise
(page 271)**

Put 1 tablespoon crème anglaise in the bottom of each glass or jar. Place a round of sponge cake on top of the crème anglaise and spoon 3 heaping tablespoons raspberries and 2 tablespoons peaches on top. Pour 2 tablespoons of the crème anglaise on top of the peaches and place the second round of cake on top. Spoon on raspberries

and peaches as before and pour over 1 tablespoon crème anglaise. Place a third round of cake on top and pour a final 2 tablespoons crème anglaise on the top of the cake. Cover and chill.

The trifle can be made in the morning to serve that evening, or it can be served the next day. Before serving, garnish with:

**Fresh peach slices and berries**

VARIATIONS

◆ For a large trifle, cut 2 circles of sponge cake. Pour ½ cup crème anglaise into the bowl, add the cake and half of each fruit, as above. Pour over ¾ cup custard. Make a second layer of fruit and pour ½ cup custard over it, add the second layer of cake, and pour over the last ½ cup custard.

◆ Use blackberries, olallieberries, boysenberries, loganberries, or marionberries instead of raspberries.

◆ Substitute Bing Cherries Roasted with Lemon Verbena (page 250) for the peaches and raspberries.

◆ Use lemon crème anglaise (page 272) and substitute blueberries for the peaches and raspberries.

◆ Use cinnamon-bourbon crème anglaise (page 272) and substitute puréed Hachiya persimmons for the peaches and raspberries.

◆ Use Marsala-flavored crème anglaise (page 272) and substitute poached pears for the peaches and raspberries. Sprinkle shavings of bittersweet chocolate over the crème anglaise layers.

◆ Use Calvados crème anglaise (page 272) and substitute Sautéed Pink Pearl Apples (page 289) and Honey Candied Walnuts (page 299) for the peaches and raspberries.

## Sponge Cake

MAKES ONE 12- × 18-INCH RECTANGULAR CAKE

This sponge cake recipe is based on a recipe from Shirley Sarvis, a dear friend of Chez Panisse. The recipe has evolved over the years—we use less sugar now—but it is still the same feather-light cake, wonderful for making layered desserts and cake crumbs.

Preheat the oven to 350°F.
Butter a half-sheet pan (12 × 18 inches) and line the bottom with parchment paper. Butter the parchment paper and dust the pan with flour, shaking out the excess.
Separate:

**5 eggs, at room temperature**
Sift together:

**1½ cups cake flour**
**½ teaspoon baking powder**
**¼ teaspoon salt**
Put the yolks into a mixing bowl and whip for 5 minutes until light in color. Add:

**½ cup cold water**
**½ teaspoon vanilla extract**
**1¼ cups sugar**
Continue whipping for 5 minutes more. The mixture will form a faint ribbon when the whisk or beater is lifted. Whip the egg whites into soft peaks with:

**½ teaspoon cream of tartar**
Gently fold the flour mixture into the egg yolks. When the flour is incorporated, gently fold in the beaten egg whites. Pour the batter into the prepared pan, smooth the top, and bake for 15 to 20 minutes, or until the cake is lightly brown and begins to pull away from the sides of the pan. Let cool completely. The cake can be made 1 or 2 days ahead, wrapped well, and held at room temperature. It also freezes well.

VARIATION
◆ For a regular round cake, bake in a buttered 9-inch cake pan for 30 to 40 minutes.

## Noyau Crème Anglaise

MAKES 2¼ CUPS

Apricot kernels give this custard a wonderful fruity, bitter almond flavor. The flavor of noyau marries perfectly with berries and stone fruit. Serve it chilled and poured over a bowl of berries or sliced fruit for a heavenly—and easy—dessert.

Separate:

**3 eggs**
Reserve the whites for another purpose. Whisk the yolks just enough to break them up. Pour into a heavy-bottomed pot:

**2 cups half-and-half**
**2 tablespoons sugar**
**8 apricot kernels, chopped**
Set a strainer over a heat-proof bowl. Heat the half-and-half over medium heat, stirring occasionally to dissolve the sugar. When hot, turn off the heat and leave to steep for 20 minutes. Reheat the half-and-half, whisk a little into the egg yolks, and then whisk the yolks into the hot half-and-half. Cook over medium heat, stirring slowly, until the mixture thickens just enough to coat the back of the spoon (about 170°F). Do not let it boil. Remove from the heat, stir, and strain. Crème anglaise can be made in advance and kept in the refrigerator for 2 or 3 days.

VARIATIONS

* For lemon crème anglaise, add the zest of 1 lemon to the hot half-and-half mixture, and let steep 15 minutes before cooking the custard.
* For vanilla crème anglaise, cut open and scrape out the seeds of a 3-inch piece of vanilla bean into the hot half-and-half mixture. Add the scraped piece of bean, too, and let steep for 15 minutes before cooking the custard. Or stir 1 teaspoon vanilla extract into the chilled crème anglaise.
* For cinnamon-bourbon crème anglaise, add a 2-inch piece of cinnamon stick to the hot half-and-half mixture and let steep 15 minutes before cooking the custard. When the crème anglaise is completely cooled, stir in 1 tablespoon bourbon (or to taste).
* For Marsala-flavored crème anglaise, add 1 to 2 tablespoons Marsala to the chilled custard.
* For Calvados (apple brandy) crème anglaise, add 1 tablespoon Calvados to chilled custard.
* Substitute milk for some or all of the half-and-half.
* Add another egg yolk for a slightly thicker custard.

# Blackberries (*Rubus fruticosus*)

In northern California wild blackberries are the easiest plant for foraging. Blackberries grow in backyards and parks, and even plants along the roadside are good for a handful of sweet berries in July and August. It is hard to resist stopping when a bush full of deep purple berries comes into view.

Blackberries are good fresh for shortcake, tarts, and compotes, by themselves or with other berries or peaches and nectarines. Cooking brings out their flavor; they are wonderful in cobblers and pies. Use blackberry purée for ice cream, sorbets, and soufflés. Wild blackberries are sometimes so sweet that they need a squeeze of lemon juice for balance. *Boysen*, *Marion*, and *Ollalie* are tasty varieties. *Black Satin* is a thornless variety with large tasty berries.

Though wild blackberries are frequently considered an invasive weed, there are many better-behaved cultivated varieties that grow well in home gardens. Most cultivated blackberries are hybrids of one or more of the naturally occurring species with larger berries and smaller seeds. Most varieties bear fruit in summer, although there are some that bear in fall as well. In general, blackberries are not as hardy as some of the other berries, so be sure to check which varieties will grow in your region. Western trailing varieties are hardy down to about 0°F. Eastern erect varieties can tolerate more cold.

Plant in well-amended soil, keep the plants watered and fed with compost, and mulch to keep the soil moist and the plants protected during winter. Prune according to the type grown. Ripe blackberries are plump, juicy, and colorful. They should come off the stem with a gentle tug. If you are using the fruit for jam, a few underripe berries will help the jam to jell better. Store blackberries like other berries, in a single layer on a paper-lined baking sheet. Refrigerate them if it will be more than a few hours before you use them. They freeze well, too.

*Golden and red raspberries*

*Huckleberries*

*Blackberries*

## Blackberry and Honey Compote with Tarragon

Sweet juicy blackberries have just a hint of wild herbs in their fragrance. Try this compote of warm berries drizzled with honey and scented with 1 tarragon sprig. They are mighty fine spooned over whole-grain pancakes and yogurt or on a cut biscuit with loads of freshly whipped cream.

Preheat the oven to 400°F. Pour a pint of blackberries into a baking dish that just holds them comfortably in a single layer. Look them over and discard any moldy or blemished ones. Break up 1 tarragon sprig and tuck it down among the berries. Drizzle 2 teaspoons honey over the berries. If the honey is thick, set the jar in hot water to thin it out. Roast the berries for 5 to 8 minutes (6 minutes if they are in a metal dish). Remove from the oven and let sit a few minutes in the warm pan. Serve warm or at room temperature.

If you like these berries, try them with rosemary, scented geranium, anise hyssop, or lemon verbena, all of which are delicious.

## Blackberry Coulis

This is a very simple fruit sauce that can be served over ice cream, under a poached peach, next to a simple pound cake, stirred into a bowl of mixed berries, or poured into a hot soufflé. Any soft berry makes a delicious coulis.

Purée together with a food mill or in a food processor:

> **1½ cups blackberries**
> **2 tablespoons sugar**
> **A pinch of salt**

Look for and discard any moldy or blemished berries as you put them in the food mill or processor bowl. Strain the purée through a fine-mesh nonreactive sieve, pressing the berries with the back of a spoon to extract as much juice as possible.

Stir in, if desired:

> **1 teaspoon blackberry liqueur or**
> **framboise**

Taste for sugar and adjust as needed. Blackberry coulis can be kept in the refrigerator for up to 3 days.

# Blackberry Soufflé

MAKES 5 INDIVIDUAL SOUFFLÉS

Wild blackberries are abundant in northern California during the months of July and August, when one can easily pick a few pounds of these delicious berries on a short hike through almost any parkland. Berries from the market work just fine, too. This soufflé is relatively simple to make, filled with intense blackberry flavor, and quite beautiful to look at, with its deep purple hue.

The pastry cream for the soufflé can be made a day ahead. In a small saucepan, heat until steaming:

**½ cup milk**
**Zest of ½ lemon, grated**

In a small bowl, stir together:

**1½ tablespoons sugar**
**1½ tablespoons unbleached all-**
**   purpose flour**
**A pinch of salt**

Turn off the heat and sprinkle the flour mixture into the steaming milk. Stir the mixture until smooth. Turn the heat back on to medium and stir slowly until very thick. Turn off the heat.

In a small bowl, whisk:

**2 egg yolks**

Add one quarter of the milk and flour mixture to the yolks, a spoonful at a time, whisking all the while. Pour the egg mixture back into the saucepan and whisk together thoroughly. Turn the heat back on to medium and cook until the mixture thickens, stirring slowly and scraping the sides and bottom of the pan to prevent scorching. Do not boil. Remove the pan from the heat and add:

**1½ teaspoons butter**

Stir until the butter is well incorporated. Pass the hot mixture through a fine sieve to strain out the lemon zest. Place plastic wrap right on the surface to prevent a skin from forming and chill thoroughly before using. Purée, in a food mill or food processor:

**1½ cups freshly picked blackberries**
**Juice of 1 lemon**

Strain the purée through a fine-mesh nonreactive sieve, pressing the berries with the back of a spoon to extract as much juice as possible. This will yield ¾ cup thick purée.

Generously butter five 5-ounce ramekins, leaving a lip of butter on the inside rim of the ramekins for better rising. Coat the buttered ramekins with a fine layer of sugar.

Preheat the oven to 450°F.

Mix together in a mixing bowl the chilled pastry cream, blackberry purée, and:

**2 tablespoons blackberry liqueur or**
**   framboise**

Mix well and set aside. (If the pastry cream is quite thick and curdled, smooth it with an immersion blender or pass it through a food mill.) Measure into a copper or stainless steel mixing bowl:

**5 egg whites**
**¼ teaspoon cream of tartar**
**A pinch of salt**
**1½ tablespoons cornstarch**

Whisk until frothy. Sprinkle on:

**⅓ cup sugar**

Keep whisking until the peaks are firm and glossy but not dry. Gently fold half the whites into the blackberry mixture until they are partially incorporated, then add the rest of the whites and fold until all the whites are incorporated. Spoon the soufflé mixture into the prepared ramekins, filling them just to the lip. Drag your finger around the top and outer edge of each ramekin to clean up any splattered soufflé mixture. This ensures that the soufflé will rise straight up without sticking to the sides. Let the soufflé mixture rest in the ramekins for 5 minutes before baking. Sprinkle a thin layer of sugar on the top of each soufflé right before putting them in the oven. Bake for 8 to 9 minutes, until the soufflés are tall, golden brown on top, and still slightly soft to the touch in the center. Remove the baking sheet from the oven and dust the tops with powdered sugar.

Serve immediately on individual plates lined with napkins, doilies, or grape leaves (to prevent the ramekin from sliding). As an option, you can drizzle 1 teaspoonful Blackberry Coulis (page 273) on top of the soufflé before serving, or pass around a pitcher of the coulis to pour into the center of the soufflé.

## Blueberries (*Vaccinium* spp.)
## Huckleberries
(*Vaccinium* spp. *Gaylussacia* spp.)

Blueberries and their close relatives huckleberries add another dimension to the berry story. Huckleberries grow wild all over northern California. They seem to have an affinity for nectarines; you can combine the two in cobblers, crisps, or pies—although they will taste just fine on their own, too.

When used alone in a tart or a sauce, blueberries often need brightening with a bit of lemon juice and zest. They make great jam, and freeze well, too. And you can't forget blueberries or huckleberries in muffins or buttermilk pancakes.

Blueberries and huckleberries are ornamental shrubs that fit in any landscape. In addition to their beautiful fruits, the foliage of many varieties turns bright red in the fall. Blueberries need very acid soil conditions; you will probably have to amend your soil to meet their requirements. A more practical solution may be to grow them in containers, in an acid soil mix. Plant breeders have been very active developing varieties of blueberries for all parts of the country, so you should be able to find a variety that will flourish where you garden. In general, highbush types are cold hardy and need winter chill in order to fruit, while rabbit-eye and southern highbush types are suitable for warmer southern and coastal climates.

It is preferable to plant at least two varieties in your garden. Though some blueberries are self-pollinating, they all produce better-tasting, larger crops with a partner. Amend regularly to keep the soil acid. The bushes do best in full sun, but they will tolerate some shade. Feed with compost and keep watered.

Blueberries and huckleberries are ready to pick when they have developed their characteristic hazy "bloom" and they come off the stems easily. The plants ripen fruit over a longer period of time than other berries, often for four to six weeks. They hold well on the plants, so you don't have to pick every day, and they are fine for several days in the refrigerator.

## Blueberry and Poppyseed Butter Cake

MAKES ONE 9-INCH CAKE

This simple tender cake is loaded with fresh blueberries. The nutmeg deepens the blueberry flavor.

Preheat the oven to 350°F. Butter a 9-inch springform pan and dust with flour.
Take out of the refrigerator to come to room temperature:

**1 egg**

Grate the zest (about 2 teaspoons) from:

**2 lemons**

Gently stir together:

**2 cups blueberries, stems removed**
**2 tablespoons sugar**
**¼ teaspoon freshly grated nutmeg**

In another bowl, stir until well mixed:

**1½ cups unbleached all-purpose flour**
**2 tablespoons poppyseeds**
**½ teaspoon baking soda**
**½ teaspoon salt**

Measure:

**½ cup crème fraîche**

In another bowl or in a stand mixer, beat together until light and fluffy:

**8 tablesoons (1 stick) butter, softened**
**½ cup sugar**

Add the egg and lemon zest and keep mixing. When well mixed, add the flour mixture alternately with the crème fraîche, starting and ending with one third of the flour. Stir just until the flour is incorporated. Spread the batter into the prepared pan, spreading the mixture 1 inch up the sides of the pan to make a depression in the center.
Stir the blueberries and add:

**1 tablespoon unbleached all-purpose flour**

Pour the blueberries into the center of the batter. Bake for 45 to 50 minutes.
While the cake is baking prepare a glaze. Mix together:

**⅓ cup powdered sugar**
**2 tablespoons lemon juice**
**1 tablespoon milk (or just enough to reach a drizzling consistency)**

Drizzle the glaze over the warm cake. When cool, run a knife around the edge of the pan and lift out of the form.

VARIATIONS

‣ Stir 2 tablespoons finely chopped candied lemon peel into the blueberries with the nutmeg.
‣ Use raspberries, blackberries, or mulberries in place of blueberries, fold in the sugar at the last minute, and omit the nutmeg.

## Almond Ice Milk with Huckleberry Sauce

MAKES 1 QUART

This light ice milk made with fresh almonds is delicious with the deep rich purple huckleberry sauce. Together they taste of long summer days filled with sun and fruit.

Measure into a bowl:

**1 cup almonds**
**3½ cups water**

Cover the bowl and soak the almonds overnight. (This softens them and makes them easier to purée.) The next day, drain the almonds and save the liquid. Peel off the skins and discard. In a blender, purée the almonds with all the soaking water. Line a strainer with cheesecloth and strain the blended mixture. Once most of the liquid has drained through, gather up the corners of the cheesecloth and squeeze the almond pulp to extract the remaining liquid. Measure 4 cups almond milk. Save any extra for another use.

Pour 1 cup of the almond milk into a small heavy-bottomed pan along with:

**½ cup sugar**
**A pinch of salt**

Heat until steaming, stirring to dissolve the sugar. Remove from the heat and stir back into the rest of the almond milk. Chill thoroughly.

Measure into a bowl:

**⅓ cup sugar**
**3 egg whites**

Beat until the whites are shiny and form stiff peaks. Fold the egg whites into the chilled almond milk. Freeze in an ice-cream maker according to the manufacturer's instructions. Transfer the frozen ice milk into a clean dry container, cover, and freeze for several hours before serving, to firm up.

For the huckleberry sauce, heat together until tender in a heavy-bottomed pot:

**1½ cups huckleberries, stems removed**
**3 tablespoons sugar**
**¼ cup water**

Stir to dissolve the sugar. Pass the berries through a food mill. Taste for sugar and adjust as needed. Chill.

To serve, spoon huckleberry sauce into individual serving bowls and top with a scoop of ice milk. Garnish with slices of peaches if desired.

## Mulberries *(Morus nigra, Morus rubra)*

Ripe mulberries are fragile and special. Don't try to keep them—not even overnight in the refrigerator. Either use them right away or freeze them. A plate of freshly picked mulberries is a very special dessert. Mulberry ice cream balances the sweet juiciness of the fruit with the richness of cream. It is my favorite ice cream.

Climb up into your tree and pick the fruit when it is black and starting to fall. Bring the berries indoors and spread them out on a paper-lined baking sheet until you are ready to use them the same day, or pack them into airtight containers and freeze. One mulberry tree will probably produce more than you can use. But what a flavorful indulgence!

If you live where winter temperatures seldom drop below 0° or −10°F, plant black mulberries, *Morus nigra*. Oscar and *Black Beauty* are two named varieties. Red mulberry, *Morus rubra*, is a good choice for colder climates where winter temperatures go as low as −40°F. Red mulberry trees are larger and need more room than black. A hybrid of black and red mulberry, *Illinois Everbearing*, has high quality fruit and is hardy down to −25°F.

Don't ever plant white mulberries! The fruit is insipid and the trees are very invasive.

# Mulberry Ice Cream

MAKES 1½ QUARTS

This is my favorite flavor of ice cream during the summer months. To make an especially fruity and flavorful ice cream, I use equal parts fruit purée and an ice-cream base with a nice creamy texture.

Purée with a food mill or in a food processor:

**3½ pints mulberries**

Look for and discard any moldy or blemished berries as you are adding them to the food mill or processor bowl. Strain the berries through a fine-mesh strainer into a clean bowl. If you like a bit of texture in your ice cream, add a small amount of seeds (too many can give a bitter flavor) back into the purée. You should have 2½ cups mulberry purée.

Measure into a medium pot:

**¾ cup cream**

**½ cup sugar**

Heat until the sugar is dissolved and the cream is steaming.

Meanwhile, separate into a heat-proof bowl (reserve the whites for another purpose):

**4 egg yolks**

Whisk to break up the yolks and set aside. When the sugar is dissolved and the cream is hot, add a small amount of the hot liquid to the egg yolks to temper them. Gradually add the hot cream and sugar mixture to the yolks, whisking the entire time to make sure you are not cooking the yolks too fast. Once all the cream is added to the yolks, pour the mixture back into the pot. Cook over medium heat, stirring constantly, until the mixture thickens and coats the back of the spoon (170°F). Do not let it boil. Remove from the heat and strain. Stir in:

**1½ cups cream**

Cool the ice-cream base to room temperature and add the mulberry purée. Chill thoroughly in the refrigerator and freeze in an ice-cream maker according to the manufacturer's instructions. Transfer the frozen ice cream into a clean dry container, cover, and store in the freezer for several hours before serving to firm up.

VARIATIONS

• For raspberry or blackberry ice cream, substitute 2¼ cups of raspberry or blackberry purée for the mulberry purée.

• For strawberry ice cream, substitute ¾ cup half-and-half for the first ¾ cup cream and 2¼ cups strawberry purée for the mulberry purée.

# Red Currants  *(Ribes rubrum)*

Currants were once a very popular fruit and easy to find. They don't travel well and taste good only when dead ripe. And do they taste good! Currants are well worth looking for. Red currant season comes and goes very quickly. The brilliant glossy red berries look like tiny ornaments. Their flavor is tart and sweet and is fantastic mixed with other summer fruit or frozen into a granita or made into a crystal clear jelly.

Red currants are beautiful in the garden. Green lobed leaves turn crimson in fall and the striking berries pop out in the landscape. The bushes are cold hardy and, if protected from afternoon sun, will tolerate plenty of heat. Plant in well-draining soil, feed with compost, and water consistently and you will be rewarded with plenty of fruit. Currants do well in containers, too. Harvest when the fruit are highly colored and sweet. Pick whole clusters as opposed to single berries. Birds are fond of the ripe fruit so keep an eye on them or protect the fruit under netting.

# Red Currant Granita

MAKES ABOUT 1 QUART

Sweet-tart currants can be paired with almost any other summer fruit—strawberries, peaches, nectarines, blackberries, or other berries. Pile this brilliant vermilion fluffy ice into pretty little bowls or glasses and garnish another favorite summer fruit.

Rinse and remove from their stems:

**4 cups red currants**

Put the currants in a nonreactive pot and add enough water to just cover. Cook the currants over medium heat for about 5 minutes, or until they have released their juices. Press the currants with a whisk or potato masher to burst the berries. Pass the fruit and liquid through a fine-mesh strainer or a colander lined with cheesecloth, pressing the fruit with the back of a wooden spoon to extract as much of the juice as possible. (If you are using cheesecloth, pick up the corners of the cloth and squeeze to extract the juice.)

Measure into a nonreactive mixing bowl:

**2 cups red currant juice**

**1½ cups water**

**3 tablespoons lemon juice**

**½ cup rosé wine (or water if you prefer not to use wine)**

**⅔ cup sugar**

Stir until the sugar is dissolved. Pour the mixture into a square metal or glass baking dish and set in the freezer. Give the mixture a stir with a whisk every hour until it is completely set and frozen. Alternatively, you can let the mixture freeze solid and then scrape it with a fork, but it will not form the nice big ice crystals that come from stirring it as it freezes.

Once frozen, cover tightly with plastic wrap. Granita will keep for up to a week in the freezer. Fluff with a fork before serving.

VARIATIONS

♦ For pomegranate granita, combine 2 cups pomegranate juice (see page 296 for instructions on how to extract pomegranate juice), 1 cup plus 1 tablespoon water, 2 tablespoons lemon juice, and 7 tablespoons sugar.

♦ For mulberry granita, combine 2 cups mulberry juice (see page 297 for instructions on how to extract mulberry juice), 1 cup water, and 6 tablespoons sugar.

# Summer Pudding

8 SERVINGS

One of the most vivid of berry desserts, summer pudding is very simple to assemble and serve. The season for red currants is rather short, so don't miss out!

Remove the crust from:

**½ loaf fine-textured white sandwich bread**

Cut into ¼-inch slices. Line the bottom and sides of a 1-quart glass or other nonreactive bowl. Overlap the slices so the whole surface is covered.

Measure into a nonreactive heavy-bottomed pot:

**1 cup red currants, stems removed**

**2 cups raspberries**

**½ cup blackberries**

**½ cup boysenberries**

**¼ cup sugar**

Look for and discard any moldy or blemished berries as you add them to the pot. Gently warm the berries and sugar until the berries just begin to give off juice. Remove from the heat. Spoon half the warm berries into the bread-lined bowl. Top with a layer of sliced bread. Add the rest of the berries and finish with a final layer of bread. Cover with plastic wrap and place a weight on top. (A small plate that just fits inside the bowl with a stone or can of tomatoes on top works well.) Set the bowl on a plate or tray to catch any juices that might leak out and refrigerate overnight. The berry juice will completely soak the bread, changing it to a wonderful deep purple color.

Unmold to serve. Remove the weight and plastic wrap, place a larger plate upside down over the bowl, and together, turn over both of them. Remove the bowl. Cut slices of the pudding and serve with any extra juices and:

**Lightly whipped sweetened cream**

VARIATIONS

◆ Instead of making 1 large pudding, use 8 ramekins, cutting the bread to fit inside. Don't worry about lining the edges. Run a knife around the edges of the ramekins before unmolding.

◆ To make it easier to unmold the pudding, line the bowl with plastic wrap before lining it with bread.

◆ Huckleberries, black raspberries, black currants, and mulberries can be substituted for some of the fruit. Because of their juiciness, keep the proportion of raspberries high.

# Autumn Fruits and Nuts

## Figs, Grapes, Apples, Pears, Quince, Persimmons, Pomegranates, Walnuts, Hazelnuts, and Almonds

AS LEAVES CHANGE COLORS, the markets fill with a multitude of apple and pear varieties; clusters of purple, red, and green grapes; succulent teardrop-shaped purple and green figs; golden quinces; bright orange persimmons; and ruby red pomegranates. Creamy sweet, early-crop walnuts, hazelnuts, pecans, and almonds appear, just barely off the trees. It is time for autumn salads filled with fresh fruit and nuts, cheese plates with toasted nuts and fruit jams and pastes, and poached quinces, roasted figs, sautéed apples, apple pies, and fig galettes to finish warm meals. But maybe best of all is the simple pleasure of eating each fruit fresh out of hand.

# Recipes

Adriatic Figs with Honey, Mint, and Ricotta  284

Black Mission Figs Roasted with Wild Fennel  285

Sierra Beauty Apple Pie  288

Sautéed Pink Pearl Apples  289

Bosc Pear Tarte Tatin  291

Comice Pears Baked with Nocino  292

Baked Quince with Crème Fraîche  293

Quince and Apple Galette  293

Quince-Orange Sorbet  294

Frozen Hachiya Persimmons  295

Fuyu Persimmons with Lime  295

Pomegranate Gelée  296

Olive, Pomegranate, and Walnut Relish  298

Walnut and Date Galette  299

Honey Candied Walnuts  299

Crispy Hazelnut Meringues  301

Hazelnut Floating Island  302

Almond Milk Panna Cotta  304

Soft Almond Meringues  305

Chocolate Candies with Dried Fruits and Nuts  306

# Autumn Fruit and Nut Trees in the Garden

The trees that produce fruit or nuts in the fall are some of the most versatile in the kitchen and in the home landscape. The colors of their fall foliage are an added attraction. The leaves of apple, pear, and quince trees turn golden yellow. Persimmon trees range from yellow through orange to shades of red.

Like most fruit trees, the autumn bearers grow well in moderately deep, well-drained soil, but persimmons, pears, and figs will tolerate wet soil, especially in the spring. Walnuts and pecans need your best deep, well-drained topsoil. With a few exceptions, notably walnuts, the trees can be kept small by pruning or planting dwarf varieties. But if you have the space, a well-grown walnut or pecan tree can provide some shade.

When choosing trees for autumn harvest, consider any special needs they may have. Apples and pears are widely adapted; you can find varieties that will grow well in any state. Walnuts and hazelnuts are good for cold climates, but almonds, figs, and pomegranates all love summer heat and struggle where there is real winter chill. A trip to a local nursery in the spring will help you decide which trees will provide abundant crops in your area.

Grapevines bring a feeling of serenity to the garden, especially when they are with clusters of fruit. Don't feel you have to train them on wires as the big producers do. A single vine can be tied to a stake to develop a two- to three-foot trunk as it grows. Each winter, cut off side growth and thin out and shorten top growth. When the trunk is self-supporting, the stake can be removed. If you have an overhead trellis or other arched garden framework, you can plant a grapevine near each support post and train the vines to cover the structure. Pruning will still be necessary to thin out tangled growth and keep the vines healthy.

## Figs  (*Ficus carica*)

Figs are the most sensual of fruits when completely ripe: sweet, soft, and seductive. They can be served quartered and baked on a galette crust, cut in half and roasted with a little sweet wine and sugar, or cooked down with sugar and lemon zest to make jam. They pair especially well with candied citrus peel or fresh berries. Their leaves lend a wonderful coconut-like aroma when heated. Wrap a piece of goat cheese or a fillet of fish in a fig leaf before baking or grilling it—for protection from the heat and a delicious infusion of flavor.

*Black Mission* is a very dependable variety with purple-black skin and sweet pink flesh that has long been a standard in California. The fruit of *Adriatic* figs has bright green skin and strawberry red flesh. *Genoa*, with greenish yellow skin and reddish flesh, and *Celeste*, with bronzy skin and rosy flesh, are popular varieties for the more humid East and Southeast.

Figs are ready to pick when they feel very soft; the skin may be cracked, and they will hang from the branch with a pliant stem. They should come off with an easy snap when grasped where they attach to the branch. Ripe figs can be stored in the refrigerator for a day or two in a single layer in a shallow pan with good air circulation. They need little preparation for cooking or eating fresh. Just snip off the little tough part of the stem and give the fruits a rinse in cold water. Only those with the thickest skin need to be peeled.

To preserve backyard figs, let the ripe fruits hang on the tree until wrinkled and partially dried, then finish drying on trays set in the sun or in a dehydrator. Fruit that falls from the tree is okay to dry if picked up soon after it falls.

Fig trees' whimsical growth pattern and small size add charm to any space. Large deeply lobed leaves cast dense shade in the summer, and silvery gray branches make an interesting silhouette in winter. Most fig varieties have a small summer crop, borne on growth from the previous season. The main crop forms on the current season's twigs in late summer and fall. In cold regions, grow figs in containers or trained against a south-facing wall.

## Adriatic Figs with Honey, Mint, and Ricotta

Ripe plump Adriatic figs are a gorgeous lime green with brilliant ruby red flesh. They are delicious on their own and a decadent luxury drizzled with a bit of honey and mint. Creamy fresh ricotta completes the dish.

Allow two figs for each person. Wipe them clean with a damp cloth, cut off the stem ends, and cut in half lengthwise. Arrange the halves prettily on a plate, leaving a hole in the center of the design. Fill the hole with a spoonful of ricotta per person. Drizzle with honey and scatter a fine chiffonade of fresh mint over the dish. Finish with a grind of black pepper, and if you desire, a drizzle of extra-virgin olive oil. Serve with grilled toasts or butter cookies depending on whether they are served at the beginning or the end of the meal.

# Black Mission Figs Roasted with Wild Fennel

4 SERVINGS

Roasted figs are delicious and can be served either sweet or savory. Try them on a grilled piece of bread with a slice of prosciutto and a dollop of mascarpone, next to roasted duck or pork, or nestled into a salad of rocket and garden lettuce. For dessert, spoon vanilla ice cream over them (or ice cream scented with a few roasted fig leaves) or line them up in a baked sweet tart shell filled with whipped cream. Roast extra figs and have them in the morning with Yogurt (page 183).

Preheat the oven to 375°F.
Remove the stems and cut in half lengthwise:
> **8 Black Mission figs**

Lay the figs, cut side up, in a single layer in a baking dish that just holds them comfortably. Tuck in among the figs:
> **4 to 6 wild fennel fronds**

Measure into a small bowl:
> **1 tablespoon red wine vinegar**
> **2 tablespoons red wine**
> **1 tablespoon extra-virgin olive oil**
> **1 tablespoon honey (optional)**
> **Fresh-ground black pepper**
> **A large pinch of salt**
> **2 wild fennel flower heads, yellow**
>     **flower tops only**

Mix well and spoon over the figs. Bake for 15 minutes or until soft and puffed. Serve warm or at room temperature.

VARIATIONS

• Add a few drops of Pernod to the red wine mixture.

• Use purple basil in place of the fennel fronds and omit the fennel tops.
• Roast small clusters of grapes instead of figs.

# Grapes  (*Vitis* sp.)

Late summer and fall bring grapes to the market. Many stores are limited to only those green and red table grapes that ship easily. But local farmers' markets offer the tender tasty varieties I love, whether eaten right out of hand, tossed into fall salads, made into smooth sweet sorbets, or roasted and served over ice cream or next to a grilled duck breast. I get very excited when *Bronx* grapes arrive on the scene. They are a cross between *Concord* and *Thompson Seedless*. They are mindblowingly delicious: sweet, tender, and juicy, with a touch of the unique flavor of Concord grapes. *Muscat* grapes have a fantastic aromatic and spiced flavor. Try purple *Muscat Hamburg*, small green *Early Muscat*, and early ripening golden *Queen of the Vineyard*. Some other tried and true varieties are *Concord, Swenson Red, Flame*, and *Crimson Seedless*. Wine grapes, though usually not good for eating out of hand, are good for cooking, though they are harder to find at the market.

When young, grape leaves can be cut into a number of salsas, and I like to toss warm olives with them for a tart marinade. Goat cheese, and sardines and other little fish, are delicious wrapped in a grape leaf and grilled. The leaves help keep pickles crisp. And if you grow your own grapes you can pick some while still green and make your own verjus (verjuice) to add a splash of fruit tang to dressings, sauces, and sliced fruits and vegetables.

Raisins are dried grapes, and when freshly made they are in their own class. Poach them with other winter fruit for a delightful compote or add them to fresh scones and other baked goods.

Grape varieties are divided into three categories: European, American, and French-American hybrid. European varieties are quite cold sensitive, while American varieties are fairly cold hardy. The hybrids share the cold hardiness of the American type. All the well-known wine grapes are European, as are the muscats and Thompson Seedless grapes. The American varieties include the Concord and other similarly flavored grapes. Ask around to find the best-flavored grapes that do well in your area.

Grapes need sunlight and room to ramble. They do well in large containers, with sturdy support for the vines to climb. Keep grapes well fed with compost and compost tea and prune them annually. Harvest grapes when they are plump, juicy, colorful, and delicious.

# Apples (*Malus domestica*)

There are apple varieties that can be grown from coast to coast, and some that will only grow in a specific climate; there are apples that hold their shape when cooked, others that turn into a luscious purée; there are tart apples, sweet apples, green apples, red apples, striped apples, and more. The choice of apple varieties is exciting, enormous, and possibly bewildering—autumn at the farmers' market offers bins and bins of colorful fruit to taste, learn about, and choose from.

California's *Gravenstein*, which ripens in August, is close to my heart—it is supremely good for cooking and delicious right off the tree. It is a notoriously bad choice for storage or shipping, though, and Gravensteins are getting harder and harder to find. *Pink Pearl*, another notable apple, arrives in late summer. Their firm, marvelous deep pink flesh, under nearly translucent white skin, is tart and berrylike. They make pretty pink applesauce and are good in pies and tarts combined with wild blackberries or raspberries. *Sierra Beauty*, a green apple with red stripes, has a perfect balance of tart and sweet flavor and crisp texture. At Chez Panisse we use them for cooking or sliced raw into a salad. They hold their shape beautifully for tarte Tatin and make the best old-fashioned apple pie. Heirloom *Cox's Orange Pippin* and *Ashmead's Kernel* are both tasty and crunchy tart-sweet apples. These are only a select few of the extraordinary variety of apples that is available.

All apples need some winter chill, and nearly all need a pollenizer, so choose at least two apple trees for your local climate, or plant a tree that has at least two compatible varieties grafted onto the rootstock. Extend your harvest with varieties that ripen early, midseason, and late. I have three in my yard: an early Gravenstein, a midseason dwarf *McIntosh*, and a late *Pink Lady*. Choosing varieties that have a history in your area is fun and gives meaning to your plantings. You should also think about planting varieties resistant to local disease

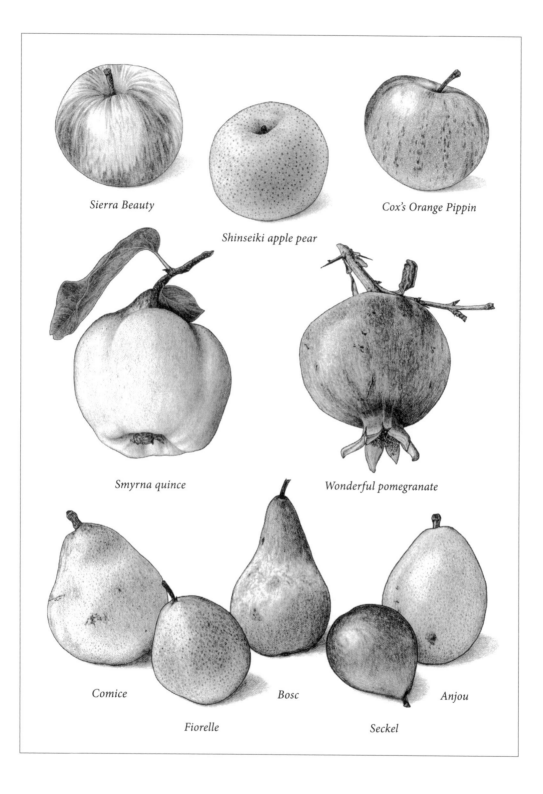

Sierra Beauty

Shinseiki apple pear

Cox's Orange Pippin

Smyrna quince

Wonderful pomegranate

Comice

Fiorelle

Bosc

Seckel

Anjou

and insect pests, which seem to love apples.

Apple trees tend to set more fruit than they can comfortably carry to maturity, so thin the fruit and prop up the branches as needed. Taste is the best indicator of apple maturity. Bear in mind that apples produce fruit on short fruiting branchlike spurs that develop on older branches and last for several years. To harvest without damaging the fruiting spur, twist the apple and lift gently. A ripe apple will come off the tree easily. The texture and flavor of most apples improves after a week or more in cool storage. A general rule of thumb is that early apples have the shortest storage potential and late varieties the longest.

## Sierra Beauty Apple Pie

MAKES ONE 9-INCH PIE

The success of a dessert as simple as apple pie depends on using perfect ingredients: tart, flavorful apples like Sierra Beauty, good buttery pie dough, and just enough sugar to bring out the flavor of the apples. You can always make a double-crusted pie, but for something different, try this one with its crumb topping.

Roll out on a cool, lightly floured surface into a 12-inch round about ⅛ inch thick:

**One 10-ounce disk Pie Dough
(page 248)**

Line a 9-inch pie pan with the dough. Trim the dough about ½ inch beyond the edge of the pan. Fold under the edge of the dough and crimp with a fork or use your thumb and finger to make a decorative edge. Refrigerate the dough in its pan.

Position a rack in the middle level of the oven. Preheat the oven to 375°F in time to bake the pie.

Quarter, peel, and core:

**2 pounds Sierra Beauty or other crisp, tart apples**

Slice the apples about ¼ inch thick and put them in a large bowl. You should have about 6 cups. Sprinkle with:

**2 tablespoons granulated sugar**

Toss the apples and sugar together to mix well. Taste for sweetness and add a squeeze of lemon juice if the apples seem bland. Set apples aside while making the topping.

Chop fine:

**½ cup almonds, walnuts, or pecans**

Mix with:

**1 cup unbleached all-purpose flour**
**½ cup firmly packed light brown sugar**
**¼ teaspoon salt**
**½ teaspoon cinnamon**

Add:

**8 tablespoons cool unsalted butter, cut in ¼-inch pieces**

Work the butter into the flour mixture with your fingers, a pastry blender, or a stand mixer fitted with the paddle attachment. Work just until the mixture comes together and has a crumbly, but not sandy, texture.

(If you prefer to use a food processor, process the nuts with several tablespoons of the flour until chopped fine. Add the remaining dry ingredients and pulse to mix well. Add the butter and pulse until the mixture has the texture of very coarse meal. Transfer to a bowl and finish working with your fingers until crumbly.)

Pile the apples and accumulated juice

into the refrigerated crust and smooth the top, leaving it slightly higher in the center. Cover with the topping, making sure no bits of apple show through.

Bake in the middle level of the oven for 40 minutes. Test for doneness with a small sharp knife. If the knife goes in easily, the pie is ready. If not, continue baking until the fruit is tender and the topping is brown. Cover the pie loosely with foil if the crust and topping get too brown.

Let the pie cool for about 1 hour before serving with whipped cream or vanilla ice cream.

VARIATIONS

• Add to the apples ⅓ cup dried fruit (cranberries, cherries, or apricots) soaked overnight in 2 tablespoons water or Cognac.
• Add ½ cup huckleberries to the apples before tossing with the sugar.
• To make a crisp instead of a pie, omit the dough, and add 1 tablespoon flour to the apples when tossing them with the sugar. Assemble and bake as above.
• Omit the topping and make a 2-crust pie, following the directions for Sour Cherry Pie (page 251). Season the apples with ⅓ cup sugar, ½ teaspoon cinnamon (if desired), and a sprinkle of lemon juice or Cognac. Dot the apples with 2 tablespoons butter before putting on the top crust.
• Make a 2-crust pie, reduce the sugar to ¼ cup, and add ⅓ cup candied lemon zest.
• Make a 2-crust pie and substitute slices of poached or baked quince for one quarter of the apples.

# Sautéed Pink Pearl Apples

4 SERVINGS

Pink Pearl apples are a stunning pink, and when sautéed they make a simple and elegant dessert. Serve them with a dollop of lightly whipped crème fraîche. The apples also make a great accompaniment to roasted pork or duck.

Peel, core, and slice about ⅓ inch thick:

**3 medium Pink Pearl apples (about ¾ pound)**

Melt in a large, heavy-bottomed sauté pan over medium-high heat:

**1 tablespoon unsalted butter**

Add enough apple slices to cover the bottom of the pan in a single layer. It's best to do this in multiple batches so the apples cook evenly.

Sprinkle over the apples:

**1 tablespoon sugar**

Shake the pan to coat the apples with the sugar. Cook until the apple slices start to caramelize on the bottom, about 2 minutes. Turn the apples with a spatula and continue cooking. The apples are done when they are soft and slightly translucent but still retain their shape. Remove the apples to a baking dish and cover with foil to keep them warm while you finish sautéing the rest of the apples. Before you sauté the next batch, return the pan to the heat and carefully pour in:

**1 tablespoon Calvados (apple brandy)**

The liquor will ignite. Cook until the flame dies down and then pour over the cooked apples. Repeat the process until all the apples are cooked. Serve immediately, or cover with aluminum foil and rewarm them in a low oven when you are ready to serve.

VARIATIONS

◆ Use Gravenstein, Sierra Beauty, Pink Lady, or another cooking apple instead of Pink Pearl.

◆ Skip the Calvados and continue cooking the apples until all are cooked.

◆ Use apple juice instead of Calvados to deglaze the pan.

◆ Roast the apples instead of sautéing them. Preheat the oven to 500°F. Lay the apple slices in a single layer in a baking pan. Drizzle 2 to 3 tablespoons melted butter over them and sprinkle with 2 tablespoons sugar. If you want to add Calvados, add a generous splash before baking. Bake apples uncovered for 10 minutes. Turn the slices over, rotate the pan, and bake for an additional 3 to 5 minutes, or until they are soft and slightly translucent but still retain their shape.

# Pears   (*Pyrus communis*)

The rich, nectarlike flavor of a ripe pear is one of the supreme rewards of fall. Slice fresh pears for fall salads or serve them after dinner with a good blue cheese and a few walnuts. Pears poached in red or white wine are very good alone or in a compote with poached quince or dried apricots. Roast pear halves in the oven with a sprinkling of sweet wine and sugar. A tender, juicy *Comice* can stand alone on any table at dessert time. The late-summer standby *Bartlett* is good for fresh eating as well as for canning or in preserves. Both make wonderfully smooth sorbet when the flesh is cooked until just tender with lemon juice and sugar before being puréed. *Bosc*, with its long, ele-

gant neck, holds its shape well when baked or poached. *Seckel* is small, but very sweet and aromatic. It makes a very pretty dessert poached with the skin on. *Warren, Winter Nelis*, and *Anjou* are tasty, too.

Asian pears (*Pyrus pyrifolia* and *Pyrus ussuriensis*) are firmer, crisper, and rounder than European varieties. Many of them have a slightly pronounced granular texture that is not at all unpleasant. Sweet and crisp, they are perfect sliced into salads and fruit compotes, and they pair very nicely with nuts and cheese. Large *Shinko* has golden brown skin with juicy, crisp flesh; *Hosui* has particularly russeted skin and outstanding sweet flesh; and *Kikusui* is extra juicy and sweet.

When you see local pears at the farmers' market, ask the grower for advice about varieties. Pears are not as cold hardy as apples, but they do need winter chill to produce fruit. Asian pears need less chill than European varieties. Most pear varieties require pollination by a compatible variety to bear fruit, and though Asian pears can pollenize European pears, their bloom period is so much earlier that it does not really work.

Pears are unique in that they must be harvested green, before they completely ripen. If left to hang on the tree, they turn brown and mealy in the center. To test for ripeness, gently lift one or two of the largest fruits. The stem of ripe fruit will snap cleanly and easily off the branch; if not, wait a few days and try again. Pears should be kept in a cool cellar or in the refrigerator and brought out to finish ripening at room temperature as needed. Asian pears and Seckel pears are ripened on the tree. Taste for the best moment to harvest.

# Bosc Pear Tarte Tatin

MAKES ONE 9-INCH TART

This is a variation of the traditional tarte Tatin, which is typically made with apples. The cooking time will vary according to how tender the pears are.

Roll out on a cool, lightly floured surface into a 12-inch round, about ⅛ inch thick:

**One 10-ounce disk Pie Dough (page 248)**

Place a 9- or 10-inch cast-iron skillet upside down on the dough and trim the dough to leave a ½-inch border. Brush off any excess flour, transfer the dough to a parchment-paper-lined baking sheet, and refrigerate while preparing the fruit.

Position a rack in the middle level of the oven. Preheat the oven to 400°F. Have ready a large pan of ice and water that will accommodate the skillet.

Melt in the skillet over medium-high heat:

**2 tablespoons unsalted butter**

**½ cup sugar**

Stir with a wooden spoon to combine the melting butter and sugar. The mixture will gradually begin to caramelize. Continue cooking and stirring until the mixture turns dark brown and just begins to smoke. Immediately place the skillet in the ice-water bath to stop the cooking.

Peel, quarter, and core:

**6 firm, ripe Bosc pears**

Place the pear quarters in a large bowl and toss gently to moisten with:

**2 tablespoons rum, Cognac, or water**

Arrange the cut pears in the caramel-lined skillet, with the pointed ends toward the center and the larger ends just touching the side. Fit the fruit together as snugly as possible. Place the refrigerated dough on top of the pears and let it soften a bit to become pliable. Tuck the edges of the dough down between the pears and the side of the pan. Cut 3 or 4 slashes through the dough to allow steam to escape, and sprinkle with:

**1 tablespoon sugar**

Bake in the middle level of the oven. After 30 minutes, start checking on the pears. Poke a sharp knife through one of the steam vents. If the knife goes into the fruit easily, the tart is ready. If not, continue baking until the fruit is tender and the crust is brown.

When the tart is done, remove from the oven, set on a heat-proof surface, and give the pan a couple of short, quick twists to the right and left, until you see the contents shift in the pan. Let the pan cool for 1 or 2 minutes, then reverse a serving plate on top of the pan and, holding the plate tightly against the top of the pan, flip both over together to unmold the tart. Remove the pan and replace any fruit that has stuck to the bottom of the pan back on the tart. Let the tart cool for about an hour before serving with whipped cream, crème fraîche, or vanilla ice cream.

VARIATIONS

◆ Use Comice, Bartlett, or another firm, juicy pear instead of Bosc.

◆ Use apples in place of the pears and omit the Cognac. Cut the apples into quarters and arrange as above. Cut the quarters in half to fill in the gaps.

## Comice Pears Baked with Nocino

4 SERVINGS

Pears and walnuts make a good couple, especially with rich, winey winter pears like Comice. *Nocino* (page 353) is a liqueur made from green walnuts, lemon zest, and sweet spices.

Preheat the oven to 375°F. Peel, halve, and core:

**2 firm, ripe, juicy Comice pears**

Arrange the pear halves, rounded side down, in a shallow baking dish rubbed generously with unsalted butter. Fill the cavity of each pear with:

**2 teaspoons nocino**

Sprinkle the pears lightly with:

**Sugar**

Dot with:

**2 tablespoons unsalted butter**

Bake for 25 to 30 minutes, until a sharp knife inserted into the fruit goes in easily.

While the pears are baking, toast until golden, about 8 minutes:

**3 tablespoons walnut halves**

Chop walnuts and set aside.

Remove the roasted pears to a serving dish, pouring any nocino remaining in each cavity into the baking dish. Transfer the accumulated juices to a small saucepan and add:

**1½ tablespoons nocino**

**A few drops of fresh lemon juice**

Bring to a boil and pour the juices over the fruit. Sprinkle with the chopped walnuts. Serve as is or with vanilla ice cream.

## Quince  (*Cydonia oblonga*)

I would grow quinces if only for their scattering of beautiful pale pink flowers in the spring and their unpredictably twisting branch pattern. But a better reason to grow them is for their intensely aromatic, golden yellow fruits. I don't know why today they are considered an unusual or rare fruit. Quince trees were a backyard fixture in America from the time of the earliest European settlements until around the turn of the twentieth century.

Quinces define the concept of "slow food." Even when completely ripe, raw quinces are hard and astringent. They must be cooked before eating. This may explain their decline in popularity in our age of instant gratification. *Smyrna* and *Orange* (sometimes called *Apple*) are the best, most productive varieties. They both turn a gorgeous red when fully cooked.

To prepare quinces, rinse in cold water and rub off as much fuzz as you can. If you will be using the fruit in slices, quarter, core, and peel as you would an apple, keeping in mind that quinces are very hard.

In the garden, quince trees have a similar culture to apple trees. They don't need much winter chill, but they need a long period of good fall weather to mature. Quinces bloom after apples, and are seldom bothered by late-spring frost. Quince trees are small and reliably self-fertile; they can be trained either as a small tree or a multistemmed large shrub.

The best way to determine harvest time is by color; a ripe quince is a true golden yellow. Or wait until a few fruits fall from the tree, and the rest snap off the branch easily. The rock-hard fruits bruise easily, so handle with care when harvesting. The fruit can be stored in a cool place for several weeks before cooking. Put one on the countertop in the kitchen and it will perfume the whole room.

# Baked Quince with Crème Fraîche

4 SERVINGS

Quinces are so tannic when raw that they are basically inedible, but a simple slow poaching in syrup renders them sweet, tender, and compellingly aromatic. Baked quince makes an elegant dessert with a dollop of crème fraîche. It is also delicious added to a fruit compote or layered into a Quince and Apple Galette (recipe follows). The quince can be stored in its syrup and refrigerated for up to 2 weeks.

Preheat the oven to 300°F.
Pour into a baking dish:
> ¾ **cup sugar**
> **3 cups water**
> ½ **lemon, cut into slices**
> **2-inch piece of vanilla bean, split and scraped**

Peel, quarter, core, and cut into ½-inch slices:
> **4 medium quinces (about 1½ pounds)**

Go slowly when cutting and coring the fruit. Quince is quite hard and requires a bit of muscle. As the slices are cut, put them in the baking dish. When all the slices have been added, stir well to be sure they are all coated with the lemony sugar water. Cover

tightly with foil or a lid, and bake until tender and rosy, about 1½ hours. Leave the fruit in its syrup to cool. To serve, arrange the quince slices in a serving bowl using a slotted spoon. Drizzle with a bit of the poaching liquid. Garnish with:
> **A spoonful of crème fraîche**

VARIATIONS
• Use ½ cup honey instead of the sugar.
• Add some sweet spices to the sugar mixture, such as a few cloves, a star anise, a cinnamon stick, or a few allspice berries.
• The fruit may be poached on the stove top instead of baked in the oven. The process is quicker, but it takes supervision as they cook. Double the ingredients for the poaching syrup and heat in a heavy-bottomed pot. Add the quince slices and poach at a very slow simmer until tender, about 45 minutes. Keep adding water as needed to keep the slices submerged in the liquid.

# Quince and Apple Galette

8 SERVINGS

Firm, slightly tart baking apples such as Gravenstein, Sierra Beauty, Pink Pearl, or Pink Lady are best for making a galette. The slices of russet orangey red quince are beautiful when interspersed among the apple slices. Serve the galette with sweetened cream, crème fraîche, or à la mode.

Preheat the oven to 400°F.
On a lightly floured surface, roll out to a 14-inch circle:
> **One 10-ounce disk Galette Dough (page 246)**

Brush off any excess flour and transfer the dough to a baking sheet lined with parchment paper and set in the refrigerator to chill. Peel, quarter, core, and slice ¼ inch thick:

**2½ pounds apples**

Drain and slice in half:

**1 cup Baked Quince (page 293)**

Take the dough out of the refrigerator and lay apple slices end to end in a circle around the circumference, leaving a 1½-inch border. Arrange the remaining apple slices within this circle in tight overlapping concentric circles adding a slice of quince after every 7 or so apple slices. If you need more quince slices, drain and cut a few more. For a rustic look, fold the edges of the dough over the apple slices toward the center. For a more composed look, twist the dough edge over itself toward the center, creating a rope pattern, pinching the beginning turn and the final turn together. Sprinkle the apples with:

**1 to 2 tablespoons sugar**

The amount of sugar depends on the tartness of the apples. A good way to test is to use a small amount, taste an apple slice halfway through baking, and add more sugar as needed.

Brush the crust with:

**2 tablespoons melted butter**

Drizzle any remaining butter over the apple and quince slices. Sprinkle the crust with:

**1½ tablespoons sugar**

The butter and sugar will caramelize as the galette bakes, giving the crust a nice sweet crunch. Bake on the bottom rack of the oven for 45 to 50 minutes, until the crust is golden brown on the bottom. Slide off the pan and cool on a rack.

Brush the fruit with a bit of quince syrup for a little shine and quince flavor. Serve warm or at room temperature with sweetened cream, crème fraîche, or à la mode.

VARIATION

◆ For a different look, arrange the fruit in overlapping rows instead of circles. A herringbone pattern can be achieved by pointing the ends of the apples of each row in the opposite direction of the adjacent rows.

# Quince–Orange Sorbet
MAKES ABOUT 1 QUART

The floral sweetness of the quince is complemented by the tartness of the freshly squeezed orange juice. Serve the sorbet with a few slices of Baked Quince (page 293) or Sautéed Pink Pearl Apples (page 289).

Peel, quarter, and core:

**3 quinces**

Put in a heavy-bottomed pot with:

**1½ cups water**
**¾ cup sugar**
**A pinch of salt**
**Zest of 1 orange**

Bring to a boil, reduce the heat, and simmer until the quince is soft and falling apart, about 45 minutes. Start checking after 30 minutes. Let the mixture cool and pass it through a food mill or purée it in a food processor. Whisk into the cooled purée:

**2 cups freshly squeezed orange juice**

Strain the mixture through a sieve. Use a plastic spatula to work (turning and pressing) all the liquid out of the fruit pulp. Chill thoroughly. Freeze in your ice-cream maker according to the manufacturer's instructions.

# Persimmons

*(Diospyros kaki, Diospyros virginiana)*

A tree full of ripe persimmons glowing orange long after all the colorful autumn leaves have fallen is a stunning sight. I have one planted in my backyard that glows with fruit every autumn. The persimmons we commonly see on our tables, varieties of *Diospyros kaki*, are originally from China and Japan. The most common Asian variety, *Hachiya*, bears large, pointy, orange fruit on a very attractive tree. They can be harvested while firm or soft but after picking must be allowed to soften until the texture of pudding; otherwise they are impossibly astringent.

When they are very soft, freeze them whole to eat as sorbet, or slit the skin and scoop out the flesh; strain out any seeds and use the purée to make cookies, steamed puddings, and cakes. *Fuyu* and *Chocolate* can be eaten when just-picked or slightly soft. Slice them for salads or as a dessert, peeled or not, as you please.

American persimmons, *Diospyros virginiana*, are native to the East and South, and will grow as far north as southern New England, Michigan, and much of the Midwest. They were important food for Native Americans. The fruit, which is smaller than that of the Asian varieties, is astringent until soft-ripe, at which point they become very sweet and delicious. *Meader* has great flavor and *Early Golden* has larger fruit.

Asian persimmons are more susceptible to winter cold; they do well in the Southeast and Southwest. Either species grows into a small tree perfect for a home landscape.

They adapt to wet soil in winter and summer drought but do better with occasional deep watering in summer. Persimmons bloom late, often not until early summer, so spring frost is not a problem. Most persimmons are self-fertile, but planting two trees will give a more abundant crop and more seeds in the fruit.

## Frozen Hachiya Persimmons

This is as easy as it gets. Put one clean, ripe Hachiya persimmon in the freezer per person. Freeze until hard. When ready to eat, remove from the freezer, pull off the pretty green stem (calyx), and eat, spooning the frozen soft flesh right out of the skin. Delicious.

## Fuyu Persimmons with Lime

Fuyu persimmons are a beautiful pumpkin orange and have a crisp texture and sweet flesh with a hint of spice. I like them peeled and tossed into frisée and chicory salads. They make a delicious dessert as well, cut into wedges and served with a spritz of lime. For an even more luscious treat, peel the slices before serving.

## Pomegranates *(Punica granatum)*

I'm always surprised when I break open a pomegranate and rediscover the beauty of the ivory-colored, paper-thin pulp cradling hundreds of tiny scarlet fruits, each encasing one seed. Their sweet-tart juice is perfectly refreshing, and the crunchy texture of the seeds is part of the experience. A sprinkling of pomegranate seeds is an easy garnish for a fall fruit salad or a slice of lemon tart. The juice makes terrific granita or gelée. Add a tablespoon of juice to an autumn white wine spritzer.

*Parfainka* has dark red seeds with loads of sweet-tart flavor. *Angel Red,* a newer variety, is early ripening, with soft seeds and dark red skin. *Wonderful* is the most commonly grown pomegranate; it has crimson-red seeds in large fruits with greenish red skin. *White* has light pink skin and pink, almost white, sweet fruit within.

To remove pomegranate seeds without getting covered with juice, cut the whole fruit into quarters and gently break the pieces apart underwater in a large bowl, releasing the seeds. The skin and white pulp will float to the top where it can be skimmed off. Strain the seeds out of the water and discard any bits of pulp. The seeds will keep in the refrigerator for a day or so. I find the easiest way to extract the juice is to roll the whole pomegranate on a kitchen counter until soft, then carefully pierce a hole with a paring knife, and squeeze the juice into a bowl.

Pomegranates grow on big shrubs with small, shiny green leaves that contrast beautifully with their extravagant 2- to 3-inch crêpe-paper-like orange and red flowers and glossy red fruit. The plants thrive where winter temperatures don't fall below 15°F, and there is a long, hot growing season. They are sensitive to late frost in spring and early frost in fall. In marginal areas, they are still worth growing for their landscape value, but they may fail to produce fruit. Pomegranates ripen in October and should be picked as soon as they are ready and then refrigerated. The skin tends to split if allowed to hang on the branches. The plants do quite well in containers.

## Pomegranate Gelée

6 SERVINGS

Gelée is a great way to feature pomegranates and it is very simple to make. Garnish the gelée with more pomegranate seeds and serve it on its own or with a scoop of Quince-Orange Sorbet (page 294).

Remove the seeds from:

**6 medium pomegranates**

Pass the seeds through a food mill fitted with the large-holed plate. Strain the juice through a fine-mesh strainer or cheesecloth. Press the pulp with the back of a wooden spoon or squeeze the cheesecloth to extract all the juice. Measure and set aside 1½ cups juice.

Measure into a small metal or heat-proof bowl:

**¼ cup water**

Sprinkle over the top of the water in an even layer:

**One ¼-ounce packet unflavored gelatin**

Set aside to let the gelatin "bloom."

Measure into a small pot:

**1½ cups water**

**½ cup plus 2 tablespoons sugar**

Bring to a boil, stirring to dissolve the sugar. Remove from the heat. Set the bowl of bloomed gelatin on top of the pot of sugar water to melt the gelatin. Once the gelatin is melted, stir it into the pomegranate juice. Pour in the warm sugar water and stir again to combine. Taste the mixture. Add, if desired:

**A squeeze of lemon juice**

**A splash of rosé wine**

Pour the mixture into an 8-inch-square baking dish and put in the refrigerator. (Make sure you have a flat surface in the refrigerator to set the dish on.) Let the mixture jell completely before serving. Once it has set, cover tightly with plastic wrap. Gelée will keep for up to 3 days in the refrigerator.

To serve, drag a knife through the gelée lengthwise and crosswise to cut it into cubes and spoon them into small bowls. Garnish with slices of peach, nectarine, strawberries, or other summer berries.

VARIATIONS

◆ Mulberry gelée: Use 2 cups mulberry juice, 1 cup water, and ½ cup plus 2 tablespoons sugar. Depending on the tartness of the berries, before the gelée sets, taste, and adjust with more sugar, if needed. To make mulberry juice, put mulberries in a pot with a small amount of water to cover the bottom, which prevents the mulberries from scorching. Warm the berries over low heat until warmed through (not boiling) and beginning to burst. Strain the berries through a fine-mesh strainer or cheesecloth, pressing the berries with the back of a spoon to extract as much juice as possible.

◆ Red currant gelée: Use 2 cups currant juice, 1 cup water, and ½ cup plus 2 tablespoons sugar. To make 2 cups currant juice, you will need 3 pints of currants. Pick the currants off their stems, putting them in a nonreactive pot, and add just enough water to cover them. Cook the currants over medium heat for about 5 minutes, or until they have released their juices. Then press the currants with the back of a wooden spoon or potato masher until most of them have burst. Strain the currants through a fine-mesh strainer or a cheesecloth, pressing the berries with the back of a spoon to extract as much juice as possible.

◆ Tangerine gelée: Use 3 cups tangerine juice and ¼ cup sugar. It takes about 12 tangerines to yield 3 cups juice. Heat the sugar with ½ cup juice to dissolve it.

## Olive, Pomegranate, and Walnut Relish

4 SERVINGS

This relish is a vibrant mix of colors, flavors, and textures: creamy nuts, crunchy sweet pomegranates, pungent scallions, and briny olives. Add a pinch of deep sweet Aleppo pepper and some chopped parsley and you have a fantastic relish to garnish roasted chicken, grilled fish, a rocket salad, or even a heady piece of cheese.

Preheat the oven to 350°F and lightly toast:
> **½ cup walnuts**

Let cool. Rub the nuts in your hands to remove some of the tannic skin, and coarsely chop.

Pit and coarsely chop:
> **½ cup green olives (about 3 ounces)**

Stir in the walnuts and:
> **1 scallion, trimmed and thinly sliced**
> **¼ cup chopped parsley**
> **⅛ teaspoon Aleppo pepper**
> **½ cup fresh pomegranate seeds**
> **2 teaspoons lemon juice**
> **1½ tablespoons extra-virgin olive oil**
> **Salt**
> **Fresh-ground black pepper**

Let sit for 10 minutes or so for the flavors to marry.

## Walnuts  (*Juglans regia*)

Walnuts are a staple for baking; used in cakes, bread, pastry filling, cookies, and candies. They are a welcome addition to salads and cheese plates, and when toasted with herbs they are an easy hors d'oeuvre to serve with an apéritif. And it's always nice to have some around in the winter to crack and enjoy with a glass of Port. Harvest green nuts in early summer, before the inner shell has hardened, to make the Italian green walnut liqueur Nocino (page 353). *Hartley* and *Chandler* are delicious varieties; *Hansen*, which is self-fruitful, and *Lake* are both very hardy.

Stately walnut trees provide shade in the summer, a bountiful harvest in the fall, and a grand silhouette in winter. They need lots of space in the garden, and prefer good, deep soil and regular water. Fast-growing when young, they can eventually reach a height and width of sixty feet. Walnuts have separate male and female flowers on the same tree, but they usually don't open at the same time, so pollination can be uncertain with only a single tree. Best to plant two. Choose varieties that will grow in your climate.

Walnuts mature inside a green husk, which splits open in late summer and early fall, letting the nuts fall to the ground. They should be picked up frequently as they fall, or they may be shaken from the tree limbs with a pole to harvest all at once. (Walnut husks make a great natural dye; they will stain your hands black.) Cure freshly harvested nuts for several days to a week in a shaded area. Crack one open from time to time; they are ready to store when the kernel is brittle and tastes nutty.

# Walnut and Date Galette

MAKES ONE 10-INCH DOUBLE-CRUSTED GALETTE

Preheat the oven to 400°F.

Put in a food processor (or chop finely):

**2 cups pitted Barhi or another variety
of soft dates**

Process the dates into a coarse paste, about 1 minute or so. If the dates remain too chunky, add a little milk to soften the paste. Put the date purée in a medium mixing bowl with:

**1 tablespoon unsalted butter, melted**
**½ cup walnuts, coarsely chopped**
**Zest of ½ orange**
**½ cup orange juice**
**1 teaspoon orange blossom water**
**1 tablespoon honey**
**A pinch of salt**

Mix well and set aside.

On a lightly floured surface, roll out into two 14-inch circles:

**Two 10-ounce disks Galette Dough
(page 246)**

Brush off any excess flour and transfer the dough circles onto a parchment-paper-lined baking sheet. Put the baking sheet in the refrigerator for 10 to 15 minutes to allow the dough to firm up. Remove the dough from the refrigerator. Set 1 piece aside on another piece of parchment paper. Spread the date filling evenly over the dough, leaving a 1-inch border. Brush the border with water and cover the galette with the other circle. Press the edges together, gently smoothing out any air pockets. Trim the edge evenly and crimp with a fork or pinch with your fingers. Cut a few decorative slits on the top to let steam escape during baking.

Brush the top of the galette generously with:

**3 tablespoons melted butter**

Sprinkle evenly with:

**¼ cup sugar**

Bake on a pizza stone on the floor of the oven or on a pan on the lowest rack, until well browned, 30 to 40 minutes. Cool to room temperature before serving.

VARIATION

◆ For a fragrant Middle Eastern flavor, substitute 2 teaspoons rose water for the orange blossom water and add ½ teaspoon ground cardamom and ½ teaspoon ground cinnamon to the filling.

# Honey Candied Walnuts

MAKES 2 CUPS

These lightly sweetened nuts are delicious on their own, with cheese and fresh fruit, tossed in salads, or sprinkled over Sautéed Pink Pearl Apples (page 289) or a bowl of cinnamon ice cream.

Preheat the oven to 325°F.

Measure into a small saucepan:

**½ cup sugar**
**¼ cup water**
**¼ cup honey**

Bring the syrup to a boil over medium heat, stirring. Add:

**2 cups walnuts**

Stir, mixing well, for 1 minute. Turn off the heat and let the nuts steep in the syrup for 2 to 3 minutes. Pour the nuts into a strainer and drain well. Spread the drained nuts in a single layer on a baking sheet lined with parchment paper. Bake for 10 to 15 minutes, stirring every 5 minutes. Properly candied nuts should feel slightly sticky and look light golden and shiny. Remove the nuts from the oven and cool completely before using. The nuts can be stored in an airtight container in the pantry for up to a month.

VARIATIONS

• Substitute pecans or pistachios for the walnuts.

• Substitute hazelnuts for the walnuts, toasting them for 10 to 12 minutes, stirring every 5 minutes or so. They are ready when they are slightly colored. Put the toasted nuts on a clean kitchen towel and wrap loosely. Let the nuts cool for a couple minutes and rub the nuts with the towel to remove the skins.

• Substitute almonds for the walnuts, toasting them for 10 to 12 minutes, stirring every 5 minutes or so. No need to remove the skins.

# Hazelnuts and Filberts
(*Corylus* spp.)

Hazelnuts have a rich, complex flavor that informs meringue-based cakes, cookies, and fillings. They are delicious paired with chocolate. Infused into hot milk and cream, they make a sensational ice cream and custard. I like to stuff baked apples or pears with chopped, roasted hazelnuts, mixed with sugar, butter, spices, and breadcrumbs. Uncured hazelnuts, fresh off the tree, are a treat, cracked and sliced (without roasting) and sprinkled over fall salads.

Filberts and hazelnuts belong to two separate species in the same family. Filberts (*Corylus avellana*) originated in southern Europe; their cousin, the smaller hazelnut (*Corylus americana*), is from North America, growing wild from the northern United States to southern Canada. Most cultivated nuts, the ones found in markets, are filberts, even though the culinary convention is to say hazelnut.

The recent expansion of eastern filbert blight across the country has made cultivation of the older, most desirable varieties nearly impossible for home gardeners. You should only plant varieties that are listed in catalogs as immune or highly resistant to the blight. Two good varieties that are considered immune are *Santiam* and *Jefferson*. *Yamhill*, another immune variety, will pollenize either, and produce its own delicious crop, too. Check with your local Cooperative Extension office for up-to-date advice.

Because they are naturally big and nicely shaped shrubs, hazelnuts are useful in a home garden for hedges or windbreaks. In the warmest climates, they appreciate afternoon shade. Hazelnuts require cross-pollination and will not set a crop without a compatible companion. Hazelnuts ripen in a pretty frilly husk. They are ready to harvest in the late summer or early fall, when they begin to drop from the trees. Pick the nuts from their husks on the tree, before the squirrels or birds do, and lay out the nuts to cure for several days or a week until completely dry. Store hazelnuts in their shells until ready to use, or crack them open and refrigerate the kernels.

# Crispy Hazelnut Meringues

MAKES ABOUT 6 DOZEN 2-INCH-ROUND COOKIES

This simple meringue cookie can be served alone with a cup of tea or coffee or used to make the desserts suggested at the variations at the end of the recipe.

Make a template for piping the meringue cookies. Use a 2-inch-diameter cookie cutter and trace 24 circles on a piece of parchment paper cut to fit on a 13- × 18-inch baking sheet (make 4 rows of 6 circles).

Preheat the oven to 350°F.

Toast, on separate baking sheets:

**⅓ cup almonds**
**½ cup hazelnuts**

Toast the almonds for 10 to 15 minutes, stirring every 5 minutes, until light golden brown. Remove from the oven and let cool completely. Toast the hazelnuts at the same time (they may take 2 or 3 minutes more, depending on their size). Remove the hazelnuts from the oven, tip them onto a clean kitchen towel, wrap loosely, and let cool for 2 to 3 minutes. Rub the skins off the hazelnuts and let the nuts cool completely.

Reduce the oven temperature to 325°F. Grind the almonds in a coffee or spice grinder until they resemble fine coffee grounds. (If you do not have a coffee or spice grinder, use a food processor. This will take longer, 2 to 3 minutes, and the grind will be coarser.) Transfer the ground almonds to a medium mixing bowl.

Finely grind the hazelnuts in the same grinder with:

**¼ cup sugar**

Add the ground hazelnuts to the ground almonds and mix well.

Measure into another mixing bowl:

**5 egg whites (6 ounces), room temperature**
**A pinch of salt**
**⅛ teaspoon cream of tartar**

With a clean whisk, beat the whites until they are foamy. Continue whisking, gradually adding:

**½ cup sugar**

Keep whisking until the whites hold a firm and glossy peak. Gently fold half the whites into the nut mixture, then fold in the remaining whites until there are no white streaks visible. Spoon half the mixture into a pastry bag fitted with a ½-inch piping tip. Line a baking sheet with the prepared template and cover it with another piece of parchment paper over it (you should be able to see the traced circles through the upper piece of paper). Pipe the meringue mixture onto each circle, starting at the center and spiraling outward. The thickness of the piped circles should be relatively even. Use an offset spatula to even out the disks before baking. Pull out the template from under the completed sheet of meringue circles, put it on another baking sheet, cover with another piece of parchment paper, and pipe another sheet of meringues. Depending on how thick you pipe the meringues you will end up with 2 to 3 baking sheets. Dust the disks lightly with:

**Confectioners' sugar**

Let them dry on the counter for 10 to 15 minutes. Bake for 15 to 20 minutes, until evenly brown all the way through. Cool on a rack. When they are cool, the cookies should lift off the parchment easily without sticking. If they are sticky, put them back in the oven and bake for a few more minutes until they can be lifted off the parchment. Store them in an airtight container for 2 to 3 days, or freeze them for up to a month.

VARIATIONS

* Chocolate sandwich cookies (makes 12): Melt 3½ ounces coarsely chopped bittersweet chocolate in a bowl over simmering water. Let the melted chocolate cool, stirring occasionally, until it is thick enough to pipe. Spoon the chocolate into a piping bag with a small piping tip. Lay out 12 meringue cookies on the counter, smooth side up, and pipe a dollop of chocolate ½ inch in diameter onto the center of each cookie. Place another meringue, smooth side down, on top of the chocolate and press gently to spread out the chocolate dollop.

* Chocolate ganache sandwich cookies (makes 12): Coarsely chop 3½ ounces bittersweet chocolate and put in small mixing bowl. Bring ¼ cup cream to a boil and pour the cream on the chocolate. Wait about 1 minute to let the chocolate melt into the cream. Stirring slowly and working from the center of the bowl out, stir until all the cream and chocolate is combined into a shiny mixture. This is called a ganache. Spoon the ganache into a piping bag with a small piping tip. Lay out 12 meringue cookies on the counter, smooth side up, and pipe a dollop of ganache 1 inch in diameter onto the center of each cookie. Place another meringue, smooth side down, gently, on top of the chocolate, to spread out the ganache.

* Raspberry chocolate ganache sandwich cookies (makes 12): Follow the instructions for the chocolate ganache sandwich cookies, but pipe slightly less ganache and "glue" 5 or 6 raspberries around it. Top with another cookie and press gently to make the sandwich.

* Ice-cream sandwich: Put a small scoop of any ice cream on the smooth side of a meringue cookie and top with another cookie.

## Hazelnut Floating Island

4 SERVINGS

Floating island is a classic French dessert of poached meringues served in a bowl of crème anglaise. You can make a deeply flavored, nutty crème anglaise by using hazelnuts that have been toasted until they are a rich dark brown and ground so fine they become a butter.

Preheat the oven to 350°F.
Spread out on a small baking sheet:

**½ cup hazelnuts**

Toast the nuts, stirring every 5 minutes or so, until dark brown, about 12 to 15 minutes. Cool slightly and rub in a kitchen towel to remove any loosened skin. In a food processor, grind the warm nuts to the consistency of butter with:

**2 tablespoons sugar**

Separate:

**4 eggs**

Reserve the whites. Whisk the yolks just enough to break them up.

Measure into a heavy-bottomed pot:

**2 cups milk**

**2 tablespoons sugar**

**A pinch of salt**

Set a strainer over a heat-proof bowl. Heat the milk over medium heat, stirring occasionally to dissolve the sugar. When the milk is hot, whisk a little into the egg yolks and then whisk the yolks into the rest of the hot milk. Cook over medium heat, stirring slowly, until the mixture thickens just enough to coat the back of the spoon (170°F). Do not let it boil. Remove the pan from the heat and add the nut butter to the custard. Whisk gently until all the butter is completely incorporated. Let the mixture cool for 5 minutes and strain. Chill completely in the refrigerator before serving.

For the meringues, fill a shallow pan with:

**2 cups cold nonfat milk**

**2 cups ice**

It is important to use nonfat milk because any fat in the milk will cause the meringues to break down.

Pour into a pot with a large diameter:

**2 cups nonfat milk**

**2 cups water**

Whisk the egg whites until frothy with:

**A pinch of salt**

**1 teaspoon cream of tartar**

Slowly add:

**¾ cup sugar**

Beat the whites with the sugar until they form shiny, stiff peaks. Heat the milk and water to a simmer.

Poach the meringues in batches. Slip spoonfuls of beaten egg white about the size of an egg into the hot milk and poach until puffed, 2 to 3 minutes, making 12 meringues in all. With a slotted spoon, transfer the poached meringues to the cold milk. Chill the meringues before serving. Poached meringues can be stored in the refrigerator for up to 8 hours.

For each serving, ladle ¼ cup of the cold hazelnut anglaise into a chilled bowl and float 3 meringues on top. If desired, garnish with:

**Candied Orange Peel (page 349), chopped**

VARIATIONS

◆ For a denser, browned meringue, pour the hot milk and water mixture into a low-sided baking dish. Spoon in the meringues and bake in a 400°F oven for 5 to 8 minutes until the tops of the meringues are nicely browned. Transfer the meringues to the cold milk with a slotted spoon. Don't let them be submerged.

◆ The hazelnut crème anglaise can be made into a sublime ice cream. Use 1 cup hazelnuts and ¼ cup sugar when making the hazelnut butter. When making the custard, substitute half-and-half for the milk and increase the amount of sugar to ¼ cup. Add 2 cups cream after stirring in the hazelnut butter. Strain, chill, and freeze in an ice-cream maker according to the manufacturer's instructions. Makes 1½ quarts of ice cream.

## Almonds (*Prunus dulcis*)

At Chez Panisse, a little plate of almonds toasted to a rich golden brown and tossed with herbs is frequently the first thing people see when they sit down for dinner. This dish is a delight. Almonds are a close cousin of the stone fruits, and they add flavor and depth to desserts made with peaches, nectarines, apricots, cherries, and plums. I like to make a filling for baked peaches with chopped almonds, butter, and sugar. A few slivered almonds transform plum ice cream. We also add almonds to the topping for peach and nectarine crisps.

*Mission* has small nuts with plenty of fruity noyau flavor. *Ne Plus Ultra* has large pointy nuts with good flavor. *All-in-One* is a garden favorite, with very tasty nuts on small self-pollinating trees. *Garden Prince*, another self-pollinating variety, has tasty, soft-shelled nuts.

Almonds on the tree look like small pale green peaches. If you grow your own almonds, pick some in spring when the fruits have formed, but the inner shell has not hardened. Carefully cut around the soft pit and release the tender, crisp immature kernel or nut. If it is still soft and jellylike, wait a week and try again. When they are ready, take out the kernel, peel off the thin skin, and use them right away. They are delicious in a spring salad or slivered and served over vanilla ice cream with fresh berries or a stone fruit compote.

Almond trees burst into bloom in late spring with showy pink-white flowers. Although they need some winter chill, they also need a mild climate that will support their early bloom. The nuts ripen best in dry, hot summer weather. If you garden in a marginal area, choose late-blooming varieties. Most varieties require another variety planted nearby for cross-pollination.

When the nuts ripen in the late summer their green hulls crack open and reveal the nut inside. Spread a tarp under the tree and use a pole to shake the nuts from the branches. Remove the hulls and spread out the nuts to cure in an airy location out of the sun. They should be ready to store after a week or so. Check by shaking the nuts; the kernels should rattle in the shell. Store in a cool place, where they will keep for six months. Shelled almonds should be refrigerated or frozen.

## Almond Milk Panna Cotta

8 SERVINGS

Making your own almond milk is very simple and is what makes this dessert fresh, light, and utterly compelling. Add a few slices of peach, nectarine, or other stone fruits for a perfect finish, and a spoonful of raspberry or chocolate sauce will make this dessert quite elegant indeed.

Measure into a bowl:

**⅔ cup almonds**

**2⅓ cups water**

Cover the bowl and soak the almonds over-night. The next day, strain the almonds and save the liquid. Peel off the skins and discard. In a blender, purée the almonds with all the soaking water. Line a strainer with cheese-cloth and strain the blended mixture. Once most of the liquid has drained through, gather up the corners of the cheesecloth and squeeze the almond pulp to extract the remaining liquid.

Measure 1¾ cups of the almond milk and set aside.

Lightly brush eight 4-ounce ramekins or custard cups with:

**Almond oil or a flavorless vegetable oil**

Measure into a small heat-proof bowl:

**2 tablespoons water**

Sprinkle over the surface of the water to "bloom":

**One ¼-ounce packet unflavored gelatin**

If there are any dry spots on the gelatin, sprinkle them with a few of drops of water to saturate. Set the bowl aside.

Measure into a heavy-bottomed pot:

**1¾ cups heavy cream**

**4½ tablespoons sugar**

**A small pinch of salt**

Heat the mixture over medium heat to 170°F, stirring to dissolve the sugar and salt. Remove from the heat and let the mixture cool.

Once the cream mixture has cooled to 130°F, gently dissolve the bloomed gelatin by placing your heat-proof bowl into a pan of shallow hot water. Stir gently, and when the gelatin is completely liquefied add it to the warm cream mixture. Stir in the almond milk and:

**2 to 3 drops of almond extract, if desired**

Strain the mixture and pour into the pre-pared ramekins or custard cups and put them in the refrigerator to chill until set, about 4 to 5 hours, or overnight.

To serve, run a small knife around the inside of each ramekin. Turn each ramekin over onto a small serving plate, shake gently, and lift off the ramekin.

VARIATION

♦ Use the extra almond milk to make a fan-tastic smoothie with a handful of berries, a few slices of peaches, and a couple dates.

## Soft Almond Meringues

MAKES 2 DOZEN MERINGUES

Crunchy on the outside and chewy in the center, these meringues are absolutely deli-cious, either eaten on their own or served with a scoop of ice cream or sorbet.

Preheat the oven to 325°F.

Spread out on a baking sheet:

**1⅓ cups sliced almonds**

Toast lightly (about 5 minutes) and set aside to cool.

Put a small pot of water on the stove to boil. Whisk together in a heat-proof nonreactive metal bowl:

**4 ounces powdered sugar, sifted**

**2 large egg whites**

Set the bowl over the pot of boiling water.

Whisk until the mixture is warm, remove from the heat, and continue whisking until the egg whites form stiff peaks. (This can easily be done by hand or in the bowl of a stand mixer if you have one.)

Gently fold in the cooled sliced almonds and:

**¼ teaspoon vanilla extract**
**A pinch of salt**

Line a baking sheet with parchment paper and pipe out or drop spoonfuls of meringue onto the pan leaving at least 1½ inches of space between them. Bake in the oven until the meringues look dry and you can lift them slightly off the parchment, about 15 minutes. Remove from the oven and let cool completely before putting them away. These will keep in an airtight container for up to 1 week.

VARIATIONS
◆ Substitute chopped toasted hazelnuts, pecans, walnuts, or pistachios for the almonds.
◆ Along with the toasted nuts, add to the meringue mixture the same amount of toasted coconut or bits of chopped bittersweet chocolate.

# Chocolate Candies with Dried Fruits and Nuts

MAKES ABOUT 25 CANDIES

These candies are made with a drop of melted chocolate and topped with dried fruits and nuts. In France, they are called *mendiants*, "beggars," because these chocolates are carrying their belongings (dried fruits and nuts) on their backs!

Gather together:

**25 dried sour cherries**
**13 toasted almonds (cut into halves)**
**¼ cup Candied Orange Peel (page 349), cut into 25 small pieces**

Coarsely chop into same-size pieces:

**½ pound bittersweet chocolate**

Put into a small heat-proof mixing bowl. Set the bowl over a pot of boiling water to melt the chocolate. Stir constantly and once the chocolate is melted, remove the bowl from the pot and let the chocolate cool and thicken, stirring occasionally. It should feel just cool to the lips. Transfer to a piping bag with a small piping tip and pipe coin-size drops (about the size of a quarter) onto a parchment-paper-lined sheet tray. (You can also use a small spoon to make the drops.) Quickly place 1 cherry, 1 almond half, and 1 piece of candied orange peel onto each chocolate coin. Refrigerate the candies before serving.

NOTE
◆ You can temper the chocolate and keep the mendiants at room temperature for up to 1 week. Tempering chocolate is a tedious and finicky process. It usually takes a few tries to get the technique down. For complete instructions, refer to a good chocolate cookbook such as Alice Medrich's *Seriously Bitter Sweet*, David Lebovitz's *The Great Book of Chocolate*, or Dorie Greenspan's *Chocolate Desserts by Pierre Hermé*.

VARIATIONS
◆ Substitute any dried fruit and toasted nuts for the dried cherries and almonds.
◆ Use Candied Mint Leaves (page 30) or rose petals in place of the nut or one of the fruits.

# Sweet and Savory Citrus

## Lemons, Limes, Oranges, Grapefruit, Kumquats, Mandarin Oranges, and Citron

CITRUS ARE POSSIBLY the most versatile of fruits, satisfying our desires for sweetness and sourness at the same time. Unless they are way too sour, they are delicious eaten out of hand and in desserts, but I also count on them to provide flavor and balance in the savory kitchen. A squeeze of lemon juice or a sprinkle of grated zest is often the best way to brighten a vinaigrette or mayonnaise, perk up a sauce or soup, or provide the finishing touch to a plate of grilled fish. Because they mostly ripen in wintertime, they are the beautiful jewels of the cold months, bringing flavor and color to an otherwise dark and dreary season. Tiny orange kumquats and kishu tangerines, brilliant blood oranges, fragrant citron, tangy rangpur and *yuzu*, sweet satsumas, and juicy tangelos add to the standard list of seductive citrus.

Recipes

Creamy Meyer Lemon Dressing  312

Meyer Lemon Soufflé  312

Fettuccine with Roasted Purple Asparagus,
Lemon Zest, and Parmesan  313

Farro Tagliatelle  313

Lime Spritzer  315

Halibut Ceviche with Lime  315

Blood Orange and Golden Beet Salad  317

Panforte with Candied Orange Peel and Chocolate  318

Panforte Candies  318

Cara Cara Campari Cocktail  319

Pink Grapefruit Granita  320

Kumquat Relish  321

Tangerine Ice Cream  322

Rangpur Curd  322

Yuzu Marmalade Thumbprint Cookies  323

Fish Tartare with Pickled Buddha's Hand  324

# Citrus in the Garden

With their lush, glossy evergreen leaves, righly fragrant blossoms, and brightly colored fruit, citrus trees make a delightful addition to a kitchen garden. The world of citrus includes tart yellow lemons, fragrant green limes, sweet juicy oranges, and pink sweet-tart grapefruit, not to mention kishus, kumquats, yuzu, tangelos, citrons, and many more enticing varieties. They are all heat lovers and can tolerate little, if any, chill or frost, but perhaps to make up for that fact they are especially easy to grow, requiring very little care to thrive and make fruit.

If you live in the warm belt of southern states, you are gardening where citrus trees can thrive. With a little care and planning, many varieties can be grown in other parts of the country, especially on a small scale. If a permanent place in the garden is not an option for you, consider growing citrus in containers. Dwarf citrus and varieties that are naturally shrubby are great for container culture and bear fruit even though they are small. I have two kumquat trees on the covered porch at the entryway to my house; they flourish with very little attention and their beauty regularly attracts comments.

Whether planted in containers or in the ground, citrus trees should be grown in a sunny spot protected from strong winds, with well-draining soil. If possible, place the plants near a patio or path to enjoy the charm of their fragrant flowers and colorful fruit. Before planting, amend the soil with plenty of compost and organic material. Feed the trees regularly with compost and compost tea early in the growing season. Stop feed-ing them in the fall and winter, when their growth slows naturally. Harvest citrus fruit when it is fully colored and filled with flavor. Taste often to determine when the fruit is at its peak of flavor, as it may have colored but not yet be fully ripe. When harvesting, twist or cut the fruit from the tree. Citrus needs little pruning other than shaping the plants and keeping them within bounds.

If your climate is marginal for citrus, choose a small tree and take advantage of microclimates. Choose a place sheltered from cold north winds and situate your plant near a south-facing wall that has solar-absorbing pavement nearby or on a south-facing slope where frosty night air will flow away to lower areas. Protect the plants from occasional severe cold weather. Build a simple wooden framework around the tree to support burlap fabric or clear plastic sheeting that can be put in place on nights when frost threatens. Inside the enclosure, provide a heat lamp or a few incandescent lightbulbs that can be turned on at night. In an emergency, a string of Christmas lights will keep the temperature up a few degrees (so long as they are not the LED kind, which are too efficient). A bedsheet or lightweight blanket thrown over a small tree could also do the job. I do have to state a caveat, one gained from personal experience in my foggy yard: sometimes a tree will thrive and bear plenty of fruit that just does not taste sweet because of lack of heat. However, it will still be beautiful and its blossoms fragrant. That fruit needn't be wasted: candied zest or other preserves are always a possibility.

In cold climates, follow the system perfected by French royal gardeners for their *orangeries*. Keep the trees in containers outdoors in the warm months, and then move them to a cool, bright sunny room indoors during the winter. Choose containers on wheels for ease of movement. A small greenhouse also works well as a place to protect and overwinter citrus. Some citrus varieties will bear fruit when grown indoors year-round.

## Lemons  (*Citrus limon*)

I can't imagine cooking without lemons. The tart juice and the fragrant oil in the zest flavor countless dishes, both savory and sweet. I reach for a lemon whenever a dish needs a final lift—the fruity acid helps bring out the natural flavors of a dish and adds freshness at the same time. A squeeze of lemon juice may give the final flourish to a soup, brighten a grilled piece of chicken, steak, or fish, or perfect a bubbling pot of apricot jam. Lemon zest on the other hand brings the essence of lemon without the acidity. I use it in tandem with lemon juice or by itself where only the essential perfume of lemon is wanted. A grating of zest brings a simple glass of lemonade to new heights, adds pizzazz to salsa verde, and gives depth of flavor to a lemon curd tart. Salads, sauces, pastas, braises, sorbets, tarts, soufflés, cookies, pies, cakes—these are all preparations to which I might add a little or a lot of lemon. The high level of citric acid in lemon juice is also useful to prevent oxidation and discoloration of fruits and vegetables, particularly artichokes, cardoons, pears, and apples. And half a lemon dipped in salt and rubbed on your copper pots will keep them gleaming.

Tree-ripened lemons, either homegrown or fresh from a local farmer, are remarkably better than store-bought. (Most commercial lemons have been harvested green, before they ripen, so they can be held in storage for long periods.) Smooth, shiny, rounded *Meyer* lemons (probably a hybrid of lemons and mandarins) are perennial favorites at Chez Panisse. Their flesh has a milder acidity than regular lemon, and the zest is more complexly aromatic. The white, inner part of the peel is not nearly as bitter as other citrus, and the skin is thinner, so the entire fruit can be used. To make a quick relish for cold meat or fish, chop a whole Meyer lemon, either fresh or preserved in the Moroccan way, and add some chopped shallot, olive oil, salt, and pepper.

*Lisbon* and *Eureka* are the two most common varieties of conventional lemons. They are quite similar, but I am partial to the juicy smooth-skinned Lisbon. The juice and flesh is typically sour, and the zest is slightly bitter. Be careful when zesting these lemons to avoid the underlying white, acrid part of the rind. A tree-ripened Lisbon lemon has an extraordinarily delicious floral quality that is divine when the lemon is sliced extra thin and added to a radish sandwich or used as a relish for a piece of grilled fish.

If you have room and time for only one citrus tree, plant a Meyer lemon. The dwarf varieties are small and compact, perfect for containers, and the fruit is incredibly versatile. Meyer lemons are the most cold hardy of the lemons, followed by Lisbon and then Eureka. Lisbon and Eureka lemon trees grow to be quite tall.

Meyer lemons

Pink lemons

Kishu mandarins

Nagami kumquats

Mexican limes

Bearss lime

Oroblanco grapefruit

Buddha's Hand citron

# Creamy Meyer Lemon Dressing

MAKES ABOUT ½ CUP

This is a creamy dressing that coats lettuce in a luscious way. The flavor is light and sprightly filled with lemon juice and zest. I especially like it on sweet lettuces such as butterhead or romaine or a mix of small chicories and radicchio.

Stir together in a large bowl:

**1 tablespoon Meyer lemon juice**
**1 tablespoon white wine vinegar**
**Grated zest of 1 Meyer lemon**
**Salt**
**Fresh-ground black pepper**

Taste, and adjust as needed. Whisk in:

**3 tablespoons extra-virgin olive oil**
**3 tablespoons heavy cream**

Taste for salt and acid and adjust as needed.

VARIATIONS

• Add a pinch of cayenne along with the salt for a bit of spice.

• Stir in a tablespoon of chopped tender herbs such as chives, chervil, parsley, dill, tarragon, summer savory, or anise hyssop to the finished dressing.

• Try rangpur lime, bitter orange, lemon, lime, or another sour citrus instead of Meyer lemon.

• Use red wine vinegar instead of white wine vinegar.

• Omit the cream and use 5 tablespoons olive oil.

• Substitute 2 tablespoons buttermilk or crème fraîche for 2 tablespoons of the cream.

• Add a few chopped salt-cured anchovy fillets to the lemon juice and vinegar.

# Meyer Lemon Soufflé

6 SERVINGS

A bit of homemade candied lemon peel stirred in and a little fresh juice sprinkled on top before baking make this extraordinary soufflé lovely and bright.

Generously butter a 1-quart soufflé dish and sprinkle with a light coating of sugar. Preheat the oven to 425°F and position an oven rack in the center of the oven. In a medium bowl stir together:

**½ cup plus 1 tablespoon pastry cream (see page 274)**
**3 tablespoons Meyer lemon juice**
**1½ teaspoons kirsch (optional)**
**1½ tablespoons chopped candied Meyer lemon peel (see page 350)**
**¼ teaspoon grated lemon zest**

Into a large stainless-steel or copper mixing bowl, add:

**4 egg whites**
**A pinch of salt**

Whisk until the egg whites are foamy. Add:

**1½ teaspoons cornstarch**

Continue whisking and add in a steady stream:

**¼ cup sugar**

Whisk until the whites are slightly stiffer than soft peaks. Fold a small amount of the egg whites into the Meyer lemon mixture to loosen the mixture, and then gently fold in the remaining egg whites until just blended. Pour into the prepared dish and drizzle over:

**1 tablespoon Meyer lemon juice**
**A large pinch of sugar**

Place the dish in the middle of the oven and bake for 20 to 25 minutes until the soufflé is puffed and browned. Serve immediately.

• For individual soufflés, prepare 6 individual ramekins and bake for 7 to 8 minutes.
• Use lemon instead of Meyer lemon.

# Fettuccine with Roasted Purple Asparagus, Lemon Zest, and Parmesan

4 SERVINGS

Roll out and cut into ½-inch-wide noodles:

**1 recipe Farro Tagliatelle (this page)**

Toss the noodles with extra flour, lay them out on a plate or baking sheet, cover with a towel, and refrigerate until ready to use. Preheat the oven to 425°F. Break off and discard the stem ends and peel:

**A 1-pound bunch of purple asparagus**

Toss with:

**Salt**

**A drizzle of olive oil**

**3 lemon thyme sprigs, leaves only**

Lay out in a single layer on a parchment-paper-lined baking sheet and roast until just tender and caramelized, about 9 minutes. Let cool slightly, and then cut on a diagonal into bite-size pieces. Leave the tips 1½ inches long and cut them in half lengthwise. Toss with:

**Finely grated zest from 1 lemon**

**Salt, if needed**

Bring a pot of salted water to a boil. Add the noodles and cook until al dente, about 3 to 4 minutes, depending on how thin the noodles are. While the noodles are cooking, heat a heavy-bottomed pan over medium heat. Pour in:

**2 tablespoons extra-virgin olive oil**

Add the asparagus and toss, and once the pan begins to sizzle, turn off the heat. Drain the noodles, reserving ½ cup of the cooking water. Toss the noodles with the asparagus, ¼ cup of the cooking liquid, and:

**A squeeze of lemon juice**

**¼ cup grated Parmesan cheese**

Taste a noodle for salt and adjust as needed. Add more cooking water if the pasta seems dry. Plate the pasta and sprinkle with:

**Grated Parmesan cheese**

# Farro Tagliatelle

4 SERVINGS

I love the flavor farro gives to pasta. Farro is an ancient variety of wheat and has a distinct nuttiness that complements tomatoes, broccoli rabe, sausage, and chicories—some of my favorite pasta dishes. Using a combination of whole-grain and all-purpose flour allows the dough to have plenty of flavor and stay smooth and silky, with enough stretch for stuffed pasta dishes, too.

Mix together in a medium bowl:

**1½ cups farro flour**

**½ cup unbleached all-purpose flour**

Lightly mix together in another bowl:

**2 eggs**

**2 egg yolks**

Make a well in the flour and pour in the eggs. Mix with a fork, as though scrambling eggs, incorporating the flour bit by bit. When the flour is too stiff to mix with a fork, finish the mixing by hand. Turn the dough out onto a floured surface and knead lightly.

Or make in a stand mixer fitted with the paddle attachment. Measure the flour into the mixer bowl, and pour in the eggs while mixing at low speed. Mix until the dough just starts to come together, adding a few drops of water if the dough is dry and crumbly. Turn out onto a floured surface and knead lightly. Shape the dough into a disk and wrap in plastic. Let it rest at least 1 hour before rolling. Refrigerate if not using within 2 hours.

Roll the dough out by hand on a lightly floured board or with a pasta machine. When using a machine, roll the pasta through the widest setting, fold into thirds, and pass through the machine again. Repeat two more times. Then roll, decreasing the setting on the machine one notch at a time, until the pasta is the desired thickness. Cut the pasta into 16-inch lengths and stack them, flouring liberally between each sheet. Fold the stack in half lengthwise, and then in half again (always lengthwise). Cut crosswise into ¼-inch slices. Toss the noodles with more flour to separate and unfold them. Place on a plate and cover with a towel. Refrigerate if not using immediately.

To cook, bring a large pot of salted water to a boil. Add the noodles and cook until al dente, from 3 to 5 minutes. The time will vary with the thickness of the noodles.

VARIATIONS

◆ Use whole-wheat instead of farro flour, or use a greater ratio of all-purpose flour.
◆ Cut the noodles into thicker or thinner noodles, or keep them in sheets for lasagne, ravioli, or cannelloni.

# Limes  (*Citrus latifolia*)

If lemons are the everyday workers in the kitchen, then limes are the specialists. Their aroma is stronger and more complex than lemons, yet their flavor accommodates the mild flavors of avocado, chicken, and fish quite nicely. Limes also accent the subdued flavors of tropical fruits such as papayas, guavas, and mangos, and their assertive character pairs well with spicy chiles and exotic spices. Guacamole, ceviche, and salsa are all better made with lime. And limes enhance cold refreshing beverages from sparkling water to carefully crafted cocktails. Lime is found in the dishes of Central America, the Caribbean, Africa, India, and all tropical areas where the trees thrive.

*Bearss* limes (*Tahiti*) are fantastic when tree-ripened and fresh. They are large, seedless, and filled with plenty of tart lime juice. *Mexican* or *Key* limes (*Citrus aurantifolia*) are small and filled with bold flavor. Some say that guacamole is not right without them, and bartenders prefer them for margaritas and *mojitos. Kieffer* or *Kaffir* limes (*Citrus hystrix*) have highly aromatic double, or hourglass-shaped, leaves that are much used in Thai cuisine. Try a Kaffir lime leaf instead of a bay leaf in your next chicken or turkey soup for an interesting lift. The zest of the bumpy-skinned fruit is full of aromatic oils and is common in many Southeast Asian curry pastes, and the juice, though scant, is quite tart and tasty.

Limes grow well outdoors in only the warmest climates; Bearss are the least cold sensitive. Dwarf Kieffer and Key limes will grow nicely in containers.

# Lime Spritzer

MAKES 1 DRINK

Homemade lime syrup made with fresh juice mixed with sparkling water is the perfect drink for a hot summer's day. Add a little rum or *shoju* and a very refreshing cocktail is ready to serve.

Fill a 10-ounce glass with ice and measure in:

**3 tablespoons Lime Syrup (page 348)**
**2 tablespoons lime juice**

Stir and top with sparkling water. Stir. Taste and add more syrup or juice if needed. Garnish with:

**A slice of lime**

VARIATIONS

✦ Add 3 or 4 mint leaves to the glass with the syrup and juice and stir well to release the flavor into the drink.

✦ Use only 2 tablespoons syrup and add 1½ ounces shoju or rum with the lime juice. Pour in half the amount of water, or to taste.

*Kaffir lime*

# Halibut Ceviche with Lime

4 SERVINGS

Ceviche is a refreshing salad made with pristinely fresh fish marinated in lime juice. The juice "cooks" the fish, turning it opaque and firm, while flavoring it with the unmistakable, fragrant tang of lime. Halibut makes a fantastic ceviche but any fresh, firm-fleshed fish will work.

Cut into ¼-inch cubes:

**¾ pound halibut**

Put in a nonreactive bowl and season with:

**Salt**

Pour over:

**⅓ cup Key or other lime juice**

Mix well and press the fish down so it is submerged in the juice. Cover and refrigerate for 1 hour, or until the fish is opaque and firm.

Meanwhile, cut the stem ends from:

**2 jalapeño or other hot peppers**

Slice in half lengthwise and remove the seeds and veins. Slice thinly. Peel and dice:

**1 small red or white onion**

Chop coarsely:

**6 cilantro sprigs**

When the fish is ready, drain off and discard the lime juice. Stir in half the hot peppers, the onion, and cilantro. Season with:

**Salt**

Taste and add salt and more hot peppers as desired. Serve on:

**A bed of romaine or butter lettuce**

And garnish with:

**Sliced radishes**
**Sliced avocado**
**Tortilla chips**

## Oranges *(Citrus sinensis)*

Fresh-squeezed orange juice from your own backyard may be the most compelling reason to grow sweet oranges. Add sweet navel oranges to eat in the fall and winter, and the brilliant color of blood oranges in early spring, and you have citrus for almost all seasons. I like to slice oranges into salads both savory and sweet and use the zest to flavor sauces and tapenade. Oranges make delicious cakes, sorbets, and ice creams, and orange tart, with beautiful segments arranged on pastry cream, is one of the best tarts of the winter season. Candied orange peel, chopped fine and sprinkled over any dessert that wants a hint of orange or dipped in chocolate to have with an espresso, is like gold in the pantry.

*Washington* navel is the best variety for eating fresh, out of hand. It is seedless, easy to peel, and the segments separate without trouble. The *Cara Cara* navel has salmon pink flesh and the same delicious flavor as Washington. Both ripen in late fall and early winter. Don't try to use navel oranges for juice. They aren't very juicy, and they contain a chemical compound (limonin) that makes the juice bitter within a few minutes. *Valencia* oranges and their relatives are the "juice oranges" in the market. They are in season from late winter through early summer. At the restaurant we use Valencias for sorbet—with Armagnac in spring, strawberries in summer, and chocolate whenever we want. Valencia oranges make the best, most tender candied peel, so we save every bit of peel left from juicing. Valencia is the most popular variety in my area. *Midknight*

is a practically seedless Valencia that ripens earlier.

Blood oranges, as their name suggests, have some degree of red flesh. They ripen from late winter into spring, and their tart flesh and juice often hint of the flavor of raspberries. *Tarocco*, bright orange and red; *Moro*, with deep wine red–colored flesh; and the aptly named *Sanguinelli*, which has orange flesh shot through with red, and beautiful red rind, are the best varieties. Blood oranges make brilliant juice and sorbet, and they are the best oranges to use for upside-down cake, where their acidity is an asset. They are also nice in salads and vinaigrettes that need an acid bite.

Sweet oranges will grow in climates where winter temperatures don't fall below the upper 20s. Navel oranges need more summer heat to ripen than Valencia oranges, but their fruit will be ripe and off the tree before the most severe winter cold. Valencia oranges may be left on the tree for some time without losing flavor or freshness.

Sour or bitter oranges are not good for eating out of hand, but they make perfect orange marmalade and their sour juice is great for making marinades, vinaigrettes, and sauces. Pebbly-skinned *Seville* (*Bigarade*) oranges are filled with seeds that have a high pectin content. These are the oranges for marmalade. *Bergamot* orange has a highly aromatic rind. It is best known as the flavoring in Earl Grey tea. *Chinotto* will do well in containers. Bitter oranges are more cold hardy than sweet oranges and the trees are filled with exceptionally fragrant blossoms. The fruit is ripe from December through February.

# Blood Orange and Golden Beet Salad

4 SERVINGS

Tangy red blood oranges complement tender golden beets in this beautiful sweet and savory salad. Scatter Fried Rosemary (page 27) over the top for a taste and texture sensation.

Preheat the oven to 375°F.
Trim the tops off:

**8 small or 4 medium golden beets**

Wash them well and put them in a baking dish that just holds them comfortably. Pour in water to cover the bottom of the pan to a depth of ⅛ inch. Sprinkle over:

**Salt**

**A drizzle of olive oil**

**A large pinch of fennel seeds (optional)**

Cover tightly and bake until tender, about 45 minutes to 1 hour, depending on their size. Let the beets cool, then peel. Slice the beets into ¼-inch rounds or cut in half lengthwise and then into wedges. Or do a little of both. Sprinkle with:

**2 teaspoons red wine vinegar**

**Salt**

Let the beets sit to absorb the flavors. Taste and add more salt as needed. Toss with:

**2 teaspoons extra-virgin olive oil**

Meanwhile, remove the peel and membrane, exposing the juicy flesh of:

**4 small or 3 medium Moro blood oranges**

Using a small sharp knife, slice off the top and bottom of the oranges. Then carefully cut away strips of peel, cutting down from top to bottom, following the contours of the fruit. Cut the sections free, slicing along the partitioning membranes. Squeeze the juice from the membranes. Measure 1 tablespoon of the juice into a small bowl. Stir in:

**1 teaspoon red wine vinegar**

**Salt**

**Fresh-ground black pepper**

Whisk in:

**1½ tablespoons extra-virgin olive oil**

Taste for salt and acid and adjust as needed. Arrange the beets and orange segments on a plate and spoon the dressing over. Garnish with:

**Watercress, curly cress, or chervil sprigs**

VARIATIONS

◆ Cut the oranges into ¼-inch slices instead of cutting into sections.

◆ Use different colors of beets. When using red beets, dress them separately so their color does not bleed all over the others.

## Panforte with Candied Orange Peel and Chocolate

MAKES ONE 9-INCH CAKE

There are many versions of this traditional Italian confection. This one is spicy and rich with chocolate. Use the best-quality cocoa powder and bittersweet chocolate you can find and candied orange peel that is moist and fresh. A wedge of panforte makes a special holiday gift, and it will keep for months, if you can resist eating it up.

Preheat the oven to 300°F. Generously butter a 9- or 10-inch springform pan and dust with:

**2 teaspoons cocoa powder**

Toast until fragrant and lightly browned, about 12 to 15 minutes:

**1 cup hazelnuts**
**1½ cups almonds**

Rub the skins off the hazelnuts (see page 301), and chop the nuts coarsely.
Chop and melt in a bowl set over simmering water:

**3 ounces bittersweet chocolate**

In a large bowl, stir together the nuts with:

**¾ cup unbleached all-purpose flour**
**5 tablespoons cocoa powder**
**1 cup Candied Orange Peel (page 349), coarsely chopped**
**1 tablespoon ground cinnamon**
**2 teaspoons ground ginger**
**1½ teaspoons fresh-ground black pepper**
**¼ teaspoon freshly grated nutmeg**

Measure into a heavy saucepan:

**1 cup sugar**
**¾ cup honey**

Heat the mixture until the temperature reaches 240°F on a candy thermometer. Add the melted chocolate to the nut and flour mixture in the bowl, and pour in the honey mixture. Stir to mix well; it will thicken and stiffen quickly. Turn the batter out into the springform pan. Dampen your hands with water, and press and spread the batter evenly in the pan.

Bake for 50 minutes on the center rack of the oven. Remove from the oven and cool on a rack. After 45 minutes or so, while still warm, loosen the edge from the pan with a knife and remove the springform. Use a spatula to remove the panforte from the bottom of the pan and let cool completely. If you like, before storing, sprinkle with:

**Powdered sugar**

Cut in quarters or wedges, wrap in plastic, and store in a cool dark place.

## Panforte Candies

MAKES ABOUT 4 DOZEN 1-INCH-SQUARE CANDIES

This is a milder flavored version of panforte. Use a mix of candied peels for good flavor.

Preheat the oven to 300°F. Generously butter and flour a quarter sheet pan (9 × 13 × 1 inches ) and set aside.
Toast until golden brown, about 14 minutes:

**2¼ cups almonds**

Stir the nuts now and then to ensure even browning. Let cool.
Chop medium-fine:

**2¼ cups of candied peel (¾ cup grapefruit peel and 1½ cups orange or tangerine peel; see page 350)**

Measure into a large bowl:

**¾ cup unbleached all-purpose flour**
**1 teaspoon ground cinnamon**
**¼ teaspoon freshly grated nutmeg**
**¼ teaspoon ground cloves**

Add the cooled toasted nuts and chopped peel, making sure to break up any clumps of peel.

Measure into a heavy saucepan:

**¾ cup sugar**
**½ cup honey**
**¼ cup corn syrup**

Bring to a boil and cook until the temperature reaches 250°F on a candy thermometer (soft ball stage). Remove from the heat and carefully pour the syrup over the nut and peel mixture. Working quickly, stir the whole mass together to evenly distribute the syrup. Keep stirring until well mixed. Spoon the mixture into the prepared pan, a spoonful in each corner, and then distribute spoonfuls around the pan. Flatten the candy evenly in the pan with a lightly oiled spatula or dampened hands. (You can keep a bowl of cold water handy to cool off your hands.) If you find holes, take a nut or two from somewhere else in the pan and fill it in. Bake for 30 minutes, rotating the pan halfway through. The candy should be bubbly all over. Remove from the oven and let cool. Run a knife around the edges of the pan and lift out the panforte. Wrap in parchment paper or plastic wrap and cut as needed. Panforte will keep for months stored in a cool, dark place.

VARIATION

✦ Instead of almonds, use a combination of nuts such as hazelnuts and pistachios.

# Cara Cara Campari Cocktail

MAKES 2 DRINKS

This is a beautiful and refreshing drink, lovely for a celebratory brunch or a holiday gathering.

Fill 2 pretty glasses with ice. Pour into each:

**2 ounces Cara Cara orange juice,**
**freshly squeezed**
**2 ounces Prosecco or Champagne**
**1 ounce Campari**

Stir together and garnish with:

**1 strip of orange rind**

VARIATIONS

✦ Use blood orange juice or another sweet orange juice in place of Cara Cara juice.
✦ For a stronger cocktail, replace the sparkling wine with 1 ounce gin.

# Grapefruit (*Citrus paradisi*)

When I was growing up we always had white grapefruit (probably *Marsh*, still the best of the white varieties). The red varieties *Rio Red* and *Flame* provide gorgeous, ruby-colored segments to eat by themselves or to pair with avocados and onions in a salad or with oranges and other citrus in fruit compotes, or to freeze into beautifully colored sorbet and granita. Sweet seedless *Oroblanco* is a pummelo-grapefruit cross with white flesh. It makes extraordinary sorbet as well.

Not every gardener can grow grapefruit in their backyard or greenhouse. Grapefruit trees love heat. They grow best in the hottest climates: in the southern California and Arizona deserts, along the Rio Grande in Texas, and in the Indian River Valley in Florida. Trees in mild, frost-free coastal climates produce fruit that can prove disappointingly sour. Oroblanco needs less heat than its grapefruit cousins and could be a good choice.

# Pink Grapefruit Granita

MAKES 2 CUPS

Grapefruit granita is one of the easiest desserts to make—find the best-tasting fruit available, juice it, mix it with a bit of sugar if needed, and freeze it. When it becomes hard, scrape it with a fork or chop it with a pastry scraper to a crumbly sweet icy confection. I like to serve it sprinkled over vanilla ice cream.

Once you have mastered the recipe, experiment with all the other citrus that you like to eat. It is fun, and pretty, to make and you can serve two or three flavors at a time.

Put a small plate in the freezer. Wash and dry:

**2½ pounds Rio Red or Flame grapefruit**
Using a vegetable peeler, cut 3 or 4 long strips of zest from one of the fruits. Use only the colorful part of the peel. If there is any white on the strips scrape it away with a spoon. Juice the grapefruit for about 2 cups of juice. Pour ½ cup of the juice into a saucepan with the zest and:

**¼ cup sugar**
**A tiny pinch of salt**
Heat, stirring, until the sugar is just dissolved. Pour into the remaining juice. Stir in:

**2 tablespoons lemon juice**

Put a small amount of sweetened juice on the frozen plate. Taste for sweetness. Add more sugar as needed. Pour into a shallow nonreactive pan and freeze. Stir after 1 hour or when the sides and top have developed ice crystals. Stir again after 2 hours or when slushy. Chop or scrape when solid but not hard. Transfer to a chilled container.

VARIATIONS
• Garnish with peeled grapefruit sections.
• Stir in ¼ cup Campari before freezing.
• Garnish with a chiffonade of mint.

# Kumquats  (*Fortunella* sp.)

Kumquats look like tiny oranges, but they are a fruit unto themselves. Their skin is quite thin and sweet, while the juicy flesh within is tart. Just pop one into your mouth and enjoy the sweet-tart burst of flavor. Because they are tiny and have tasty peel, the whole kumquat fruit is used in cooking. Slice them into salads, chop them for relish, and salt them like lemons to preserve. Cook them in sugar syrup for a gorgeous garnish or chop into ice cream or a soufflé. The most common variety, *Nagami*, has small oval fruit with few seeds. Sweet, juicy *Meiwa* has larger, more rounded fruit.

Kumquats are among the most cold-hardy citrus and can be planted outdoors in areas where winter temperatures fall into the upper teens. The small, bushy plants are well-behaved ornamentals, with a symmetrical growth habit, small, intensely green leaves, and tiny bright orange fruits. The fruits ripen in late fall through early winter. Dwarf kumquats are ideal for containers.

# Kumquat Relish

MAKES ABOUT 1 CUP

This sweet-and-sour relish goes well with fish. I also like it on steamed asparagus and spooned over an avocado and grapefruit salad.

Cut crosswise into thin slices:
> **10 kumquats (about ¼ pound)**

Stir together in a small bowl:
> **1 small red or white onion, sliced thin**
> **1 tablespoon chopped chervil or**
> **cilantro**
> **Salt**
> **Fresh-ground black pepper**
> **A pinch of cayenne or Marash pepper**
> **(optional)**

Stir in the kumquats along with:
> **1 tablespoon extra-virgin olive oil**

Taste for salt and adjust as needed.

# Mandarin Oranges

*(Citrus reticulata)*

Mandarin oranges form the largest group of citrus fruits; the many different kinds include tangerines, clementines, satsumas, and hybrids such as tangelos and rangpur limes. Mandarins are ideal for eating fresh—their rind is usually easy to peel (sometimes charmingly referred to as zipper skin), the segments separate without trouble, and many are seedless. Their color and lively flavor partner well on the savory side, in salads and Asian-inspired dishes, and in desserts such as mandarin sorbet with crêpes Suzette or mandarins arranged in a pastry shell and topped with meringue.

Mixed with Champagne, mandarin juice makes an eye-opening mimosa.

*Satsumas* are the classic small seedless mandarins with sweet, low-acid fruit. Delicious clementines are easy to peel and most are seedless. Both are early ripening and are the first mandarins to reach the markets in winter. *Page*, a clementine and tangelo hybrid, though not as easy to peel, has the best-tasting juice; it is perfect for sorbet. They come to market in midwinter. *Kishu* mandarins are tiny, flavorful, seedless midwinter mandarins. They come in little clusters with their leaves still attached and are so charming and delicious that we serve them at Chez Panisse, plain, in a fruit bowl, for as long as they are in season. I send them to all my friends back East in January and they write me love letters. Delightfully sweet *Pixie* is one of the latest-ripening mandarins; its small fruit extends the mandarin season into late spring. *Minneola* tangelos are a cross between a mandarin and a grapefruit. They are deep orange, with delicious sweet-tart flesh. *Rangpur*, frequently called a lime because of its acidic flesh, is actually a cross between a mandarin and a lemon. Rangpurs have highly aromatic skin. Candy their zest or preserve them in salt for a taste treat.

Mandarins grow well in mild temperate climates. Satsumas are particularly cold hardy. Most fruit can be held on the tree for some time, making the plants both ornamental and functional through the winter. Many varieties need a pollinizer to be fruitful or productive.

# Tangerine Ice Cream

MAKES 1 QUART

This ice cream gets its lively flavor from both the juice and zest of the fruit. It has a beautiful pastel color and light body. Be sure to avoid the bitter white pith (albedo) when taking the zest from the fruit. A long hand-held plane grater (Microplane) makes the zesting process quick and easy. If you like, serve the ice cream garnished with one or two Confited Tangerine Slices (page 349).

Combine in a small, nonreactive heavy-bottomed pot:

**Zest of 4 tangerines**
**¾ cup sugar**
**1¼ cups half-and-half**
**A pinch of salt**

Heat until steaming, stirring to dissolve the suger. Turn off the heat and let steep for 30 minutes. Meanwhile, separate:

**4 eggs**

Whisk the yolks just enough to break them up. Save the whites to make meringue.

Strain the steeping half-and-half and return to the pot. Stir in the egg yolks and cook over medium heat, stirring constantly until the mixture thickens and coats the back of the spoon (170°F). Do not let it boil. When done, remove from the heat and strain. Pour in:

**1¼ cups cream**

And add:

**Grated zest of 2 tangerines**

Chill thoroughly. When cold add:

**1 cup cold tangerine juice (from**
**8 tangerines)**

Freeze in an ice-cream maker according to the manufacturer's instructions. Transfer the frozen ice cream into a clean, dry container, cover, and store in the freezer for several hours before serving to firm up.

VARIATIONS

◆ For blood orange ice cream, add the zest of 2 oranges to the steeping half-and-half. Add the zest of 2 oranges to the thickened ice-cream base. Use 1 cup blood orange juice.

◆ For lemon ice cream, add the zest of 2 Meyer lemons and 1 Lisbon or Eureka lemon to the steeping half-and-half. Increase the sugar to 1 cup and add the zest of 1 Meyer lemon and ½ regular lemon to the thickened ice-cream base. Use ¾ cup Meyer lemon juice and 3 tablespoons lemon juice.

◆ For grapefruit ice cream, use 1 cup of grapefruit juice but don't use any zest.

# Rangpur Curd

MAKES 2 CUPS

Wash and dry:

**6 rangpurs**

Finely grate the zest of 2 of the rangpurs on the small holes of a grater or with a Microplane. Juice the rangpur; there should be about ½ cup juice.

Beat until just mixed:

**2 eggs**
**3 egg yolks**
**2 tablespoons milk**
**⅓ cup sugar**
**¼ teaspoon salt (omit if using salted**
**butter)**

Stir in the rangpur juice and zest and add:

**6 tablespoons butter, cut into small**
**pieces**

Cook the mixture in a small, nonreactive heavy-bottomed pan over medium heat, stirring constantly, until thick enough to coat a spoon. Do not boil or the eggs will curdle. When thick, pour into a bowl or glass jars to cool. Cover and refrigerate.

VARIATIONS

• Use Key or Persian lime juice instead of rangpurs. You may need a few more limes to get ½ cup juice. Roll the limes on the countertop to soften them before juicing.
• For blood orange curd, use 2 blood oranges instead of the rangpurs. Zest 1 orange and reduce the sugar to ¼ cup.
• For lemon curd, use 4 Meyer or Lisbon lemons instead of the rangpurs, and the zest of 1 lemon.

# Yuzu, Calamondin, and Other Cold-Hardy Citrus

Yuzu (*Citrus junos*) is popular in Japan where its distinctively flavored peel and juice are used in dipping sauces. The blocky orange fruit itself is rather dry and seedy, but the peel can add flavor to soups and vinegar. I love it made into marmalade.

The calamondin or calamansi (*Citrus madurensis*) is a hybrid between a mandarin and a kumquat that is very popular in Southeast Asia and the Philippines. It is high in acid and a squeeze of its juice adds spark to food, much as lemon and lime do. A small tree will produce hundreds of fruits throughout most of the year. A large tree at maturity, it can easily be grown in containers or kept landscape-size with pruning.

Try growing limequat, orangequat, or citrangequat—all hybrids of kumquat—in containers or near your patio. The plants have all the charms of a kumquat, are hardy in winter temperatures as low as the midteens, and make delicious sauces and marmalades.

# Yuzu Marmalade Thumbprint Cookies
MAKES 30 COOKIES

These simple cookies are marvelous at the end of a meal or with an afternoon cup of tea. The cookie dough can double as tart dough.

Beat together until creamy:
> **8 tablespoons (1 stick) butter at room temperature**
> **¼ cup sugar**

Add and mix until completely combined:
> **¼ teaspoon salt**
> **¼ teaspoon vanilla extract**
> **1 egg yolk**

Add:
> **1¼ cups unbleached all-purpose flour**

Mix well, stirring and folding, until there are no dry patches. Chill until slightly firm. Preheat the oven to 350°F. Roll the dough into 1-inch balls. Place on two baking sheets lined with parchment paper, about 1 inch apart. Press your thumb (or your finger if your thumb is very large) into the top of each cookie to a make a depression. Bake the cookies for 12 minutes, rotating the baking sheets halfway through for even baking. While the cookies are baking, measure into a small bowl:

**½ cup Yuzu Marmalade (page 344)**
Remove the cookies from the oven and fill each depression with ¾ teaspoon marmalade. Bake for another 5 minutes, until light golden. Let cool before serving.

VARIATION
• When using the dough for a tart shell, wrap the dough in plastic wrap and flatten into a disk. Chill overnight, or for at least 4 hours, before rolling out.

# Citron  (*Citrus medica*)

Citrons are large beautiful golden-yellow citrus fruits with a penetrating, sweet fragrance. The fruits have very little flesh or juice—it is the thick aromatic rind, both the colorful zest and the white pith (albedo) beneath, that is used in the kitchen. Most often it is candied for use in desserts and pastries, but I also like it sliced thin or grated coarsely in salads, relishes and vinaigrettes, or transformed into delicious pickles. *Buddha's Hand* is a natural marvel with bright yellow long fingerlike extensions. A tree full of ripe fruit is an astonishing sight. I like to cook with it, but also keep one in the kitchen, for its beauty and fragrance. *Etrog* (or *Ethrog*) citron looks like a big, heavily ridged lemon and has a fine aromatic rind.

Grow citron outdoors in areas with frost-free winters or in containers that can be brought indoors when frost threatens. Both varieties bloom throughout the year with the main crop ripening in fall. The trees themselves can be a bit straggly, with thin limbs and big leaves. Turn their drawbacks into assets by training them as an espaliered tree.

# Fish Tartare with Pickled Buddha's Hand
4 SERVINGS

Halibut, snapper, bluefish, or small local albacore are my top choices for tartare. Be sure to purchase sparkling fresh fish for this dish and keep it cold while you are working with it. I like to keep the cut fish in a bowl nested into a larger bowl filled with ice, even when it is in the refrigerator. Serve spooned onto a toasted crouton, a lettuce leaf, or a cucumber slice.

Trim away any skin and dark flesh from:
**6 ounces fish fillet**
Cut the fish into thin slices, and then cut the slices into thin sticks. Cut across the sticks to make a fine dice. Put the cut fish into a nonreactive bowl and refrigerate.
When ready to serve, remove from the refrigerator and add:
**1 tablespoon Pickled Buddha's Hand (page 347), larger circles cut in half**
**2 teaspoons lemon juice**
**1 tablespoon chopped shiso**
**2 teaspoons extra-virgin olive oil**
**Salt**
**A pinch of cayenne**
Mix together, stirring gently. Garnish with:
**Herb flowers**

VARIATIONS
• Add sliced or julienned radishes to the mix.
• Chop 1 teaspoon green radish seedpods and mix in.

# Preserving Vegetables and Fruits

## Home Canning, Pickles, Jams and Jellies, Candied Fruit, Liqueurs, and Dried Fruit

A PANTRY STOCKED with colorful jars filled with seasonal abundance is comforting and inspiring, especially when they have come from your own kitchen. Many vegetables and most fruits ripen all at once bringing copious quantities that cannot be eaten before their prime has passed. Preserving them when they taste the best provides seasonal flavors to be savored throughout the year. You will find that your preserves are far superior than most you can buy. A full pantry is also a treasure trove for sharing—a pretty jar of jam, tomatoes, pickles, or homemade liqueur makes a wonderful and appreciated gift.

# Preserving Vegetables

Canned Tomatoes 328

Dried Tomatoes 329

Tomato Conserve 330

Cornichons 331

Quick Dill Pickles 331

Pickled Onions 332

Pickled Okra 333

Pickled Carrots 333

Dilly Beans 334

Traditional Dill Pickles 336

Lacto-Fermented Dilly Beans 337

Indian-Spiced Sauerkraut 338

Kimchi 338

# Home Canning

Canning and pickling are traditional ways of saving seasonal abundance. Preserving vegetables in jars to be shelf stable (no refrigeration necessary) is quite easy and the jars are gorgeous, sparkling like jewels in the pantry. Get a group of people together and make a day of it. Canning or pickling with friends makes the work go by quickly and allows you to buy at bulk prices or process a large harvest before it spoils. There is lots of time to chat and share recipes, and in the end there will be plenty of jars to fill everyone's pantry.

There are a few basic rules to follow to keep the vegetables fresh and safe. You will need: heat-proof jars; new canning jar lids that are rimmed with a gasket or gaskets that snap onto the lids, screw-on rings, or clips; and a large pot to boil the jars in. The pot does not have to be heavy-bottomed. Inexpensive enamelware pots along with jars, extra lids, and gaskets can be found at the local hardware or kitchen supply store. A few handy accessories are a jar lifter for handling the hot jars and a canning funnel with a wide mouth to fill the jars cleanly.

Canned fruits and vegetables must have a certain amount of acid to inhibit any growth of harmful anaerobic bacteria. Pickles and most fruit have plenty of acid, but many vegetables don't. Low-acid vegetables and meat must be canned using a high-pressure canner. All the recipes in this book are for the low-pressure canning process. Please look online or in detailed books on pressure canning if you are interested in that type of preserving. Preserve only healthy, unbruised, undamaged produce, which will have the best flavor and texture and will not introduce unhealthy bacteria to the mix.

The basic procedure for canning is as follows. Wash the jars and lids and place in a pot of boiling water and boil at least 5 minutes to sterilize. Leave the jars in the hot water. Wash and dry the produce well, and cook it as needed according to the recipe. Remove the jars from the water and if there are any spices required for the recipe, put them in while the jars are still hot. Next pack in the prepared fruits or vegetables, and pour over the hot brine or syrup called for. Don't fill the jars completely full; instead fill them to one-half to one-quarter inch below the rim of the jars. This empty space, called the headspace, is important because it allows for the expansion of air and mass in the sealed jar as it is heated in the boiling water. Wipe the rims clean, retrieve a lid or gasket from the boiling water, and place it on the jar. Seal with a screw-on ring or clips. Lower the sealed jar into the hot-water bath. The water should cover the jars by a least an inch; two is even better. Bring the water to a boil and from that moment process (boil) for the amount of time given in the recipe. Higher altitudes require longer times. Look online for conversion charts.

Lift the jars from the water and allow to cool on a countertop. I like to put a kitchen towel down before placing the jars, especially if the countertop is stone or another hard surface. The jars are more fragile when very hot. As the jars cool, you will hear the pop of lids sucking in as a result of shrinking cooling air (the little tab of the gasket that sticks out from the lid will point down). This creates an airtight vacuum seal to protect the contents in the jars. To test the seal push on the top of the lid; it should be concave. To test a gasket seal, remove the clip or clips and lift the jar by the lid a few inches off the countertop. If the jar stays shut the seal is in place. Refrigerate any unsealed jars and use them first. Canned fruits and vegetables have a shelf life of at least one year. For better flavor, keep the jars stored in a cool dark place. It is suggested to store the jars without their rings or clips. That way, if a seal is broken by off-gassing or another mishap, you will be aware of it right away.

## Canned Tomatoes

MAKES 3 OR 4 PINTS

Home-canned tomatoes are remarkably better—off-the-charts better—than any you can buy in a tin can. Only use fresh tomatoes at their pinnacle of flavor and ripeness. There's no sense going through the effort of preserving for ho-hum tomatoes. My favorite tomato for canning is a high-acid red full-flavored type—the same one I love to cook with fresh. I cold-pack these tomatoes, which means they are not cooked before being canned. It is a simple process of dipping the tomatoes into boiling water to peel them, cutting them in half to remove the seeds (the strained juice is saved), and packing them into jars. I really press on the tomatoes while packing them so the jars are quite full of tomatoes. Juice is added as needed to fill the jars. Any extra juice is delicious fresh, or it can be canned alone.

Roma, or paste-type tomatoes, are less juicy. I like to turn them into sauce before canning them. This is called hot packing. An added bonus of cooking the tomatoes first is that they don't have to be peeled or seeded. Both the peel and seeds are removed when the sauce is puréed through a food mill before the hot sauce is ladled into hot jars.

Slicing tomatoes are fine to can, too. Just be sure you like to cook with the variety you are choosing to can. Many slicing tomatoes are grouped under the category of heirloom tomatoes and they tend, overall, to be juicier and lower in acid. These are good facts to know when canning. It means that they will give off a lot of juice (sometimes the end product will look like half tomatoes, half juice), and it is highly recommended to add lemon juice to the jar before closing it, to guarantee there is enough acid to make them shelf stable.

Bring a large pot of water to a boil and add:
**4 pint jars with their lids to sterilize**
Wash and remove the core from:
**5 pounds high-acid tomatoes**
Plunge the tomatoes (in batches) into a separate pot of boiling water until the skins slip, about 15 to 30 seconds. Cool the tomatoes in an ice bath. Slip off the skins and discard. Place a strainer over a nonreactive bowl. Cut the tomatoes in half crosswise and remove

the seeds and pulp into the strainer. Rub the seeds in the strainer to remove all the juice. Pack the tomato halves into the hot jars, pressing firmly as they are added. Fill to ½ inch below the rim. Pour in juice to the same level. Slide a dinner knife down the sides of the jars to help release any air bubbles. Wipe the rims clean and top with a hot lid. Screw on the ring and immerse in the hot water bath (the water can be quite hot but not boiling). Pour the extra juice into a sterilized pint jar and process, too (or drink it fresh with a pinch of salt). Bring to a boil and process for 20 minutes.

NOTE

✦ Recently, 100 pounds of Early Girl tomatoes yielded 60 pints of very tightly packed tomatoes and 20 pints of juice. It took three people 9½ hours start to finish. A very productive way to pass a day home canning with friends.

VARIATIONS

✦ Pack the tomatoes into two 1-quart jars and process for 35 minutes.
✦ Don't peel the tomatoes. Instead, cut them into large chunks and cook them for 15 minutes until they are tender and falling apart. Pass through a food mill. Can the purée directly, or return it to the pan and reduce to the desired consistency before pouring into the hot jars. Process as above.
✦ Use low-acid slicer or heirloom tomatoes and add 1 tablespoon lemon juice to each pint before sealing (2 tablespoons for each quart).
✦ Instead of canning the tomatoes, fill freezer bags with peeled and seeded tomatoes, and freeze for up to 1 year. Freeze tomatoes in different-size bags for a variety of needs.

# Dried Tomatoes

MAKES 1 PINT

Dried tomatoes were once solely made under the hot summer sun—set out on screens for a few hot days to dry and concentrate for winter cooking. Today I make them in an oven set to the lowest temperature possible. They are quite delicious cut into salads, pasta sauces, and salsas; or laid on grilled bread, in sandwiches, or on onion tarts before they bake. The trick, I find, is to dry them to a chewy, slightly moist texture, stopping before they are crispy or leathery. Store them under olive oil to enjoy year-round. Roma, or paste tomatoes, and cherry tomatoes are good choices for drying.

Preheat the oven to 200°F or as low as it will go. Cut in half:
    **4 pounds Roma or cherry tomatoes**
Lay out in a single layer, cut side up on cooling racks placed on baking sheets or on parchment-paper-lined baking sheets. The tomatoes will dry more evenly on the racks. Dry the tomatoes in the oven overnight, or until they are shriveled and dry with the texture you like. Some pieces may dry before others; take those out first. Allow to cool thoroughly, a good 2 hours, then pack into 2 sterilized ½-pint jars. Sprinkle over each layer:
    **Sea salt**
When the jars are full, pour over:
    **Extra-virgin olive oil**
Gently tap the jars and slide a knife down the sides of the jars to help release any air bubbles. The tomatoes should be fully covered by the oil. Store in the refrigerator up to 1 year.

## Tomato Conserve

MAKES 1¼ CUPS

This is a recipe for Sicilian-style dried extra-thick tomato conserve. In Sicily, it is dried on the rooftop in the hot summer sun and stirred daily until the right consistency is reached. In Berkeley, I make it in the oven, drying it slowly over a number of hours instead of a number of days. The tomatoes are concentrated into a paste that is more like jam than standard tomato paste. Try it stirred into a stew, soup, or pasta sauce, or spread it on some garlic toast for an easy and delicious treat. Roma tomatoes have less juice and sweeter flavor, while conventional red tomatoes are juicy with a bit more acid. Both will work (the juicy tomatoes will need to cook longer); just be sure to choose tomatoes that are fully ripe and delicious.

Preheat the oven to 300°F.
Remove the cores from:

**5 pounds ripe tomatoes**

Cut coarsely and add to a heavy-bottomed pan with:

**½ teaspoon salt**
**2 tablespoons olive oil**

Bring to a boil, stirring now and then, reduce to a simmer, and cook for 5 minutes, or until soft. Pass through a food mill fitted with the finest plate. Pour the purée onto a rimmed nonreactive sheet pan or low-sided baking dish. Bake, for 3 to 5 hours, stirring every half hour (the time depends on how juicy the purée is). Be sure to stir any thickened mass at the sides into the middle. If the purée starts to burn on the sides before 3 hours, transfer it to a smaller dish. When the puree is quite thick, lower the oven to 250°F, and cook for another 1½ to 2 hours. The conserve should be quite thick, shiny, and brick red. Pack into 4 sterilized ¼-pint (4-ounce) jars and cover with ½ inch of olive oil. Store in the refrigerator. Keep the level of olive oil at ½ inch after each use.

## Pickles

Pickling is a great way to preserve vegetables and fruit. The vinegar adds flavor and acidity so any vegetable can be preserved and lots of seasonings can be added for flavor. I love the bright taste of a pickle with rich meats and fish, in a sandwich, or as an appetizer before dinner. The pickle juice in the jars is delicious to cook with, too. Add it to sauces, mayonnaise, and salad dressings.

The process is basically the same for most pickles: a brine is made with vinegar, water, salt, and sometimes sugar. Spices and herbs are added to sterilized jars and then vegetables or fruit are packed into the jar, leaving the required headspace. Hot brine is poured over, the jar is sealed, and processed for the required amount of time. It is important to use quality vinegar that tastes good. Different vinegars have different levels of acidity.

Commercial vinegars have the percentage written on the label. Most commercial wine vinegars are 6 to 7 percent and cider and distilled vinegars are usually around 5 percent. When heat processing for long storage, homemade vinegar must be tested to find its level of acidity. Home tests for pH are easily found online.

Grape leaves, if available, are a good addition to the jar. They contain alum and tannins that help keep the vegetables crisp. Cherry leaves, oak leaves, and horseradish leaves will work in the same way. When processed in a hot-water bath, vinegar pickles will last for at least a year.

Pickles can also be made without a hot-water processing and stored in the refrigerator. Some vegetables will require a short amount of preliminary cooking time in the brine as they will not have any cooking time in a hot-water bath. Refrigerated, they will last for four months to a year.

## Cornichons

MAKES 4 PINTS

Cornichons are tiny, intensely flavored pickles—a classic accompaniment to pâté and charcuterie in France. They are typically made with undiluted white wine vinegar, but I prefer a milder version and add some water to the brine.

Wash well:
   **2 pounds small cornichon cucumbers**
Mix with:
   **3 tablespoons sea salt or kosher salt**
Let the cornichons stand for 4 hours, and then rinse and drain.

Wash and sterilize four 1-pint canning jars with lids.
Bring to a simmer:
   **3 cups white wine or champagne vinegar (7% acidity)**
   **2 cups water**
Distribute equally among the 4 warm jars:
   **1 teaspoon black peppercorns**
   **1 teaspoon mustard seeds**
   **4 bay leaves**
   **8 large tarragon sprigs**
   **4 small dried chiles**
   **8 shallots or pearl onions, peeled**
   **4 grape leaves, washed (optional)**
Pack the jars with the cornichons. Fill the jars with simmering vinegar to within ¼ inch of the top, then seal with the lids and bands. Store in a cool, dark place and allow to cure 1 month before eating. Refrigerate any jars that fail to make a tight seal.

## Quick Dill Pickles

MAKES 6 QUARTS

Quick pickles are an easy and delicious alternative to traditional fermented pickles. The proportions of pickles and brine may not be exact, depending on the size of the cucumbers and how they fill the jars. It is important to remove any blossoms still clinging to the end of the cucumbers. They are filled with an enzyme that makes the pickles mushy and unpleasant.

Wash well, making sure to remove any blossoms remaining on the ends of the cucumbers, and soak in cold water:
   **50 to 60 cucumbers, 3 to 4 inches long (about 20 pounds)**

Combine in a pan and bring to a simmer:

**1 quart white wine vinegar
(7% acidity)**
**¾ cup sea salt or kosher salt**
**2½ cups water**

Wash and sterilize six 1-quart canning jars with lids.

Measure into each warm jar:

**½ teaspoon black peppercorns**
**½ teaspoon coriander seeds**
**1 bay leaf**
**2 fresh dill flower heads
(or 2 large tarragon sprigs)**
**1 small dried chile**
**2 garlic cloves, peeled**
**1 grape leaf, washed (optional)**

Drain the cucumbers and pack into the warm jars. Fill with simmering brine to within ¼ inch of the top, and seal with lids and bands. Store in a cool, dark place and allow to cure 1 month before eating. Refrigerate any jars that fail to make a tight seal.

## Pickled Onions

MAKES 2 PINTS

Onions can be pickled simply by slicing them and pouring vinegar over them. Stir in some salt and let them steep a few minutes and they are good to go. They will last a few months in the refrigerator and are a good garnish for a chicken liver toast. For more complexity of flavor, make a brine and pour it over sliced onions or whole little pearl onions. I like to add a touch of sugar to this brine, but it is not necessary. Pick fresh and unsprouted onions; smaller ones (2½ inches or less) make the prettiest pickles.

Peel and slice into ¼-inch rings:

**½ pound onions**

Measure into a small pot:

**1 cup red or white wine vinegar**
**1½ cups water**
**1 tablespoon salt**
**1 tablespoon sugar**

Bring to a boil, turn off the heat, and stir to dissolve the salt and sugar. Bring a large pot half filled with water to a boil. Wash and sterilize two 1-pint jars in the boiling water. Distribute equally between the jars:

**½ teaspoon black peppercorns**
**2 small whole dried chiles**
**4 allspice berries**
**6 cloves garlic, sliced thick**
**4 thyme or savory sprigs**
**2 bay leaves**

Pack the sliced onions into the jars. Heat the brine back up to a boil and then pour it over the onions, filling to ½ inch below the rim. Wipe the rims clean and dry, and cap with a fresh lid and screw-on ring. Process for 10 minutes in a hot-water bath—start timing from the moment the water comes to a boil. Carefully remove the jars from the water and let cool on a towel. Refrigerate after opening.

VARIATIONS

◆ To make a refrigerator pickle, add the spices to the brine, and when it has boiled, add the sliced onions. Return to a boil, scoop out the onions, and cool both the brine and onions for 5 to 10 minutes. Combine and store in the refrigerator for up to a year or more (be sure the onions are submerged in the brine).

◆ For small whole onions, blanch the onions for 3 minutes and carefully peel. The blanching will make the peeling much easier and soften the onions. For refrigerator pickles, cook the peeled onions in the brine for a few minutes or until just cooked through. Remove from the brine as above.

◆ Add ¼-inch-thick sliced carrots or carrot sticks, garlic, or ¼-inch-thick sliced fennel to the onions.

## Pickled Okra

MAKES 4 PINTS

Whole okra pods make a delicious and beautiful crisp pickle. If your okra is long, pack them into the tall thin jars sold for jelly.

Heat in a nonreactive pot:

> **2 cups white wine vinegar**
> **3 cups water**
> **2 tablespoons salt**

Bring to a boil and then turn off the heat. Stir to dissolve the salt.

Wash, dry, and trim the very tip of the stem from:

> **2 pounds small okra pods**

Wash and sterilize four 1-pint jars. Distribute equally among the 4 jars:

> **½ teaspoon yellow mustard seeds**
> **½ teaspoon brown mustard seeds**
> **½ teaspoon black peppercorns**
> **½ teaspoon coriander seeds**
> **4 bay leaves**
> **4 cloves**
> **4 allspice berries**
> **One 2-inch piece cassia**
> **4 whole fresh or dried cayenne**
>    **peppers**
> **4 garlic cloves, sliced thick**
> **4 small grape leaves, washed**

Fill the jars with the okra, sliding them in lengthwise, with some tips pointing up and some down. All the okra should be ½ inch below the rim of the jars. Bring the brine back to a boil and pour over the okra, leaving ½ inch of headspace. Wipe the rims clean and dry, and cap tightly. Put the jars in the pot of hot water, making sure the water is 2 inches over the tops of the jars. Bring to a boil, and process the pickles for 10 minutes. Carefully remove the jars from the water and let cool on a towel. Refrigerate after opening.

## Pickled Carrots

MAKES 2 PINTS

These are a simple quick pickle that can be eaten in a couple of days or sealed and stored for months to come. I like to serve these pickles as an hors d'oeuvre on their own or as a garnish for a salad or a grilled cheese sandwich. They are quite tasty in the morning, too.

Peel and trim:

> **1 pound carrots cut into pretty shapes**
>    **(¼-inch slices or sticks)**

Measure into a nonreactive pan:

**2 cups water**

**1⅓ cups red or white wine vinegar**

**2 tablespoons salt**

**1 small bay leaf**

**½ teaspoon black peppercorns**

**1 teaspoon coriander seeds**

**2 allspice berries**

**4 cloves**

**6 thyme or savory sprigs (or some of each)**

Bring to a boil, turn down to a simmer, and cook for 1 minute. Add the carrots, bring back to a boil, and back down to a simmer. Remove when they are softening but still crisp, about 1 to 2 minutes. Turn off the heat and pour the brine into a bowl. Let the carrots cool for 5 minutes, then add back to the brine. Let the carrots sit for 1 day before eating. Store the carrots tightly sealed and submerged in their brine in the refrigerator for 1 year or more.

VARIATIONS

• To seal for shelf storage in the pantry: Heat the vinegar, water, and salt to a boil and then turn off. Distribute the herbs and spices between 2 sterilized 1-pint jars. Pack the carrots into the jars. Reheat the brine and pour over the carrots leaving ½ inch of headspace. Wipe the rims and seal with new sterilized lids. Process for 8 minutes in a boiling water bath. Cool and test the seal. Refrigerate after opening.

• Add a few peeled garlic cloves to the brine.

• Add sliced fennel, sliced onions, rutabaga slices or sticks to the mix. Cook the vegetables separately as they will all have different cooking times. (When sealing for storage, pack them all together into the jars.)

# Dilly Beans

MAKES 4 PINTS

Green beans make a delightful pickle, and dilly beans with loads of dill are a classic.

First prepare the brine. Combine in a heavy-bottomed pot:

**2 cups white wine vinegar**

**3 cups water**

**2 tablespoons salt**

Bring to a boil, stirring to dissolve the salt. Turn off the heat.

Bring a large pot of water to a boil. Wash well, and trim the stem end from:

**1 pound just-picked green beans (Kentucky Wonder, Blue Lake, or another meaty green bean)**

Gather:

**1 teaspoon black peppercorns**

**4 dill flower heads, or 16 large dill sprigs and 1 teaspoon dill seeds**

**4 small whole dried chiles**

**1 teaspoon coriander seeds (optional)**

**5 garlic cloves, sliced thick**

**4 fresh grape leaves**

Wash four 1-pint jars and sterilize by immersing in the boiling water for a few minutes. Distribute the herbs, spices, garlic, and grape leaves equally among the 4 jars. Then pack the jars with green beans, placing them lengthwise, trimmed side up. Trim them if necessary to fit ½ inch below the rim of the jar. Heat the brine back up to a boil and then pour it over the beans filling to ½ inch below the rim. Wipe the rims clean and dry, and seal well. Place in the pot of hot water, bring to a boil, and process for 6 minutes from the moment the water comes to a boil. Carefully remove the jars from the water and let cool on a towel. Store for at least 2 weeks in a cool dark place before eating. Refrigerate after opening.

VARIATIONS

* Use other herbs such as rosemary, marjoram, or wild fennel sprigs and other spices such as fennel, cumin, or ajwain seed.
* Preserve other vegetables this way: green tomatoes, peppers, eggplant, and more.

# Fermented Pickles

Lacto-fermentation is an age-old way of preserving food. Sauerkraut and dill pickles are the best-known examples, but almost any vegetable may be pickled this way. Though it seems like alchemy, it is a simple process using salt and the naturally occurring bacteria found in the vegetables and the air. The salt creates an environment that obliterates harmful bacteria and encourages beneficial microbes that eat the natural sugars of the vegetables and turn them into lactic acid. This acidic environment preserves the vegetables and supplies the sour taste to the pickles. These beneficial bacteria are probiotics, similar to those living in yogurt, and are quite important to our health.

There are basically two ways to ferment with salt. With one, the vegetables are cut into small pieces and tossed with salt. The salt extracts the juices from the produce to create a brine that covers and protects the pickle as it ferments. With the other, whole vegetables are submerged in a prepared brine—a mixture of salt and water. Chlorine will inhibit and kill natural bacteria. Use filtered tap water for the brine, or let the water sit out uncovered overnight to allow the chlorine to evaporate. Once the vegetables are salted, weight is added to the jar or crock to keep them submerged in the brine so they don't spoil. The weight can be anything clean and heavy: a rock resting on a plate slightly smaller in diameter than the container, a jar filled with brine, or a brine-filled plastic bag (which, if it were to leak, won't dilute the brine with water).

Herbs and spices are added for flavoring. Mixtures of different vegetables can be pickled together, such as grated carrots or apples in sauerkraut, or sliced beets and turnips pickled together, or ground sweet and hot peppers (which make a delicious salsa). When pickling whole vegetables, grape leaves are a good addition if they are available. They contain tannins that help keep the vegetables crisp. Cherry leaves, oak leaves, and horseradish leaves will work in the same way.

Fermentation occurs at room temperature in contact with oxygen, so the jar and weight are left open to the air. A towel draped over the opening keeps dust out. When fermentation starts, carbon dioxide is emitted. You will see bubbles rising in the brine, a sign of escaping gas. Scum, or bloom, as some fermenters like to call it, will form on the surface of the brine. This is a harmless by-product. Skim it off and rinse the weight. The pickles will be done in a week or up to six, depending on what is being pickled and how sour you like it. The sour flavor deepens as the amount of lactic acid increases over the weeks. When you are happy with the flavor, remove the weight, cap the jar, and refrigerate. Cold slows down the fermentation but does not stop it. Pickles and kraut will last up to six months or more in the refrigerator.

Fermentation is affected by salt and weather. It speeds up in hot weather and an increased level of salt slows it. The salt level can be adjusted to the weather, adding more in hot weather and less in cold. The ratio of salt to water in the recipes below works well for a normal ambient temperature of 65° to 75°F. If the pickles get mushy or smelly, throw them out and start over. They won't hurt you; they are just unpleasant. A reassuring fact to know is that there has never been a reported case of sickness caused by eating lacto-fermented food: a pretty amazing track record.

## Traditional Dill Pickles

MAKES 2 QUARTS

This is the quintessential dill pickle, the kind that was once seen floating in large barrels in general stores in the olden days. They are the same pickle as the half-sours that top-notch Jewish delicatessens serve. No vinegar is used; only salt, water, herbs, and spices. Natural fermentation supplies the sour, and fresh just-picked cucumbers bring the crunch. Look for pickling cucumbers at the farmers' market, or grow some in your yard or in a container. A single rambling plant will give plenty of cucumbers to pickle.

Wash, dry, and gently rub off any spines from:

**2 pounds just-picked small pickling cucumbers**

Carefully check the blossom end of each cucumber to be sure all the bloom has been removed. If the cucumbers are not fresh picked, soak them in cold water for a few hours to revive them.

Wash and dry two 1-quart jars or one half-gallon jar. Divide equally between the jars:

**6 garlic cloves, peeled**
**4 to 8 dill flower heads (depending on their size)**
**1 teaspoon black peppercorns**
**4 small whole dried chiles**
**1 teaspoon coriander seeds (optional)**
**1 teaspoon yellow mustard seeds (optional)**
**2 grape leaves**

Carefully pack the cucumbers into the jars. Mix together:

**6 cups filtered or dechlorinated water**
**¼ cup sea salt**

Stir until the salt is dissolved. Pour over the cucumbers to cover. Fill smaller jars or plastic bags with extra brine and place them over the cucumbers to submerge them while they ferment. Cover them with a clean cloth to keep dust out. Store at room temperature out of direct sunlight. Bubbles should begin to rise after 2 days, which shows that fermentation is happening. Skim off any scum that appears and rinse off the jars or plastic bags. Allow to ferment for 1 to 3 weeks. Taste the pickles after 1 week. Cap and refrigerate when they are cured all the way through (no white parts in the middle) and you are happy with the flavor. The pickles will last a few months refrigerated.

VARIATION

+ Substitute 16 large dill sprigs and 1 teaspoon dill seeds for the dill flower heads.

# Lacto-Fermented Dilly Beans

MAKES 4 PINTS

These are an especially addictive pickle. Kids love them. Pack them in a lunch box and you will hear stories about lunchtime bartering you thought was limited to sweets.

Wash well, drain, and trim the stem end from:

**1 pound just-picked green beans (Kentucky Wonder, Blue Lake, or another meaty green bean)**

Wash and dry four 1-pint jars. Distribute equally among the 4 jars:

**1 teaspoon black peppercorns**
**4 dill flower heads or 16 large dill sprigs and 1 teaspoon dill seed**
**4 small whole dried chiles**
**1 teaspoon coriander seeds (optional)**
**5 garlic cloves, sliced thick**

Then pack the green beans lengthwise into the jars. Trim them, if necessary, to fit ½ inch below the rim. Mix together:

**6 cups filtered or dechlorinated water**
**¼ cup sea salt**

Stir until the salt is dissolved. Pour over the green beans to cover. Top with:

**1 fresh grape leaf**

Use smaller jars that will fit into the opening of each jar or fill 4 small sealable plastic bags half full with any extra brine. Fit the smaller jar into the larger, or snuggle the bags into the tops of the jars, to weigh down the beans below the level of the brine. Cover the tops with a clean cloth to keep dust out. Store at room temperature out of direct sunlight. Bubbles should begin to rise after 2 days, which shows that fermentation is happening. Skim off any scum that appears

and rinse off the jar or plastic bag. The beans should be done fermenting after 10 days to 2 weeks (the beans will ferment faster in hot weather). Taste a bean; it should be sour, soft but still crisp, and the bubbling should have stopped in the brine. The fermentation process is slowed when refrigerated, so when you are happy with their flavor and texture, remove the plastic bags, cap the jars, and keep in the fridge.

VARIATIONS

♦ Use other herbs and spices such as rosemary, marjoram, wild fennel, fennel seed, cumin seed, or ajwain seed.
♦ Other vegetables can be preserved this way: green tomatoes, peppers, eggplant, and more.

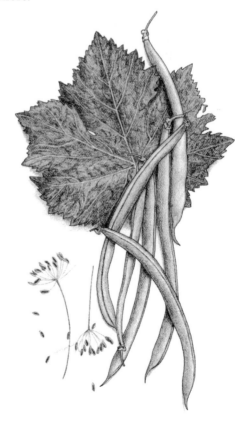

# Indian–Spiced Sauerkraut

MAKES 1 QUART

This sauerkraut recipe is based on one by pickle maker Alex Hozven of Cultured, a local shop in Berkeley. She makes a number of delicious sauerkrauts, and this bright yellow one is my favorite. Try experimenting by using different spices to make krauts with different flavors, or for a plain kraut leave out all the spices.

Remove any outer damaged leaves from:

> **1 large, firm green or red cabbage**
> **(about 1¼ pounds)**

Cut the cabbage in half and remove the core. Cut the halves into quarters and slice the quarters as thinly as possible. You should have about 5 cups of shredded cabbage. Put the shredded cabbage into a bowl with:

> **3½ teaspoons sea salt**
> **1½ teaspoons cumin seeds**
> **1½ teaspoons coriander seeds**
> **¾ teaspoon fennel seeds**
> **¾ teaspoon black peppercorns**
> **½ teaspoon brown mustard seeds**
> **½ teaspoon fenugreek**
> **½ teaspoon turmeric**

Thoroughly work the salt into the cabbage with your fingers until it begins to release juices. Pack the cabbage into a nonreactive container. Press down the cabbage as you pack it in. Place a weight over the cabbage to keep it submerged under the brine. Cover the container loosely with a dish towel. Let it rest for 1 day. Take the weight off the cabbage and (with clean hands) massage the cabbage again. Press it down. There should be enough liquid to cover the cabbage. If not, top it up with a brine made from:

> **1 cup filtered or dechlorinated water**
> **1 tablespoon salt**

Replace the weight. Let the cabbage ferment at room temperature for up to 5 weeks. Remove any scum that may appear on the surface of the brine and wash the weight as necessary. Start tasting the kraut after a week. When you are happy with the flavor, remove the weight, cover the container, and refrigerate. The sauerkraut will keep in the refrigerator for up to 6 months.

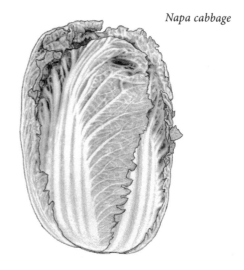

*Napa cabbage*

# Kimchi

MAKES 1 QUART

This is Korea's number one condiment, and it is simple to make. One disclaimer: kimchi is addictive. Try some with a glass of rosé or a cold beer for an apéritif, spoon some into your hot grilled cheese sandwich, or use some to perk up a simple bowl of brown rice. You may just find yourself eating it right out of the jar while standing in front of the open refrigerator. That is when you know you are hooked. Not to worry: kimchi is filled with many more vitamins than fresh cabbage and is teeming with probiotics.

*Gochugaru*, crushed dried peppers, is the fundamental seasoning of kimchi. Gochugaru is usually translated as chile powder, but the texture is more like a coarse ground freshly dried pepper than an actual powder. Gochugaru is hot, with plenty of sweet flavor, too. It is easy to find at Korean and Asian groceries. Look for bright red color. Price tends to reflect quality, which is helpful to know if you cannot read the label. Most other chile powders are not good substitutes.

Although purists might object, I have successfully made a substitute for gochugaru using local freshly ground organic peppers, inspired by my friend the fantastic chef Russell Moore of Camino Restaurant in Oakland. A mixture of Espelette and New Mexico chiles is especially good. Try growing and drying the gochugaru at home, which is certainly the traditional way. There are a few seed companies that carry Korean pepper seeds.

Cut in half lengthwise:

> **1 large or 2 smaller napa cabbages**
> **(about 1 pound)**

Remove the core and cut crosswise into ½-inch slices. Wash and drain well. Prepare a brine. Mix together:

> **5 cups water**
> **3 tablespoons salt**

Place the drained cabbage in a large mixing bowl and cover with the brine. Place a plate or other large flat weight on the cabbage to submerge it. Let it sit a few hours or overnight, to soften. Drain, reserving the brine. Return the cabbage to the bowl and add:

> **1 tablespoon minced garlic**
> **1 teaspoon minced peeled ginger**
> **6 scallions, trimmed and thinly sliced**
> **1 tablespoon fish sauce**
> **A large pinch of sugar**
> **2 tablespoons gochugaru or dried**
> **chile flakes**

Mix thoroughly to evenly distribute all the flavorings. Pack into sterilized jars. Press down on the cabbage to pack tightly. The cabbage should be submerged; if necessary, pour in some of the reserved brine. To keep the cabbage under the brine, weight it with smaller brine-filled jars that just fit into the neck of the kimchi jars, or a resealable plastic bag filled with brine. Keep the jars in a dark place at room temperature and let the kimchi ferment for 2 to 6 days. Taste daily and refrigerate when the kimchi is the right sourness for your taste. Kimchee will keep for months in the refrigerator. It will continue to ferment and get more sour, but in the cold environment of the refrigerator this will happen very slowly.

VARIATIONS

✦ Grate a small daikon radish and add with the scallions.

✦ Grate 2 medium carrots and add with the scallions. Omit the sugar.

✦ Add whole small radishes to the soaking brine.

✦ Use daikon, either sliced or cut into chunks, instead of the cabbage. Soak until softened.

✦ Add 4 fresh-shucked oysters instead of fish sauce.

# Preserving Fruits

Wild Plum Jam  342

Rose Hip Jam  343

Fig Jam  343

Crab Apple Jelly  344

Yuzu Marmalade  344

Apple Butter  345

Pickled Persimmons  346

Pickled Cherries  346

Pickled Buddha's Hand  347

Brandied Cherries  347

Apricots in Syrup  348

Lime Syrup  348

Confited Tangerine Slices  349

Candied Orange Peel  349

Candied Melon  350

Candied Kumquats  351

Salt-Preserved Kumquats  352

Vin d'Orange  352

Nocino  353

Crab Apple Liqueur  354

Apricot Liqueur  354

Hazelnut Liqueur  354

Dried Fruit  355

## Jams and Jellies

Making fruit jam, jelly, or marmalade is the easiest way to preserve fruit, and all these things are delightful to have in the pantry. Their starring roles may be when they are spread on breakfast toast, but there are many other uses for them in the kitchen. Mix preserves into a marinade or stir them into a sauce for duck or pork. Spread them between layers of a cake, fill turnovers (see page 259) or thumbprint cookies (see page 323) with them, or use as a glaze on fruit tarts. Just about any fruit imaginable can be cooked into preserves. The fruit is combined with sugar, which draws out the moisture from the fruit, and the resulting juices are cooked until thickened. The sugar helps preserve the fruit and thicken the juices, and though it is a necessity, I do like to keep it to a minimum. My rule of thumb is to use

30 percent sugar, which works out to about 1 cup of sugar for every pound of fresh fruit. Depending on its natural sweetness, some fruit may require more.

Clear jellies and marmalades are thickened by naturally occurring pectin as well as by sugar. The best jellies are made with fruits with a high level of pectin such as crab apples, gooseberries, red and black currants, plums, blackberries, apples, and citrus rind. When in solution with water and sugar, pectin binds to itself and produces the signature quivering gel of fine jelly and marmalade.

For jam, choose undamaged, fresh ripe fruit. I like to cut the fruit and toss it with the sugar and then let it sit overnight. The sugar draws the juice from the fruit without heat. The next day small batches of the fruit are cooked rapidly in a broad, fairly low-sided pot to facilitate evaporation. These steps help the jam cook quickly and keep the fruit tasting as fresh as possible. At the beginning, when the fruit is very juicy, the jam is cooked at a rapid boil and the fruit is stirred now and then to keep it from sticking and scorching. As the mixture thickens, the heat is lowered and the fruit stirred frequently. The jam is done when it becomes shiny and thick.

A good way to test it is to keep a small plate in the freezer and put a spoonful of jam on it to cool rapidly. Once the jam is cool, the consistency can be judged. The jam is ready when the cooled sample forms a skin and does not pour easily when the cold plate is tipped. Keep in mind that jam made with less sugar will not set to a sturdy gel—a small price to pay for getting so much delicious natural fruit flavor.

Jelly is made by cooking fruit with water and sugar until very soft. A muslin jelly bag is fitted on a stand that is set over a bowl. The fruit and its liquid are poured into the jelly bag and left for a few hours to drip slowly through the filter. Don't press on the fruit or puréed fruit will seep through the bag and cloud the jelly. The resulting liquid is reduced at a rapid boil until it reaches the proper consistency, or a temperature of 220°F.

Marmalade is made by boiling citrus rind in water to soften it and extract the pectin. All the seeds and membranes are collected into a small sack that cooks along with the rind for their added pectin. Once the rind is soft, sugar and citrus juice are added and the mixture is boiled to the consistency that results in a crystal-clear jelly with pieces of rind in suspension.

Finished preserves are poured into hot sterilized jars. My dear friend and artisan preserve-maker June Taylor has taught me how to sterilize jars in the oven, which is much easier than using boiling water. Lay the jars and new lids on baking sheets and slide them into a 225°F oven for at least fifteen minutes. (Or the jars can be sterilized in boiling water for six minutes.) Fill the hot jars with the hot jam, leaving very little headspace. Wipe the rims clean before placing on fresh lids. There is enough sugar and acid in fruit jams and jellies to prevent harmful bacterial colonies from forming under the naturally occurring vacuum seal that develops as the hot jam and jars cool. Any jars that don't seal properly should be refrigerated. Sealed jars will keep one year or more stored in a cool dark place. If you prefer, you may process the jars in a hot-water bath. Boil pint jars for ten minutes or return them to the 225°F oven for fifteen minutes. When processing the jam leave ¼ inch of headspace.

# Wild Plum Jam
MAKES ABOUT 6 PINTS

I am particularly fond of the sweet-tart jam made with small purple wild plums that are not much bigger than cherries. They grow all over Berkeley where I live. Cook the beautiful little plums whole. The pits can be easily removed as the jam is used.

Wash and drain:

**6 pounds wild plums (a little under 5 quarts)**

Put in a bowl with:

**4½ cups sugar**

Stir together, cover, and let sit overnight. Transfer the juicy plums and sugar to a large, heavy jam-making pot. Put a small plate in the freezer. Cook the plums at a rapid boil, stirring now and then, until the fruit begins to thicken, about 40 minutes. The time depends on how deep the level of fruit is in the pan and how juicy it is. Lower the temperature and stir frequently as the jam thickens. Use the cold plate to test the jam for doneness. While the jam is cooking, sterilize six 1-pint jars and new lids by heating in a 225°F oven for 15 minutes or in boiling water for 6 minutes.

Ladle the hot jam into hot sterilized jars, wipe the rims clean, and cap. Allow to cool and seal. Sealed jars will keep 1 year stored in a cool, dark place. Refrigerate after opening.

# Rose Hip Jam

MAKES 2 PINTS

Rose hips are the fruit left after a rose has finished its bloom. They make a marvelous jam, thick and smooth, with a slight tang. Collecting rose hips and making them into a purée does take some effort, but the rewards are great and quite delicious. Pick ripe rose hips after the first frost in the fall when they have turned dark red. The frost makes the flavor sweeter.

Rinse and remove the stems from:

**2 pounds (about 6 cups) rose hips**

Put them in a saucepan and add enough water to cover. Bring to a boil, lower the heat to a simmer, and cook for 30 minutes, or until quite soft. Pass the rose hips through a food mill to remove the seeds. Put a plate in the freezer. Weigh the purée and put it in a heavy-bottomed nonreactive pot. For every 1¼ pounds of purée add:

**1½ cups sugar**
**Juice of 1 lemon**

Bring to a boil, turn down the heat, and simmer for 5 minutes. Skim off and discard any foam that rises to the top. Check the consistency by putting a spoonful of jam on the chilled plate. Keep cooking until the jam is the thickness you want. While the jam is cooking, sterilize two 1-pint jars and new lids by heating in a 225°F oven for 15 minutes or in boiling water for 6 minutes.

Ladle the hot jam into the hot jars, wipe the rims clean, and cap. Allow to cool and seal. Sealed jars will keep for 1 year stored in a cool, dark place. Refrigerate after opening.

# Fig Jam

MAKES 6 PINTS

Figs of any type make a thick and luxurious jam. I don't bother peeling the figs; I like the color the peels give to the jam.

Cut off and discard the stems from:

**3 pounds figs**

Cut the figs into 1-inch pieces. You should have a little less than 5 cups of fruit. Put the cut fruit into a nonreactive bowl with:

**2 cups sugar**

Stir to coat the figs well. Cover and leave overnight to juice. The next day, pour the figs and sugar into a wide, heavy-bottomed pot. Heat to a boil and simmer until thick. Stir frequently to keep the figs from sticking to the bottom of the pot and burning. While the figs are cooking, put a small plate in the freezer and sterilize six 1-pint jars and new lids by heating in a 225°F oven for 15 minutes or in boiling water for 6 minutes.

As the jam thickens, test it on the cold plate. When the desired thickness is achieved, stir in:

**Juice of 1 lemon**

Cook for a minute more. Ladle the hot jam into the hot jars, wipe the rims clean, and cap. Allow to cool and seal. Sealed jars will keep 1 year stored in a cool, dark place. Refrigerate after opening.

VARIATIONS
◆ For fig-raspberry jam, use 2 pounds figs and 1 pound raspberries and use the same method as above.
◆ For a chunkier jam, cut the figs only in half, instead of in smaller pieces.

# Crab Apple Jelly

MAKES 8 PINTS

In late July, the crab apple tree at the Edible Schoolyard in Berkeley is loaded with rosy red crab apples. The flavorful fruit make a beautiful clear red jelly. Crab apples are filled with pectin, perfect for a quick-setting jelly.

Wash, stem, and quarter:

**5 pounds crab apples**

You should have about 10 cups of quartered fruit. Put the cut fruit in a large pot and add just enough water to cover. Bring to a boil and cook until the apples are soft and breaking apart. Have a jelly bag fitted on its frame over a ceramic bowl or stainless steel pot. Carefully ladle the cooked apples into the bag and let it drip, undisturbed. Avoid pressing the pulp in the bag, as this will make a cloudy jelly. You should have about 9 cups of apple juice. Divide equally between 2 large, heavy-bottomed pots. Cooking in smaller batches is much easier and tastier than trying to do it all at once. Bring both pots to a boil and add to each:

**3 cups sugar**

**1 tablespoon lemon juice**

Boil, skimming off any scum that rises to the top, until the temperature registers 220°F on a candy thermometer (soft ball stage). While the jelly is cooking, sterilize eight 1-pint jars and new lids by heating them in a 225°F oven for 15 minutes or in boiling water for 6 minutes. Fill the hot jars, wipe the rims clean, and cap. Allow to cool and seal. Sealed jars will keep for 1 year when stored in a cool, dark place. Refrigerate after opening.

# Yuzu Marmalade

MAKES 2 PINTS

Marmalade is a beautiful suspension of tender citrus zest in sparkling citrus jelly. Any citrus will work, but I am particularly fond of bitter citrus marmalades such as yuzu and Seville orange.

Cut in half and juice:

**9 to 10 medium-size yuzus**

You should have 1 cup of juice. If the yuzus didn't yield enough juice, supplement with lemon juice. Strain the juice into a large, heavy-bottomed nonreactive bowl and set aside. Put the contents of the strainer (seeds and pulp) into a jelly bag or on a square of muslin. With a teaspoon, scoop out all the membranes and pith from the juiced fruit and add to the seeds and pulp. Tie up the bag or piece of muslin and set aside. Cut the yuzu peel into small same-size pieces and put into a heavy-bottomed nonreactive pot with the tied-up bag of seeds and pith. Pour in:

**2½ cups water**

The water should cover the citrus by half an inch. Add more if needed. Bring to a boil, turn the heat down to a simmer, and cook until the peel is tender, about 20 minutes. Remove the pectin bag and put it in the refrigerator to cool. Strain the peel, saving the water. Measure it and add enough water to make 3 cups. Wash out the pot. Pour the water back into the pot and add the cooked yuzu peel, the yuzu juice, and:

**2½ cups sugar**

Heat the oven to 225° F. Put a small plate in the freezer. Wash and dry four ½-pint jars and new lids and put them on a baking sheet. Place them in the warm oven to heat for at least 15 minutes while the marmalade cooks. Squeeze the cooled pectin bag; massage it thoroughly into the pot extracting as much pectin as possible. Take your time; this is an important part of the recipe. Heat the liquid over medium to high heat, stirring to dissolve the sugar. Taste for sweetness and add more sugar if necessary. (The juice should taste well-balanced.) Clip a candy thermometer onto the side of the pot. Bring the citrus to a rolling boil, and cook, stirring occasionally, until the temperature reaches 220°F. Skim off any foam that forms. To check the set of the marmalade, place a small amount on the chilled plate and push on the cold marmalade. Keep cooking until you are happy with the consistency, but be sure not to let the fruit caramelize. Ladle into the hot jars leaving ¼ inch of headspace, wipe the rims clean, and cap. Allow to cool and seal. Sealed jars will keep for 1 year when stored in a cool, dark place. Refrigerate after opening.

## Apple Butter

MAKES 1 PINT

Thick velvety apple butter is a great way to preserve apples, especially when you have a lot on hand. It is also delicious spread over the bottom of an apple galette for a little extra apple flavor. I use tart apples such as Gravenstein and Sierra Beauty. If your apples are on the sweeter side, start with less sugar and add more as needed.

Combine in a medium pot:
  **1 pound apples (about 4) cut into quarters**
  **2½ cups water**
Bring to a boil. Reduce heat to a simmer and cook until the fruit is very soft and falling apart, about 10 to 15 minutes. Let cool, and press the fruit into a bowl through a strainer (or pass through a food mill). Discard the peels and seeds.

Put a small plate in the freezer. Put the apple mash back into the pot with:
  **½ to ¾ cup sugar**
  **A pinch of salt**
  **½ teaspoon ground cinnamon (optional)**
  **⅛ teaspoon ground cloves (optional)**
  **⅛ teaspoon ground ginger (optional)**
Stir together and simmer over medium-low heat, stirring frequently, until thick, about 30 minutes. To test the thickness of the apple butter, place a small amount on the chilled plate. Continue cooking until you are happy with the consistency. Sterilize two ½-pint jars and new lids (see page 342) while the apple butter is cooking. Ladle the hot apple butter into the hot jars, wipe the rims clean, and cap. Allow to cool and seal. Sealed jars will keep for 1 year stored in a cool, dark place. Refrigerate after opening.

VARIATION
◆ For pear butter use 4 pears (Comice, D'Anjou, or Bosc) instead of apples. Use ¼ cup sugar and add the juice of ½ lemon while the pear butter is cooking.

# Pickled Persimmons

MAKES 2 CUPS

Choose ripe, but still firm, Fuyu persimmons for this pickle. I recommend cooling the brine completely so the persimmons do not get too soft. The flavors are very much like a chutney and go well with roasted chicken, turkey, and duck. I like the pickle with lobster, too, especially cold in a salad.

Measure into a small nonreactive pot:

> **1 cup water**
> **⅔ cup cider vinegar**
> **1 teaspoon salt**
> **2 tablespoons sugar**
> **2 marjoram sprigs**
> **One 2-inch piece cinnamon stick**
> **½ teaspoon coriander seeds**
> **1 small dried hot chile**
> **2 cloves**
> **1 small bay leaf**
> **A pinch of black peppercorns**

Bring to a boil, turn down to a simmer, and cook for 1 minute. Pour into a heat-proof nonreactive bowl and let cool completely. Remove the stems from:

> **4 Fuyu persimmons (about 1 pound)**

Cut into quarters and peel. Cut the quarters into ¼-inch wedges. You should have about 2 cups of cut fruit. Put in a jar and cover with the cooled brine. Let sit for one day before eating. Keep in the refrigerator for up to 4 months. The fruit will become quite soft over time.

# Pickled Cherries

MAKES 4 PINTS

These are a bright sweet and savory pickle. Red wine mellows the vinegar, and the sweet is mostly from the fruit itself. Serve the cherries with rich meats such as pork rillettes and prosciutto or cheese.

Put on a pot of water to boil. Put two 1-quart or four 1-pint jars with new lids in the water. Turn off the heat after it has boiled for 4 minutes.
Wash and drain:

> **3 pounds cherries (Bing or other sweet variety)**

Trim the stems, leaving about 1 inch.
Measure into a pot:

> **4 cups water**
> **1 cup red wine**
> **¾ cup red wine vinegar**
> **2½ teaspoons salt**
> **3 tablespoons sugar**
> **One 2-inch piece cinnamon stick**
> **½ teaspoon black peppercorns**
> **1 teaspoon coriander seeds**
> **4 allspice berries**
> **2 small hot chile pods**
> **5 cloves**
> **2 marjoram sprigs**
> **4 thyme sprigs**
> **2 savory sprigs**

Bring to a boil, turn down to simmer, and cook for 1 minute. Pack the hot jars with cherries, distribute the herbs and spices evenly among the jars, and pour over the hot brine, leaving ¼ inch of headspace. Wipe the rims and cap. Wait a week before eating to let the brine penetrate the cherries. The cherries will keep for 1 year in the refrigerator.

# Pickled Buddha's Hand

MAKES 2 CUPS

Beautiful Buddha's Hand makes a lovely pickle. The lemony fragrance is captured and spiked by the vinegar brine. The little circles are charming stirred into chopped fish tartare, salsa verde, tapenade, and marinated greens.

Cut into thin rings:
**½ pound Buddha's Hand fingers**
You should have about 2 cups. Measure into a small pot:
**¾ cup water**
**½ cup white wine vinegar**
**1½ teaspoons salt**
**4 cloves**
**1 small bay leaf (optional)**
**1 small dried hot chile**
**4 thyme sprigs**
**¼ teaspoon black peppercorns**
Bring to a boil, turn down to a simmer, and cook for 1 minute. Stir to dissolve the salt. Pour the hot brine over the cut citrus and let cool. Store refrigerated in a tightly sealed jar for up to 1 year. Or pour into sterilized jars and process in a hot-water bath for 10 minutes.

VARIATION
• Use other spices such as cassia, star anise, Marash pepper, or cardamom for a more exotic flavor.

# Brandied Cherries

MAKES 2 PINTS

Serve these cherries with cured meats or over vanilla ice cream. They make a good garnish for a cocktail as well. When the cherries are gone, enjoy the brandy as a liqueur. Canning jars with sloped shoulders will help keep the fruit submerged in the liquor.

Wash and drain:
**1½ pounds cherries (Bing or other sweet variety)**
Trim the stems, leaving about 1 inch. Wash and dry two 1-pint jars. Divide equally between the jars:
**4 cloves**
**½ teaspoon black peppercorns**
Mix together:
**1½ cups brandy**
**½ cup sugar**
Pour over the cherries. Let the cherries sit in a cool dark place for 1 week, agitating the cherries every couple of days. Store in the refrigerator or a cool, dark place for up to 2 years.

VARIATIONS
• Other fruits that can be brandied: small Champagne grapes, red currants on the branch, small prune plums, and gooseberries.
• Put 2 strips lemon zest (remove all the white pith) into each jar with the spices.
• Add a cardamom pod or a star anise to each jar with the spices.
• Substitute ¼ cup red wine for ¼ cup brandy.

# Apricots in Syrup

MAKES 2 QUARTS

Apricots can be preserved in a light syrup. The jars are beautiful in the pantry and the tender fruit is a welcome treat in the months when apricots are not in season. An apricot kernel or two is added to each jar for flavor. Save the rest of the pits for Noyau Crème Anglaise (page 271). Ascorbic acid is added to preserve the bright orange color of the fruit. Pure ascorbic acid may be found where vitamins are sold.

Make a light simple syrup. Measure into a medium-size pot:

**3 cups water**

**1½ cups sugar**

Bring to a boil, stirring to dissolve the sugar. Set aside. Sterilize two 1-quart jars and new lids in a large pot of water.
Wash and drain well:

**3 pounds apricots**

Cut in half and remove the pits. Crack open 4 pits and extract the kernels. Bring the syrup back to a boil and blanch the apricot halves for 2 minutes, or just until they start to soften. Do this in batches. Pack the warm apricots into the jars cut side down. Pour hot syrup over the apricots to cover, leaving ½ inch of headspace below the rim of the jar. Add to each quart jar:

**¼ teaspoon pure ascorbic acid**

Wipe the rims of the jars clean and cap. Process in the hot water for 25 minutes. Let cool and store in a cool, dark place for up to 1 year.

VARIATIONS

◆ Use pint jars. Add only ¹⁄₁₆ teaspoon ascorbic acid and process for 20 minutes.

◆ Peaches and nectarines can be canned exactly the same way. Dip the peaches in boiling water to loosen their skins and peel them before cutting and blanching in syrup.
◆ Blackberries can be canned using the same method. Be sure to carefully look over the berries, to remove any moldy or blemished berries. Make a lighter syrup with only 1 cup of sugar to 3 cups water if desired. Do not blanch the berries in the syrup; instead, pack them straight into the jars without crushing, pour over the hot syrup, and cap. Ascorbic acid is not needed. Process the quart jars for 20 minutes and pints for 15 minutes.

# Lime Syrup

MAKES ABOUT 2 CUPS

Cut in half and juice:

**12 large limes or 15 Key or Bearss limes**

You should have 1 cup lime juice. Strain through a fine mesh sieve or cheesecloth. Set this aside.
Measure into a heavy-bottomed pot:

**1 cup water**

**1 cup sugar**

Bring to a boil. Stir to dissolve the sugar and cook until the mixture thickens enough to coat the back of a spoon without immediately running off (220°F on a candy thermometer). Stir in the lime juice, mix well, and let cool.

The syrup will keep in the refrigerator in a sealed sterile container for up to 1 month. If you would like to keep it longer or give the syrup as a gift, pour it into sterilized pint jars and process in a boiling water bath for 10 minutes.

VARIATIONS

⁎ For blood orange syrup, use 1½ cups blood orange juice, ½ cup sugar, and ½ cup water.
⁎ For tangerine syrup, use 1½ cups tangerine juice, 2½ tablespoons lemon juice, ½ cup sugar, and ½ cup water.
⁎ For lemon-lime syrup, use ½ cup lime juice, ½ cup lemon juice, 1 cup sugar, and 1 cup water.
⁎ For Meyer lemon syrup, use 1 cup Meyer lemon juice, ½ cup water, and ¾ cup sugar.

## Confited Tangerine Slices

MAKES ABOUT 2 CUPS

Slices of sweet tangerines become beautifully translucent and tender when slowly poached in a simple syrup. Use the slices to garnish cakes, ice cream, or a lemon curd tart. Choose firm tangerines with a tight skin; Pixie, Clementine, and Fairchild all work well.

Preheat the oven to 300°F.
In a saucepan, combine:
>   **2 cups sugar**
>   **1 cup water**

Bring to a boil, stir to dissolve the sugar, and set aside.
Wash and thinly slice (about ¹⁄₁₆ inch thick):
>   **2 to 3 medium tangerines**

Lay the slices in a small baking dish, overlapping them by two thirds like shingles on a roof. Gently pour three quarters of the sugar syrup over the arranged slices. Cut a piece of parchment the size of your dish and

place it on top of the slices. Pour the remaining syrup over the parchment and cover the dish tightly with foil. Bake until translucent, about 1 hour. (The timing will depend on the thickness of the slices.)

Once the slices are translucent, remove the foil and return the dish to the oven. Bake until the slices are tender and thoroughly candied, about 30 minutes. Let cool and then pack into a container with the syrup. Refrigerate for up to 1 month.

VARIATIONS

⁎ Use Meyer lemons or kumquats instead of tangerines.
⁎ For blood oranges, oranges, grapefruit, and other citrus fruit that have a thicker rind, reduce the sugar by ½ cup and increase the initial cooking time by ½ hour.

## Candied Orange Peel

MAKES ABOUT 1 CUP

Candied citrus is a wonderful way to make use of citrus peel after the fruit has been juiced. At Chez Panisse, we use candied peel on its own as a delightful candy or chopped as a garnish on many of our desserts throughout the year. The candies also make a lovely and much appreciated gift.

Candying zest is a little time-consuming, but the steps are easy. The most important point is blanching the fresh peels. We like to keep a layer of the white pith, or albedo, on the peel to give the candy a soft chewy quality. The water is changed in the blanching process to leach the bitterness out of the pith. The degree of softness to which the peel is cooked is also important. Too soft and the peel will fall apart, but not soft enough and the candies become hard and overly chewy. This recipe can be easily scaled up to make a bigger batch.

Put in a pot:

**12 juiced orange halves**
**(6 oranges cut in half and juiced)**

Cover with cold water by 1 inch and bring to a boil, lower the heat, and simmer for 15 minutes. Drain off the water, cover the orange halves with more cold water, and repeat the process. Do this again, for a total of 3 times. At the end of the third simmer, make sure that the peels can easily be pierced by a knife. Continue cooking if needed. Drain the peels and let cool. Using a teaspoon, scoop out and discard the inner membrane, leaving a thin layer of the white pith attached to the colorful zest. Cut the cooked peels into strips or triangles.

Make a simple syrup. Measure into a 2-quart pan:

**2 cups water**
**4 cups sugar**

Bring to a gentle boil, stirring to dissolve the sugar. Add the orange peel and lower the heat to a simmer. Be sure to keep the syrup simmering slowly while the peels are cooking. Do not let it boil rapidly or the peels will become tough and chewy. Cook until the peel is translucent and the sugar syrup is thickened (220°F). Take out a piece of peel to test—it should be translucent all the way through. If you find that your syrup is reducing too fast in the pot, cover the surface of the peels with a piece of parchment paper.

Place a cooling rack over a baking sheet or plate. Remove the peel from the syrup with a slotted spoon, drain well, and lay out on the rack in a single layer. Let the peels air-dry overnight, or until they are no longer tacky. Toss the dry peels in sugar, shake off any excess, and store in an airtight container. Candied peels will keep for up to a year if stored in airtight containers in the refrigerator.

VARIATIONS

◆ The quantity of simple syrup can be adjusted to accommodate a batch of any size: the ratio is 2 parts sugar to 1 part water.
◆ When candying Meyer lemon peel, blanch and simmer a total of 2 times.
◆ For grapefruit, yuzu, rangpur, or blood orange peels, blanch and simmer a total of 5 times.

## Candied Melon

MAKES 1 POUND

Most varieties of melons such as honeydew, Charentais, cantaloupe, casaba, and Chinese winter melon can be candied using this method. Watermelon's moisture content is too high for it to be candied.

Peel, leaving as little firm skin as possible on the flesh:

**1 ripe but firm melon (about 2 pounds)**

Cut the melon into halves and remove the seeds and soft tissues in the seed cavity. Slice each half into 4 equal-size pieces; you will have 8 slices all together.

Bring to a boil:

**4 cups water**
**1 tablespoon baking soda**

Have a large bowl of ice water ready. Put the

melon slices into the boiling water and blanch for 1 minute. Remove melon slices and immediately put them in the cold water. Submerge until the slices are cool. Remove from the water and pat dry with a towel.

Make a heavy simple syrup. Measure into a 2-quart pan:

**3 cups sugar**

**1 cup water**

Bring to a gentle boil stirring to dissolve the sugar. (Be very careful if using organic sugar. It boils at a much higher temperature than conventional granulated sugar, and the impurities in organic sugar cause the syrup to become very foamy when boiled. If the syrup boils over it will catch fire and burn.)

Put the melon slices into the syrup and stir gently. Bring the syrup to a gentle boil again. As soon as it comes to a boil, turn off the heat. Put a piece of parchment paper over the melon slices and weigh them down with a plate. Let the fruits macerate in the syrup for 8 hours or overnight. Remove the fruit and lay the slices on paper towels to absorb the syrup. Bring the syrup to a boil and reduce for 15 to 20 minutes until it has returned to its original consistency. Put the melon pieces back into the syrup and repeat the heating and macerating one more time.

Remove the candied melon slices, put them on a cooling rack, and let them dry in a warm, dry place for a few days, turning the slices every now and then. Alternatively, if you have a food dehydrator, dry in the dehydrator for 1 or 2 days. Properly candied melons should feel moist in the middle and dry and slightly crystallized on the outside. Store in a clean dry jar. Keep the syrup for flavoring and to sweeten beverages.

# Candied Kumquats

MAKES 1 POUND

Candied kumquats look like glistening orange jewels, and they are quite delicious, too. It is a slow process to candy fruit. The secret to plump translucent fruit is slow steeping in hot syrup. Be patient and don't let the syrup get too hot. The kumquat syrup can be used to sweeten apéritifs or other drinks.

Wash:

**1 pound kumquats**

Measure into a 2-quart pan:

**4 cups sugar**

**2 cups water**

Bring to a gentle boil stirring to dissolve the sugar.

Using a skewer, puncture the skin of each kumquat, making 5 or more holes in each fruit. Add the punctured fruits to the boiling syrup and give them a good stir. Bring the syrup back to a gentle boil, and immediately turn off the heat. Put a piece of parchment paper over the fruits and weigh them down with a plate. Let the fruit sit in the syrup for 8 hours or overnight. The kumquats should look slightly translucent. Remove the kumquats from the syrup. Bring the syrup to a gentle boil, add the kumquats, return to a boil, and immediately turn off the heat. Cover and let sit for another 8 hours. The candied kumquats should look plump with syrup and slightly translucent. If the fruits look wrinkled or shriveled, that means you are boiling the fruit too hard.

Repeat the whole process one more time, for a total of 3 steepings. Refrigerate the candied fruit in their syrup in a jar. Or let the fruits air-dry on a rack and coat them with granulated sugar when they have dried. Store in an airtight container for up to 1 year in the refrigerator.

VARIATION

◆ Other small citrus such as calamansi, Kishu mandarins, or sour Chinotto oranges can be candied the same way.

## Salt-Preserved Kumquats

Salt-cured lemons are a Moroccan condiment that adds a unique flavor to many dishes. Recently I have started experimenting with other citrus. I like salt-cured kumquats, yuzu, and rangpur. I make them plain or spice them up with a bit of coriander, cardamom, and chile. You could add ginger and star anise, too. Try the Lacinato Kale Salad with Salt-Preserved Kumquats and Parmesan (page 210). Kumquats also make a good addition to a relish, a marinade, or a sauce. In Vietnam, they are made into a refreshing drink with water and a spoonful of sugar. The citrus becomes quite soft with the preserving and the whole fruit, except for the seeds, is used.

Choose a jar that will just barely fit the amount of kumquats you have. Wash and dry the kumquats. I recommend using sea salt or kosher salt for the best flavor. Sprinkle a ⅛-inch layer of salt over the bottom of the clean jar. Cut a longitudinal slit down the side of each fruit. Pinch the kumquats open, fill the slit with salt, and pack into the jar. Press on the fruits as you add them to help release their juice. If the kumquats don't give off much juice, or not enough to

cover them, pour in Meyer lemon or lemon juice to the top of the fruit. Sprinkle another ⅛-inch layer of salt on the top and cap the jar. Let it rest at room temperature for a few days and then store in the refrigerator for 1 or 2 weeks before eating—but you can always sneak a taste before then. They will keep up to a year (they will begin to soften after a few months).

If you would like to add spices, use whole seeds and sprinkle them in between every few layers of fruit. Remember that cardamom and star anise are very aromatic and a little goes a long way. Follow the same recipe for yuzu, rangpurs, and lemons. Make 2 slits in the medium-size fruit and 4 in the larger lemons.

## Vin d'Orange

MAKES ABOUT 3 LITERS

Wash and cut into ½-inch slices:
    **½ lemon**
    **½ sweet orange**
    **5 Seville or bitter oranges**
Put the cut citrus into a nonreactive crock or container with:
    **3 bottles dry white wine
        (such as sauvignon blanc)**
    **1½ cups vodka**
    **½ vanilla bean, split open**
    **1½ cups sugar**
Stir to dissolve the sugar. Cover and let rest in a cool dark place for up to 6 weeks. Start tasting the infusion after 3 weeks. It is ready when you are happy with the contrast of bitter and sweet (longer steeping increases the bitter flavor). Strain the liquid and let it set-

tle for 24 hours. Pour off the liquid through a fine sieve, leaving behind the sediment. Repeat until the vin d'orange is as clear as you like. The final straining can be through fine muslin. Pour into clean wine bottles and cork. Store the wine for up to 6 months unrefrigerated or up to 1 year refrigerated.

VARIATION

♦ Experiment with other citrus such as rangpur, grapefruit, yuzu, orange, and lemon; cut the sugar in half if using sweet citrus such as grapefruit or sweet oranges.

## Liqueurs

A liqueur is an infusion of fruit or nuts into an alcohol base along with sugar and other flavorings such as citrus zest and spices. Liqueurs are a useful form of preservation and are a gold mine for the dessert kitchen. A small splash of liqueur over fruit will help intensify its aromas. I also find the sharp taste of alcohol is a great foil for the cloying nature of sugar. In fact, because alcohol forms a bond between water and fat, it helps marry the flavors of fruit, cream, and sugar together. Try a spoonful of liqueur in your ice cream, whipped cream, crème anglaise, or soufflé. Add some to simple syrups to paint on a cake before filling it with fruit and cream. A touch of nocino in maple syrup makes an incredible pancake topper. Start with teaspoons and tablespoons; the idea is to support flavors, not take them over—although there are moments when the taste of the liqueur is what we are looking for. A soufflé flavored with apricot li-

queur is a delicious treat and a trifle spiked with crab apple liqueur can dazzle at the end of a meal. A small glass of liqueur as a digestif at the end of a meal is a pleasure, too, especially when it is from your own pantry and maybe even from your own garden.

## Nocino

MAKES 1 QUART

Nocino is an apéritif made from immature green walnuts. The walnuts should be about 1½ inches around and still soft enough to cut open. According to foragers in Italy and France, St. John's Day, June 24, is said to be the best day to harvest green walnuts for nocino, or *vin de noix*.

Combine in a clean 2-quart glass container:

**30 green walnuts (about 2 pounds),
    cut in halves or quarters
5 whole cloves
2 cinnamon sticks
Zest of 1 lemon
Zest of ½ orange
1 teaspoon anise seeds
1 liter vodka**

Store in a cool, dark place for 4 weeks. Shake every few days. After 4 weeks, add:

**2 cups sugar**

Shake to dissolve. Store an additional 2 weeks and shake daily. Strain out the walnuts and spices and filter the nocino through cheesecloth or muslin. Decant into bottles and cork tightly. Age the nocino for a few months in a cool, dark place before using. The flavors will develop and mellow as the nocino ages.

# Crab Apple Liqueur

MAKES ABOUT 1 QUART

Put into a sterilized 4-quart glass jar:

**4 quarts ripe crab apples (about
    4 pounds), washed and quartered**

Pour over:

**1 bottle vodka (about 3 cups)**

The fruit should be covered by the vodka, and if it is not, add more. Screw the lid on tightly. Store the jar for 2 weeks in a cool, dark place and shake daily. After 2 weeks, strain out the crab apples and filter the liqueur through multiple layers of cheesecloth or coffee filters.

Add:

**2 cups sugar**

Stir until the sugar is dissolved. Depending on the variety of crab apples, you may need more sugar. Taste and add sugar as needed. Decant into bottles and cork tightly. Store the liqueur in a cool, dark place for 2 months before using.

VARIATION

◆ For raspberry or blackberry liqueur, substitute berries for the crab apples and brandy for the vodka. Add only 1 cup sugar after straining. Taste and adjust as needed.

# Apricot Liqueur

MAKES ABOUT 1 QUART

Cut in half and remove pits from:

**16 ripe apricots (about 1¼ pounds)**

Combine in a heavy-bottomed pot:

**4½ cups dry white wine**

**2 cups sugar**

**1 cinnamon stick (optional)**

Bring ingredients to a boil to dissolve the sugar. Remove from the heat and add the apricots and:

**2¼ cups vodka**

Cover, and let the mixture infuse for 4 days at room temperature.

After 4 days, remove the apricots and the cinnamon stick. Strain the liquid through multiple layers of cheesecloth and decant into bottles. Cork tightly. The liqueur is ready to drink. Store in a cool, dark place.

# Hazelnut Liqueur

MAKES ABOUT 1 QUART

Preheat the oven to 350°F. Toast until deep golden brown:

**1⅓ cups (about 6½ ounces) hazelnuts**

Rub to remove skins and chop coarsely. Put the nuts into a sterilized glass jar or container large enough to hold 6 cups of liquid.

Bring to a boil:

**2 cups water**

Pour over the hazelnuts and let cool completely. Add:

**2½ cups vodka**

**½ vanilla bean, cut in half and scraped**

Cover and let the mixture steep in the refrigerator for 2 weeks.

Measure into a pot:

**½ cup water**

**¾ cup sugar**

Bring to a boil and cool completely. Add to the steeping hazelnuts and mix well. Strain out the hazelnuts and vanilla bean, then filter through multiple layers of cheesecloth or a coffee filter. Decant into bottles and cork tightly. Store in a cool, dark place.

# Dried Fruit

Drying, or dehydrating, is another way to preserve the bounty of the seasons. Dried fruits are naturally sweet and delicious, so no additional sugar is needed. Drying fruit at home allows you to choose high-quality premium fruit, which will taste markedly better than most dried fruit you can purchase. Raisins and prunes are the most commonly found dried fruit but persimmons and figs are very good, too. Apricots, apples, pears, and cherries are easily dried as well.

The key point in drying fruit is to maintain consistent low heat with good air circulation. Originally, fruit was dried on screens in the sun, but today there are a few more options available: your home oven, a food dehydrator, or a solar dehydrator. A conventional oven will work only if the thermostat can be held between 130° and 140°F. Food dehydrators are made specifically for drying produce and come with built-in screen shelves and easy-to-control low temperature settings. Before investing in your own dehydrator, check to see if your local tool-lending library or your community's schools have any available to rent or borrow. Solar dehydrators are fairly easy to make and there are plenty of plans available online. They make sun-dried fruit possible, even in climates that could not normally support drying in the sun; plus, there is no energy cost.

Choose fruit to dry that is unblemished and perfectly ripe but not soft. Wash it and dry it well before starting. Cut the fruit into consistent same-size pieces so they dry in more or less the same amount of time. Slice apples, pears, Asian pears, and persimmons into ¼-inch slices. Remove any seeds. Pierce prune plums to speed their drying. Cut other stone fruit in half. Apricots and Japanese plums (Santa Rosa and others) can be dried in halves, cut side up, while nectarines and peaches do better cut into ⅓-inch wedges. (Peaches can be peeled before drying by dunking in boiling water and then straight into cold. The skin will slip off.)

Some fruit oxidizes and browns as it dries, particularly peaches, apricots, and nectarines. A dip to keep fruit from oxidizing can be prepared from ascorbic acid and water at a ratio of ½ teaspoon ascorbic acid (or 3 crushed 500 mg vitamin C tablets) to 1 quart of water. Mix well and dip the cut fruit in the solution for no longer than 5 minutes.

Lay out the pieces of cut fruit on racks or drying trays in a single layer without touching each other. Dry at 130°F. Start checking thinly sliced, drier fruit, such as apples, after 8 hours; juicier fruit may take as long as 3 days. Fruit varies in moisture content, so use these times as guidelines and check the fruit from time to time during the drying process. Cool the fruit for a few minutes before testing for doneness. Cut the fruit in half to see if has dried all the way through. Properly dried fruit should be pliable and no longer tacky. If it is moist or sticky it needs longer drying. Be careful also to not overdry the fruit or it may become unpleasantly brittle and brown. Let the fruit stand at room temperature for a few hours to cool completely before storing. Storing warm fruit will cause condensation and any residual moisture could cause the fruit to mold. Store in airtight containers in a dark, cool, dry place for up to 1 year.

# Part II

## Seed to Seed

### Growing the New Kitchen Garden

# Plant Wherever You Are

I THINK THE MOST IMPORTANT piece of gardening advice is to start small. Just as I would never send a novice cook into the kitchen to prepare a four-course dinner, I wouldn't suggest starting a whole victory garden in one season. My next piece of advice is to start simply. Begin with a few herbs and some leafy greens—things that make a big difference when they're just picked. Then begin to expand outward: your backyard, side yard, front yard, stoop containers, window boxes, deck, rooftop, community garden.

A kitchen garden can be anywhere. Traditionally, it would have been planted as a single entity as close to the kitchen as possible. But factors such as urbanization, climate change, and dwindling open space have changed how we approach growing food for ourselves. Despite these limitations, planting a few seeds (and then a few more) is the best way to get fresh, healthy, delicious food—practically for free!

Even if you feel you don't have the space or time to garden, a single planter of herbs will bring you closer to nature and to those growing your food. It is essential that we remember our interconnectedness; farmers and the land sustain us. As Wendell Berry says: "Eating is an agricultural act." What we choose to buy and put on our table makes a difference every day. We can participate in the preservation of both the land and our health by buying directly from local farmers at farmers' markets, asking for organic produce at our grocers, and requiring food labeling that is explicit about how it is grown.

As eaters we are reliant on a mere two feet of topsoil. That is the source of all agriculture; this is where our food is grown. Bob Cannard has opened my eyes to the wonder of living soil. He has taught me that by observing, mimicking, and working with nature we can maintain and even increase the soil's natural fertility, rather than strip it away by using chemicals. We must all become caretakers of the soil. We can do this by cultivating our gardens, by composting to return nutrients to the earth, and by supporting and protecting the people who care for our farmlands. It is up to us to demand the use of practices that will ensure that our farmlands are full of life for our grandchildren and their children, too.

# It's All About the Soil

B OB CANNARD of Cannard Farm in Sonoma has been supplying Chez Panisse with irresistible vegetables, herbs, and fruit for over twenty-five years. Tasting his harvests has convinced me that Bob's gardening path is the one to follow. When he told me that his vegetables were much more nutritious than supermarket vegetables, I did not believe him at first. I soon learned it to be true. He has become my gardening guru.

The most fascinating and important fact I have learned from Bob is that well-tended garden soil is filled with a vast, teeming underground ecosystem of tiny creatures that work together to create the nutrient-rich conditions in which his delicious produce grows. Keeping this underground community alive and happy is the first priority of gardening. The requirements are basic and easy to supply: sunlight, air, water, organic matter, and minerals. Fertility is an ongoing process; with regular tending and feeding, soil will continue to improve year after year. The results are healthy plants that taste better and are less likely to be plagued by pests and disease.

# Soil

The soil in our gardens supplies both a home for the plants we grow and their food. Good garden soil—dark, rich, and well draining—is much more than dirt. It is filled with a complex underground ecosystem of insects, fungi, bacteria, and other beneficial organisms and microorganisms. There are literally billions of beneficial microbes in a teaspoon of fertile soil. Organic matter, minerals, water, and air supply the environment they need to thrive.

Organic matter is nothing more than decomposed plant and animal litter. Think of a forest floor covered with fallen leaves, needles, branches, and spent flowers. These all slowly turn into organic matter that, when fully decomposed, is called humus. Humus is both the home of the soil's micro-community and its diet. And as all those microorganisms eat, they convert organic matter into valuable nutrients, holding them in place and keeping them from leaching—that is, from washing out of the soil. These nutrients are then slowly made available to the plants, like a natural time-release fertilizer, as these tiny creatures digest and decompose. Water is needed to facilitate the exchange of nutrients, and many microorganisms help aggregate the soil—or stick it together—which helps increase the soil's water retention and buffer its pH. The whole mix is stirred and tilled by earthworms that distribute the organic matter and nutrients throughout the soil and aerate it with tunnels, which improve the overall structure and drainage.

As it turns out, these soil microbes are the same ones that break down our kitchen and garden scraps into compost. Compost is a universal soil amendment that improves and maintains both fertility and structure regardless of the soil type. It is a mix of partially decomposed organic matter and the microbes that do the decomposing. The soil food web is fed by the organic matter and rejuvenated by the influx of new microbes. The nutrients and microbes, in all their various forms, enhance plant growth and flavor, and suppress disease.

# Soil Type

Loam is prime garden soil. It is a loose, crumbly, sweet-smelling, balanced mix of sand, silt, clay, organic matter, air, and water. Depending on the region where you live there may be a preponderance of sand or clay in the local soil. Sandy soil is light and drains quickly; it needs to be watered often and has a hard time retaining nutrients. Clay soil is heavy and compact; it drains slowly and retains nutrients but lacks good airflow. The soil, regardless of its makeup, may have been overly compacted by construction and other heavy work. Here is an easy test to evaluate what type of soil is in your garden.

Dig from the top 12 inches of your garden soil and collect:

**2 cups soil**
Wet it thoroughly with:
**Water**
Take the wet soil into your hand and compact it into a ball. Open your hand and look at the structure of the ball.

Clay soil: A sticky ball that holds together.

Sandy soil: A ball that cannot hold its shape.

Loam soil: A ball that holds shape but is easily broken apart.

There are many gradations of these basic types, such as sandy loam, loamy clay, and so on. Each has advantages and disadvantages in drainage, nutrient and water retention, and percentage of organic material. The further the soil is from loam, the more often more compost should be added.

## Compost

Compost is the number-one food for soil. Compost is a perfect natural system in which nutrients taken by plants from the soil, water, and air are returned back to the soil. Making compost diverts our food and garden waste from landfill and turns it into a valuable natural resource and powerful plant food. Everyone can compost and it is important to do so.

Learning to compost was a revelation to me. I had felt uncomfortable—guilty, really—throwing out all the trimmings from my kitchen prep and the occasional spoiled fruits and vegetables. When I discovered that I could recycle them into compost, one of the best ways to provide food for the garden, I was thrilled. My guilt was transformed into inspired action. I immediately began composting at home, and thanks to Bob, Chez Panisse started sending bins of vegetable scraps from the restaurant to Cannard Farm. He turns all our peelings and trimmings into food for the very produce he sends us to cook. Being part of this full-circle cycle that turns garbage into garden gold deepened my connection to cooking and gardening and continues to do so today.

Start saving your fruit and vegetable scraps for your own compost pile or worm bin. Keep a small bowl or bucket near the sink to toss your scraps in as you prepare your meals. Start a compost pile outdoors, or if you have a small space, start a worm composter inside. Worm composters are odorless and will fit under a kitchen sink or other convenient place. If you don't have much use for compost, or if you have more compost than you can use, become a guerrilla composter and scatter worm castings and mature compost in a local park, on street trees, or in empty lots. It is gratifying to remediate the land around you and connect to the local ecosystem. Many municipalities are catching on and have started composting programs that take food scraps and garden waste to produce vast amounts of compost for local landscapes and gardens; and many farmers' markets have compost stations where people can bring their fruit and vegetable scraps.

A balanced compost pile consists of brown, carbon-rich elements (straw, dried plants, dried leaves) and green, nitrogen-rich elements (fresh or wilted plants, vegetable and fruit scraps, coffee grounds, tea leaves, manure from grass-eating animals). The brown material is the slow-burning fuel, and the green material is quick-burning ignition. Home composters may find brown ingredients harder to come by. A bale of straw is a great source of brown material; and each straw is hollow, which improves aeration. Water, air, bacteria, fungi, and earthworms are the other ingredients. The microbes needed for decomposition are present in the materials added to the pile. Water is essential for the bacteria and fungi to do their job. Earthworms and other beneficial insects will find the pile. Worms help accelerate the composting process and improve the compost's quality. They are also a good indicator of the pile's moisture level: they will not hang out in compost that is too dry or too wet.

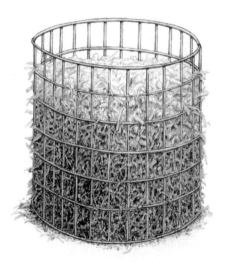

# Building a Compost Pile

Making a compost pile is a straightforward and enjoyable process; even if there is a hiccup here or there, in the end, you will have compost. The pile is built of alternating layers of brown and green elements, just as if you were making a large layer cake. A well-made compost pile is odorless and discreet.

Locate your pile out of direct sunlight; a shady area will help keep the pile moist. A compost bin is not necessary, especially if you live in a mild climate and have lots of room. You can make a bin or buy one. Look online for plans and descriptions and check your local municipalities, as many subsidize the cost of first-time bin purchases.

Spread over the bottom of a compost bin or the bottom of the pile location:

**A 4-inch layer of brown material (straw, dried grass clippings)**

Moisten with:

**Water (a fine spray from the hose or a watering can)**

Use enough water on the layer to make it damp, but not soggy or dripping. Spread on top a 2-inch layer of:

**Green material (vegetable scraps, garden trimmings, grass clippings)**

Don't worry if you don't have enough greens; the layer can be made incrementally. Spread the unfinished layer with straw or other browns to keep flies away. Push aside the brown when adding more greens. When the layer is complete, cover with:

**A 4-inch layer of brown material**

Moisten as above and keep building the pile, alternating layers just as if you were making a large layer cake, until the bin is filled or the pile is a few feet high.

If desired, sprinkle the green layers with:

**Rock dust or other minerals**
**(see page 368)**

After 3 months in warm weather, or 6 months in cold, turn the layers over into a second bin or pile, until you reach compost that has matured. (The compost on the bottom will be mature first.) Compost is ready and mature when none of its ingredients are recognizable and it is dark brown and easily crumbled. Sift the mature compost before adding it to the garden, returning any large pieces back into the pile, and continue the ongoing process of layering, turning, and making more compost.

NOTES

+ If you are making compost for the first time, or would like to rejuvenate the microbial life of your soil, throw in a handful or two of locally occurring compost (take a bag with you on a walk in the woods or in a park and gather a handful of soil from under a log, a forest floor, or alongside a creek); or add compost from a neighbor's bin to introduce some new soil microbes.

+ Add as many diverse ingredients to your pile as possible. This will give the compost a fuller spectrum of nutrients and microbes for the garden. Green ingredient options include organic coffee grounds from your local café; spent vegetables from the farmers' market or other organic food shops; and small amounts of litter from organically fed hamsters, guinea pigs, or chickens.

+ Do not add weeds that have seeds (they will germinate and take over your garden);

diseased plants; grass (or anything else) that has been treated with herbicide; manure from carnivores (dogs, cats, people); or meat and dairy products (which will compost, but also attract vermin).

+ Compost should never smell bad. Smelliness is a sign of lack of oxygen due to compaction, too much green material, or too much moisture. To correct this problem, turn the pile to aerate it, and if it is too moist, add layers of brown material.

+ Grass clippings can get matted together and become anaerobic and stinky. Let them dry for a day or two and add them to the pile in thin layers; or premix them with other brown materials before adding to the pile.

+ If the compost does not seem to be breaking down, it is probably too dry. Turn it, moistening the layers as you go.

+ To speed up the composting process, scatter compost from a previous pile or a purchased bag of live compost every layer or so to inoculate your pile with beneficial microorganisms.

+ Use a long sturdy stick or metal pole (rebar) to poke holes in the pile for added aeration. Plunge the stick all the way to the bottom of the pile at intervals of about 5 inches. Aerate the pile again after turning.

+ Only use mature compost in a growing garden; unfinished compost will continue to decompose, but it will tie up the nutrients in the soil. Coarse, unfinished compost can be used in the fall as mulch over beds that are wintering over.

VARIATIONS

+ If you have a lot of material to compost, you can build the pile all at once. Make the pile a minimum of 3 feet square. Dampen the layers of green and brown evenly. The pile will become quite hot (up to 160°F) within a few days. (The heat is the product of the feeding activities of bacteria.) Once the heat begins to subside, turn the pile to aerate it and it will heat up again. Turn again, until the pile no longer heats up. The compost will usually be ready in about 6 weeks to 3 months.

• Leaves may be composted separately into leaf mold. Leaf mold is a marvelous aid for soil structure and water and air retention. Carbon-eating microbes love it. It is also a great ingredient for homemade potting soil and makes fantastic mulch. (Leaf mold is not high in nutrients, so regular compost should be added to soil and containers, too.) A large pile of leaves is needed to create the right environment for composting—4 to 5 feet square is recommended. Make the pile in layers, moistening them as you go. Let sit for 6 months to 2 years. To speed up the process run over the leaves a few times with a lawn mower before piling them up and turn the pile every few months, wetting the layers as needed. Leaf mold is ready when it is dark brown, soft, and crumbly.

## Worm Composting

An outdoor compost pile is not the only way to transform household and garden green waste into plant food. Vermiculture, or worm composting, makes composting possible for households without a lot of outdoor space. A worm composter is also a good way to compost in the winter, if cold and snow keep you from going out to your compost pile. The worms are housed in bins and odorlessly turn food scraps into worm castings. The worms used are not the big earthworms that are found in the soil, but red worms—*Eisenia fetida* or *Lumbricus rubellus*, also called red wiggler, brandling, or manure worms. The worms eat up to their weight in food scraps every day, filling up a bin with nutrient-rich castings in just a few months. The nutrient-rich castings are filled with microorganisms and are particularly well suited for meeting the needs of container gardens and houseplants. Tending a worm composter is a great project for the whole family. Kids find worms and worm composting fascinating and fun.

Just like regular composting, worm composting depends on a balanced mix of browns and greens. The browns act as a bedding and food for the worms and are supplied in the form of damp shredded newspaper, cardboard, dried leaves, or straw. The worms appreciate a diverse mix and make better compost with it. The greens are what you feed them. They like all vegetable and fruit scraps (except for citrus, which they eat eventually, but at a much slower rate), coffee grounds, tea leaves, and broken up eggshells. Avoid feeding worms large amounts of meat, dairy, and oily foods, as they are all eaten at a very slow rate.

Worms need a well-ventilated, moist, and dark environment. There are all sorts of plans and ideas for homemade bins on the Internet and plenty of places that sell ready-made bins. Worms can be purchased from a local source or by mail order.

## Starting and Feeding a Worm Composter

Locate your bin in a warm place out of direct sunlight. The worms require a habitat with temperatures between 55° and 77°F.

Spread, on the bottom of a worm bin, a 4-inch layer of:

**Newspaper, shredded into ½-inch strips**

Sprinkle the paper with:

**Water**

Toss the paper and continue to sprinkle and toss the paper until is damp. Do not let it get soggy. If it does, start over. Sprinkle over the damp newspaper:

**A handful of clean soil or sand**

(Worms have a gizzard just like birds and need a little grit to digest their food.) Add:

**Red worms**

Cover with:

**A layer of dry bedding or a piece of moist cardboard**

This will help keep in the moisture and keep away fruit flies. Let the worms get used to their new home for 2 days before feeding. To feed the worms, pull aside the bedding and bury:

**A handful of food scraps, chopped into smaller pieces**

Cover with bedding and close the bin. Wait a few days and look in to see if the worms are eating the food. When it is mostly gone, add to another section of the bin:

**A handful of food scraps, chopped into smaller pieces**

Keep adding food scraps as they are needed to different parts of the bin. It is easiest if the bin is divided into a few zones (worm composters usually recommend six), and scraps are added to one of them at a time; the worms will move from section to section. Monitor the composter and if food is not being eaten, add the food more slowly. The worms will quickly begin to reproduce and the population and its appetite will increase.

The compost, or castings, will be ready for harvest after about 4 months. All the bedding should look dark and crumbly and all the food should be eaten. To harvest, push everything to one side and add new bedding in the vacant space. Start adding food to the fresh bedding. After a couple weeks, all the worms will have made their way over to the new side. Remove the compost and fill the space with new bedding. Sprinkle the castings into containers or around plants in the garden, or use them to make a nutrient-rich tea for feeding the soil or leaves (see page 397).

NOTES

♦ If the bedding dries out, moisten it with water; worms will perish if their environment is too dry.

♦ If the composter starts to smell, check the moisture level of the bedding. If soggy, add some dry bedding to help absorb the excess moisture and keep the lid off the bin for a couple of days. If there is rotting food in the bin, remove it. Gently stir up the bedding to bring air to the mix, and do not add any more food until all the existing food has been eaten.

• Worms do not require consistent feeding, because they have their bedding to eat as well. If you are leaving for a while (up to a couple of weeks), check to be sure there is some food to be eaten and a good supply of dry bedding on top to help keep the system moist.

## Minerals

The underground soil community transforms chemical elements into food for plants. Nitrogen, potassium, and phosphorus are the elements most often associated with gardening, but plants and soil microbes need many more than that. Just as we need a full spectrum of nutrients, so do plants. Calcium, magnesium, copper, iron, molybdenum, and many more play a crucial role in health and flavor. A balanced diet is essential. A deficiency or surplus of any of these can result in issues in the garden.

All soil contains minerals, and every geographic region has specific soils because of geologic activity and weather. Supplemental mineral nutrients can be supplied in the form of finely ground rocks and shells.

## Mineral Soil Foods

Rock dust: After compost, Bob's favorite soil and plant food is rock dust. Rock dust, especially dust from quick forming volcanic ash and cinder, supplies a vast array of micronutrients and trace minerals, which are often depleted or deficient in soils. Both plants and the soil ecosystem respond rapidly to its benefits. Bob is confident that this is where the flavor and nutrition in his vegetables comes from. Rock dust may be found at farm supply and garden stores. Local quarries and gravel pits are other possible sources. Ask what kind of rock they are mining—volcanic rock is the best, but glacial gravel works, too. Add it directly to the soil and the compost pile.

Oyster-shell meal or ground limestone: These both add much needed calcium to the soil.

Charcoal: Another readily available plant food—if you have a fireplace or wood stove—are the pieces of charcoal that you find as you clear the ashes. Break them up and add to the compost pile or directly to the soil. They are a gold mine of nutrients.

Greensand (glauconite): A good mineral source of potassium. Potassium supports vigor and disease resistance. A great additional sprinkle for the compost pile.

Soft rock (colloidal) phosphate: An effective source of phosphorus. Phosphorus is necessary for fruit and flowers. (Slow acting and long lasting, phosphate usually only needs to be applied every few years.)

Wood ash: A good source of potassium, but it should be added to the compost heap and not to growing plants, especially babies.

Leguminous cover crop: Not a mineral, but the best way, after compost, to add nitrogen to the soil. (See the next page for planting and harvesting instructions.)

# pH

The pH scale measures the acid or alkali (base) level of a substance. The scale is based on pure water, which is neutral and assigned a value of 7. (Numbers above 7 indicate alkalinity and numbers below indicate acidity.) The ideal environment for most edible plants is a range of slightly acidic to neutral—somewhere between 6 and 7. It is interesting to note that well-maintained soil with a good quantity of organic matter and a healthy living ecosystem will buffer pH in soil, making it viable even when its pH is outside the prescribed bounds. Therefore adding compost is the best place to begin any correction.

If the soil is too acidic or alkaline (too sour or too sweet as gardeners of old used to say), the biological activity slows and soil nutrients become fixed and unavailable. The ideal pH range also supports the beneficial nitrogen-fixing relationship between legumes and bacteria. Home garden pH tests are reliable and easy to use.

Oyster-shell meal and ground limestone have the added benefit of raising, or sweetening the pH of acidic soil, while pine needles, peat moss, and aged sawdust work to balance high alkaline soils. Soil sulfur helps lower pH in high alkaline soils, too, but it does not last as long as the organic matter additions. When adjusting for pH, add the amendments to the soil in the fall. Cover with compost and plant a cover crop to help them assimilate more quickly.

# Cover Crops

Bare soil quickly loses its healthy structure and microbial colonies. Consistent moisture and good aeration are necessary to keep the underground ecosystem alive and well. Cover crops—plants grown for the sole purpose of soil fertility and enhancement—have been a vital part of sustainable agriculture and gardening for centuries, and they are still one of the best ways to improve soil life and structure and protect fallow garden soil.

A cover crop can be sown as a single variety or a mix of plants, such as fava beans, bell beans, vetches, alfalfa, clovers, and rye. Some cover crops consist of plants that have deep root systems to break up hard soil and bring vital nutrients from deeper strata, some are legumes that fix nitrogen in the soil as they grow, and others have a strong network of roots that hold soil in place. They all have a dense leaf cover that suppresses weed growth, and their blooms attract beneficial pollinators. The leaves, stalks, and roots are composted back into the soil, adding nutrients and soil-loosening biomass. Seasonal cover crops prevent nutrients from leaching out of the soil, add organic matter, expand earthworm and beneficial microorganism populations, increase available plant nutrition, reduce soil compaction, increase air flow and drainage, suppress weeds, and control erosion. They are well worth planting.

The common practice is to sow cover crops in bare ground, but they can also be sown between other crops to act as a living mulch that enhances fertility. A cover crop can be cut down at any time, though their benefits are increased if they are allowed to blossom.

## Growing a Cover Crop

Choose a cover crop that is suited for your growing region, the season, and your soil's specific needs. Many local seed catalogs offer mixes that have been created especially for a specific region's soil.

Clear the bed or container of any growth, weed or otherwise. Loosen the soil with a hoe or cultivator. Broadcast over the bed:

**Cover crop seeds**
Systematically sprinkle, or cast, seed evenly over the soil's surface. Water well. Spread over:

**A light layer of straw for mulch**
Water as needed to keep the soil moist until germination has occurred, usually in 14 to 20 days.

To harvest, use a hoe, sickle, or pruners to chop off the tops at the soil surface. (Some cover crops will grow back if cut before they have fully flowered; read your seed package or catalog for full information.) Chop the plants into smaller pieces, while harvesting or after, for quicker decomposition. The plant matter can be left on top of the soil to act as nourishing mulch, lightly turned into the soil to decompose, or composted separately in the compost pile.

NOTE
◆ When mulching with a harvested cover crop or digging one in, allow 2 to 3 weeks for the plants to decompose before sowing or transplanting the next crop. As green nitrogen-rich plants decompose, they tie up the nutrients in the soil, which inhibits both seed germination and plant growth. The bed may be planted right away if the cover crop is composted separately in the compost pile.

VARIATION
◆ Sprinkle other plant foods over the seeds and soil, such as rock dust, wood ash, and oyster-shell lime.

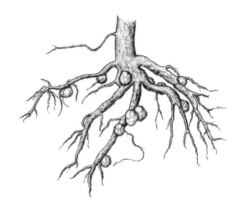

*Nodules of nitrogen-fixing bacteria on cover crop legume roots*

# Mature Cover Crops

Cannard Farm has an unusual approach to cover crops. Bob intercrops all his fields and beds and allows the cover crop to mature fully and produce seed. In the early days of Chez Panisse, we enlisted my father to help us find a farmer who could supply the restaurant with local organic produce. When he came back from visiting Bob's farm, he could not stop talking about how unusual it looked. My dad had majored in agricultural engineering when he was in college and expected to see orderly rows of plants in well-tended beds. The farm looked like a field of weeds to him, with no recognizable rows. He was amazed when Bob pulled the tall "weeds" aside to reveal the healthy food crops growing beneath. He spoke about that first visit for the rest of his life: "I couldn't believe what was underneath all those weeds!"

Bob believes adamantly that intercropping his vegetables with cover crops is both better for the soil and closer to the natural rhythms of nature than conventional organic farming. He says the secondary crop offers a habitat for beneficial insects and food for the pests, keeping them away from the primary crop being grown for harvest. His visitors still comment on his habit of letting the weeds grow, but they are not accidental weeds; they are specific crops, deliberately planted so that his vegetables will thrive and have fantastic flavor.

When interplanting cover crops, bear in mind that timing is important. The initial crop must be established before the cover crop is sowed in order to avoid adverse competition for water and nutrition. Do not plant alfalfa or other invasive crops when following this practice. There are cover crops for different seasons and climate zones. Look in seed catalogs to find a seed or seed mixture that is suitable for your growing zone and the time of year and keep experimenting until you find the perfect balance.

# Soil for Containers

Garden soil, even the best topsoil, cannot be used for container growing or starting seedlings. It will compact in the pot, stopping airflow and water drainage, and eventually the plant (and the microorgansims of the soil) will suffocate or drown. Potting soil must be made or bought. For healthy plants and flavorful produce, it pays to buy good ingredients, organic when available, or else buy already prepared potting soil (which doesn't actually contain any soil). It is a mix of natural components that supply the aeration, drainage, nutrition, and moisture retention that are needed for plants to thrive. Organic matter must be present to create a healthy soil ecosystem and to nourish the plant. Fully mature compost and worm castings are the best ingredients for this: they supply plenty of micronutrients and microbes to feed the plants, and compost boosts both water retention and soil porosity for good aeration. Minerals need to be added to help offset the loss of nutrients from the runoff that happens when containers are watered.

Making your own potting soil is less expensive than buying it especially if you have lots of containers to fill. But there are reputable products on the market. Price is usually a good indicator of quality. When buying prepared soil, read the ingredients on the bag, and if possible, look at the soil itself. It should be a fine (not coarse and chunky) mix of materials that holds water, which helps maintain the soil's moisture and keeps it separated and fluffy for airflow and drainage. I recommend adding 15 percent compost to the soil if it already contains some nutrients, and 25 percent if it does not.

## Potting Soil

MAKES ABOUT 2½ GALLONS

This mixture makes a good, light-textured growing medium for containers of all sizes. If you are reusing containers, wash them with mild soap and water before filling with new potting soil. Scale up the quantities to make enough to fill large containers. The ingredients are easy to find at a good nursery or garden supply site.

Mix together well:

**16 cups (1 gallon) prewet coconut coir**
**5 cups coarse sand (builders' sand)**
**5 cups rice hulls (heat-treated)**
**¼ cup greensand (glauconite)**
**¼ cup colloidal phosphate**
**¼ cup rock dust**
**2 tablespoons alfalfa meal**
**10 cups mature compost, screened to remove large bits**
**1 cup worm castings (optional)**

NOTES

• As the compost is utilized by the plants, the soil level will fall in the container. Just top up with compost once or twice a year.

• The soil may be reused if the previous plants were healthy. Turn out the soil, mix in 25 percent new compost and re-pot.

VARIATIONS

• Use well-rotted leaf mold instead of the coconut coir.

• Use peat moss (sphagnum peat) instead of the coconut coir. Mix with ½ cup oystershell meal to balance the pH of acidic peat.

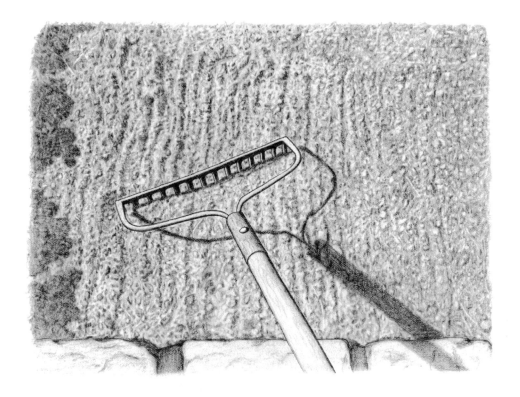

# Preparing the Beds

ONCE YOU KNOW WHERE you are going to put your garden beds or containers, there is much to discover about the exact spot where you are planting. What grows the very best there? During what time of year? How far can you push the seasons? Are there some new plants that might thrive there that you would love to try? Raised beds and containers filled with well-conditioned soil amended with compost and minerals allow for high-density planting and full-flavored harvests. Trellises and poles may be added to grow plants up for space. Mulch, cold frames, and row covers help to protect the plants as they grow.

## Plant Intensively

A small garden is efficient and productive when divided into densely planted beds with pathways in between. Raised beds (blocks of soil above the natural soil line) piled with deep, fertile soil support dense plantings that can be spaced close together for greater production, mutual support, and shade, which hinders weeds and evaporation. Beds can be positioned wherever there is a good amount of sunshine.

Because the soil is in discrete beds, it does not get walked upon and compacted. The root systems of the plants can stretch out in the loose soil and gather more nutrients and water. The soil will warm up more quickly in the spring as well, which permits earlier planting. No digging or tilling is required, which makes the beds easier to maintain and better for sustaining soil fertility. Raised beds also make gardening more accessible for those who find kneeling and bending a challenge.

## A Garden Plan

It is a good idea to draw up a planting plan each season. With organization and planning, a small space can be turned into a bountiful garden. Grow crops that produce a large harvest, such as chard, pole beans, summer squash, carrots, cherry tomatoes, and lettuce. Look for the smaller varieties of plants that require lots of space, such as melons and winter squash. Whenever possible, grow vertically; choose pole beans over bush beans and train tomatoes, cucumbers, and other climbers up trellises and poles. Cut-and-come-again plantings of lettuce, rocket, and tender greens can produce a lot of salad from a small space, and leafy greens such as chard, collards, and kale can be harvested over a long period of time. Keep a journal to keep track of what does well and where. Get creative with your planning and your garden will become busier, producing a tasty and prodigious harvest throughout more and more of the year.

You can also weave your kitchen garden into the existing landscape. Intermixing edibles and flowers creates a habitat that will bring beneficial insects and birds into the garden to pollinate flowers and ward off pests. Herbs blend naturally into flowerbeds, adding fragrance and beauty. Lettuces, showy rainbow chard, strawberries, and colorful peppers look striking when interplanted among ornamentals. Perennial edibles such as artichokes, scarlet runner beans, dwarf citrus, and rhubarb make quite a show in any landscape.

NOTES

✦ A garden journal can be as simple as a binder divided into months. Enter what you planted, how the plants fared, and how the harvest was from year to year. Or make a page for each bed and write dated entries with each planting in it.

✦ Place tall plants at the back of the garden or on the north side to keep them from casting shade over the rest of the bed.

✦ Don't forget to plan garden paths so you can walk between the beds.

✦ If you are growing perennials such as asparagus, artichokes, and rhubarb in the same bed as annuals, place them on the perimeter of the growing area so their roots won't be disturbed as annuals are rotated through.

✦ Place edible trees and shrubs carefully, remembering that they will continue to grow, taking up space and creating shade.

✦ Consider a watering plan, and whether to use a hose and watering can or to put in drip irrigation lines or soaker hoses before planting.

## What to Grow

The best answer to the question of what to grow is, grow what you love to eat, what is hard to find, or what tastes best just picked from the garden—tiny peas, young lettuces, fresh raspberries, alpine strawberries, lacy red mustards, chervil, Fino Verde basil, even rocket. Rocket will grow just about anywhere, and quickly, too. You may be able to buy it but not minutes after it was harvested. You can see, feel, and taste the freshness and life within it as you toss it in a dressing and eat it. You'll see; it's indescribable.

Once you know what you love to eat, consider the size and the specific microclimate of your growing space. I don't grow large onions or cabbages because I don't have the space, and I cannot grow large tomatoes because I don't have enough sun in foggy Berkeley. My garden is filled with lettuces, herbs, leafy greens, cherry tomatoes, and raspberries. That is what I love to eat and what grows best in my locale.

## Sun and Air

Plants need sun to grow. They use the energy from the sun in conjunction with water and carbon dioxide to make carbohydrates—food. Leafy plants like lettuce, chard, kale, and parsley can grow in partial shade, but plants like tomatoes, peppers, melons, squash, eggplant, peaches, and raspberries need a lot of sun to support all the leaves and fruit they are making. Most garden plants can be categorized by the number of hours of sunlight they need in a day to thrive. The hours of sunlight do not have to happen consecutively; there could be a few hours in the morning and a couple more in the afternoon, or vice versa.

Full sun: 6 hours.

Part sun: 4 to 6 hours.

Part shade: 2 to 4 hours.

Shade: Very little to no direct sunlight.

Many urban gardens are challenged by trees, neighboring buildings, and other architectural structures that cast shade at certain times of day. Before planting beds or setting up large containers, it is a good idea to track the sun throughout the day (and if there is time, through the seasons) to see what locations get the most sunlight. When challenged by the lack of sunlight, be creative in scouting for planting locations. Driveways, rooftops, balconies, and side yards may have the required sun. White walls and other reflective surfaces can help, too.

Also, a garden does not have to be all in one place. Sunny fences and walls are good places for climbing plants. Small salad crops can be sown in beds of ornamentals and among slower-growing plants. Portable containers are a good way to catch the sun as it moves through the seasons, especially on a deck or fire escape. Once you are familiar with the microclimates of your garden, you can bend the rules and try a plant that you really want in a less-than-perfect location. Experimenting is part of the fun of gardening.

Though the lack of sunlight is the most common issue, too much sun, especially where it is very hot, can also be a problem. Look for locations that have filtered light or shade in the hottest part of the afternoon, or erect a shade cloth or plant a bushy shrub to provide a little needed shade.

Plants also need air to thrive. Good air circulation brings the leaves in contact with fresh air, but high winds will quickly dry out plants. Locate your garden beds in a sheltered area or plant a hedge or other windbreak to protect them. A trellis thickly planted with peas and beans can protect more delicate plants below.

## Local Climate

How the sun falls in your growing area determines your own personal microclimate, while your geographic location determines the macroclimate. Coastal areas are always cooler than inland areas in the summer and warmer in the winter. Northern states have longer summer days, but that means longer winter nights, too. The length and warmth of sunny days depends on the seasons and the latitude. Median temperature, first and last frost dates, and length of day all influence what you can grow.

Last frost date: The date when all danger of frost has passed in the spring.

First frost date: The date when frost is expected to arrive in the fall.

There are maps online and in gardening books that divide the United States into basic growing regions with similar frost dates. Consult regional almanacs and your local Cooperative Extension office about the best times to get seeds or plants into the ground; local farmers, neighborhood gardeners, and nearby nurseries are also useful resources.

Planting too early may result in plants freezing or rotting in the ground while waiting for the weather to get warm enough for them to grow; planting too late may result in cool weather crops bolting under the hot sun or failing to reach maturity before cold weather arrives.

Timing influences flavor as well. Melons planted in time to fully ripen in the warm sun are superior to those that ripen as the days recede into autumn. Seed packets and catalogs will tell you how long it takes for a plant to reach maturity. From there, you can decide if seedlings need to be started indoors, or if there is time to sow directly into the garden. But you are not limited to planting only between the two frost dates. Many plants will survive the rigors of frost and snow and taste better for it.

## Cold-Weather Gardening

Many of us think of gardening as an exclusively summertime pursuit, but there is no reason not to take advantage of as much of the growing season as possible. In fact, with a few simple aids (see pages 382–384) it is possible to start many crops quite early in the spring and to grow many more late into the winter.

My friend farmer-gastronome Eliot Coleman is a master of cold-weather gardening in his home state of Maine. He has shared his knowledge in several invaluable books.

Cold weather is not an enemy to all garden vegetables. Cabbage, kale, carrots, endive, and turnips all taste better when they are harvested after a touch of frost. Radicchio becomes redder, and all the other chicories become tenderer and sweeter as the days turn colder. And many cool weather plants can be grown in both early spring and late summer for two full seasons of harvests. Plant in the early springtime before the frost has gone, so the plants have a chance to mature before the heat arrives. Plant again late in summer, so they will mature when the days are shortening and the weather is cooling down. Weeds and pests are less numerous during this time of year, too.

Use the local frost dates as guideposts for when to plant. Again, seed catalogs and seed packets list the number of days required for plants to reach maturity. If planting seedlings, subtract three weeks from the time required. If you live where the winters are mild, many plants will grow all winter long. Plant a few succession sowings of turnips, carrots, chicories, and kale and enjoy the fresh produce all through the winter. Research the temperature requirements for seed germination.

In zones where the weather is cold, with temperatures as low as −10°F, you can experiment with storing root vegetables in the ground. Parsnips are well suited to this treatment and taste much better after a couple of frosts (see page 82). Carrots, celeriac, beets, and turnips can all be left in the ground this way.

## Succession Planting

Succession planting is a great way to put timing to work and take advantage of your space. Once a crop is finished, fill the empty spot in the garden with seedlings you have grown or purchased. For example, start in early spring with plantings of peas, lettuce, and broccoli; replace these with beans, tomatoes, and squash; and then follow up with beets, carrots, and chicories. For inspiration, look at the many succession-planting guides posted online. Keep crop rotation guidelines in mind as you plan each planting.

## Crop Rotation

Families of plants tend to share the same needs. There are a few basic plant families in the garden: brassicas, nightshades (solanum), alliums, umbellifers, legumes, and cucurbits plus a few other miscellaneous ones. Don't worry; this doesn't mean you have to learn the Latin name of every plant, just the Latin name of the family it belongs to. Some families are obvious, as in the case of melons and squash (they look a lot alike as they grow), but others are less so, as with tomatoes (*Solanum lycospersicum*) and potatoes (*Solanum tuberosum*). If you are unsure, look at the seed packet, catalog, or plant tag and the Latin name will be there. The first part of the name indicates its family. Growing the same plant, or type of plant, continually in the same place will deplete the soil of specific nutrients and create a nutritional imbalance.

It is wise to rotate, or move, varieties and families of plants in the garden so they are not grown in the same spot every year. This will keep the soil in better balance and the plants healthier. Also, pests partial to the plant will be confused—many bugs won't travel very far at all and are fairly easily deterred if they must go and look for their plants of choice each year.

A four-crop rotation is ideal, but a two-crop is still a good goal. The four families that benefit the most from rotation are: legumes, brassicas, solanums, and cucurbits. This is a good order of rotation to follow as well. If your garden is small enough that you are not planting melons or squash, lump the cucumbers with the solanums and make the fourth family be a combination of leafy greens (lettuce, chard, chicories), the alliums, carrots, and beets. Otherwise these last four can be planted among the beds (and along the sides, etc.) and rotated along with their companions. Use your garden journal to keep track of the rotations.

# Raised Beds

Free-form raised beds give a natural look to the garden and can be made to follow any line or shape. Raised beds can also be enclosed in a frame to make them higher, for both ease of working and to keep plants clear of any unhealthy (contaminated) soil below. The bed construction can range from an elaborate wood frame surrounded by a bench around the top for sitting while gardening, to a simple wood frame or supporting edge of stacked bricks, chunks of broken concrete, or other recycled materials. Whatever materials you use, make sure that they are free of toxic chemicals. Only use food-quality plastics, and don't use railroad ties or wood that has been pressure-treated. Redwood and cedar are more expensive wood choices but will not rot as quickly as other types of wood.

A typical raised bed is no more than four feet wide (to keep the center of the bed easily accessible) and three to eight feet long. The height can vary from four inches to four feet. To make a basic bed in an existing garden, mark off the perimeter of the plot and dig up the surrounding paths a few inches deep, depositing the soil to the surface of the plot. Break up the bigger clods of soil and cover with a two-inch layer of compost. If the paths around the bed are bare, mulch them with a thick layer of wood chips or straw to keep down the weeds. If the soil is particularly bad, follow the instructions for establishing a new bed (see below).

Taller beds may be filled with organic compost or a mix of good loamy soil and compost that won't compact and that has plenty of organic matter and good drainage and water retention. For filling small beds, bagged soil is fine. For larger beds, it is worthwhile to locate a local soil dealer who sells bulk quantities for pick up or delivery. It takes about a quarter of a cubic yard to fill a twelve-inch-deep bed that measures four by eight feet.

# Starting a Bed from Scratch

If you do not yet have an established bed, or would like to start another one, here is an easy recipe for reclaiming a patch of lawn or an overgrown, weedy plot for a garden. Count on a minimum of four months for the whole process. In the fall, try to start 6 weeks before the first frost comes so that the cover crop plants can establish themselves.

Stamp down (or cut down) any tall weeds or grass as flat as possible. If the plot is dry, soak it well with:

**Water**

Let sit for a few hours. Cover the plot with:

**A thin layer of compost**

Over the top of the compost, lay down:

**A 4- to 6-inch layer of newspaper (no colored or glossy paper), or plain corrugated cardboard**

Overlap the edges so no light will shine through. This helps eradicate the weeds or grass. Wet the paper and cover with:

**3 to 4 inches of compost**

Tamp down the bed. Broadcast over the compost:

**Cover crop seeds (see page 369)**

Water well and mulch with a light layer of:

**Straw**

When spring arrives, cut down the cover crop plants. Leave them for mulch or dig them lightly into the soil and wait 2 to 3 weeks before planting to allow the plants to decompose (green plants tie up soil nutrients as they break down).

VARIATIONS

• If you missed the fall deadline for the cover crop, or if the plants don't do well, spread a thicker layer of straw mulch.

• To increase the nutrients in the soil, sprinkle the first thin layer of compost with rock dust and oyster-shell meal (see page 368).

• If you have access to good-quality composted horse or cow manure from healthy well-fed animals spread 2 inches on the wet paper and cover with only 2 to 3 inches of compost.

• For an established plot that is not performing as well as you'd like, proceed as above, but skip the newspaper (unless you have lots of weeds).

• If you need to plant right away, put the cut cover crop plants in the compost bin.

## Sheet Mulching

An alternative to using mature compost to create a new garden bed is to spread layers of uncomposted organic materials over the newspaper or cardboard to decompose over time. This is also referred to as sheet composting. Spread alternating layers of green and brown materials, just as though building a compost pile (see page 364), moistening each layer as needed. Build to a height of at least 6 and up to 10 inches to inhibit the weeds below. Skip sowing the cover crop

and finish with a final layer of straw or dried leaves for mulch. The optimum time to do this is in the fall, giving the materials a full season to break down and decompose.

NOTES

• Starting a garden bed or filling containers may require more compost than you have on hand. Keep building your compost pile for the future, and in the meantime, look for a source of good-quality organic compost.

• Do not buy compost with sewage sludge or grass clippings that might have been treated with herbicide (stick to organic).

• Good compost is dark brown and even textured, with a good earthy aroma. It should contain a broad spectrum of whole ingredients such as food scraps, manure, straw, sawdust, and rice hulls. Quality compost is well worth the extra expense. The success of your garden depends on it.

## Preparing to Plant

Preparing the soil is the first step of sowing seed. I recommend aerating and spreading organic matter and minerals on the surface of the soil rather than digging and deep tilling. The soil's structure and living ecosystem are easily damaged or even destroyed by the disturbance of deep repeated digging. In nature, the land is rarely if ever disturbed and plants flourish. I have learned from my farming friends that the best gardening practices come from observing nature and following her example.

The best time to work the soil is when it is moist. First, remove all the plant matter from the previous crop. (Seasonal cover crop roots can be left in place.) Send it to the compost pile to recycle the minerals and nutrients it has taken from the soil. Using a pronged cultivator, rake out all the stones or sticks and break up clumps and clods of soil. Use your hands to smooth and tamp the surface. The bed is ready to plant.

NOTES

• If the soil is still quite wet or soggy, wait until it dries before getting started. Squeeze some soil in your hand to see how wet it is. If it balls up tight and firm, it is too wet.

• If the soil is dry and powdery, give the bed a long, slow soaking and let it sit for a few hours or overnight to allow the water to be absorbed.

• If the soil is compacted and hard, lighten and aerate it with a long-handled digging fork or what is known as a broadfork (a two-handled U-shaped garden fork used to aerate and loosen soil). Push down the fork into the soil and rock it back and forth a bit to open the soil. Continue the process over the whole bed. (This is an annual job at most.)

• If your garden bed is quite large, use a garden rake or a long-handled pronged cultivator to remove the detritus and break up clumped soil. Use the back of the rake to smooth the surface and the front to tamp it down.

• If you are not planting right away (if winter is coming or you are leaving for a while), plant a cover crop, or spread a layer of mature or semifinished compost, and top with straw or dry leaves to mulch. It is important to protect the fertility of the soil and continue building it up, especially when a bed is lying fallow.

# Growing Vertically

Growing vining plants on poles or trellises saves space in the garden, and keeps vegetables clean and healthy and off the ground. It provides more exposure to the sun for quicker, more even ripening, and it makes the harvest easier to reach and pick. Tall spires of blooming beans and leaf-covered trellises of peas and cucumbers add pleasing visual variety, too. There are many edibles that can be grown upright: peas and beans, cucumbers, small squash and melons, and tomatoes.

Set up poles or trellises when the seeds or seedlings are planted. Supports can be as simple or elaborate as you choose; many can be made from recycled materials. Portable structures are especially practical because they can be moved around the garden for crop rotations and put away when not in use.

Peas, cucumbers, and small varieties of melons and squash all grow well on trellises and small tomato cages. Wooden or bamboo frames can be fashioned and strung with vertical and horizontal lengths of twine every eight inches or so, or prunings of hedges and trees can be shoved in the ground, weaving and entwining their twiggy branches. When trellising melons and squash, choose varieties that produce smaller fruit. Hammocks made with squares of soft, breathable material can be tied to the trellis to support the fruit. Tie the hammocks in place when the squashes or melons are about four inches in diameter.

Indeterminate tomatoes grow very tall and need good support to keep them from trailing over the ground. There are a variety of ways to keep them supported. Tie them to sturdy stakes or make or buy tall (six- to eight-feet) wire cages built from sturdy concrete reinforcement netting with large, four-inch holes.

## Pole Bean or Snap Pea Tepee

Pole beans and sugar snap peas grow quite tall and are heavy when filled with ripening beans and peas. A tall tepee made of bamboo poles is a good way to support them.

Plant three to six 8-foot bamboo poles six to eight inches deep in a circle about three to five feet around. Lash the polls together at the top. You can make a separation between two of the poles to create an entrance to a shady hideaway for kids. Plant a few seeds or seedlings around each pole, and train, or loosely tie, the young plants up the poles. Once established, they will climb up by themselves. Cut the ends of the vines when they reach the top for a tidier look, or let them tumble over and down, as they will.

## Extending the Seasons

Season extension starts with seed catalogs. Many varieties of fruits and vegetables have been bred to withstand both extremes of hot and cold weather. Breeding for hardiness has been going on for millennia and continues today. Push the boundaries of your growing season with varieties bred for climatic limits. When you grow a variety that you really like, try saving seed (see page 402) from the plants that grew and tasted the best to plant again the following year. This will be seed that is especially well suited to your local microclimate.

## Mulch

Mulch is a great help in keeping soil and plants protected from the extremes of hot and cold weather. The best mulch is dry organic matter: dried grass clippings, old leaves, straw, and mature, well-rotted compost. Spread mulch thickly around the base of plants and it will retard water evaporation, suppress the germination of weed seeds, and keep the soil temperature static. Organic mulch has the extra bonus of providing nutrients to the soil as it decomposes. (Soil should be weeded and watered before mulch is applied. Leave a couple of inches around the stems of the plants, and add more as it settles and breaks down.)

## Row Covers

Row covers and shade cloth can be used to temper hot and cold. They can be draped directly over plants or installed over hoops, creating a low tunnel and providing the plants with a protected environment. These coverings also protect plants from pests, but pollinators will not be able to enter, either, so they have to be opened when the plants are flowering. In zones with sporadic cold spells, burlap sacks can be laid over beds to protect them. It is marvelous to pull back the cloth and find a healthy bed of chicories or lettuce waiting to be harvested.

*Sungold cherry tomatoes climbing a trellis on a sunny wall*

## Cold Frames

A cold frame is a great addition to a small garden. It is essentially a bottomless box with a clear top that can be opened. By trapping the sun's heat, a cold frame makes early seed propagation possible, facilitates the hardening off of seedlings, and provides protection for plants in cold weather. A cold frame can also be used as a greenhouse in the summer to grow plants that might not otherwise grow in your zone.

Cold frames can be purchased ready-made or they can be constructed out of new or recycled materials. Many ingenious designs can be found on the Internet. Be sure to use nontoxic materials; otherwise toxins may leach into the soil and into the plants.

For best results, the clear top of a cold frame should be facing south. Just a little sunshine can make a cold frame very hot, even in the dead of winter, so the internal temperature needs to be monitored and the lid propped open during the day and closed at night. Solar-powered automatic vent openers are available that are reasonably priced and easy to install.

## Growing Vegetables and Fruits in Containers

Freshly picked, garden-ripe fruits and vegetables are not just for those who have a large plot of land to dig in. With a little care, most any fruit or vegetable can be grown in a container. Make (see page 372) or purchase good-quality potting soil to grow your plants in. Container plants need a growing medium that supplies lots of organic matter, nutrients, and lofty material that will supply good drainage, water retention, and air circulation for the roots.

Sunshine is a necessity and it is the one ingredient of gardening that cannot be

made—it has to be in place. A great advantage of containers is that they are portable; small containers are easily moved, and larger ones can be put on wheels to follow the sun through the seasons if need be. Keep in mind that the roots of container plants are not underground and the soil heats easily; the roots suffer when they get too warm. As a result, container plants frequently need less sun than ones in the ground. Look after your plants and adjust their sun exposure if they look like they are shriveling or burning. A larger sun-loving plant or an adjustable screen can create shade. In very hot climates and especially sunny locations, a container can be placed into another larger pot, and the space between the two filled with insulation (newspaper, for example) to keep the soil cooler.

Container plants need lots of water. There are a number of reasons for this. First, the pot confines the roots of the plant—there is nowhere else for them to grow in search of water. Second, sun and wind quickly dry the soil in a pot through evaporation and transpiration. And last, the drainage hole in the pot that keeps the plant from drowning also allows the water to run right through the pot. Vegetables grow quickly, and in order to produce a large harvest they need consistent water. If the soil is allowed to dry out, the plant will go into shock and won't recover easily—nor will the ecosystem of soil flora and fauna that feeds the plant. Containers need to be watered frequently, up to twice a day in hot dry weather. It is a wise idea to have a water source near where your containers are set up, or watering may become an onerous chore. An automatic drip irrigation system makes watering easier and more consistent. It will need to be monitored and adjusted as the weather changes. Make sure that the plants don't dry out and that the soil doesn't get soggy.

Nutrients are stripped from the soil as the water drains away, which is why potting soil needs to be rich in nutrients. For additional nutrition, container plants should be watered with compost tea (see page 397) every two weeks and the leaves sprayed.

Air circulation is important for plant health, but container plants are quite susceptible to being dried out by the wind. If necessary, set up some kind of a barrier or windbreak for them, with air holes in it so that there is still some air circulation. And finally, when selecting your plants, choose smaller varieties such as cherry tomatoes, mini-cucumbers, small squash, and so on, which are all easier to grow in containers than their larger cousins.

## Containers

First and foremost, the container you choose needs to supply proper drainage. Size is another important consideration: vegetables and fruits need a good amount of soil and water to support rapid growth and high productivity. Choose a container that is deep enough and wide enough to accommodate the root system of the mature plant. Containers can be made of terra-cotta, glazed ceramic pottery, wood, plastic, metal, or fiberglass. Recycling and reusing containers for your garden is a great idea both for the environment and the budget.

These containers can be quite creative and beautiful, but please remember that you will be eating what you grow, so do not use toxic materials.

If you are planning on growing a few plants, consider planting them together in a larger pot as opposed to singly in a few pots. Small pots dry out much more quickly than a large pot that holds more soil. Group large, heavy feeders, cucumbers and tomatoes, for example, with smaller, less hungry plants, such as lettuce and basil. Herbs, most of which have similar sun and water requirements, can be packed together for a gorgeous and efficient effect.

Large containers, if not on wheels, are much less portable (if movable at all), so be sure to research the amount of sunlight in the area where you are planning to place them.

CONTAINER CHECKLIST

• There must be a hole somewhere at the bottom of the pot for the water to exit or else the plant will drown in the soggy soil.

• Most plants need soil that is a minimum of eight to nine inches deep, and some heavy feeders such as tomatoes and cucumbers, need even more depth to flourish. Of course, there are a few exceptions to this rule, notably lettuce, which can get by in soil with a depth of only four inches.

• Don't use containers made from toxic materials. Avoid old wooden containers that may have been painted with lead-based paint, and don't use plastics that have been used for non-food-grade products or that

have PVCs in them. Look for the small recycling triangle with a number on the base of the pot (use only numbers 1, 2, 4, and 5).

• Large containers dry out more slowly than small ones.

• Many plastic containers are aesthetically challenged. Grass matting, bamboo blinds, and other natural material can be wrapped around plastic buckets and other less attractive containers to improve their looks.

## Self-Watering Containers

Many container gardeners are starting to use self-watering containers (sometimes called self-irrigating containers). These are a double container system in which one container holds a reservoir of water that is connected via a perforated tube or other vehicle to another container that holds the soil. The soil can wick the water from the reservoir as needed to maintain a consistently moist, but not overly wet, environment. Since there is no water runoff, nutrients stay in place in the soil.

Water still has to be supplied to the plants. Large, quick-growing plants may need water added to their containers daily in hot, dry weather, while smaller, slower growing plants may need only weekly attention. There are several online sites offering self-watering containers for sale and providing instructions on how to construct your own. These sites are frequently updated with tips and new ideas.

# Seeds, Seedlings, and Healthy Plants

THERE ARE TWO WAYS to introduce annual vegetables and fruits into the garden: direct sowing and transplanting seedlings. Direct sowing is the act of planting a seed where it is expected to germinate and grow. Seedlings, started at home or purchased from a nursery, are small plants grown separately and transplanted to their place in the garden. Each has its advantages. Seeds offer the excitement of seeing a plant come to life and poke its head above the soil. Seedlings provide the immediate gratification of living plants growing in your garden soil. With a good start, you can nurture healthy plants to grow to their full potential.

## Seed Catalogs

Growing plants from seed gives an enormous amount of choice. There are many wonderful seed houses across the nation. A local supplier should list seeds that will do particularly well in your growing area. There is a list of some of my favorite seed catalogs on pages 414–415. Seed catalogs give a basic description of the plant, and many list the number of days it takes for the plant to grow to maturity. Some will give in-depth sowing and growing information. I especially like catalogs that discuss the flavor of different varieties and give anecdotes of how the plants did in trial gardens. All reputable catalogs have gardens and gardeners testing their plants annually. Many varieties have been bred to grow in specific climates and seasons: hot-weather lettuce, frost-tolerant kale, short-day onions, and more. Read about the seeds before purchasing to make sure they will do well in your local climate.

## Open-Pollinated, Heirloom, and Hybrid Seeds

Choosing open-pollinated seeds helps increase the biodiversity of our food system. Genetic diversity is shrinking rapidly and diversity is important for flavor and plant health. The more varieties of plants there are, the less likely they are to succumb to a single disease.

Open-pollinated (OP) seeds: These are seeds from a plant bred naturally (by bees, self-pollination, or the wind). The plant produced from the seed will mature and create more seed that will be stable and viable and, when planted, will grow another plant very like its parents.

Heirloom seeds: These are seeds of plant varieties that have been grown for many generations and that are revered for their flavor and vigor. All heirloom seeds are open-pollinated.

Hybrid (F1) seeds: Hybrid seeds are the result of cross-breeding two parent plants that have been very specifically bred for superior traits of growth and production. The resulting seed takes on and surpasses the parental traits. This is called hybrid vigor. Most seed from hybrid plants is not worth saving and planting since it is either sterile or unstable and will not produce a plant identical to its parent.

## Direct Sowing

Planting seeds where they are meant to grow is the easiest way to start a garden. For root vegetables it is the best way, because their sensitive long central root makes them difficult to transplant. Before starting, read the seed packet to learn what the seeds require. Be sure the soil is well prepared; as seeds start to grow, they need a loose, easily crumbled (or friable) soil to push their tiny roots and sprouts through.

Sprinkle over the block or area where the seeds will be planted:

**A 1-inch layer of compost (more if the soil is poor quality)**

Consult the directions on the seed packet and make drills or holes to the correct depth, if necessary.

Sow:

**Seeds**

Cover and tamp the compost down over the seeds and water well with a gentle spray. Keep the soil consistently moist until germination.

NOTES

⬩ In general, plant seeds as deep as they are wide. Tiny seeds will need almost no soil to cover them, while larger seeds may need to be buried under as much as an inch of soil.

⬩ Consult the seed packet for how far apart to plant the seeds. Raised beds make it possible to plant in small blocks spaced closer together than the packets may recommend.

⬩ Sowing the seeds in staggered rows makes it possible to plant more in a small space. Each row of plants is offset, or triangulated, from the other. The plants will grow together and help retain moisture and suppress weeds.

⬩ Once the seeds have started to emerge, keep an eye out for pests. This is when the plants are most vulnerable and they can disappear overnight. A routine nightly survey with a flashlight will help you locate nocturnal slugs and snails for removal.

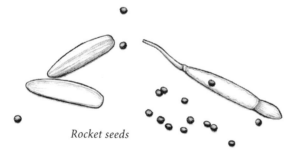

*Rocket seeds*

# Thinning

It is a wise practice when direct seeding to sow more seeds than is needed, to make up for germination failure and other mishaps. This often results in a surplus of plants that need to be thinned. Painful as it may be, it is actually beneficial to the overall crop to remove a few plants and make room for the remaining ones to thrive. Refer to the seed directions for the suggested space between plants. (When planting in blocks, the plants can be thinned less than the seed packet suggests, leaving the plants spaced equally apart in all directions.)

Cut or pinch off the plants at the soil surface to avoid disturbing the roots of neighboring plants. Root vegetables can be pulled out because their roots do not spread and get entangled with the roots of their neighbors. Pull them strategically, thinning plants at intervals to allow the roots left behind to grow and expand. Picture the size of the carrot or beet you want at harvest and leave that much space around the plants. Tiny beets, radishes, and turnips are fabulous in salads; try them with their leaves still attached.

# Broadcasting Seed

Broadcasting is the process of scattering seed evenly over tilled soil. It is one of the oldest ways to sow seed. Grain fields were sown this way for centuries. Broadcasting can be used when a dense bed of plants is wanted for a cover crop or a bed of cutting lettuce or other quick-growing salad greens and herbs. Lettuce seed can be sown in the ground or in a container. Carrots, radishes, and small turnips can be sown the same way, but some thinning will be necessary as the plants grow.

Pour into the palm of your hand:

**Seeds**

Take pinches of seed with the other hand and sprinkle the seed evenly and lightly over the whole surface of the prepared bed, just as you would season a dish with salt, holding your sprinkling hand about a foot above the surface. The goal is to have the seeds fall about ½ to ¼ inch apart. Cover the sown area with:

**A sparse layer of fine compost or soil, no more than ⅛ inch deep (this is a perfect use for extra potting soil)**

Lightly tamp down the soil to make it firm. Water with a gentle sprinkle so as not to wash away the soil or dislodge the seeds. Keep the bed evenly moist but not soggy until the seeds have germinated, about 7 to 10 days.

NOTES

⬩ To help ward off digging cats and hungry birds, cover the freshly seeded bed with bird netting, twiggy branches, or chicken wire.

⬩ Sow seeds as individual varieties or in a mix.

⬩ One gram of mixed lettuce seed is sufficient to plant an area about 2 feet square—plenty of lettuce to harvest cut-and-come-again style for a family of 3 or 4.

⬩ For a constant supply of salad greens, sow seed in a new location or container every 3 to 5 weeks throughout the year.

⬩ Lettuce, radishes, rocket, and other quick-growing crops can be broadcast among other, slower-growing crops.

## Seedlings

Sprouted seedlings transplanted into the garden have a head start and are better equipped for survival than those grown from seed sown in the ground. (Where I garden, a snail can take down a whole crop of tiny sprouts in one night.) They also give spring planting a jump-start, allowing you to grow plants that might not otherwise have enough time to grow to maturity (tomatoes and peppers, for example) and making succession plantings a smooth process.

I direct sow seeds for lettuces and herbs, but I also buy seedlings at the farmers' market. I am lucky to have Flatland Farms from Sebastopol at my market. Dan Lehrer combs the world for interesting and flavorful seeds. He mixes his own potting soil, tends his plants organically, and brings them to market when they are vibrant and healthy, at just the right time when I know they will thrive when planted in my garden. Look for locally grown organic seedlings at your farmers' market and local nursery; if they don't have organic seedlings, encourage the nursery to bring them in.

## Starting Seedlings

Seedlings are easily started at home, or they can be purchased from farmers' markets or local nurseries. There are advantages to growing your own seedlings: it is less expensive, you can choose from a greater selection of varieties, and, perhaps best of all, sprouting your own offers you the deep enjoyment of watching the magic of seeds coming to life.

Before starting, read the seed packet to learn what's required. Calculate the appropriate timing for starting the seedlings using your local frost date information and the information on the seed packet.
Gather:

> **Small pots or growing cells with drain holes**

Fill the pots with:

> **Good-quality organic potting soil that contains compost or other organic matter, homemade (see page 372) or store-bought**

Tap the containers lightly to level, but don't press the soil down. Place on the surface:

> **2 (at most 3) seeds per pot**

Cover with a small amount of soil, or tuck in the seeds below the surface. (The depth of planting depends on what you are sowing.) Don't tamp down the soil. Label your containers with the variety and date right away so you don't forget what you have planted.

Water well with a fine spray or a watering can with small holes for a gentle shower. A large stream of water can dislodge the seeds. Place the pots in a warm sunny spot indoors or outdoors in a cold frame or greenhouse. Keep moist until germination.

The first two leaves to appear are called the cotyledons; then come the true leaves. Once the true leaves are well established, thin out the seedlings in each cell, leaving only the largest, healthiest plant. Snip off the plants with sharp scissors at the level of the soil to avoid disturbing the tender roots.

Transplant into the ground or a larger pot after the second set of true leaves has emerged. It is important to move the seedlings out of the little pots before their roots become overly crowded and tangled, or root-bound. Once they are root-bound, seedlings have a much harder time growing. Before seedlings can go to the garden, they need to be acclimated to the outdoors (or "hardened off") or they may die from the shock of direct sun and cold. Take them outside during the day for a few hours, avoiding full, hot sun at first. Extend the hours outside and in the sun each day, and after a week, leave them out overnight. Then the seedlings are ready to be tucked into their new home.

NOTES
• Recycle seedling pots from a nursery or a friend; wash them with soap and a bit of vinegar before using. You can make your own biodegradable seed cells from toilet paper rolls (great for long roots) or from sheets of newspaper. (Wrap a sheet of newspaper around a jar and tape it; fold the bottom under, then remove the jar.)

⬩ Plain dirt, even very fertile soil from the garden, will not work for starting seedlings. It will quickly compact and suffocate the tender shoots. Use potting soil, a mix of natural components that supply the aeration, drainage, nutrition, and moisture retention that seeds need to germinate and grow.

⬩ Timing is important when starting seeds because you want the plants to be ready to be moved outside when favorable weather has arrived (although frost dates are less predictable than they once were). This date will vary for each type of seedling, because different plants need different amounts of indoor growing time and have different outside temperature needs. Do not be tempted to start sooner than recommended; plants set out too early or grown for too long in a small container will not thrive. Seed catalogs and seed packets will provide this information.

⬩ Consistent moisture is the key to germination. Potting soil looks dark when moist; if it looks light it has dried out and needs water.

⬩ Germination will take anywhere from 5 days to 2 weeks; consult the seed packet for more precise information.

⬩ Thinning your brand-new seedlings may seem harsh, but there needs to be enough room for a single robust seedling that will thrive when it is transplanted.

⬩ Tomatoes and peppers need to grow for many weeks, developing several sets of leaves, before they are planted outdoors. Start these seeds in larger, 4-inch containers, or transfer them into larger containers when they have their first 2 sets of true leaves.

⬩ Radishes and carrots grow best when seeded directly.

VARIATIONS

⬩ Instead of thinning tiny seedlings, transplant them. Fill small or medium pots with moist potting soil and make a large hole in the soil with your finger, a dibble, or a pencil. Hold on to the leaves of the plant while loosening the soil with the dibble or pencil, and pull out the seedling, trying to retain as much of the root system as possible. Carefully guide the roots into the hole made in the soil, gently tamp down the soil down around the plant. Label the pot and water well.

⬩ Start seedlings outdoors in an easily protected nursery zone in a corner of the garden or in a cold frame. Sow them far enough apart that they are easily dug up. When they are large enough to transplant, gently dig them out and move them to their new home.

## Transplanting Seedlings

The roots are the most sensitive part of the plant. When transplanting, try to avoid disturbing or handling the roots and keep the root ball and its soil as intact as possible.

Be sure the garden bed is well prepared. Dig a hole a bit bigger around than the pot and at least as deep. Add:

**A handful of compost or worm castings**
Squeeze the pot to loosen the soil, grasp the plant by its leaves, and carefully remove it from the pot. Gently place the plant in the hole. Fill in the hole with soil, firm the soil around the plant, and water thoroughly.

NOTES

⬩ When purchasing seedlings, select sturdy, healthy specimens that are not root-bound.

Check the bottom of the pots: any roots growing out of the drainage holes are a sign of overgrowth.

✦ Don't take the plants out of biodegradable toilet paper or newspaper pots. Instead, just peel back the cardboard or the bottom layers of newspaper, and put pot and plant directly into the hole.

✦ To cover all your bases when transplanting homegrown seedlings, plant a few seeds at the same time you plant out the small plants. Thin to the strongest plants.

## Self-Sowing Plants and Volunteers

As you garden you will begin to notice the gifts that arrive on their own, popping up unheralded—parsley plants, a patch of rocket, a snaking watermelon vine, a few kale plants, or a scattering of borage. I love the spontaneity these volunteer plants offer and I have come to depend on some of them reappearing; especially rocket, mâche, chervil, parsley, and other herbs that keep certain corners of my garden pretty and are always ready to pick for the kitchen.

Self-seeding requires that the plants run to flower and ripen seeds before they are pulled up. The flowers are quite delicious and attract beneficial insects and other pollinators to the garden. The seedpods will open when they are mature and naturally scatter seeds about. If you need the space where the plants are growing, move a plant or two to another spot to mature and go to seed.

If you are only saving one plant to go to seed, choose the finest example available from among the ones you have. This will be the beginning of your own selective breeding project for the local microclimate of your garden—the plants that thrive will continue to do so. Once the seedpods are mature and dry, break them open in place or sprinkle them where you would like the plants to grow. Once sprouted, the seedlings can be left to grow where they are or transplanted to other parts of the garden. If they come up densely, thin them periodically and use the thinnings in the kitchen.

Volunteers can be a surprise from the compost pile—sprouting from seeds that survived the heat of decomposition. Melons, tomatoes, squash, and tomatillos are the ones I see the most. If you have the room and the growing time—let them mature to find out what they have to offer.

*Mâche and chervil volunteers*

# Water

Water is a necessity of life, and of course that includes plant life. Edible plants in general require a generous amount of water—juicy tomatoes, crisp lettuce, and sweet watermelon are up to 90 percent water. Plants access water through their roots. It travels up the plant and exits through the leaves in exchange for carbon dioxide in a process called transpiration. Water facilitates the transfer of nutrients from the soil to the plant. It is also the catalyst for germination in seeds. Without water, plants begin to wilt and go into shock; when watered again, they begin to race to maturity and the making of seeds. Additionally, water-stressed plants are targets for pests and pathogens. On the other hand, too much water will make plants weak, with shallow roots, or even cause them to suffocate in soggy soil.

Plants depend on their immediate environment for water. The amount of water available to a plant depends on rainfall, irrigation, and soil type. Add lots of organic matter to the soil in the form of compost and leaf mold to maximize its water retention and drainage abilities. Locate your garden near a water source so that it is easy to water.

The stage of life that the plant is in will influence its water needs. When seeds are first sown, or seedlings are transplanted, plenty of water is needed for the plants to germinate and for the tiny roots to grow. The soil should be moist but not soggy. This may require watering two or more times a day in hot and windy weather. The color of the soil can tell you when to water. Moist soil is a deeper brown, dry soil is light brown.

Once plants are established, water deeply to encourage maximum root growth. A strong, deep root system makes a greater range of nutrients available to the plant, and gives the plant better support and the ability to adapt to changing weather conditions. To check how deep the water is going, dig a small hole with a trowel after watering. This will give you an idea of how much water needs to be applied to reach one foot down. Allow the soil to drain and dry to a depth of one inch before watering again. To monitor soil moisture between waterings, poke a finger into the first inch or more of the soil next to the plant. If moist, then there is no need for water; if dry, it is time to water. Weather affects the need to water, too. Hot, sunny days cause water to evaporate and transpire much more quickly than cool, foggy ones.

NOTES

♦ Choose the cooler times of day to water—morning and early evening. Try to water directly onto the soil and not onto the leaves. Damp leaves are prone to disease.

♦ To conserve water, use a gentle spray or trickle at the base of plants. The water will soak into the soil, instead of running off.

♦ Putting mulch around plants keeps the soil cool over the roots and inhibits evaporation. Using a natural mulch like straw, leaves, or grass clippings adds to the fertility of the soil while conserving water.

♦ Drip irrigation on a timer is a way to water consistently and conserve water. Keep track through the days and seasons and adjust as needed. Set up a rainwater catchment system to water the garden for free.

## Growing Healthy Plants

The plants growing in your garden are direct indicators of their own health and the state of the soil. Watch as they emerge from seed and grow. Use your intuition to gauge their progress. Health is palpable, as is sickness. A healthy plant is strong, vibrant, symmetrical, and well-balanced in its growth. If a plant is drooping, growing crookedly, discolored, tough, or covered with bugs, it is not healthy. Give the plant a gentle tug; if it is loose, the roots are not growing well. A healthy root system will keep a plant firmly anchored in the soil. Check the soil for moisture. Look at the amount of sunlight the plant is getting. These observations will tell you what the plant's needs are: sun, water, or food.

## Plant Food Versus Fertilizers

Whenever I use the word *fertilizer* with Bob Cannard, he is quick to say he does not fertilize his crops; he feeds them. Organic amendments are whole foods made of compost, finely-ground minerals, sea plants, and herbivore manure. They supply the full spectrum of nutrients needed to support both the soil and plants: the nutrients added to the soil are made available to the plants through the activity of the microbes in the soil. Organic plant foods do not wash away readily or burn the plants, even if over-applied. They are both slow-acting and long-lasting and help build a self-sustaining fertility.

Most modern fertilizers are synthetic, man-made, concentrated solutions of water-soluble chemicals. Think of them as fast food for plants. They cause plants to grow quickly and, quite literally, get fat, with very little internal structure to provide strength and defense against disease—effects quite similar to the effects of fast food on us. Nor do quick-growing plants develop as much flavor. Furthermore, the chemicals are toxic and must be used with caution. Their overuse will literally burn plants and rapidly suppress beneficial soil life and also pollute the environment as they are washed away by rain and irrigation.

For the health of your plants, I strongly encourage you to choose organic methods to improve your soil and maintain its fertility. That is the best way to grow food with the most flavor. And remember, the basis of fertility is well-tended, healthy, living soil.

# Using Compost and Minerals as Plant Food

Growing plants need food. Not a lot and not all at once. As Bob would say, feed your plants many light meals, just as you would feed a child. The first "meal" is best applied after the small plants are established in the soil. When feeding growing plants, sprinkle a small amount of compost or minerals around each plant. Sprinkle them over the leaves and around the plant. No need to dig the amendments in; in fact, it is better not to. Earthworms and other soil creatures will do the work of mixing them into the soil.

The food is to replace what the plants are taking, or needing, from the soil's micro-community. A balance is what you are ultimately trying to achieve. Only apply plant foods as needed. The plants won't burn, but if, for example, you have an over abundance of nitrogen, your tomatoes will grow into beautiful leafy plants with few flowers and fewer fruits.

When using compost as a food for new plants, start with a small handful per plant. Or water, or spray, the plants with compost tea (see page 397). Less compost will be needed when planting in a bed that has just been used for peas or beans or any other leguminous plants that take nitrogen from the air and hold it in nodules at their roots. Watch the new plants: as they begin to leaf out they will tell you if they need more nutrition. Yellowing older leaves (cotyledons and lower leaves) and pale green growth signals a nitrogen deficiency, while a deep green color throughout the whole plant along with graceful growth shows good nutrition.

When applying mineral amendments to the garden, Bob mixes rock dust and oyster-shell meal together in equal parts. Once again, you do not need pounds of material. Sprinkle no more than one tablespoon of the mineral mixture over and around the young plants. Water well and the amendments will be directly available to the roots. Observe the plants as they grow over the next few weeks to decide if they need more. Different families of plants use these minerals in different quantities and will need more in varying rates. Observation is the best way to take note of their need.

# Feeding the Leaves

Foliar feeding is the process of applying a fine spray of diluted compost tea to the foliage of plants. The leaves absorb the nutrients directly; in fact, plants absorb trace minerals and some micronutrients more efficiently and quickly through their leaves than through their roots. The spray deters chewing insects, such as aphids and leaf borers, and some bacterial diseases as well. It is an effective immune system booster to supplement good soil practices.

Do not use chemical fertilizers as a foliar spray, as they can easily burn the plants and they contain none of the trace minerals and micronutrients that leaves can absorb.

A handheld plant mister works well for small jobs, and a regular garden sprayer for larger ones. Strain the tea before using so it does not plug up the sprayer. Spray all parts of the plants, including both sides of the leaves. The nutrients are absorbed through the stomata—the small openings, or pores, on the plants' surfaces. The best time for foliar feeding is in the late afternoon or early morning. Do not spray in the heat of the day: stomata open in cooler temperatures and close when it is hot and dry. Use any leftover tea to water the plants. Your lawn, trees, shrubs, perennial flowers, and houseplants will also benefit from foliar feeding.

# Compost Tea

Bob is constantly brewing compost tea to feed to his plants. The mixture is aerated to build up a large quantity of microbes in the solution. When ready, the liquid is strained and added directly to the irrigation lines to feed the growing plants. The solution is dense with microbes that bolster the existing community and nutrients in solution ready for absorption by plant roots.

Aerated compost tea is easy to make at home with a 45-liter-per-minute aquarium pump and air stones in a 5-gallon bucket. Only a small amount of compost is needed to inoculate a large amount of water. Once the tea is ready, dilute it to 1 part tea to 4 or 5 parts water. Use it to water plants right away, as the microcommunity will begin to diminish rapidly.

Different plants have different nutritional requirements, but a general recommendation for heavy feeders, such as cucumbers and other fruiting plants, is to feed as often as every two or three weeks after the first true leaves appear; for less needy plants, such as leafy greens, every four weeks may be enough.

If you don't have a pump, use only worm compost (see page 366) instead of regular compost and stir the solution often to help aerate it. The microbes need oxygen to survive, and as they multiply they will use up the existing air in the water.

Set up the pump with tubing and air stones. Fill a bucket with:

**4 gallons water**

If using tap water let it sit out for 24 hours or run the pump for 2 hours to allow the chlorine to evaporate; otherwise it will reduce the population of microorganisms living in the compost. Add:

**4 cups mature compost, or ¾ cup worm castings**

Put the air stones into the water and turn on the pump. Stir in:

**1 tablespoon unsulfured blackstrap molasses**

Steep for 2 days. Stir vigorously now and then to encourage the microorganisms to grow. Strain the tea and put it into a watering can or clean sprayer. Clean the airstones, tubing, and bucket right away. The tea may be used full strength or diluted to extend it throughout the garden. Use the tea within the hour; the microorganisms dissipate quickly. Put the strained castings or compost back on the compost pile or in the worm bin, or dig them into a container or your garden; they still have lots of good nutrients in them.

NOTES

⬥ Use fresh, moist worm castings and fully mature compost to get the greatest amount of active microbial life.

⬥ Compost tea should be sweet-smelling. If

your tea becomes unpleasant-smelling or stinky, don't use it. A bad smell indicates that unfriendly anaerobic bacteria have taken over friendly aerobic bacteria.

• Another nutrient-rich tea can be made from plants. Chop comfrey leaves and add to the bucket of water (about one-third to one-half full). Weigh them down with a rock or another similar weight. Fill with water and let steep 2 to 3 weeks. Keep covered. This will make a highly aromatic tea filled with nutrients, but without microorganisms, so it can be used over time. Dilute 1 part tea to 10 parts water. Nettles and sea kelp tea are made in the same manner.

## Cultivation

Cultivation is the act of breaking up the top of the soil and opening it up to air. Soil microbes need air to thrive; occasional cultivation gives them a breath of fresh air to keep them healthy and active. Use a pronged cultivator or other tool to lightly break up the surface of the soil in beds. Be gentle around the growing plants to avoid disturbing or harming their roots. Do this just before watering and watch the water absorb into the soil instead of running off. In fact, seeing water run off the surface of the soil is a good indicator of the need to cultivate.

## Weeding

Unwanted plants or weeds need to be removed or they will compete for sun, water, nutrients, and air. The best tools for weeding are a long-handled collinear hoe or a handheld swan-neck hoe or CobraHead tool. These tools are small enough to get between the crops in densely planted beds and slice off weeds at the soil's surface. Don't go deep enough to harm the crop's root system. Whenever possible, it is best to inhibit weeds from growing in the first place.

Here is a good weeding program to follow:

• Clear beds of all weeds before planting.
• Don't turn or till the soil. This can bring weed seeds to the surface of the soil, allowing them to germinate.
• Spread mulch around young plants to inhibit weed growth.
• Pull or remove all weeds when young, before they have established a deep root system.
• Plant densely. As the plants grow, their leaf cover acts as a living mulch.
• Interplant with quick-growing plants such as lettuce and radishes.
• Don't allow weeds to go to seed nearby.
• Don't put weeds that are blooming or have gone to seed in the compost pile.

# Harvesting Flavor

Anticipation is a large part of gardening—watching and waiting as the plants germinate, grow, flower, and set fruit. Then, suddenly, lettuce is big enough to cut, tomatoes begin to turn red, and shell beans get plump—and the time has finally come to harvest! Nothing tastes better than perfectly ripe produce straight from the garden. That is the sweet luxury enjoyed by everyone who grows some of their own food. The flavor is enhanced for the growers by the wonder and pride they feel as each fruit and vegetable is harvested. My connections to the land and the cycles of nature get deeper and deeper as I harvest, cook, and eat from my garden. And the quality of the ingredients is truly as good as it can get.

# Peak Harvest

Almost every fruit and vegetable has a prime moment when it tastes best and has the best texture—although some plants have more than one moment because they are delicious at different states of maturity (green beans and shell beans) or because different parts of the plant are eaten (squash blossoms and summer squash). Decide what tastes good as the plants begin to ripen and follow your own counsel. Maybe you feel like eating fried green tomatoes, or you would like your jalapeños red, not green. Don't hesitate to act on your curiosity. How does eggplant taste when it is really tiny? Which tastes better, a three-inch cucumber or a five-inch one? Don't ever feel you have to follow the harvest instructions on the seed packet; I almost always pick things much younger and smaller than the instructions recommend. It would be a shame to miss out on what could be your favorite way to eat your harvest.

There are many vegetables that taste better when they are young and tender—bright green and yellow summer squash, firm glossy eggplant, tiny haricots verts, and sweet juicy cucumbers, to name a few. These vegetables can go from perfect to overly mature in a matter of a day or two, turning bitter, tough, and seedy. Not only do the vegetables lose their fine flavor, their maturity causes the plant to think it is done with its phase of producing seed, and it will stop producing flowers and die. But if you continually harvest young and tender vegetables, the plant will keep flowering and setting fruit in hopes of reproducing, and your plants will yield more delicious vegetables for the kitchen over a longer period of time. Eventually, of course, the plant gets played out, or the season changes and production stops; but until then, it is best to harvest frequently and enjoy the vegetables at their best. To avoid being overwhelmed at harvest time, stagger your plantings of crops a few weeks apart so they mature over a period of time.

Most fruit—and some vegetables—taste much better when they are allowed to fully ripen and sweeten on the vine or tree. Sample and taste as they ripen—you will find the sweet spot. A perfectly ripe tomato or peach is incomparable, and shell beans allowed to reach their full color and plumpness are richer and creamier than any other kind. Peppers, winter squash, melons, stone fruit, and apples are other examples of produce that taste best when picked ripe.

For specifics on the harvest of fruit, see page 409.

# All the Parts of the Plant

As gardeners, we have access to the whole growing plant. Many times there are delicious parts not sold at market. Tender young broccoli and cauliflower leaves can be harvested as the plants are growing. The young leaves of garlic and onions may be snipped now and again to season a sauce or soup. Turnip and beet greens are wonderful. Don't throw them out when you harvest the roots; cook them just as you would other leafy greens. Cauliflower stems, pea tops, fava bean leaves, and sweet potato leaves are all delicious.

Most edible plants are not grown for their flowers, but they all produce them, and many are notable for their beauty and fragrance. Some are quite delicious as well. Herb blossoms are delightful scattered on salads, pastas, desserts, and even cocktails. Rocket bolts easily and its flowers make a beautiful sweet and spicy garnish. The blossoms of scarlet runner beans have an amazing sweet, beany flavor and are a sight to behold on a bowl of buttered beans. Squash blossoms are delightful stuffed or chopped and folded into frittatas, quesadillas, vegetable sautés, and soups.

Take a peek in ethnic markets. Maybe they are selling a part of a plant you are growing that you never knew you could eat—a flower, a seed, a leaf. I first learned about shelling beans when I went to Italy, I found out about baby lettuces in France, and I started cooking and eating pea tops after trying them at my favorite Chinese restaurant.

## Curing and Storing

Many fruits and vegetables must be canned, dried, or frozen to be stored for later consumption. But some produce can be stored in a dark cupboard or cool garage and eaten later. (Once thought of as old-fashioned, root cellars are becoming popular again; there are many plans online for building one at home.) Onions, garlic, shallots, winter squash, potatoes, and sweet potatoes are all vegetables that store well. A good indicator of their storage capabilities is that they are all sold unrefrigerated. They all have a thick, dry outer skin that helps slow moisture loss and degradation. To develop the skin, they are dried—or "cured," to use the gardening term. (But do note that not all onion varieties are good for storing; check before you get started.)

The curing process starts with a cessation of watering when the plants are mature, usually about two weeks before harvesting. Potatoes are left in the ground for an additional two weeks to toughen the skin. The alliums (as onions, garlic, and shallots are known) are harvested and air-dried at room temperature, which turns their outer layers into papery skins. Winter squash are air-dried for a few days after harvest to heal the stem and further harden the skin.

Be very gentle while harvesting vegetables intended for storage; any bruising or cuts make them susceptible to rot. Brush—don't wash—the dirt from the vegetables: water inhibits the drying process. A thin layer of (dry) soil increases storing potential, especially on potatoes. When the vegetables are cured and ready for storage, keep them in a cool, dark place that has good air circulation. Too moist an environment will cause the vegetables to rot, and very dry air will cause them to shrivel. Temperatures may range between 28°F and 50°F. For alliums, 40°F is optimal, but sweet potatoes and winter squash store better at 50°F. Air circulation is important to keep the stored vegetables healthy.

# Saving Seeds

It is astonishing how many seeds there are in the pods from a single plant: often more than in a seed packet. Many are easy to save, to plant again for another crop. First, do a little research to be sure that the seed you are going to save will grow into the plant you want. Open-pollinated varieties will grow true to type, which means their seed will produce a new plant like the one it came from. Hybrids will not grow true to type, so don't bother saving those seeds. And keep in mind that plants of the same species can cross-pollinate, so if your goal is to save seeds, you should grow plants of the same species (say, two varieties of melon) as far apart as possible, or grow only one variety.

A good place to start seed saving is with beans, peas, tomatoes, chicories, and lettuces. These are self-pollinators (they pollinate themselves from the same flower or from another flower on the same plant) so there is less probability of cross-pollination. Heirloom squash and melon seeds are also very easy to save. The vegetables will have to be fully mature, so save seed at the end of the season to get the full harvest from your plants. If there is a choice, save seed from the finest plant with the best-tasting produce.

Try saving seed from the local produce you especially love; it may grow true to type. If it does, it will probably thrive in your microclimate.

Here are a few seed-saving pointers:

◆ The pods of beans and peas and lettuces should be dry and brittle. Shell the seeds and let them continue to dry.

◆ If you are growing bush beans, the whole plant can be pulled up and hung upside down to dry.

◆ Take tomato seeds from slightly overripe, but not rotting, fruit. Scoop out the seeds and let them dry completely. Or soak them in water for a few days: they will ferment and lose all their surrounding pulp. Drain off the scum and liquid, rinse well, and lay out on newspaper or plates to dry. Scoop the seeds from mature melons and squash, rinse off all the pulp, and dry.

◆ Store dry seeds in sealed, labeled envelopes in glass jars in a cool, dry place. Seeds that have not been fully dried or that are exposed to moisture will mold.

◆ Most seeds will stay viable for up to three years.

There are many seed libraries and exchanges popping up all over the country. Check with your local library, ecology center, or search online for a seed library near you. They are filled with an enormous inventory of local favorites and old heirloom varieties with a rich history. These varieties are almost always the tastiest, because flavor is a powerful motivator for gardeners to save seed.

Saving seeds helps ensure the genetic diversity of our plant world and is an important practice in a time when supermarkets are full of vegetables and fruits grown from sterile hybrid seeds in large monocultures.

# Fruit in the Garden

FRUIT TREES, BUSHES, AND VINES are true edible ornamentals, embellishing the landscape with showers of springtime blossoms, colorful fruit, and stunning autumnal
leaves, while filling your kitchen with delectable garden-ripe fruit. Kitchen gardeners
have perfected growing fruit in small spaces: training apricot and cherry trees to grow on
sunny walls and grape and kiwi vines along fences, filling hanging baskets with strawberries, growing hedges of gooseberries and currants, and tucking dwarf apple and lemon
trees in containers. If you have a bit of room, you have the opportunity to plant multiple
trees, vines, and bushes and have fruit ready to harvest all through the growing season.

## Selecting the Right Variety

Fruit trees and bushes are perennials that grow and expand to become part of your landscape for decades. Selecting a variety and growing location requires more thought than most garden annuals. The parameters might seem overwhelming at first, but it really takes only a little research to find out what grows best where you live. Local farmers, neighbors, nurseries, and catalogs will fill you in on all you need to know.

Many antique and heirloom varieties are renowned for their tasty fruit—fruit that is rarely seen at the supermarket because it does not ship well or is not perfect-looking. Farmers' markets are filled with interesting varieties (and farmers to talk to about them), and some nurseries and botanical gardens have annual tastings. It is worth the effort to research the tastiest variety that will thrive in your growing area.

## Rootstock and Size

All fruit trees are sold grafted onto a specific rootstock. The graft joint is easy to spot: it is a joint that looks like an elbow located a couple of inches above the soil line. It is important that this joint is never buried and stands clear of soil or mulch, never touching them. Rootstock determines the size that the tree will grow (dwarf, semidwarf, or standard) and how adaptable it will be to the soil environment in your growing area. Some rootstock tolerates drought while others are more adaptable to heavy soils with poor drainage. Certain rootstock is bred for resistance to disease and others will promote vigorous growth and early fruit bearing. Fruit trees should have two tags, one that describes the fruit variety and one that describes the rootstock variety. Check with your local nursery for advice on desirable rootstock for your growing area.

Dwarf and semidwarf trees are smaller in size, but the fruit they bear is the same as standard trees'. Standard trees can become quite tall (up to thirty feet). Fruit trees tend to grow taller than stated, but their size can easily be controlled with conscientious pruning. Dwarf and semidwarf trees are good choices for smaller gardens. They don't take up as much room and are easier to prune and harvest. Dwarf trees are the best choice for containers.

Blackberries, raspberries, and other caning berries and grapes take up less room in the garden than fruit trees, but if left on their own they will stretch and grow; and many of them reproduce by suckers (brambles) or runners (strawberries). Except for some very vigorous blackberries, these fruits can be trained to fit most any space. Learn the natural tendencies of your chosen varieties before planting them.

## Chill Hours

In order to produce fruit, many fruit tree varieties (cherries, apples, apricots, and plums, for example) need a certain amount of exposure to cold temperatures when dormant. The designation "low chill" identifies varieties that will produce fruit in warmer climates. All nurseries and catalogs should list or know the chill hours required for every variety.

## Bloom Time

Bloom time is important information for colder, rainier climes. If the tree blooms before the last frost date, there is a chance that the fruit will not "set," and the tree will bear no fruit that year. Heavy rains can ruin fruit set as well. Choose later as opposed to early varietals (but not so late that the fruit isn't mature before the first frost date).

## Ripening Date

The ripening date refers to the approximate date when the fruit is expected to ripen. This is invaluable information when planting trees where there is a short growing season. Planting varieties with different ripening dates can result in a longer harvest.

## Pollination

Fruit and nuts are either self-pollinating, which means they are able to bear fruit on their own (with the help of bees), or cross-pollinating, in which case they require pollen from another tree or plant of the same type close by. If you select a fruit that requires cross-pollinating, plant two trees or bushes of the same fruit that bloom in the same period, or look around the neighborhood to see if there is another nearby. A family tree, which is a tree that has several varieties of a fruit grafted onto the same rootstock, will ensure pollination, as will planting more than one kind of tree in the same hole (see page 407). In this way, not only is pollination achieved, but the different branches yield an enticing selection of fruit—a mini-orchard on a single tree or from a single high-density planting. You can get creative with pollinating your trees by bringing a bucket of blossoming branches from a compatible faraway tree.

## Planting

The requirements for growing perennial fruit and nuts are very similar. They all do best in positions that are sunny (at least six hours a day during the growing season), sheltered (away from driving winds), and have rich soil with good drainage. When choosing a site for a tree, keep in mind how much shade the tree will cast, and when and where the shadow will fall, especially if planting the tree near your kitchen garden. If you discover after a year or two that the site does not suit the plant or that a tree is taking up too much sun, carefully dig it up while it is dormant and transplant it to another area.

It is best to plant fruit and nut trees when they are young, as they are more easily shaped and trained during their initial growth. Plants come bare root, with no soil around the roots (which must be kept moist until planted), or in a pot. If there is time the season before, sow a cover crop and dig it in a few weeks before you plant. This, along with the addition of compost in the greater growing area, will make a big difference in the vitality and long life of your perennial fruits. Bare-root plants are planted when still dormant. Early spring is the best time to plant.

Water is important, especially in the first years while root systems are being developed. Water deeply and consistently to encourage deep root growth, but be very sure not to overwater. Check the soil with your finger, and water only once the soil feels dry one inch down. A thick mulch will greatly lessen the need for watering.

Test the drainage of your soil before planting. Dig a hole one foot deep. Fill with water and when it has drained, fill again. Time how long it takes the hole to empty. If it drains in less than four hours, the soil is fine for planting; if it takes over four hours, the soil needs some help with drainage. If your soil does not drain well, consider an alternative planting method such as mound planting (see page 407) or raised beds, put in a drainage system—or choose another planting spot.

# Planting a Bare-Root Tree, Vine, or Cane

Dig a hole that will allow plenty of room for the roots of the plant. The hole should be large enough around to easily accommodate the roots and the right depth to hold the plant at the same soil level at which it grew. You can easily see this demarcation by the color change on the trunk about 1 inch above the topmost roots.

Mix the soil from the hole with:

    **Compost**

Add some amended soil back to the hole in the shape of a small mound. Center the plant over the mound. Position the tree to your liking and spread the roots out around the mounded soil. Fill in the hole with the amended soil, tamping it down against the roots every few shovelfuls. Keep the tree straight as you fill the hole. Fill with soil to where the plant was growing originally. Create a ridge of soil in a ring around the hole to help keep water in place. Water deeply. To help keep the roots moist, spread around the tree, in at least a 2-foot diameter:

    **A 4-inch layer of mulch (unsifted compost, leaf mold, wood chips, or other natural mulch)**

Keep the mulch from actually touching the tree so there is air circulation at the base of the trunk.

NOTE

✦ Once planted, cut small bare-root whip trees (about ¾ inch around or smaller) off at knee height. This may seem drastic, but it will cause the tree to send out lateral growth at the proper height.

VARIATIONS

• In areas of poor drainage, plant the trees, canes, and vines at soil level. Bring in well-amended soil with good drainage. Build a mound with its center scooped out. Plant the tree as above, creating a ridge around the edge of the mound. Mulch around the tree and around the mound itself.

• To plant a tree, vine, or cane in a container, proceed as above, but instead of creating a mound, make a flat-bottomed hole. Try not to disturb the root ball as much as possible. If the plant is in a plastic pot, cut away the pot with strong shears. If there are any circling roots, straighten them out or prune them.

• To plant a bare-root tree in a container, proceed as above using a high-quality potting soil amended with 25 percent compost. In very cold and very hot climates, choose thick terra-cotta or wooden pots to help protect the soil from extreme temperatures. Larger containers are best: 15 gallons is the minimum size recommended.

## Planting Multiple Trees in One Hole

Multiple, or high-density, planting is another way to save space, extend the harvest, and assure pollination. Two to four trees of similar varieties (with similar cultivation needs) can be planted in a single hole. A four-foot square hole can be planted with up to four trees, eighteen to twenty-four inches apart. Trees on dwarf stock should be used and shaped with regular summer pruning to keep air and light available to all the trees. Trees may also be planted in a row, with holes spaced at regular intervals, two trees to a hole. Dave Wilson Nursery, a founding proponent of high-density planting, has a wonderful online article, "Backyard Orchard Culture" (see page 415), that outlines the whole process as well as listing groupings of fruit that work well together for flavor, color, and extended harvest.

## Fruit Tree Mulch

Mulch will inhibit water evaporation and keep the roots in a temperature-stable environment. Mulch made from wood chips and leaves (leaf mold) contains fungi that fruit trees greatly benefit from. Fruit trees also prefer a compost high in fungi as opposed to bacteria. A greater proportion of brown materials will help boost the fungal population of a compost heap.

Minerals can be added along with the mulch: oyster-shell meal for calcium, rock dust for trace minerals, and gypsum to help with soil compaction. Don't dig in the minerals, but scatter them and let them sit on the soil surface with the mulch to attract beneficial worms and microbes to boost the soils nutrients. Compost tea (see page 397) will also significantly boost the microbial community and improve the nutrient content and structure of the soil.

# Pruning and Shaping Fruit Trees

As fruit trees, vines, and canes grow, they require pruning. This is the process of shaping the structure of a tree to control its size and create a sturdy shape that will support abundant harvests and allow for adequate airflow and sunshine to ripen the fruit. The first years of growth are spent training and shaping the branches into a healthy growing pattern. Pruning is a broad subject, too broad to cover in detail here. There are wonderful resources for learning more about pruning, both in the library and online (see page 415), but in the end, the best way to learn to prune is by pruning. Each year, you will see the results and learn as you go. If you have experienced friends or local orchardists, visit them during pruning season or ask them over to guide you.

Pruning and training is best started right away. There are two main times to prune trees: when they are actively growing (summer pruning) and when they are dormant (winter pruning). Regular cleaning, which includes the removal of dead wood, broken branches, disease, old fruit, and crossed branches, happens at both times of the year. Keep in mind that any cuts to the tree will stimulate growth, so prune close to the end of the dormant period, after the coldest months of winter, and in the summer before fall sets in.

Keep the base of the tree cleaned of fallen fruit and diseased leaves. It is important to maintain healthy conditions for the trees.

*Vertically pruned columnar apple tree*

## Summer Pruning

Summer cuts control size. The branches are shortened, or topped, to keep the tree the proper size for its space. This pruning is especially useful for trees in small spaces, family trees, and high-density plantings. Any dominant types need to be cut back so they don't overtake and shade out the less vigorous varieties. Summer pruning also opens up the tree for sun and air.

Citrus trees are an exception to this advice. They are evergreen trees that need little pruning except to neaten and tidy the plants or keep the size reduced.

## Winter Pruning

Winter cuts are meant to establish the overall shape of the tree. This is especially important in the early years of the tree's life. Winter pruning encourages new growth. Young limbs are cut at an angle just above a bud. Before making major cuts on large branches, research good cutting practices to avoid breaking and tearing wounds to the bark and trunk of the tree. When removing branches, leave a one-inch collar, or piece of branch, on the tree.

## Espaliers

Espaliered trees are trained flat onto wire or fences. Training trees to grow this way saves space and decreases the amount of shade they cast in the garden. The process is fairly easy. Basically all the growth is cut except for that growing in a flat two-dimensional plane. The limbs are tied to a supporting trellis or wire to help train their growth pattern. Espaliered and other specially trained trees need continual summer and winter pruning to control their growth and retain their shape.

## Soft Fruit Pruning

The bushes, canes, and vines of most soft fruits need annual pruning as well. Each has different needs based on how they grow and how the fruit is set on the plant. Some plants, including raspberries and other bramble fruit, set fruit on second-year canes; others set fruit on new growth (currants and blueberries); and some will grow wild without vigorous pruning, which results in diminishing harvests (grapes). This may sound confusing, but it is easy to find out what treatment your plants need and learn to care for them over the years.

Caning and vining fruits frequently need support for their growth. Tall and trailing brambles need a sturdy trellis for their flourishing canes, while the vines of grapes and kiwis can be trained on stakes, fences, or arbors. Trellises or other support systems are best put in place when the plants are first put in the ground.

## Harvest

Delectable fruit is the garden's most delayed gratification. Fruit trees and bushes don't produce fruit the first season, so one must wait until abundant harvests are ready to pick. Dwarf and semidwarf trees will begin to produce fruit the second or third season after they are planted; standard trees will take a few years longer. Other than strawberries, most soft fruits (grapes and berries) require a few seasons to bear a full harvest.

When trees begin to bear fruit, it is wise to keep an eye on the tree. As hard as it may be to do, abundant fruit needs to be thinned. Removing fruit when it is still small makes room for larger, better-quality fruit, maintains consistently large annual harvests (otherwise small harvests will follow bumper crop years), and helps keep branches from breaking and splitting from too much weight. If branches do start to bend down from the weight of the fruit, tie up smaller ones to the trunk of the tree with rope and support larger ones on wooden poles or crutches to keep them from breaking and possibly splitting the tree.

You won't be the only one eyeing your fruit as it ripens. Birds, squirrels, and other animals have an uncanny knack of knowing just when fruit is ready to pick. Netting or caging the harvest may be necessary if there is a lot of competition for your fruit. (This is another good reason to keep trees fairly small.)

Except for pears, fruit tastes best when it is ripened on the tree or bush. Keep tasting the fruit to decide the best time to harvest. Most fruit ripens all at once. Get ready to eat, bake, can, and freeze to preserve the bounty for the rest of the year. If your harvests are large, invite friends to help, or barter with other fruit growers to share your surpluses, and help one another preserve the abundance. If you don't have fruit trees, keep an eye on neighborhood trees; if they are going unpicked, it is worth asking if you can harvest the fruit. In return, a few jars of jam or fruit in syrup are always greatly appreciated. There are websites in some areas that have lists of trees belonging to people who are interested in barter or who would like someone to come and help harvest. Local food banks are grateful for any excess fruit in good shape that you can't use.

# Tools and Resources

J UST AS I DON'T RECOMMEND a lot of complicated equipment in the kitchen (my mortar and pestle, a few knives, a cutting board, and a few heavy pots and pans are all I really ever need), I don't recommend a lot of fancy tools for the garden. Less is more, and a lot easier to keep track of, reach for, and store. Along with a garden journal and some tools, you will also need seeds or plants, compost, minerals, and a few good books. Your local farmers, neighborhood gardeners, brick-and-mortar nurseries, and public libraries are invaluable resources for information and guidance. The Internet is filled with videos, articles, forums, and more on just about any subject you care to research.

# Tools

### FOR COMPOST

**Manure fork**: A lightweight fork that makes turning compost a breeze.

**Compost sifter**: This is easily made with a wooden frame and sturdy ¾-inch wire mesh.

**Sprayer for foliar feeding**: This can be as small as a spray bottle or as large as a backpack version.

### FOR CONTAINER GARDENING

**Trowel**: A small handheld shovel for planting, digging, and cultivating.

**Handheld cultivator**: The three to five curved tines of this tool make cultivating and weeding easy and efficient.

**Clippers**: Essential for pruning and harvesting.

### FOR SMALL GARDENS (ALL OF THE ABOVE PLUS)

**Handheld hoe**: Choose a tool that has a narrow blade so you can easily weed between tightly spaced plants.

**Spading fork**: A long-tined fork used to aerate and break up hard-packed soil.

### FOR LARGER GARDENS (ALL OF THE ABOVE PLUS)

**Long-handled hoe**: For weeding.

**Soil rake**: A stiff-tined rake useful for smoothing garden beds.

**Shovel**: Very helpful for digging and moving compost.

**Wheelbarrow**: Good for larger gardening projects, especially moving large quantities of compost and soil.

**Broadfork**: Useful for loosening and aerating soil that is not in raised beds.

### FOR FRUIT TREES

**Clippers** (shears): Great for small pruning cuts.

**Folding saw**: A sharp saw is essential for pruning, and a folding saw is a handy way to keep the blade safely folded away.

**Loppers**: For making cuts on larger branches.

### EXTRAS THAT ARE NICE

**Weed carrier**: A lightweight collapsible container makes collecting and carrying garden matter neat and easy.

**Hand tool carrier**: Convenient for keeping your hand tools easy to find and at your side.

**Harvest basket**: Very handy for collecting and bringing in the harvest.

# Books

This is a list of books filled with useful information on gardening, soil, season extension, growing fruit, and saving seeds.

*Backyard Fruits and Berries: Everything You Need to Know About Planting Fruits and Berries in Your Own Backyard* by Miranda Smith

*Botany for Gardeners: An Introduction and Guide* by Brian Capon

*Build Your Own Earth Oven: A Low-Cost, Wood-Fired, Mud Oven, Simple Sourdough Bread, Perfect Loaves* by Kiko Denzer with Hannah Field

*Creative Vegetable Gardening* and *The Organic Salad Garden* by Joy Larkcom

*Edible Estates: Attack on the Front Lawn* by Fritz Haeg

*The Edible Garden: The Complete A to Z Guide to Growing Your Own Vegetables, Herbs, and Fruit* by the editors of Sunset Books

*Edible Landscaping* by Rosalind Creasy

*The Essential Urban Farmer* by Novella Carpenter and Willow Rosenthal

*Fruit Trees in Small Spaces: Abundant Harvests from Your Own Backyard* by Colby Eierman

*Grow Great Grub: Organic Food from Small Spaces* by Gayla Trail

*Heirloom Vegetable Gardening: A Master Gardener's Guide to Planting, Seed Saving, and Cultural History* by William Woys Weaver

*How to Grow Winter Vegetables* by Charles Dowding

*The Kitchen Garden: A Passionate Gardener's Comprehensive Guide to Growing Good Things to Eat* by Sylvia Thompson

*The New Organic Grower: A Master's Manual of Tools and Techniques for the Home and Market Gardener* and *The Winter Harvest Handbook: Year-Round Vegetable Production Using Deep-Organic Techniques and Unheated Greenhouses* by Eliot Coleman

*The One-Straw Revolution: An Introduction to Natural Farming* by Masanobu Fukuoka

*Seed to Seed: Seed Saving and Growing Techniques for Vegetable Gardeners* by Suzanne Ashworth

*Teaming with Microbes: The Organic Gardener's Guide to the Soil Food Web* by Jeff Lowenfels and Wayne Lewis

*The Vegetable Gardener's Bible* and *The Vegetable Gardener's Container Bible: How to Grow a Bounty of Food in Pots, Tubs, and Other Containers* by Edward C. Smith

# Seed and Garden Supply Catalogs

**Baker Creek Heirloom Seeds** (www.RareSeeds.com)
Many unusual and delicious open-pollinated varieties.

**Fedco Seeds** (www.FedcoSeeds.com)
Interesting seeds especially suited to the Northeast, with lots of specific growing information.

**Filaree Garlic Farm** (www.FilareeFarm.com)
An extensive offering of organic garlic.

**Four Winds Growers** (www.FourWindsGrowers.com)
Specializes in citrus trees, with lots of great growing information.

**Johnny's Selected Seeds** (www.JohnnySeeds.com)
A large selection of seed, also available in bulk, and a great selection of garden tools.

**Kitazawa Seed Co.** (www.KitazawaSeed.com)
Specializing in Asian seeds, almost all open-pollinated.

**Native Seeds/SEARCH** (www.NativeSeeds.org)
Many interesting varieties, especially those adapted to the Southwest.

**Nichols Garden Nursery** (www.NicholsGardenNursery.com)
A large selection of herbs and vegetable varieties.

**Peaceful Valley Farm & Garden Supply** (www.GrowOrganic.com)
Organic garden supplies, tools, and information; vegetable and cover crop seeds; many helpful videos on organic gardening (www.YouTube.com/user/groworganic).

**Renee's Garden** (www.ReneesGarden.com)
A select collection of tasty varieties.

**Richters Herbs** (www.Richters.com)
An extensive catalog of herb seeds and plants.

**Seed Savers Exchange** (www.SeedSavers.org)
A wonderful catalog of seeds and community of seed savers.

**Seeds of Change** (www.SeedsOfChange.com)
An extensive catalog of organic seeds, gardening supplies, and apple trees.

**Seeds of Italy** (www.GrowItalian.com)
Italian heirloom seeds, with many varieties of chicories and other greens.
The U.S. distributor for Franchi Seeds.

**South Carolina Foundation Seed Association** (www.Virtual.Clemson.edu/groups/seed)
An interesting selection of beans, crowder peas, and okra.

**Southern Exposure Seed Exchange** (www.SouthernExposure.com)
  Organic seeds.

**Southmeadow Fruit Gardens** (www.SouthmeadowFruitGardens.com)
  A large selection of fruit trees.

**Territorial Seed Company** (www.TerritorialSeed.com)
  A large selection of organic seeds and garden supplies.

**Trees of Antiquity** (www.TreesOfAntiquity.com)
  Many heirloom varieties of fruit trees and bushes.

## Forums and Newsletters

**Dave Wilson Nursery** (www.DaveWilson.com)
  A great resource for fruit tree planting and pruning information, including videos (www.youtube.com/user/davewilsontrees).

**GardenWeb** (www.GardenWeb.com)
  Internet garden community

**Green String Farm** (www.GreenStringFarm.com)
  Farmer Bob Cannard

**Ladybug Newsletter** (www.LadybugLetter.com)
  Farmer Andy Griffin at Mariquita Farm

## Seed Saving

To find seed libraries near you, search "seed lending libraries" online.

Here is a good article on how to start your own public seed-lending library:
  (www.shareable.net/blog/how-to-create-your-own-seed-lending-library)

## Urban Foraging and Fruit Exchange

Asiya Wadud started Forage Oakland, which is a great source for general information; for more localized information and groups, search online. (www.ForageOakland.wordpress.com)

## Cooperative Extension Offices

This website will direct you to the office nearest you. (www.csrees.usda.gov/extension)

# Glossary

## FOOD-LABELING TERMS

**Biodynamic** includes all the requirements of organic as well as those stating that the whole farm must be certified biodynamic (instead of a sole plot), a certain percentage of plant diversity must be intact, and the farm must be a self-sustaining closed system. For animals, at least 50 percent of the feed must be produced on the farm. The standards for processed biodynamic foods require minimal processing and a high content of biodynamic ingredients. Demeter, an international certification, is the only biodynamic certification available.

**Cage free** refers to chickens that can move freely in a hen house or barn instead of held in cramped cages. The chickens do not necessarily have access to the outdoors. Conditions can range from light and airy to cramped and dirty. There is no certification in conjunction with this labeling.

**Conventional** fruits, vegetables, and meat are raised allowing the use of chemical fertilizers, pesticides, herbicides, fungicides, antibiotics, and hormones. The use of irradiation, solvents, and chemical additives is allowed as well.

**Dry farming** is a water-saving agricultural technique most commonly used for fruits and tomatoes. Young plants are watered until well established and then not watered again apart from natural rainfall. The lack of water can concentrate the flavor in dry-farmed fruits and vegetables.

**Factory farm**, also referred to as a CAFO (Concentrated Animal Feeding Operation), is a very large, densely populated operation that provides animals no room to move about naturally or much quality of life. The animals are frequently maimed (debeaked, tails removed, etc.) to lessen infighting that damages the product. Antibiotics are typically necessary and regularly administered to curb diseases caused by overcrowding. Waste produced by the animals is commonly stored in enormous, volatile pits called lagoons that can erupt and leak into the local watershed.

**Free range** refers to how animals are held while being raised for meat. Though the impression given is that the animals roam freely outdoors, there are no regulations on the size, quality of, or access to the space (it could be a whole pasture or a small door onto a tiny pad of concrete). Free range does not refer at all to what the animal eats.

**GMO (genetically modified organism)** is a plant or animal that has had a gene or genes inserted into its DNA that changes the actual genetic makeup of the organism. There have been very few long-term studies of these foods; potential risks include "genetic drift," the spread of novel genes into conventional plants by cross-pollination, and the development of resistant weeds and pathogens. All GMOs are patented and may only be used by purchase—it is illegal to save seeds from GMO plants or use seeds that were not purchased from the manufacturer. In the United States there are no requirements to label foods made with GMO ingredients.

**Grain fed** refers to meat that is from animals that have been raised, or in the case of beef, sometimes finished (fed for the last few months of growth) on grains, most often corn, soy, and barley. Grazing animals grow and fatten much faster on grain than on grass. Grain is not the natural diet for cows or other grazing animals.

**Grain finishing** is a method of raising cattle. The animals are grown on pasture or provided forage and then for the last few months of their lives, they are fed a diet high in grains, most often in large crowded feed lots, to quickly increase their final weight.

**Grass-fed** animals eat grass from grazing pasture or provided forage (hay or silage). No grain is fed to the animals. Grass is the natural diet of cows, sheep, goats, and other grazing animals. Grass-fed certification is voluntary, though to get the USDA shield, the production must be verified. USDA certification requires the animals be fed 100 percent grass or forage and have access to pasture during the growing season. The American Grassfed Association (AGA) offers certification that requires the animals to be pastured their whole life and bans the use of antibiotics and hormones. Organic grass-fed meat is from animals fed organic pasture or forage. One hundred percent grass fed or grass finished means the animals were fed grass their whole life. Some uncertified grass-fed beef has been grain finished.

**Heirloom** plants are domesticated varieties that have been grown for many generations. They were saved most often for their flavor or vigor, though they are not usually plants that work best for commodity shipping or large-scale conventional farming. Originally seeds were handed down from family to family, and some still are. Now many heirloom plants and seeds may be bought from catalogs and nurseries. Most heirloom plants are open pollinated.

**Heritage-breed** livestock animals are those that have been raised by farmers for generations. Most of these breeds are dying out due to the use of a few main breeds in large-scale ranching and farming. Heritage breeds are important for genetic diversity and are frequently raised for unique attributes, good flavor, and the ability to survive outdoors in local climates.

**Hormone free** states that the meat or milk comes from animals that were never administered any hormones, growth or otherwise.

**Humanely raised** refers to the way in which animals that produce dairy, eggs, and meat are treated while alive and while slaughtered. Humane provisions include: room to move and engage in natural habits (wing flapping, rooting, etc.), quality food and water, access to shelter, clean living areas, no administering of antibiotics and hormones, and the careful handling of animals en route to and during slaughter. There is no USDA standardized definition. Any producer can label their food with this adjective, but there are respected, independent nonprofit groups (such as Certified Humane) that have established viable certifications that can be applied for and displayed on labels. Researching the certification group on the Internet will tell you about their protocol.

**Natural** is an adjective frequently used in conjunction with meat and other foods. It implies that the food is healthy, and in the case of meat, that no hormones or other chemicals have been used during production, but in fact there is no government, or any other, control whatsoever over the use of the word. It really means nothing specific on a label, except in the case of meat, where it indicates only that the meat has not been processed with any additives after slaughter.

**Organic** is a federal certification that requires that no synthetic pesticides, fungicides, or chemical fertilizers be used when growing plants or added to feed for domesticated animals that are intended for food. Antibiotics and hormones are not permitted, nor are the foods allowed to be subjected to irradiation, chemical solvents, or mixed with synthetic chemical additives. There have been some agricultural pesticides and food additives developed that fall under the category of organic and are permitted in organic food production. Originally, certification was awarded by independent state groups (some with more stringent standards than the federal requirements), but now there is also a USDA organic certification. Look for a certification stamp on the label.

**Pasture raised** indicates animals that are raised free roaming on pastureland with access to protective shelter. Grazing animals are not fed any additional grain, forage, or silage. Chickens are fed some grain in addition to the insects and grass provided by the pasture. There are no government or state regulations for pasture-raised animals. Organic pasture-raised meat and eggs are raised on pasture that has been organically certified.

**Pesticide free** states that no pesticide has been used on the plant or in the soil during the growth cycle of the plant. Commercial fertilizer may have been used. This nomenclature is frequently used by farmers who farm organically and are in transition to certification, or cannot afford the certification process. There is no government or state regulation of pesticide free.

**RBGH-free** or **rBST-free** on milk and dairy product labels means that the dairy cow in question was not administered bovine growth hormone. It does not indicate the absence of any other hormone.

**Whole grain** refers to a grain or flour that contains all the naturally occurring essential parts of the grain—the bran, germ, and starchy endosperm—though a food labeled whole grain may contain as little as 51 percent whole grain. The other 49 percent may comprise refined flours, sugars, trans fats, and other additives. Multigrain means a mixture of grains but not necessarily whole grains. Look for products with whole grains and whole-grain flours as the first ingredient. Read the entire ingredients list to know what makes up the rest of the product.

## GARDENING AND AGRICULTURAL TERMS

**Amendments** are materials added to soil to improve tilth, water retention, and fertility.

**Annual** refers to a plant that completes its life cycle in one year. It sprouts from seed, grows its vegetative state, and produces flowers and seeds, all in one year.

**Biennial** refers to a plant that usually requires two years to complete its life cycle. The first year is spent producing roots and leaves. The second year it flowers and produces seeds.

**Biodynamic gardening** is a philosophy and practice of organic gardening introduced by Rudolf Steiner in Germany in the 1920s. It considers the garden as a single organism, promoting the interrelationship of plants, animals, and soil.

**Biointensive gardening** merges aspects of organic, biodynamic, and French intensive gardening, introduced in California by Alan Chadwick and developed by John Jeavons. It emphasizes the production of high yields from a small piece of land, while improving the soil.

**Bolting** is when an annual, leafy, or root vegetable begins to send up a flower stalk and go to seed. Most of the energy of the plant goes into the flower-bearing stalk and the quality of the rest of the plant declines. Bolting can be hastened by water stress.

**Cold frame** refers to a small enclosure with a removable translucent lid, usually glass or plastic, designed for protecting young plants from cold temperatures. Tender plants in a cold frame will get a head start on the growing season.

**Companion planting** is the planting of herbs, flowers, or other non-crop plants among crop plants that attract beneficial insects or repel insect pests.

**Compost** is decomposed organic material that is used as a mulch or soil amendment. Compost diverts food and garden waste from landfill and turns it into a valuable natural resource and powerful soil and plant food.

**Cover crop** refers to a crop, usually planted by broadcast seeding, that is grown to improve soil fertility, control erosion, and improve soil structure, but not intended for harvest. Also referred to as green manure.

**Crop diversity** refers to planting a number of different crops in the same area to help increase populations of beneficial insects, decrease the prevalence of plant diseases, and improve soil fertility.

**Direct sowing** is the planting of seeds where the plant will complete its life cycle, without transplanting.

**Double digging** is a system of gardening sometimes called French intensive gardening. In its simplest form, this cultivation practice requires digging a deep trench, then filling that trench with manure or compost, and soil from an adjacent trench. The soil is aerated and more permeable to water, providing a better environment for plant growth.

**Espalier** is a method of training plants to grow flat against a wall or trellis, to conserve space and provide more light or warmth for plant growth.

**Exposure** is the environmental situation of a plant with regard to temperature, sunlight, and wind.

**F-1 hybrid** refers to a plant produced from seed by cross-pollination of its parents. The seed from this first generation grows into the desired plant; subsequent generations do not, which renders their seeds undesirable for saving and planting. This is different from seeds ultimately produced by cross-pollination of several generations of parents, which will grow true to type.

**Friable** refers to the condition of a soil that breaks apart when it is tilled and is easily worked. It is crumbly, even textured, and resists being compacted.

**Germination** is the physiological process whereby a seed breaks dormancy in response to temperature, moisture, and light and begins to grow.

**Greenhouse** refers to a building with roof and walls of glass or other transluscent material that captures heat from the sun. A greenhouse is used to start seeds, grow plants, or house fragile varieties during cold weather.

**Hybrid** refers to a plant or animal produced by cross-fertilization that did not happen in the wild.

**Microbial activity** is the beneficial activity of bacteria, fungi, and other microorganisms in the soil to decompose organic matter and release nutrients in a form that plants can use.

**Monoculture** is large-scale farming of the same crop in the same field year after year. The efficiencies of this form of farming are offset by greater susceptibility to pest and disease outbreaks, the need to treat crops with large amounts of chemicals over a large area, reduced diversity of beneficial organisms, and the depletion of soil nutrients.

**No-till** or **no-dig gardening** is a practice of organic gardening that depends on the natural soil life and structure to cultivate the soil. All amendments are placed on top of the garden to be naturally worked into the soil by earthworms and other soil organisms. The soil is not disturbed by digging, tilling, or disking before planting. Instead the soil is loosened and aerated only a few inches down before planting. Most no-dig beds are started by a deep layer of sheet compost that is added to between each planting.

**Open pollination** is pollination that occurs naturally by wind, birds, insects, or other natural exchanges of pollen between flowers, or by self-pollination within the same flower. As long as open-pollinated plants are isolated from others with which they can cross-breed, they will produce seed that is true to type, and when planted will produce a plant the same as the parent. The term OP is used to signify open-pollinated seed in catalogs.

**Organic gardening** uses growing practices that replicate nature, encouraging the activity of soil microorganisms and beneficial insects, growing different species together, and providing plant nutrition and pest control with naturally occurring materials.

**Perennial** refers to a plant that lives more than two years, producing flowers, fruits, and seeds for many years.

**Permaculture** is an organic gardening system that strives to mimic the ecology of the natural environment and minimizes any external inputs. Bill Mollison and David Holmgren developed the Permaculture Institute in Tasmania. In permaculture, waste becomes food for other organisms. Its successful implementation requires careful attention to and understanding of the order of the natural world.

**Propagation** is the production of individual plants from their parents. This may be done by sowing seeds, taking divisions or cuttings, grafting, or budding.

**Row cover** is a fabric placed over plants to protect them from frost and increase soil temperature. Some types also provide insect and disease control. They may be designed to be supported above the plants or lie directly on the plants.

**Sustainable** refers to cultural practices that ensure long-term productivity of plants and animals by increasing crop diversity and using biological methods of pest control and soil-fertility maintenance. The main tenet of sustainability is to return more to the soil than is being taken away.

**Tilth** is the physical structure of soil as it relates to plant growth. Soil with good tilth allows water to penetrate, while maintaining good aeration.

**Topsoil** is the thin, uppermost layer of soil with the greatest value. It usually contains the greatest concentration of plant nutrients and has the best tilth. Topsoil is where all agriculture takes place.

**Viable** refers to the condition of seeds that will have a high percentage of germination.

# Index

Acorn squash, 151, 152. *See also* winter squash
agua fresca, cucumber, 141–42
aïoli (garlic mayonnaise), 55
alliums, 51–65, 401. *See also specific types*
    about, 51, 54
    recipe list, 52
almond(s), 281, 283, 304
    almond, marjoram, and red wine vinegar sauce, 235
    almond milk panna cotta, 304–5
    apricot almond-custard tart, 255–56
    chocolate candies with dried fruits and nuts, 306
    ice milk, with huckleberry sauce, 276–77
    meringues, soft, 305–6
    panforte candies, 318–19
    panforte with candied orange peel and chocolate, 318
    pounded almond and mint pasta sauce, 29
almond paste: frangipane, 246, 247
amaranth, 219
    and ricotta cannelloni, 220
anchovy(ies)
    crostini with dried tomatoes, capers, and, 167
    dandelion greens with garlic croutons and, 49

and parsley sauce, 235
    puntarelle with lemon, garlic, and, 203
anise hyssop, 10, 20
    and cucumber salad, 20
apple(s), 281, 283, 286–88
    apple butter, 345
    chicory salad with celery root, walnuts, and, 199
    drying, 355
    kohlrabi, carrot, and apple slaw, 238–39
    Pink Pearl, sautéed, 289–90
    and quince galette, 293–94
    Sierra Beauty pie, 288–89
apricot(s), 245, 252
    apricot almond-custard tart, 255–56
    apricot aperitif, 256
    drying, 355
    galette, 254
    liqueur, 354
    Royal Blenheim sorbet, 254–55
    in syrup, 348
apricot kernels, 243
    noyau crème anglaise, 271–72
artichokes, 106
arugula. *See* rocket
Asian greens, 208, 220–21. *See also* bok choy; mustard greens
Asian pears, 290
    drying, 355
    red mustard salad with pecans and, 222
asparagus, 25, 97, 100, 105
    purple, roasted, fettuccine with lemon zest, Parmesan, and, 313

and spring vegetable ragout, Moroccan, 105

Bacon
    leek tart with crème fraîche and, 63–64
    sautéed spigarello broccoli with, 232–33
basil, 10, 12
    basil mayonnaise, 13
    basil-squash blossom butter, 187
    rocket salad with peaches and, 44
    vinaigrette, grilled crookneck squash fans with, 148
bay laurel, 10, 33
bean(s), 111, 119–21, 124–25, 382, 402. *See also* chickpea(s); fava beans
    black bean and epazote tostadas, 18
    black-eyed peas with sautéed okra and peppers, 130
    cannellini bean purée, 126–27
    chile con carne, 129–30
    cranberry bean and tomato salad with summer savory salsa, 126
    crowder pea and greens soup, 131
    dilly beans, 334–35; lacto-fermented, 337
    fresh flageolet beans with spicy lamb sausage, 127–28

haricots verts with toasted pecans and purple basil, 122

Rio Zape beans cooked in the coals with garlic and chiles, 129

three-bean salad à la Chez Panisse, 123

white beans with duck confit, 128

yellow romano beans in tomato sauce, 122

beet(s), 70, 79–80

blood orange and golden beet salad, 317

butter lettuce salad with Gruyère, walnuts, and, 42–43

Chioggia beet and carrot salad, 80

cooked in the coals, 80

soup, with dill, chilled, 14

Belgian endive, 198, 199

Belgian endive leaf hors d'oeuvres, 202

red, crab salad with tarragon and, 21

berries, 263–80, 404–5, 409. *See also specific types*

about, 263, 265

recipe list, 264

blackberry(ies), 265, 272

coulis, 273

and honey compote, with tarragon, 273

and nectarine galette, 262

soufflé, 274–75

summer pudding, 280

black-eyed peas, 124–25

with sautéed okra and peppers, 130

black trumpet and Yellow Finn potato gratin, 91

blood orange and golden beet salad, 317

blueberry(ies), 265, 275

and poppyseed butter cake, 276

bok choy, 220

sautéed with ginger and garlic, 221

borage, 10, 30

borage cocktail, 31

brandied cherries, 347

brassicas. *See* cabbage family; *specific types*

bread. *See* crostini; pita bread, whole-wheat; sandwiches

broccoli, 223, 226, 231

Calabrese, and green garlic frittata, 232

spigarello, sautéed, with bacon, 232–33

sprouting, with anchovies and garlic, 231–32

broccoli rabe, 208, 212, 226, 240

and chickpea soup, 214

and ricotta pancakes with lemon-coriander butter, 213

sautéed, with sherry vinegar, 240

Brussels sprouts, 223, 226

roasted, with sesame seeds and ginger, 241

sautéed, with sherry vinegar, 240

Buddha's Hand citron, 324

pickled, 347; fish tartare with, 324

bulgur

and golden chard pilaf, 215

salad, with roasted Sheepnose pimientos and cilantro, 176–77

butter

basil-squash blossom, 187

lemon-coriander, 213–14

butternut squash, 151. *See also* winter squash

and celery root gratin, 155–56

Cabbage(s), 223, 226–27

kimchi, 223, 227, 338–39; spicy Korean pork stew with, 229–30

red cabbage salad with Medjool dates and kumquats, 227–28

sauerkraut, 223, 226; Indian-spiced, 338; sautéed with parsnips and juniper, 230

spicy napa cabbage slaw, 228

sweet and hot green cabbage, 228–29

cabbage family, 223–41. *See also specific vegetables*

about, 223, 226

recipe list, 224

cake

blueberry and poppyseed, 276

Santa Rosa plum cake, 258

sponge cake, 271

calamondin (calamansi), 323

candies

candied kumquats, 351–52

candied melon, 350–51

candies (*continued*)
candied mint leaves, 30
candied orange peel, 316,
349–50
candied rose petals, 30
chocolate, with dried fruits
and nuts, 306
honey candied walnuts,
299–300
panforte candies, 318–19
panforte with candied
orange peel and
chocolate, 318
Cannard, Bob, 360, 361,
363, 368, 371, 395, 396,
397
cannellini beans, 124
cannellini bean purée,
126–27
white beans with duck
confit, 128
cannelloni, ricotta and
amaranth, 220
canning, 327–28
apricots in syrup, 348
canned tomatoes, 328–29
lime syrup, 348–49
cantaloupe, 142
capers, fried, orange
cauliflower salad with
rocket and, 237
cardoon(s), 97, 100, 106
braised with olive oil and
lacinato kale, 107–8
gratin, with béchamel and
Parmesan cheese, 108
salad, with lemon, anchovy,
and black olives, 106–7
carpaccio, wild salmon,
with chervil and green
coriander seeds, 16–17

carrot(s), 70, 71, 392
carrot curls, 71
chicken braised with
coriander and, 72
and Chioggia beet salad, 80
colorful, with butter and
honey, 72–73
grilled pork sandwiches with
radishes, chiles, and, 76
kohlrabi, carrot, and apple
slaw, 238–39
pickled, 333–34
pickled jalapeños and, 185
spiced carrot raita, 73
cauliflower, 223, 226, 234, 400
orange cauliflower salad
with fried capers and
rocket, 237
Romanesco, deep-fried,
235–36
spicy Indian cauliflower
stems, 236–37
whole roasted, 234
celery, 97, 100, 104
celery root soup with
buttered croutons and,
81–82
and Comice pear salad, 104
celery root, 70, 81
and butternut squash
gratin, 155–56
chicory salad with apples,
walnuts, and, 199
soup, with celery and
buttered croutons, 81–82
ceviche, halibut, with lime, 315
chard, 208, 214–15
golden chard and bulgur
pilaf, 215
and shaved rhubarb
crostini, 109

cherries, 245, 249–50
Bing, roasted with lemon
verbena, 250
black cherry galette, 250–51
brandied, 347
dried: chocolate candies
with dried fruits and
nuts, 306
pickled, 346; mâche with
duck liver croutons and,
47
sour cherry pie, 251–52
cherry tomatoes. *See*
tomato(es)
chervil, 9, 10, 14
herb noodles, 15
parsley and herb salad,
11–12
wild salmon carpaccio with
green coriander seeds
and, 16–17
Chiang, Cecilia, 228
chicken
braised with carrots and
coriander, 72
braised with tomatoes and
vinegar, 166
with 40 cloves of garlic, 57
lovage meatballs, 28
meatballs, puntarelle soup
with, 204
paella with pimientos and
chorizo, 180–81
yogurt-spiced chicken
skewers, 183
chicken broth, 61
chickpea(s), 125
braised leeks with saffron,
dried marjoram, and, 64
and broccoli rabe soup,
214

hummus with preserved
lemon, 132
Moroccan asparagus and
spring vegetable ragout,
105
chicories, 191–204. *See also
specific types*
about, 191, 194, 198–99
Castelfranco salad with
celery root, apples, and
walnuts, 199
chopped Pan di Zucchero
salad, 202
recipe list, 192
chile(s), 173–74. *See also* salsa
ancho, grilled pork
shoulder with, 182–83
chile con carne, 129–30
chile verde, 26, 181–82
grilled pork sandwiches
with radishes, carrots,
and, 76
pickled jalapeños and
carrots, 185
Rio Zape beans cooked in
the coals with garlic and,
129
sliced melon with salt, lime,
and, 143–44
spicy napa cabbage slaw,
228
sweet and hot green
cabbage, 228–29
sweet and spicy peppers
pizza, 178
yogurt-spiced chicken
skewers, 183
chips, sunchoke, 95
chives, 10, 14, 33, 41
parsley and herb salad,
11–12

roast leg of lamb with
spring herbs, 22
salt-roasted potatoes
with crème fraîche and,
92
chocolate
candies, with dried fruits
and nuts, 306
chocolate-dipped candied
mint leaves, 30
panforte with candied
orange peel and, 318
chorizo, paella with pimientos
and, 180–81
cilantro, 10, 15. *See also
coriander seeds*
bulgur salad with roasted
pimientos and, 176–77
green rice pilaf with onions
and, 17
parsley and herb salad,
11–12
citrons, 324
pickled Buddha's Hand,
347; fish tartare with,
324
citrus fruits, 307–24. *See also
specific types*
about, 307, 309–10
recipe list, 308
clams: paella with pimientos
and chorizo, 180–81
cocktails. *See* drinks
Coleman, Eliot, 216, 377
collard greens, 208–9
with cumin and black
mustard seeds, 211
compote
blackberry and honey, with
tarragon, 273
rhubarb, 110

cookies
crispy hazelnut meringues,
301–2
yuzu marmalade
thumbprint, 323–24
coriander seeds, 9, 15. *See also*
cilantro
chicken braised with
carrots and, 72
lemon-coriander butter,
broccoli rabe and ricotta
pancakes with, 213–14
wild salmon carpaccio with
chervil and, 16–17
corn, 157, 185–86
creamed, 188
fresh corn tamales, 187–88
Padrón peppers stuffed with
queso fresco and, 179
and summer squash soup,
186
cornichons, 138, 331
corn salad. *See* mâche
coulis, blackberry, 273
cowpeas, 124–25
crab apple jelly, 344
crab apple liqueur, 354
crab salad with tarragon and
red Belgian endive, 21
cranberry bean(s), 124
chile con carne, 129–30
and tomato salad, with
summer savory salsa, 126
crème anglaise
hazelnut floating island,
302–3
noyau, 271–72
crème fraîche
and bacon, leek tart with,
63–64
baked quince with, 293

crème fraîche (*continued*)
salt-roasted potatoes with
chives and, 92
Crenshaw melon, 142
sliced, with salt, chile, and
lime, 143–44
crépinettes, spinach and pork,
217–18
crostini
with dried tomatoes,
anchovies, and capers,
167
shaved rhubarb and chard,
109
winter squash antipasto
on, 152
crowder pea(s), 124–25
and greens soup, 131
cucumber(s), 135, 137, 138–40
and anise hyssop salad,
20
cornichons, 138, 331
cucumber agua fresca,
141–42
dill pickles, 335; quick,
331–32; traditional, 336
lemon cucumber, purslane,
and cherry tomato salad,
141
and yogurt raita, 140
cucurbits, 135–56. *See also*
*specific plants*
about, 135, 137–38
recipe list, 136
curd, rangpur, 322–23
curly endive. *See* frisée
currants. *See* red currant(s)
custard. *See also* crème
anglaise
apricot almond-custard
tart, 255–56

Daikon radish, 74
braised with miso and soy,
75
dal, kohlrabi and red lentil,
239
dandelion greens, 49
with anchovies and garlic
croutons, 49
date(s)
Medjool, red cabbage salad
with kumquats and,
227–28
and walnut galette, 299
Delicata squash, 151, 152. *See*
*also* winter squash
dill, 9, 10, 13
beet soup with, chilled,
14
dilly beans, 334–35; lacto-
fermented, 337
pickles, 335; quick, 331–32;
traditional, 336
dill seeds, 9, 13
doughs. *See also* pita bread,
whole-wheat; tortillas,
whole-wheat
farro tagliatelle, 313–14
galette dough, 246–47
pie dough, 248
pizza dough, 147–48
sweet tart dough, 248–49
dried beans, 124, 125. *See also*
chickpea(s)
Rio Zape beans cooked in
the coals with garlic and
chiles, 129
dried fruit, 355
chocolate candies with nuts
and, 306
persimmons, radicchio and
farro salad with, 200

dried peppers and chiles,
174
grilled pork shoulder with
ancho chiles, 182–83
yogurt-spiced chicken
skewers, 183
dried tomatoes, 329
crostini with anchovies,
capers, and, 167
drinks, 353. *See also* liqueur(s)
apricot aperitif, 256
borage cocktail, 31
Cara Cara Campari
cocktail, 319
cucumber agua fresca,
141–42
lime spritzer, 315
vin d'orange, 352–53
duck confit, white beans with,
128
duck fat
fingerling potatoes roasted
in, 92
warm frisée salad, 196
duck liver croutons, mâche
with pickled cherries and,
47

Edible flowers, 9, 401. *See also*
*specific plants*
Edible Schoolyard, 5, 344
egg(s)
baked in spicy tomato
sauce, 166–67
broccoli and green garlic
frittata, 232
chopped, garden cress and
lettuce with, 48–49
poached, escarole soup
with, 197–98

eggplant, 15, 157, 160, 169
canapés, 169
Moroccan braised, 172–73
Rosa Bianca, roasted, with
feta and mint, 171
simple eggplant Parmesan,
171–72
slices, roasted or grilled,
169, 171
endive. *See* Belgian endive;
frisée
epazote, 10, 18
and black bean tostadas, 18
escarole, 194–95
salad, with hazelnut
vinaigrette, 196–97
soup, with poached egg,
197–98

Farro, 313
and radicchio salad, with
dried persimmons, 200
tagliatelle, 313–14
fava beans, 117
fava greens, 118
potato and green garlic
ravioli with, 56–57
squid and, with garlic and
parsley, 118–19
young, roasted whole,
118
fennel, 9, 97, 100–101
fronds, roasted striped bass
with, 102–3
and Meyer lemon relish,
102
pollen and seeds, pork
tenderloin with, 103
and sunchoke soup, 95
wild, figs roasted with, 285

fermented pickles, 335–36
Indian-spiced sauerkraut,
338
kimchi, 223, 227, 338–39
lacto-fermented dilly beans,
337
traditional dill pickles, 336
feta and mint, roasted
eggplant with, 171
fettuccine with roasted purple
asparagus, lemon zest,
and Parmesan, 313
figs, 281, 283, 284
Adriatic, with honey, mint,
and ricotta, 284
Black Mission, roasted with
wild fennel, 285
fig jam, 343
roasted, frisée salad with
pancetta croutons and,
195
filberts, 300. *See also*
hazelnut(s)
fines herbes, 14
lettuce wedges with shaved
radish and, 41
fish
halibut ceviche with lime,
315
roasted striped bass with
fennel fronds, 102–3
sautéed salted fish and
peppers, 177–78
tartare, with pickled
Buddha's Hand, 324
wild salmon carpaccio
with chervil and green
coriander seeds, 16–17
flageolet beans, 124
with spicy lamb sausage,
127–28

floating island, hazelnut,
302–3
flowers, 9, 401. *See also specific
plants*
fool, golden and red
raspberry, 268–69
frangipane, 246, 247
frisée, 194–95
salad, with roasted figs and
pancetta croutons, 195
warm frisée salad, 196
frittata, broccoli and green
garlic, 232
fruits. *See also specific fruits*
growing, 4, 403–10
preserving, 340–55

Galette(s), 246
apricot, 254
black cherry, 250–51
dough for, 246–47
nectarine and blackberry,
262
pluot and raspberry, 257–58
quince and apple, 293–94
walnut and date, 299
garbanzo beans. *See*
chickpea(s)
garden cress, 48
and lettuce salad with
chopped egg, 48–49
gardens. *See* kitchen gardens
garlic, 11, 54–55, 401
broccoli and green garlic
frittata, 232
chicken with 40 cloves of, 57
croutons, warm frisée salad
with, 196
lamb kebabs with oregano
and, 26–27

garlic (*continued*)
  marjoram, garlic, and
    Marash pepper sauce, 23
  mayonnaise (aïoli), 55
  potato and green garlic
    ravioli with fava beans,
    56–57
gelée, pomegranate, 296–97
ginger and sesame seeds,
    roasted Brussels sprouts
    with, 241
goat cheese and garden greens
    pasta, 209
granita
  pink grapefruit, 320
  red currant, 279
  watermelon, 145
grapefruit, 319–20
  pink grapefruit granita, 320
grapes, 281, 283, 285–86
  grape leaves, 285–86, 331, 335
gratin
  butternut squash and celery
    root, 155–56
  cardoon, with béchamel
    and Parmesan cheese,
    108
  parsnip and rutabaga,
    84–85
  potato and black trumpet,
    91
green beans, 111, 119, 120–21.
    *See also* bean(s)
green garlic. *See* garlic
greens, 205–22. *See also*
    chicories; salad greens;
    *other specific types*
  about, 205, 208
  recipe list, 206
green tomatoes, fried, 163
gremolata, 11, 189

Griffin, Andy, 133
growing information. *See*
    kitchen gardens; *specific
    plants*
Gruyère, butter lettuce salad
    with beets, walnuts, and,
    42–43

Halibut ceviche with lime,
    315
haricots verts, 111, 120, 121. *See
    also* bean(s)
  with toasted pecans and
    purple basil, 122
hazelnut(s), 281, 283, 300
  floating island, 302–3
  liqueur, 354
  meringues, crispy, 301–2
  panforte with candied
    orange peel and
    chocolate, 318
  vinaigrette, escarole salad
    with, 196–97
herb(s), 7–33. *See also specific
    herbs*
  about, 4, 7, 9–10
  cut-and-come-again salad,
    40
  fines herbes, 14; lettuce
    wedges with shaved
    radish and, 41
  garden salad tortilla, 40
  herb noodles, 15
  and parsley salad, 11–12
  recipe list, 8
  spring, roast leg of lamb
    with, 22
honey
  and blackberry compote
    with tarragon, 273

colorful carrots with butter
    and, 72–73
  figs with mint, ricotta, and,
    284
  honey candied walnuts,
    299–300
horseradish, 20, 86
  and tarragon salsa, 86
Hozven, Alex, 338
huckleberry(ies), 265, 275
  sauce, almond ice milk
    with, 276–77
hummus with preserved
    lemon, 132
hyssop, 10, 20, 33. *See also*
    anise hyssop

Ice cream
  lemon verbena, 32
  mulberry, 278
  peach leaf, 261–62
  tangerine, 322
ice milk, almond, with
    huckleberry sauce, 276–77
Indian cauliflower stems,
    spicy, 236–37
Indian-spiced sauerkraut, 338

Jalapeños, 173. *See also*
    chile(s)
  pickled carrots and, 185
jams, 341–42
  fig jam, 343
  rose hip jam, 343
  wild plum jam, 342
  yuzu marmalade, 344–45
Jefferson, Thomas, 5–6
jelly, 342
  crab apple, 344

Jerusalem artichokes. *See* sunchoke(s)
jus, strawberry, 266

K affir limes, 314
kale, 208–9
    garden greens and goat cheese pasta, 209
    lacinato, cardoons braised with olive oil and, 107–8
    lacinato salad with salt-preserved kumquats and Parmesan, 210–11
    Red Russian, green polenta with, 210
kimchi, 223, 227, 338–39
    spicy Korean pork stew with, 229–30
kitchen gardens, 3–6, 359–415. *See also specific plants*
    choosing what to plant, 375, 388
    climate and exposure, 375–77, 384–85
    cold frames, 384
    cold-weather gardening, 377
    compost and compost tea, 363–68, 379–80, 396–98, 407
    container gardens, 360, 371–72, 384–86
    cover crops, 117, 368, 369–71, 379–80
    cultivation and weeding, 398
    direct sowing and thinning, 387, 388–90
    extending the season, 382, 384

feeding and fertilizing, 385, 395–98, 407
garden plans, 374–75
growing fruits and nuts, 403–10
growing vertically, 381–82
harvesting and storage, 399–401, 409–10
healthy plants, 361, 395
intensive planting, 374, 398
minerals, 368, 369, 371, 396, 407
mulching, 380, 382, 398, 407
preparing to plant, 379–81
raised beds, 374, 379
row covers and shade cloth, 382
saving seed, 382, 393, 402
self-sowing and volunteer plants, 393
soils and soil amendments, 361–72, 374, 379, 382, 406–7
starting and transplanting seedlings, 387, 390–93
succession planting and crop rotation, 378
tools and resources, 411–15
using the whole plant, 400–401
watering, 385, 386, 394–95
where to plant, 375–76
kohlrabi, 223, 226, 238
    kohlrabi, carrot, and apple slaw, 238–39
    and red lentil dal, 239
Korean pork stew, spicy, with kimchi, 229–30
kumquat(s), 320
    candied, 351–52

red cabbage salad with Medjool dates and, 227–28
relish, 321
salt-preserved, 352; lacinato kale salad with Parmesan and, 210–11

L acinato kale, 208, 209
    cardoons braised with olive oil and, 107–8
    salad, with salt-preserved kumquats and Parmesan, 210–11
lacto-fermentation. *See* fermented pickles
lamb
    kebabs, with oregano and garlic, 26–27
    roast leg of, with spring herbs, 22
    sausage, spicy, fresh flageolet beans with, 127–28
lamb's lettuce. *See* mâche
leek(s), 54, 62
    braised, with chickpeas, saffron, and dried marjoram, 64
    tart, with crème fraîche and bacon, 63–64
legumes. *See* bean(s); peanuts; peas
lemon(s), 310
    creamy Meyer lemon dressing, 312
    gremolata, 11, 189
    lemon-coriander butter, broccoli rabe and ricotta pancakes with, 213–14

lemon(s) (*continued*)
  Meyer lemon soufflé,
    312–13
  preserved, hummus with,
    132
  zest, fettuccine with
    roasted purple asparagus,
    Parmesan, and, 313
lemon thyme, 25
  roast leg of lamb with
    spring herbs, 22
  strawberries roasted with,
    267
lemon verbena, 10, 32
  Bing cherries roasted with,
    250
  ice cream, 32
Lenderink, Annabelle, 151
lettuces, 3, 4, 6, 35, 37–38, 390,
    402. *See also* salad(s)
lima beans, 124
lime(s), 314. *See also* rangpur
    limes
  halibut ceviche with, 315
  lime spritzer, 315
  lime syrup, 348–49
liqueur(s), 353
  apricot, 354
  crab apple, 354
  hazelnut, 354
  nocino, 353
lovage, 10, 28
  lovage meatballs, 28

Mâche, 46
  with pickled cherries and
    duck liver croutons, 47
mandarin oranges, 321. *See
    also* rangpur limes;
    tangerine(s)

Marash pepper, 174. *See also*
    chile(s)
  marjoram, garlic, and
    Marash pepper sauce, 23
marjoram, 10, 22
  almond, marjoram, and red
    wine vinegar sauce, 235
  dried, braised leeks with
    chickpeas, saffron, and,
    64
  marjoram, garlic, and
    Marash pepper sauce, 23
  roast leg of lamb with
    spring herbs, 22
  sauce, grilled sweet potatoes
    with, 94
  summer squash pizza with
    fresh ricotta and, 147
marmalade, 342, 344
  yuzu, 344–45; thumbprint
    cookies with, 323–24
Masumoto, Mas, 245
mayonnaise
  basil, 13
  garlic (aïoli), 55
meatballs
  chicken, puntarelle soup
    with, 204
  lovage, 28
melon(s), 20, 135, 137, 138,
    142–43
  candied, 350–51
  Crenshaw, sliced, with salt,
    chile, and lime, 143–44
  soup, chilled, with mint,
    144
  watermelon granita, 145
merguez sausage
  fresh flageolet beans with
    spicy lamb sausage,
    127–28

  whole-wheat spaghetti with
    radicchio and, 200–201
meringues
  almond, soft, 305–6
  hazelnut, crispy, 301–2
  hazelnut floating island,
    302–3
mesclun, 3, 14
  cut-and-come-again salad,
    40
Mexican oregano, 26
Meyer lemon(s), 310
  dressing, creamy, 312
  and fennel relish, 102
  soufflé, 312–13
miner's lettuce, 50
  miner's lettuce salad, 50
mint, 10, 29
  candied mint leaves, 30
  chilled melon soup with, 144
  and feta, roasted eggplant
    with, 171
  figs with honey, ricotta, and,
    284
  parsley and herb salad, 11–12
  pounded almond and mint
    pasta sauce, 29
miso and soy, daikon radish
    braised with, 75
Moore, Russell, 339
Moroccan asparagus and
    spring vegetable ragout,
    105
Moroccan braised eggplant,
    172–73
mulberry(ies), 265, 277
  ice cream, 278
mushrooms: potato and black
    trumpet gratin, 91
mustard flowers, salumi with,
    221

mustard greens, 208, 220–21
and crowder pea soup, 131
red mustard salad with
Asian pears and pecans,
222

Napa cabbage, 227. *See also*
cabbage(s)
slaw, spicy, 228
nectarine(s), 245, 260–61
and blackberry galette, 262
nocino, 353
Comice pears baked with,
292
noyaux, 243
noyau crème anglaise,
271–72
nuts, 281, 298–306. *See also*
*specific types*
chocolate candies with
dried fruits and, 306
panforte with candied
orange peel and
chocolate, 318
recipe list, 282

Okra, 157, 188
cornmeal-fried, 189
pickled, 333
sautéed, black-eyed peas
with peppers and, 130
sautéed spiced okra with
tomatoes, 189
olives
cardoon salad with lemon,
anchovy, and, 106–7
olive, pomegranate, and
walnut relish, 298
Olney, Richard, 33

onion(s), 54, 58, 401
green rice pilaf with
cilantro and, 17
grilled scallions, 60
onion rings, 60
onion soup, 61
pickled, 332–33
spring onions in cream, 59
orange(s), 316
blood orange and golden
beet salad, 317
Cara Cara Campari
cocktail, 319
peel, candied, 316, 349–50;
chocolate candies with
dried fruits and nuts, 306;
panforte candies, 318–19;
panforte with chocolate
and, 318
quince-orange sorbet, 294
vin d'orange, 352–53
oregano, 10, 26
lamb kebabs with garlic
and, 26–27

Paella with pimientos and
chorizo, 180–81
pancakes, broccoli rabe and
ricotta, with lemon-
coriander butter, 213
pancetta
croutons, frisée salad with
roasted figs and, 195
roasted radicchio pizza
with fried rosemary and,
201
paneer cheese, 219
fried, spiced spinach with,
218
panforte candies, 318–19

panforte with candied orange
peel and chocolate, 318
panna cotta, almond milk,
304–5
parsley, 10, 11, 14, 41
and anchovy sauce, 235
green rice pilaf with
cilantro and onions, 17
herb noodles, 15
and herb salad, 11–12
parsnip(s), 70, 82–83
and rutabaga gratin, 84–85
sauerkraut sautéed with
juniper and, 230
soup, with sage and toasted
walnuts, 83
pasta
farro tagliatelle, 313–14
fettuccine with roasted
purple asparagus, lemon
zest, and Parmesan, 313
garden greens and goat
cheese pasta, 209
herb noodles, 15
potato and green garlic
ravioli with fava beans,
56–57
radicchio, merguez sausage,
and whole-wheat
spaghetti, 200–201
ricotta and amaranth
cannelloni, 220
pasta sauce, pounded almond
and mint, 29
peach(es), 245, 260–61
Babcock, rocket salad with
basil and, 44
drying, 355
peach leaf ice cream, 261–62
and raspberry trifle, 270
Rio Oso, grilled, 262

peanuts, 133
  boiled, with star anise and
    soy, 134
  fresh roasted, 134
  spicy napa cabbage slaw,
    228
pears, 281, 283, 290. *See also*
    Asian pears
  Bosc tarte Tatin, 291
  celery and Comice pear
    salad, 104
  Comice, baked with nocino,
    292
  drying, 355
peas, 111, 114–15, 382, 402
  Moroccan asparagus and
    spring vegetable ragout,
    105
  pea tops sautéed with garlic,
    116
  sugar snap pea slaw, 116
pecans, 281, 283
  toasted, haricots verts with
    purple basil and, 122
peppers, 157, 160, 173–74, 392.
    *See also* chile(s)
  bulgur salad with roasted
    Sheepnose pimientos and
    cilantro, 176–77
  grilled Jimmy Nardello and
    Padrón peppers, 179
  Jimmy Nardello, black-eyed
    peas with sautéed okra
    and, 130
  julienned Gypsy pepper
    salad, 176
  Padrón, stuffed with corn
    and queso fresco, 179
  paella with pimientos and
    chorizo, 180–81
  roasting and peeling, 176

sautéed salted fish and,
    177–78
  sweet and spicy peppers
    pizza, 178
persimmons, 281, 283, 295
  dried, 355; radicchio and
    farro salad with, 200
  Fuyu, with lime, 295
  Hachiya, frozen, 295
  pickled, 346
pesto, rocket, 45
Petrini, Carlo, 5
pickles, 138, 330–31, 335–36
  cornichons, 331
  dill, 335; quick, 331–32;
    traditional, 336
  dilly beans, 334–35; lacto-
    fermented, 337
  kimchi, 223, 227, 338–39
  pickled Buddha's Hand, 347
  pickled carrots, 333–34
  pickled cherries, 346
  pickled jalapeños and
    carrots, 185
  pickled okra, 333
  pickled onions, 332–33
  pickled persimmons, 346
  sauerkraut, 223, 226; Indian-
    spiced, 338
  Tokyo turnip pickles, 77–78
pie
  pie dough, 248
  Sierra Beauty apple, 288–89
  sour cherry, 251–52
pilaf
  golden chard and bulgur, 215
  green rice, with cilantro
    and onions, 17
pimientos. *See* peppers
pita bread, whole-wheat,
    132–33

tomato and toasted pita
    bread salad, 164
pizza
  dough, 147–48
  roasted radicchio, with
    pancetta and fried
    rosemary, 201
  summer squash, with
    marjoram and fresh
    ricotta, 147
  sweet and spicy peppers
    pizza, 178
plums, 245, 257
  drying, 355
  roasted Italian prune plums
    and rosemary, 260
  Santa Rosa plum cake, 258
  wild plum jam, 342
  wild plum jam turnovers,
    259
pluot(s), 257
  and raspberry galette, 257–58
polenta, green, with Red
    Russian kale, 210
pomegranates, 281, 283, 296
  olive, pomegranate, and
    walnut relish, 298
  pomegranate gelée, 296–97
poppyseed and blueberry
    butter cake, 276
pork
  chile con carne, 129–30
  chile verde, 26, 181–82
  grilled pork sandwiches
    with radishes, carrots,
    and chiles, 76
  lovage meatballs, 28
  shoulder, braised in milk
    with sage, 23–24
  shoulder, grilled, with
    ancho chiles, 182–83

spicy Korean pork stew
with kimchi, 229–30
and spinach crépinettes,
217–18
tenderloin, with fresh
fennel pollen and seeds,
103
thyme-scented baby back
ribs, 25
potato(es), 88–89, 401
Cranberry Red, salt-
roasted, with crème
fraîche and chives, 92
fingerling, roasted in duck
fat, 92
German Butterball,
smashed and fried, 90
and green garlic ravioli with
fava beans, 56–57
new potatoes with butter
and thyme, 90
Yellow Finn and black
trumpet gratin, 91
preserving, 325–55. *See
also specific fruits and
vegetables*
about canning, 327–28
about jams and jellies,
341–42
about liqueurs, 353
about pickling, 330–31,
335–36
drying fruit or tomatoes,
329, 355
recipe lists, 326, 340
prune plums, 257
drying, 355
roasted, with rosemary,
260
pumpkins, 151. *See also* winter
squash

puntarelle, 198, 199
with lemon, garlic, and
anchovies, 203
soup, with chicken
meatballs, 204
purslane, lemon cucumber,
and cherry tomato salad,
141

Quesadillas, squash blos-
som, 149
quince(s), 281, 283, 292–93
and apple galette, 293–94
baked, with crème fraîche,
293
quince-orange sorbet,
294
quinoa: orange cauliflower
salad with fried capers
and rocket, 237

Radicchio, 198–99
roasted radicchio pizza
with pancetta and fried
rosemary, 201
Tardivo radicchio and
farro salad with dried
persimmons, 200
Treviso radicchio, merguez
sausage, and whole-wheat
spaghetti, 200–201
radish(es), 70, 73–74, 392
daikon braised with miso
and soy, 75
French Breakfast, sautéed,
75
grilled pork sandwiches
with carrots, chiles, and,
76

shaved, lettuce wedges with
fines herbes and, 41
shaved watermelon radish
with lime and sea salt, 74
ragout, Moroccan asparagus
and spring vegetable, 105
raita
cucumber and yogurt, 140
spiced carrot, 73
rangpur limes, 321
rangpur curd, 322–23
raspberry(ies), 265, 268
golden and red raspberry
fool, 268–69
and peach trifle, 270
and pluot galette, 257–58
summer pudding, 280
turnovers, 269
ravioli, potato and green
garlic, with fava beans,
56–57
red currant(s), 278–79
granita, 279
summer pudding, 280
Red Kuri squash soup, 154–55
red lentil and kohlrabi dal, 239
relish
fennel and Meyer lemon,
102
kumquat, 321
olive, pomegranate, and
walnut, 298
rhubarb, 97, 100, 109
compote, 110
shaved rhubarb and chard
crostini, 109
rice. *See also* risotto
paella with pimientos and
chorizo, 180–81
pilaf, green, with cilantro
and onions, 17

ricotta
   and amaranth cannelloni,
     220
   and broccoli rabe pancakes
     with lemon-coriander
     butter, 213
   figs with honey, mint, and,
     284
   summer squash pizza with
     marjoram and, 147
risotto, scarlet turnip, with
   red wine, 78–79
rocket, 4, 43–44
   orange cauliflower salad
     with fried capers and, 237
   roasted Delicata squash
     salad with scallions and,
     152, 154
   rocket pesto, 45
   salad, with peaches and
     basil, 44
rocket, wild, 45
   with balsamic vinegar and
     speck, 40
romano beans, 120–21
   in tomato sauce, 122
roots and tubers, 67–95. See
   also specific types
   about, 67, 70, 88, 377
   recipe lists, 68, 87
rose hip jam, 343
rosemary, 9, 10, 27
   fried, 27; roasted radicchio
     pizza with pancetta and,
     201
   roasted Italian prune plums
     and, 260
rose petals, candied, 30
rutabaga, 84
   à la grecque, 85
   and parsnip gratin, 84–85

Sage, 9, 10, 23
   parsnip soup with toasted
     walnuts and, 83
   pork shoulder braised in
     milk with, 23–24
salad(s), 35–50. See also salad
   greens; slaw
   anise hyssop and cucumber,
     20
   beet and carrot, 80
   blood orange and golden
     beet, 317
   bulgur, with roasted
     pimientos and cilantro,
     176–77
   butter lettuce, with beets,
     Gruyère, and walnuts,
     42–43
   cardoon, with lemon,
     anchovy, and black olives,
     106–7
   celery and Comice pear,
     104
   chicory, chopped, 202
   chicory, with celery root,
     apples, and walnuts, 199
   crab, with tarragon and red
     Belgian endive, 21
   cranberry bean and tomato,
     with summer savory
     salsa, 126
   cut-and-come-again salad,
     40
   dandelion greens with
     anchovies and garlic
     croutons, 49
   escarole, with hazelnut
     vinaigrette, 196–97
   frisée, warm, 196
   frisée, with roasted figs and
     pancetta croutons, 195

   garden cress and lettuce
     with chopped egg, 48–49
   garden salad tortilla, 40
   julienned Gypsy pepper, 176
   lacinato kale, with salt-
     preserved kumquats and
     Parmesan, 210–11
   lemon cucumber, purslane,
     and cherry tomato, 141
   lettuce wedges with fines
     herbes and shaved radish,
     41
   mâche with pickled cherries
     and duck liver croutons,
     47
   miner's lettuce, 50
   orange cauliflower, with
     fried capers and rocket,
     237
   parsley and herb, 11–12
   radicchio and farro, with
     dried persimmons, 200
   red cabbage, with Medjool
     dates and kumquats,
     227–28
   red mustard, with Asian
     pears and pecans, 222
   red romaine, with sherry
     vinegar and garlic, 42
   roasted Delicata squash,
     with scallions and rocket,
     152, 154
   rocket, with peaches and
     basil, 44
   rutabaga à la grecque, 85
   three-bean salad à la Chez
     Panisse, 123
   tomato and toasted pita
     bread, 164
   wild rocket with balsamic
     vinegar and speck, 46

salad dressing, creamy Meyer
  lemon, 312
salad greens, 35–50, 390. *See
  also* salad(s); *specific types*
  about, 35, 37
  fava greens, 118
  kale as, 208
  recipe list, 36
salmon carpaccio with chervil
  and green coriander
  seeds, 16–17
salsa
  horseradish and tarragon,
    86
  roasted tomatillo, 168
  summer savory, cranberry
    bean and tomato salad
    with, 126
  Sungold cherry tomato, 165
salsa verde, 11
salted fish and peppers,
  sautéed, 177–78
salt-preserved kumquats, 352
  lacinato kale salad with
    Parmesan and, 210–11
salt-roasted potatoes with
  crème fraîche and chives,
  92
salumi with mustard flowers,
  221
sandwiches, grilled pork, with
  radishes, carrots, and
  chiles, 76
Sarvis, Shirley, 271
sauce(s). *See also* mayonnaise;
    tomato sauce
  almond, marjoram, and red
    wine vinegar, 235
  blackberry coulis, 273
  huckleberry, almond ice
    milk with, 276–77

marjoram, garlic, and
    Marash pepper, 23
  parsley and anchovy, 235
  pounded almond and mint
    pasta sauce, 29
  rocket pesto, 45
  salsa verde, 11
  sorrel cream sauce, 19
  strawberry jus, 266
sauerkraut, 223, 226
  Indian-spiced, 338
  sautéed with parsnips and
    juniper, 230
sausage(s)
  lamb, spicy, fresh flageolet
    beans with, 127–28
  paella with pimientos and
    chorizo, 180
  spinach and pork
    crépinettes, 217–18
  Treviso radicchio, merguez,
    and whole-wheat
    spaghetti, 200–201
savory. *See* summer savory;
    winter savory
savoy cabbage, 226. *See also*
    cabbage(s)
scallions, 58. *See also* onion(s)
  grilled, 60
sesame seeds and ginger,
    roasted Brussels sprouts
    with, 241
sformato, Bloomsdale
    spinach, 216
shallot(s), 54, 65, 401
  crispy fried, 65
  sweet-and-sour, 65
shell beans, 111, 119, 124–25. *See
    also* bean(s); chickpea(s)
shiso, 10, 33
  parsley and herb salad, 11–12

slaw
  kohlrabi, carrot, and apple,
    238–39
  spicy napa cabbage, 228
  sugar snap pea, 116
sorbet
  apricot, 254–55
  quince-orange, 294
sorrel, 10, 19
  sorrel cream sauce, 19
soufflé
  blackberry, 274–75
  Meyer lemon, 312–13
soup
  beet, with dill, chilled, 14
  celery root, with celery and
    buttered croutons, 81–82
  chickpea and broccoli rabe,
    214
  corn and summer squash,
    186
  crowder pea and greens, 131
  escarole, with poached egg,
    197–98
  Golden Jubilee tomato, with
    spiced yogurt, 164–65
  melon, with mint, chilled,
    144
  onion, 61
  parsnip, with sage and
    toasted walnuts, 83
  puntarelle, with chicken
    meatballs, 204
  Red Kuri squash, 154–55
  sunchoke and fennel, 95
soy
  and miso, daikon radish
    braised with, 75
  and star anise, boiled
    peanuts with, 134
spaghetti. *See* pasta

speck, wild rocket with
    balsamic vinegar and,
    40, 46
spigarello broccoli, 231
    sautéed, with bacon, 232–33
spinach, 216
    Bloomsdale spinach
        sformato, 216
    Moroccan asparagus and
        spring vegetable ragout,
        105
    and pork crépinettes, 217–18
    spiced, with fried paneer
        cheese, 218
sponge cake, 271
spring onions. *See* onion(s)
squash, 135, 137, 138. *See also*
    summer squash; winter
    squash
squash blossoms, 145, 146
    basil-squash blossom
        butter, 187
    squash blossom quesadillas,
        149
    stuffed and fried, 150–51
squid and fava beans with
    garlic and parsley, 118–19
star anise and soy, boiled
    peanuts with, 134
stone fruits, 243–62. *See also*
    *specific types*
    about, 243, 245
    recipe list, 244
strawberries, 265–66
    alpine strawberry tartlets
        with crab apple glaze, 267
    roasted with lemon thyme,
        267
    strawberry jus, 266
striped bass, roasted, with
    fennel fronds, 102–3

sugar snap peas, 114, 115
    sugar snap pea slaw, 116
summer pudding, 280
summer savory, 31
    salsa, cranberry bean and
        tomato salad with, 126
summer squash, 135, 137,
    145–46. *See also* squash
    blossoms
    and corn soup, 186
    fresh corn tamales with,
        187–88
    grilled crookneck fans with
        basil vinaigrette, 148
    pizza, with marjoram and
        fresh ricotta, 147
    zucchini ribbons with
        lemon and basil, 146
sunchoke(s), 88, 94
    chips, 95
    chopped chicory salad with,
        202
    and fennel soup, 95
sweet potato(es), 88, 93, 400,
    401
    grilled, with marjoram
        sauce, 94
    straw sweet potato cakes,
        93–94
Swiss chard. *See* chard
syrup
    apricots in, 348
    lime, 348–49

Tagliatelle, farro, 313–14. *See
    also* pasta
tamales, fresh corn, 187–88
tangerine(s), 321
    ice cream, 322
    slices, confited, 349

tarragon, 10, 14, 20, 41
    blackberry and honey
        compote with, 273
    crab salad with red Belgian
        endive and, 21
    and horseradish salsa, 86
    parsley and herb salad, 11–12
tart(s). *See also* galette(s)
    alpine strawberry tartlets
        with crab apple glaze,
        267
    apricot almond-custard,
        255–56
    Bosc pear tarte Tatin, 291
    leek, with crème fraîche and
        bacon, 63–64
    sweet tart dough, 248–49
Taylor, June, 342
thumbprint cookies, yuzu
    marmalade, 323–24
thyme, 9, 10, 24–25. *See also*
    lemon thyme
    new potatoes with butter
        and, 90
    thyme-scented baby back
        ribs, 25
tomatillos, 157, 168
    roasted tomatillo salsa, 168
tomato(es), 157, 160–62,
    381–82, 392, 402. *See also*
    tomato sauce
    canning, 328–29
    chicken braised with
        vinegar and, 166
    and cranberry bean salad,
        with summer savory
        salsa, 126
    dried, 329; crostini with
        anchovies, capers, and,
        167
    fried green tomatoes, 163

Golden Jubilee soup with
spiced yogurt, 164–65
lemon cucumber, purslane,
and cherry tomato salad,
141
peeling and seeding, 163
sautéed spiced okra with,
189
Sungold cherry tomato
salsa, 165
and toasted pita bread
salad, 164
tomato sauce
simple eggplant Parmesan,
171–72
spicy, eggs baked in, 166–67
yellow romano beans in, 122
tortillas, whole-wheat, 149–50
garden salad tortilla, 40
squash blossom quesadillas,
149
tostadas, black bean and
epazote, 18
trifle, raspberry and peach,
270
tubers. *See* roots and tubers;
*specific types*
turnip(s), 70, 77
purple top, caramelized, 78
scarlet turnip risotto with
red wine, 78–79
Tokyo turnip pickles, 77–78
turnovers
raspberry, 269
wild plum jam, 259
Tuscan flat black cabbage. *See*
lacinato kale

Vinaigrette(s), 35, 40, 65. *See
also* salad(s)

basil, grilled crookneck
squash fans with, 148
hazelnut, escarole salad
with, 196–97
vin d'orange, 352–53
Vitali, Benedetta, 216

Walnut(s), 281, 283, 298
butter lettuce salad with
beets, Gruyère, and,
42–43
chicory salad with celery
root, apples, and, 199
and date galette, 299
honey candied, 299–300
nocino, 353
olive, pomegranate, and
walnut relish, 298
rocket pesto, 45
toasted, parsnip soup with
sage and, 83
watermelon, 142, 143
granita, 145
watermelon radish, shaved,
with lime and sea salt,
74
white beans. *See* cannellini
beans
whole-wheat pita bread,
132–33
whole-wheat spaghetti with
radicchio and merguez
sausage, 200–201
whole-wheat tortillas, 149–50
garden salad tortilla, 40
wild rocket, 45
with balsamic vinegar and
speck, 46
wine: vin d'orange, 352–53
winter savory, 10, 31

winter squash, 135, 137, 138,
151–52, 401
butternut squash and celery
root gratin, 155–56
Red Kuri squash soup,
154–55
roasted Delicata squash
salad with scallions and
rocket, 152, 154
toasted squash seeds, 155
winter squash antipasto,
152

Yogurt
coating for frying, 235
and cucumber raita, 140
homemade, 183–84
spiced, Golden Jubilee
tomato soup with, 164–65
spiced carrot raita, 73
yogurt-spiced chicken
skewers, 183
yuzu, 323
marmalade, 344–45;
thumbprint cookies with,
323–24

Za'atar, 26
zucchini, 145. *See also*
summer squash
ribbons, with lemon and
basil, 146

Restaurateur ALICE WATERS was born in New Jersey in 1944. She graduated from the University of California at Berkeley in 1967 and from the International Montessori School in London. Her daughter, Fanny, was born in 1983.

Chez Panisse Restaurant opened in Berkeley in 1971, serving a single fixed-price menu that changed daily. The set menu format has remained at the heart of the restaurant philosophy for more than forty years. A network of local farmers and ranchers dedicated to sustainable agriculture assures Chez Panisse a steady supply of pure, fresh ingredients. The upstairs café at Chez Panisse opened in 1980 with an open kitchen, a wood-burning pizza oven, and an à la carte menu.

In 1996, in celebration of the restaurant's twenty-fifth anniversary, Alice founded the Edible Schoolyard, a one-acre garden and kitchen classroom at Berkeley's Martin Luther King Jr. Middle School where students are given the knowledge and values to make food choices that are healthy for them, their communities, and the environment. To support the program, Waters started the Edible Schoolyard Project, a nonprofit organization with the goal of building and sharing an edible education curriculum from kindergarten through high school. Its website, EdibleSchoolyard.org, serves as a resource for like-minded programs around the world, and gathers and maps best practices for an edible education curriculum.

Alice is vice-president of Slow Food International, and is the author of ten books, including *New York Times* bestsellers *40 Years of Chez Panisse* and *The Art of Simple Food*, as well as *In the Green Kitchen* and *Edible Schoolyard: A Universal Idea*.